Eckhard Dittrich, Heiko Schrader (Eds.)

“When Salary is not Enough …”

Gesellschaftliche Transformationen
Societal Transformations

herausgegeben von/edited by

Eckhard Dittrich, Jakob Fruchtmann,
Nikolai Genov, Raj Kollmorgen, Heiko Schrader,
Thomas Steger, Tatjana Thelen

Band/Volume 20

LIT

“When Salary is not Enough ...”

Private Households in Central Asia

edited by

Eckhard Dittrich and Heiko Schrader

LIT

Cover images:
Above: Village in Chui Region, Kyrgyzstan (Heiko Schrader)
Below: Astana, Capital of Kazakhstan (Heiko Schrader)

Published with the kind support of the The Volkswagen Foundation (VolkswagenStiftung)

This book is printed on acid-free paper.

Bibliographic information published by the Deutsche Nationalbibliothek
The Deutsche Nationalbibliothek lists this publication in the Deutsche Nationalbibliografie; detailed bibliographic data are available in the Internet at http://dnb.d-nb.de.

ISBN 978-3-643-90525-3

A catalogue record for this book is available from the British Library

Klosbachstr. 107
CH-8032 Zürich
Tel. +41 (0) 44-251 75 05 Fax +41 (0) 44-251 75 06
E-Mail: zuerich@lit-verlag.ch http://www.lit-verlag.ch
Distribution:
In the UK: Global Book Marketing, e-mail: mo@centralbooks.com
In North America: International Specialized Book Services, e-mail: orders@isbs.com
In Germany: LIT Verlag Fresnostr. 2, D-48159 Münster
Tel. +49 (0) 2 51-620 32 22, Fax +49 (0) 2 51-922 60 99, E-mail: vertrieb@lit-verlag.de
In Austria: Medienlogistik Pichler-ÖBZ, e-mail: mlo@medien-logistik.at
e-books are available at www.litwebshop.de

Contents

List of Figures

List of Tables

1. Sustainable Livelihoods in Central Asia: a Comparison from Kazakhstan and Kyrgyzstan

Eckhard DITTRICH and Heiko SCHRADER

1.1. Introduction

More than 20 years ago the Soviet Union collapsed. Ever since, the question, which direction of development the former Soviet Union and the resulting republics would take, has become a standing topic in scientific debates. These debates concern nation building and the political and economic regimes to come. Today it seems clear, that nation building is a difficult process that – by no means – necessarily evolves into stable and enduring statehood. Democracy as a proclaimed idea has been achieved only by a few of the successor states of the former Soviet Union and market society in its full sense seems to be taking shape only in those countries, which are members of the European Union. In general, the three topics seem to be interwoven in multiple forms, appear to experience repercussions and contradictions, advantages and backlashes. For the republics at the periphery of the former Soviet Union the transformation was especially difficult. They had not known modern statehood in their history, no economic drive towards market society existed and groups favoring democratization could hardly be found. Economically, the countries are very differently equipped. Kazakhstan and Turkmenistan e.g. are resource rich countries and the former had gone through industrialization of parts of its economy already in Soviet times. Nevertheless, as compared with the Western republics of the Soviet Union, all of the new states belonged to the poorer regions. In their rhetoric, most of the old and new elites tried to tie up with the glorious past of the silk road in order to create a vision for the development of their now independent countries (Halbach 2007). Nursultan Nazarbaev, the President of Kazakhstan e.g. thought and thinks of his country as being developed into a new center in a globalizing world, being situated at major crossroads of the modern Eurasian trade routes connecting China, Europe, Russia and the Arab Sea region (Nazarbaev 2008a). While such a vision has some plausibility because of Kazakhstan's rich resource base, for other countries in the region like Kyrgyzstan, Tajikistan and Uzbekistan such a perspective does not exist. Apart from their ideas of development, all Central Asian countries underwent deep changes in all segments of their societies. In the study presented here, we want to investigate some of these changes from a bottom up perspective.

The study, financed by the Volkswagen-Foundation during the years 2011-2014, investigates the socioeconomic situation of private households in Kazakhstan and Kyrgyzstan. The economic situation of these two countries is very dissimilar. They were therefore chosen to be studied, because we hoped to get a deeper insight by studying two most dissimilar cases. In Kazakhstan GNI per capita in US$ according to World Bank Data e.g. is 7,590 US$ while in Kyrgyzstan it is 840 US$. Kazakhstan is rich in resources (predominantly oil, gas, uranium) but with limited secondary-sector development and sparsely populated. Apart from natural resources, "in 2010 Kazakhstan, Russia and Ukraine produced around 10 percent of wheat and coarse grains, and contributed around 20 percent of the global trade in these products" (European Bank of Reconstruction and Development 2012: 23). Incomes in Kazakhstan – but also living expenses – are much higher than in Kyrgyzstan. As a result of economic growth in recent years, a middle class has emerged, notably at least in the urban centers Almaty and Astana, as well as in the main oil-producing cities in the Caspian region. Unemployment is lower than in other Central Asian countries. Kazakhstan is a country of in-migration. Politically, it shows a stable soft-authoritarian regime of the development-state type (Schrader 2010) and a comparatively mild nationalist Kazakh orientation. It seems that clan adherence still plays a role among the titular group and that it shapes social exchange. The overall situation is in flux.

Kyrgyzstan is a mountainous, mainly agro-pastoralist country with only little primary resources except water and some gold. Industrialization during Soviet times was and is still very limited. The country belonged to the poorest regions of the former SU. Today, it is politically rather unstable. While initially being the only promising democratic state in Central Asia, it is now touched by deep conflicts. State authority is weak. There are conflicts between the South (Osh and Jalalabad regions) and the North, between ethnic Russians and Kyrgyz. Several more or less peaceful "revolutions" have occurred. Political unrest followed by ethnical disputes in 2010 caused a sharp drop in economic wellbeing and the GNI fell, contrary to the situation in Kazakhstan and the other Central Asian countries, where it has displayed a continuous rise since 2007, if we follow World Bank Data. There is a lot of labor migration directed towards the big neighbor as well as to Russia and to other countries. Shuttle trade especially to the Kazakhstani city of Almaty, as well as to China or to Turkey, offers other opportunities for making a living. Remittances play a considerable role for the GNI and for the survival of many households. According to Kraay (2010), Kyrgyzstan is among the six countries with the lowest governance score and can't be looked upon as a consolidated state – despite all efforts at improvement undertaken by the present government.

This study investigates how households in Kazakhstan and Kyrgyzstan, confronted by very different economic, political and national environments try to achieve sustainable livelihoods. The core underlying question is whether the households have taken responsibility for their own conduct of life ("Lebensführung") or whether they still display attitudes of relying on the "nanny" state concerning their survival strategies. That is, the core question concerns the achieved transformation from Soviet conditions. More concretely, we investigate which life strategies the households take to achieve sustainable livelihoods and how far they utilize the organizations of the evolving markets such as banks, insurance companies, etc.

The research followed a mixed team approach concerning international comparative investigations. It was conducted by research teams from North Kazakhstan headed by Aigul Zabirova (L.N. Gumilev Eurasian National University Astana), South Kazakhstan headed by Nazym Shedenova (Al-Farabi University Almaty) and Kyrgyzstan headed by Galina Gorborukova (University of Central Asia Bishkek). The German group was represented by Eckhard Dittrich, Heiko Schrader and by Nigina Avganova, Batima Mambetalina and Aikokul Maksutova. The research consists of a non-representative household survey based on 450 questionnaires (first stage), and of 121 qualitative interviews (second stage). The interviews were conducted both in urban and rural regions: in the major economic centers of the two countries Astana, Almaty and Bishkek and their rural environments. The research teams in Kazakhstan and Kyrgyzstan obtained research training concerning the different types of interviews and their analysis. In common workshops questionnaires and interview guidelines were developed, reporting was conducted and practical and theoretical questions discussed.

This book is the outcome of that research project. We shall start with some theoretical considerations about the transformation from Soviet societies to the present countries. We then present the sustainable livelihoods approach, which represents the general framework of our research. What follows is a deeper look into the profiles of the countries and the regions. We continue with the quantitative analysis of the survey and the qualitative analysis of the deep interviews. Finally, we draw some conclusions in a chapter on sustainable livelihoods and household life strategies.

The book represents a joint effort of the four research teams.

We are very thankful to the Volkswagen Foundation for financing this research. Special thanks go to Wolfgang Levermann for his cooperation. All teams would like to thank Markus Kaiser, who gave us valuable input for the study, and Denis Gruber, who took a major role in the research trainings and in the analysis of the sustainable livelihoods strategies. Special thanks go to Aigul Beimisheva and Daurenbek Kuleimenov from the Almaty and Astana teams. Last, but not least, thanks to John und Antje Bateman for proofreading of the manuscript.

1.2. Transformation of Post-Communist Societies

The transformation from a communist to a post – communist society is a long-term process (Dittrich 2001; Kollmorgen and Schrader 2003) during which the transformations of everyday life are equally important as the systemic transformations from above. These transformations touch upon all spheres of society: the political, the social, the cultural, the economic etc. Many authors have argued that the difficulties of change in these societies stem from the contemporaneousness of nation building, and of setting up a new political and economic order. On the economic level the change concerns the transition from a centrally planned to a market economy, which implies a process of institution building: the implementation of new formal, market-systemic institutions. Market society is more than institution building dealing with financial organizations like banks, labor and commodity markets, exchange rates etc. It also refers to the process of internalization of norms and values among the population, without which the functioning of the organizations is threatened and market orientated actions are endangered (Hollingsworth and Boyer 1997).

Part of our philosophy of transformation is the path dependency concept (David 2008, Stark 1994, 1996).[1] In line with North (1988, 1995) we assume that formal organizations can be institutionalized rather quickly in the process of systemic change, while informal institutions like the thickened norms and values and codes of conduct change rather slowly with the changing cohorts and their position in society (Inglehart 2003).

Critics of the path dependency concept hold that it is deterministic. We argue that developments can only take place upon the foundations of the past, while it

[1] Goldschmidt/Zweynert define path dependency as follows: "[...] the significance of historical and social contexts, as well as the necessity to take these contexts into consideration in economic policy-making [...] it is one of the prerequisites of successful political agenda-setting to be aware of the informal rules that form the soil in which newly established formal rules must strike roots. Specific institutional cultures [...] are not necessarily successful when transferred to other social environments [...] Path dependencies appear to be due mainly to informal rules. Because informal constraints are created through a long-term process, they provide *'fertile ground'* for path dependent developments" (Zweynert and Goldschmidt 2005:5)

is, however, over simplistic to assume that all post–socialist societies are and were on the same development path. Their pre-communist past is too diverse for simple comparisons. For example, some societies, that have broken with the Soviet period, may nowadays connect to the pre-Soviet and Russian colonial history in their nation-building (cf. Anderson 1983; Roy 2000) by considering the communist period as an unsuccessful experiment. In Central Asia, however, the history of nation-states is rather recent. Uzbekistan e.g. refers to its history of sedentary settlements along the Silk Road and the river systems, while Kazakhstan and Kyrgyzstan refer to their mainly nomadic pasts (cf. George 2009; Sancak 2001). In these cases nation building processes are post-Soviet and difficult. Often national identities compete with ethnic identities, and access to important political and economic positions is often based on ethnic lines or, as in Kazakhstan, on hordes. Here we can observe Kazakhization and Kyrgyzization processes linking to the historical heritage of nomadic lifestyle, the Golden Horde, and Turkic ancestry (Fuller 1994; Hiro 2009).

During the Soviet period development occurred according to a central development plan independent from mainly artificially drawn republic boundaries, and different economic roles were designed for different regions. Some e.g. became mainly agro-industrial producers (kolkhoz and sovjos;cf. Szporluk 1994), others industrial producers. Likewise road and rail construction was directed to the centers of the Soviet Union to extract resources from the periphery and support industrialization in the Soviet centers. This nowadays hampers regional development in the new nation states. Concerning center – periphery relations, the economic policy of the Soviet Union was at least partly a continuation of the Tsarist colonial period (cf. Soucek 2001).

The heritage as well as the geopolitical situation constitutes both starting conditions and development opportunities for the present situation. The collapse of the Soviet Union put the former Republics into the position of independent states. While every former Soviet Republic experienced hardship, effects on Central Asia were severe. Kyrgyzstan, Tajikistan and Uzbekistan experienced levels of output and wellbeing, which were comparable to low–income countries in sub–Saharan Africa, while Turkmenistan and Kazakhstan are much better off (Brück 2012). The two countries being studied here, Kazakhstan and Kyrgyzstan constitute most dissimilar cases in Central Asia (see Chapter 2).

Table 1: Selected development indicators for Kazakhstan and Kyrgyzstan

Development Indicators / Country	**Kazakhstan**	**Kyrgyzstan**	**Low Income Countries**
Population (million)	16.6	5.5	–
Annual Population Growth %	1.4	1.1	2.1
Fertility Rate	2.6	2.9	4.1
Rural Population (%)	46.4	64.6	72.0
GDP p.c. in US$	11,245.0	1,075.0	581
Poverty Headcount at National Poverty Line %	8.2	33.7	–
Gini Index	29.0	26.2	–
Life Expectancy at Birth	68.3	69.4	58.8
Literacy Rate, Females 15 and above (%)	99.6	89.0	56.4
Secondary School Enrolment, Female (%)	98.3	83.5	38.5

Source: Brück (2012)

We have assumed interdependencies between transformation paths, macroeconomic conditions and life strategies of private households. Therefore we have investigated the people's economy –the economy of everyday life of households and their members. During the communist period the omnipresence of the state meant that households were usually not required to take on their own responsibilities; neither for the present survival nor for the future concerning education, old age, unemployment or sickness. People were given a certain place in society by the state and the party and obtained their education for that particular role; children were hosted in kindergartens; healthcare provision was free-of-charge; pensions were safe; their own initiative and private planning were not required and not in line with the communist ideology of the "nanny state" and the *Homo Sovieticus* (cf. Oswald 2000). Due to the shortages in supply, however, informal networks were nevertheless important for making a living as well as for the functioning of state enterprises. Once the communist regime collapsed, many 'normal' people experienced a disorientation and a need for help (cf. Demszky 2005: 258). Others, who already had had important logistic functions in the party system or in state enterprises during Soviet times, could much more easily adapt to the new conditions and even benefit from them. The biggest challenge for the private households was to adapt to the requirements, norms and practices of the emerging new market system and to cope with specific capitalist problems that were rather unknown, such as unemployment, poverty, increasing stratification, as well as self-responsibility for one's own life and planning for the future.

Rural – urban migration is an important issue for all societies in the process of modernization and urbanization, as cities provide the better labor and educational opportunities. In Central Asia foreign labor migration also plays an important role – first of all within Central Asia, for example from poor Kyrgyzstan or Tajikistan to Kazakhstan. Secondly there is migration from these countries particularly to Russia but also to other places such as Turkey or China. Studies from many world regions have shown that remittances of migrants not only play an important function for the survival of private households but also in making entire states function because these remittances might even exceed the gross national product of a given country (Musabaeva 2008; Ronsijn 2006). Migration of household members is a strategy that the household may take to stabilize its resources(cf. Haug and Pointner 2007). The term 'household strategy'[2] (de Haan and Zoomers 2005; Lokshin et al. 2001; Wallace 2002) implies that not only individuals apply strategies, but that households may decide[3] that different household members may take over different roles or economic functions so that only the mix may provide for security and survival. Households reflect upon their economic, human and social capital provisions, investments and expenditures. The strategies that may be pursued by a household and its members are somewhere in between the two poles of risk averse behavior with probably low but hopefully stable returns on one hand and high risk involvement with potentially high returns but also high potential losses on the other. Cultural norms concerning gender and age may determine the specific household roles (Gubhaju and De Jong 2009; Holzmann 2003). Furthermore, short-term and long-term strategies can be distinguished. Typical coping strategies of poorer households are the combination of formal, informal and subsistence incomes (Elwert, Evers, and Wilkens 1983; Schrader 1999) to spread risks Studies on poorer households, in different regions of the world, have discovered subsistence production not only in rural regions but also in cities ('ruralization of the city'; cf. Stren 1986).

---

2 We should not assume that the term "strategy" requires strategic planning and rationalization in a strict sense. In another context Lindblom (1969) described the strategy of "muddling through" by arguing that the complexity of everyday life requires a reduction of decision-making (cf. Luhmann 1988b). With reference to Lindblom, Scott called such actions to do the right things in the right moment "practical knowledge" (Scott 1998). It is not necessarily conscious, but represents a flexible adaptation to the environment. In poverty research scholars prefer the term "coping" (Benda-Beckmann 2000; Lokshin et al. 2001; Ronsijn 2006).

3 Of course, such decisions are not always smooth, discursive and democratic but underlie cultural norms and power relations (age, gender, etc.), as De Haan and Zoomers (2005) emphasize.

1.3. Sustainable Livelihoods and Life Strategies of Private Households

The sustainable livelihoods approach (SLA) is less a theoretical approach but rather a practical frame of analyses for development intervention. It provides an orientation towards a more holistic approach, towards systematization and interpretation of complex social structures. This approach was developed for investigating the possibilities of reproduction and the capacities of people close to the poverty line in a world subject to rapid change. The approach takes a bottom-up perspective to consider the multiple dimensions influencing the livelihoods of people in rather insecure living conditions: their social, political, cultural, economic and natural embeddedness. It looks at constraints as well as potentially successful strategies for making a living. Initially the SLA was applied to rural regions only (Asian Development Bank 2008; Chambers 1992, 1994), more recently also to urban contexts (Espling 1999; Evans 2002a, 2002b; Mukherjee 2001; Tacoli 1998).[4]

In this research project, we do not research poverty as such, but research the transformation processes. As we acknowledge that societies are stabilized by developing middle classes with corresponding orientations, we investigated how middle class households stabilize their lives or aim at doing so in the future. We selected private households in urban as well as in rural regions because of the big differences in life styles in the urban and in the rural regions of the two countries. While in Kazakhstan the official poverty headcount per USD 2 a day is rather low (in 2009: 0.18),[5] in Kyrgyzstan, however, in 2010 it concerns 23% of the population.[6] This means that in the Kyrgyzstan sample we will find households that can be classified as "poorer" or even "poor" particularly in rural regions if being compared with Kazakhstan.

For the households in the urban and rural regions of Kazakhstan and Kyrgyzstan, the post-socialist transformation implies first of all a "redefining and renegotiating of economic and social scopes of the space of action" (Yurkova 2004). Legal regulations and public norms have been shifted, and accustomed practices have been changed or retained their character. The sustainable livelihoods approach links the micro with the macro level, since household's (survival) strategies are connected with their resource basis, their macro-context (institutions' scope of ac-

4 For critique of the concept see (Morse and McNamara 2013; Small 2007).

5 http://www.indexmundi.com/facts/kazakhstan/poverty-gap#SI.POV.GAP2; access date 19-08-13

6 http://www.indexmundi.com/facts/kyrgyz-republic/poverty-headcount-ratio; access date 19-08-13

tion and their practices) and their vulnerability context.[7] The level of vulnerability is especially high, when households due to misfortunes and unforeseen problems, national or international developments (unrest, civil wars, international economic crises, etc.) are threatened in their achieved level of subsistence and are no more able to secure their livelihoods as done before. Considering the households' resource basis, the SLA is closely connected with Bourdieu's (1986) concept of forms of capital. The SLA refers to physical capital, financial capital, human capital, social capital and natural capital. With regard to natural and physical capital this approach widens Bourdieu's conception, while at the same time it narrows the scope by referring to human capital (a term being avoided by Bourdieu and replaced by the term of cultural capital). It is worth discussing the difference between these two terms. Human capital, which is used by international organizations such as the World Bank, has been scrutinized as being too instrumental in that which regards investment into it. Bourdieu, on the other hand, is less interested in the economic perspective of investment, but rather in power relations and reproduction of social structure. Cultural capital includes education and titles being related to it, but it is more than that. It is also an expression of "civilization" (which he additionally identifies as symbolic capital) of a class, being represented in a certain habitus (Bourdieu) in difference to other classes. Insofar, Bourdieu's approach is more politically economic than the SLA which is more instrumentally economic. While we chose the latter terminology in our approach to household behavior due to the fact that we are mainly concerned with socioeconomic topics such as income, monetary security, etc., we nevertheless also have the former in mind when we talk about middle class as distinct from lower and upper class. Symbolic capital, as used by Bourdieu is inherent in all other forms of capital and cuts across classes. It is close to Weber's idea of status. Of course it can be observed in the middle class. But we decided not to research into it separately, but to deal with this form when we look at the other forms. Operationally this was more suitable for us. Another major difference between both approaches is that the SLA refers to the asset mix which determines the vulnerability of households, social groups, villages or regions, while Bourdieu emphasizes social structure and

7 "Vulnerability" describes the fact that households and individuals are often ill-equipped to cushion risks (Moser 1996: 2). "Because people move into and out of poverty, vulnerability better captures processes of change than more statistic measures of poverty" (ibid). We share Moser's view that the extent of vulnerability is directly connected with the types and size of available resources.

its access to capital forms, the reproduction of social classes, convertibility of capital forms into others, and vertical mobility between classes.[8]

According to Portes (2010: 35ff) in addition to instrumental action social capital includes mechanisms of social control, family support, and nonfamily benefits. He emphasizes that social capital has both positive and negative effects being found within the same mechanisms. Solidarity and reciprocity/mutual help provide useful security mechanisms, however may restrict the building of "weak ties" (Granovetter 1983) beyond the narrow structures of kin or colleagues or "bridges", (cf. Burt 2004), because of self-exclusion and social exclusion of people from outside of the group. He refers to Simmel (1978) who emphasized the ambiguity between individual freedom and group solidarity. Family ties bind, and this can be an advantage for support as well as a disadvantage, constituting a type of bondage which includes claims on redistribution of wealth among the network members (ibid. 42).

But let us have a closer look at the terminology of the SLA. These forms of capital provide "assets" for the households or for a specific group of households in a particular setting. To some degree, the forms may substitute for each other if they are scarce (Brad 2008). We characterize the five forms of capital as follows:

Natural capital: represents an essential component of subsistence particularly in rural regions: all the natural resources to which households have access (water, wood, agricultural produce) and which are significant for subsistence production. It can reduce expenditure of the households for food, and increase their income through trade/exchange of the subsistence products of the direct producers.

Physical capital: Infrastructure (transportation, streets, buildings, water supply, sanitation, energy supply and telecommunication) and technologies (instruments, production conditions, technical equipment). The physical capital plays an important role in the rural/urban comparison.

Social capital: combination of the current and potential resources that are connected with having a permanent network of more or less institutionalized rela-

---

8 Following Portes (2010: 77ff) we argue that the class concept makes sense even now when we drop the assumption of class consciousness. Classes are midrange theoretical constructs for analyses of social change and even revolution. Classes provide deep structures of society being defined by long-lasting inequalities between large social aggregates. Classes are defined by different forms of control over resources within a certain social system. Portes therefore believes that in contemporary societies we may empirically find more than two or three classes (he prefers the terminologies of dominant classes and subordinate classes). And, class structures are reproduced within society, as well as the class position of a single household, as has already argued Bourdieu.

tionships of mutual recognition. Such networks are usually based on the affiliation to a specific group. The positions taken are connected with the authority to and ability of action. This means, an individual's position in the social structure determines to which authority and ability of action he/she will have access. Social capital refers here to a potential benefit from affiliation to a specific group (e.g. religious group, ethnic group, kinship group, social group etc.). The scope of social capital depends on the extension of the network of relationships, which a household or an individual of the household can mobilize, as well as the scope of (physical, natural, economic, cultural or symbolic) capital of those with whom the individual is related. The existence of the network is neither a natural nor a social "reality" that exists once for all, but rather a product of individual or collective investment strategies that are consciously or unconsciously focused on creation and maintenance of social relationships that can sooner or later yield a benefit (cf. Bourdieu 1986).

Human capital may have two forms. The form of a permanent disposition of an individual: incorporated cultural capital, and the form of titles and credits (secondary school completion, diplomas, professional examinations, certificates) as an institutionalized form. The latter form is necessary to receive 'licenses' whenever they are necessary to operate a business e.g. (ibid.).

Financial capital (economic capital as per Bourdieu) may consist of money in the wider sense or of property that is possessed. Property represents money in an objectified condition, in form of goods, instruments and machines. The latter is directly convertible into money and especially suitable for institutionalization in form of lasting property rights.

In Bourdieu's concept, convertibility of the different forms of capital is basic. Among the assets of a household a scarcity of one capital can to some degree be substituted by other capital what implies choices and risks. Natural capital, for example, can to some degree compensate for scarce financial capital. However, often vulnerable households may lack several forms of capital simultaneously, so that substitution becomes impossible. A rural household, lacking physical capital due to the location of the village, may also lack access to human capital formation and therefore in the long run will lack financial capital, too. This renders the household more vulnerable.

We assume that households mix different forms of capital in order to secure their livelihood.[9] Due to the differences of rural and urban households, but also due to age cohorts and macro-conditions, the mixtures may take different expressions.

[9] Tu Dang (2008) defines vulnerability as the present probability of being in poverty in future.

Specific life strategies to overcome vulnerabilities and to make a good living stem from these mixtures and their underlying convertibility. In order to make the concept of capital forms usable for empirical research, it must be made operational. Indicators like professional positions and educational levels of household members, household's structure and its income composition (formal, informal and subsistence income), property and network relationships of the household (personal and institutionalized relationships) give information about its sustainability and should allow the deciphering of past strategies that have led to the present level of livelihoods. They should also allow hypothesizing on the future to maintain or improve the situation. This also concerns advance planning for crises, sickness, old-age, social events such as marriages and funerals, investments in human capital such as children's education, etc. The available quantitative household surveys conducted in Kazakhstan and Kyrgyzstan collected a lot of information on specific household issues; however, they lack an identification of strategies that households take, or have taken in the past, to overcome vulnerabilities and to make a better living. We believe that quantitative investigations can quite well collect information on the assets of households. However, we agree with Brück (2012) that qualitative deep interviews are required to learn more about the pathways and trajectories of households to achieve stability and well-being. The question of strategies needs qualitative in-depth interviews to learn about the motives, practices and actions of households and their members and to answer the question whether one can find strategies middle-class households employ in order to adjust, to improve or to fail in the course of their survival.

How have households in Kazakhstan and Kyrgyzstan adapted to the market economy? Have they developed a corresponding market-economy-based behavior by balancing risk-taking and risk avoidance to achieve sustainable livelihoods?

With regard to sustainability of private households, Zoomers (Zoomers and Kleinpenning 1996; Zoomers 1999) distinguishes four class-dependent strategies: accumulation, consolidation, compensation and security.

- *Accumulation* is a long-term strategy to create a resource base in order to enable future actions of the households being more 'profitable' than the present one (e.g. by deposits, investment in child education etc.).
- *Consolidation* aims at security of existing resources and efforts by purposeful investments (e.g., in house building, purchases of cars, buying hay in summer, etc.).
- *Compensation* describes how negative developments or unexpected problems resp. shocks are compensated through the use of social resources (social capi-

tal, friends, acquaintances, network relationships) or the sale of economic valuables.

- *Security* is a sustainable strategy especially for those households that are near to the subsistence minimum. We assume that through diversification of activities, by referring to subsistence production, by using close reciprocity networks, and resorting to successful past crisis management etc. the households organize their survival. This kind of preventive risk management may be looked upon as a rational strategy of action if it is reflected upon or if it represents a relatively successful "muddling through" against the background of "limited rationality" in regard to the complexity of everyday life. These households use past experiences as guidelines to secure their survival.

In contrast to Zoomers, we put more stress on the convertibility of the forms of capital. Convertibility implies flexibility that is a general orientation in the life course that helps households to adjust to different constellations they may enter or be pushed into. Convertibility is especially important for crisis situations. Households e.g. may resort to (re)activating of private security networks they have invested into in the past. Or, they may reactivate subsistence production to make themselves more independent from the market by slaughtering cattle they have raised. Or, they may use up their deposit accounts in order to pay for expenses stemming from a marriage or a funeral.

The central hypothesis of the given actor-related concept of action is that we assess private households of the two Central Asian societies as capable of making decisions and processing experiences. As social actors they are competent within the practical knowledge that is at their disposal. However, they are often overwhelmed with the complexity of everyday life and prone to households' internal as well as external shocks.

We assume that the choice and specific arrangement of strategies largely depend on the context. In compliance with the vulnerability context and action frameworks established by institutions (see Fig. 1) we consider economic, geographic, social, political, historic and cultural factors as impacting on private households to form their options of action.

Based on De Haan and Zoomers (2005), we distinguish between "pathway" and "trajectory". Under the former, we understand observable regularities in the behavior of group members (e.g. private households in certain localities in our empirical research) which are determined by similar abilities, authorities, resources, social norms and particularly the same history. The path dependencies may refer to the common socialist heritage, as well as country specificities (resources, cultures, level of development / average income, etc.). The "trajectory" is about the

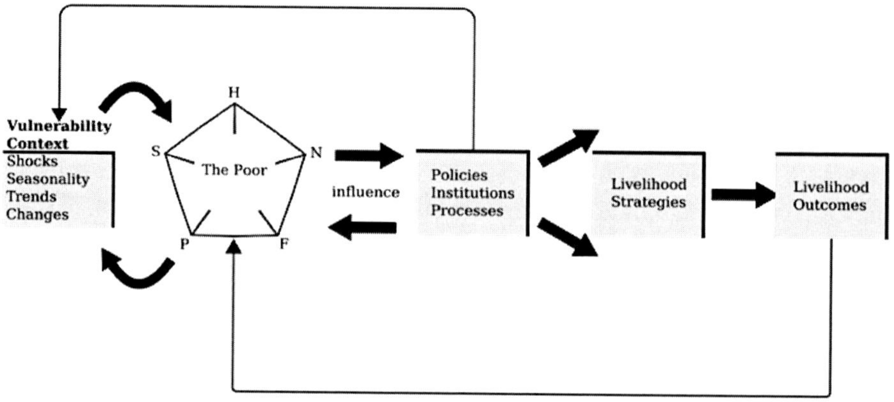

Figure 1: The Sustainable Livelihoods Framework
Source: cf. http://www.ifad.org/sla/; 22.03.13

individual scope of action and decisions of households, therefore they represent a specifically arranged combination of the forms of capital.

With regard to these aspects of transformation, we want to examine, whether 20 years of post-socialist development in the two countries in Central Asia, the households have developed necessary adaptations towards the new livelihood conditions and the handling of insecurities and risks of the new market economies.

We deal with the "vulnerability context" of households (Bonnen 2007) that belong to the middle classes. To fight vulnerabilities and to be prepared to do so in our view is the test for adaptation to the new living conditions 20 years after the breakdown of communism. According to the central hypothesis of Watts/Bohle (1993), vulnerability is determined through the specific position of individuals and groups in their network of relationships, especially by power relations and disposal rights. Actions towards livelihood security under risk can infer only from the logic of societal conditions and processes, in which the actors are imbedded. Chambers (1994) defines vulnerability as a space of tensions between outer threats and inner coping mechanisms. According to Chambers, individual efforts of a vulnerable person in the field of diversification, security and risk management must be systematically supported, and moreover the observation and indicator systems must be additionally developed for fighting vulnerabilities, for developing coping mechanisms and life support systems.

Vulnerabilities can be of temporary and of chronic nature. Crises in livelihoods are caused on the one hand by calamities (death of the bread winner, divorce), individual mistakes or poor skills of household members (e.g. low education). On the other hand they are caused by macro-developments (national and international) which the households have to react to (e.g. unemployment, loss of deposits, labor migration, ethnic conflicts, civil wars, international economic and financial crises, etc.). Conversely, improvements in the political and economic realms can positively influence the resource basis and scope of action of actors: e.g. concerning financial capital through better interest rates, better paid employment or concerning physical capital through improvements in the infrastructure that allows for commuting. The introduction of state-based security systems, especially health security, pension funds, and unemployment insurance, directly influences the vulnerability of households. If a household is not able to overcome temporary vulnerabilities, and if they become chronic, this may lead into a downward spiral of deteriorating living conditions and into poverty.

Survival and the strategies taken to secure it, imply complex decisions. They concern savings and consumption decisions, private investments in property and human capital, professional orientation, and insurances (commercial as well as kinship security networks), migration, credits, and the use of institutional arrangements in the private setting (family, relatives, friends). Middle and long-term strategies (planning) are represented for example by provisions for old-age and health, private insurances, money deposits, long-term capital accumulation and investments, purchase of apartments or houses, human capital formations of children, professional and advanced education. They contribute to stability and improvement of livelihoods.

With regard to rural strategies and patterns of lifestyle, extended notions of "capital" and "strategies" must be used (cf. Kandiyoti 1999) because of the different contexts. In rural areas e.g. raising a cattle herd represents a form of saving with the chances of accumulation by breeding, and additionally it represents symbolic capital, which is convertible into economic capital. Moreover, the same strategy may deliver subsistence products and implies insurance in case of emergency (food). The households are part of functioning networks that imply reciprocity patterns representing both social capital and securities (cf. Kuehnast and Dudwick 2004). Households in rural and urban areas are expected to have different strategies.

But there are also strategic elements that cut across rural, urban and even interregional or international space and may support or even facilitate the convertibility of capital forms: kin networks. For example, urban family members may remit financial capital to rural ones, or they may support the education of rural children while they receive subsistence produce from their relatives.

That is, with regard to social capital, we open up for network relationships beyond the household boundaries: our open household concept.) The networks influence the household situation (transfers from family members, labor migration, etc.) in such a way that – in theory – a certain interface/gap appears between the household concept and the family concept.

We investigate how private households from the middle-class cope with their everyday life in the view of macro developments of their societies. We assume that households in a similar social position cope with insecurity in similar ways. Here we shall bring the class aspect into the SLA. But we assume – in line with Portes (2010) – that an aggregation of the middle class is perhaps too broad but would cover different sub-classes. In the analysis of our data we will try to identify a differentiation of the middle class into sub-classes mainly according to their access to and their utilization of resources.

Since the beginning of the new millennium, a new tendency seems to appear in many post-socialist societies according to which the ongoing consolidation in the political, economic and social fields of certain transformation states influences the livelihoods of private households. Whether this is relevant to all countries in Central Asia, whether these developments take place equally in the rural and urban areas, whether all age groups are affected, and whether micro- and macro-social factors have an impact on these developments remain open questions empirically.

2. Country Profiles

2.1. Kazakhstan

Aigul ZABIROVA, Eckhard DITTRICH and Heiko SCHRADER[10]

Regional Profile[11]

Capital City: Astana (capital, since 1998, pop. 814 000 (2014)), Other Cities: Almaty (former capital) 1.2 million, Karaganda 440,000, Shymkent 370,000, Taraz 340,000, Ust-Kamenogorsk 310,000, Pavlodar 300,000.

Government: Republic; authoritarian presidential regime. Independence: December, 16 th, 1991 (from the Soviet Union). Declaration of sovereignty: October, 25 th, 1990. The area was conquered by Russia in the 18th century and Kazakhstan became a Soviet Republic in 1936.

Geography: area 2.7 million km^2; ninth-largest country in the world. Terrain: Extends east to west from the Caspian Sea to the Altay Mountains and north to south from the plains of Western Siberia to the oasis and deserts of Central Asia.

Climate: Continental; cold winters and hot summers; arid and semi-arid.

Population: 16.7 million (2012); Ethnic groups: Kazakhs 51.8%, Russians 31.4%, Ukrainians 4.4%, Tatars 1.7%, Germans 1.6%. There are over 100 other nationalities.

Religion: Sunni Muslim 47%, Russian Orthodox 44%, Protestant 2%, other 7%.

Languages: Kazakh language has the status of the "state" language, while Russian is declared the "official" language. Russian is used routinely in business and science; only 52% of the population speaks Kazakh. Literacy: 98%.

Natural resources: Major deposits of petroleum, natural gas, coal, iron ore, manganese, chrome ore, nickel, cobalt, copper, molybdenum, lead, zinc, bauxite, gold, uranium. Kazakhstan is a country rich in resources.

Agricultural products: Grain (mostly spring wheat), feed and oil crops, cotton; livestock.

---

[10] A preliminary paper for Almaty and Almaty region was provided by Nazym Shedenova; part of her material was integrated in the report from Astana. The integration as well as the adjustment was done by Eckhard Dittrich and Heiko Schrader. Batima Mambetalina was helpful in providing additional statistics.

[11] Nations Online: http://www.nationsonline.org/oneworld/kazakhstan.htm, access 30-7-13

Industrial products: Oil, iron and steel; tractors and other agricultural machinery, electric motors, construction materials.

Currency: Tenge (KZT); 1 Tenge = 0.004 Euro or 0.005 USD (2014)

Figure 2: Political map of Kazakhstan[12]

Demographic Aspects

In spite of its large surface area[13] Kazakhstan is a sparsely populated country. In 2012 the number of people was 16.7 million, having slightly increased over the last years.[14] In 2010 life expectancy at birth reached 62 years for males and 72 for females, the probability of dying under five (per 1,000 live births) was 28.[15] The map above shows the provinces of Kazakhstan. According to official statistics, on January 1, 2011 the Republic of Kazakhstan consists of 40 cities, 45 towns, and 6,982 villages.

This research on sustainable livelihoods concerns two regions in Kazakhstan: (a) Akmola region in North Kazakhstan, which on January 1, 2011 includes 2

[12] Wikipedia online: https://en.wikipedia.org/wiki/Provinces_of_Kazakhstan; access 27-3-13

[13] 2,724,900 sqkm; UN Data – A World of Information, Kazakhstan, World Statistics Pocketbook, 2013, Online: http://data.un.org/CountryProfile.aspx?crName=Kazakhstan; access 27-7-13

[14] Average population growth for 2010-2015 is 1%; UN Data – A World of Information, Kazakhstan, World Statistics Pocketbook, 2013, Online: http://data.un.org/CountryProfile.aspx?crName=Kazakhstan; access 27-7-13

[15] World Health Organization, Country Profiles; http://www.who.int/countries/kaz/en/; access 27-7-13

cities – one of these being the capital Astana – 8 towns and 628 villages; (b) Almaty region in South Kazakhstan, and Almaty city, being the largest city of Kazakhstan, the former capital Alma-Ata during Tsarist and Soviet times. Almaty provides the highest population density in the country.[16] The following table provides data on the area and population size.

Table 2: The provinces Akmola, Almaty region, Astana and Almaty in Kazakhstan[17]

Province	Capital	Area (km^2)	Population
Akmola	Kokshetau	121,400.0	829,000
Astana(1)	Astana	710.2	600,200
Almaty Province	Taldykorgan	224,000.0	860,000
Almaty(1)	Almaty	324.8	1,226,300

Note: Almaty and Astana, the two primary cities, have the status of 'state importance' and do not relate to any province.

Kazakhstan is a very young country. The following figure shows the age pyramid for the year 2009.

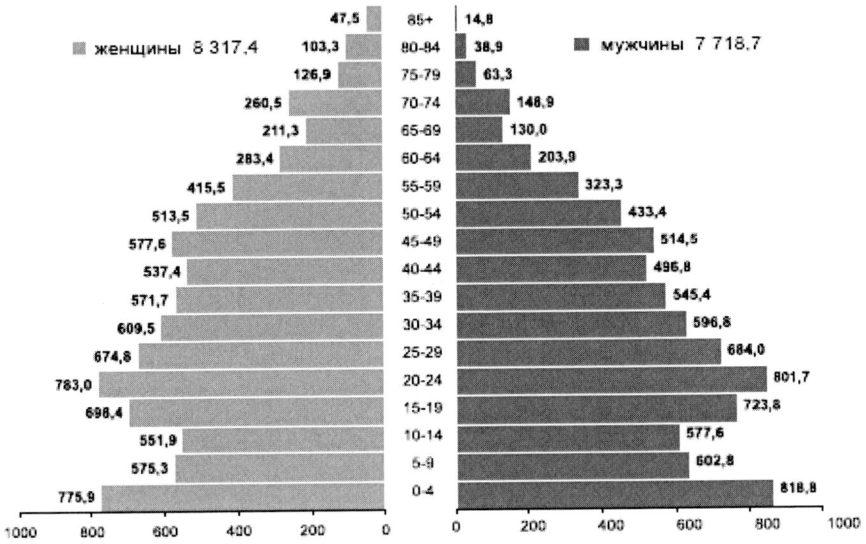

Figure 3: Age pyramid in Kazakhstan, 2009[18]
Legend: left female, right male

---

16 The population of Almaty, Department of Statistics, 19 May 2009

17 Wikipedia online: https://en.wikipedia.org/wiki/Provinces_of_Kazakhstan; access 27-3-13

18 "Zhen'shchiny i muzhchiny Kazakhstana" (Men and women in Kazakhstan) Statistical year-

The Economy

Kazakhstan has the most advanced economy in Central Asia and counts among the middle-income countries according to international statistics. In 2012 the GDP comprised USD 201.7 billion. GDP and GDP development throughout the period 2000-2010 can be seen from the following figure.[19] Since 2010 it has quickly recovered again.

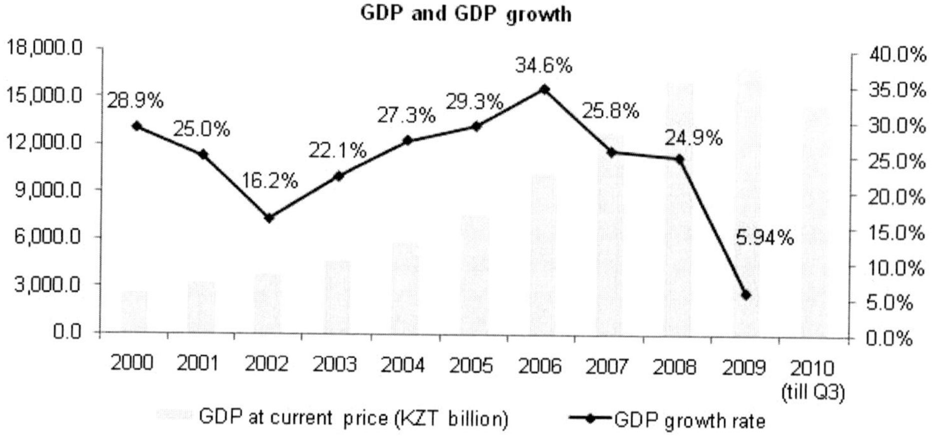

Figure 4: GDP and GDP growth in Kazakhstan, 2000-2010[20]

In 2010 foreign exports accounted for 57,244.1 million USD, imports for 24,023.6, so that a positive balance of trade was achieved. For exports (2010) the major trading partners are China (17.7%), Italy (16.7%) and France (7.7%), for imports the Russian Federation (22.8%), China (16.5%) and Germany (7.6%).[21]

book, in ed. Smailov A.A. / The Agency of Statistics of the Republic of Kazakhstan, Astana, 2010 – p. 7

19 ECR Euro money Country Risk, online: http://www.euromoneycountryrisk.com/Wiki/Kazakhstan; access 27-7-13

20 Ibid.

21 UN Data -A World of information, Kazakhstan, World Statistics Pocketbook, 2013, Online: http://data.un.org/CountryProfile.aspx?crName=Kazakhstan; access 27-7-13

Table 3: Gross regional product per capita, Kazakhstan 2001-2012[22]

Year	**2001**	**2002**	**2003**	**2004**	**2005**	**2006**
Republic of Kazakhstan	218,8	254,1	309,3	391,0	501,1	667,2
Akmola region	140,6	155,2	189,1	222,1	263,4	340,0
Almaty region	102,1	119,2	147,3	163,5	202,1	253,5
Astana city	438,1	463,8	596,8	901,7	1.318,0	1.701,8
Almaty city	504,9	603,3	695,8	924,4	1.218,6	1.792,9
Year	**2007**	**2008**	**2009**	**2010**	**2011**	**2012***
Republic of Kazakhstan	829,9	1.024,2	1.056,8	1.336,5	1.665,1	1.799,4
Akmola region	543,2	641,4	712,1	798,1	1.105,3	1.113,4
Almaty region	337,4	409,2	424,8	537,9	658,9	757,0
Astana city	1.927,0	2.080,2	2.189,4	2.635,7	2.904,1	3.573,0
Almaty city	2.048,9	2.193,2	2.306,8	2.797,3	3.418,8	3.856,1

* preliminary

The table shows a constant increase of GRP per capita over the period observed. However, we can see from the data that the GRP per capita in Almaty region is much lower than that in Akmola region, while the GRPs per capita in the cities are nowadays close to each other. Comparing the cities with their regions: While in 2012 the GRP per capita in Akmola was one third of that in Astana, that of Almaty region was only one fifth compared to Almaty city. In both regions investigated, there is a clear difference between the cities and the countryside, a phenomenon we find throughout the country and also in Kyrgyzstan.

While in 2005 the official unemployment rate in Kazakhstan was 8.1%, in 2010 only 5.8 percent were measured. Labor force participation of females was 64.4% and 66.4% respectively, of males 75.0 and 76.8%. For these two years the employment rate in the industrial sector was 18.0 and 18.9 percent, in the agricultural sector 32.4 and 29.4%.[23] That means that ~~a~~ roughly half of employment is in the service sector.

The inflation rate and the consumer price index in Kazakhstan for the period 2000-2010 can be seen in the following graphs. For households they imply a problem that touches on savings especially. And poorer households that normally spend a higher share of their budget on consumption may face adjustment problems with regard to the increase of the consumer price index.

22 The Agency of Statistics of the Republic of Kazakhstan 2008. National accounts. Online: http://www.eng.stat.kz/National%20accounts/Integrated%20accounts/Pages/default.aspx; access 27-7-2013

23 UN Data -A World of information, Kazakhstan, World Statistics Pocketbook, 2013, Online: http://data.un.org/CountryProfile.aspx?crName=Kazakhstan; access 27-7-2013

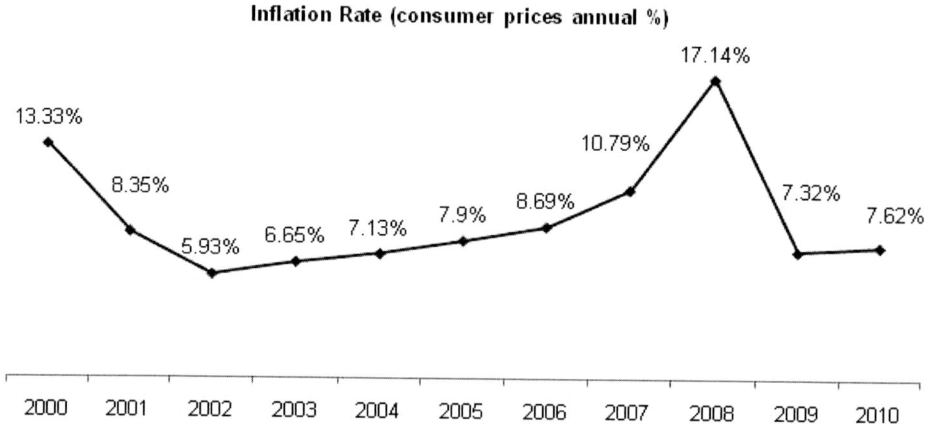

Figure 5: Inflation rate Kazakhstan 2000-2010[24]

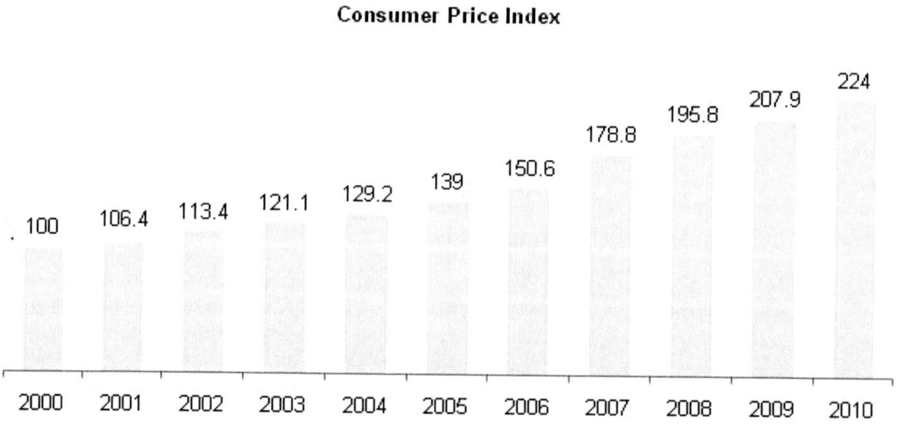

Figure 6: Consumer price index in Kazakhstan 2000-2010[25]
Base, 2000 = 100

[24] ECR – euro money country risk, Kazakhstan, 2013. Online: http://www.euromoneycountryrisk .com/Wiki/Kazakhstan; access 27-7-13

[25] Ibid., access 27-7-13

Regional economic development

According to the data of The Agency of Statistics of the Republic of Kazakhstan,[26] all sectors of the economy are at present experiencing growth. The most rapid rise in comparison with previous years is in agricultural production (22.8%) and transport (26.2%); other strongly growing areas are trade and communication (14.2% and 17.8%). Lagging behind are all types of industry (mining industry, manufacturing industry and electric, water power supply industry and construction (average growth rates 3-4%).

Akmola region is the largest agricultural and industrial region in the country.

Astana is first of all an administrative, business and educational city that originally was a small industrial town of minor importance. Population growth and overall national importance increased dramatically when President Nazarbaev decided to move the capital from Almaty in the South to North Kazakhstan.

Almaty city provides 44.5% of the republic's volume of trade. The major financial institutions and resources of the country are concentrated in Almaty. It accounts for 37% of all financial-sector employees, 50.5% of total deposits volume, and 69.3% of all loans. The National Bank, financial regulatory authorities, the stock exchange, 33 second-tier banks out of 34, 12 from 14 saving retirement funds, and 36 of 41 insurance companies are located within the territory of the city. It is also the largest transport, logistics and communications hub of the country, accounting for 26.4% of services in transport and communications of the republic.[27]

In 2010, the largest contribution to GDP (gross domestic product) of the country was by Almaty (18.2%). As any big city, Almaty has a highly diversified structure of the gross regional product (GRP). Essential items here are the provision of services (33%), wholesale and retail trade (29.4%), information and communication (11.7%) and real estate activities (10.5%). Almaty is the leader in the

---

26 Social-economic development of the Republic of Kazakhstan/ Statistical yearbook, in ed. Smailov A.A. / Agency of Statistics of the Republic of Kazakhstan, Astana, 2010 –Vol 1. – p. 130.

27 The state development program for Almaty in 2010-2015. Online: http://www.mga.kz /uploads/prog_2011-2015.pdf; access 21.10.2013 and http://www.zakon.kz/100059-utverzhd eny-strategija-razvitija-almaty.html; access 21.01.2013. 'The development of Almaty as a big regional center of financial and business activities' was also one of the long-term goals in the program of "Strategy of the development of Kazakhstan to a one of 50 competitive countries in the world", announced by the President Nazarbaev in 2006. See http://www.akorda.kz/ru/page/page_poslanie-prezidenta-respubliki-kazakhstan-n-a-index{Nazarbaev}nazarbaeva-narodu-kazakhstana-mart-2006-g_1343986805; access 23-10-.2013

development of tourism of the country; it accounts for 50% of the national work and services performed in the tourism industry. Tourist routes cover wild life and nature sanctuaries in the region.[28]

In terms of regional economic activity per capita, Almaty is gradually losing its leadership to the oil-bearing regions in the west. But International transport and communication segments of the Southern Transport Corridor will be developed within the territory of the region within the frame of the Project "West China – Western Europe" which may enhance its standing within the regional position again.

The shift of the capital to Astana has made this administrative-cum-educational city a migrational goal. While 2001-2010 the overall increase of the population in Kazakhstan was 21%, in Astana it was 105%. Not all migrants find employment in the city, so that the unemployment rate is slightly higher than in the country.

A structural difference between urban and rural economic activity is that the self-employment in rural regions is particularly higher.[29] On a whole, the self-employment rate decreased over the period considered, which is due to the improved employment conditions in the urban economies. Unemployment is higher among women than among men.

From the 1990 onward in Kazakhstan, as in most former Soviet countries, industrial employment has been declining, while the service sector has particularly grown. The number of highly skilled professionals has been decreasing, that of semi-skilled professionals increasing. The services are mostly found in commerce/trade, both in formal (shops, malls etc.) as well as informal (markets/flea markets, street vendors) sectors of the urban economy, office jobs in banks, universities, firms, enterprises, hospitals, museums, etc. Informal self-employment is found in private transport, as well as in street and market sales.[30] The share of people employed in the service sector is slightly less than half of all employed people in the economy (43.8%), while agricultural employment amounts to one third (30.2%). With regard to the latter, poor technical equipment capability of farms, lack of modern approaches, low availability of credit due to small and

28 The state development program for Almaty in 2010-2015. Online: http://www.mga.kz/uploads/prog_2011-2015.pdf; access 21-10-2013 and http://www.zakon.kz/100059-utverzhdeny-strategija-razvitija-almaty.html; access 21-01-2013.

29 Agency of Statistics of the Republic of Kazakhstan (2011): Living standards in Kazakhstan, 2006-2010. Astana. Online: http://www.stat.kz/publishing/2011/UrovJizniEnd.pdf; access 22-10-2013

30 Data about the informal sector are not available in the official statistics.

unstable incomes, and low levels of domestic comfort due to bad village infrastructure occurs as one of the realities of rural life. In the villages 43.3% have no social security in their self-employment.

According to its economic importance Almaty has at least remained on equal terms with Astana – the new capital of the Republic of Kazakhstan. In the regional development plan of the country both cities are seen as post-industrial zones with a strong concentration of trade, finance, innovation and education, transport logistics and recreation centers which stimulate the inflow of human capital.

Social and economic situation of households

According to data of the Statistics Agency of RK[31] from 2010 the average size of households in Kazakhstan is 3.4 persons. In urban areas, the average size is 3 persons, in rural areas 4 persons. 59% of the households comprise one to three persons, in half of the households with children (under 18 years) there is only one child, and in 18%, there are 3 or more children. The distribution in rural areas is similar.

The following figure shows the development of the nominal salary in Kazakhstan during the period 2001-2010. The constant increase was interrupted by the world economic crisis in 2008.

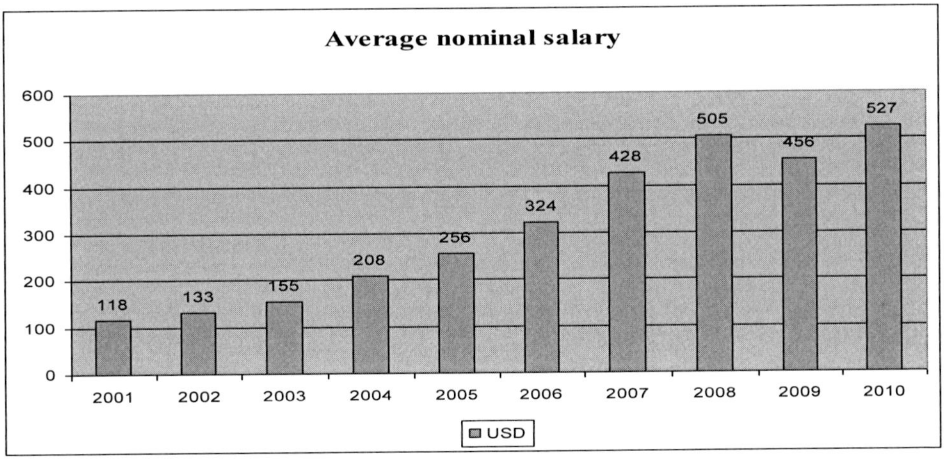

Figure 7: Average nominal salary in Kazakhstan in USD, 2001-2010[32]

[31] The Agency of Statistics of the Republic of Kazakhstan (2011): Living standards in Kazakhstan, 2006-2010. Astana. Online: http://www.stat.kz/publishing/2011/UrovJizniEnd.pdf; access 22-10-2013

Sectoral average nominal wages differ considerably. In 2010[33] the lowest labor remuneration was in fishing, fish farming, agriculture, hunting and forestry, and education. It ranged from 44 to 62% of the national average salary. The highest average salary was observed in extraterritorial organizations (323.3%), finance (201.4%), mining (183.1%), real estate, renting and services to consumers (155.3%), construction (133.3%), transport and communication (131%).[34] Positive changes occurred in the fields of health and social services due to wage increases to workers of these budgetary sectors. Also, the number of paid services in private hospitals increased (from 58.7% to 62.3% compared to the average in the period 2006-2010). Also decreases happened: employees engaged in "hotels and restaurants" (119.5% to 99.2%) and in "transport and communications" from 144.3% to 131%. This reflects the impact of the economic crisis and the slowdown in salary growth.

In 2010 the lowest average monthly nominal wages in comparison to the national average level were observed in such regions as North Kazakhstan (66.6%), Akmola region (70.3%), Almaty region (75.3%), South Kazakhstan (74.1%), East-Kazakhstan (79.1%). The average wage is significantly higher in Almaty city (137.3%), Astana (142.8%), Mangistau (171.6%), Atyrau region (191.1%). On the subject of wages the vast gap between urban and rural regions is again evident. In 2010, the minimum subsistence income was set at 13,487 KZT, and the minimum food basket at 8,092 KZT.

On the whole data show an increase of nominal average incomes and a decrease of income inequality. Average welfare of the population has increased between 2001 and 2010. As far as the weakest income groups are concerned, poverty has decreased. Incomes from self-employment and entrepreneurship are important for roughly 10 % of citizens.[35] They are almost twice as high in rural areas due to self-employment. This includes self-employment of family members in farming activities. However, the vast majority of farms are small and have low profitability.

---

32 Website of The National Agency of Statistics of the Republic of Kazakhstan http://www.eng.stat.kz/digital/Labour/Pages/default.aspx; access 15-09-2013

33 Agency of Statistics of the Republic of Kazakhstan (2011): Living standards in Kazakhstan, 2006-2010. Astana. Online: http://www.stat.kz/publishing/2011/UrovJizniEnd.pdf; access 22-10-2013

34 Agency of Statistics of the Republic of Kazakhstan (2011): Living standards in Kazakhstan, 2006-2010. Astana. Online: http://www.stat.kz/publishing/2011/UrovJizniEnd.pdf; access 22-10-2013

35 Agency of Statistics of the Republic of Kazakhstan (2011): Living standards in Kazakhstan, 2006-2010. Astana. Online: http://www.stat.kz/publishing/2011/UrovJizniEnd.pdf; access 22-10-2013

Housing availability

In the 1990s, as the result of policies of denationalization and privatization, housing in Kazakhstan has become almost completely private property. However, the price of real estate in the expensive cities like Almaty and Astana exceeds the purchasing ability of the majority of the population. In the end, "the housing policy, dropped from the shoulders of the State to the family and the market, leaving many people without affordable homes" (Panarin 2008). Affordable housing is of high demand especially as most ethnic Kazakhs prefer individually owned houses to live in. Housing constitutes an immense problem for many citizens.

State programs for cheap mortgages and housing construction have only slightly eased the situation. Limited solutions to the housing problem have led to an increase of illegal practices such as squatting and "self-construction", which have already engendered shanty or migrant towns. Their citizens are mostly recent rural migrants, generally with lower education and low incomes, making their living in the informal sector of the urban economy. Decent and affordable housing is one of the most pressing social problems in Kazakhstan.

Migration

In the post-Soviet period, the state no longer regulates urbanization and demographic processes by administrative methods. Major migratory moves occurred in independent Kazakhstan. Many ethnic Russians as well as ethnic Germans left the country. The Russian out-migration made Kazakhs the majority in the ethnic composition of the country. At the same time in-migration from other Central Asian states and rural-urban migration took and takes place, the latter of which accounts for 68.5% of all migration. The urban centers of attraction for internal migrants are particularly Almaty and Astana as the most dynamic economic centers.[36]

The main causes of contemporary migration of rural residents to cities lie in the low living standard, limited labor options and low incomes in rural areas. Over recent years, the depth of poverty in rural areas has become 2.2 times higher than in the city.[37] Rural-urban migration particularly concentrates in two cities,

36 Results of the 2009 National population census of the Republic of Kazakhstan. Analytical Report. The Agency of Statistics of the Republic of Kazakhstan. Astana 2011. pp. 38-42.; http://www.eng.stat.kz/publishing/DocLib/2011/%D0%90%D0%9E%20%D0%BD%D0%B0%20%D0%B0%D0%BD%D0%B3%D0%BB%D0%B8%D0%B9%D1%81%D0%BA%D0%BE%D0%BC.pdf; access 21-20-2013

37 Agency of Statistics of the Republic of Kazakhstan (2011): Living standards in Kazakhstan, 2006-2010, Astana, p. 80. Online: http://www.stat.kz/publishing/2011/UrovJizniEnd.pdf; access 22-10-2013

Almaty and Astana, whose share of net migration growth of the country in 2008 accounted for 86.6%. Almaty e.g. is dominated by rural migrants from the nearby southern regions.[38] In the period 2005-2009 Kazakhs share, in the inflow of internal migrants, was 83.2%, while their share in the number of outflow was also considerable – 63%. This suggests that a high percentage of people come for temporary, seasonal earnings; they are pendulous migrants looking for employment and education.

While initially after independence Almaty experienced a migration loss, this could soon be compensated. Interestingly, migratory flows show a higher number of women in migration movements than men. International migration from Kazakhstan to other countries, particularly Russia, Turkey and China is less frequent than in other Central Asian countries, while migration from other Central Asian countries to Kazakhstan is high.

Porous borders especially with Kyrgyzstan allow for a large influx of temporary as well as enduring immigration from this country. These migrants work especially in construction and in vast parts of the low paid service sector. Much of the migratory influx is illegal.

Social Security

The Kazakh pension system[39] is presently in a process of reformation to build a safe system for the future. It is based on three pillars combining mechanisms of solidary and accumulation. The first pillar was inherited from the Soviet Union. Pensions are paid from the state budget by taxes from the working population and other receipts, according to the duration of employment. The second pillar is a compulsory accumulative pension system. The working population has to pay 10% of its monthly incomes into this fund. The third pillar, also accumulative, rests on voluntary payments. The reorganization of the pension-system is an ongoing process which will be completed by 2040. Most recently the state pension fund was reorganized,[40] and another pillar of the pension system – a company pension – started to be discussed.[41]

38 http://i-news.kz/news/2011/04/13/4397910.htm

39 GNPF Kazakhstan: About Pension System; online: http://www.gnpf.kz/1369; access 28-8-13

40 In August 2013 a new – the only – state pension fund was set up which is controlled by the National Bank of RK. Till the end of 2013 all other non-state pension funds ("Oil & Gas ", "GRANTUM", "Halyk Bank of Kazakhstan" "Atameken", "SAPF", "YlarYmit", "Kazakhmys", "Otan", "Astana", "AMANAT KAZAKHSTAN", "Republic ", "Capital") will be transferred into this newly created national pension fund. News on website "zakon.kz" from August, 9, 2013: http://www.zakon.kz/4570615-v-kazakhstane-sozdan-edinyjj.html; access 21-10-2013

41 The plan is an introduction of 5% payments from the employers' side, especially for employees

Referring to official statistics, the retirement age gradually increased during the post-socialist period. At present retirement age is 63 years for men and 58 for women, while it is planned to raise the women's retirement age to 63 too.[42] As a consequence of this the number of pension recipients has diminished. It constituted 1,695,301 in 2010. Among the older generation, however, we find a lot of pensioners who have retired quite early according to the Soviet standards.

The government guarantees basic pensions for all pensioners and people with disabilities who have reached the retirement age regardless of their work experience and previous income, as well as state social benefits for people with disabilities, those who have lost their breadwinner and those who have reached the retirement age but have no work experience.[43]

The present social support system[44] includes:

1. Social support of maternity and childhood: childbirth allowance paid for the first, second and third child independent from income, homecare allowance for children under 1 year regardless of income, allowance for parents with disabled children equal to a minimum wage, and allowances for low-income families with children below 18 years. The introduction of this system has had a positive effect on the birth rate.
2. Social support to low-income families below 40% of the subsistence level.
3. Special social benefits for people in difficult life situations in accordance with the law of Kazakhstan "On special social services".

Health and Health Care

In the post-Soviet period a decrease in quality and accessibility of health care can be observed, which led to poor health conditions for the citizens. With the split of the health care system in public and private health care institutions, unequal

with unhealthy work conditions. The employers would not have extra costs because they shall be compensated by taxation. Source: Interfax Ukraine News Website from July, 7, 2013: http://interfax.com.ua/news/political/156312.html; access 22-10-2013.

42 The idea was to start a step-by step increase in January 2014. However, as the feelings got high in society, the president suggested postponing its start for 4 years to 2018. Source: Interfax Ukraine News Website from July, 7, 2013: http://interfax.com.ua/news/political/156312.html; access 22-10-2013

43 Prime Minister of Kazakhstan, Serik Akhmetov, An extract from the Strategic Plan of the Kazakh Ministry of Labor and Social Protection of the Population for 2011-2015, 2012-2013. Online: http://www.primeminister.kz/page/article_item-110?lang=en; access 28-8-13

44 Ibid.

opportunities for the citizens have emerged depending on location and economic status[45].

According to the National Statistic Agency[46], during the past 10 years healthcare infrastructure in Kazakhstan as a whole shows a constant positive trend. The number of medical doctors in Kazakhstan grew from 51,300 in 2001 to 63,800 in 2010. There is also an increase in the number of nurses (from 109,400 in 2001 to 143,800 in 2010). But the number of hospitals showed an increase until 2004 (1,042) followed by a decline until 2010 (998).

On the regional level healthcare infrastructure in Astana shows a steady growth. In contrast to Astana, Akmola region reached a peak in 2006, but then there was a gradual decline of the healthcare conditions up to the present day. The city of Almaty has the largest infrastructure in the country for the delivery of health services: there are hundreds of specialized diagnostic, outpatient clinics and institutions, research organizations and sanatoriums and various treatment centers. Despite the relatively satisfactory quantitative indicators of medical care compared with the national level, health quality in the city is at a fairly low level. Mortality of working age people as well as infant mortality remains high, which in 2010 amounted to 16.54 casualties per 1,000 births.[47] Drug and mental diseases exceed the average in Kazakhstan by 3.2 and 2.6 times, the level of oncology diseases by 1.3 times. Incidence of malignant neoplasms in Almaty is among the highest along with such regions as East Kazakhstan, Pavlodar, Kostanai, North-Kazakhstan regions, Astana and Akmola region.[48] It should be noted that these regions have a more developed industrial sector in comparison with other regions and therefore higher environmental pollution. One of the causes of disease is the high degree of contamination of the urban environment which exceeds by several times the permissible level. "Civilization diseases" as a result of the urban way of life – everyday stress, commuting, traffic jam, noise, etc. decrease the life quality further.[49] It seems that health provisions can be a major challenge for households.

---

45 Zhusupov B.S./Alimbekova G.T. 2002: Medical service in Kazakhstan: realities and evaluation. http://ciom.kz/assets/files/Nashi%20publikacii/Med_obsluzhivanie.pdf; access 23-10-2013

46 Website of The National Agency of Statistics of the Republic of Kazakhstan, http://www.eng.stat.kz/digital/index{Health}Health%20care/Pages/default.aspx; access 15-09-2013

47 Agency of Statistics of the Republic of Kazakhstan (2011): Living standards in Kazakhstan, 2006-2010. Astana. Online: http://www.stat.kz/publishing/2011/UrovJizniEnd.pdf; access 22-10-2013

48 Epidemiology of malignant tumors of the child population of the Republic of Kazakhstan (review)//Bulletin KazNMU. – November 16, 2011

49 Ikonnikov A.//Center for Asia. – 2009. – 13 (13). Online: http://asiakz.com/rus/article/305

Education

According to official statistics, the number of kindergartens in Kazakhstan has steadily grown during the past 10 years (1,103 in 2001 4,781 in 2010).[50] The number of children taken care of increased from 140,400 to 390,800. Many of these kindergartens are nowadays privately owned. During the past ten years we observed a decline in the number of primary schools (8,408 schools in 2001, 7,755 in 2010). Within the past three years, however, the number of teaching staff in primary schools has grown from 276,850 in 2008 to 286,733 to 2010. The number of colleges has increased from 318 in 2001 to 803 in 2010, the enrolment of students from 196,200 in 2001 to 604,200 in 2010. There is also an increasing number of students – about one fifth in 2010 – who study with state grants (increase from 47,200 in 2001 to 130,700 in 2011). The number of Masters students (5,410 in 2001, 16,586 in 2010) and the number of PhD students has increased from 285 to 960 during the past ten years.

Looking at the Astana and the Akmola regions, we observe a growing number of children in kindergartens (Akmola: 5,507 in 2003; 11,007 in 2010; Astana: 9,239 in 2001; 18,973 in 2010), and a slight growth in the number of kindergartens. In the Akmola region there has been a decrease in the number of primary schools (from 736 in 2001 to 648 in 2010). The same trend is observable in the countryside over the whole country. On the contrary, in Astana the number of primary schools has grown from 61 in 2001 to 85 in 2010. In the Akmola region the number of pupils in primary schools has decreased during the past 10 years from 154,800 to 110,000. In Astana the number of pupils in primary schools increased from 57,500 to 76,400. The number of colleges in the Akmola region slowly increased from 19 in 2001 to 25 in 2009, in Astana from 14 in 2001 to 28 in 2010. There is also a strong increase in the number of students. The number of universities in the Akmola region and in Astana demonstrates 2 opposed trends. In the Akmola region the number of universities has decreased from 14 in 2001 to 6 in 2009. On the contrary, in Astana the number of universities grew from 7 in 2001 to 12 in 2009. The number of students at universities in Astana has grown from 24,300 in 2001 to 39,298 in 2009. The Akmola region has a slowly growing number of students.

Let us now look at the situation in Almaty and the Almaty region. One of the reasons for Almaty's comparatively good adaptation to the market economy lies in its strength in knowledge and educational fields. Not only that one-third of the

---

50 Website of The National Agency of Statistics of the Republic of Kazakhstan; http://www.eng.stat.kz/digital/index{Education}Education/Pages/default.aspx, access date 15-09-2013

country's universities and students are concentrated in Almaty;[51] these students also find employment in the city and increase the advantages of the city if compared to other regions and the countryside. Almaty has a concentration of more than 35% of all institutions of higher education and of 30.7% of all Kazakh university students across the country.[52] As in the field of medical services, education has also found its market value. In addition to the numerous public kindergartens, schools, and institutions of higher education, the number of which has decreased during the post-socialist period, private institutions have spread. Those who can afford to, quite often send their children to such institutions, which are believed to provide better education and thus labor market options.[53]

However, many observers complain about a sharp decline in the quality of education compared to the Soviet period including the level of students' training. The system of higher education has turned into a machine printing diplomas, despite state attempts to set international standards in control. But there is a widespread practice of paying for favorable educational ratings and titles; bribery of teachers, etc.[54] Furthermore, educational output and suitability for market needs appears to be weak. Apart from this general problem, employment positions are also heavily distributed by 'f-connections' (Ben-Porath 1978) and bribery.

Cultural Identity: National Origin, Minority/Majority

Emigration was the dominant form of mobility in the immediate post-Soviet period. In 2009 however, the population of Kazakhstan almost reached the level of 1989 again, but its ethnic composition has changed dramatically. Since 1989 the number of Turkish ethnic groups, Kazakhs, Uzbeks, and Uyghurs, has increased by 1.5 times and in 2009 amounted to 67.4% of the population of the country (compared to 42.9% in 1989). European ethnic groups (Russians, Ukrainians, Tatars, and Germans) during the same period decreased by 1.9 times. Their share

51 Regions of Kazakhstan – Astana: The Agency of Statistics of the Republic of Kazakhstan, 2009. Online: http://www.eng.stat.kz/publishing/DocLib/Region_%D0%B0%D0%BD%D0%B3%D0%BB_09.pdf, access 25-10-2013

52 Almaty after 10 years of independence. (Almaty za gody Nezavistimosti) – Almaty, 2001 – p. 153

53 The state development program for Almaty in 2010-2015. Online: http://www.mga.kz/uploads/prog_2011-2015.pdf; access 21-10-2013 and http://www.zakon.kz/100059-utverzhdeny-strategija-razvitija-almaty.html; access 21-01-2013.

54 Ministry of Education and Science of the Republic of Kazakhstan. Online: www.edu.gov.kz/ru/news/; access 15-9-13

has been falling from 51.0% in 1989 to only 28.2% in 2009. This is also related to the governmental policy of 'Kazakhization'.[55]

In the post-Soviet period, despite the government policy of promoting and enhancing the role of Kazakh as the state language, the Russian language is widely used in business and higher education. Also internet users prefer sites in the Russian language[56]. However, the symbolic significance of 'the Kazakh' has been enhanced. The presence of the Kazakh language has become more visible in the streets; constant inflow of rural Kazakhs changes the language environment of the big cities. But the scale of '*kazahizatsii*' has not led to open ethnic quarrels as in neighboring countries. The president particularly stresses the necessity of the country's unity apart from ethnicity and religious beliefs, the latter being another touchy topic in Central Asia.

Environmental Quality

The environment is part of the real wealth of a society, and demands careful protection. Oil and gas, metallurgical and mining industries can be very dangerous for the environment. These are the most profitable industries in Kazakhstan today. Furthermore, todays Kazakhstan has inherited many ecological problems from the Soviet period, such as the Aral Sea problem or the atomic legacy from the nuclear test area of the Soviet Union. In addition to industrial exploitation water scarcity, global warming, desertification and salinization particularly in West Kazakhstan, but also the environmental consequences of modernization and modern life provide an enormous threat to the country.

According to National Statistic Agency during the period 2001 to 2010 the rates of the emissions of harmful air pollutants fluctuated slightly,[57] but in the two

---

55 Agency of Statistics of Kazakhstan: Demography Bulletin for 2010. Online: http://www.stat.kz/publishing/DocLib4/2010/%D0%94%D0%B5%D0%BC%D0%BE%D0%B3%D1%80%D0%B0%D1%84%D0%B8%D1%8F/Bull_Hsany2010.rar; access 24-10-2013, see also http://www.stat.gov.kz/publishing/Pages/demo_2011.aspx; access 24-10-2013; http://demoscope.ru/weekly/2002/057/analit04.php; access 24-10-2013

56 Results of the 2009 National population census of the Republic of Kazakhstan. Analytical Report. Agency on Statistics of the Republic of Kazakhstan. pp. 25Astana 2011.; http://www.eng.stat.kz/publishing/DocLib/2011/%D0%90%D0%9E%20%D0%BD%D0%B0%20%D0%B0%D0%BD%D0%B3%D0%BB%D0%B8%D0%B9%D1%81%D0%BA%D0%BE%D0%BC.pdf; access 21-20-2013; see also http://www.eng.stat.kz/publishing/DocLib/Region_%D0%B0%D0%BD%D0%B3%D0%BB_09.pdf; access 25-10-2013

57 Website of The National Agency of Statistics of the Republic of Kazakhstan; http://www.eng.stat.kz/digital/index{Environment}Environmental%20protection/Pages/default.aspx;accessdate15-09-2013

cities concentration of pollutants in the air is several times above the standard. One reason is the sharp decline in public transport and the simultaneous growth in private car ownership. State policy is aiming at reducing the emissions step by step.[58]

There are also complex environmental problems in many parts of the country associated with an inadequate drainage system, resulting in pollution of groundwater sources of drinking water, which impairs quality of life. There is an urgent need for repairs and improvements in the water provision sector and sewage system. In all localities the water supply systems have been operating for more than 30 years without substantial renovation.

Safety/Crime

The number of registered crimes in Kazakhstan diminished from 152,168 in 2001 to 121,667 in 2009. In the whole country, the data show a drop in the crime level.

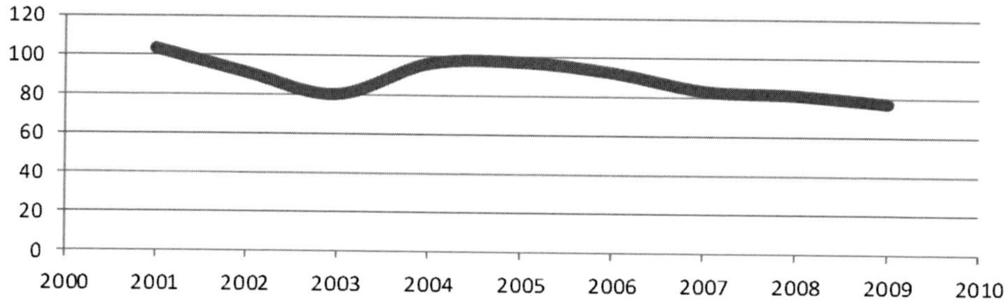

Figure 8: Level of crime in Kazakhstan[59]
Note: basic year 2001

According to the data of the Committee on Legal Statistics and Special Accounting of the General Prosecutor's Office of the Republic of Kazakhstan, the regional distribution of crimes in 2011 was as follows: Almaty (4,887 cases, ranking first in the country, East-Kazakhstan (4,113), Karaganda (3,375), South-Kazakhstan

[58] For the environmental programs see *cng.kz/wp-content/uploads/.../ecoprogramm.doc*?; Ohrana okruzhajushej sredy i ustojchivoe razvitie Kazahstana/Ecology and sustainable development of Kazakhstan. – Astana 2010. pp. 117-147; http://www.stat.kz/publishing/2010/%D0%9E%D1%85%D1%80%D0%B0%D0%BD%D0%B0_%D0%BE%D0%BA%D1%80%D1%83_%D0%B8%D0%BD%D1%82.pdf; access 21-20-2013; http://www.meta.kz/60555-gazovaja-ataka.html; access date 21-10-2013)

[59] Website of The National Agency of Statistics of the Republic of Kazakhstan 18.09.2013 http://www.stat.kz/digital/pravo/Pages/default.aspx; access 15-09-2013

(3,492), Almaty region (2,094), Kostanai (1,980), Pavlodar (1,914) and Akmola (1,741).

Corruption

The annual Corruption Perceptions Index (CPI) was, for the first time, outlined in 1995. According to the Transparency International data, in 2010 Kazakhstan took the 104th place of world ranking with 2.9 points,[60] which means that the perception of corruption in Kazakhstan is quite high. Throughout the period 1999-2010 corruption increased from 2.3 to 2.9 points.

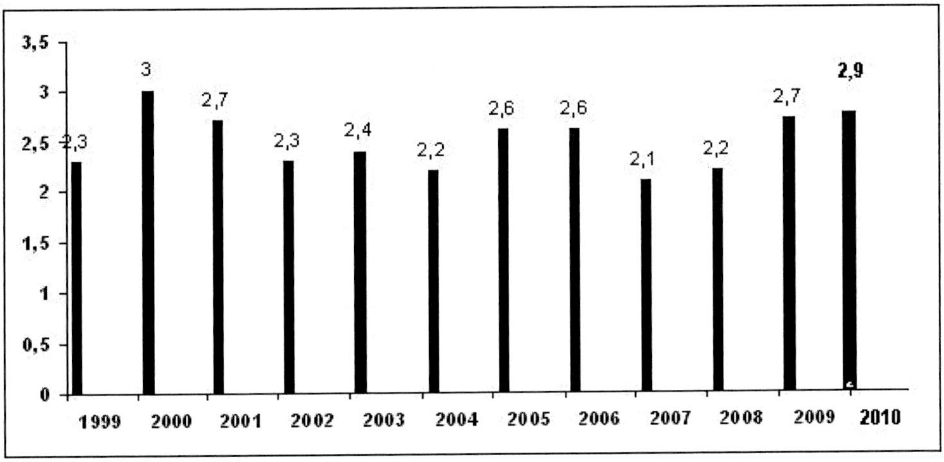

Figure 9: Corruption perception index for Kazakhstan, 1999-2010
Note: The scale ranges from 10 – corruption almost absent – to 0 – the highest level of corruption.

Life Satisfaction

According to a non-representative study with the title "The level of social conflict: the potential risks and threats" from 2010,[61] the material conditions of the

60 The scale ranges from 10 – corruption almost absent – to 0 – the highest level of corruption.

61 Shaukenova, Z.K./Morozov, A.A./Buluktaev, Ju.O. (2010): Uroven' social'noj konfliktnosti: potencial'nye riski I ugrozy (na osnove sociologičeskogo issledovanija). Almaty: KISI pri Prezidente RK. Online: http://kisi.kz/img/docs/5048.pdf; access 21-20-2013. The question concerned the satisfaction with the financial situation of their families.

Kazakhstani population may be called satisfactory. More than half of the respondents (61.7%) rated their financial situation as average, a quarter as good (24.0%) and 2.7% as excellent. Only one tenth (11.5% was dissatisfied with their level of wealth, and 1% describes their own living conditions as very poor. According to a study on social and political stratification of 2011, 71.6% of respondents refer to themselves as middle class, 2.1% well-off, 26.3% low-income class. The following social factors for poverty were proposed in the study of 2010:

1. The gap in living standards between urban and rural areas. Among the respondents which have rated the welfare of their families as poor and very poor, urban residents amount to 10.4%, but rural ones to 12.8%;
2. Regional differences;
3. The relationship between poverty and age: the percentage of poor people consistently increases with age groups: from 6.4% in the age group 18-29 years to 16.4% in the age group of 60 years and older;
4. Inverse dependence between education and poverty. Among the poor, 7.1% have higher education, 10.7% secondary special, 13.2% secondary and notably 29.5% incomplete secondary education.
5. A weakening of the "poverty – gender" bias, because many women have found their ways into well-paid jobs.

According to the same source, for the past year, material condition of families of the majority of respondents either did not change (41%), or changed for the better (38.4%). 20.5% of respondents noted negative changes. Positive changes correlate to higher-income households, negative changes to lower-income households. We find similar regional assessments as already mentioned above. But it seems to be clear that urban-rural differences and gender play a considerable role concerning poverty and life satisfaction. We shall see whether this also holds true for our own quantitative and qualitative results.

2.2. Kyrgyz Republic

Galina GORBORUKOVA[62]

Regional profile[63]

Capital City: Bishkek (formerly Frunze), 825,000 inhabitants. Other important cities: Osh, Jalalabad, Cholpon Ata, Karakol.

Government Type: Republic; Authoritarian presidential regime; bicameral parliament with 60 deputies in upper (legislative) chamber, 45 in lower (representative) chamber. Administrative divisions: 7 oblasts: Batken oblast (Batken), Chui oblast (Bishkek), Jalalabad oblast (Jalalabad), Naryn oblast (Naryn), Osh oblast (Osh), Talas oblast (Talas), Issyk-Kul oblast (Karakol). Annexed by Russia in 1864; independence from the Soviet Union: August, 31, 1991. Constitution: May, 5, 1993.

Geography: Kyrgyzstan is a mountainous country of 200,000 km^2. The Tien Shan mountain range covering approximately 95% of the surface. The country is adjacent to China in the East, Kazakhstan in the North, Uzbekistan in the West and Tajikistan in the South. The level of economic development is much lower than in Kazakhstan.

Population and ethnic composition: 5.5 million (2012): Kyrgyz 52.4%, Russian 18%, Uzbek 12.9%, Ukrainian 2.5%, German 2.4%, others 11.8%. On the whole more than 90 ethnic groups.

Main religions: Islam: 75%; Russian Orthodox: 20%; other: 5%.

Languages: Kyrgyz and Russian.

Natural resources: hydropower; gold and rare earth metals; locally exploitable coal, oil, and natural gas; other deposits of nepheline, mercury, bismuth, lead, and zinc. In general, Kyrgyzstan is a country poor in natural resources.

Economy: Currency: Som (KGS) 1 USD = 47 KGS; 1 Euro = 65 KGS (2014); Wages: 960 KGS monthly average salary by 2014; budget deficit: 23 billion Soms equivalent 7% of GDP (2009); GDP: 320,000 USD; (2009).

Agricultural products: Tobacco, cotton, potatoes, vegetables, grapes, fruits and berries; sheep, goats, cattle, wool.

Industries: Small machinery, textiles, food processing, cement, shoes, sawn logging, refrigerators, furniture, electric motors, gold, rare earth metals. In general,

[62] Revised by Eckhard Dittrich

[63] Nations Online, Kyrgyzstan

the industry is not very developed and has not recovered from the transitional changes.

Human Development Index: rank 121 (middle human development); Kazakhstan rank 69 (2012).

Corruption: rank 154; Kazakhstan: rank 133; Russia: 133 (Corruption Perception Index) (2012)

Figure 10: Political map of Kyrgyzstan[64]

Demographic aspects

At the end of 2010, the population of the Kyrgyz Republic was 5,477,600 people, 1,861,700 of which belonged to the urban population and 3,615,900 to the rural population. That is, the majority of the population has a rural background. Three main factors influence the population growth: birth rate, mortality, and migration.

Since the migration balance is negative due to out-migration, population growth results from a high birth rate. In 2009, the average growth rate was 1.3%. A higher growth rate than average was observed in South Kyrgyzstan (1.5-1.6). At the beginning of 2010 the age pyramid was as follows: 32.3% children and teenagers, 59.9% working age population, 8.2% beyond working age. Kyrgyzstan is a young society.

64 E photo Pix, Kyrgyzstan Political Map

65 Kyrgyzstan v sifrah. Statisticheskiy sbornik. Bishkek 2011. p. 46.

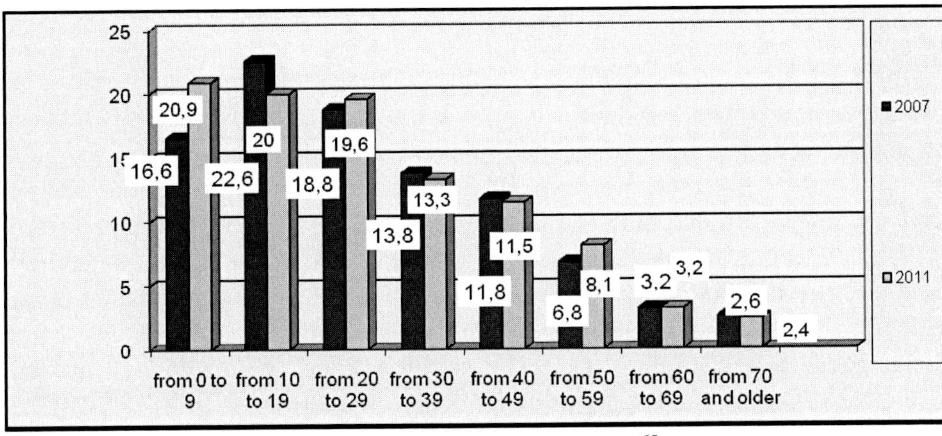

Figure 11: Age structure of Kyrgyzstan, 2007 and 2011 compared[65]
Note: percent

By the end of 2010 the migration outflow was 9.3%.[66] Population density by January, 1st of 2011 was 27.4 people per square kilometer. In 2011, males made up for 49.9%, females 50.6%[67] of the total population. The gender imbalance is attributed to the lower life expectancy of males.[68] During the 2000s there was a steady population growth because of an increasing number of women having reached childbearing age. These women represent the 1980s' and 1990s' baby boomers. Thus, women's fertility coefficient increased from 2.5 in 2005 to 2.9 in 2009. It is worth noticing that children born outside of marriage account for almost 1/3 of the total number of newborn children (31.0% in 2009).[69]

In 2009, the overall mortality coefficient was 6.7 per thousand people. The highest death ratio occurred in Narin, Chuy, and Issyk-Kul oblasts since they have a majority of old people. As in many countries of Central Asia, the major cause of death is blood circulation deceases which account for 49.0% of the total death rate. Traumas, poisoning, and influence of external reasons are the second major cause of death (9.7% of all deaths in 2009). Suicides and intentional killings are also included in this number.[70]

66 Kyrgyzstan v sifrah. Statisticheskiy sbornik. Bishkek 2011. p. 44.
67 Kyrgyzstan v sifrah. Statisticheskiy sbornik. Bishkek 2011. p. 45.
68 Kyrgyzstan v sifrah. Statisticheskiy sbornik. Bishkek 2011. p. 48.
69 Uroving jizni naseleniya Kyrgyzskopy respubliki 2005-2009. Godovaya Publikasiya. p. 9.
70 Uroving jizni naseleniya Kyrgyzskopy respubliki 2005-2009. Godovaya Publikasiya. p. 10.

The Economy

"Kyrgyzstan is a poor, mountainous country with a dominant agricultural sector. Cotton, wool, and meat are the main agricultural products, although only tobacco and cotton are exported in any quantity. Industrial exports include gold, mercury, uranium, natural gas, and electricity. The economy depends heavily on gold exports – mainly from output at the Kumtor gold mine – and on remittances from Kyrgyzstani migrant workers primarily in Russia".[71] After transition, the country faced a severe drop in output but was also prompt in inaugurating market orientated reforms. Slight signs of recovery were to be seen from 1995 on. The country had some success in boosting economic growth and in reducing its financial deficit. Nevertheless, industrial output remained on a low level. In April 2010, the government of Kyrgyzstan was overthrown. Social tension grew very high, especially in the south of the country, and in cruel ethnic conflicts that affected Osh and Jalal-Abad especially. The ethnic conflict, along with theft, looting, and fires, destroyed parts of the industrial sector and caused a lot of casualties. These events undoubtedly influenced the general economic situation and the living standard. The absence of legal power, looting and closing of borders after these events aggravated business and economic development. "Shrinking trade and agricultural production, as well as political instability, caused GDP to contract 5% in 2010. The fiscal deficit widened to 11% of the GDP, reflecting significant increases in crises-related spending, including both rehabilitation of damaged infrastructure and bank recapitalization. The economy grew 5.7% in 2011, but slowed to around 1% in 2012, primarily because of decreased production from Kumtor; the budget deficit has been reduced to fewer than 8% of the GDP. Progress in reconstruction, fighting corruption, restructuring domestic industry, and attracting foreign aid and investment are key to future growth.[72] In many fields international aid helped and helps the country. Judging by data from the World Bank, humanitarian aid reached 1.1 million people including 255,000 children aged between 7 and 15 as well as 72,000 refuges. The conflicts also resulted in large scale damage to dwelling places. Victims lost almost all of their belongings including school books, school uniforms, supplements and computers. The events caused a large migration of people from the South to the North of the country since it was a safer place to stay. However, it led to a large financial drain on families that had to flee.[73]

Today, the economic, political, and social situation is still precarious.

---

[71] Index mundi,_country comparisons, Kazakhstan vs. Kyrgyzstan; see also Nation Master op cit.

[72] Index mundi, op cit, infrastructure for peace.

[73] Kyrgyzskaya respublica. Vtoroy otchyot o progresse v dostijenie seley razvitiya tisyachiletiya.

Living Standard: GDP, Income, (Un)Employment

Transition to a market economy caused a devastating economic decline in the 90's, from which the economy and the country as a whole are only recovering gradually – if so at all. The GDP remains precarious. Poverty is very high although data from various sources are sometimes contradictory. They vary between 31 and 41% of the population. Based on UNDP data and UNICEF reports 22% of the population is living below USD 2.00 a day.[74] "Income inequality in the country has risen, with an increase in the Gini coefficient from .31 in 1990 to .47 in 1999. Youth unemployment remains high at 15% and total unemployment is about 10%. ... The country is ranked 116th out of 177 countries on the Human Development Index, which is toward the bottom for the region and situated between Tajikistan and Uzbekistan in the sub-region".[75] In 2009, the GDP in current market prices was 201.1 billion KGS, while in 2005 it was 100.9 billion KGS (39.2 and 20.2 thousand KGS per capita[76] respectively). Within the five years period 2005-2009, its real growth reached 24.5%, with an average 4.5% annual growth, 20.3% per capita growth or 3.8% total growth on average annually. The economic growth seems to be unstable as is the inflation rate: 1999: 37%, 2005: 5.2%, 2010: 4.8%, and 2011 16.6% (Kazakhstan 2011: 8.4%). Which structural changes have occurred during the period from 2005 to 2009 affecting the GDP? The share of services increased by 5.9% against the total share of 46.6%. In addition, during the five years the share of educational services (3.8%-4.5%) and public health services (2.0-2.6%) remained stable. The major growth was observed in the transportation and communication sectors. The production of consumer goods decreased by 6.1% making up 42.2% of the GDP. The GDP of agriculture, 18.8% in 2009, decreased from the level of 2005 by 9.7%. The share of industry decreased from 17.3% in 2005 to 16.9% in 2009.[77]

According to the Integrated Inspection of Households "Employment and Unemployment"[78] the number of economically active people (above 15 years) reached 2,420.1 thousand people, out of which 2,216.4 thousand were employed and 203.7 thousand unemployed. Among the economically active population 35% (855.4 thousand people) were urban, 65% (1,564.6 thousand people) were rural in 2009.

---

74 UNICEF, country profile, Education in Kyrgyzstan, acc. 09.09.2013, 11.40 h, p. 1

75 UNICEF, country profile, education in Kyrgyzstan, access 09.09.2013, p. 1.

76 UNICEF, country profile, education in Kyrgyzstan, acc. 09.09. 2013, 11.29 h, p. 1; Dec. 2009: 884 USD per capita, Dec. 2005: 488 USD per capita

77 Socialnye tendensii KR 2005-2009. Vypusk 6. Bishkek. 2010. p. 79.

78 Socialnye tendensii KR 2005-2009. Vypusk 6. Bishkek. 2010. p. 49.

The economically active population at the age of 15 and older was 64%. Males are more active in the labor market than females (three quarters of all males of the economically active population, compared to half of all females). In urban areas, the level of the economically active population is lower than in rural areas. This results from a large number of university and high school students. The age group of 40-44 (88%) makes up the biggest share of the economically active population.[79]

From 2005 to 2009 the situation in the labor market was unstable. It was determined by changes in the socio-economic spheres. In 2009 the level of people being employed at the age of 15 and older was 59%. In urban areas, the level of economic activity was lower than it was in rural areas (55% and 61% respectively). This is due to the fact that in rural areas, businesses usually are done by all family members of working age.

As it was shown by the results of the Integrated Inspection of Households "Employment and Unemployment",[80] the average monthly income of the Kyrgyz population in 2009 was 2,311.6 KGS per capita. Incomes of the population involve salaries and social transfers (such as pensions, scholarships, social payments, insurance payments etc.), incomes from businesses, property incomes (dividends, securities and rent payments), and incomes form private farms and livestock.

The structure of urban population's income differs from that of the rural population. Urban residents' income share of the overall amount of income was 78.1%, whereas the share of rural residents was 61.0%. The relative weight of income by sale of agricultural goods produced on individual farms in rural areas was 23.4%, in urban areas it reached only 2.1%. The share of social transfers does not differ much between urban and rural residents making up for 10.1 and 9.8% respectively.

The average income in the city of Bishkek is higher than the country average reaching 2,889.4 KGS. In the Chuy region, the rural area where our research was conducted, it amounts to 2,582.7 KGS. Comparing the data from other districts: Osh 2,371.2 KGS, Batken and Djalalabad regions' 2,142.7 and 2,115.7 KGS respectively, Issyk-Kul region 1,761.1 KGS, Naryn 1,747.6 KGS, Talas 1,762.9 KGS. The incomes of people above the poverty line are twice as high as that of poor people. This fact is present in both rural and urban regions. The poor urban population survives mainly due to incomes from employment (share of 75.1%). In rural regions, the poor population survives due to incomes from employment (60.3%) and agricultural activities (25.9%).[81]

---

79 Socialnye tendensii KR 2005-2009. Vypusk 6. Bishkek. 2010. P. 49. i.e. 52 USD (Dec., 2009 rate).

80 Uroving jizni naseleniya Kyrgyzskopy respubliki 2005-2009. Godovaya Publikasiya. p. 14.

81 Uroving jizni naseleniya Kyrgyzskopy respubliki 2005-2009. Godovaya Publikasiya. p. 14.

According to the Population and Housing Census of 2009, there are about 1,145,000 individual farms throughout the country; 41% belong to urban areas and 59% belong to rural areas. The majority of the total population or 5,329,000 people (99%) live in privatized houses, and less than 1% lives in specialized settings for collective living such as homes for disabled and old people, child care houses, orphanages, and other institutions.

The average size of households is 4.6 people. In urban settlements it is 3.8 people, and in rural area 5.2 people. Most common are households consisting of four or five people. In villages, households of more than four people constitute 77%. This is due to significant differences in daily routines of urban and rural residents. In urban areas, the birth rate is significantly lower, and cohabitation with relatives and parents is less frequent, whereas single households are common (almost 100,000 households).[82]

The number of unemployed, according to the labor force survey conducted in 2009,[83] reached 203.7 thousand people, male's share being 51% and females share 49%. The unemployment rate was 8.4% (women (9.8%); men 7.4%). Urban unemployment reached 10.4%, rural unemployment 7.3%. Unemployment is prevalent and disproportionately high among younger people. The average age of unemployed was 25 and that of the employed people 35 years, with hardly any difference in urban and rural regions. The highest unemployment rate was in the age group of 15-24 (16.8%). Not only is it difficult to enter the labor market; in comparison to older people, young people are more likely to change their jobs, having unstable employments. One-fifths of the unemployed people, men and women, have higher education or vocational training. The unemployment rate among people with higher education was, however, lower than average (4.4%). The unemployment rate among the people with only secondary education was higher than average.

In 2009, on the basis of the national indicators for poverty,[84] the National Bank counted almost one-third (31.7%) of the total population living in poverty: 1.7 million people out of 5.5 million. Like in other mostly agricultural countries, the poverty rate in rural areas is higher than in the urban areas (37.1% against 22%).

---

82 Socialnye tendensii KR 2005-2009. Vypusk 6. Bishkek. 2010. p. 32-33.

83 Unemployment in Kyrgyzstan, http://works.doklad.ru/view/MHUaci6D6Rg.html

84 The level of 'absolute poverty' and 'abject poverty' are the terms used by National Statistical Committee. They mean the upper and the lower level of poverty respectively.

Migration

International migration

Figure 12: International net migration in Kyrgyzstan, 1960-2005[85]

Up to 1959, the official statistics do not disclose figures on migration. A decreasing in-migration occurred until the early 1970s where in- and out-migration reached a balance. Due to the collapse of the SU, independence brought about a steep decrease between 1990 and 1994. But since 1995 the situation has become balanced again. Since the turn of the century the situation has meanwhile changed again in a dramatic way. Nowadays, a negative balance characterizes migration, due to increased labor migration. The following numbers illustrate the situation: in 2007 4,000 people arrived, but 54,600 people left. In 2009, the migratory outflow amounted to 29,600 people. In 2010, the number of those who arrived in the Kyrgyz Republic was 3,903 people against 54,531 who left. In 2012, the net migration rate (migrants per 1000 of the population) was -8.1, while in Kazakhstan it was + 0.43. Most of the migrants leave for Russia, CIS, notably Kazakhstan and other countries. According to an official statement of the Kyrgyz government, in 2009, 52% of the population work outside of the country. The main reason is the disastrous economic situation. Many of the migrants work illegally. Half of them are female migrants. In 2008, concerning remittances, Kyrgyzstan ranked 4th in

[85] National Statistical Committee, Bishkek. p. 24.

the world. These remittances made up for 27% of the GDP, which is USD 322 Mio. In other words, the state budget, as well as many private households relies on income earned abroad. In her study on migration, based on data of the International Organization for Migration (IOM), Erica Marat estimated, that remittances and shadow economy accounted for 50-60% of the Kyrgyz GDP. "Some 71% of Kyrgyz migrants to Kazakhstan and Russia are seasonal, leaving each spring and returning home during winter months. . . .over 16% of the households in Kyrgyzstan received remittances in 2006. The average annual remittance income was USD 1,331 per household; while average domestic earnings were about $ 400 per month . . . most remittances are spent on consumer goods. According to IOM data, only 10% of remittances are spent on healthcare and education. The rest goes to everyday needs" (Marat 2009:15f.). Marat believes that the remittances have a low internal developmental impact, that they help to boost real estate prices in the capital cities and that they are "often squandered on traditional celebrations such as weddings, birthdays, funerals and other commemorations" (ibid: 20).

Internal migration

The poor economic situation especially in the countryside has spurred the internal migration. From 2006 to 2010, intensive migration from rural areas to urban settlements could be observed. Chui region which is adjacent to the capital Bishkek with its employment opportunities is particularly affected. From the World Bank's report: "internal migration plays an important role in households' well-being. As the data shows, 26% of the household heads migrated from the other regions of the country. It has been noted already that poverty reallocation according to the "city-village" principle demonstrates more favorable economic perspectives in cities. This is one of the possible reasons of one-end migration from villages to cities. According to the data of statistical research, in Bishkek and Chui region there is the highest relative weight of household heads born in other regions (71% and 60% respectively); in Jalal-Abad and Batken regions the relative weight of household heads born in different regions is the lowest (1% and 4% respectively). As the data shows, in line with the growth in consumption rate per capita, the number of migrating household heads from rural to urban places (to Bishkek particularly) also increases. This, however, does not indicate that internal migration from villages to towns is tied to a lower poverty level in the cities. Nevertheless, everything being equal, and assuming that the particular connection between consumption per capita and migration level is directed towards poor rural citizens, migration can be observed as one of the strategies of the poor to overcome obstacles".[86] The consequences of this development in respect of family structures and relations are hardly known by now.

With the breakdown of the SU, the social systems in all Central Asian countries ran into a deep crisis. Since then, all countries have tried to reform them. Nevertheless, all countries involved, Kazakhstan and Kyrgyzstan included, still live on the social policy and infrastructural heritage of the Soviet time. "According to official statistics literacy rates in the Kyrgyz Soviet Socialist Republic increased from 3.5% in 1924 to 57.1% in 1935, and by the end of the 1980s, were close to 100% (…). It is fair to say, therefore, that higher education in Kyrgyzstan is a Soviet creation as are the provision of universal primary education and the virtual elimination of illiteracy by the post war era" (Reeves 2005:10). The same holds true for primary health care and the whole health system. Both countries inherited a tight net of educational institutions and health organizations, nowadays being" inefficient and underfinanced"(Gilster and Hättich 2007:511). "The education system, together with the successful provision of primary health care, is commonly identified in Kyrgyzstani political discourse as having been critical in propelling Kyrgyzstan from a 'backward' nomadic country into a 'civilized', modern Soviet republic (Reeves 2005:10). Before independence both systems were financed from Moscow so that afterwards, new financial as well as market economy orientated organizational and curricular models had to be developed. Today, salaries are low, so that the fields lack incentives for engagement. All countries are young countries, which imply that the educational subsystem receives a lot of attention, and that all societies have a large pool of potential high manpower if it is developed in a way that it can compete within the globalizing economy. A last remark concerning data; official data are sometimes unreliable, so that assessments are difficult and sometimes only plausible evaluations can be made.

Social Security

Kyrgyzstan has a state based pension system. In 2012, it meant 1,000 KGS (USD 21) per month. The equivalent in Kazakhstan meant 8,000 KGT, which is 54 USD. In both countries men are eligible at 63, women at 58. With a life expectancy on average in 2010 of 65 in Kyrgyzstan and 64 in Kazakhstan, it is obvious, that the

86 Profile and dynamics of poverty and inequality 2009. Department of poverty reduction and management of the economy, European and Central Asian region. The World Bank document, 3 October, 2011. p. 36; see also Schuler (2009).

vast majority of the populations does not merit from state pensions. Additionally, the pensions have to be called at best rudimentary.

In 2009, the number of social security recipients was 433,900 people. The recipients of monthly aid designated to those in need comprised 125, 500 families or 370,800 people in need, such as the disabled, who do not receive pensions but are defined as people in need of additional aid. They make up 63,100 people. The number on public relief grew by 14% between 2005 and 2010. The poor economic situation of many people in the country is closely related to health problems: early mortality, high maternal and high child mortality rate etc.

Health and Health Care

Independent Kyrgyzstan inherited its health system from the former SU and has ever since tried to reform it. "In the post-Soviet era, Kyrgyzstan's health system has suffered increasing shortages of health professionals and medicine. Kyrgyzstan must import nearly all its pharmaceuticals. The increasing role of private health services has supplemented the deteriorating state-supported system. In the early 2000s, public expenditure on health care decreased as a percentage of total expenditure, and the ratio of the population to number of doctors increased substantially, from 296 per 10,000 inhabitants in 1996 to 355 in 2001. A national primary-care health system, the Manas Program, was adopted in 1996 to restructure the Soviet system that Kyrgyzstan had inherited. The number of people participating in this program has expanded gradually, and province-level family medicine training centers retrain medical personnel. A mandatory medical insurance fund was established in 1997. Largely because of drug shortages, in the late 1990s and early 2000s the incidence of infectious diseases, especially tuberculosis has increased. The major causes of death are cardiovascular and respiratory conditions....The maternal mortality rate rose by more than 15% to 62 deaths per 100,000 births from 2008 to 2009. According to non-governmental studies, things are worse than the official data indicate".[87] In 2009, a restructuring of the medical sector was begun. 72 family medical centers (FMC) were introduced. FMC included 595 groups of family doctors (GFD) and 20 GFDs as independent judicial persons. 182 medical institutions (182 hospitals) were running (148 of which belonged to the health ministry. Rural hospitals were incorporated into the larger group of territorial hospitals as structural branches and were transformed into FMCs. Family doctors were united into bigger groups for the sake of a more

[87] Wikipedia, health in Kyrgyzstan, acc. 09.09. 2013.

rational use of financial resources. On the bases of territorial hospitals and centers of family medical care, around 26 centers of general medical practice were established. Nevertheless, the number of medical staff decreased. In 2009 the number of doctors per 10,000 inhabitants was finally 24. A similar decrease is observed among the average medical staff (2009: 59). One reason for the decline is low salaries. The budget for public health care in the government budget was 10-12%, the expenses for public health care per capita 1,168 KGS in 2009. In 2011, the government initiated an improvement of the system by ordering pay increases for medical workers and better working conditions. Thus, it reacted to a massive shortage of doctors and medical staff especially in rural areas. The responsible Health Minister explained that 1,500 medical workers had left their profession only in the last year, mostly working in other industries, only 200 moving abroad. Many NGOs work in the field for its betterment.[88] It seems clear that the reform has to go on, if a sustainable betterment of the system and a better health status of the population is the aim (Ibraimova 2011). Gilster/Hättich (2007:521) sum up the situation by declaring, that in the past, the decline of life expectancy of the 1990s has been stopped, what in their eyes is a first success. But there are many challenges ahead.

The latest reform was also fuelled by the low health status of children in the country. By the end of 2009, there were about 21,000 children of 18 or younger with disabilities, comprising almost 17% of all disabled people. In comparison to 2005, the number of children with disabilities increased by 14.5%, although there was a decline in recent years. This can be explained by improvements of diagnostics. Health problems of mothers, like anemia and deficits in iodine, exposure to diseases during pregnancy (intrauterine infections, flu) contaminated environment, result in births of unhealthy or prematurely born children who either die or develop disabilities. "Government statistics for 2002 show that 52 infants in 1,000 die before, during, or just after birth and the maternal mortality rate for the same year was 110 per 100,000 women.…Along with the high death rates is the fact that six out of 10 births in rural Kyrgyzstan result in complications and illnesses that can negatively affect the mother and child, often permanently. The poverty of the rural population, the lack of medicine and gynecological equipment and poorly trained medical personnel are the main reasons for birth being such a risk for mother and child in Kyrgyzstan,"…. "A general lack of contraceptives and poor knowledge of how to use them means birth rates remain high, further endangering women with each subsequent birth". In 2009, child mortality was down:

[88] Central Asia online.

nevertheless, 32 children died within the first year, compared to Russia 11, Brazil 17, Poland 6 and Kazakhstan 26. In 2009, the average amount of monthly public relief per child was 961.6 KGS. However, the size of public relief is only 34% from the minimal consumer budget per child.[89] Physician density and their low pay play an additional role for low health standards in the country. In 2007, the density was 2.301 per 1,000 of the population (Kazakhstan 3.877) and the hospital bed density was 5.06 (Kazakhstan 7.6).

Education

Education in the country is compulsory for nine years, between ages 7 and 15. Following four years of primary and five years of lower secondary school, the system offers two years of upper secondary school, specialized secondary school, or vocational/technical school. ... The majority of primary and secondary schools teach in Kyrgyz, but the language of instruction in the higher institutions is Russian. Budget cuts that have reduced teacher salaries and equipment availability are reflected disproportionally in reduced numbers of female students".[90] In 2005 some 5.5 percent of the GDP was spent on education while in 2000 it was only 3.9%. This doesn't look too bad. But as considerable sums come from non-budget sources (tutoring, parents fees, NGOs), this has helped to increase inequality because "poor children can't afford to pay the informal fees, which are often inflated to compensate for teachers' low salaries" (ibid.). With his financing of the educational system, Kyrgyzstan is below average in the region.[91]

Of course, the country has tried to reform the system. New types of educational institutions with different types of ownership have recently emerged. At the beginning of the 2009/2010 academic year, there were 2.2 thousand day schools of general education throughout the republic. But the number of children at secondary schools has decreased from the 1990s onward. This is largely due to a lower birth rate, migration, and poverty that don't allow some children to attend schools at all. According to World Bank data not all children will be able to obtain elementary school education or reading skills.[92] The primary school net enrolment ratio is at 87%, the enrolment in secondary schools is 80%, and pre-school

89 IRIN, Humanitarian news and analysis, a service of the UN office for the Coordination of Humanitarian Affairs, 06. Sept., 2013; Index mundi; Uroving jizni naseleniya Kyrgyzskopy respubliki 2005-2009. Godovaya Publikasiya. p. 39-40.

90 UNICEF 2009, p. 4

91 From Wikipedia, education in Kyrgyzstan; and Gilster, Hättich 2007, p. 527.

92 Socialnye tendensii KR 2005-2009. Vypusk 6. Bishkek. 2010. p. 38-48.

enrolment is only 10%. "According to UNICEF, enrolment figures in the Kyrgyz republic have actually consistently decreased during the past five years, although figures vary. Reasons for the decline could be rising formal and informal costs of schooling, poor educational quality and reduced private returns of school completion. Additionally, the disintegration of school infrastructures and poor conditions in schools may act as a deterrent. The government created new obstacles to educational access in 2007. The government decreed that a school uniform is compulsory for all primary school students beginning in the 2008-2009 school year. The uniforms must be purchased by the parents. This contradicts the government's policy of free education and creates a barrier of access to education for all children, especially the poorest children who cannot afford the uniform".[93] Equity in school attendance is largely influenced by the rural-urban divide but also wealth.

Understaffed, badly paid teachers, under-resourced materials and infrastructure, decreasing investments also lead to bad academic results and quality of education. In the PISA assessment of 2006, Kyrgyzstan performed worst from all participating CEE/CIS countries in all fields: reading ability, mathematics, science.

In the 2009-2010 academic years, private institutions comprised 42% of the professional training institutions (PTI) with a students' share of 11%. In 2009, 3,000 students attended seven combined branches of foreign PTIs.

In recent years, as a result of attempts to develop the infrastructure, new and additional pre-school institutions with innovative programs have been established. This resulted from a severe drop in pre-school education since independence. Between 1990 and 1999 the reduction meant 71,9%. There is a severe shortage of pre-schools in the republic. The number of children attending public pre-schools amounted to 76,000 children in 2009. The number of children under the age of 7 attending preschools remained small with only 10% (cf. Gilster and Hättich 2007:522). The number of children attending pre-schools is five times higher in urban areas than in rural areas. In recent years, demand on pre-school institutions has increased, which eventually affects the quality of education. Due to the overcrowded pre-schools, a high sickness rate among pre-school children is observed. As lack of early education has a negative impact on advancement in primary education, the deteriorated situation in this field affects education as a whole (ibid.).

As in health, the salaries in the educational field are low. They are not only low, but the social image is bad too. Teachers "are looked at as incompetent and corrupt..." (ibid: 528). This is the case in all Central Asian countries. But while

---

93 UNICEF 2009, Education in Kyrgyzstan, Country profile, access 09.09.2013, p. 2.

in Kazakhstan e.g. the income is 25% below the average earning, in Kyrgyzstan it is 42% which makes it "the least value out of all Central Asian States".[94] This has resulted in a brain drain worsening the overall gloomy situation and its further development.

Civil, Political and Religious Aspects

"Kyrgyzstan's democratic credentials were regarded as relatively strong in the immediate post-Soviet era, but this reputation was lost when corruption and nepotism took hold during President Akayev's years in office. Parliamentary and presidential elections were flawed, opposition figures faced harassment and imprisonment, and opposition newspapers were closed... His successor after the 2005 revolt, Kurmanbek Bakiyev, failed to restore full confidence in state institutions at home or abroad. His time in office was marred by political instability and an almost constant struggle with parliament over the constitutional balance of power. Elections held under Mr. Bakiyev were criticized as being undemocratic, and human rights groups expressed concern over the curtailing of civil liberties and attacks on the media. Civil tensions again came to a head in April 2010, when Mr. Bakiyev himself was toppled and an interim government was set up under the leadership of former Foreign Minister Roza Otunbayeva".[95] She served as transitional president until Almazbek Atambaev was inaugurated in December 2011. But major problems have not changed: the path to democratization – freedom of press included –, endemic corruption, nationalism, and terrorism. Instability has become an everyday phenomenon with an enduring character.[96]

Nevertheless, many observers suppose Kyrgyzstan to be the most democratic of the Central Asian countries, all of which represent authoritarian presidential regimes. By January 1st 2011, 71 political parties were registered,[97] most of which are located in big cities – Bishkek, Osh, and Chuy regions. The number of non-government organizations grows from year to year. Throughout the republic 48 independent radio and TV companies were registered at the beginning of 2010. Also, 2,200 religious units and organizations were registered by January 1st, 2010. The mobile phone services made up more than 80% of the sector of electronic communications services. Private enterprises occupy more than half of communications users.

---

94 UNICEF 2009, p. 3.

95 BBC News, Kyrgyzstan profile.

96 Index mundi, country comparisons Kazakhstan vs. Kyrgyzstan.

97 Kyrgyzstan v sifrah. Statisticheskiy sbornik. Bishkek 2011. p. 46

All this sounds quite democratic, but there are also other indices that change the formal picture into one of a struggle about democracy and freedom of press. Reporters without borders in its press freedom index ranks Kyrgyzstan best among all Central Asian States: position 108 out of 179. But despite this, also under the new presidency the political tensions remain, polarization and disorders still undermine media freedom. There are frequent attacks on journalists, which are not always thoroughly investigated into by the police. "Nationalism is a hot issue and several of the dozen journalists physically attacked in recent times have been ethnic Russian Kyrgyz citizens".[98]

The overall instability in the country is so high, that hardly anybody, any social unit, including family households, is not influenced by it.

Environmental Quality

Air and water pollution factors

Water pollution is far spread in Kyrgyzstan especially in the countryside. Many households get their drinking as well as their irrigation water directly from contaminated wells and streams. "As a result, water-borne diseases are prevalent".[99] In some parts of the country increasing soil salinity from faulty irrigation practices is also reported. The emission of contaminating substances into the air is increasing. In 2009 it reached 118,100 tons. Such growth is caused by significant increase of emission of gas-like contaminating substances, related to the oil-field development in the Jalal-Abad region.

Safety: crime, corruption

We don't want to go into the details about crime statistics here; we only want to mention a specialty of a state near to failure: lack of providing basic trust in peaceful social relations among citizens. Kyrgyzstan, nowadays, is a weak state with de facto low enforcement responsibilities for its citizens. State's weakness fuels an overall feeling of insecurity among the population. State weakness, organized crime and corruption are linked with each other, the state administration included, as Erica Marat could convincingly show (Marat 2006).[100] This situation has led to an overall uncertainty among the population and a loss of systemic trust,

[98] www.reporters without borders.press freedom index 2011-2012.1043html, acc. 12.09. 2013; for an overview see also Bensmann (2007:531 ff.).

[99] Index mundi op cit

[100] see also Nation Master; Infrastructure for peace.

which can be felt everywhere in the Kyrgyz society. Although a certain improvement has been reported in recent years, a deep anxiety about the future prevails as many people don't believe, that safety in the direct social relations among citizens can be guaranteed by the state. In 2012 Kyrgyzstan was ranked as the 154th in the Corruption Perceptions Index. Corruption penetrates all levels of society, including the presidency and caused the two presidents Askar Akayev and Kurmanbek Bakiyev to resign in 2005 and 2010, respectively. "Nepotism and corruption have also led to a great deal of pressure on journalists and civil society activists. After reporting the arrest in Italy of businessman Yevgeny Gurevich, close to the government and suspected of ties to the mafia, several media outlets have been suspended, some heavily fined, and their existence threatened. The *BBC* has been inaccessible inside the country since March, 15 and *Radio Free Europe / Radio Liberty (Aztatyk)* programs can no longer be heard" (reporters without borders, op cit).

3. The Quantitative Research

3.1. Questionnaire and Data Set

Heiko SCHRADER, Eckhard DITTRICH

The first part of the research project consists of a quantitative study. It was designed as an explorative one. We wanted to get an overview about household related questions in the two countries before we turned to in-depth interviews in order to have some insight into the understanding of our respondents about their life world (second part). To avoid low rates of return, the interviews were taken personally and the answers were recorded and written down by the interviewers. We worked with three research teams, two in Kazakhstan (one in the new capital Astana, another in the equally important old capital in Almaty and one in Kyrgyzstan (in the capital Bishkek). The entire sample consists of 451 questionnaires, 150 each from the two Kazakhstan teams and 151 from the Kyrgyzstan team. In every research region 100 questionnaires were taken from the urban area and 50 from the rural area (in Kyrgyzstan 51). The rural sample was taken from villages which were sufficiently far away from the urban centers so that daily commuting for the villagers was not possible. The teams were asked to select "normal" villages with regard to employment opportunities, infrastructure, and ethnic composition. In the different locations the researchers selected the respondents according to the snowball system.

The core unit of our analysis is the private household. Household research implies a certain basic methodological problem: who is supposed to be interviewed? While older studies ask the formal head of the household, because he or she is assumed to have the best knowledge and decides about household affairs, the empirical question is whether these assumptions are true. Newer studies reveal that the formal head of a household may not necessarily be the main breadwinner and that in many regions in the world women are responsible for the household budgets and best understand household procedures. Additionally, in some more traditional societies, the role of decision making is attributed to the oldest male, whether he is the main bread winner or not.

The more recent approaches in household research try to avoid these problems by arguing that it is not important who reports on the household, because we are interested in the research entity and not the respondent. The so-called "household-level approach". (Hess and al. 2000) therefore does not pre-define who shall provide answers. The respondent is looked upon as an "expert on his own behalf" (Meuser and Nagel 1991). The questionnaire we used in this first part of our research was developed in English by studying a number of other household surveys and discussing their cultural orientation. We took in those questions which seemed appropriate for our research design and for our cultural context, others we added ourselves. In the first workshop with all research teams the questionnaire was discussed and improved. Country-specific comments played a major role in these revisions. Then the questionnaire was translated into Russian.[101] This implied constant interchange because of semantic differences in the languages. Some vagueness and related problems became only clear on that level in the development of the research instrument. Therefore we additionally checked the appropriateness of the research instrument in 15 pilot interviews. New revisions of the instrument followed.

Doing interviews on that basis took around one hour (for the questionnaire see appendix). As already discussed in the theoretical part we decided to use the household concept instead of the family concept. Nevertheless, as will be seen, both concepts are often but not always overlapping.

The first and most complex part of the questionnaire concerns household composition, household activities and household revenues. The terms "household activities" and "household revenues" have to be explained. As we worked in both urban and rural regions household incomes can be both monetary and in kind. The latter usually don't show up in official statistics, be they viable or not. The term "activities" was intended not to predefine occupations but to give the opportunity for the respondents to address other household roles also and related activities such as "housework" and other work on the subsistence level outside formal and informal wage labor contracts such as for example pensioners looking after the garden, the cattle or their grandchildren. Already during the discussions among the research teams and after the pilot interviews it had become obvious that the question about activities might cause misunderstandings due to semantic problems. Indeed, many people reported on occupations only and neglected additional subsistence activities. Therefore the results from that part of our research are not very far-reaching and lead to a special emphasis in the qualitative interviews in order to find more appropriate answers concerning the question of pooled incomes.

Due to the fact that incomes in post-socialist countries are difficult to measure, since official and unofficial incomes differ from each other and people often have

[101] In those cases in which the respondents' knowledge of Russian was insufficient, the interviewers translated the questions into Kazakh, Kyrgyz or sometimes even Uighur and the answers back into Russian.

several (formal and informal) jobs we took a very rough measure of broad household income to assess which economic stratum the household belongs to. Here we should already emphasize that the incomes and price levels in Kazakhstan and Kyrgyzstan differ a great deal from each other.

Furthermore, as a matter of fact, scarcity of income in a number of post-socialist countries causes household members to migrate. As we knew from secondary material this implies rural – urban migration and international migration to other countries with better employment opportunities, first of all to Russia, Kazakhstan and Turkey. The consequence of this is that only an open household concept makes sense as it allows consideration for the household being embedded in a resource network. Although from our design it is possible to apply household-centered network analysis we did not go deeper in that direction and only formed a network-type household category later on (closed, giving, receiving household).

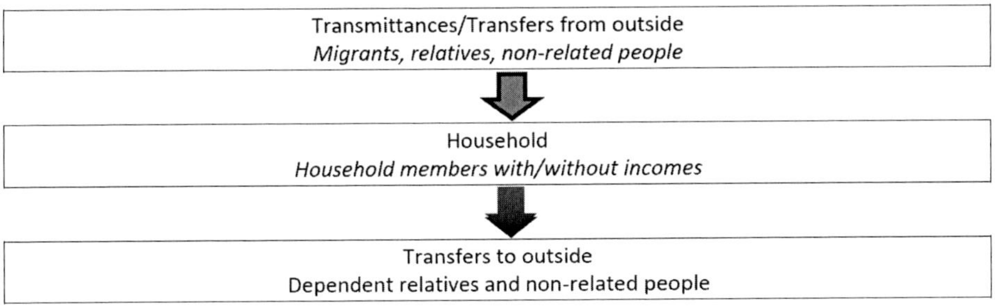

Figure 13: The private household as a resource network

The above figure already schematizes how the household is connected to family/kinship. One can easily imagine the types of transfers that may occur: transfers into the household from family members working abroad, transfers to dependents such as students living in a university city being funded by their parents, monetary transfers to dependent old age people living in the countryside, transfers in kind to urban dwellers etc. We strongly believe that any concept of households should allow for the integration of these relations. We call this concept an open-household concept.

The second part of the questionnaire concerns the living conditions including problems as perceived, assistances given and received, and vulnerabilities. Questions concerning self-assessments about the economic conditions, about the public infrastructure, about decision making and support structures, about the living standard and tensions occurring in the household belong to this part of the questionnaire.

The third part addresses questions about savings, credits, and investments. The key issue is of whether the household relies more on personal networks or also on market structures such as banks or insurance companies.

The fourth part considers values of the household as well as the assessment of the future. It aims at addressing certain values and responsibilities. We aimed at topics such as old age security, and unemployment. We asked the respondents about their responsibilities for these topics. The value issue is important in order to assess the general orientation of the respondents. The answers, we hoped, would fit into the ongoing discussion about value change which needs more clarifications in the view of the ongoing changes in post socialist societies (Inglehart 2003). The responsibility issue was supposed to address the question of public goods versus market regulations.

On the whole, the idea of the questionnaire is to define a number of variables from which different household types with different problems can be deduced. We aimed at a better understanding of households 20 years after the breakdown of the Soviet Union and their embeddedness into the new socio-economic conditions they face. Additionally, the questionnaire was aimed at giving us hints about those social problems of the households that were worthwhile exploring in more detail during in-depth interviews.

In general, the questionnaire worked well and most respondents answered all questions as intended, so that only very little information is missing. The research teams compiled these data in three regional matrices. Later on, these were integrated into one single matrix consisting of all 451 cases. Recoding led to 445 variables to be analyzed with SPSS 21. Most variables constitute categories of nominal and ordinal measure. The final matrix was again split up into the three regional matrices to be analyzed in more detail. We used univariate and bivariate methods.

In what follows, we start with certain aspects of the entire sample,[102] followed by the three reports of the research teams on their regions (Astana and Akmola region, Almaty and Almaty region, and Bishkek and Chui region). We conclude with a comparison of the three locations of the sample.

[102] For the full analysis of the 451 cases and the SPSS outputs see Schrader/Dittrich (2012).

3.2. Data Analysis of the Full Sample[103]

Heiko SCHRADER, Eckhard DITTRICH

Although the open household approach in general allows for a change of the respondent in the course of the interview, this hardly ever happened. This can be attributed to the fact that the interviews most often took place during daytime when not every member of the household was at home. And usually only one person, if others were also present, felt obliged to answer the questions. The age of the respondents covered a wide spectrum from 17 to 78 years (mean: 39.7, standard deviation: 12.4; in the Kyrgyzstan sample the mean is slightly higher than in the two other samples: 41.7 compared to 38.7). The majority of the respondents (76%) are between 25 and 55 years old. Due to the fact that we did not predefine any gender quotas as a consequence of the household level approach the sample is gender biased (81% female, 19% male). This may be a result of presence during the time of the interview or of competence to answer questions about the household. One could also argue that this represents the 'normal' division of labor in the households according to which women are 'responsible' for the closer household, budget affairs included. We shall come back to this later.

Household structure

The first part of the questions concerns the household structure. Our aim was to find out different household types. From the answers of the respondents we could identify the number of people living in the household, the household size, the generations living together, and the household age (taken as the mean of the age of all people living in the household). Also a certain type showed up easily: one that is normally considered to be more vulnerable, the single–headed household with dependent children. Asking for the activities pursued by all household members we could analyze another household variable: employment diversity.[104] This implies one indicator for the vulnerability of households.

The households in the sample are rather homogeneous with regard to ethnicity.

103 In the text we make descriptions of the variables. For bivariate analysis we made cross-tabulation, Chi-square tests, and a comparison of grouped means. We chose the significance level of 0.05. Highest significance means a Pearson Chi-square of 0.00. High significance is between 0.00 and 0.02. Significance is between 0.02 and 0.05.

104 Employment diversity was measured along the criteria of number of monetary income sources and types of employment (formal/informal/public/private). The households were then grouped into three categories (see table).

Only 7% of the households have mixed ethnic background.[105] Among the Kazakhstan sample these households amount to 10% (predominantly Kazakh-Russian intermarriages), in the Kyrgyzstan sample we find less than 1% mixed households.

The household characteristics are summarized in the following table.

Table 4: Household characteristics of the sample households

Household characteristics acc. to...		**Percent**	**Urban**	**Rural**
Size	One or two persons	18	22	12
	Three persons	22	23	21
	Four persons	28	23	26
	Five persons	17	24	19
	Six and more persons	11	21	15
Generations	One generation	13	17	6
	Two generations	69	67	77
	Three and more	15	16	17
	Single headed	9	10	8
	Single	4	5	1
Household Age	Up to 25	32	34	36
	26-35	39	37	43
	36-45	19	18	19
	46-55	5	5	5
	56-65	4	4	5
	More than 66	2	1	2
No of HH Members with Monetary Incomes	No	1	1	1
	One	17	18	15
	Two	43	43	44
	Three	21	22	19
	Four	11	10	13
	More than four	7	7	7
Employment Diversity	Not diverse	24	24	26
	Diverse	39	40	38
	Highly diverse	36	36	36
	No classification	1	1	1
Resource Network	Closed household	64	67	60
	Only giving	22	19	27
	Only receiving	9	10	7
	Giving and receiving	5	4	6

Note: N=451, urban N=300, rural N=151

[105] Due to semantic problems, the Russian questionnaire chose the term "nationality" which corresponds to the English term ethnicity.

The household age is taken to be the mean age of all household members. To some degree, it may help us to understand special problems the household may be confronted with. Young households for example usually have high expenses for consumer goods as well as for small children. Households consisting of two pensioners usually have the problem of low pensions and high expenses for healthcare. We calculated this variable from the data gained.

We also consider employment diversity, a variable that we introduced as a result of the activities referred to and with which we try to approach the problem of vulnerability of households. About 3 out of four households show employment diversity, more than one third are highly diverse concerning employment that hints at the labor market and income options and necessities.

With the open household concept we investigate both transfers into and from the household. The combination of the two variables transfer and employment diversity persuaded us to introduce a new variable: the household resource network type. 64% of all households are from the "closed household" type (67% urban, 60% rural) with no inflow or outflow. We believe this number to be too low; it needs validation in the qualitative research. More households are "giving" than "receiving" (22% compared to 9%), but interestingly the percent of rural households giving is higher (27%) than among urban ones (19%), which probably indicates that rural households subsidize urban ones with food. 5% of all households (4% urban, 6% rural) have transfers into both directions ("giving and receiving"). We guess that urban households seem to provide cash transfers to others living somewhere else, be this in a city or in the countryside.

Who is supported if transfers occur? This can be several people. Firstly rank sons and daughters (41%) followed by parents/parents-in-law (21%), brothers and sisters (12%), aunts/uncles (10%), husbands (8%), and grandparents (7%) – all kinfolk. This indicates the importance of kinship networks. Considering the outflow from the household, we gain the following picture: 24% of the households provide cash support to others outside of the household. The figures for cash and non-cash support are almost the same. 20% of the sample households provide both cash and non-cash support to others. These predominantly live in the countryside. Again, it is predominantly relatives who obtain support from the households investigated.

To assess the income category of the households we constructed different scales for Kyrgyzstan and Kazakhstan, because price and income levels in these two countries differ considerably from each other.[106] 50% of the households in

[106] The pre-definition of income groups was taken from national statistics.

Kyrgyzstan have a monthly income of less than 300 USD, in Kazakhstan of less than 780 USD.[107] For the cross-tabulation we built three income categories for each country and changed these into dollar units to make incomes comparable. It is evident that average incomes in Kyrgyzstan are half the average incomes in Kazakhstan.

Table 5: Income categories in Kazakhstan and Kyrgyzstan, USD

Kyrgyzstan	**Percent**	**Cumulative Percent**
Less than 160 USD	28.5	28.5
160-<300 USD	22.5	51.0
300 USD and above	49.0	100.0
Total	100.0	
Kazakhstan	**Percent**	**Cumulative Percent**
Less than 490 USD	23.3	23.3
490-<780 USD	25.0	48.3
780 USD and above	51.7	100.0
Total	100.0	

For Kazakhstan and Kyrgyzstan the income differences between urban and rural locations are striking. The grouped urban median for Kazakhstan is 2.64, the rural one 1.65. The same figures for Kyrgyzstan are 2.56 against 1.54.[108] In Kyrgyzstan there is a high dependency between four-person households and high incomes, while one and two-person households are underrepresented among them. Such a dependency is not found in the Kazakhstan cases.

In addition to monetary incomes, subsistence incomes were analyzed. For 65% of the urban households animal husbandry and animal products are inaccessible or unimportant for their livelihoods while for 30% these are important; but for almost 60% of the rural households animal husbandry is important while 30% do not consider it as important for their revenue. For urban households gardening or agriculture show almost the same figures as for animal husbandry; two thirds of the rural households consider gardening as important for their life. We also considered other natural resources such as drinking water, grazing land and other revenues. According to the different strengths of the category mentioned we build a relevance indicator concerning subsistence, scoring the importance of revenues for the sample households.

---

107 Exchange rate autumn 2011: Kazakhstan: 1 USD=150 KZT (Tenge), Kyrgyzstan: 1 USD= 49 Som. Examples: in Kazakhstan a middle income of 155,000 Tenge in our sample amounts to 1037 USD, in Kyrgyzstan a middle income of 28,000 Soms per month amounts to 575 USD.

108 Kurskal-Wallis Test and comparison of grouped medians.

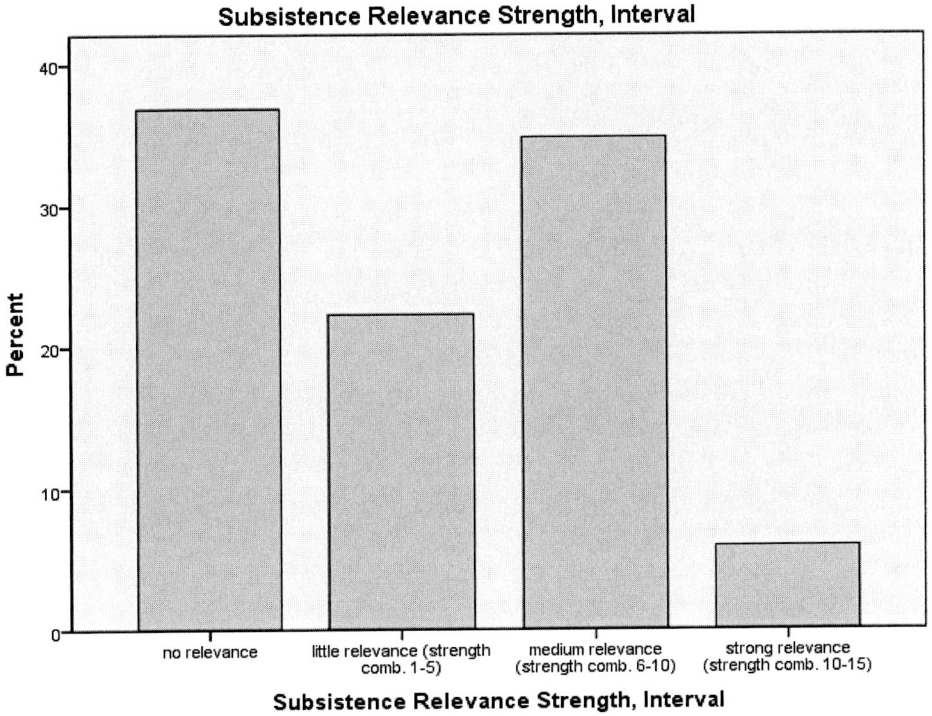

Figure 14: Relevance of subsistence

It is not astonishing that the relevance of subsistence is dependent on location. For urban household subsistence incomes are much less important than for rural ones. The rural grouped median is 1.89 compared to an urban one of 0.59 (average 1.07).[109]

The living conditions of households, main problems, the assistance provided and the vulnerability of households

The following figures give us some more information about the living conditions. Almost 50% of the households report to have a sufficient income and another 39% an almost sufficient income, but for 12% living conditions are difficult. While in Kyrgyzstan there is no significant dependence between income category and income sufficiency, significant dependence can be observed in the Kazakhstan

[109] Kurskal-Wallis Test and comparison of grouped medians.

sample. Interestingly there is no significant dependency between household size and sufficiency of incomes. However, highest dependency occurs with regard to insufficiency of incomes in the countryside, were only 1/3 of the sample households have a sufficient income. We conclude from this that poverty is more a rural than an urban issue. We have to remind the reader once again that rural households constitute only on-third of the sample.

A self-assessment of the households' living conditions compared to average shows that almost 60%, of the sample households, feel better off than average, which is probably again due to the over-representation of urban households in the primary cities. It is self-evident that self-assessment of living situations compared to average[110] is highest significantly dependent from sufficiency of income and context (rural –urban). For the latter the urban grouped median is 0.58 compared to a rural one of 0.34 (average 0.58).[111]

Asked how far the household's living conditions improved during the past 10 years, the following figure 3 shows that the improvement is more highly valued in Kazakhstan than in Kyrgyzstan.

What about the assessment of the household's future economic status? 66% believe in a better future, while 14% believe in no change and 19% believe in a worse future. Again it is the urban households that have highly significant better economic future expectations than the rural ones.[112] The grouped urban median is 0.67 compared to 0.41 for rural households.[113] Among those who already have sufficient incomes the expectations are highly significantly higher than the worse-off. With regard to the different locations, the Kyrgyzstan people are less optimistic about their economic future than the Kazakhstan population (highest significant dependency). But we should keep in mind that the results may be distorted due to the fact that the Kazakhstan cases constitute 2/3 of the sample.

[110] Three income classes: worse than average (-1), average (0), higher than average (1).

[111] Kurskal-Wallis Test and comparison of grouped medians.

[112] Three classes about expectations to economic future: worse (-1), same (0), better (1).

[113] Kurskal-Wallis Test and comparison of grouped medians.

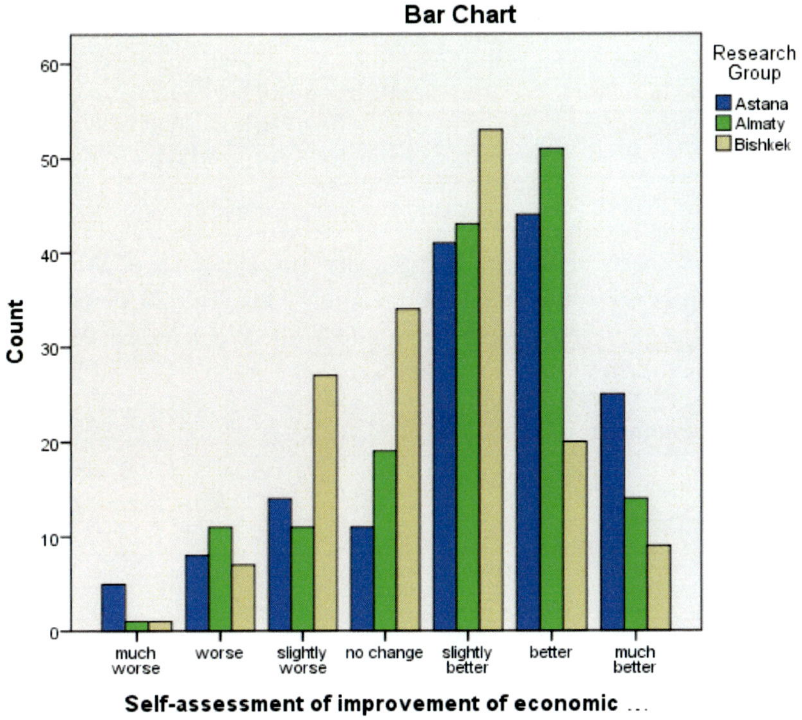

Figure 15: Improvement of economic status after ten years

Why do people have positive or negative expectations for the future? The following two tables explain their reasoning (categorized open answers).

Table 6: Grouped reasons for positive and negative expectations for the future of households

Positive Expectations	Frequency	Percent	Cumulative percent
career growth and employment/better education	86	26.3	26.3
better housing	16	4.9	31.2
opening own business and its development	27	8.3	39.4
trust in future in general	112	34.3	73.7
improved financial situation	86	26.3	100.0
Total	327	100.0	

Negative Expectations	Frequency	Percent	Cumulative percent
economic recession and instability	29	49.2	49.2
general skepticism for future	30	50.8	100.0
Total	59	100.0	

Note: N=386

An open question asked about the living space (in sqm)[114] available to the household. The mean is 66.5, the standard deviation 34.0. The 25 percentile is 44.2, the 50 percentile 58.0 and the 75 percentile 80.0. We grouped the living space into intervals as follows.

Table 7: Living space (square meters)

	Frequency	Percent	Cumulative Percent
up to 50	175	40.3	40.3
51-75	130	30.0	70.3
76-100	65	15.0	85.3
101-125	28	6.5	91.7
above 125	36	8.3	100.0
Total	434	100.0	

Living space increases very significantly with household size (category). The grouped medians are as follows:

Table 8: Living space (household size)

Living Space (Category)	Household Size (Interval)
up to 50	2.6
51–75	2.7
76–100	3.1
101 and more	3.7
Total	2.9

To assess the living standard of the households we pre-defined several consumer and investment goods and asked if these are available in the households. Interestingly, some consumer items such as washing machine or refrigerator are present in almost every household. Also visible from the data is the high value of owning a house or apartment. Such ownership provides security for the future, since par-

[114] 1 sqm is 10.764 sqf.

ticularly in the city rent prices as well as purchasing prices are constantly rising. Computers are found in more than 60% of the sample households, of course more in the cities than in the villages. Interestingly less than half own a car or motor cycle. In the cities there is a very functional transport system, so that private vehicles are not always a necessity. On the other hand, a private vehicle is seen as a prestige object. In the villages public transport services are not so well developed, but many private taxis operate between the villages and the next urban center. This also means that in rural regions ownership of a car or motorcycle is not absolutely necessary for the inhabitants. Some items mentioned are less important in the city than in the countryside. This concerns land or agricultural machinery. The following table summarizes the different items that we used for assessing the living standard of the sample population.

Table 9: Living standard

Item	% of households possessing...
Refrigerator	94.4
Washing machine	90.4
House/apartment	89.3
Computer	63.8
Land	56.2
Car/Motor Cycle	43.8
LCD/Plasma	50.1
Music Center	41.3
Euro Remont	35.8
Livestock	20.0
Dacha	9.6
Agricultural machinery	4.0

Note: "Euro Remont" is a particular way of renovation according to European standard, which is expensive and therefore prestigious.

Cross-tabulation between living standard and place of living (urban – rural) and subsequent chi-Fisher's-Exact-Test show highest or highly significant dependency for all variables, which means that the living standard differs widely between urban and rural households. Cross-tabulation between living standard categories and sufficiency of income shows highest significant dependency of car/motorbike, computer, plasma or LCD TV, music center and Euro Remont from sufficiency of income; and significant dependency of washing machine, livestock and agricultural machinery.

Highest significant correlation[115] on the 0.01 level occurs between house and

[115] Phi, correlation significance level 0.01.

washing machine (0.38), land and livestock (0.40), car/motor cycle and computer (0.30), fridge and washing machine (0.26), music center and computer (0.35), computer and LCD/Plasma TV (0.37), LCD and Euro Remont (0.37), dacha and livestock (0.14), and livestock and agricultural machinery (0.18).

The following table shows the infrastructural components available to the sample households in both urban and rural regions.

Table 10: Infrastructure available to the household

Infrastructure	General	Urban	Rural
Doctor	82%	87%	75%
Medical center	80%	80%	83%
Polyclinic	84%	94%	66%* ***
Hospital	80%	85%	64%* ***
Pre-primary education	81%	90%	65%* ***
Primary education	75%	90%	65%* ***
Secondary education	92%	95%	89%**
Vocational training	55%	68%	30%* ***
University	47%	71%	01%*
Banking service	82%	96%	54%* ***
Market, shops	96%	99%	93%** ***
Transportation service	93%	96%	90%**
Library	80%	80%	79%
Cinema	54%	74%	14%*
Theater	42%	62%	01%*
Music entertainment	60%	83%	13%* ***
Sports facilities	68%	84%	39%* ***
Internet at home	61%	75%	36%* ***
Internet café/shop	68%	87%	33%* **
Post office	95%	96%	95%
Access to phone	95%	99%	90%** ***
Gas	81%	93%	58%* ***
Regular electricity	99%	99%	99%
Free access to safe drink-ing water	80%	93%	61%* ****

*: highest significant

**: significant dependence on context (rural-urban).

***: The infrastructural gap in the Kyrgyzstan sample is much higher and will be analyzed in more detail in the regional study. Particular differences to the Kazakhstan samples occur with regard to primary education, phone and internet access.

****: The Kyrgyzstan villages are much better equipped with safe drinking water than the Kazakhstan villages.

Highest significant correlations concerning infrastructure are various and often unremarkable[116] because they are an outcome of distinct city and village infrastructures. Villages often lack gas provision so that heating with coal is necessary. Of course, higher education facilities as well as cultural services, sports facilities and internet access are lacking. Particularly in Kazakhstan free access to safe drinking water is a problem in the villages.

Savings and investments, credits and security

The questions concerning this part were aimed at finding out how the households create security under the conditions of their past experiences and the conditions society and economy makes available to them. The data for savings and their possessions must be looked upon with caution because of the high number of missing cases, as many respondents did not talk about this. Therefore we did cross-tabulation only with regard to the importance of savings.

We start with the type of savings and investments which the households consider important and those types of savings they have.

Table 11: Purposes and possessions of savings

Purposes of Saving	**Importance (%)**	**Possession of savings or investments today (%)**	**Savings or investments realized in the past (%)**
Wedding/funeral	50	7	32
Other family events	57	8	28
Apartment	78	26	39
Jewelry/gold	40	22	17
Land	46	14	22
Livestock	31	24	16
Private health insurance	33	6	17
Private old age insurance	24	2	15
Life insurance	27	3	15
Children's education	67	10	38
Vacations	56	8	58
Hadj (Pilgrimage to Mekka)	22	0	16

Note: multiple answers

Owning an apartment is considered to be important by 78% of the sample households. This is followed by savings for children's education, so that we as-

[116] Correlation significance level 0.01.

sume that the intergenerational family security system still plays an important role. This assumption is further supported by the fact that family events of the different types follow in number concerning the importance. Only vacation is ranked similarly high. This contradicts to some degree for the household types observed. Here two generation households dominate strongly. But types are only a faint indicator for practices or beliefs.

When we compare the data that is considered to be important and who already possesses such properties or savings we can see that roughly speaking only half of the sample households already possess what they consider to be important. This concerns housing facilities as well as savings for children's education, land or jewelry/gold. We can also see that a number of people who do not yet have their own landed property save for such a purpose.

Concerning differences of the three locations some can be explained. Saving for an apartment is significantly more important in the Astana sub-sample. Where saving for land and livestock is of highest significance, it is less important in the Astana/Akmola sample and highest in the Bishkek sample. All insurance savings are considered highly significantly less important in the Bishkek region. Also children's education savings are considered significantly less important in that sub-sample. The importance of savings for apartment, gold/jewelry and land is significantly dependent on income. We can see that saving for private provisions like health, old age and life insurance doesn't play a big role. One may conclude, that the social insurance sector in the two countries is assumed to be still small although present. The fact that there are some public provisions of health services free of charge and in Kazakhstan also an obligatory pension fund exists (cf. country reports) may contribute to this but also soviet experiences, which made private provisions unnecessary. Two-thirds up to three-quarters of all respondents do not consider such insurances as important. The reasons for this attitude have to be explored in more detail with help of the qualitative interviews.

We also took a look at the correlations between the different saving items.[117] The highest correlation occurs between the different savings for insurances (0.6-0.7). This means those who have an opportunity to save for such purposes do this through different kinds of insurances. The correlation between savings in land and livestock is also high (0.57) which is not unexpected – both being related to rural regions.

The following table provides data on the households and their ability to save for particular purposes.

[117] Correlation significance level 0.01.

Table 12: Household ability to save for crisis, old age and next generation

Type of saving	Percent of household being able to save for...
Crisis	42
Old age	30
Next generation	54

Nearly half of the households feel able to take some care concerning unforeseeable events of the crises type. But saving for old age occurs only in about one third of the sample. It must remain unclear of whether the respondents have taken obligatory old age insurance into consideration which exists in Kazakhstan. But provisions for old age security must be analyzed together with savings concerning the next generation. More than half of all households save for the next generation. This kind of saving seems to provide an insurance mechanism between the generations and may hint at a strong belief in education as a provision for the future among people with a middle class background. It seems that these people rely more on their kin than on their own individual attempts for old age provisions.

In rural regions the cross-tabulation shows a significant underrepresentation of savers for crisis, a highly significant one of savers for old age, and a highest significant one for savers for the next generation. That the opportunity to save for such purposes depends on the sufficiency of income is self-evident (highest significance). Between all types of savings highly significant correlations exist (0.36-0.48).[118]

Furthermore, we asked where the respondents save or invest their money. Of course we wanted to find out whether they use those organizations of the market economy which have been established in the last years and whether saving, especially in rural contexts, means something else than financial accounts in banks. Multiple answers were possible.

Table 13: Where people save

Institution	Percent
At home	44
Private property	40
Local bank	38
Livestock	15
Investment (stocks etc.)	3
Other	2
Foreign bank	1
Bank account abroad	1

[118] Correlation significance level 0.01.

The high percentage of those who save at home is striking. Whether this represents mistrust in the organizations of the market economy in the two countries and/or whether this is due to the recent financial crises that also hit the countries can be pursued further in the qualitative interviews.

The Chi-square test shows a highest significant dependency of saving in local banks from an urban setting and a highest significant saving in livestock in rural regions. Investment in private property is significantly more an urban affair. These results are hardly surprising; however, the highest significant relatedness of saving at home in urban regions was not expected by us, since here we expected a much stronger orientation at current availabilities of banks and their options. Furthermore, highest significant dependency of the rural regions and saving in livestock occurs, with Almaty region below average and Bishkek region above average. Interestingly, with regard to investment in private property the Almaty region ranges highest significantly below and Astana above average.

Households with sufficient incomes and feeling better off, save in local banks with a significantly higher degree than other households. They also invest significantly higher in private property than other groups.

The respondents were also asked about their current credit situation. We offered the possibility to mention up to five credits. The number of credits ranges from 0 to 4. The majority had only one credit, while only few households had four. Only for the first credit, households were asked to provide detailed information on the credit purpose in an open question. We categorized the answers as follows:

Table 14: Credit purpose (Category)

Category of credit	Frequency	Percent
Mortgage, buying apartment or real estate	53	17
Business investment, livestock purchase, land investment	64	21
Consumer credit	75	24
Marriage, funeral	11	4
Family needs, education	26	8
Housing repair, house construction work	34	11
Paying back debts	4	1
Car purchase	44	14
Total	311	100

From Chi-square test we can conclude that mortgages, buying apartments and real estate are mainly urban affairs (urban: 25%; rural: 2%), while business investment, livestock purchase and land investments are more often rural affairs (urban: 13%; rural: 35%).

It is important to mention that one-third (29.5%) of all respondents had not taken credit at the time of our interview. The other 70% have a distribution of credit amount (for the first credit) as follows:

Table 15: Credit amount for the first credit

Credit amount	**Frequency**	**Percent**
50-99 USD	77	17
500-999 USD	94	21
1000-4999 USD	103	23
>20000 USD	44	10
Total	318	71
No credit	133	30

Comparing urban and rural credit amounts, significantly urban dwellers are the group with the highest number found in the large credit categories. Interestingly there is no significant dependency of sufficiency of income from credit amount.

Where do the credits come from? Banks range first (81%), followed by microcredit institutions (11%). Relatives, friends, and colleagues amount to less than 4%. The result is astonishing to us, because we know from other investigations in Russia and Eastern Europe that financing with help of personal networks usually plays an important role even among businessmen (Dittrich, Schrader, and Stojanov 2008). If we look at the amount of the credits, the huge amounts are typically for mortgages for houses and apartments. The cross-tabulation shows that microcredit is more rural than urban (18% compared to 7%). Only 14% of all respondents have also taken a second credit. Also here banks and microcredit institutions account for more than 90% of all credits provided. Only 6% of the sample also mentions a third credit. Here microcredit institutions range before banks. 2% also mention a fourth credit. The answers show that the amounts of credits do not decrease with the numbers of credits. This means that some of the households might have debts ranging between USD 80,000 and 200,000, which is considerably high if compared to the general income situation of middle class people in the two countries.

What is the amount of credit interest rates? Of those who currently have taken credit, 45% report an interest rate of between 1 and 5%, 8% between 6 and 10%, 18% between 11 and 15%, 15% between 16 and 20%, 11 % between 21 and 25% and 4% above the 25%. High interest rates are not unexpected because of the high inflation rate. Mean interest rate for the first credit amounts to 11.14, the standard deviation is 30.47. For the second credit more than 90% of the relevant sample households report an interest rate between 1 and 5%. Here the mean is 3.66 only, the standard deviation 4.76. Credits of rural households are significantly the highest overrepresented in the lowest as well as in the highest category (Pearson Chi-Square 0.0).

Lending to Others

If we ask whether the households provide credits to others, 20% report on one credit, 3% on two credits and one household offered even five credits. Looking at first credits only, we discover that interest–free credits range first (90%), while another 9% of the households report on interest rates of less than 5%. Asked to whom credits are provided, here 54% of the households mention relatives, followed by friends (26%), colleagues (11.4%), and neighbors (7.6%). This means that the vast majority of low interest credits are provided to members in close personal networks. Therefore, the interest rate is zero or very low. The lending amount is as follows: 15% report an amount of less than USD 15, 10% USD between 15 and 49, 12% USD between 50 and 99, 26% between USD 100 and 499, 16% between USD 500 and 999, 15% between USD 1,000 and 4,999 and 5% of more than USD 5,000. Considering lending terms, 3% are long-term credits of 10 years and more. We may assume this to be loans for the purchase of a house or an apartment.[119] 5% report a lending period of one to three years, 47% between 1 month and a year, and 45% for less than a month. It seems that bridging acute money crises often leads to lending operations.

Looking at lending helps us to explain why the interest rates of credits in general, described above, seem so low. In the personal transactions, between relatives, friends, colleagues, and neighbors, borrowing money and being helped by a ‘credit’ does not imply interest rates as being ‘normal’ in bank transactions. Perhaps even interest-free credit is not considered as such but as “help” or “borrowing” from kinfolk. These transactions mostly represent mutual help/reciprocity with its own ethics which does not follow the rationale of the financial market.

Problems of the Households

We asked: “Which are the main problems that the household has been confronted with in the last year?” Additionally we asked the respondents to weigh the problems: weak, medium, strong. General price increases rank top with 94 %. For 19%

[119] Interestingly, there are no loans in the sample ranging from 3 to 10 years.

they are of strong and for 43% of medium importance. General price increases are followed by food price increases which are a top priority for 91% of the households. 18% feel strongly affected by them and for 41% food prices are of medium importance. The respondents also mention the prices for communal services as being a problem for them: 86%. 13% feel strongly affected and 39% explain that this topic is of medium importance to them. Costs for schooling are another topic defined as a problem by our respondents. The academic year, which implies costs for teaching material, school uniforms etc., affects half of all households (7% strong; 20% medium). Payments for education rank similar. 42% mention these payments as being a problem.

Unemployment is no issue for 57% of the sample households, while 13% have weak problems, 17% have medium problems, and 13% report to have strong problems. For illness the numbers are as follows: 12% are strongly affected, 18% medium. Death of a family member can be a shock situation for the households, particularly, if the main breadwinner is affected. 10% report that the extent of how they are affected is strong or medium. Divorce concerns 5% of all households. Marriage problems affect 9% in a medium or a strong way.

Comparing the urban and the rural situation, unemployment is significantly higher and more a rural than an urban issue, which means that the urban labor market can absorb labor demand from different segments of society much better than the rural one. A significantly higher affectedness by food prices and price increases also occurs in rural regions. Transportation problems on the other hand show no significant difference between cities and the countryside, although probably the reasons for that are different in both locations. Is it probably traffic jams in the cities that cause the result while rural citizens suffer from lack of public transport and bad roads. A highest significant dependency of the variables household size and problems with the academic year occurs, which is not astonishing when we assume that large households have a number of children of school age and therefore higher costs related to education.

Likewise it is not astonishing that the highest significant correlations[120] occur between the problems of unemployment and price increases (0.34), illness and death (0.25), food prices and price increases in general (0.82), price increases and communal services (0.62), academic year and educational payment (0.21), and problems with neighbors and criminality (0.21).

Asked about the three major problems (open question reclassified during data analysis), the first major problem concerns housing, communal services and flat prices (21%) followed by inflation, food and general prices, low salary (20%) and

[120] Correlation significance level 0.01.

traffic and transport (16%). 9% consider unemployment as their major problem, 8% bad infrastructure, 6% ecological problems, and 7% transportation (medium and strongly affected). The ranking of the second and third major problems is the same, whereas only the percent differ from each other.

With whom do the respondents discuss their problems? We offered 12 possibilities to the respondents. On a whole, these answers show that problems are predominantly discussed in the family and between husband and wife. Responsibility for the discussion of finance falls upon either all household members (41%) or husband and wife (34%). With health problems the distribution is similar (41% with all household members 28% between husband and wife and 7% with parents/parents-in-law). 39% see educational problems as an affair of all household members, 23% as one of husbands and wives. Problems with relatives, marriage, family and cultural traditions, neighbors, and community are equally a family affair. In addition to family members problems with friends are also discussed among friends (22%), while labor problems are additionally discussed with colleagues (13%). Highest significant correlations[121] occur concerning the discussion of various problems due to the fact that discussions normally happen among the family members.

Furthermore, we predefined various problems which a household may be confronted with and asked from whom it gets assistance. The results are similar to the answers about the problems. The first problem addressed was finance. 73% of the households report that assistance is provided by family and relatives, 7% by friends. Institutional support by banks or employers is negligible. With health problems the picture is slightly different. Again it is first of all family members and relatives who provide help (59%), but then follows professional help: doctors and nurses (26%). Also concerning educational problems family and relatives give assistance and range first (49%). 9% mentioned assistance from the educational administration and 4% from friends. Problems with relatives are mainly supported by members of the family themselves and relatives (80%). Problems with friends are first of all assisted by friends (39%), followed by family members (32%). Assistance in case of marriage problems is again a family affair. Also labor problems are first of all assisted by the family (35%). 17% are assisted by colleagues and 40% by employers. Then follow friends with 4%. In almost 80% of the cases, family and cultural traditions are assisted by family and relatives, and only friends play a role worth mentioning (2%). Problems with neighbors and community again are assisted by family and relatives (41%) or neighbors (12%).

[121] Correlation significance level 0.01.

State structures and local administration play a negligible role. The overall results to that block show that it is first of all the family network which provides support to the household when problems occur. Other personal relations (friends, neighbors) rank quite a way behind, while institutional/professional assistance is hardly mentioned, with the exception of the health sector. On the other hand, the percentage of those who report receiving no support in either of these problem situations is quite high. This may result from urbanization and individualization; or for those respondents for whom these problems simply do not occur.

When we asked about responsibilities for savings, credits, investments, education and migration as well as insurances other than car insurances, we offered different prefixed categories. To sum up: for the majority of the households all relevant problems are first of all a nuclear family affair or a household affair. To provide some examples: 42% of the households consider savings a nuclear family affair, 28% a household affair and 17% an individual affair. For consumer credits the picture is similar. First ranks the nuclear family (39%), followed by the household (23%). Housing investment is also predominantly a nuclear family affair (35%) or a household affair (24%). Education and higher education concern 55% of the households and are mainly a family affair. Migration is relevant for 42%, mainly being an individual affair (41% of these households), followed by the nuclear family (37%) and the household (18%). Insurances other than car insurance are relevant for only 48% of the households. They are mainly a nuclear family or household affair.

In general, in both countries the households and the nuclear families are largely self-organizing units that solve their everyday problems on their own. Husband and wives play a major role but also other household members are included in most of the decisions the households have to take. Professional help is only relevant in case of illnesses. Banks and other financial organizations as well as public administrations have no relevant role concerning the discussion and the solution of the problems.

Values and Responsibilities

Which important goals in life do the households pursue? Well-being and prosperity of children ranks first, followed by the respondent's own well-being and prosperity and that of the family. These three categories cover 90% of the answers. 8% aim at the purchase of property (vehicles or land) and 2% at peace, stability, and prosperity for the country. A cross-tabulation shows an over proportionate share of rural households aiming at the well-being of the children (52% compared to 38%). The Kyrgyzstan sample shows highest significant difference in this category when compared with the Kazakhstani sample (55% compared to 36%).

In the section on values pursued by the households we predefined various answers and offered a 4-tier scale of importance of each of these. Every value was to be considered separately. Materialist and post-materialist values were mixed, but we group them here.

Materialism is a value characteristic of social change and marketization in post-soviet societies. 37% find this value important and 58% very important. This high percentage is different to western societies where post-materialist values are in progress and materialism is perhaps already in demise (cf. Inglehart 1997).[122] The value of improving the living standard is also materialist, but less crude in expression; therefore the result is perhaps even slightly higher (36% find this value important, 62% very important). Buying a house or apartment has a special meaning in post-socialist societies because ownership provides independence, security and a form of saving. The value ranges high (28% important, 43% very important).

The value of enhancing ones competences is very much linked to the new capitalism as a system of life-long learning. 38% find this value important, 41% very important. This value ranges behind the more materialist values.

Establishing their own household is more a matter for young people who want to become independent from the household of their parents. This can be looked upon as an indicator for emergent nuclear families or couples. 52% of the respondents pursue this goal, and 15% of them find this value very important. However, these data are biased, insofar as one-generation households or nuclear family households do not necessarily consider this value to be important as they have already become independent.

Let us now have a look at the non-materialist and post-materialist values. 44% consider the value of keeping the household together as important and 22% as very important. This value is familial. In the Bishkek sample the positive link to that value has the highest significant difference to the two samples from Kazakhstan. The value of providing best education to the children is found throughout both countries (28% important, 53% very important).

[122] Inglehart argues with his scarcity hypothesis that societal scarcity has to be overcome before post-material values can emerge. In combination with his socialization hypothesis that value change takes place intergenerational – due to the fact that the most important part of socialization is during childhood and youth – people who are now still young have experienced scarcity during the socialist period and the early transformation period. Relating the argument to our cases, in spite of the increasing wealth in Kazakhstan material values predominate.

Being healthy is also a value not directly linked to materialism and often juxtaposed to it. 16% find this value important and 83% as very important which makes it the top-priority value. It is closely followed by the value of being happy (17% important, 81% very important).

We included a religious value, making a Hadj, which usually is supposed to rank high in Muslim societies. Here we have to mention that in Kazakhstan the nominal Muslim population is 47% only,[123] while it is 75% in Kyrgyzstan.[124] However, both governments take a strict attitude against Islamism. This can perhaps explain why only 14% of the sample considers that goal to be important and 6% as very important.

On the whole, rural and urban respondents don't differ in their answers concerning values. Only in the case of the two family values do we find a significant difference in that younger people in rural households would prefer building their own household.

Concerning the whole sample, the highest significant correlations[125] occur between the values building a new independent household and buying a house/apartment (0,29), earning more money and improving the living standard (0,71), enhancing skills and giving the best education to children (0.46), and being healthy and being happy (0.80).

Who should be responsible for old age security, childcare, unemployment, healthcare, the poor, school education, and higher education? The answers were predefined in the questionnaire: state, family, the individual, insurance companies, charity organizations. The findings are shown in the following table. Multiple answers were possible.

Table 16: Perceptions about responsibilities

Responsibility field	State	Family	The Individual	Insurance Companies	Charity Organizations
Old Age Security	73%	31%	39%	20%	6%
Childcare	51%	78%	22%	9%	10%
Unemployment	86%	26%	40%	8%	7%
Healthcare	91%	20%	19%	18%	8%
The Poor	88%	17%	20%	12%	41%
School education	88%	39%	20%	8%	8%
Higher Education	74%	44%	35%	5%	5%

123 http://www.nationsonline.org/oneworld/kyrgyzstan.htm; access date 3-9-13.
124 http://www.nationsonline.org/oneworld/kyrgyzstan.htm; access date 3-9-13.
125 Correlation significance level 0.01.

The results are interesting although difficult to interpret. In all fields, except for childcare, the respondents believe that the responsibility is with the state. At first sight, one may assume that the respondents cling to "socialist" attitudes of the "nanny state"-type as existed in the soviet past. But in other countries with welfare traditions, the state also guarantees at least a basic pension system, health and educational infrastructures, etc. Maybe it is possible to assume that most people wish a development towards such a type of welfare regime found in certain European countries. With regard to education people distinguish between school education and higher education. For the latter it is interesting to note that the state is considered to be less responsible. In some fields like old age security or healthcare, insurance companies cannot be neglected, which implies that some of the respondents have accepted the market for the provision of security. Those, who also attribute the responsibility to the individual, may be looked upon as having said farewell to the old nanny-state orientation. Nevertheless, the absolute number of households having insurance contracts is quite low. Charity organizations are particularly considered to be responsible for the poor ranking at second place behind the state. Interestingly the family scored 17% only. This may be due to the fact that we asked middle class households with little experience concerning "the poor".

Next we developed a kind of responsibility types by summing up the cases. 36% of the sample mentions the state in all seven categories, another 22% in six of the seven categories. Only 10% mention the family seven times and another 3% in six of the seven categories. 9% mention the individual in all seven categories, and 3% in six of the seven. Insurances are mentioned only in 3% of all categories, and 1% in six of the seven categories. Charity is selected in seven cases by 3% of the sample only. The Chi-Square test does not show any significance with regard to location or age group, which we found to be very remarkable.

Looking at the means of the different responsibility types: the state ranges highest with 5.47 and a standard deviation of 1.67. Next follows the family with a mean of 2.56 and a high standard deviation of 2.12. Then the responsibility type of individual follows with a mean of 1.91 and a standard deviation of 2.21. Insurances and charity organizations are hardly mentioned.

Despite our cautious argument at the beginning, the latter results support the argument towards the strong survival of "nanny-state" orientations even 20 years after the breakdown of the authoritarian soviet regime. In the beliefs of our respondents private responsibility as well as private insurance options both elements of market societies are hardly developed. Interestingly enough, younger age groups do not show different orientations and there is no difference concerning people living in the country side or in urban surroundings, as is the case in other behavioral norms.

Let us now have a look at the three samples. We shall start with North Kazakhstan, followed by South Kazakhstan and Kyrgyzstan.

3.3. The North Kazakhstan Survey

Aigul ZABIROVA, Daurenbek KULEIMENOV, Heiko SCHRADER

The Sample

The sample consists of 100 urban respondents from Astana, the capital of Kazakhstan, and 50 respondents from the Akmola oblast, the neighboring rural region. Data were collected during July and August, 2011. The report is structured according to four paragraphs:

- Household structure (composition, activities/occupations and income);
- Living conditions of the households (major problems, assistance provided and household vulnerability;
- Savings, credits and security;
- Values and responsibilities.

The focus of attention will be on a comparison of urban and rural households.

Household Structure

The survey involved 118 women and 31 men. It was important to interview those members of the households who would be able to provide full information about family income, decision making, savings, problem-solving, etc. As a rule, women run the household in Kazakh families, do the necessary purchases, administer the household budget, etc., which means that Gwomen were the more suitable respondents for our research, which justifies the gender bias.

The age distribution is as follows: about one third (30%) are younger than 30 years old, a quarter (25%) is between 30 and 39 years old, another quarter between 40 and 49, 15% fall into the interval between 50 and 59 and 5% are 60 and above.

The majority are two-generation households: parents and children (65%). Every fourth household (21%) includes three generations: a married couple, children and elderly parents of the husband or the wife. 15% belong to a one-generation household. The household size is as follows: every fifth household (22%) consisted of one or two people, a quarter (26%) of three people, another quarter (25%) of four people, 17% of 5 people and 11% of six and more people.

The ethnic composition of the respondents is as follows: 78% are Kazakh, 16% Russian, and 5% other nationalities. The vast majority of households (88%) are of homogeneous ethnic composition, while the rest (12%) is ethnically mixed.

Let us take a look at the average household age:[126] 43% fall into the age interval from 26 to 35 years, while 27% have an average household age below 26. 19% fall into the interval from 36 to 45, 5% from 46-55, 7% from 56 to 65 years, and less than 1% into the interval above 65 years. Combining these age groups of households, it can be seen that a considerable part (70%) can be defined as "younger" households with an average household age below 36, while another 30% belong to the "older households" with an average age above 36. We can assume that the problems of younger and older households are different.

According to the degree of involvement of respondents into various spheres of activities, it can be noted that in about half of the households (46%) respondents have more than one job. While in 3-generation households the grandparents' usually have no additional/second job, the parents do. Males work in the private sector in transport, promotion, trade, etc., or in the state sector (schools, public health). Females often have part time jobs in the state or (medicine, education) in the private sector (promotion, construction, accounting and finance, law, commerce, sports, beauty).

Incomes in urban and rural areas are significantly different, as the following table shows. Higher incomes are predominantly found in the city. Furthermore, rural households are more evenly distributed among several categories than urban households.

Table 17: Income distribution in Astana and Akmola region, Kazakhstan

Income category (KZT)	**Total, % (N=150)**	**Urban, % (N=100)**	**Rural, % (N=50)**
10,400-<27,000	1	1	2
27,000-<75,000	13	3	32
75,000-<120,000	17	10	32
120,000-<155,000	17	16	10
155,000-<310,000	37	49	12
310,000-<465,000	10	13	2
465,000-<620,000	5	8	0
Total	100	100	100

How many people per household contribute to the monetary household income and its security? In the majority of cases (both urban and rural) it is two or three people. Single-headed households have much lower incomes than other households.

[126] Mean of age of all household members.

We investigated how far access to natural capital is important for households to make a living. Or, to put it differently, how far do Kazakhstani households still rely on subsistence production to make a living? To sum up this point: natural capital is rather important for 33% of the urban and almost every rural household. 10% urban and 4% rural households refer to one, 12% each to two, 7% urban and 22% rural households to three, 4% urban and 48% rural households to four and 0% urban and 14% rural households to five different types of natural revenues[127] of the kind that can be converted into money. We don't distinguish here between animal husbandry as a farming activity and animal husbandry as a source for additional income as often practiced in rural areas. Astonishingly, also for a considerable number of urban households' incomes from natural capital plays a considerable role in making a living. How this is possible, must be left to the qualitative report.

Revenues from "animals" are important for 20% urban and 32% rural, very important for 17% urban and 28% rural households. Gardening/agriculture is important for 27% urban and 42% rural, and very important for 23% urban and 38% rural households. The collecting of revenues from nature is important for 24% urban and 38% rural households and even very important for 27% urban and 46% rural households. Grazing land plays a minor role for most of the households, particularly urban ones. The numbers given for the urban households indicate that there must be close relations between urban households and rural ones because animal husbandry especially is not normally possible in Astana.

How far do households provide support to dependents and how far do they receive support from outside? 15% urban and 30% rural households provide cash support; 10% urban and 38% rural households provide non-cash support. 9% urban and 26% rural households even provide both cash and in kind support. And what do the households obtain? 17% urban and 18% rural households obtain cash support from outside, 6% urban and 18% rural households report support in kind from outside, and 17% urban and 20% rural households both cash and in kind support from outside. We observe a stronger involvement of rural households in such support networks, as well as a negative correlation between income level and assistance from outside.

The household type "closed" fits to more than half of the researched households (68% urban and 50% rural). "Just giving" households are one in five households (16% urban and 32% rural). "Just receiving" households make up 16% ur-

[127] These five revenues are animal products, garden and agricultural products, drinking water (pipe/well), collection from nature, and grazing land.

ban and 6% rural households. 0% urban and 12% rural households are "giving and receiving" households.

Concluding the first section of report it is important to note:

- Most of those surveyed households are "young" in household age, and in general comprise two generations.
- One third of the urban and most rural households consider subsistence revenues as important for their survival. Most rural households combine different subsistence revenues from gardening, animals and nature.
- Households make/obtain fewer transfers than we assumed. Half of the households are from the "closed" type. We shall take a closer look at this topic in the qualitative part. Urban households which usually have higher incomes are less involved in transfers than rural households. Certain subsidies are transferred from rural to urban households, which is often due to children studying in the city.

The following table summarizes the household characteristics according to location (percent)

Table 18: Household characteristics, North Kazakhstan

Household Characteristics Acc. To...		**Total, %**	**Urban, %**	**Rural, %**
Respondents' sex	Male	21	25	12
	Female	79	75	88
Size	One or two persons	22	24	18
	Three persons	26	27	26
	Four persons	24	24	26
	Five persons	17	16	18
	Six and more persons	11	10	12
Generations	One generation	14	17	10
	Two generations	65	62	70
	Three and more	21	22	20
	Single headed	15	14	16
	Single	6	7	4
Household Age	Up to 25	27	29	22
	26-35	43	43	42
	36-45	18	19	18
	46-55	5	5	4
	56-65	6	3	13
	More than 66	1	1	0

No of HH Members with Monetary Incomes	No	2	2	0
	One	15	18	4
	Two	36	33	42
	Three	27	28	26
	Four	11	10	14
	More than four	9	10	9
Employment Diversity	Not diverse	18	24	8
	Diverse	36	32	44
	Highly diverse	46	45	48
Resource Network	Closed household	62	68	50
	Only giving	21	16	32
	Only receiving	13	16	6
	Giving and receiving	4	0	12

Note: N=150, urban N=100, rural N=50

Living Conditions, Major Problems, and Vulnerability of the Households

We wanted to find out how content people are with their situation and therefore we asked about their incomes and how they see their future.

Table 19: Sufficiency of incomes, North Kazakhstan

Sufficiency of incomes/region	**Total, %**	**Urban, %**	**Rural, %**
Not sufficient/hardly sufficient	14	13	16
Almost sufficient	36	27	54
Sufficient	50	60	30

Most urban Kazakhstani households believe that their income is sufficient, but rural households overwhelmingly don't believe that. But the picture changes if one asks to compare one's own household with others. 10% (both urban and rural) assess their living conditions as worse than average households; 31% urban and 40% rural households as average, and 59% urban and 50% rural households as better than average. It is interesting to note that there is a rather positive assessment of their own standard of living compared to others, both in the city and in the village. Self-assessment of the future economic development also affects the general contentment of people. Three quarters of the households (74%) see their financial situation in the next year with optimism, 18% expect a negative development and 7% believe in an unchanged situation. Again it is the urban population which is significantly (p=0.03) more optimistic than the rural population, whereas among rural households there are also more than half of whom believe that their economic future will be better.

Table 20: Expectations to future economic status, North Kazakhstan

Expectation to future economic status/region	Total, %	Urban, %	Rural, %
Worse	18	13	29
Same	7	4	14
Better	74	83	57

Looking at the household situation 10 years ago, the majority of all households see an improvement of the situation. However, this is felt stronger among urban households. Among the rural households every third household considers the present economic situation worse than 10 years ago, compared to only 12% of the urban ones. On the whole urban and rural assessments are significantly different ($p=0.05$).

What further factors determine the positive mood? Among the "social optimists", 34% have trust in the future in general, 26% believe in their own improved financial situation and another 26% in career development, employment and educational upgrade. 8% believe in an improvement or the opening / promoting of their own business, and 5% believe in better living conditions. Half of the households with negative expectations explain their feelings through critical economic conditions and instability in the country, the other half through general skepticism about their future position, without specifying any particular reason.

What about infrastructure in the households' location? There are severe differences between urban and rural households as the following table shows. Rural households are disadvantaged in almost every category. To mention some problems: medical infrastructure in villages seems to be a problem, with the exception of medical centers (health posts). 40% of rural households do not have access to pre-primary education. Access to internet information is available to less than half of rural households. Almost half of the rural households lack access to banking services, more than three quarters to cultural entertainment except library service, more than 60% of rural households do not have sports facilities in their villages. Free access to drinking water is a problem for more than 80% of the sample households.

Table 21: Access to infrastructure, North Kazakhstan

Access to infrastructure / region	Total, %	Urban, %	Rural, %
Medical Service			
doctor	17.8	54.2*	0
medical center	2.1	9.0*	22.9
polyclinic	17.7	50.0*	2.0
hospital	23.8	56.3*	8.1
Education			
pre-primary	15.0	39.6*	3.0
primary	9.5	29.2*	0
secondary	7.5	22.9*	0
vocational	44.0	77.1*	21.6
university	43.9	100.0*	17.0
Banking Services	16.2	45.8*	2.0
Market/Shops	0.7	0.0	1.0
Transport	6.8	17.0*	2.0
Cultural Services			
library	13.5	12.5	14.0
cinema	38.5	72.9*	22.0
theatre	49.3	95.8*	26.5
cultural entertainment	26.5	77.1*	2.0
Sports facilities	26.1	66.7*	9.0
Internet at home	28.1	58.3*	13.3
Internet café	20.1	52.1*	4.2
Postal service	3.4	10.4**	0.0
Phone Access	1.4	2.0	1.0
Gas	10.1	12.2	9.1
Regular electricity	0	0	0
Free access to the drinking water	31.3	81.6**	5.3

Chi-square test: *highest significant, ** highly significant difference

Considering the households vulnerability we asked about personal shocks, such as death of family members and general problems such as price increases, as well as the level of affectedness (weak, medium, strong). The following table provides the results. One can generally say that all such problems that occur through price increase/inflation have an impact on many households. It is again rural households that are more strongly affected by such, due to their lower incomes in general, and many of these expenses cannot be avoided, while some can be compensated for by subsistence production.

Table 22: Affectedness by problems during the last year, North Kazakhstan

Category / Affectedness (percent)	Weak affect-edness	Medium affect-edness	Strong affect-edness
Unemployment	6.7	16.1	13.4
Illness of a family member/treatment	10.7	20.7	12.0
Death of a family member	1.3	4.7	4.0
Divorce	3.3	0.0	0.7
Wedding	5.3	5.3	2.7
Rising food prices	21.3	48.7	21.3
General increase in prices	23.3	50	20.7
Prices for apartment services	27.3	46.7	16.0
Preparing children to school (buying school clothes, books etc.)	15.3	16.7	8.0
Payments for education	7.3	14.7	12.7
Crime	3.3	2.0	4,0
Natural disasters	2.0	1.3	0.7
Transport	19.3	5.3	3.3
Problems with neighbors	10.7	4.0	0.7

Problems of the Households

Which problems in everyday life affect the households and who discusses them? We provided a list of problems (stemming from finance, health, education, relatives, friends, marriage, labor, family, cultural traditions, neighbors, community) and a list of potential discussion partners (all household members, all male household members, all female household members, the oldest males/females, husband/wife, brother/sister, parents/step parents, father in law/mother in law, friends, colleagues, others). In one third of the households in northern Kazakhstan (urban 35%, rural 36%) issues related to finances are discussed among all household members, in another third (urban 33%, rural 40%) between husband and wife. 10% of the rural households discuss their financial problems among male members only, while such a gender bias is not found in the city. Every tenth urban respondent does not discuss financial problems with anybody. The number of rural households that do not discuss these problems can be neglected.

Many urban and rural households are discussing health problems with members of their households (26% and 38% correspondingly and between husband and wife (27% and 24% correspondingly). Again every tenth urban household member does not discuss health problems with anybody.

Many urban and rural households (29% and 38% correspondingly) prefer to discuss issues related to education only in the family. Urban households prefer to discuss family problems among all household members (28%) or between husband and wife (30%). Villagers prefer to discuss family problems in the household only (24%) or not at all (34%). They are more hesitant in the discussion of family problems with outsiders. Perhaps this is due to widespread gossip in the villages.

Urban households prefer to discuss problems with friends among husband and wife (38%) and friends (21%). Most rural households do not discuss problems with friends at all (41.7%) or among husband and wife (25%). Urban households are more open in this matter than the rural ones.

Rural and urban households gave identical answers concerning the discussion of marriage problems. Most urban and rural households (35% and 40%) prefer to discuss such problems among husband and wife only, or they do not discuss them at all (33% and 35% correspondingly).

Many urban households (34% compared to 20% rural) prefer to discuss employment problems between husband and wife or with all household members (22% compared to 20% rural), and 29% of rural households prefer to discuss such issues with no one, while this group is much smaller among urban households (16%). Among the rural households there is also a tendency to discuss employment problems with colleagues (18% compared to 6% urban). Friends (10% urban, 6% rural) are also an addressee to discuss labor problems. Urban and rural households discuss issues related to cultural traditions with members of their family: husband and wife (24% urban, 32% rural) or all family members (34% and 47% correspondingly). Generally, rural households are more open in discussing these issues at all.

Problems with neighbors/community are often not discussed at all (37% urban and 43% rural), or discussed only with family members.

Summing up, we can say that many problems are mostly discussed only within families or with no one at all. With financial problems urban households seem to be more closed (discussing with no one) than rural ones; on the contrary rural households are often hesitant to talk about social and family issues with outsiders or not at all.

Who provides assistance to the household members when they have problems? Many urban and rural households receive help from family members and relatives (56% urban, 67% rural) when they have financial problems. However, almost one-third of urban and 18% of rural households receives no help for their financial problems. For 10% of the rural and 7% of the urban households friends also provide help. These data once again suggest that social networks play an important role especially in the lives of rural households. Urban households seem to be more independent in solving their financial problems but they also seem to be embedded in larger networks of support. Financial institutions and other institutional support organizations (administration, employer) play a negligible role.

In the case of health problems most urban and rural households (55% and 68% correspondingly look for institutional help first (doctors, hospitals, etc.). Apart from the medical sector, support is sought from family/relatives (31% urban and 22% rural). It should be noted that the level of reliance on doctors by urban households is lower than in the countryside, although the quality is higher and access of medical services better in the city than in rural areas. But prices for medical services in private hospitals or for 'private' specialists are high.

In the case of educational problems most urban and rural households (42% and 51% correspondingly) do not get assistance from anybody. Family/relatives rank next (24% and 20% correspondingly). Only 17% of urban and 12% of rural households get support from the school administration. This may be due to a low level of acceptance in educational organizations and corresponding institutions or a lack of offers from them. Friends (6% urban, 8% rural) and colleagues (7% urban, 2% rural) are also mentioned by some households as being supportive.

In urban and rural households (89% and 55% correspondingly) problems with relatives are mostly assisted by family members and other relatives. A high percentage of rural households (43%, compared to 14% urban) are not assisted at all. This can perhaps be explained by more traditional behavior prevailing in the countryside. In the case of problems with friends, urban households are supported by their friends (63%), while support is much weaker in rural regions (25%). Here 54% complain of getting no support from anybody (compared to 23% urban). In both locations family/relatives are mentioned (11% urban, 17% rural). Many urban and rural households solve marriage problems with the assistance of the family and with relatives (54% and 50% correspondingly). Other categories beyond the close network of family and friends can be neglected – except that many do not get any support from others.

Most rural households have no support of any kind from others in solving employment problems (52%), compared to a much smaller number of urban households (18%). Many of those report solving their employment problems with the assistance of colleagues (27%, compared to 18% rural), family members and relatives (22% compared to 14% rural). This urban-rural divide may hint at the vainness in solving employment problems in the countryside, which seems to represent rural households as depending much more strongly on themselves than urban households.

Issues related to family/cultural traditions are mainly solved within families and among relatives in both urban and rural households (83% and 77% correspondingly).

Problems with neighbors/community are mostly solved by the household members of both urban and rural households (54% and 49% correspondingly). Family and relatives with assistance rank next (30% urban and 42%). For 11% of the urban households neighbors also provide support.

In general we may say that families and relatives form a very strong support network for solving problems of the households. Friends and colleagues are not important except in the case of employment problems. Apart from medical services, societal support is hardly asked for. Private and public financial institutions are negligible and also educational organizations do not play an important role.

Which is the most relevant sphere of problems for urban and rural households? The following table compares some answers to show the difference among the problems:

Table 23: Spheres of problems of urban and rural households, North Kazakhstan

Problem sphere	Total, %	Urban, %	Rural, %
Traffic and transport	17	20	11
Housing, communal services, flat prices	28	31	21
Inflation, food prices, general prices, low salary	17	22	7
Bad infrastructure (medical, communal, leisure)	14	3	36

One can observe that problems centered on housing (including prices for real estate) form the most relevant sphere for the urban households of Astana, while the rural households are much more concerned with their poor infrastructure. Prices and price increases are also important for urban households, but less mentioned by rural ones, maybe because of the higher degree of subsistence production which allows the rural households to be less vulnerable from the markets and thus also from price increases.

Both urban and rural households emphasize the transport problems. Urban households are dealing with traffic jams and crowded public transport while for the rural areas the problem is more related to bad or lacking transport facilities between villages and the center. These results are very much in tune with those from table 4 above, which lists the affectedness by certain problems and with the results about the addressees, with whom the households discuss their problems. Prices and price increases form the major challenges for the households. But employment and infrastructural problems should not be neglected.

The next issue, we want to address is the households' living standard. The following table provides the total numbers (percent) and the urban-rural distribution.

Table 24: Households' living standard, North Kazakhstan

Living standard	Total, %	Urban, %	Rural, %
Own house/apartment*	87	83	94
Own land***	41	23	78
Car/motor cycle	56	56	56
Refrigerator	94	93	96
Washing machine	91	98	93
Stereo equipment	43	42	46
Computer**	74	81	60
Plasma or LCD***	66	84	31
Euro Remont***	33	43	14
Dacha	10	8	14
Livestock***	19	10	36
Agricultural machinery	3	4	2

Chi-square test:
*** highest significant dependency
** highly significant dependency
* significant dependency

Housing and related problems were mentioned as the major sphere of problems for the households. In this table we can see, that the vast majority of our households have their own house or apartment. Housing is obviously of high esteem in Astana and in Akmola region and property in real estate ranks high if compared with other nation states. We should also take into account, that our respondents represent middle class people. To apply a standard, we report the figures from the EU: "In 2011, over one quarter (27,6%) of the EU-27 population lived in an owner-occupied home for which there was an outstanding loan or mortgage, while more than two fifths (43,1%) of the population lived in an owner occupied home without a loan or mortgage".[128] The quotation already indicates a possible problem, that is, loans and mortgages connected with ownership of real estate. We may assume from this that price increases for apartments and general price increases hit owners hard, renders them vulnerable and makes them judge the related problems being of high priority as done above. A small number of households (2%) own more than one apartment. We believe that the investments in apartments or houses represent insurance for old age as well as an additional income when one lets those. But it may also represent traditional orientations

[128] http://epp.eurostat.ec.europa.eu/statistics_explained/index.php?tittl, 20.08.2013.

favoring extended family formations. The latter argument only represents an assumption and needs further exploration with help of our in-depth interviews. From our data, we can also conclude that fewer households with only one source own a house or apartment than households with several incomes. In other words, if people in Astana and in the Akmola region can afford it, they invest in private property. This also refers to property of land, which is fairly wide spread, also among urban citizens. Taking into account the high prices for land plots in Astana and its suburban areas it is not astonishing that owning land in the urban region is less widespread than in the rural regions. In general the data also shows that the living conditions in our region improve with the number of income earners.

Both rural and urban households are well equipped with consumer items. However, with regard to Plasma/LCD and expensive and prestigious European refurbishment (Euro Remont) urban households are the highest significantly better equipped, than rural ones, while it is just the opposite relation with regard to livestock and land. Computer equipment shows a highly significant difference between urban and rural households, and own house/apartment a significant difference. Stereo equipment is nowadays comparatively low, due to television and computer. Livestock and land are significantly higher and more a rural than an urban issue. This is not a picture of a developing country but of one that during the survey belongs to the better off middle income countries if we compare nations.[129]

The possession of cars also indicates the well-being of households in the region. Most households with one and two income earners do not have their own vehicles (68% and 54% correspondingly), while the majority of households with three or more sources of income have. In Astana personal transport facilities are not absolutely necessary, due to a wide net of public and private (taxis of all kind) transport facilities. But of course a car is also a status symbol.

Today computers especially represent important technical equipment for households. The majority of households with different income sources have computers and also LCD or plasma TVs.

Not only ownership of real estate makes up for the standard of living but also the quality. A rough indicator is the size of available living space. 7% of the sample households have a living space of less than 25 square meters. More than one third (35%) lives in a flat or house of 26-50 square meters. The second third (31%) has a living space of 51-75 square meters. 15% amount to a space of 76 to 100 square meters, and 9% of 100 to 125 square meters. Another 3% even exceed this size. Comparing urban and rural households, the very small apartments are more

[129] http://web.worldbank.org/WBSITE/EXTERNAL/EXTOED/EXTM, 20.08.2013.

urban and related to singles or couples. A typical rural households lives in an apartment or house of the size of 26-50 square meters (44%) or 51-75 square meters (28%), compared to 31% and 33% of the urban households correspondingly. In general, living space increases with the size of the household.

Normally, in households people of different sex, generations and also of different ethnicity are living together. This may cause tensions. Some questions tried to investigate these problems. The following table provides the results.

Table 25: Household tensions, North Kazakhstan

Tensions between...	Generations, %	Males and female, %	Different nationals, %
No tensions	49	65	98
Some tensions	48	34	2
Strong tensions	3	1	0

To sum up, half of the respondents report some generational tensions, 'one third some gender tensions. Ethnic tensions do not play an important role, also due to the fact that interethnic marriage is rather low.

We asked the households about the three most severe problems in an open question and classified the answers. The following table consists of three parts. The first part provides the analysis of all households, followed by two parts for urban and rural households. We also calculated the average of each problem over the three columns and ranked the problems according to that average. However, one can also read the table in such a way that the first problem mentioned is considered to be the major problem.

Table 26: Three major household problems, North Kazakhstan

Problems, total (%)	1st	2nd	3rd	Average
Traffic and transport	17	26	19	21
Housing, communal services, flat prices	28	23	12	21
Inflation, food prices, price increasing in general, low salary	24	13	22	20
Bad infrastructure (medical, communal, leisure)	14	18	15	16
Ecology, pollution, garbage, noise	8	9	4	7
Unemployment and economy	7	4	7	6
Education, educ. Infrastructure, playgrounds	4	6	8	6
Criminality, corruption, drugs, alcoholism, homeless people	1	3	5	3

Problems, urban (%)	**1st**	**2nd**	**3rd**	**Average**
Housing, communal services, flat prices	31	24	15	23
Inflation, food prices, price increasing in general, low salary	22	16	32	23
Traffic and transport	20	26	15	20
Ecology, pollution, garbage, noise	7	11	17	12
Bad infrastructure (medical, communal, leisure)	3	6	8	6
Education, educ. Infrastructure, playgrounds	4	7	7	6
Unemployment and economy	1	4	7	4
Criminality, corruption, drugs, alcoholism, homeless people	2	4	7	4
Problems, rural (%)	**1st**	**2nd**	**3rd**	**Average**
Bad infrastructure (medical, communal, leisure)	36	43	30	36
Traffic and transport	11	27	33	24
Housing, communal services, flat prices	21	22	7	17
Ecology, pollution, garbage, noise	21	22	7	17
Unemployment and economy	21	5	7	7
Inflation, food prices, price increasing in general, low salary	7	0	7	5
Education, educ. infrastructure, playgrounds	2	3	10	5
Criminality, corruption, drugs, alcoholism, homeless people	0	0	3	1

The results of this table are more or less affirming the already gained picture. Housing and prices are top problems followed by traffic and ecological problems. Urban and rural answers don't differ much, but the bad infrastructure in rural areas attracts a lot of criticism. This is also true concerning unemployment. In Astana the labor market seems to absorb the work force pretty well while in the countryside this is not the case. In international literature, corruption shows up as a big problem in the country. But our respondents from the capital and its surrounding region don't evaluate the situation in the same way. This needs further investigation in our qualitative part of the research project.

Savings, Credits and Material Security

If one wants to get an impression about the households' living standard, it is necessary to look at the income side, but also the savings and the credits, the households have. We shall start with the question, how far and for which purposes the households take credits? With this question we also aim at exploring the link between the households and the wider economy.

In general, 89% of all households have at least one credit during the time of our interview, 94% of these only one credit, 5% two credits and 2% even had three credits. Looking at the credit amounts, for the 1st credit the households mentioned the following amounts.

Table 27: Credit amount (1st credit), North Kazakhstan

Credit amount	Total	Urban	Rural
999 USD and less	16%	15%	19%
1,000-4,999 USD	35%	21%	64%
5,000-19,999 USD	28%	35%	12%
20,000 USD and above	21%	29%	5%

The Chi-square test shows that rural households have the significantly highest number and take lower credit amounts than urban households.

Table 28: Credit purposes, North Kazakhstan

Purpose	Total	Urban	Rural
Mortgage/real estate	32%	44%	5%
Business investment, livestock, land	7%	6%	11%
Consumer credit, paying back credits	26%	23%	34%
Family needs, education, funeral, marriage	10%	9%	13%
Housing repair, house construction	6%	2%	15%
Car purchase	22%	14%	8%

The data shows a very uneven distribution between urban and rural households. Mortgage and real estate credits are significantly the highest in urban households, while consumer credits and business investments resp. investments in livestock and land as well as housing repair (construction) occur significantly more in rural households.

How much interest do the households pay for their credits? First of all, we have to mention that credit among kin is usually interest-free. 9% of the sample households state that their first credit is interest-free, even if it concerns high amounts and it is a long-term credit. The interest rates from the other households are shown in the following table.

Table 29: Interest rates, North Kazakhstan

Interest rate	Total	Urban	Rural
1-5%	3%	3%	3%
6-10%	19%	21%	13%
11-15%	28%	35%	14%
16-20%	26%	33%	11%
21-25%	20%	8%	43%
>25%	5%	0%	16%

The table shows unevenly distributed interest rates in urban and rural regions. The result may be due to a better credit infrastructure with more competition in the city. It may, however, also result from a higher risk premium for rural dwellers.

Who are the institutional credit providers for the households (excluding relatives)? They are first of all banks, followed by shops/shopping centers and, more in rural than in urban regions, microcredit institutions.

Savings may render households less vulnerable and represent rational planning concerning expenditures. How many households are able to save for crisis, old age and children?

Table 30: Saving for the future, North Kazakhstan

Purpose of saving	Total	Urban	Rural
Crisis*	41%	53%	16%
Old age**	34%	41%	20%
Children*	50%	67%	14%

* highest significant dependency from location
** highly significant dependency from location

Half of our respondents are able to save for their children. We assume that like this the parent generation builds up an emotional stock for keeping the family together, obligations for old age security included. We assume additionally, that this socio-economic behavior represents the traditional way of Kazakh familism. But both assumptions need further investigations with in-depth interviews. But as we see from the data too, the ability to save is very unevenly distributed between city dwellers and people from Akmola region. In Astana 53% are able to build up a buffer reserve for crisis compared to only 16% from Akmola region, and 67% can save for their children compared to only 14% from rural regions. Old age savings range last, 41% in Astana and 20% in Akmola region.

Where do the households save? The majority of people save at home, both in the city and in the villages. Even in Astana it is only every second household which saves with a bank. Investments with banks occur on a small scale only. It seems that these institutions of the market economy still lack acceptance among our respondents. Savings in private property are important, and are rather frequent in both locations. Interestingly, livestock investment is less a rural than an urban affair; the herd is – we assume – managed by rural relatives. One can see from the data that savings in general seem to be more difficult for rural households than for urban ones.

Table 31: Savings behavior, North Kazakhstan

Institution	Total	Urban	Rural
Local Bank*	44%	50%	31%
Foreign bank	2%	3%	0%
Bank account abroad	1%	2%	0%
Bank Investments	5%	7%	0%
Livestock investment	15%	12%	2%
Private property*	60%	67%	45%
Saving at home	69%	79%	48%

* highly significant dependency from location

In the questionnaire we provided a list of potential purposes for the savings, a mix of different investments. To avoid distortion we also asked the respondents how far they already possess such investments. The following table shows the results.

Table 32: Savings purposes for social events and security, North Kazakhstan

Category	Saving for...	Already having...
Wedding/funeral	31%	10%
Other family events	17%	13%
Apartment	33%	42%
Jewelry/gold*	33%	39%
Land	12%	21%
Livestock	4%	13%
Health insurance	5%	13%
Old age insurance	8%	3%
Life insurance	5%	8%
Children's education	27%	12%
Vacation	27%	9%
Hadj	7%	-

Data show the importance of savings for social events in the family like wedding, funerals, and other family events, this again underlines the importance of the family networks. Also the importance of an owned house or apartment is highlighted again. Insurances as institutional providers of security are rather an exception, while savings for children's education are stressed again. But our middle class respondents also save for vacation. Saving for Hadj seems to be a lip service only as nobody in our sample had any savings for that purpose.

From the many facts revealed above, we may conclude, that family relations are still strong in Kazakhstan. Let us now consider how far households provide loans to other households and whether the recipients are relatives. Every fourth household in the sample has an open financial claim on others and 3% even two. The recipients are, first of all, family members/relatives (63%), followed by friends (27%) and colleagues (7%). All loans provided are interest-free. Therefore, it is not astonishing that among the purposes mentioned in an open question, it is predominantly "help", "debt repayment" of the recipients and "some consumer purchases". Looking at the first loan from a financial viewpoint, the bulk of such credits falls into the category of 100-499 USD (33%), another 21% of 500-999 USD, and another 19% above 1,000 USD. The highest category mentioned was more than 20,000 USD in one case. But also smaller loans are provided: 17% of 50-99 USD and 10% less than 50 USD. Most of these loans are short-term in nature: less than a month (37%) or 1-3 months (32%). Another 17% fall into a 3-6-months' loan, 5% into a 6-12-months loan, 10% are a loan for more than a year. That is, lending is a very frequent activity by which urgent financial problems are solved mainly among family members and friends.

Table 33: Decision-making units in the households, North Kazakhstan

Purpose of decision	Household	Nuclear Family	Individual	Not relevant
Savings	24%	50%	13%	13%
Consumer credit	28%	52%	14%	6%
Housing investment	28%	46%	5%	21%
Other investment	22%	33%	7%	38%
School education	16%	29%	7%	48%
Higher education	18%	40%	11%	31%
Migration	18%	21%	4%	57%
Insurances other than car	15%	22%	13%	50%

Who takes the decisions for the different purposes concerning savings, credits and investments: the whole household, the nuclear family or the individual?

Data show that considerable percentage of decisions, such as making savings, investments in real estate, about insurances or taking credits and school and higher education issues, migration and other issues are taken within the nuclear family.

The household ranks next. Individuals seem to play a minor role which could be due to the fact that we asked household related questions. We should keep in mind that in many cases households and families overlap each other.

To summarize the section on savings, credits and lending:

- The majority of private households take credits from banks if we exclude relatives. The interest rates show a broad variation.
- The main credit purposes are: buying real estate and consumer goods and purchasing cars.
- Many households provide monetary assistance to relatives.
- Saving at home is the most widespread way, but every fourth household has no savings of any form.
- Three most important priorities that households save money for could be identified. The first savings' priority is to buy real estate. The second priority is to improve health and education, and finally, the third priority is just for the future. Many households keep savings in cash and gold.
- The decisions concerning savings, investing in real estate, insurances, credits, schools and higher education, and migration are mainly taken on the level of the families and the households.

Values and Responsibilities

What priority is given to different values by the households? We want to look at both rural and urban households in comparison.

Table 34: Household values, North Kazakhstan

Value	Very important (%)			Important (%)		
	Total	Urban	Rural	Total	Urban	Rural
Keeping household together	16	21	6***	35	37	32
Building new independent household	14	14	15	37	33	44
Earning much money	62	58	71	33	36	27
Improving living standard	61	55	75	37	42	26
Improving competences	33	28	43	43	43	43
Giving best education for children	53	40	80*	32	39	18
Buying a house/apartment	39	34	48	28	30	23
Being healthy	85	78	100**	13	19	0
Being happy	85	80	96***	13	17	4
Going to Hadj	6	1	21*	12	13	12

* highest significant dependency from location
** high significant dependency from location
*** significant dependency from location

Among the priority values (very important) we find good health, with 85% of the respondents and even with 100% among the rural households, and happiness with 85% of the respondents and even 96% among the rural households, to be the highest. This may perhaps be due to the lower medical infrastructure and the lower financial security in the countryside. Next follow two material values; earning more money (62%) and improving the living standard (61%), is considered even more important in the villages (71% and 75%) than in the city (58% and 55%). But also 'best education for children' ranks high. We can stress again the importance given to educational issues by our respondents which we believe to be due to the intention to foster family relations among the generations. The difference between the city and the countryside can probably be explained by worse educational infrastructure in the villages which makes 'investment' in education even more important. The material aim of buying a house ranks next (39%, and even 48% in villages). This seems to be a contradiction to our former findings, however, once households own their own private property; this goal may decrease in importance. The goal of increasing one's skills follows (33%), and here villagers again see a higher priority than urban dwellers, probably due to their lower incomes and perhaps with the wish to qualify for a city job. The aim of keeping the household together is pursued more in the city than in the villages, probably due to a stronger individualization of life in the city. The aim of building one's own household is dependent on generation; here young people who are still living with their parents/parents-in-law may be concerned. The religious value of going to Hadj is rather unimportant (6%) but is still important for every fifth village household, compared to only every tenth urban household. If this is lip service here – as remarked above – must be left open.

We also asked who should take responsibilities for certain problems.[130] We again consider rural and urban households separately. Let us begin with old age security. 76% of the urban and only 50% of the rural households consider the state responsible (average 67%).[131] However, 35% of the urban and 12% of the rural households consider the family as responsible (average 27%).[132] 53% of both household types see the responsibility with the individual. 14% urban and 28% rural households name insurance companies (average 19%).[133] 4% of the urban households also address charity organizations.

What about children's education? This is clearly a family matter (93%, 98%

[130] Multiple answers.

[131] High significant dependence from location.

[132] High significant dependence from location.

[133] Significant dependence on location.

urban and 84% rural)[134], while the state is considered to be less responsible (41% compared to 44% urban and 36% rural households). An explanation for the difference, shown locationally, is perhaps the stronger dependence of urban households on kindergartens. With 12% in both locations the individual is also held responsible.

Unemployment is looked upon as a responsibility of the state, 81 % of the Astana and 88% of the Akmola region households believe this (average 84%). In both locations, almost 50% look upon the individual as being responsible for unemployment. But in the city, the family is also held responsible to some degree (33% against 4% rural), which interestingly constitutes the highest significant dependency. This may perhaps be explained by support networks in the countryside. Interestingly none of the households consider insurance companies or charity organizations responsible for support of unemployed people.

Healthcare primarily concerns the state's responsibility; more than 90% of the households believe this. This mirrors the public health care system in Kazakhstan. Insurance companies are mentioned only by 15%. Although some people have private insurance for health care, in order to compensate for bad public services, the responsibility is believed to be with the state. With 13% for the individual and with 6% the family plays a rather unimportant role.

The poor should be supported by the state; more than 90% of the households believe this. Charity organizations are mentioned by 42% of the urban and even 60% of the rural households (average 48%).[135] It is remarkable that 12% of the rural and only 3% of the urban households hold the individual responsible (average 6%)[136], which may perhaps be due to lack of support in the villages for some dwellers.

School education is the state's responsibility (more than 90%), while one-third of the households also see a responsibility for the family. For higher education, however, only 70% see the responsibility as being the state's; it shifts more to the family (40%) and the individual (33%).

It is noteworthy that all tests on dependency concerning particularly vulnerable groups, age and gender do not provide significant differences in the answers compared to average households.

We may conclude on that part that health and happiness are the top priority values, followed by two material values, earning more money and improving one's

[134] High significant dependence on location.

[135] Significant dependence on location.

[136] Significant dependence on location.

living conditions with some gap to the top priority (more than 20%), and the goal to give 'best education for the children' (again 10% behind).

Concerning the spheres of responsibility, we assume that paternalistic attitudes combined with 'nanny-state' orientation dominate in Kazakhstani society. If it is not the state being responsible, it is the family. The belief in individual responsibility already shows up in some answers but quite weakly. The institutional sphere of insurances to care for problem situations is hardly considered in Astana and Akmola region, that is, market driven orientations and solutions for solving social problems hardly exist.

3.4. The South Kazakhstan Survey

Nazym SHEDENOVA, Aigul BEIMISHEVA, Heiko SCHRADER, Eckhard DITTRICH

The Sample

The sample consists of 100 urban and 50 rural private households. Data gathering took place in June 2011. The survey was conducted in Almaty, Kazakhstan's largest city, its business, educational and cultural center, and in villages in the region. Distance from Almaty and Taldykorgan, a regional center, served as a criterion for the selection of villages. The two townships – Turgen and Shilik – are 60 km away from Almaty and Taldykorgan, which makes it difficult for the residents of these villages to commute daily to the cities.

The majority of the respondents were female (79% in total, 81% urban, 74% rural). Most respondents are ethnic Kazakhs (84% in total, 92% urban, 67% rural). 8 % are ethnic Russian, and 8% other ethnic groups. Overall, 92% of all studied households are ethnically homogeneous families, while 6% and 12% rural households in the sample are ethnically mixed households/couples. All households represent the middle class as defined above.

Household Composition

Most households studied include only two generations both in urban and rural areas (79% and 78%, respectively. In the city there are more one- generation households (12% compared to 4% rural). In the rural areas we find more households which consist of relatives from 3 (18% rural, 9% urban) and even more generations. Whether this higher number of extended families, and also of larger families in the countryside, is due to the lower living standard or to more traditional orientation or to both, must be left open here. The following table shows the household size in urban and rural regions.

Table 35: Household size, South Kazakhstan

Household Size (Interval)	Location		
	urban	rural	Total
One or two persons	18.0%	10.0%	15.3%
Three persons	16.0%	2.0%	17.3%
Four persons	33.0%	22.0%	29.3%
Five persons	22.0%	24.0%	22.7%

Six and more persons	11.0%	24.0%	15.3%
Total	100.0%	100.0%	100.0%

Only 8% of the households are single parent families with young children in care.

The majority of the respondents (59% in the city, 50% in the countryside) belong to the "middle age" (30 to 49). Younger respondents (younger than 30) cover 22% of the sample, and 24% are 50 years and older. Particularly among the rural households, we also find respondents being 60 years and older (12% compared to 3% urban).

The most common average household age fits into the age group "26-35" (41% of urban and 46% of rural respondents) which leads us to assume that these are households with smaller children. About a third of the respondents refer to the age group "less than 25 years" – young married couples without or with one child. 15% of all respondents are between the ages of 36 and 45 years. This is probably older parents with older children, or at least three generation households.

The Living Conditions of the Households, their Socio-Economic Relations and their Vulnerability

The economic situation of the households is largely determined by the number of income-generating adults, their incomes, and their dependents. The survey shows that 15% of urban and 24% of rural households have only one income. 42% and 38%, respectively, have two incomes, 34% and 40% 3 or 4 incomes. There are only very few households in the two locations with more than four incomes.

We distinguished the households through diversity of employment in order to gain estimation for their vulnerability.[137] The idea is that the more heterogeneous the employment and related incomes are, the better the household can cope with crises, such as unemployment.

Table 36: Household type according to employment diversity, South Kazakhstan

Household type according to employment diversity	Location		Total
	urban	rural	
Not diverse	17.0%	36.0%	23.3%
Diverse	42.0%	30.0%	38.0%
Highly diverse	41.0%	34.0%	38.7%
Total	100.0%	100.0%	100.0%

137 The employment diversity was determined by the team according to number of income earners, and state vs. private employment of household member. High diversity means less vulnerability of the household and vice versa.

Now we will consider the distribution of incomes by location. As can be expected and as we can see from the following figures, the average income of urban citizens is higher than the income of rural inhabitants. 34% of urban households have an income of 75,000-120,000 KZT,[138] while only 26% of rural ones fall into this interval. A look at the lower income interval of 27,000-75,000 KZT shows that only 10% of the urban, but 54% of the rural households fall into this range. On the other hand, 51% of the urban and only 10% of rural households have an income of 120,000 KZT and higher. Urban households that are financially better off, have significantly higher incomes than rural ones.[139] Gardening and breeding of cattle allow the latter to survive in such difficult economic conditions, but these sources of "non-cash" income depend on the season. The following figure implies smaller intervals and underlines the uneven distribution of urban and rural incomes.

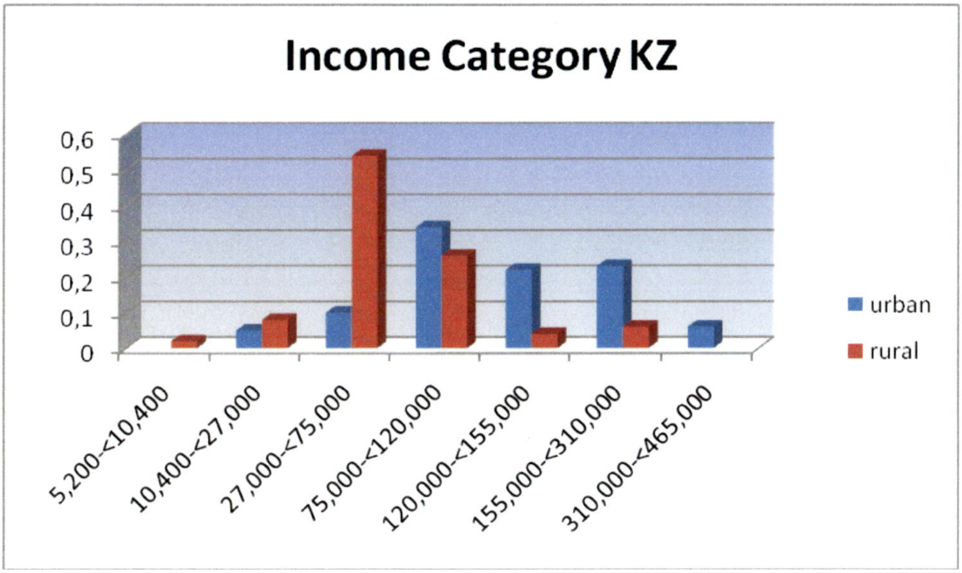

Figure 16: The distribution of income of urban and rural households, South Kazakhstan

64% of households, both in the city and rural regions, are closed households, economically independent from external recipients or providers. One-tenth of urban and rural households receive financial assistance from outside. Some house-

138 We apply the same exchange rate as in the North Kazakhstan region: Kazakhstan: 1USD=150 Tenge.

139 Pearson Chi-Square asymptotic significance 0.0. Here and in the other chi-square tests significance level 0.05.

holds also receive different non-monetary help from outside. The supporters are close family members – parents support children and vice versa, or siblings support each other, or it is uncles and aunts providing support. This kind of help may include food, clothes and durable goods, including second-hand goods.

The other side of reciprocal relations is from the household to dependents. One-third of urban households and one-fifth of rural households provide cash support to dependents, the same amount provides non-cash support. First rank children who receive support, but it is mainly the urban households who provide support to their children living outside the household. Another group that requires and deserves support from urban households is relatives of pensionable age – mainly the parents (32%). They often live apart from their adult children. Occasionally widows/widowers and other family members receive support.

The following figure shows the household resource network type.

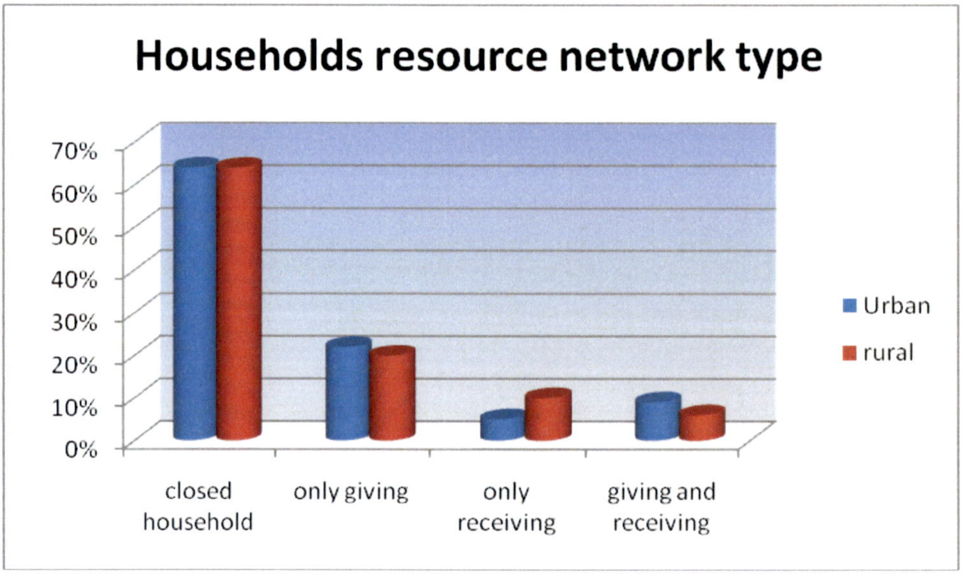

Figure 17: Households' resource network types, South Kazakhstan

Particularly in rural regions monetary and non-monetary incomes are important for economic survival. Households reduce their costs with help of natural resources for food, combustible fuel material etc. We asked the respondents about access and importance of the following subsistence goods: a) livestock and poultry, meat and dairy products; b) agricultural produce grown in their own garden or fields; c) access to drinking water (pipeline / from the well); d) natural products such as fish, mushrooms, honey, wood, coal, etc.; and e) access to grazing lands for animals.

Table 37: Importance of subsistence/natural revenues, South Kazakhstan

Subsistence/Natural Revenues	Access/ importance	Urban, %	Rural, %	Total, %
Animal products	Little important	8.0	10.0	8.7
	Important	31.0	50.0	37.3
	Very important	9.0	12.0	10.0
Garden/agricultural products	Little important	4.0	20.0	9.3
	Important	37.0	54.0	42.7
	Very important	9.0	16.0	11.3
Drinking water (pipe/well)	Little important	5.0	14.0	8.0
	Important	28.0	52.0	36.0
	Very important	28.0	18.0	24.7
Collecting from nature (including fishing)	Little important	21.0	12.0	18.0
	Important	23.0	54.0	33.3
	Very important	3.0	12.0	6.0
Grazing land	Little important	5.0	14.0	8.0
	Important	12.0	8.0	10.7
	Very important	0.0	4.0	1.3

This subsistence/natural income is much higher for the rural households than for urban ones, but urban residents also can have access to these resources. They can raise vegetables and fruits in their cottages, keep poultry and livestock (if not on a dacha, then with their relatives), use natural resources, and the like. For urban households access to subsistence production often takes place via their networks. The findings show that in general more than half of the urban residents have less direct access to subsistence revenue. But there are still more than 40% who state that animal or garden products are important or very important for their subsistence. In the rural cases it is more than 60%. Some villagers report to have no access to drinking water from pipe or well.

How far are incomes sufficient to meet basic expenses? Almost 70% of the urban households and almost half of the rural households consider their incomes to be sufficient. On the other hand, every fifth rural household reports that incomes are not or hardly sufficient for making a living – this is a highly significant difference to urban households as the chi-square test shows.

Table 38: Sufficiency of income for expenses, South Kazakhstan

Sufficiency of income for expenses	Location		Total, %
	Urban, %	Rural, %	
Not / hardly sufficient	4.0	20.0	9.4
Almost sufficient	29.0	34.0	30.7
Sufficient	67.0	46.0	60.0
Total	100,0	100.0	100.0

The households were asked to evaluate their present economic situation and their future prospects. These estimates were to reflect the positive or negative perception of their economic positions and the objective living conditions and overall socio-economic situation in the country. Undoubtedly, the economic crisis of 2008, after a prolonged period of stabilization from 2001/2002 onward, affected the rate of employment and the income growth rate, and increased the sense of insecurity and anxiety about the future. On the other hand, the state spends money for socio-economic modernization and for the development of production and business, support of rural employment and income growth of the vulnerable groups. But certain groups nevertheless rate their situation as not being rosy, to put it in a poetic way.

As can be seen from the next figure, urban residents consider their living conditions better than average, while the majority of rural households rate them worse than their counterparts in the city. This mirrors clearly the difficult living conditions in the countryside with the high dependence on subsistence production, the employment problems, the lower incomes etc. This diagnosis that could already be seen in northern Kazakhstan will find more corroboration later on.

Asked for the overall changes within the last 10 years, the majority of the respondents in both urban and rural locations of southern Kazakhstan reported that their economic situation had improved. This can also be interpreted as optimism about the future. It seems that the dynamic changes after independence have laid ground for optimistic orientations in the future. This optimism is found both in the city and the countryside (small differences). 71% expect an improvement, be it small (25%) or larger (47%), while 22% expect no change and 7% a deterioration. The 'shock' of the financial crises of 2008 seems to have faded away. The quick macro-economic recovery seems to find an equivalent in this positive future orientation.

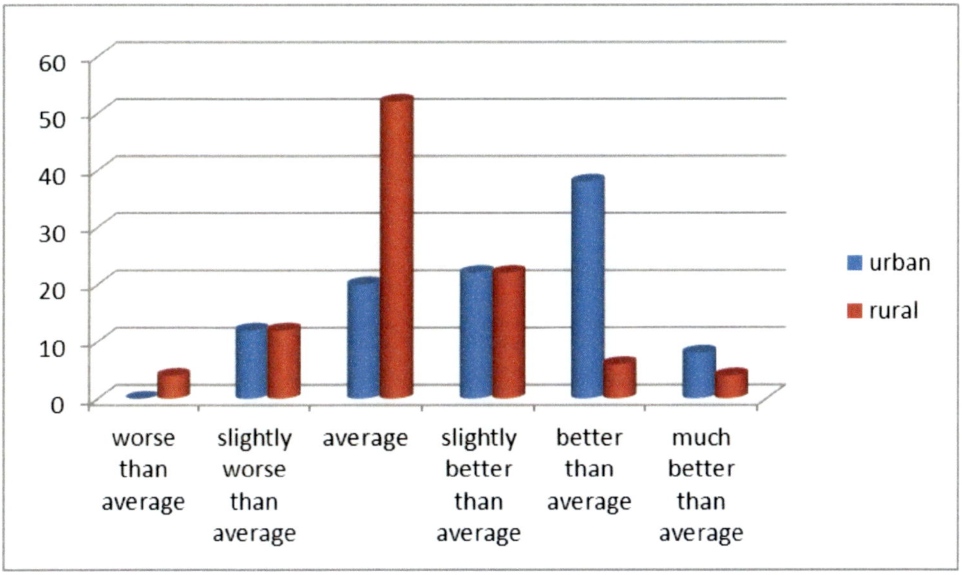

Figure 18: Self-assessment of living conditions compared to average, South Kazakhstan
Note: percent

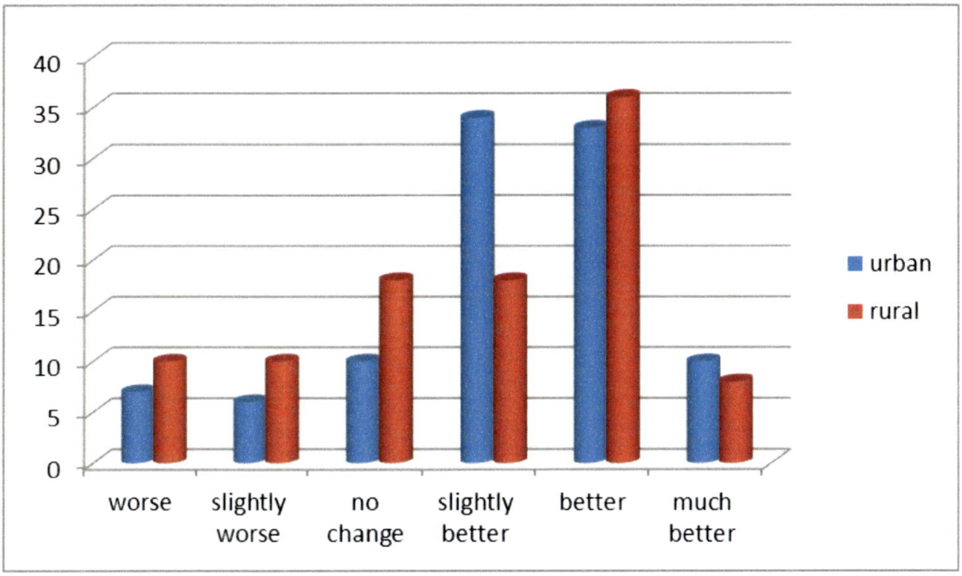

Figure 19: Self-assessment of improvement of economic status during the last 10 years, South Kazakhstan
Note: percent

What about the reasons for their assessment (open question)? 39% of the respondents with an optimistic view (city – 42%, rural – 31%) expect an improvement of their financial situation, 32% (city – 29%, rural – 40%) foresee a positive career development, employment improvement and further education. Among those 29% who foresee no improvement, external reasons (economic recession and instability and internal reasons related to the household prevail.

In literature, infrastructural differences between urban and rural locations are very often stressed. As infrastructure is closely related to a household's well-being, we wanted to know about the availability of certain public and private goods and facilities in both locations.

Table 39: Access to infrastructure in the location of living, South Kazakhstan

	Urban, %	Rural, %	Total, %
Doctor	70	96	79
Medical center	81	94	85
Polyclinic	87	96	90
Hospital	76	98	83
Pre-primary	89	84	87
Primary	91	98	93
Secondary	96	98	97
Vocational	80	66	75
University	74	2	50
Banking Services	98	66	87
Market, shops	100	100	100
Transportation services	100	90	97
Library	88	90	89
Cinema	84	0	56
Theater	80	0	53
Music entertainment	91	12	65
Sports facilities	87	58	77
Internet at home	86	66	79
Internet cafe/shop	90	50	77
Post office	94	94	94
Access to phone	99	96	98
Gas	98	76	91
Regular Electricity	100	100	100
Free access to safe drinking water	89	66	83

In general, one has to keep in mind, that the villages, where the interviews took place, represent 'regional centers' which generally have better infrastructure than 'normal' villages due to state politics.

Regarding access to *health services*: By health care we mean the territorial availability of government clinics and hospitals, private medical centers and doctors. The rural availability is a result of the type of the villages studied. The availability is even better than in Almaty, where the other interviews were taken. Some rural respondents report that certain specialized doctors are only found in the larger district towns, including the city of Almaty. With regard to health services the urban dwellers score lower – which is astonishing and can perhaps be explained in that they refer to their immediate neighborhood.

In the sphere of *early children's education* urban residents feel slightly better equipped with pre-school infrastructure. After transition to a market economy many public kindergartens were privatized and then not used for their intended purpose. Nowadays, many private kindergartens have been opened in the city, which helps to reduce the demand. In the rural areas kindergartens were opened not long ago. But because of lower female employment in the countryside, available kinfolk that may help in childcare, the need of kindergartens is lower. But, apparently, there is no large gap.

Due to the state program of compulsory *secondary education* in Kazakhstan, all children attend high schools. Virtually all respondents noted access to primary and secondary education in the community (89-98%). However some respondents in the city are dissatisfied by the distance to school, congestion or the quality of nearby schools.

In rural areas, the situation is more in need regarding *vocational training* (80% urban, 66% rural)*and university education* (74% urban, 2% rural). There is no chance for university education in the villages, even if they have the status of regional centers, but in those two third of the population may go to college. However, anyone who wishes to have university education has to move to Almaty or to another city. This increases migration of different types.

The banking system of Kazakhstan is looked upon as one of the best in the post-soviet countries. But while urban residents are fully covered by bank infrastructure (98%), only 66% of rural residents can obtain their services in their location. Concerning *Shops, markets and supermarkets* 100% of respondents note that they do not have any difficulties with their availability at least in these rural centers. *Transport* plays one of the most important roles in the infrastructure of any area, because it is responsible for the mobility of the residents. Both in the city (100%) and in the villages (90%) coverage by transport services seem well established. However, a differentiation has to be made between private and public transport. In Almaty public transport is available for everybody, but in our villages almost all public transport is abolished. The main transport is represented by private taxis.

In terms of access to *cultural services* the countryside is inferior to the city. In the villages researched, only 90% of people have access to libraries. In almost all villages in the country there are no cinemas and theatres. Only 12% of rural residents have access to music pubs, such as disco clubs. Typically, they are organized by young people themselves, who live in these villages and they do not operate on a regular basis. More than 90% of urban residents have noted the accessibility to different kinds of cultural services is no problem.

Only slightly more than half of the respondents have access to *sport services* (58%), because in the villages there is only limited access to sport clubs and groups. The urban population reports an accessibility of 87%.

At present the *internet* is one of the most powerful forms of communication. Our survey shows that 86% of urban and 66% of the rural population have access to the internet at home. The low percentage in rural areas may be explained by the fact that only a few internet providers operate in the villages because of economic reasons. Internet cafes only compensate for this for half of the rural population, while coverage in Almaty is 90%. Access to *post offices* of *"KazPost"* and *phones* is above 90 % in urban and rural areas. The fact that not all urban respondents have access to phones is connected with the building of new residential estates in the vicinity of Almaty. The installation of phones is lagging behind.

Only 76% of the rural population has access to *gas*, while the coverage in Almaty is 98%. Gas has still not reached all villages of the Almaty region. Free accesses to *safe drinking water* also still represent a problem with 89% of urban and 66% of rural availability. Not all villages have a central water supply; they use the wells. Sometimes the situation is even worse, for example, when the water has to be imported. All respondents have access to a *regular electricity supply* – 100%.

In general, one may conclude that the living conditions in Almaty and the region investigated are fairly well developed. This must be attributed, at least partially, to the status of the villages that represent 'centers' with better infrastructural facilities. One may assume that this status has positive effects on the households economic possibilities, employment included. Nevertheless this needs further investigation and a thorough comparative look at the northern region, where the villages investigated are not 'regional centers'. But despite the advantageous position, major differences between the countryside and Almaty remain.

Household Problems

The household, as any other economic and social body, is embedded in its wider social surroundings, and faces – apart from its inner problems – the problems society is confronted with. We may assume that the rural-urban divide leads to different problems, but also other social and economic as well as cultural givens will pose challenges to the households. We start with the question concerning the main problems, the households were confronted with. The respondents were asked to assess the strength of various problems that were pre-given. The respondents had four options to answer: no problem, weak, medium and strong problems. The time span was one year.

Table 40: Households' main problems during the past year, South Kazakhstan

Main problems reported / per region (percent)		Weak	Medium	Strong
Unemployment	Urban	19	17	8
	Rural	4	32	22
Illness of a family member/treatment	Urban	11	20	6
	Rural	6	24	18
Death of a family member	Urban	4	6	3
	Rural	0	6	8
Divorce	Urban	4	5	2
	Rural	0	0	0
Marriage	Urban	8	11	1
	Rural	2	4	2
Rising food prices	Urban	39	44	10
	Rural	8	60	22
General increase in prices	Urban	39	44	11
	Rural	6	66	22
Apartment Services	Urban	29	49	11
	Rural	2	72	12
Preparing children to school (buying school clothes, books, etc.)	Urban	23	36	5
	Rural	6	42	6
Payments for education	Urban	13	19	8
	Rural	2	18	8
Crime	Urban	1	2	3
	Rural	0	2	0
Natural disasters	Urban	7	1	0
	Rural	4	6	0
Transportation	Urban	16	4	2
	Rural	6	6	6
Problems with neighbors	Urban	2	0	2
	Rural	2	2	0

Note: multiple answers

On a whole, the citizens and rural people worry about general economic problems, though the strength of such concern differs. The rural people feel such problems acutely, because of the influence of institutional conditions and regional differences in employment, incomes, quality of life and economical choice of the households.

The economic problems rank first. *Price increases* of the various kinds have bothered all households. But apart from payments for education, in all fields mentioned the rural respondents feel more strongly affected: unemployment, rising food prices, general increase in prices, prices for apartment services, school outfit and equipment. This also concerns *increase in prices for public utilities.*

The next group of issues may be defined as personal and familial problems. *Illness of a member of the family and her or his treatment* concerns both urban (26%) and rural households (42%) in a medium way or strongly. It seems that middle class households despite their economic position face illness not only as a personal problem but also as a social and economic one. But this is an assumption and needs further investigation. The same is true for the death and for marriages of family members. Both represent challenges in economic, social and cultural terms. When we looked at infrastructural equipment it seemed, that transportation was a minor problem even in the countryside. But now we have to register, that transportation is problematic for 22% of the respondents in the city and 18% in the countryside. Only small parts of the respondents worry about *criminality, natural disasters and disputes with the neighbors.*

The biggest concern of the households seems to be represented with costs of living determined by prices in general and their increase, but also by unforeseeable events like death, illness and marriage.

The problems considered in the table above are discussed and solved in particular ways. The financial problems are mostly discussed within the spouses (39% of urban and 42% of rural households). The other part of the respondents prefers to discuss the financial problems among the family members (32% in the city and 46% in the villages). 6% town dwellers noted that they discuss the financial problems with their parents. 7% of town people and 4% of rural people prefer to avoid discussion of such problems with anybody.

It is interesting that 4% of respondents both in the city and in the country considered discussion of the financial issues only with the male household members, and 3% of respondents – only with female household members (no respondents in the villages). This issue exemplifies preservation of the traditions regarding the families, and separation of concerns for making decisions and family budget management.

Health problems are discussed with both the spouses (40% of urban and 26% of rural families), and all members of the households (31% and 52% respectively). Only 2.0% of rural household members can share this problem with the male relatives. 7% of town and 4% village respondents prefer to seek advice from their parents.

41.3% of the respondents noted that they discuss the educational problems with all family members, and 23.3% – with their spouses. 3.3% of the respondents prefer to rely on the advice of male relatives.

Problems with relatives are mostly discussed with all family members (39% of urban and 44% rural households). City dwellers (30%) discuss this problem with their spouses more often than the country people (24%). And in the villages people try to avoid discussions at all more often than the town people (20% of village and 7% of urban respondents).

Problems with friends are more often discussed by the town people with their friends themselves (39 % in the city and only 14% in the villages). In the villages this issue is preferably discussed with all members of households (28%). A quarter of the respondents seek advice concerning this problem with their spouse.

About one third of respondents discuss marriage problems only between the spouses (36% of town and 32% village people), the other third prefers to avoid discussions on this issue (30% and 26% respectively) while in 22% of urban and 32% of rural families the whole household is involved.

Problems at work are discussed by the urban people with their colleagues (27%), spouses (26%) and all members of the households (21%). The rural people prefer to share this problem with their families: with all members of the households (32%), with nobody (30%), with spouses (16%) and with colleagues (10%). It is obvious, that in the urban setting, colleagues play a more important role which contradicts the result from northern Kazakhstan.

Issues about family traditions and culture are considered with all members of the households (44% urban and 58% of rural). 21.0% of urban people and 26.0% rural people discuss this problem with their spouses. The following data are rather interesting: this problem is not discussed in 25% of urban and only 8% of rural households. We very much believe that in the countryside family traditions and culture preserve their influence on the everyday life of the people to a larger degree than in the urban setting of Almaty.

43% do not discuss their problems with neighbors. However, in the rural area people know each other and communicate with each other better than in the city. 20% prefer to discuss this issue only with their spouse.

Who provides assistance in case of problems? The majority of interviewed accept help from relatives in resolving financial problems (76% of urban and 70% of rural households). 12% of urban households receive help from friends in difficult situations, while rural dwellers prefer to rely more on themselves (18%). Here again, the importance of the family becomes very clear.

In order to deal with labor problems, rural households generally refer to family members. Urban dwellers have wider discussion networks. They get help from family members (29%), from colleagues at work (25%), and from employers (29%).

Concerning educational problems, the majority of help also comes from family members and relatives (55% of urban and 60% of rural households). 29% of urban and 32% of rural respondents never received help from anybody. Institutional help seems to be negligible.

Relatives also render significant help in resolving health problems (71% of urban and 76% of rural households). Interestingly, only 13% of urban respondents prefer to seek help from medical professionals and doctors (2% of rural respondents). By contrast, many rural dwellers count only on themselves and note that they do not receive help from anybody (16%). This astonishing result cannot be sorted out on the basis of our data. Maybe the question itself has been falsely understood. Perhaps the answers refer indirectly to financial aid in such cases. However in the northern Kazakh sample, the medical profession ranks first.

The majority of the households questioned seek help from family and relatives in resolving marriage issues (51% of urban and 62% of rural households). 42% of urban and 36% of rural households do not ask help from anybody. Also, problems with families are mainly an issue discussed amongst family members and relatives (88% of urban and 68% of rural households). Friends (56% of urban and 24% of rural households) and relatives (23% and 48%, respectively) render the principal help in resolving problems with friends.

Resolving problems associated with family and cultural traditions, the majority of respondents request help from family members and relatives (68% in cities and 77% in rural localities). It was found that they also help in solving problems with the neighbors (34% in cities and 53% in rural localities).

To sum up: it is mainly family and immediate relatives that provide support for problems the households face. This concerns personal, family, social, economic, and other problems. In general, urban households seek such support less frequently, trying to generate other ways of problem solving.

Families were asked an open-ended question about what they consider to be the most urgent problems they are confronted with. We grouped the answers into categories. Urban dwellers reported inflation, high prices for food products, and a poor salary level as principal problems (41%). The ranking for rural dwellers is a little different. They point firstly at the issues of unemployment and then at the general economic problem centered on prices (29%). Next ranks housing, public facilities and housing prices (21% of urban and 25% of rural households).

What about tensions in the household? The interview results demonstrate that about one fourth of the respondents (25% of urban and 20% of rural respondents) note some disagreement between different generations in their households. In this respect, 2% of rural households face quite intense disagreements. Such situations can be explained by the fact that in rural households several generations may cohabitate, as well as there being more strict control and the presence of hierarchies between the generations. One third reports gender disagreements/contradictions and only 2% face ethnic disagreements. It should be noted that the interview included only a small number of ethnically mixed families.

Consumer items such as a TV set, refrigerator and others, provide comfort for everyday life, and together with the general equipment of a household can be looked upon as the living standard in the city and in rural localities. The following table compares the living standards of the urban and rural dwellers. The quality of life in the two localities is very different.

A living place constitutes the basis of any household. Almost all interviewed households (87%) own houses or apartments (84% of urban and 94% of rural households), this may be due to privatization programs, that transferred former state property to the private sector. The smaller percentage of private ownership in Almaty might result from higher real estate prices. 72% of the rural and 38% of the urban population have landed property. In Almaty, it may be represented by the owners of private cottages and houses with plots, for which they have to pay land tax. However, some urban dwellers also possess garden patches or dachas and/or invest in land or own a place where they can spend their holidays.

Table 41: Living standards, South Kazakhstan

Living standards	**Location**		**Total, %**
	Urban, %	**Rural, %**	
House/apartment	83,8	94	87.2
Land	38	72	49.3
Car/motor cycle	74	54	67.3
Refrigerator	95	90	93.3
Washing machine	87	72	82.0
Music center	53	40	48.7
Computer	80	40	66.7
LCD/Plasma	73	48	64.7
Euro Remont	52	24	42.7

Dacha	9	2	6.7
Livestock	4	16	8.0
Agricultural machinery	2	6	3.3

City dwellers more often possess automobiles and motorcycles than rural dwellers (74% and 54%, respectively). Currently household appliances are one of the most needed devices for a comfortable life. Almost all interviewed households own a refrigerator (93%). Washing machines are no longer articles of luxury either (82%). About half of the households possess music centers (49%); almost two thirds have computers and LCD/Plasma TVs (67% and 65%, respectively). But regarding computers, the difference between urban and rural households is striking. The latter possess only half the number of this item if compared with the urban counterparts. In general, urban households own all listed types of home appliances more often.

Table 42: Households and their responsibilities concerning savings, credit and security, South Kazakhstan

Household activities	Households Decisions	Urban, %	Rural, %	Total, %
Savings	household affair	34	10	26
	nuclear family affair	45	70	53
	individual affair	20	14	18
Housing investment	household affair	24	12	20
	nuclear family affair	43	56	47
	individual affair	12	4	9
Consumer credit	household affair	24	6	18
	nuclear family affair	52	56	53
	individual affair	14	6	11
Other investments	household affair	11	14	12
	nuclear family affair	32	50	38
	individual affair	10	-	7
School education	household affair	16	8	13
	nuclear family affair	52	62	55
	individual affair	8	6	7
Higher education	household affair	21	12	18
	nuclear family affair	40	58	46
	individual affair	8	2	6
Migration	household affair	22	14	20
	nuclear family affair	22	54	33
	individual affair	7	-	5
Insurances other than car insurance	household affair	24	10	20
	nuclear family affair	17	50	28
	individual affair	12	-	8

Currently very few dwellers have dachas (9% in city and 2% in rural locality). Interestingly, only 16% of rural dwellers own livestock. An explanation is that the purchase and feeding of the livestock requires a considerable investment and labor costs.

Also the size of living space is interesting in respect to the standard of living. Around half of the interviewed respondents reside in small houses or apartments with a size of up to 50 sqm (45% of urban and 54% of rural households). Around one fourth have a living space between 51 to 75 sqm (29% of urban and 16% of rural households). 15% reside in homes of between 76 and 100 sqm (13% and 18%, respectively). Only 11% have more living space available.

Coping with insecurity is an ability to allocate resources for the saturation of one's own short-term and long-term needs. Typical coping strategies concern savings, investments and credit, but also education, migration and insurances. We aimed at analyzing whether the household, the nuclear family or the individual is concerned with which decisions. Of course, such decisions depend on the current living situation.

In most categories the nuclear family is seen to be the unit to be concerned with such issues, whereas those who refer to the household may have dependent old-age people living with them. Those living alone or living in the household but having separate incomes may take decisions individually. Secondly, insurances other than car are not relevant for 47% of the urban and 40% of the rural households.

Who is the main breadwinner? We grouped the answers and found that in most cases, both urban and rural, it is father/husband and/or mother/wife who are the main breadwinners. In some cases it is the grandparents' generation. Household heads, according to tradition in patriarchal societies are male.

Savings, Credits and Security

Let us also consider the question for which purposes households take credit. Here we have to keep in mind, that traditionally credit also concerns the family network (relatives) to help in family gatherings such as marriage or funeral, or to help with finance for the purchasing of the house. In addition to such self-finance, banks spread in urban and rural Kazakhstan to offer all sorts of credit to households – consumer and investment credits such as mortgage credits. In addition, in recent years, big trading houses have started offering sales on credit for furniture or electronic items, mainly on the basis of installments, also to make purchases flow in times of economic crisis. This consumer credit is very popular among the public now. Our data show that 40% of the households in the village and 30% in the city have one or more consumer credits. Also car purchases involve credit. 20% of the urban and 13% of the rural households have such a credit. Another important reason to take a credit is the purchase of a house, an apartment or real estate. Interestingly almost 15% of the urban households but no rural household has such a long-term credit. On the other hand, every third village household has taken a credit for house repair/construction work, while in the city this concerns only 15% of the households. Investment in business, livestock or land on credit basis only occurs among urban households (7%). Every tenth rural household takes up credit for financing a marriage or a funeral, whereas only few urban households do this. Taking up a credit for repayment of another one only occurs in rare cases among urban households.

Table 43: Credit purpose according to category, South Kazakhstan

Credit purpose according to category	Urban, %	Rural, %	Total, %
Mortgage, buying apartment or real estate	15	-	12
Business investment, livestock purchase, land investment	7	-	6
Consumer credit	30	40	32
Marriage, funeral	4	13	6
Family needs, education	7	-	6
Housing repair, house construction work	15	33	19
Paying back debts	2	-	1
Car purchase	20	14	18

Half of the urban and one third of the rural households have taken credit. The amounts range from less than 499 to more than 20,000 USD. The following table provides the results.

Table 44: Credit amounts for the first credit, South Kazakhstan

USD	Urban, %	Rural, %	Total, %
<499	6	60	17
500-999	25	13	23
1,000-4,999	44	27	40
5,000-20,000	20	0.0	16
>20,000	6	0.0	4

Rural households less often take credits, and if they do, the credit amounts are lower. 60% of all rural credits amount to less than 500 USD, and we found no household with 5,000 USD and more credit. On the contrary, among the urban households taking credits, one-fourth has a credit amount of more than 5,000 USD, 6% even of more than 20,000 USD. The highest category is usually for mortgages or for a purchase of a vehicle.

Respondents also shared their information from where they obtained their first credit. Banks are the major source of credits (85% urban compared to 75% rural). In the villages we also found stores (6%), relatives (3%), a friend (3%), a colleague (3%), and microcredit institutions (3%) as creditors.

About one third of the city respondents and almost 17% of the village respondents took an interest-free loan from their relatives and friends. Normally, these loans were given for an indefinite term or for a period of one year up to three years.

Interest rates are quite different. To judge on them, one has to keep in mind the inflation rate. Commercial interest rates fall into the categories 11-15% (50% of urban households, no rural household), 16-20% (25% urban, 40% of rural households), 21-25% (11% of urban and 60% of rural households), and above 25% (15% of urban, no rural household). Here we can see that with the exception of the highest category, rural interest rates seem to be higher than urban ones.

An important coping strategy for households for overcoming difficulties is saving. Only one fourth of the households (25%) save voluntarily for old age (28% or urban households and 18% of village households). One has to keep in mind that Kazakhstan has a mandatory pension system which is not addressed with this question. 46% of households are able to save money for a household crisis (here village households rank before urban ones: 58% compared to 40%). However, 64% report to be able to save for the next generation (71% of urban and 50% of rural respondents). This includes savings for higher education. It is striking that – with the exception of crisis savings, urban households are more able to save than rural ones.

Which are the most important goals that the households save for? The inquiry shows that the most significant saving goals are children's education (76.7%), apartments/houses (74.7%), weddings/funerals (56.7%) and other family events, like anniversaries e.g. etc. (66%). For urban households, savings for apartments/houses is more important than for rural ones (78% compared to 68%). Villagers more often save money for weddings/funerals (78% compared to 46%) and any other family events (76% compared to 61%), which means that family gatherings are important for them and that they cannot just pay such expenses from their running incomes.

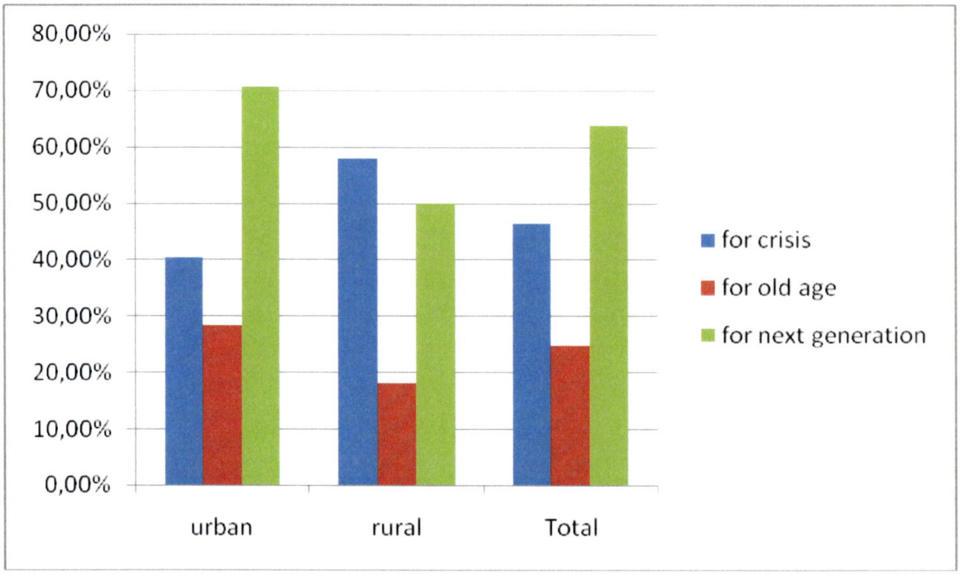

Figure 20: Ability to save for crisis, old age and for the next generation, South Kazakhstan

53% of respondents suppose that it is necessary to make savings for vacations. Interestingly, the proportion of villagers is higher (61% vs. 49%).

42% of respondents consider jewelry and gold as a reliable investment. The proportion in rural areas is higher (50% compared to 38% in the city). In rural areas, 56% of the sample households save money for the purchase of land, in the city only 42%. 52% of rural and 22% of urban respondents consider it important to save money for livestock.

Over one third of respondents specified such goals as medical insurance (38.7%), private old age insurance (36.7%), and life insurance (38.7%) as savings goals, although – as we already saw – most households do not save for such purposes yet. For one third of Kazakh families Hadj is an important goal for which they make savings.

Table 45: Important savings purposes, South Kazakhstan

Savings purposes	Urban, %	Rural, %	Total, %
Wedding/funeral	46.0	78.0	56.7
Other family events	61.0	76.0	66.0
Apartment/house	78.0	68.0	74.7
Jewelry/gold	38.0	50.0	42.0
Land	42.0	56.0	46.7
Livestock	22.0	52.0	32.0

Health insurance	33.0	50.0	38.7
Private old age insurance	31.0	48.0	36.7
Life insurance	30.0	56.0	38.7
Children's education	76.0	78.0	76.7
Vacations	49.0	61.2	53.0
Hadj	33.0	34.8	33.6

While so far we considered goals which households mentioned to be important for saving, this does not mean that they really save for them. Therefore we added the question for which purposes they really save and who of them already possesses savings for items such as a house. 50% of both urban and rural households save for weddings or funerals. 63% of urban and 37% of rural households save for other family events. 47% of urban households and 28% of rural households actually save for an apartment or house, while 22% of the urban and 3% of the rural households already possess one. 54% of the urban and 46% of the rural households save in gold and jewelry, 40% and 42% respectively for land. 17% of the urban households already possess such savings. Saving for livestock occurs among 41% of urban and 59% of the rural households. 50% in each location save for a health insurance and 50% for a life insurance; 67 % of urban and 3% of rural households save or have saved for children's education. For vacation 59% and 41% respectively save. Finally, 55% of the urban and 45% of the rural households save or have saved for Hadj. These numbers differ considerably from those from northern Kazakhstan.

Lending to Others

As we saw from the credit side, sometimes households obtain credits from relatives for the purchase of consumer items or investments. We also wanted to find out the lending behavior of households. One third of urban households and one fourth of rural households provide credits to other people. The lending amount for the first credit provided ranges from a few USD to amounts between 5,000 and 20,000 USD. Among the rural households we find 8 households providing a loan up to 50 USD, as well as 5 households providing a loan between 1,000 and 5,000 USD. Among the urban households the majority of loans are up to 50 USD (15) and between 100 and 500 USD.

Those who obtain such credits fall into the category of relatives (21), friends (12), colleagues (8) and neighbors (6). In the villages, relatives rank before neighbors, in the city relatives before friends and colleagues.

Lending purposes (open question) are far reaching: for making a living (food, education, debt repayment, crises), for family obligations (dowry, marriage, funeral, etc.), for consumer items such as a car or for investments (apartment, business).

More than 90% of these loans are interest-free and considered as help (this holds true for all rural loans and 90% of the urban loans). For the rest the interest rates range between 1 and 11%.

63% of these loans are for less than a month, 21% for 1 to 3 months, 12% for 3-12 months, 5 % for longer, the longest up to 10 years (usually house building). 40 households have provided one, five households two loans to others.

How far are banking institutions accepted among urban and rural households? 63% of all households – half of the urban and 10% of the rural households – keep savings and investments in a local bank. The Chi-Square Test shows a highest significant dependency of savings on the location in a local bank. Foreign-bank savings and investments are reported by only two households, one household even has a bank account abroad. 33% of all households, which is 40% of the urban and 20% of the rural households, save at home (significant dependency on location). Investing in livestock is important for only 4 urban and 4 rural households. 30 urban and 5 rural households invest in private property – a highly significant dependency of investment behavior on location has to be noted.

Values and Responsibilities

Values are important in respect of strategies and household behavior. What values are important and to what degree?

Respondents noted the following values as "very important" for the household: to be healthy (73%), to be happy (69%), to improve the living standard (48%), equip children with the best education (46%), earning more money (37%), buy a house/apartment (33%), and improve education, knowledge and skills (30%). Summing up the categories "important" and "very important", we have to mark the following ranking: be healthy (100%), improve living standard (100%), be happy (99%), earn much money (95%), equip children with the best education (85%), improve education, knowledge and skills (83%), and buy a house/apartment (73%).

Table 46: Importance of values for the household, South Kazakhstan

Values	Level of importance	Urban, %	Rural, %	Total, %
Keeping the household together	not important	10.0	14.0	11.3
	less important	20.0	2.0	14.0
	important	52.0	66.0	56.7
	very important	18.0	18.0	18.0
Building new independent households	not important	20.0	22.0	20.7
	less important	19.0	8.0	15.3
	important	47.0	62.0	52.0
	very important	14.0	8.0	12.0
Earning much money	not important	1.0	2.0	1.3
	less important	4.0	2.0	3.3
	important	59.0	58.0	58.7
	very important	36.0	38.0	36.7
Improving living standards	important	52.0	52.0	52.0
	very important	48.0	48.0	48.0
Enhancing skills	not important	7.1	8.0	7.4
	less important	13.1	2.0	9.4
	important	49.5	62.0	53.7
	very important	30.3	28.0	29.5
Giving best education to children	not important	11.0	12.0	11.3
	less important	5.0	0.0	3.3
	important	31.0	56.0	39.3
	very important	53.0	32.0	46.0
Buying a house/apartment	not important	11.0	16.0	12.7
	less important	14.0	16.0	14.7
	important	36.0	48.0	40.0
	very important	39.0	20.0	32.7
Being healthy	important	22.0	38.0	27.3
	very important	78.0	62.0	72.7
Being happy	less important	1.0	0.0	0.7
	important	27.0	38.0	30.7
	very important	72.0	62.0	68.7
Going to Hadj	not important	25.0	51.1	33.3
	less important	35.0	19.1	29.9
	important	32.0	23.4	29.3
	very important	8.0	6.4	7.5

As is evident, the first places are occupied by the universal values of health and happiness, then – values of improving the living standard follow, including securing the future of children and reaching a stable survival for the household by growth of income, purchase of a house/an apartment, improvement of the occupational status. Comparing the city and the villages, there are only slight differences in the rates of competence improvement (city – 80%, village – 90%) and purchase of house/apartment (city – 75%, village – 68%).

Values concerned with the family are also important: keeping the household together (75%) and creation of a new, independent household (64%). Family integrity maintenance (city – 70%, village – 84%) and creation of conditions for the separation of young families (city – 61%, village – 70%) appeared to be more important for the rural households. This seems to be related to an ample quantity of economic difficulties for their realization.

Religious values, in particular, going to Hadj is significant for one third of respondents (37%); being more important for urbanites (city – 40%, village – 30%). The city has become the center of recovery and dissemination of religious practices; moreover, only independent and economically better off families may afford going to Hadj.

Respondents were also asked to name their most important life goals in an open question. We grouped the answers into categories. 46% specified their own prosperity and welfare and 8% – family prosperity. 36% specified prosperity and welfare of their children. 10% mentioned purchases of movable and immovable property. 1% aimed at peace, stability and prosperity for the whole country. Looking at the rural and urban distributions: while the most mentioned value for rural households is the well-being and prosperity of the children (41% compared to 33% urban) or the family (10% compared to 7% urban), for the urban ones it is their own well-being and prosperity (52% compared to 35% rural).

The last block of questions was related to what institutions and groups bear responsibility for various life situations.

Table 47: Assessment of responsibilities in life situations, South Kazakhstan

Life situations	**State**	**Family network**	**The Individual**	**Insurance companies**	**Charity organizations**
For old age security	67.8	27.3	34.7	21.3	6.7
For child care	41.3	84.0	20.0	9.3	8.0
For unemployment	84.0	21.3	36.0	8.1	6.7
For healthcare provision	90.7	18.0	18.0	18.0	6.7
For the poor	79.9	16.7	19.3	12.1	48.0
For school education	85.2	36.7	27.3	8.7	12.0
For higher education	78.0	38.7	36.0	6.7	6.0

Note: percent

The inquiry shows that the government is looked upon as still being responsible for social services and social security. The nanny state of soviet times seems still very much alive. Concerning state responsibility healthcare ranks first (91%), followed by school education (85%), unemployment (91%), the poor (80%), higher education (78%) and old age security (68%).

Only with regard to child care, the majority of respondents suppose that family and wider family networks bear prime responsibility (84%). According to one third of respondents, the family as an institution is responsible for providing its members with school and higher education. Also, about one third of respondents suppose that the family is responsible for old age insurance, care of elderly family members. The family network is responsible for job security of its members according to 21.3% of respondents, medical services – 18%, poverty protection – 16.7%.

The last twenty years of market transformation in Kazakhstan has been aimed at making people responsible for their lives. About one third of respondents believe that they bear personal responsibility for old age insurance, for jobs resp. unemployment, for their advancement via school and higher education. One in five agrees with the position of personal responsibility for care for children, health and poverty. On one hand, one may say that the soviet beliefs still seem to be pretty much alive, but on the other hand, at least among these middle class people, new orientations appear to have grown that put more importance on the individual. One may speculate that a certain proportion of the nanny state orientation is transformed into the responsibilities of the family.

The inquiry clearly shows that institutions of the market, such as insurances of all kind, play a marginal role in organizing the life of the people. Only one in five of the respondents specified responsibility for old age insurances. Many people dealing with self-employment, working in small companies, or those being employed occasionally, have no insurance deductions for old age pensions. Even the government is now worried with the weakness of the pension system. Institutionally, voluntary health insurance is comparatively developed; many big companies provide their employees with additional packages of medical services. Individual health insurance is however uncommon. Only 18% believe in insurance companies for the protection of health.

The majority of respondents also have little faith in charity organizations helping in the different everyday living situations they may face. According to them, their main role is limited to relief for the poor (48%).

Comparisons of answers of urban citizens and villagers about responsibility of various institutions for the solution of important social issues showed that there are only few significant dependencies of the answers on the location.

Table 48: Perception of responsibilities, South Kazakhstan

Life situations	State		Family network		The Individual		Insurance companies		Charity organizations	
	urban	rural	urban	rural	urban	rural	urban	rural	urban	rural
For old age security	66	72	24	34	37	30	20	24	3	*14
For child care	38	48	88	76	18	24	4	**20	4	*16
For unemployment	82	88	19	26	39	30	7	10	5	10
For health-care provision	91	90	14	26	16	22	19	16	3	14
For the poor	76	88	13	24	18	22	13	10	55	*34
For school education	81	94	41	28	27	28	8	10	11	14
For higher education	74	86	43	30	40	28	6	8	6	6

Notes: percent;
* Chi-square: significant dependency on location;
** highly significant dependency on location

But it should be noted that rural households trust more in governmental assistance concerning all items, especially in issues of access to education and poverty. Only in health care do urbanites have a negligible lead (91% vs.90%). Urban citizens more often suppose that the family itself should provide its members with good education and child care. Villagers suppose that the family is responsible for elderly people, health care, care of the poor and unemployed. This indicates both local economic problems in rural areas, its "abandonment" by the government, and the maintenance of stronger family supportive networks in the countryside. People in the city often tend to speak about individual responsibility for higher education, jobs and old age protection. People in the rural settlements tend to stress more the responsibility of insurance companies and charitable organizations in child care issues. Urban citizens more often note responsibility of charity providers for the solution of poverty issues which reflects the activity of these organizations in the city. But all these differences touch only very few respondents.

Overwhelmingly the responsibilities for 'social policy' issues are seen to be with the state, then followed by the family and the individual.

Conclusions

The results of this empirical research in South Kazakhstan demonstrate the mix of traditional and market-based ways to cope with social and economic problems in urban and rural areas. Private households tend to use all possible survival strategies – depending on their capabilities. These range from "muddling through", i.e. always spontaneously reacting on problems, to planning for the future.

Data demonstrate, to a certain extent, the preservation of the role of social networks, despite their significant weakening in recent years as a result of the influence of the market economy, the growth of economic differentiation of families and the reducing of guarantees to return the debts by relatives and friends. Nevertheless, particularly intergenerational solidarity within the household, which is regulated according to tradition (the youngest son living with his parents) is still more important than individual security provided by market institutions such as insurances, and mainly designed for individuals, couples and nuclear families. This refers to ethnic Kazakhs. However, urban life shows that the weakening of this pattern of behavior can already be observed from the quantitative data, with regard to the constitution of households.

However, the economic strategies of the monetary mutual support of households in a wider network of relatives (on a regular basis and on event-based basis) is gradually losing its leading position and individual strategies gain importance, the strategies directed at the autonomy of nuclear families.

3.5. The Kyrgyzstan Survey

Galina GORBORUKOVA

The Sample

Transformational processes, economic crises and social unrest have strongly affected the major social institutions of Kyrgyz society, families and households. Within the framework of households all social resources of survival expressed in the different capital forms of the sustainable livelihoods matrix are activated. Among these is mutual assistance among household and family members, friends, colleagues and neighbors. The sustainable livelihoods of private households are investigated in 100 urban households from the capital Bishkek and 51 rural households in the Chui region, sufficiently far away from the city so that these still have a typical rural structure.

Household Composition

According to the set quota for the questionnaire, 66% of respondents were from Bishkek city and 34% of respondents from villages. 15 % of respondents were men and 85% women. 87% of those interviewees were representatives of the Kyrgyz ethnic group, 8% were from the Russian ethnic group, 1% from the Uzbek ethnic group and 4% of other nationalities. The demographic distribution in the sample households is as follows: 48% males and 52% females live in the sample households, covering a range of 1 to 10 household members. The distribution of these household types is uneven between urban and rural regions. In rural regions one-or two-person households are significantly underrepresented ($p= 0.003$).[140] The distribution is shown in the following table.

Table 49: Household type according to size, Kyrgyzstan

Household Size	Location		Total
	Urban	Rural	
One or two persons	24.0%	7.8%	18.5%
Three persons	25.0%	15.7%	21.9%
Four persons	26.0%	19.6%	23.8%
Five persons	12.0%	29.4%	17.9%
Six and more persons	13.0%	27.5%	17.9%
Total	100.0%	100.0%	100.0%

[140] Here and in the other chi-square tests on independence we chose a significance level of 0.05.

the majority of households do not have a culture or a tradition concerning revenues and expenditures. As a result, the study relies on what respondents know and keep in mind. To keep in mind constant transfers is much easier than to assess all non-recurrent and seasonal revenues.

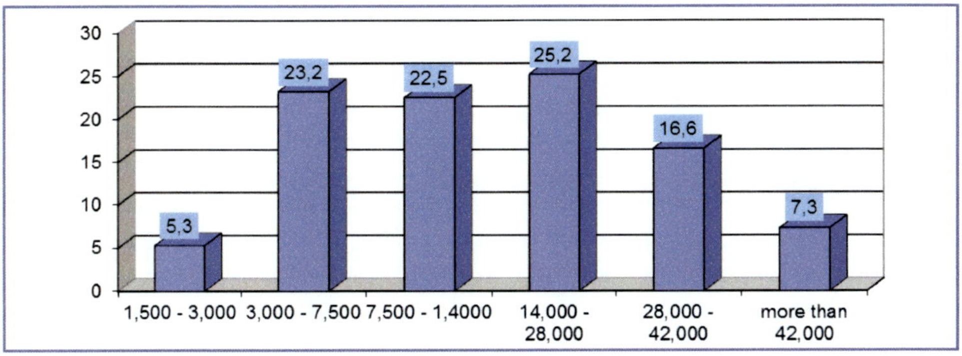

Figure 22: Household income in Som, Kyrgyzstan
Note: percent. Exchange rate on Jan 1st, 2012: 1,000 Som = 16.60 € = 21.50 US.

51% of the households in our sample live on less than 14,000 Som. We should keep in mind here, that normally, the households have more than one member. The latter households usually have to live on less than 301 USD. 49% have an income above 28,000 Som, an equivalent of USD 651. The majority of those (25.2 %) have an income roughly between 301 and 651 USD. In international comparative statistics, Kyrgyzstan shows up as one of the poorest countries on the globe. Our sample approves this.

The comparison of monetary incomes of urban and rural households shows much lower incomes of rural households on average. However, while monetary incomes in the countryside are extremely low, we should not forget that Kyrgyzstan is still an agricultural country with predominance of subsistence agriculture which – in economic terms – is helping rural, and also to some degree urban areas to survive. By growing crops and breeding livestock rural dwellers can sell surplus and buy necessary goods or barter among each other. At the same time gardening in the city helps improving the living situation of urban households. Agricultural subsistence production counts among natural capital and provides an important asset in addition to financial capital.

A third component of the asset mix is social capital. Respondents pointed out that they receive financial help from relatives living outside the households. Normally this may be children, parents, grandparents, other kin who receive financial support or in kind and who also give support.

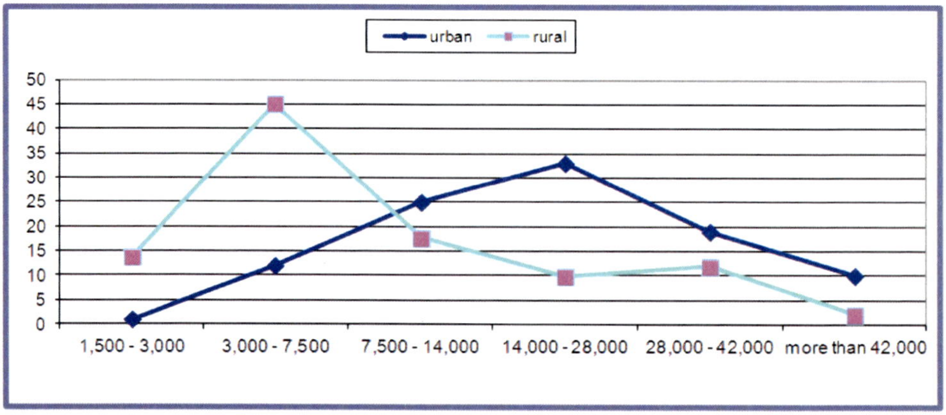

Figure 23: Comparison of average household income in the city and village, Kyrgyzstan
Note: percent

Generally speaking 10% of rural and 14% of urban households obtain contributions from outside. While this may look like a paradox it is often found that rural households subsidize urban ones and not the other way round. Distinguishing support in cash and kind, 10% of rural and 14% of urban households obtains cash contributions from others, compared to 4% and 10% contributions in kind, respectively. The figure below illustrates the exchanges.

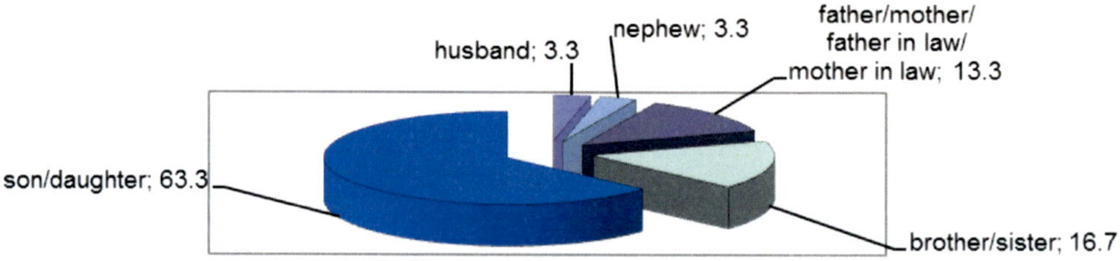

Figure 24: Aid sources received by the household, Kyrgyzstan
Note: percent

The aid mostly (80%) comes from foreign countries where relatives live; only 13% of the respondents receive support from relatives in the capital Bishkek and remaining 4% comes from other regions of Kyrgyzstan. It is known that some of the families are forced to live on remittances from relatives, working in Kazakhstan's fields or on job sites in Russia or elsewhere.[143]

[143] "Labor migrants send $1.5 billion in 2011 from Russia to Kyrgyzstan" – says the Central Bank of Russia. – site http://www.kyrtag.kg/?q=ru/news/18870; access date 20-08-13.

22% of the urban and 30% of the rural sample households provide help to relatives outside the household in cash. The bulk of the recipients are students and pupils (62%), followed by pensioners (29%). Various other relatives amount to 9%. 18% of the urban and 30% of the rural households provide support in kind.

The following table characterizes the households of our sample and their sharing of incomes:

Table 52: Network type of sample households, Kyrgyzstan

Network type / location	Location		Total
	Urban	Rural	
Closed household	68.0%	64.7%	66.9%
Only giving	19.0%	29.4%	22.5%
Only receiving	9.0%	5.9%	7.9%
Giving and receiving	4.0%	–	2.6%
Total	100.0%	100.0%	100.0%

In virtue of the agrarian nature of the economy of Kyrgyzstan, animal husbandry and crop production are the main areas of the country's income-generating activities of households. While during Soviet times farming and agriculture were mainly industrialized in kolkhoz form, privatization and transformation of the agricultural sector engendered a small peasant production pattern which is nowadays crucial not only for survival of rural households but also a factor in the development of key areas of the agriculture. In recent years a number of institutions and international organizations working on poverty reduction in rural areas carried out interventions to enhance diversification of rural entrepreneurship, to increase off-farm production and employment in the manufacturing/reprocessing of agricultural products.

State programs for the employment of the rural population have limited the influence on formal unemployment rates on the people's lives. The vast majority of rural dwellers are engaged in subsistence agriculture for their own consumption and for limited exchange to cover their basic needs. Frequently, these largely self-sufficient households are legally formalized as peasant-farmer households.

The income structure of households in or at the edge of poverty is directed at overcoming risks of economic instability and at saturation of basic needs. A strategy that has often been observed is a de-linking from market structures and relying on subsistence production. Therefore, the majority of households are combining several production lines such as crops, animal and poultry husbandries, and non-farm income-generating activity at the same time. Often different household members take up farm and non-farm activities. Although we have very detailed data on the household composition of monetary and non-monetary incomes, data are not good enough to measure monetary and non-monetary incomes. One reason is that part of subsistence produce is also sold in the market. Nevertheless, the importance of cattle breeding and raising crops for subsistence is high.

The following figure summarizes the importance of natural capital for both urban and rural households.

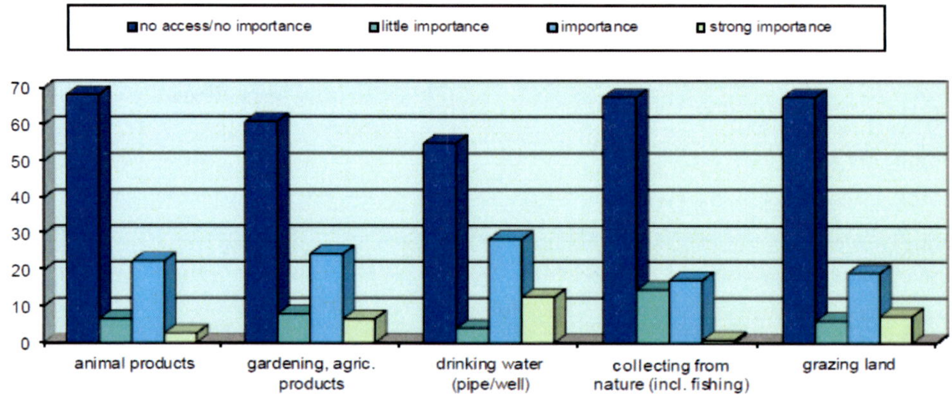

Figure 25: Importance of natural capital for the households, Kyrgyzstan
Note: percent

Let us now take a closer look at the poverty situation. Only 39% of the sample households are able to cover all necessary expenses, while the rest suffer to different degrees: While still for 49% the income is almost sufficient, 12% report to really suffer from insufficient incomes so that they cannot satisfy their basic needs.

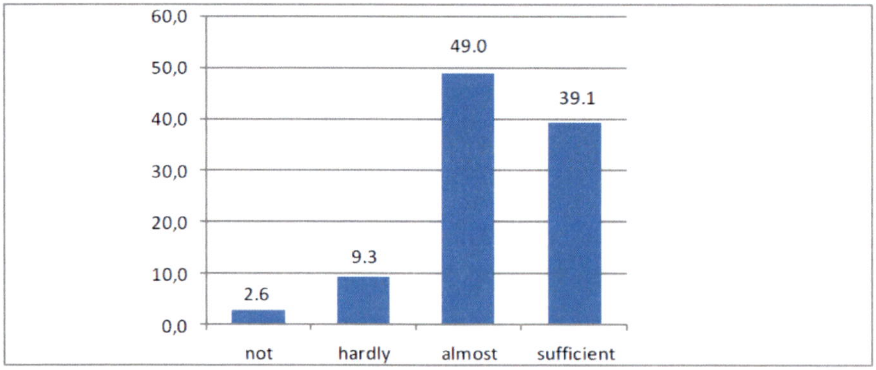

Figure 26: Sufficiency of income for the saturation of basic needs, Kyrgyzstan
Note: percent

Comparing urban and rural households, 41% of urban and 35% of rural households consider their incomes sufficient for the satisfaction of basic needs, while 1% of urban and 6% of rural households consider it to be insufficient, and 8% and 12%, respectively as hardly sufficient. This hints at higher rural poverty than urban one, although the sample is too small to make valid generalizations.

The self-assessment of the investigated households compared to average population is provided by the following table.

Table 53: Self-assessment of the living conditions compared to average population, Kyrgyzstan

Improvement of economic status after ten years	Location		Total
	Urban	Rural	
Worse than average	9.0%	11.8%	9.9%
Average	31.0%	43.1%	35.1%
Better than average	60.0%	45.1%	55.0%
Total	100.0%	100.0%	100.0%

Interestingly, the vast majority of urban (60%) and even 45% of the rural households believe themselves to be better off than average households, compared to the 41% of urban and 35% of rural households stating that they have sufficient income for making a living.

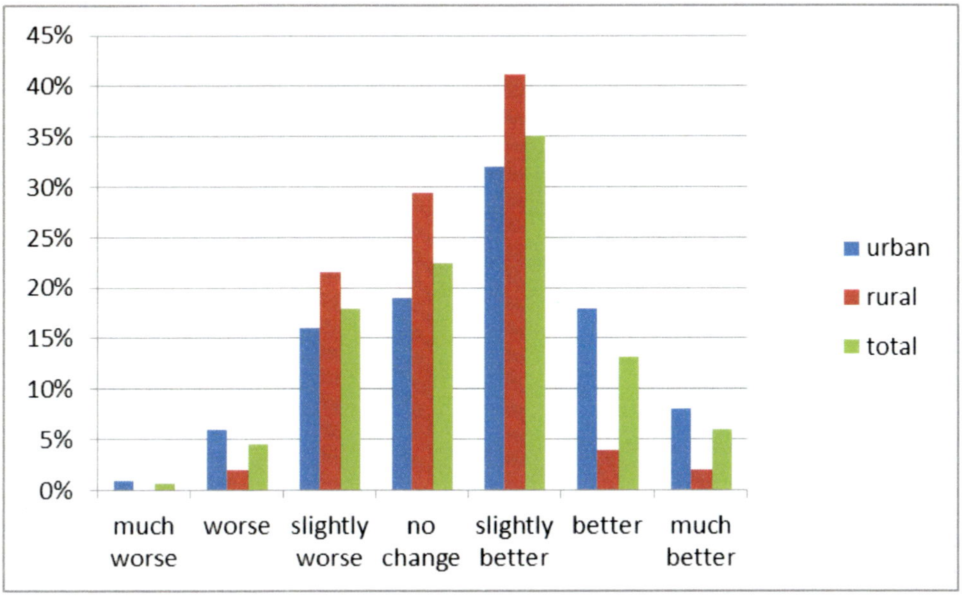

Figure 27: Expectation of economic situation of household in the future, Kyrgyzstan

In spite of hardly sufficient incomes the sample respondents are in general more optimistic than pessimistic about the future development of their household and are expecting betterment. 8% point out that the economic situation of the household will deteriorate while 38% believe that life will improve slightly while 20% believe in an improvement. However, the rural households lag behind to the optimism of the urban ones.

Reasons for this optimism are as follows: the majority (57%) believes that life will get better in general and the households will prosper. 17% are planning to start an additional business which will give hope for a better life; 13% are expecting improvement in their financial situation. Respondents, who do not believe in improvement of their households, attribute this situation to the uncertainty about the future development of the country (55%) and the economic instability in Kyrgyzstan (45%).

Household Problems

One of the research objectives was to identify sets of problems encountered by households during 2010. Survey results show that the most noticeable problems for households were overall price increases across the country, particularly increase of the prices for food and communal services, thus negatively affecting the way of live. Lack of jobs and high unemployment is also a serious problem and significantly higher in rural regions (felt strongly by 24% compared to 8% urban households; p=0.032). Respondents also mention the health issue, meaning that there is a lack of access to high quality health care and high costs for medication. Natural disasters and crime are the items surveyed families hardly suffered from; they also did not have problems with neighbors, transportation services and divorces. The small sample size and the type of sampling do not allow us to generalize the findings and to speak about the overall population of Kyrgyzstan. But the ubiquitous increase in prices for goods and services that was observed by the respondents is severely felt in the whole country. This can be generalized.

Table 54: Households encountering problems, Kyrgyzstan

Household Problem	Medium	Strong
Unemployment	13.2%	13.2%
Illness of family member/medical treatment	12.6%	12.6%
Death of family member	2.6%	5.3%
Divorce	0.7%	1.3%
Marriage	3.3%	4.6%

Food price increases	25.8%	19.9%
Overall price increases	27.2%	22.5%
Prices of communal service	13.2%	12.6%
Prepare kids for new academic year (clothes, books etc.)	6.6%	7.9%
Payment for Education	13.2%	8.6%
Criminality	0.7%	2.0%
Natural disaster	0%	0%
Transportation	2.0%	3.3%
Problems with neighbors	0.7%	0%

We also asked who discusses the problems of the household. Considering different types of problems we found that the entire household members or husband and wife are the most common discussion partners. Gender or age specific discussions concerning household issues are not frequent. The problem fields addressed were finance, health, education, relationships with other relatives, problems at work, conservation and maintenance of practices of family rituals and traditions. Problems with friends are usually discussed among household members, for example with brothers or sisters, once this concerns partner relationships. Marriage and other family planning issues are also deliberated in a circle of close relatives. Interestingly, however, quite a large number of respondents do not discuss the problems with anybody.

As respondents pointed out, they often expect and receive assistance in solving previously mentioned problems from family members and relatives.

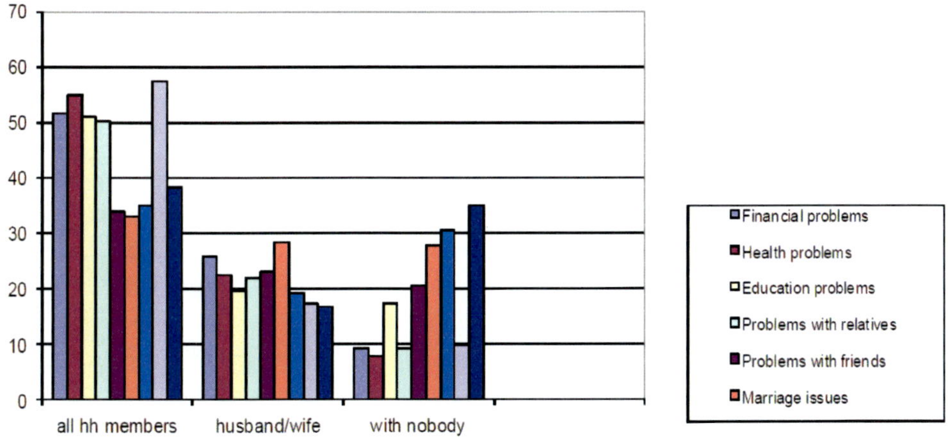

Figure 28: With whom do you discuss the following household problems? Kyrgyzstan
Note: percent

Tensions between generations occur in 46% and between males and females in 40% of the households, while only 2% reported about tensions between different nationals within the household.

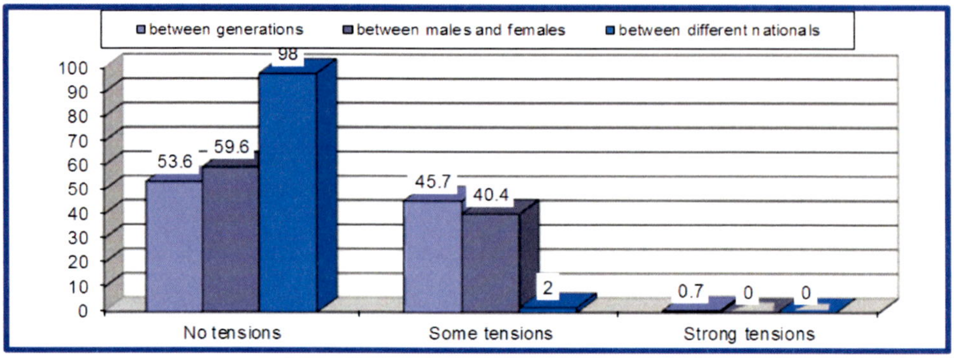

Figure 29: Household tensions, Kyrgyzstan
Note: percent

The analysis of property/possessions of consumer goods makes it possible to classify households as poorer or better off. Modern household technology helps to make housework easier, more efficient and less labor-intensive. The latter circumstance is especially important considering the tradition of a gender-based division of labor in Kyrgyzstan.

Following possessions were noted as existing. A significant majority of the respondents (94%) have their own home. At the same time living space of households varies from 16 to 205 square meters. Almost all respondents also noted the presence of refrigerators and washing machines. But only half of all respondents have computers, which is perhaps due to lack of internet access. All residents interviewed in the rural areas have their own livestock.

The possession of land is highest significantly unevenly distributed between urban and rural households (39% compared to 96%, p= 0.0). The same holds true for livestock (10% compared to 80%). With consumer goods the relation is just the other way around: car/motorcycle (56% urban compared to 24% rural, p=0.0) and computers (69% compared to 14%, p=0,000) and LCD/Plasma TV (29% compared to 0%, p=0.0), Euro Remont (43% compared to 8%, p=0.0). Electric equipment such as e.g. air conditioners and personal computers are still recognized as unaffordable objects of desire for rural residents.

The categorization of consumer items shows functional/investment orientated purposes as well as mere consumptive ones; while the possession of a house or an apartment, a refrigerator or a washing machine is generally important and pos-

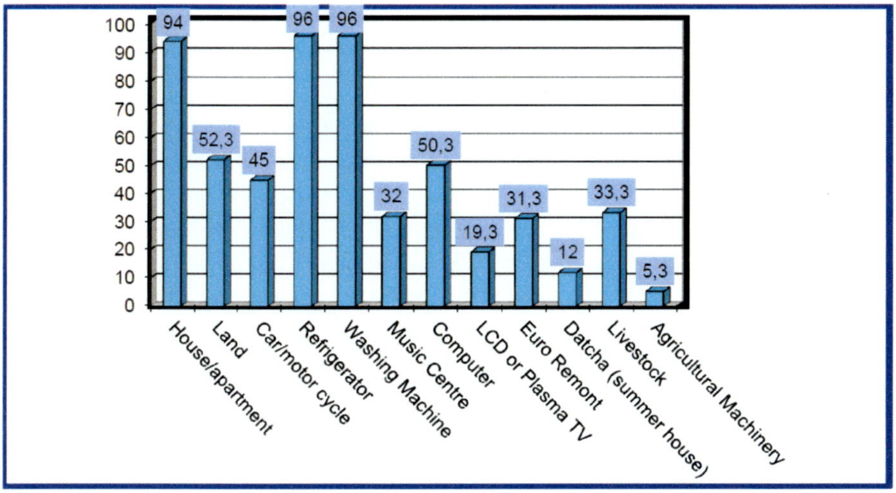

Figure 30: Household possessions, Kyrgyzstan
Note: percent

sessed by almost every household; rural households particularly consider livestock as important and necessary for making a living (subsistence production as well as sale of produce and animals). But also prestigious belongings and conspicuous consumption (big cars, celebrating magnificent ceremonial events) can be found; middle class people have often just overcome poverty and they start to purchase goods that can demonstrate their status as high and prestigious. The purchase of gold and jewelry is also a form of saving and serves as a possible dowry for the girls.

The main breadwinners in the families are usually from the parents' generation (83.7% of all households).

Savings, Credits and Security

Which role do credits play among our households? 78% of all households have taken at least one credit, the majority of them one or two. The number of credits is significantly (0.009) unevenly distributed among urban and rural households. 64% of the urban households have only one credit, another 23% two credits and 11% three credits, and only 3% four credits, while 33% of the rural households have one, 37% two, 18% three and 12% four credits. Interestingly, not all credit intervals are found in the Kyrgyzstan sample.[144] 43% of the households have a credit amount for the first credit in the interval from 500-999 USD, another 25% between 1,000 and 4,999 USD, 21% between 50 and 99 USD and 11% above 20,000 USD. There is a weak significant (0.046) dependency of credit amount to location: Small credits up to 99 USD and large credits above 20,000 USD are significantly more often found among urban households. The latter probably falls into the category of purchase of a house or an apartment.

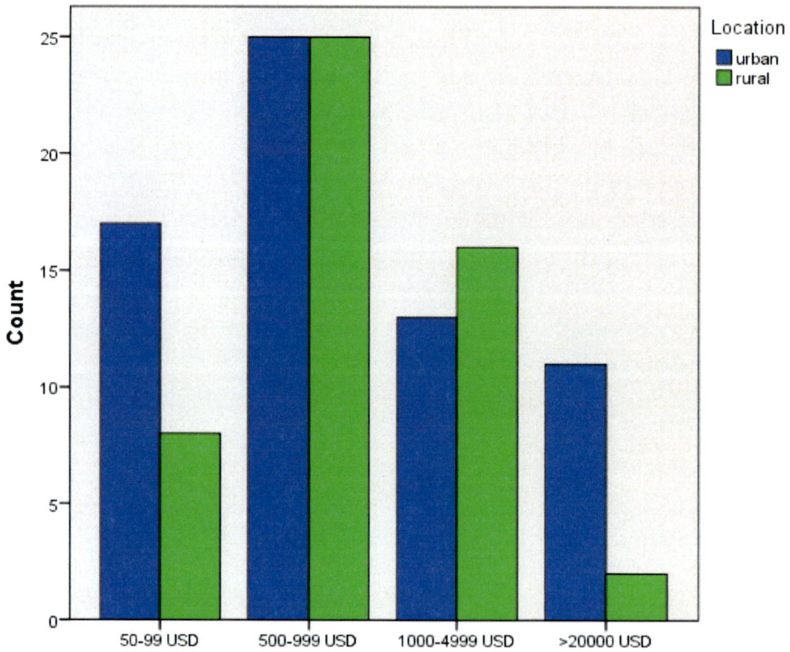

Figure 31: Credit amount (first credit), Kyrgyzstan

[144] No household has a first credit amounting to 100-500 USD or 5,000-19,999 USD.

The different loan purposes for the first credit are shown in the following figure.

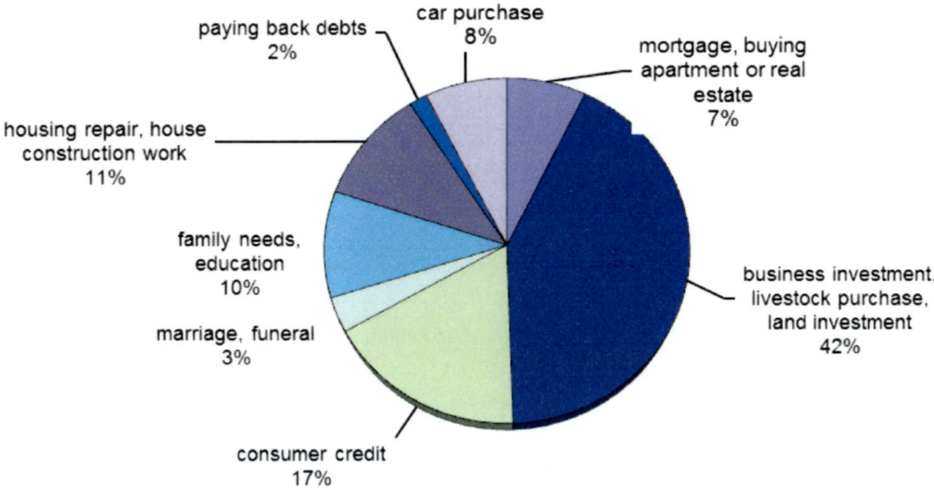

Figure 32: Loan purposes (first credit), Kyrgyzstan

The following figure outlines the different loan purposes according to region. It can be generalized that business investment, purchase of livestock and land is much more important in rural regions than in the city.

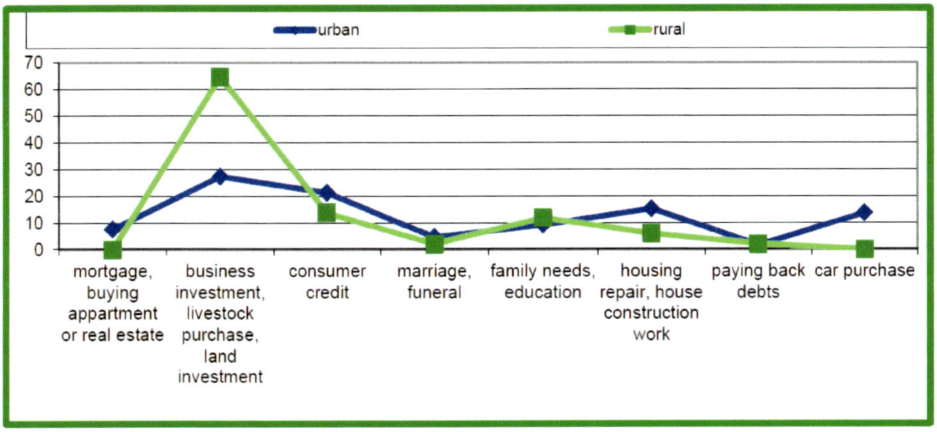

Figure 33: Loan purposes (first credit), Kyrgyzstan
Note: percent

From which credit sources do Kyrgyzstan citizens take their loans? Banks range before micro credit institutions. The latter being a more rural issue. But also rural households have access to bank credits, so that there is no difference between urban and rural households. Interestingly enough, credit support from relatives is not very common in the sample. One reason is probably that most households are at the edge of poverty so that they cannot provide loans. In a private conversation one of the respondents complained that traditional ties between relatives do not work anymore, because, on the one hand, relatives do not want to commercialize relationships, on the other traditional levels of trust among tribesmen and clan have collapsed. If this is a valid account of the situation, can only be answered by our qualitative data.

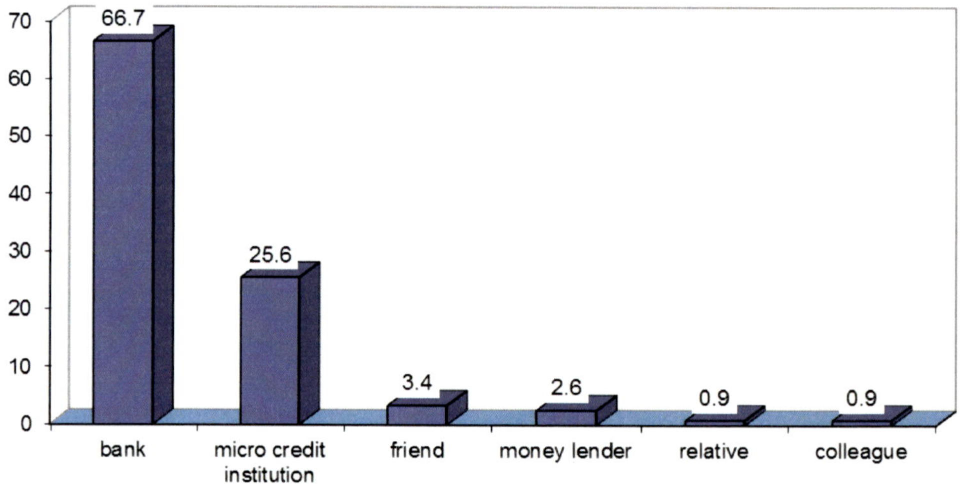

Figure 34: Credit sources (first credit), Kyrgyzstan
Note: percent

Interestingly, there is no correlation between credit amount and credit institution. Also with small credits banks range first, and micro credit institutions are also involved in large credits above 20,000 USD.

According to the study, the surveyed households are extremely liable to economic crisis, because they do not have an opportunity to put up, save and deposit money. Only 40% are engaged in putting money by for a rainy day, 30% are concerned about upcoming retirement and 47% are saving money for children's and grandchildren's education. Among top priorities for savings was business maintenance, land or apartment purchasing, education of children, health care and payment of the current loan. The latter is popular among poorer households. Few respondents pointed out about upcoming indebtedness, the so called "a life of loan", where a person continuously takes up credits to repay another credit. Crucial factors for such a development are functional illiteracy of particularly rural residents and lacking cultural patterns to repay loans on time. Providing loans to other people was reported by only 1/10 of the sample, all urban households except one. Those who provide credits to others mentioned the target group to be relatives, followed by friends. The majority of loans are in the categories up to 5,000 USD.

Where do the sample households save? 31% save at home in form of cash or jewelry. One third (33%) keeps their savings in local banks, and less than 1% have accounts in foreign banks. Also bank investments are rather the exception. The majority invest money in private property (38%), 23% in livestock.

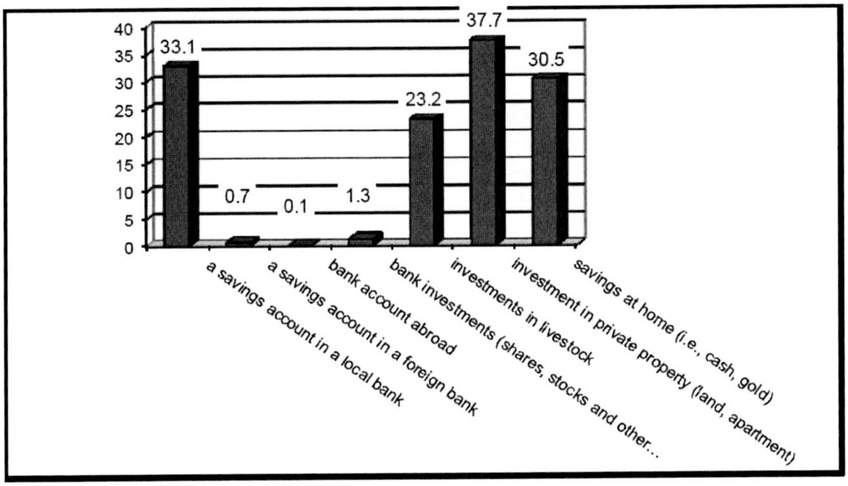

Figure 35: Where households save, Kyrgyzstan
Note: percent

Respondents were asked about their opinion on which purposes savings are important and which purposes they have already saved or which goods they already possess. Houses and apartments are highest in priority, both in importance for saving (74%) as well as in possession (19%). Savings for children's education rank next, but only 7% have such savings. These are followed by saving for land purchase/lease (56%) and possession (13%). At the end of the ranking are insurances, whereas health insurance is still considered important by 21%, old age insurance is only considered important by 13%. However, hardly any household possesses health insurance (3%), not to mention life insurance or old age insurance. The strong difference between the importance of saving and real savings is probably due to the rather poor living conditions of many households in our sample. Only a few respondents said that they have the financial means to save for specific purposes. In Kyrgyzstan only a very small part of the community can talk about property ownership, possession of livestock and land tenure. The bulk of the population – even of the middle class – lives on the brink of poverty or in poverty. In these cases money is often barely enough for food, medication and necessary clothing.

Table 55: Purposes which are important to save for and savings possessions, Kyrgyzstan

Savings purposes	Important (%)	Savings possession or possessions (%)
Apartment/house	73.5	19.2
Children's education	58.9	7.3
Land	55.6	12.6
Vacations	49.0	6.6
Other family events	48.3	6.6
Livestock	45.0	11.9
Wedding/funeral	37.1	4.6
Jewelry /Gold	37.1	15.9
Life insurance	17.9	0.7
Perform Hadj	14.6	–
Private old age insurance	12.6	0.7
Health insurance	21.2	2.6

Interestingly, there are some variations between rural regions and the city. For example, 42% of urban households find saving for funeral/marriage important compared to 28% villagers. A similar difference appears in the importance of saving for other family festivities. As can be expected, saving for land is considered particularly important in villagers (92% compared to 37% in the city); the figures for savings in livestock are similar: 86% compared to 22%. Saving for children's education is considered to be more important among urban households.

Savings for wedding/funeral and other family festivities or possessions of such are only found in the city. The savings for and possession of land and livestock is more frequent among the rural households. Saving for and possession of health insurance or children's education is more an urban issue.

According to this study, loans, savings and accumulation issues are either an individual affair or discussed and resolved in the household and/or with different family members outside of the household. Respondents unanimously replied that such vital questions as the necessity of and the possibility of savings, children's education, and labor migration are discussed and decisions are made at the household level with participation of all family members.

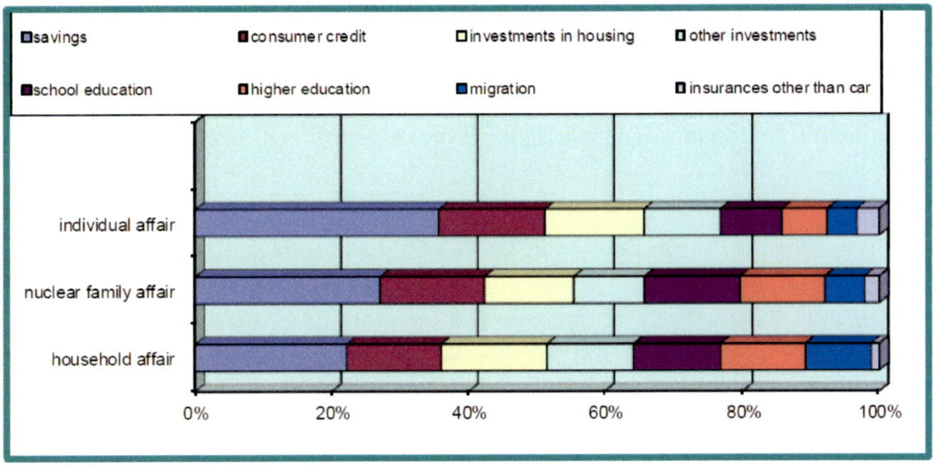

Figure 36: Decision-making on loans, investments, education, migration, security, Kyrgyzstan
Note: percent

Important life objectives for respondents are such common values as a good, stable standard of living for their families, children's prosperous future, peace and stability in the society.

Values and Responsibilities

The market society is usually associated with self-responsibility of individuals and households, while socialism was state dominated in almost all spheres of life. To whom do the households nowadays attribute responsibility for these spheres? We addressed different spheres that can usually be responsible to supply the households with public or private goods. The following table provides the answers.

Table 56: Perceptions about responsibility, Kyrgyzstan

Spheres of life / Sphere of Responsibility (%)	State	Family network	The individual	Insurance companies	Charity organizations
For old age security	84.1	39.1	31.8	18.5	15.2
For child care	69.5	59.6	32.5	15.9	17.2
For unemployment	91.4	33.1	36.4	16.6	14.6
For healthcare prov.	92.7	37.7	27.8	21.2	16.6
For the poor	92.1	31.1	35.8	21.2	27.8
For school education	89.4	48.3	27.8	13.9	11.3
For higher education	72.8	53.6	35.8	7.9	7.3

In all spheres of life the state is considered to be the responsible institution. Only in child care does the family network come close to it. That is, in the poor country of Kyrgyzstan, an overwhelming group is still orientating itself toward the nanny state of the soviet past. Next comes the family; only relief for the poor and unemployment are issues where the responsibility of the individual surmounts the responsibility of the family. Insurance companies and charity organizations only play a small role concerning the organization of certain spheres of life.

Conclusions

In recent years, experts pointed out that the following trends are threatening the development of the region: [145] poverty and income and property differentiations; deformed structures of national economies, the slow pace of development and utilization of production capacity; expansion of criminal activities; increasing anthropogenic stress, particularly for poor people; environmental degradation; economic disintegration and conflicts over the use of land, water resources and others.

Experts remarked that in recent years the most significant patterns at the local level are the following: slowdown in economic growth and social development decline, structural changes of GDP by increasing share of agriculture; negative impact of global and local financial crises, including the crisis 2009, as well as political and economic pressure by neighboring countries (including customs union regulations); revolutionary disturbance; ethnic and border conflicts; food and energy crises due to regional economic disintegration problems and occasional border closure with neighboring countries, and so on.

Our study has not taken the top-down approach starting from the macroeconomic figures, but we aimed at taking a bottom-up view from the perspective of the household. The results from our questionnaire are not representative, nor do they cover every aspect of everyday life. Nevertheless, they give us some insight about the living situation of households in Kyrgyzstan, both in urban and rural regions. A number of the findings will be further investigated and studied in more detail in the qualitative research following this quantitative phase.

---

[145] W. Niyatbekov: Faktori, Sposobstvuyushye Koordina'zii Internazionnich prozessov w Zentral'noi Asii, http://www.easttime.ru/reganalitic/1/278.html.

3.6. Comparison of the Results from Northern, Southern Kazakhstan and from Kyrgyzstan

Heiko SCHRADER and Eckhard DITTRICH

In the last section of this quantitative data analysis we shall have a look at those indicators where differences between the research teams occur. They concern differences between North and South Kazakhstan, between Kazakhstan and Kyrgyzstan, and between urban and rural regions. Due to our household approach, there is no data concerning generations valid enough for generalization.

Household Characteristics

To begin with there is a striking difference between the three samples with regard to ethnic homogeneity of the households. In the North Kazakhstan sample 10% of the urban and 16% of the rural households are ethnically heterogeneous. The South Kazakhstan sample is in the middle with 6% urban and 12% rural households. The Kyrgyzstan sample is very homogeneous in nature, with only 1% urban households being ethnically heterogeneous. The reasons – if it is not a mere accident – can't be sorted out here.

A look at the households' sizes shows that in all places the two – generation household is the majority. However, in urban Astana every fifth household is a three – and more generation household, in Almaty only every 10th household. Maybe this is a result from the rural migration to Astana which has taken place in recent years. In the rural locations of Kyrgyzstan the three – and more generation households (14%) are underrepresented, while Akmola and Almaty regions are at 20% and 18%. Anyhow, most of the households are populated by nuclear families which have to organize their way of life on their own but maybe not alone.

This can already be observed looking at the in- and outflows of contributions. Considering, which household obtains contributions from outside, it is around 15% in all urban cases, but while in rural Kazakhstan every fifth household obtains cash or kind from outside it is only every 10th household in Kyrgyzstan. In the Akmola region almost every fifth household obtains monetary support from outside, but only every 10th household in the Chui region of Kyrgyzstan is supported.

Among the households providing cash and non-cash to dependents we find the following situation: for the urban households, Almaty city ranks first (27%) followed by Bishkek (18%) and Astana (9%). Among the rural households it is almost every third household in Chui region and Astana providing both kinds of support, compared to every 5th household in Almaty region. These results are very much in tune with the numbers concerning household sizes. Nuclear families being dominant, their members act on behalf of themselves. Only a limited number of households are embedded in broader exchange relations with others.

Incomes and Future Expectations

We already showed earlier that the monetary income median in Kyrgyzstan is about 300 USD, compared to more than 780 USD in Kazakhstan. But the income level alone does not say very much about household survival strategies because we have to take the living conditions and price levels into consideration. Additionally, material household and family constellations have a strong subjective element and can't be measured appropriately by looking at incomes of the different kind only. The following figure shows us how the households consider their income situation themselves.

For the urban situation the figure shows that in Bishkek the smallest number of households (about one-fourth) considers their income as sufficient, and the majority (one-third) considers their income as almost sufficient. In Almaty almost half of the households consider their income as sufficient, another 25 households as almost sufficient. The Astana households are close to these figures. Interesting is that among those households that consider their incomes as not sufficient or hardly sufficient, the Astana households provide the majority. That is, the overall view of the respondents mirrors the overall economic conditions.

The rural situation is much different. Sufficiency is lower than in the urban areas. Here it is interestingly the households of the Akmola region feeling worst. Only 15 households of 150 consider their incomes as sufficient, compared to 27 that consider it as almost sufficient and 8 households that consider their incomes as not sufficient or hardly sufficient. The households from Chui region are in the middle position, whereas the households from Almaty region are comparatively the best off, with 15 having a sufficient and 27 having an almost sufficient, but 8 having a not sufficient/hardly sufficient income. We assume that especially the worse living conditions in the country side play a considerable role concerning these results. Comparisons with the boom town Astana might have been responsible for the northern Kazakhstan data.

Related to the perception of the household's sufficiency of income are comparisons with an average household.

On a whole the majority of urban households believe that they are better off than the average, while rural households consider their position as average or bet-

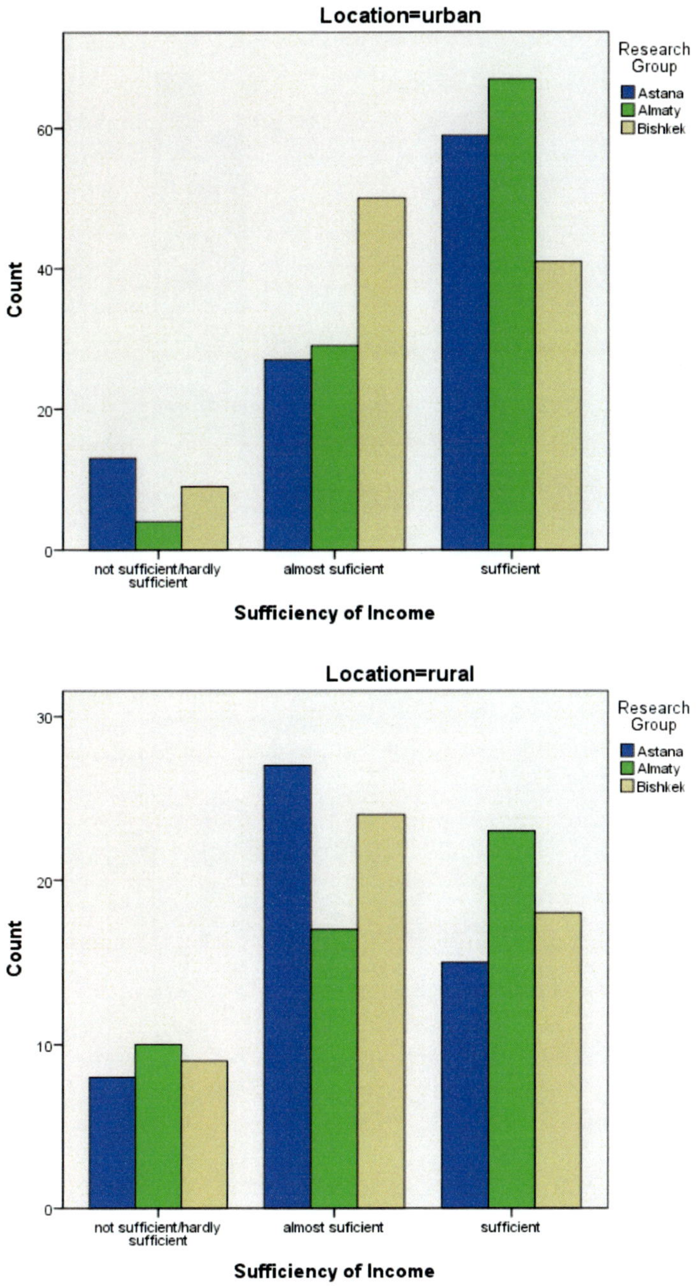

Figure 37: Income sufficiency per regional sample

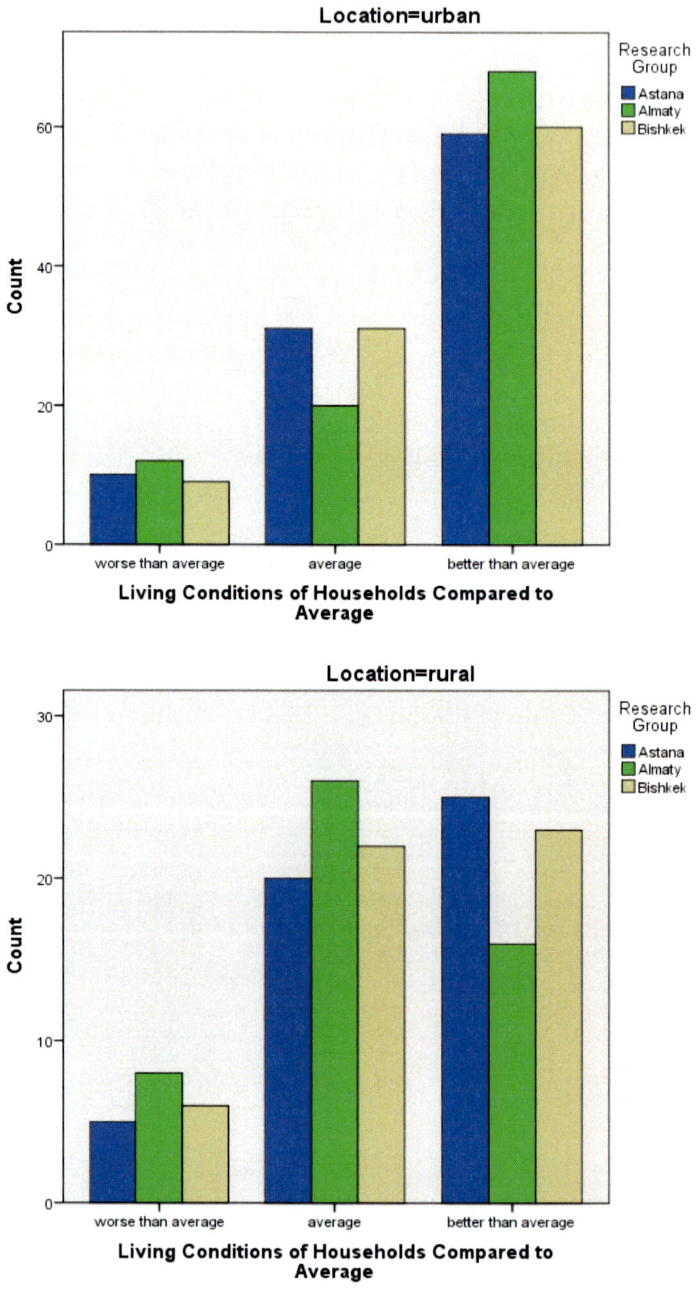

Figure 38: Living conditions compared to average per regional sample

ter than average. Almaty region households depart from the general pattern in that the majority believes to be as average.

Let us now take a look at the subsistence revenue situation. Among the cities it is interestingly Astana (67%) and Bishkek (62%) where the majority has no access to the subsistence revenue, while in Almaty city this group is considerably smaller (36%). In the latter 40% combine four or five subsistence revenue sources, compared to the average of 18%. In the rural regions 12% of the Chui households have no access to subsistence revenues at all. On the other hand more than 60% of the Akmola and Chui households combine four or five subsistence revenues, compared to 54% in the Almaty region. The difference in future expectations between Kazakhstan and Kyrgyzstan households is striking. The latter are less optimistic than their counterparts in Kazakhstan, both in the city and in the countryside. This seems not to be astonishing if we compare the economic situation and the overall political situation of the two neighboring countries. In general, rural households are less optimistic than urban ones, and rural households in the Akmola region have the largest number that even believes it will become worse in the future.

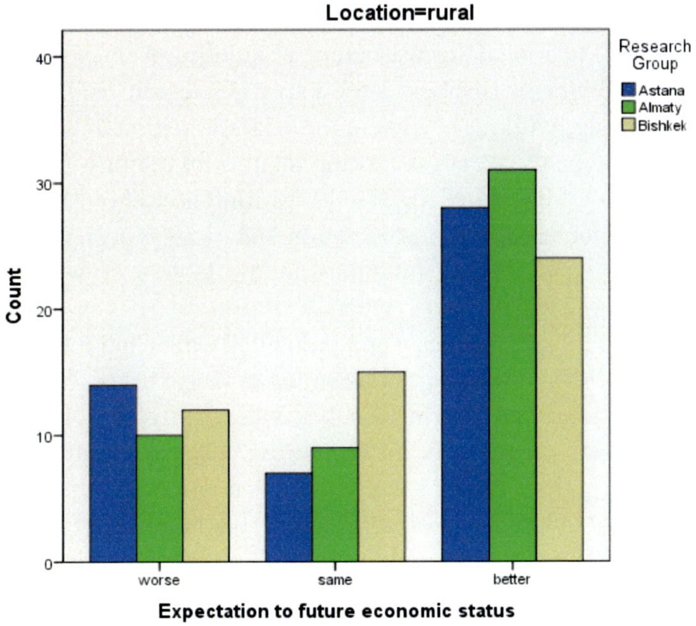

Figure 39: Expectation to future economic status of the household, per regional sample

Infrastructure

What follows is an analysis of the infrastructure. Let us begin with the *rural regions*.

Medical aspects: From the rural households in Akmola region half report to have no access to doctors, while the situation in the Chui (21%) and particularly Almaty region (4%) is much better. 22% of rural households in the Akmola and Chui regions also complain about lack of access to medical centers, and every second household in both regions also complain about lack of access to a polyclinic or hospital. In the Almaty region, on the other hand, there seems to be much better access.

Educational access is also unevenly distributed across the countries and the country sides. In Chui regions every second household has complaints while in the Akmola region 40% complain. Primary education also seems to be a problem in Bishkek where 43% complain about lack of access. In the Chui region it is even as low as 14% who have access, compared to 98% in the Almaty region and 71% in the Akmola region. Secondary education is available everywhere in the cities, and in the Almaty and Chui regions, while 23% in Akmola region complain of having no access. Vocational infrastructure is quite high in Almaty and Astana (80%) it is much lower in Bishkek (45%). In Chui region only 2% have access to vocational training, while it is 23% in the Akmola region and even 66% in the Almaty region. University access is lacking in all rural regions.

Banking services are lacking for 34% of the rural households from the Almaty region, for 46% of those from Akmola region and of 59% from Chui region. *Post offices* which often have banking functions are available everywhere. Also transportation services are available everywhere. *Cultural services* are weak in Bishkek (33% complain about lack of access) and particularly the Chui region (61%) while they are offered to 90% of the rural households in Kazakhstan. Cinemas are lacking in all rural regions, but also in Bishkek where only 60% have access. The results are even worse for theaters. In Bishkek two thirds complain about lack of access. In the rural regions of our sample there is no access to theaters at all. Also music entertainment is less available for Kyrgyzstan households – both urban and rural. *Sports facilities* are lacking behind in rural regions: the least in Chui region (24%), followed by Akmola region (33%) and Almaty region (58%). Only every 2nd household in Bishkek has *access to internet* at home, while it is more than 85% in Almaty and Astana. From the rural households none in the Chui region, 42% in the Akmola region and 66% in the Almaty region have internet access at home. But also internet shops or cafés are absent in Kyrgyzstan, so that the rural population is cut off from internet. *Access to a phone* is lacking for 24% of the households in the Chui region. *Gas provision* is also a problem for almost 90% of these households, while 76% in Almaty region and even 88% in Akmola region have access to gas. In the three cities gas is available everywhere. Regular electricity supply is found in every village. *Access to safe drinking water* is a particular problem in the Akmola region (81% lack such), less in Almaty region (34% lack such), while the villages in Chui region are well equipped.

The *urban infrastructural situation* in the three cities is similar except some spheres. Primary education and vocational training facilities in Bishkek seem to be less frequent in the neighborhood than in the two cities in Kazakhstan. Also cultural services (libraries, theatres, musical entertainment) and sports facilities seem nowadays to be less available in Bishkek than in Almaty or Astana. This may be an expression of strong constraints in the provision of public goods in Kyrgyzstan, even in the cities, or – when private goods are concerned – that a sufficiently large purchasing power of consumers is not available. This also holds true for internet access at home or in internet cafés – being less frequent in Bishkek than in Almaty or Astana.

Problems of the Households

Let us now compare the major problems of the households in the three samples.[146] Prices and their increases play a very important role in the two countries and in the locations investigated. Food prices and general price increases rank equally high and are a touchy issue for the vast majority of all households in the sample. In Kazakhstan food prices are more an issue for rural households than urban ones, in spite of subsistence production. While in Bishkek food price increases are felt stronger by a comparable number of households than in Astana and Almaty, interestingly rural households in the Chui region are much less affected than those in the cities and particularly in the Kazakhstan countryside. The same relations occur when we consider prices for other consumer goods and communal services, but here also the Bishkek citizens are much less affected. This can perhaps be explained by different price levels of food and consumer goods in the two countries considered; perhaps the consumption level in Kyrgyzstan is also lower. And maybe rural households in the Chui region seem to be less dependent on purchases than rural households in Kazakhstan. While in all samples unemployment concerns less urban than rural households (Astana 29%, Almaty 25%, Bishkek

[146] We summed up the percentage of households feeling the particular problems medium and strongly.

21%), the affectedness in Almaty region concerns 54%, in Chui region 37% and in Akmola region 31%. Other comparisons can be taken from the following table.

Table 57: Problem affectedness per regional sample

Problem / Region	North Kazakhstan		South Kazakhstan		Kyrgyzstan	
	Urban	Rural	Urban	Rural	Urban	Rural
Unemployment	29%	31%	23%	54%	21%	37%
Illness	28%	42%	26%	42%	28%	20%
Death	9%	8%	9%	14%	7%	10%
Divorce	1%	0%	7%	0%	2%	2%
Marriage	8%	8%	12%	6%	8%	8%
Food prices	62%	86%	54%	82%	56%	35%
General prices	62%	88%	55%	88%	56%	37%
Com. services	57%	79%	60%	84%	28%	22%
Academic year	24%	33%	41%	48%	16%	12%
Education exp.	25%	34%	27%	24%	27%	12%
Criminality	5%	8%	5%	2%	4%	3%
Natural disasters	0%	8%	1%	6%	0%	0%
Transportation	10%	6%	6%	12%	5%	6%
Neighbors	5%	4%	2%	2%	0%	6%

With whom do the respondents discuss particular problems? Most problems are discussed within the households or among husbands and wives. This holds true for financial issues, health problems, problems with relatives, marriage problems, labor problems, family/cultural traditions, problems with friends or neighbors. Individuals are of less importance concerning the discussions about household problems. This is even stronger the case concerning friends. The Chui households show a particular tendency that problems are discussed with male members of the households only (14-17%).

Let us now compare the forms of assistance households can rely on when they have problems. With regard to financial issues it is families and relatives that play a strong role everywhere, stronger in the rural than in the urban contexts, strongest in Kyrgyzstan (urban: 83%, rural 92%), followed by South Kazakhstan (76% urban, 70% rural[147]) and North Kazakhstan (urban: 56%, rural 67%). In urban Astana every third household, however, reports getting no support in such cases, compared to 12% in Bishkek and 8% in Almaty, 18% in the Akmola and Almaty regions and only 6% in Chui region. That is, at least with the crucial issue of financial assistance, networks of kin are very much intact. But these social

[147] Here the urban-rural relation is reversed.

ties are also functioning in other social fields: we find a similar tendency concerning e.g. support in health problems. But interestingly, in this field the respondents of the North Kazakhstan sample refer to institutional help (doctors/nurses) with highest priority (urban 55%, rural 68%) compared to 13% in Almaty and 20% in Bishkek and a negligible number in the neighboring rural regions. A similar difference occurs with regard to institutional help in educational problems. Assistance concerning problems with relatives or with marriages is also received from the family/relative network. Assistance concerning problems with friends is, first of all, given by friends in Kazakhstan, followed by the family, while in Kyrgyzstan family help ranks first and friends are ranked second, but particularly in the Chui region on a much smaller scale (family: 73%, friends: 13%). Only in the field of labor problems assistance by colleagues plays a certain, but minor role. Assistance concerning cultural traditions again occurs within the kinship network, however, 28% in Almaty city and 22% in Almaty region report to get no such help, compared to only 12% in Astana and 17% in Akmola region, 11% in Bishkek and 8% in Chui region. A high percentage reports no assistance in problems with neighbors or the community (Astana: 54%, Almaty 35%, Bishkek 41%, Akmola region 49%, Almaty region 33%, Chui region 27%), followed by the kinship network. Thus, our comparison shows, that kinship networks are very much intact and in use for discussing and solving problems the households face. Only in education and health, where professional advice and help usually plays a role concerning problems, social ties of the kinship type do not strongly dominate the structure of assistance. But there are some indications that the kinship ties are weakening. The number of households receiving no help may be looked upon as such an indication though a weak one. This topic needs further exploration by qualitative research.

What about tensions in the households from a comparative view? Generational tensions[148] do not concern about 50% in Bishkek, 60% in Astana and 75% in Almaty, 28% in the Akmola region, 75% in the Almaty region and 51% in the Chui region. This is a quite mixed result, so that we cannot identify a general trend here. Gender tensions have similar ratings. In the Akmola region stronger tensions occur than elsewhere. Nevertheless, we can conclude that tensions exist in the households. Concerning general tensions and gender tensions about half of all households in Kyrgyzstan are affected. It does not seem to be farfetched to relate this result to the economic problems, the political instability, and the social rifts in the country. Astonishingly, ethnic tensions can be neglected in all sub-samples.

[148] We compare those who report no tensions.

Which types of problems occur in which sub-samples? In Astana and Bishkek the problems concern various categories (particularly housing related issues, inflation and food prices, traffic and transport), while in Almaty they particularly concern food prices and inflation. In Bishkek criminality, drug and alcohol problems are also worth mentioning. The picture is different in the rural regions. Respondents in the Akmola region mention first of all infrastructural problems, which are felt much stronger than in other rural regions. Unemployment and housing related problems rank next, but they are felt much stronger in Kazakhstan than in Kyrgyzstan. In the Almaty region the ecology also seems to play a stronger role than elsewhere. Traffic and transport problems are felt stronger in the Akmola region than in the other two regions.

A comparison of the living standard shows that 83% in urban Kazakhstan (Astana and Almaty and 93% in urban Kyrgyzstan have a *house or an apartment*. In the rural regions the rate is even higher (94% in Kazakhstan, 96% in Kyrgyzstan). Land possession is predominantly a rural issue. In Akmola region 78% own *land*, in Almaty region 92%, and in Chui region even 96%. Between 56% (Astana and Bishkek) and 74% own a *car or motorcycle*. Looking at the rural regions there is a striking difference: 56% and 54% in Akmola and Almaty regions, compared to 24% in the Chui region. As already mentioned, public transport in rural Kyrgyzstan is considered less of a problem than in rural Kazakhstan, and furthermore, many of those who own a car offer private taxi service to make an (additional) income. But the availability of a privately owned vehicle says nothing about its age and condition. Our observations in Kazakhstan and Kyrgyzstan show that cars in Kyrgyzstan are much older than in Kazakhstan. *Refrigerators* belong to the standards in both countries, urban and rural (>93%). The same holds true for *washing machines* (>87% except in Almaty region: 72%). *Computers* are frequent in the households in Kazakh cities (>80%), less frequent in Bishkek (69%). In the countryside, however, the frequency is much lower and significantly different in Kyrgyzstan: in the Akmola region 60%, in the Almaty region 40%, and in the Chui region only 14%. This underlines the lower living standard in Kyrgyzstan. Expensive Euro Remonts have been chosen by 43% in Astana and in Bishkek, 52% in Almaty. In the countryside the Almaty region ranges first (24%), followed by the Akmola region (14%) and the Chui region (8%). *Dacha* possessions, roughly speaking, are not very frequent (10%). They are found in Kyrgyzstan and Kazakhstan, both in urban and rural regions. In Kyrgyzstan dacha possession is slightly more frequent than in Kazakhstan, which may reflect the higher dependency from subsistence incomes. *Livestock* possession is of course more a rural phenomenon, but highest significantly more frequent in Kyrgyzstan (Akmola region 36%, Almaty region 16%, Chui region 80%). But also in Almaty and Bishkek every 10th household possesses their own livestock, compared to only 4% in Almaty. We assume that many rural households in Kyrgyzstan are more involved in livestock and also agricultural activity than in Kazakhstan, which can also be seen from higher possessions of agricultural machinery (8% compared to 2% and 4% in Akmola and Almaty regions).

Living space is not much different in the entire sample, this we believe is due to path dependency from soviet housing and apartment construction and apportioning which were kept during the first transformation period. In many cases the apartments are overcrowded.

Credits, Savings, Investments and Households' Decision-Making

Let us now look at the credits households have.[149] In Astana, interestingly, mortgage credits range first (44%), compared to only 15% in Almaty and 8% in Bishkek. Except in the Akmola region (5%) such credits do not play any role in rural regions.

Next follows consumer credits (urban 21-30%, rural 14-40%). In both cases Kyrgyzstan shows the lowest percentage, which may be an expression of the lower income/living standard situation. The latter is also supported when we look at credits for car purchases, which play a role in the cities (again in Bishkek to a lesser degree) and in rural regions except in Kyrgyzstan. In rural regions family needs/education as well as family events such as marriages or funerals are paid to a larger extent on credits. The exception seems to be the results concerning business/land/livestock investments in rural Kyrgyzstan with 65%, compared to 11% in the Akmola region and 0% in the Almaty region. Also Bishkek citizens invest in these categories to a much larger extent than their Kazakh counterparts (27% compared to 6 and 7%). No clear-cut picture emerges from the credit amounts with regard to country wise as well as rural-urban considerations. Urban and rural people predominantly take their credits from banks (Kazakhstan 75-91%, Kyrgyzstan 68%). In Kyrgyzstan institutes that are involved with microcredits are also important (Bishkek 18%, Chui region 35%). This may account for the much lower interest rates in Kyrgyzstan compared to Kazakhstan.

The ability to save for crisis does not differ much in the urban context. 47% of the respondents in Astana, 56% in Bishkek and 59% in Almaty state that they cannot save for crisis. A difference, however, occurs in the rural context. In the

149 We shall only compare the first credit mentioned, because we believe that this is the most important one.

Akmola region it is 84% who state that they cannot save for crisis, compared to 67% in Bishkek and 42% in Almaty region. Saving for old age cannot be done by 60% in Astana, 67% in Bishkek and 72% in Almaty, compared to 77% in Chui region, 80% in Akmola region and 82% in Almaty region. While it is obvious that incomes in rural regions are much lower than in urban ones and therefore rural dwellers have much less capacities to save in general, we can explain the situation in urban regions insofar that both countries have pension schemes which bring at least a minimum though often insufficient security. The capacity to save for the next generation is different. Here it is only around 30% in urban Kazakhstan who cannot do so, and 56% in Bishkek. In Akmola region, 86% state that they cannot save for the next generation, compared to 50% in the Almaty region and 45% in the Chui region. From these data and earlier data the impression given is that for many households in the Akmola region the living conditions are even harder than in the Chui region, while in the rural region of Almaty the living conditions seem to be better. Probably this must be related to the regional centers we researched.

For which purposes do the households save?[150] In all cities savings for real estate as well as its repairs and communal services rank first, followed by health and education and the future in general. Interestingly savings for funerals and marriages do not play any role in Bishkek, compared to the Kazakhstani cities (11 and 7%). In Astana 14% save for repayment of credits, which does not play any role in the two other cities. In rural regions savings for real estate, repairs and communal services rank highest in the Chui region (63% compared to 29% in the Akmola region and 39% in the Almaty region). In the two rural Kazakhstan regions savings for health and education are equally important (37% compared to 10% in the Chui region). It is again North Kazakhstan where 14% of the rural households save for the repayment of debts.

How many households lend to others? In Astana it is 25%, in Almaty 20% and in Bishkek 10%. In rural regions only the Almaty region is worth mentioning (10%). In all cases lending to relatives ranks first, followed by lending to friends. In urban regions the majority of lending is up to 1,000 USD, in few cases up to 20,000 USD. In the Almaty region the lending amounts are either up to 50 USD (8 cases) or up to 5,000 USD (5 cases). Most credits are short-term (up to 3 months) and interest-free. The majority lends to other households only.

Most savings are in a local bank or at home. Savings in private property occur

[150] We shall look again into the first savings. The second savings purpose confirms the relations outlined, however, adds another important category: material property.

both in urban and rural families. Savings in livestock occur in every sixth household in the Chui region, in rural Kazakhstan less frequently.

Decisions on *savings, investment and credits* are predominantly a nuclear family affair, ranking before 'household affairs'. Often households have a certain common budget for the everyday expenses, whereas certain subgroups (e.g. older generation or children with own incomes) administer their own budget. Asked for the main breadwinner in the households, we have to state that he or she usually stems from the middle age generation and often also from their children. Decisions on education/higher education also predominantly concern the nuclear family. Interestingly in Kazakhstan decisions on *migration*[151] concern households and nuclear families to the same extent, while in Kyrgyzstan the decisions are taken by the whole household.

Responsibility for Selected Problems

We asked the respondents whom they consider to be responsible for certain social fields:[152] state, family, individuals, insurances or charity organizations. In all fields the state is addressed by the overwhelming majority to be responsible, followed by the family. Individuals as well as insurances and civil society are hardly addressed. At best they can be taken as faint indication for a small change. Respondents referring to the state are particularly strong in rural and urban Kyrgyzstan. The family is given stronger responsibility in Kyrgyzstan than in Kazakhstan. In Kyrgyzstan and in Almaty also the individual is considered to have responsibilities in certain fields, but not in North Kazakhstan. On a whole, the state is considered to be responsible in most fields, except in childcare and education where also the family is considered to be responsible.

Provisional Results from the Statistical Research

The majority of the households are represented by nuclear families (69% two generation households). That is why we assume that the modernization of the soviet period has not been replaced by an increase of extended families as some nationalist rhetoric in the two countries suggests. The scientific assumptions about long

[151] We did not distinguish rural-urban and international migration. For Kazakhstan mainly rural-urban migration is relevant, while for the other Central Asian countries interregional/international migration is equally important.

[152] This concerned the provision of old age security, child care, unemployment, healthcare, the poor, education, and higher education.

term modernization and the development of the family structure are confirmed. This also holds true if we look at our two countries and some differences that occur. In urban Astana every fifth household is a three or more generation household. We argue that this is the result of rural-urban migration plus scarcity of housing in the new capital. And also the fact, that in the country side the number of nuclear families is lower, if compared with the cities, does not contradict the assumption about long term change. Also in Western countries, rural areas have lacked and lagged behind concerning the change of family size and structure. In our opinion this does not indicate a new trend. These households – two generation households being the vast majority – usually have at their disposal two and more incomes and secure their survival by a high employment diversity. That means, for the majority of cases we can assume that women are included in the workforce. A further confirming indicator for the ongoing long term change is the high number of closed households (64% across the two countries). Closed households have no economic exchange with relatives, friends etc. Concerning their economic activity they rely on themselves and are not embedded in a wider kin network. It is nuclear families that form the basis of the societies in Kazakhstan and Kyrgyzstan.

The overall living conditions in the two countries are very different which is affirmed by all data from international statistics. This forced us to construct different income categories for the two countries. To be middle class means a different income margin in Kazakhstan and Kyrgyzstan. But despite these differences, for a considerable number of these middle class households subsistence production and natural resources play a considerable role for their survival. For around one third of the urban and two third of the rural households these revenues are part of their household budget. Our indicator on the relevance of subsistence shows that only for about one third of households' subsistence income is irrelevant. We conclude from this, that many incomes in both countries are believed to be rather unstable, scarce and insecure. Otherwise households would not try to stabilize their incomes with subsistence revenues. That is, this group of the middle class households in our sample feels vulnerable. About the reasons for this diagnosis we can only speculate; but we believe that the reasons are connected with the macroeconomic context of the two societies. Especially in Kyrgyzstan but also to a lesser degree in Kazakhstan, the overall development has resulted in a general feeling of instability among these middle class respondents. This assumption can be supported by those answers of the respondents that claim that their income is almost sufficient (39%) or not sufficient (12%). A rough 40% declare that they are not better off than average and concerning the experience of the last ten years, 14% declare that there was no improvement, and 19% that their economic situation is worse now. Also the expectations for the future show that only a good 60% are optimistically orientated. Those better off show a significantly higher optimism than those with lower incomes. We believe that the assumption can be upheld that we articulated above. Many of the middle class households believe that their incomes are insecure and that they live under vulnerable conditions with a gloomy future.

How do the middle class households in our sample secure their wellbeing? Concerning the living standard, we can conclude that the households are well equipped with basic appliances like refrigerators, washing machines etc. The high degree of ownership of the houses or apartments the households live in (89%) is remarkable. This property can help them to render their livelihoods more secure. Internet access and computers though are not available to everybody. It seems that this is a result of the bad infrastructure, especially in the countryside but not only there. The middle class households in our sample are able to save and they do save. Saving as a form of postponed consumption helps the households to render them more secure against the risky conditions of the market economy. For a large part, the savings are for different events within the families that can't be calculated but that might occur, for real estate, for vacation and for children's education. The latter is an investment in the future of the children themselves but also for the future of the investors. In both countries, old age 'security' plays an important role especially in the belief systems of ethnic Kazakhs and Kyrgyz which form the bulk of our respondents. According to this belief, it is the children who have to guarantee the elders' generations lives. Public and private insurances have not replaced this traditional orientation on a mass level. Taken as an indicator for adjustment to the market economy, we may conclude that the households know fairly well about the insecurities and risks of such an economic system and try to arm themselves against it. Of course, not all of them do that or do that sufficiently. And partially, they do this with means the importance of which is unclear. Investment in children's education is one of the weapons to challenge the market economy by the means of traditional conduct. Other investments and savings serve the same purpose. Family ties have to be upheld in order to reduce household vulnerabilities. This strategic orientation is less followed by the use of the means of the market or by relying on public security offers, but by supporting and knitting family ties. Therefore the ability to save is mainly directed towards the next generation (54%) and not towards old age directly (30%). This strategic orientation of the households also discloses to us something about the relations of the respondents concerning trust in the organizations of the market economy. It seems to be still limited and therefore strategies of survival based on kin are plausible to many of our middle class people interviewed. Therefore these people save their money at home. And a remarkable number save in gold and jewelry, assets convertible in dowry and usually looked upon as more safe than most offers by banks. Also the high orientation on private property as a form of saving, the saving in livestock or credits taken for family affairs support our thesis about the high importance of family ties for survival strategies of households. Twenty years of capitalist market economy have not led to economic exchange relations mainly between individuals and institutions of the market economy but have to be viewed also as relations between families and the organizations of the economy because of the lack of trust the institutions of the market have by now been able to produce. If we generalize our results we may say, that in the new economic system money, contracts and family based trust are the major steering instruments. As the diachronic elements of our study are weak we can't really argue in favor of a trend. Nevertheless, we speculate that economic kin relations will coexist with market organizations still for some time to come but they will decrease in importance. The existence of many nuclear families, many closed households with no economic exchange relations receiving inputs from or giving inputs to kin networks makes us put forward this speculation. Whether in the younger generation these orientations get weaker can't be answered by our statistical data.

The importance of families as economic space goes hand in hand with a strong state orientation among many of our middle class respondents. They believe that the state is responsible for nearly all social policy issues in a wide sense: old age and health insurance, employment and infrastructure etc. The regulation of these issues by market forces or the individual itself is not very prominent. Only educational problems are believed to be an issue where the regulatory power is attributed to another social aggregate: the family. It seems that 'nanny state' orientations being dominant under the communist regimes have not receded very much and do still impinge their influence on policy issues and private behavior. But such an interpretation of our data seems too simple. In the last twenty years, the respondents have hardly experienced a stable and well-functioning market economy but one, that in a first period impoverished parts of the populations and caused much hardship for them concerning new behavioral challenges. In addition, the respondents had to face globalization and financial crises. After these experiences low trust in market institutions to regulate these developments is not astonishing. To make the state the addressee to solve these problems seems plausible. Additionally, our statistical data don't show relevant opposition to the market economy as such. To the contrary, the majority of the respondents sees economic improvement in the last 10 years and expects further improvement. Maybe the strong state orientation expresses something else that is a state being competent to solve the threatening problems of the population. It may hint at a welfare state regime in which the state provides and guarantees certain common goods.

Urban-rural differences are strong and influence the impulses towards acceptance and adjustment of the market economy. The rural households are poorer, family orientations among them are stronger, and reliance on subsistence production is higher. In general, their economic vulnerability is greater.

Much of what is said above, especially what we called speculation about modernization and acceptance and adjustment to the market economy needs further investigation. This will follow next because the research we undertook comprises a country comparison, a statistical analysis and a qualitative analysis. Therefore above conclusions represent provisional results. With the following qualitative research we hope to get better insights and to find better answers concerning the livelihoods of middle class households in the region, their sustainability, their survival strategies, their vulnerabilities and their embeddedness in the wider economy and society.

4. The Qualitative Research

Eckhard DITTRICH, Heiko SCHRADER

4.1. Research Design and Practical Research Process

The following sub-chapters present the results of the qualitative research of our project – the second stage of empirical investigation. Achieving these results involved a long common discussion process in and between the teams which we would like to summarize here.

Based on the results of the first quantitative stage of the research project, its questionnaire, the Sustainable Livelihoods Approach and secondary material, the mixed team from the different locations developed an interview guideline, which was empirically tested and modified.[153] Moreover, the Magdeburgian team provided research trainings to the team leaders and interviewers – professionals, PhD and master students – in which we taught techniques and practice of qualitative interviewing,[154] transcription and data analysis (coding and content analysis).[155] This training also aimed at a common understanding of the research project itself so that intelligent repeated inquiries by the interviewers were made possible. The training intended to introduce international standards of research for the participating universities, staff and students.

According to our research design each of the three Central Asian research teams headed by Aigul Zabirova (L.N. Gumilev Eurasian National University Astana), Nazym Shedenova (Al-Farabi University Almaty) and Galina Gorborukova (University of Central Asia Bishkek) took 25 interviews in the economic centers Astana (North Kazakhstan), Almaty (South Kazakhstan) and Bishkek (Kyrgyzstan) and an additional 15 in the adjacent rural regions Akmola Oblast (North Kazakhstan), Almaty Oblast (South Kazakhstan) and Chui region (Kyrgyzstan). The research design required villages and small towns that were sufficiently far away from the cities so that they did not constitute suburbs and people could not commute for their daily work. This should allow us getting an insight into the problems of rural life. Furthermore, another requirement was that these regions should be "normal" regarding social structure and rural problems.

153 This phase provided a particular challenge when translating the key English terms into adequate terms of languages being applied in the interviews (Russian, Kazakh and Kyrgyz, Uighur).

154 We applied the method of semi-structured expert interview according to Meuser/Nagel (cf. Meuser & Nagel, 1991), and content analysis according to Mayring (2010).

155 For these trainings we also invited Denis Gruber and Markus Kaiser to provide their inputs.

The interviews took place during summer 2013. The interview languages were Russian, Kazakh and Kyrgyz, even Uyghur. If necessary, the recorded interviews were translated into Russian, later on into English, the lingua franca of the project. The entire text corpus constitutes far more than 1,000 pages. They represent a very rich raw material which by far exceeds our focus of analysis here.[156]

As already outlined in Chapter 3.1 (quantitative methodology) we applied the household-level approach (Hess), which does not pre-define who will be asked, and the open-household approach which considers transfers from and to the households.

For data analysis the mixed team developed a hierarchical code book, in which categories and codes were deduced from the interview guideline, theory and secondary material observations. The researchers were also motivated to code inductively (from the transcripts) beyond the pre-defined codes. Coding was done by the research teams on their own by using the analysis program MaxQdata, while the Magdeburgian team accompanied them in this process. Wherever the English translation provided problems of understanding we asked our Magdeburgian team members Nigina Avganova, Batima Mambetalina and Aikokul Maksutova (Central Asian scholars who all finished their MA of social science in Magdeburg) to get into the original transcripts and find more adequate translations.

Finally, the Magdeburgian team leaders Eckhard Dittrich and Heiko Schrader developed a structure for bringing the coded material into a report and a guideline for data interpretation. Despite all attempts at standardization of the qualitative reports in order to reach a basis for comparison, the individual traits of the reporters still can be deciphered in the following chapters. For this book the Astana and Bishkek reports were revised by the editors, while part of the coding and writing of the Almaty report was done by the Magdeburgian team.[157]

A half year stay of Eckhard Dittrich in Astana eased the entire coordination work as well as the stays of two doctoral students Aigul Beimisheva and Daurenbek Kuleimenov in Magdeburg. The presence of Markus Kaiser in Bishkek and a comparative research of Denis Gruber in Russia also belonged to the frame constituting the working relations.

[156] The length of the interviews ranged from 3 to almost 40 pages, depending on the skills of the interviewers and the household where the interviews took place.

[157] Of course, the research was influenced by the conditions of academic everyday life of the scientists in charge. Nazym Shedenova, team leader of the Almaty team, won a scholarship and was absent during critical phases of the qualitative part of the project and had to be replaced by an advanced doctoral student (Aigul Beimisheva).

4.2. Qualitative Report from North Kazakhstan

Aigul ZABIROVA, shortened and edited by E. DITTRICH and H. SCHRADER

According to UN statistics, the path to market conditions in Kazakhstan has led to the country become one of the middle-income countries in the world. Economically and politically it has an outstanding position among all the Central Asian countries. An authoritarian rule is combined with a strong economic policy of development, the model of which is Singapore. In the following quotation, the president himself explains this general orientation: "'Political stability is what matters most. In Asian society discipline and order are more important than democracy, which has to develop over time'. This was the credo of Lee Kwan Yew. I never concealed the fact that this approach appealed to me. 'Economics before politics' was what I always used to say. I was criticized for saying so. But I had seen the disintegration of the USSR with my very own eyes, when politics had taken precedent over peoples' prosperity and peace of mind" (Nazarbayev 2008:26).

The development of Kazakhstan is a success story in economic terms. But despite the undeniable success, the development also shows a deep cleavage between the living situation in urban and rural areas. While in many urban settings – notably in Astana and Almaty – one can discover the results of the economically successful exploitation of the natural resources like oil, gas, and metals, in rural areas no equivalent development has happened. Living conditions in the latter are much worse than in the cities. Thus, for parts of the population, urban rural migration has become a reality and a prospect for personal achievement (cf. Mathijs and Swinnen 1998).

Most of Kazakhstani villages face severe problems with unemployment, outmigration of the economically active population, an underdeveloped infrastructure, especially drinking water etc. E.g. 55% of rural inhabitants do not have access to drinking water at home and 11% are dependent on supply of drinking water from outside of their village[158]. The poverty rate in rural areas is three times higher than in urban areas. 10.1 % of the rural population has an income below subsistence level, while in urban areas these people account for 3.7 % of the population[159].

158 Agency on Statistics of the Republic of Kazakhstan: "Results of the 2009 national population census of the Republic of Kazakhstan", Analytical report. Available at http://liportal.giz.de/fileadmin/user_upload/oeffentlich/Kasachstan/40_gesellschaft/Kaz2009_Analytical_report.pdf; access date 10-11-2014

159 Agency on Statistics of the Republic of Kazakhstan: "Osnovnye pokazateli differenciacii dochodov naselenija za 2001-2010 gody" [Principle indicators of income differentiation of the population for the period of 2001-2010], Bulletin. Astana, 2011

Kazakhstani governments have tried to improve the situation in rural areas. E.g. the governmental program of employment for graduated youths in rural areas centers around incentives to make young specialists stay in the countryside by means of different financial allowances as loans for housing etc. There also exists a State Program of Industrial and Innovative Development for 2011-2015. In general, cities in Kazakhstan like Astana and Almaty have financial, institutional and political support in order to spur development while country centers or regional centers (mostly former industrial cities) are not in the same situation. But in very recent times, the social conditions of the rural population are getting slightly better. According to President Nazarbayev this results from new possibilities: "If we want to get 1st level of export of products in agriculture, we should pay attention to villages. Earlier we did not have enough possibilities for that, but now we have gained resources for it".[160]

Household Structure and Marital Status

If we look at the total number of rural and urban households that are represented in our sample in north Kazakhstan, nuclear families (30 households) hold the clear majority. Extended households are only represented by 10 households. It is important to emphasize that this type of extended household is equally distributed in urban as well as in rural areas. One household does not belong to any of the listed types, being composed of two sisters. This household is not listed in the following table.

Table 58: Household type in the qualitative sample, North Kazakhstan

	Nuclear household	Extended household	Total
Astana	18	6	24
Akmola region	12	4	16
Total:	30	10	40

Note: frequencies

The average number of children in the observed households is 2.7 kids. In our sample there are only few families with more children than average. In general, adult children don't stay in their parent's households after being married but found

160 Forbes Kazakhstan: "Nazarbaev: V Kazachstane neobchodimo prinjat' socialnuju programmu vozrozhdenija sela" [Nazarbaev: It is necessary to adopt the rural revival program in Kazakhstan], Interview as of 11-04-2013. Available at http://forbes.kz/news/2013/04/11/newsid_247 56; access date 18-07-2013

a household on their own. There are 4 households with widows, belonging to the older generation. Three households include divorced persons. The average age of the divorced persons is 31 years. Three households are single-parent households in which women bring up children by themselves. Also, there is an interesting case of one household, in which four of its members live in different cities. In the household's locality, there is constantly living only a married spouse. There are four singles among our interviewees. In addition to this, there are many households with adult children. These households are bound together by a common budget although the household members have locally split up, working, studying and partly living in separate locations. With the expected further rise of rural to city migration, and the rise of children studying at universities, the number of such households is likely to increase.

The structures of our households mirror demographic trends, we can observe in Kazakhstan and partly worldwide: continued fertility declines, further acceleration of the speed of aging, growing numbers of divorces, single parent families and small families, and the key role of education and human capital in further development as will be disclosed later on in our research.

General Orientation of the Interviewees

Most interviewees show an overall satisfaction with their current living conditions, despite their critical positions concerning details. We will discuss this topic in the following chapter. This general satisfaction can be observed especially among older ethnic Kazakh respondents who show a strong identification with their new statehood. We sincerely believe that this has to do with the collective memory that considers the past as a 'colonial' period with harsh crises in the 1930s, after the Second World War and with stagnation during the Brezhnev era and the threatening challenges of the perestroika period. Additionally a comparison is quite often drawn with neighboring countries. The respondents talk about this context by explaining that Kazakhstan is comparatively well off, economically as well as politically. Improvements – even if they take place gradually – nourish a positive mood. Also 'strong' religious Muslim orientations seem to have an appeasing influence on the level of satisfaction, although they are not mentioned often. They are nearly always directed towards health. The younger cohorts seem to be more critical concerning their own socio-economic conditions. Nevertheless, there seem to be very pressing problems for both groups such as the rise of prices, education of the next generation, housing, and with an undertone of resignation concern about corruption. All groups talk about the bad living conditions in rural areas. The following are some quotations to highlight the general mood.

"Everything is getting better. We have a middle financial position. We are not poor, also we are not so rich, we are somewhere in the middle. We economize our income, pay utilities, buy products, dress and somehow live from one salary to the next one" (Ast int 11: 19, rural, male).[161]

"All expenses and finances of our household are calculated in advance. We don't have property as security. We are satisfied by our monthly income. We never buy goods, which can create problems for our family budget" (Ast int 7: 17, rural, female).

"Now, since the last five years all members of the family are working, and this is enough for us. We are not rich, but we are content. However, we can't travel abroad every week" (Ast int 17: 45, urban, female).

"Our house is heated with a stove and we have to use coal and firewood, which we buy. Since this year we have water directly in the street, but earlier we hauled water from a kilometer away. We are glad that water is near now; we want to have water in our house, which demands huge expenses. We want to equip our house for women, because in the winter period our outside toilets can lead to illnesses of women. We plan to do so, but I don't know how it turns out. Such possibilities are restricted still" (Ast int 11: 13, rural, male).

"We live here for a long time and have got accustomed to here. We have even drinking water and stable electricity at home. We heat our home ourselves. Additionally, we have 2 cars for both communicating within the village and going to the city. We are satisfied by our living conditions" (Ast int 11: 13, rural, male).

"There is a good school and three kindergartens here! It is well like this. In general all questions are solvable. The main thing is to approach the right person. I am such person who never swears. I just think we redeemed the credit. We wanted the baby; he was born on February, 14th. I hope we will continue to work and to raise our children" (Ast int 29: 55-56, urban, female).

"Well... I think, it is normal, we are somewhere in the middle, it is not bad and it is not good. The main thing is we don't fall behind people. The main thing is health" (Ast int 6: 254, rural, female).

---

[161] The reference to the interview paragraphs reads as follows: Astana interview 11, paragraph 19. Sometimes, if gender (male, female), location (urban, rural), age or ethnicity (e.g. Kazakh) is important, we add this information, too. Correspondingly, in the latter qualitative parts read Alm: Almaty, Bishkek Ast: Astana.

"We live at average. We are not rich, not poor. We live like many others" (Ast int 33: 28, urban, male).

"Thanks to Allah every member of the household is healthy" (Ast int 1: 18, rural, male,).

"I have already told you, the main problem of living here is the high cost of living. ... Basically the main products like meat, butter, bread and utilities are the most expensive in Kazakhstan" (Ast int 9: 25, rural female).

"The main problem was to find suitable accommodation that will serve us concerning quality, capacity and location ... Here, half of the working people are public servants. For example, bedroom apartments cost at least USD 100,000. A good apartment costs USD 120,000-130,000. And with our salary how can one buy an apartment; what do you think? ... We applied for the public program; there were 26,000 people in the queue for 2000 flats. ... The biggest problem – it is the price of housing" (Ast int 24: 38, urban, female).

In general, of course, there are households that are content with state services. But the majority has many complaints concerning services. Many households in rural areas complain about the local infrastructural conditions they have to live in, while urban households express their concerns especially about housing. Rural households also criticize the state services that are supposed to provide social allowances to socially vulnerable groups, the system of *blat* (cf. Ledeneva 1998), without which hardly any services seem to function, and the bureaucracy in general. Urban households are not satisfied with the traffic, with street cleaning.

"I don't trust our local administration. They don't support us as a young family. I think the main problem for living in a rural area is 'blat' and informal relationships. All depends on the strength of your networks" (Ast int 15: 24, rural, female).

"There are very different types of authorities, some are able to solve our problems and others are not able to do so. Our local authority is not capable in the case of cleaning streets and solving the problems of ordinary urban residents. I think they don't know about commuting" (Ast int 40: 24, urban, female).

Criminality is often mentioned when the people talk about their problems, but only seldom is it also seen as a problem of the administration.

"I feel secure myself here. I have never seen any problems during I live here. I am secure" (Ast int 7: 25, rural, female).

"I feel safe, but it depends on where I am, which part of the city. I consider myself in full safety during day time. Our country develops, especially Astana. It is the economic and political center of the country. It is safer but in the evenings it is dangerous to be alone in outer districts. Strangers can beat or rob you. I try to avoid such a situation and don't go late to criminal areas. I try to go with friends" (Ast int 39: 29, urban, male).

"I don't feel safe, because it is a resort zone, where there are a lot of visitors. They come and go at any moment. The local police is not able to put policemen at every corner, so I can't feel secure" (Ast int 9: rural, female).

"Now there are a lot of drug addicts here and I am anxious. I'm afraid of terrorists, Wahhabis and afraid of people with beard, but I respect the religion, Islam. How to explain, I respect, I am a Muslim. But I do not approve fanatics of religion. I do not want to have the situation like in Zhanaozen. They started the same at Adai[162] I know well. That's what I'm afraid of and also I do not want to have terrorism in our country" (Ast int 19: urban, female).

Corruption is one of the main problems for Kazakhstani society. It seems to be present at all levels. But it also finds public attention and the state spends a great deal of money to fight against it. A state agency, the RK (financial police) is in charge of fighting corruption. In Kazakhstan, corruption is deeply interconnected with giving gifts as elements of 'traditional' social exchanges. Drawing the line between gifts, 'blat' and corruption is quite often difficult.

In 2012, according to official statistics of the financial police, the amount of damage from corruption was 7.8 billion KZT. In that year, 784 civil servants were involved in criminal liability suits on the charge of being corrupt. 1,828 new cases of corruption were revealed. The most widespread corruption crimes were abuse of power in office (389 cases) and receiving of bribes (367 cases). The majority of corruption crimes involved employees of local administrations in cities and in regions.[163]

"The mentality of our village has been changed. ... Currently money and networks play the main role" (Ast int 26: 24, rural, female).

"There is corruption, which is unlike corruption in the South, where money plays the main role. Here all problems are solved through acquaintances and networks. For example, if any of my relatives goes to the authorities with certain problems, he firstly will look for acquaintances among his relatives" (Ast int 10: 26, rural, male).

"Of course, I think there is a corruption problem. Perhaps this corruption disturbs our activities. Many traffic policemen demand small bribes from us due to our informal taxi

---

[162] Adai is a Kazakh tribe in the Western region of Kazakhstan.

[163] Galat, Irina: "Infografika: Korrupcia v Kazachstane" Info-graphics: Corruption in Kazakhstan]. In: Vlast, 17.04.2013. Available at http://vlast.kz/?art=1606; access date 10-11-2014

service. ... We can only hope and wait that the situation is improving" (Ast int 5: 24, rural, male).

"I should formalize my flat right now. I think with scary about the future informal expenses, because you have to either wait 3-4 months or pay a certain sum, the height of which I don't know" (Ast int 26: 24, urban, female).

"It seems that corruption becomes an everyday practice. You have to give a bribe for getting a job or improving your living conditions. This has become the only means to solve one's problems" (Ast int 40: 24, urban, female).

"Difficulties ... ? Probably, it is the circulation in offices, bureaucracy in banks ... I could work in a bank as well... but it is a question of being promoted. You need to pay for that. It happened that I gave bribes ... the greatest I gave is 100 dollars to solve a question with property registration. But in general I do not like to give bribes" (Ast int 29: 51, urban, female).

Under these circumstances, the development of public "trust" as a resource of social relations is difficult to achieve (cf. Putnam, 2007).

We cross checked these general orientations by asking about life goals. They center on a decent living without financial problems, a good education for the next generation, good relations with friends and relatives and a decent house. In so far, these goals of life – partly ex negativo – support the general orientation described above.

Household Positions and Decision Making

"A man must toil from sun to sun, but a woman's work is never done" (Kazakh proverb).

As in all modern societies, in Kazakhstan the value of work is measured by money and the society attributes more value to the work generating a monetary income. Work done in the household – overwhelmingly done by women – is largely 'invisible' and its contribution to the society's and the household's wellbeing is often overlooked or underevaluated. Even nowadays, most working mothers still come home in time to fulfill their duties: taking care of their children, husbands and parents or parentsin-law. They have to shoulder a double burden: caring for their family and relatives and making money.

In the observed households, the traditional division of labor is still very much intact. While women typically do regular necessary indoor household tasks like cooking, child care, washing, cleaning, and additionally shopping, the male persons in the households are mostly responsible for the outdoor and the 'heavy' activities. Women typically plan and enlist other family members' help. This constellation is absolutely dominant in the rural households while in the urban ones some variations can be observed.

"My husband mainly does the outside works like work in the shed, deals with livestock, sometime he makes the heavy works in the house with our son when he comes from the city" (Ast int 4: 9, rural, female).

"I don't do the female work like cleaning, washing, whitewashing and painting the house ... construction work, deconstruction, moving something and everything else related with housekeeping is men's duty" (Int Ast 5: 8, rural, male).

"In general my husband does all masculine works like rising heavy things, replacing something, but the rest of the obligations are mine: cleaning, washing etc. Of course, my children help me" (Ast int 9: 9, rural, female).

The responsibility for education of children as well as for the household budget is usually attributed to women:

"My wife used to run issues of child's education. ... Also she runs the family budget" (Ast int 13: 4, rural, male).

Children are strongly involved in this gendered labor division.

"My younger son is responsible for sustaining of the livestock... he also deals with preparing, bringing the fuel, heating the house, since there is no central heating system" (Ast int 3: 10, rural, female).

"My granddaughter A. helps her mother with the housework" (Ast int 2: 10, rural, female).

"I work every day till evening without any holidays in summer time. Therefore cooking, washing by machine, watering flours and cleaning are duties of my second daughter. I don't let her do hand washing because it is hard work for her and usually I do it myself ... The duties of my son are taking out the garbage, going for bread" (Ast int 9: 9, rural, female).

But there are also households where the division of labor is not strictly based on gender.

"Who has time and the ability does the tasks" (Ast int 5: 8, rural, female).

"My daughter comes back from work very tired, then we have a dinner together, and after that I can wash dishes. It is not a shame for me. I buried my wife 7 years ago. ... she [my daughter] cleans, washes and vacuums on the weekends. Sometimes she calls me and says: 'Daddy, fry something, cut or boil something.' There is no fixed labor division. I do all difficult works, because women's health is weak" (Ast int 10: 9, rural, male).

"No, there are no fixed duties in the household. We do everything jointly. My obligation is earning money for the household and that is all. My wife and the elder daughter cook. We clean the flat jointly. There is no duty division on male and female works" (Ast int 12: 9, rural, female).

The typical form of the division of labor in the households as well as the deviations from them is not disputed. No respondent complains about unfairness concerning his or her tasks.

We also wanted to learn about the decision making processes. Concerning the latter element, we find orientations at traditional values according to which males and age play the decisive roles, but also orientations at socio-economic status, giving those who earn most the main power in decision making. But there are also situational factors that impinge on decision making. The following are some citations that intend to show the varieties:

"I'm the head of our household. Definitely. Therefore I make the main decisions in the household" (Ast int 5: 4, rural, male).

"I am head of the household and usually run all issues at home. I am a main breadwinner as well" (Ast int 1: 4, rural, male).

Nevertheless, sometimes women have a strong position:

"If there are some urgent problems, we solve these questions with my husband. My decision is more crucial" (Ast int 41: 3, urban, female).

"I manage the family budget. As I'm a woman I should calculate all expenses of the household" (Ast int 40: 3, urban, female).

Especially in urban families, there can be observed that in more well-off families the role division and domination in decision making depends on earnings.

"I think that the one who contributes most to the income of the household is the main decision maker" (Ast int 4: 5, rural, female).

"I am the main breadwinner in the household. My family severely depends on my salary. For this reason I am the main decision maker in our household" (Ast int 7: 5, rural female divorced).

In some better-off families, respondents stress joint decision making.

"The family budget is administered by both me and my wife. .... She manages all expenses concerning food stuff and everyday needs, and I run the issues of farm's expenses" (Ast int 1: 4, rural, male).

"We jointly make the decisions about the education of the children after having discussed the issues" (Ast int 2: 5 rural, female).

Historically, in Kazakh nomadic households the important decisions were made by the elders. Despite serious social and cultural transformations during the Soviet time, this structure remained particularly intact especially in the countryside.

"Our household consists of my husband's mother, me, my son, my daughter-in-law, and four grandchildren. I am the main decision maker in the household. I am a pensioner now. We jointly take the decisions about the education of the children after discussing them. I manage the family budget" (Ast int 2: 5, rural, female).

"I am the oldest member of our household. I am the 'ot anasy' (mother of the fire place). I make the main decisions in the household" (Ast int 3: 5, rural, female).

"I am the oldest member of the household. I am the head of the household and main decision maker. ... The crucial decisions are mine" (Ast int 8: 4, rural, male).

There are cases in which the priorities of adult children do not coincide with priorities of their parents. In these cases children make the disputable decisions, which hints at changes in the traditional orientations.

It is difficult to give a definite interpretation on decision making because in some interviews the notion of decision making and the one about the head of household are completely confounded. In other interviews, the traditional task of being responsible for the budget of the household is misunderstood as being the main decision maker. And of course also situational aspects play a role when e.g. females have to take a decision because their husbands are absent. Nevertheless, in general one may say, that decision making usually follows traditional gender and age roles. With a growing labor market, the participation of women and their crucial role in supporting the households with their salaries, leads to what we can also observe in some interviews, a growing influence of women on decisions in the households, joint decision making included. There also seems to be a certain tendency to reduce the decisive role of the elderly on decisions in the households.

Tensions in the Household

We also asked our respondents about tensions in their households. The background for this were reflections on the new challenges, the market economy has brought about concerning new economic behavior but also concerning traditional orientations among many Kazakh families. If traditional behavior is concerned, we refer to ethnic Kazakh households not to other minorities. Of course, a certain degree of tensions and quarrels in households is normal and many respondents say so and thus relativize their opinions, but it seems that for other households certain tensions exceed this normality. Additionally, there are certain problems, many households face, which are also presented here. They include the 'generational gap', alcoholism of male members and inner-ethnic changes in Kazakh households. In reality, the issues are often not separated as it appears here in the quotations because of space restrictions.

"Sometimes, we think differently. My husband wants to do something, and I too, but in a different way. Then we try to find a compromise between these issues. Either I agree with the decision of my husband, or he agrees with me. Well, it depends on the circumstances. Sometimes my husband says that I am right, and agrees with me. Sometimes he says 'no' and decides in his own way. He says that it is correct and that I should agree with him" (Ast int 24: 21, urban, female).

"We have disputes on education, on financing the children" (Ast int 9: 21 rural, female).

For many households financial problems are important. Women, often in charge of the budget sometimes seem to find their own ways in which to handle 'misunderstandings' as the following quotation shows:

"Yes, misunderstandings. Earlier, I recorded on everything I bought and how much it cost" (Ast int 6: 85, rural, female).

"Conflicts happen for various reasons: lack of money for personal needs or different opinions on life. Usually, we try to find a compromise" (Ast int 39: 11, urban, male).

Another field of tensions is obligations concerning gender roles. This contradicts the above mentioned 'peace' concerning the question about the division of labor in the households.

"There are also some cases of tensions based on male and female obligations. The frequency of those conflicts depends on our mood. If she doesn't clean the house, I can express my opinion concerning this. It happens not so often" (Ast int 11: 11, rural, male).

Sometimes the new economic conditions (unemployment) have endangered the role of men as breadwinners and household heads and also the traditional age hierarchy. The first quotation represents a classical conflict in ethnic Kazakh households known as *"kyshik kyyeu"* (a husband lives at the expense of a wife and her relatives).

"The only thing is that my husband doesn't respect my relatives. Sometimes I think that he has complexes due to living with my father in an apartment owned by me. My sister also thinks so. On the other hand nobody rebukes him. When my relatives come, he does not sit down with them and does not talk with them. He stays in another room. But when his relatives arrive, I meet them, we talk together" (Ast int 18: 18, urban, female).

"I am the eldest. I am like a father for them. I try to give advice to them, to guide them based on my own experience. They do not like to be cramped in strict frames... I want them to think ahead. I have my own plans for them, and I want them to follow this plan (Ast int 34: 19, urban, male).

But not only men reclaim the adherence to traditions but also women:

"I believe that there are no bad men, there are bad wives. All women should endure" (Ast int 21: 23, urban, female).

Men's addiction to alcohol is a major problem in Kazakhstani households and especially in rural areas. Although ethnic Kazakhs are the focus of this chapter, we can conclude from the interviews with household heads of other ethnicities, that they face similar problems.

"My father left his work because of an accident... He began to drink. I came home and argued with him, screamed at him. Now, many years later, my father explained that he was afraid of me at that time" (Ast int 20: 17 urban, female).

"I stopped drinking alcohol in 1995, because I had one very disgraceful incident. I don't drink even a beer after that" (Ast int 10: 13, rural, male, widower).

In some rural areas, the security situation seems to be quite dramatic as an old women reports that lives alone with her husband in a village 100 km north of Astana:

"I: What about roads, transport and is it dangerous to live here?

R: Definitely it is dangerous, many drug users, drunkards and they ask money from us.

I: Do they knock at a door?

R: They do knock! They do come, if you will not give them money – it is dangerous, they will set fire to our house. They have set fire recently to the neighbor's house [...] There are drug addicts; we know many of them... It's the guys who have stayed in prison ... If you do not give them, you will be an enemy to them. They knock and go home. You give them money and they come anyway.

I: Come again?

R: Yes, when my husband works at night, I stay alone and I'm afraid to sleep. I say him to lock the door. But if someone wants to enter, one will enter, break a window! Or at first they will cut off the phone ... there is an area 'Shanghai', it is terrible there, always fighting, last night somebody was killed and brought away by the 'ambulance' car (Ast int 6: 196-203, rural, female).

The clash of generations is represented by adherence to different values. In the first following quotation, they are expressed by the use of an ethnic Kazakh proverb:

"Till 7 years keep children as kings, from 7 to 17 keep them as slaves, after 17 keep them as equal to you" (Ast int 19: 19, urban, female).

"This is obvious, since we are from the twentieth century, and they are from the twenty first century. My kids say, now everything is not the same as in the XXth century... For example, my child wants to engage in business, but the financial situation doesn't allow us to do so at this time. I say that in our times no one had made appropriate conditions for us, my parents didn't leave us any patrimonies" (Ast int 28: 9, urban, female).

"Sometimes such debates appear between me and my daughter. She says: 'Daddy, you live like in a former century. ... Today you must live for yourself. You were brought up in that time, but today it is another time. Everything is different and we must live only for ourselves. Everything is like commerce now.' I reply to her: 'Daughter, we should always be human in any circumstances. We must respect elder persons.' Then she replies me with a laugh: 'Of course, you are so well-bred. I can't change your mind, but today everyone must live only for himself'" (Ast int 10: 11, rural, male).

"Mostly the younger generation wants to have more material things than they can afford" (Ast int 26: 9, urban, female).

"In our household our only child has failed to comply with his obligations, he doesn't want to learn. We are quite different. I am studious but my daughter always runs somewhere" (Ast int 31: 20, urban, female).

Nevertheless, some parents treat children as adults, considering them as equal.

"Earlier in the Soviet Union, children did what their parents told them; it was believed that parents are always right. Probably, this way of thinking has its advantages. But now, times have changed. We teach our children to express their opinions and stick to them. They can also give advice to us" (Ast int 24: 21, urban, female).

There is a custom among Kazakh people called "*Atalyk*", what implies that the first child is brought up by the grandparents. In all interviews, that report on that praxis, it is connected with severe adaptation problems and sometimes with psychological disorders concerning mothers.

"When my oldest daughter was born, we gave her to be educated by my parents. She grew up with them. At that time, she didn't like to spend time with us. She couldn't get used to us. After the ninth class, middle school, my mother began to send her to live with us for some time as she understood that she wasn't young any longer and she needed to get used to her native parents and sisters. Now she has already accustomed to us because she is adult" (Int Ast 32: 11, urban, female).

"One of my sons was brought up by his grandmother. He has different opinions from all other household members. Sometimes it seems to me that he doesn't consider us as his parents. I often think about this. Therefore I assume that my grandchildren must be brought up by their parents" (Ast int 40: 10, urban, female).

Also the obligations of mutual help among the wider family in Kazakh networks come under pressure and seem to lose their coherence:

"As we live in the capital many relatives come to study or to work here. This is very inconvenient for us, because we want to live on ourselves" (Ast int 30: 12, urban, female).

"Even if you know that this relative has money, he denies helping you. He finds any reason in order to refuse it to you" (Ast int 39: 11, urban, male).

"My relatives offended me because I did not lend them money" (Ast int 11: 11, urban, female).

To sum up this section:

1. Tensions in the household may involve all members. Coping abilities seem to be different as some feel tensions to be 'normal', others not. Underlying the latter attitude seems to be a notion of harmony.
2. Tensions concern adaptation to the new economic conditions. Quite often the financial attitudes are at the base of controversial relations among household members.
3. Many tensions center on traditional obligations concerning gender roles but also concerning traditional customs among ethnic Kazakhs.
4. Alcoholism seems to be a widespread problem, especially in rural area.

Income and Employment of Households

Our respondents view employment as one of the most pressing problems over the last 20 years. All people interviewed stress this point, even if they currently have a job about which they do not complain and even if they admit that the situation in their region is not bad. As the experience of life-long employment security has been lost, many respondents are afraid that their jobs might be endangered in the future, might not fit the labor market needs because of age or specialty. Therefore households have tried to diversify their incomes.

According to households' employment, we can divide our sample in several groups: households with a sole income source and those with many, households with stable employment in state organizations, and those with less stable employment in private enterprises, households with and without subsistence production. We start with quotations that represent opinions of satisfaction.

"We are coping with our problems and we don't have large weaknesses. Our income allows us to overcome these problems, but not so much. Nevertheless our income is sufficient for us. Currently I and my wife work. We have stable salaries" (Ast int 11: 13, rural, male).

"Now I have no difficulties at all, because I have been working in one place since 2006. It is the 6th year in the centre and, I am satisfied with my wage" (Ast int 31: 22, urban, female).

"We don't have any constraints in sustaining our household. We are just budget workers. Although our salary is not so high, it is stable. I would like to say, have a stable job and stable salary. Therefore I can't see any constraints in the realisation of our life" (Ast int 7: 23, rural, female).

The arguments mentioned above are not representative of a majority opinion. Many interviewees have mixed employment and an income biography with good and bad times. In general, for all respondents it is clear that it is a burden to be taken up individually to make a household keep going. Second jobs might be necessary, income pooling, bridging times of financial crises with credits etc.

In soviet times households mostly lived on formal incomes (salaries, pensions, scholarships, etc.); today many households in Kazakhstan seek to combine formal (official income) and informal (temporal incomes, additional sources of income) types of incomes to reach financial stability. Informal income sources are derived from employment in the large informal economy, which is considered as out of the state regulations like registration, tax payment, conditions of employment and operating licenses (Becker 2004:12). Current Kazakhstani households have many options to pool different sources of income in order to fulfill their needs.

Nowadays the levels of income of rural and urban households are very different. The average level of salaries and the options to combine different sources of income seem to be higher among urban households.

"In the city most people have enough time for doing some works simultaneously, and I envy them. In rural areas, people don't have such opportunities due to unemployment problems. Therefore we even don't look for additional work" (Ast int 15: 20, rural, female).

Rural and urban households have specific problems involved in their efforts to make a living. Two major differences show up in the following quotations:

"Particularly in the season of stocking fuel and hay we have financial problems. We seek to sell some livestock in order to overcome these problems, but sometimes we can't sell it. In that case we usually suffer. It is seasonal problems, which occur only in autumn. We buy a lorry of hay and a lorry of coal in that period" (Ast int 4: 13, rural, female).

Many urban households have financial problems concerning housing, because rents in Astana are comparatively high.

"In general, our regular income is about 350,000 KZT per month. But it happens that this money is not enough, because we rent an apartment. Each month we have to pay 70.000 KZT for rent. There are also public utilities and our son studies elsewhere. He is living in a dormitory, and we have to pay for it. We pay 23,000 KZT for his living in a dormitory; food and studying is free" (Ast int 24: 17, urban, female).

Very rarely households have a sole income. Usually, the households have different income sources.

"Currently in our household, there are 4 persons with permanent incomes: me and my mother-in-law, who has a 2-nd grade of invalidity. We have pensions; my son and daughter-in-law, they have salaries. If we calculate the income of the household members, it will be about 170,000 KZT (1034 USD) per month. It is not sufficient for us, but it keeps us alive until the next salary" (Ast int 2: 14, rural, female).

Well-off households with their own housing or stable incomes acquire flats in order to rent them out which implies a prosperous business.

"We are a normal household. We rent out an apartment. This brings us some income. We are renting it out for 100,000 KZT. It is on the left bank near the pyramid. We rent out this apartment during 2 months for 100,000 KZT. The previous renting price was 75,000

KZT. This apartment belongs to our parents. It is our daughter's apartment" (Ast int 23: 37, urban, male).

Sometimes, the people are very ingenious to find additional income sources. The following example is a very remarkable one from a women living alone with her children:

"At present, thanks to my two higher educational degrees, I always have work. For example, my sports degree serves me in three jobs. The first job is a teacher at the university with a maximum of hours. I also work as a manager in sports. It is a separate division of the university. In addition, I work at a special educational center for youth's promotion of sport as a trainer. Thus, I earn 120,000 KZT (810 USD) as a teacher at the university. It is the main income. I earn 33,000 KZT (225 USD) as a manager in sports. I earn 28,000 KZT (190 USD) at a children's sport school. I also train people in self-defense. With these lessons I earn about 45-50,000 KZT (305-340 USD) a month. Additionally I draw up legal contracts, sometimes I work out statements of claim. I earn about 200 USD or 30,000 KZT. In total my income makes up for 250,000 KZT (1,700 USD)" (Ast int 22: 17, urban, female).

In this household survey, on the base of narrative sequences in the interviews, we tried to get accurate descriptions of the households. Holding multiple jobs is typical for middleclass households. Usually Kazakhstani households try to differentiate the sources of income to render their financial situation more secure. This diversification of income sources depends on social and territorial peculiarities of the households.

Furthermore, incomes are not only monetary but also in kind. The SLA considers natural capital of households, which consists of produce and assets derived from surrounding natural resources like water, earth, etc. In case of the Kazakhstani society, we have to take into account e.g. cattle or poultry, produce from dachas and gardens (subsistence production), which was already part of the household's economy in soviet times. Natural capital is more widely spread among rural and suburban households due to the lack of access to natural resources in cities. In the case of Astana, earlier there were huge arrays of dachas and gardens in the outskirts and a lot of land houses within the city. But with the extension of the city most dachas and gardens were demolished or stopped their function as providing natural capital, because they were transformed into financial capital by renting them out or selling the property. Rural households may use their natural capital income to compensate for lack of financial income.

"We plant potatoes in our vegetable garden only for self-consumption. We don't have an additional source of income" (Ast int 10: 14, rural, male).

"We have chicken; we buy 20 pieces of chicks, ducklings during spring and raise them to fall. This is enough for winter and to share with our children" (Ast int 6: 18, rural, female).

But there are poorer rural households without any financial opportunity to buy land for cultivation, to buy cattle and seeds, so that they cannot decrease their living expenses by subsistence production.

"Our family doesn't have any other additional sources of income. We don't have self-provisioning and a vegetable garden, because we live in an apartment. We don't have a dacha. Moreover we don't have enough time for maintaining these activities" (Ast int 12: 13, rural, male).

Very often there is no more 'pure' subsistence production but natural capital is converted into financial capital. This may concern sales from the subsistence produce (dairy products, vegetables, eggs etc.) but also concerns sales of cattle and meat.

"My wife's monthly salary is 60,000 KZT (402 USD). Together with my elder son, I earn 150-160,000 KZT (1,006-1,073 USD) per month owing to selling milk, meat and butter. ... We earn about 400-500,000 KZT (2,684-3,355 USD) every fall by selling cattle ... We can buy the winter stock for the cattle from this money" (Ast int 1:12, rural, male).

Slaughtering may also help as a coping strategy to overcome difficulties.

"I asked (credit manager) what I should do in order to pay off this credit, and he said that I had to pay 180,000 KZT (1,200 USD) at once [...]. I went and slaughtered one cow, although we need this cow. I slaughtered the cow and redeemed the credit of 180,000 KZT at once" (Ast int 5: 14, rural, male, household consisting of 7 members).

One's own labor being calculated as costs, also subsistence production needs thorough calculations, as the following quotation shows.

"Because of that I have continued to work with cattle and forgot about my diploma. Concerning the decision of further work this priority was more favorable ... We have a lot of acquaintances, whose parents stayed at home and are engaged in cattle-breeding. They earn not badly. This earns you 5,000-7,000 KZT a day from the sale of milk or the sale of a matured bull. Certainly, this is a quite profitable business, but it demands much strength, patience and time. We had 2-3 cows, but there were a maximum of 5-6 calves plus 3-4 sheep at least. Currently we have a vegetable garden, and we keep hens. Earlier we sold part of crop from cucumbers and tomatoes, but now we work and there is no time to sell these products. We use them for ourselves and distribute them to acquaintances, relatives and friends. We explain them that it is our surplus ... Sometimes we use surplus of a crop for exchange. We haven't exchanged crop products in this year, but we used our crop for exchange last year. For example, our acquaintances grow apples, and we change our cucumbers for apples. We changed eggs for a certain quantity of apples. We use products from poultry farming: eggs and meat of birds for sale and for our own consumption. This is not such a big income. The price for eggs is much cheaper in the shops. We earn on it approximately less than 5,000 KZT in a month. Therefore we use products from poultry farming only for ourselves now. We consume these products, and distribute surpluses to the relatives, acquaintances, and friends" (Ast int 39: 13, urban, male).

In addition to subsistence production with or without partial sales rural and urban households try to combine e.g. an official salary with informal income.

"My husband is an ambulance driver. And from time to time he makes extra money with his truck. For example, a customer needs sand, he brings it for 6,000 KZT; 2,000 KZT goes for refueling the car, 2,000 KZT for loaders and 2,000 KZT remains for himself, and this helps us to buy 3 sacks of bran for 300 KZT and one sack of offal" (Ast int 6:24,30-31, rural, female).

High levels of unemployment or underemployment and absence of private enterprises in rural areas are the main constraints for diversifying the income sources of rural households. Urban households have better opportunities to use different sources of income and to combine them in order to secure their households.

"My salary is 75,000 KZT (507 USD). When my husband has extra work, he gets about 75,000-77,000 KZT (507-520 USD). Without it he earns 55,000 KZT (372 USD). Well, during the period of exam and graduation at the university. In addition, I have extra work during organizing the government purchases. People ask me to help them with it. I can earn little money, about 5,000 – 10,000 KZT (34-68 USD). When I earn extra money, I don't tell my husband. My money is my money. His money is our money" (she is laughing) (Ast int 18: 34, urban, female).

Pensions are another important financial source of Kazakhstanis' households which subsidize the income when several generations live together.

"Also my dad lives with us. He receives a pension, but I don't ask his money. We almost do not pay utilities. My father pays for the utilities" (Ast int 18: 14, urban, female).

Other transfer payments from the state concern allowances for child care being paid under certain conditions for one year:

"At present my husband is the main source of income, because I don't work. Thus the income of our household is 90,000 KZT (600 USD) per month: 80,000 KZT (533 USD) is the salary of my husband and 10,000 KZT (66 USD) is temporal subsidies from the government for looking after the baby" (Ast int 15: 12, rural, female).

"Our approximate income amounts to some 400,000 KZT (2684 USD). There are my income, apartment rentals of 100,000 KZT (671 USD), my wife's scholarship of 40,000 KZT (268 USD) and the allowance for a child of 35,000 KZT (234 USD)" (Ast int 23: 14, urban, male).

Households also receive other kinds of social fees like labor veteran's fees (3,000 KZT = 20$), allowances for disability depending on the level of invalidity (16,234 – 24,378 KZT (109 USD – 196 USD) per year.[164] In all these cases both urban and rural households receive the same amount.

In addition to strategies of making additional incomes, physical capital (property, cars, etc.) can be converted into financial capital in emergency situations such as life crises or financial crises.

"I sold all my possessions in order to overcome this financial crisis and redeemed the loan. My aim was to quickly redeem the credit, even if I would remain homeless and without my apartments. I sold my vehicles, shops, sold all that I had to redeem the loan. But I haven't been homeless. At one time my family supported me very well. The children said: 'Mom, why are you so upset? This is not your last business; you will open a new one again'" (Ast int 28: 19, urban, female, business women).

A farmer from a village uses cattle as his 'savings account'. He sells cattle once he needs money.

"We earn about 400-500,000 KZT (2,684-3,355 USD) every fall by selling cattle ... We can buy winter stock of hay for the cattle for this money. The rest of the money is spent for ourselves, for clothes, for material help for the children in the city. We send meat, milk and butter, and some surplus money to our children every month. We also pay for A's education about 300,000 KZT (2,013 USD) per year" (Ast int 1: 12, rural, male).

To sum up briefly the evidence in this:

1. Incomes in urban and in rural areas are different. Rural incomes take often a non-monetary form of natural capital, which can in turn be converted into financial capital.
2. Urban households have much better opportunities for high paid jobs and better chances of gaining additional money via additional jobs in formal and informal

[164] Law of the Republic of Kazakhstan No 126-I as of 16.06.1997 "O gosudarstvennych social'nych posobijach po invalidnosti, po slučaju poteri kormi'lca i po vozrastu" [On state social benefits for disability, loss of the provider and the old age]", Article 12. Available at: http://online.zakon.kz/Document/?doc_id=1007927; access date 10-11-2014

settings. This makes city life very attractive for rural people and is the 'pull' factor for a high rate of rural to urban migration (from the Akmola region to Astana).

3. Natural capital/property can be converted into financial capital in emergency situations and is used like that.

Expenditures

Incomes, expenditures, savings, and credit are connected to each other. A full picture of the living standard of the households can only be gained if all of the mentioned aspects are looked at. When salaries are not enough to make a living people have to find ways to adapt their everyday life to the consecutive constraints. As we already mentioned above, key factors of expenses are housing, food expenses, maintenance costs/utilities (gas, electricity, etc.), and education. Each of these major expenses can be a potential adjustment factor of a household for coping with his living conditions.

Housing in the two primary cities Astana and Almaty is a big social challenge for many residents.[165] Concerning Astana, between 1999 and 2009 the population of Astana doubled. Owning a house or apartment is held in high esteem among ethnic Kazakhs and contributes to household security. Due to enormous migration into the city and an insufficient supply, demand is high both for rent and for purchase and consequently market prices for apartments rocket. Furthermore, the housing market in the two cities offers apartments which are more designed for nuclear families than extended ones. This offers opportunities for independent nuclear family lives. But Kazakh custom also claims that old parents should stay together with their youngest son which causes problems for many families.

"I wish that my sons will live in their own house in the future, because all of them have their own family. If they live separately, they will get used to an independent life. Otherwise they will just rely on each other. They have to be ready to make own decisions in their life and to overcome difficulties. We lived by this rules for a long time already. My children should take into account these rules. We are going to live together with my youngest son as it is considered to be our custom" (Ast int 40: 26, urban, female).

---

165 Agency on Statistics of the Republic of Kazakhstan: "Migratsia naselenija. Itogi Nacionalnoi perepisi naselenija Respubliki Kazachstan 2009 goda" [Migration of the population. Results of the census in the Republic of Kazakhstan in 2009]. Edited by Smailov A.A., 2010 p. 192. Available at http://www.stat.gov.kz/faces/wcnav_externalId/p_perepis?_afrLoop=16797994110690#%40%3F_afrLoop%3D16797994110690%26_adf.ctrl-state%3D1agozx3if5_186; access date 10-11-2014

While this respondent's younger son follows the Kazakh custom, in other cases space constraints may undermine these responsibilities.

The purchase of a house or an apartment is usually financed by credits, what we will discuss later on separately.

The housing shortage has not been sufficiently dealt with despite state programs and subsidies. High rents or mortgage payments may cause financial problems for the households. The strong idea of private property of housing and the constant immigration to Astana and Almaty given, mortgages are not always a secure way to reach ones housing aim. Mortgages represent expenses with which to cope can imply severe difficulties:

"It became difficult for us to pay the mortgage and therefore we have invited the parents of my husband to live with us. It was so hard that I fell ill ... The shortage of money was visible in me. All time I thought of money and worried. As a result I was ill with hernia and I lay in hospital for two months" (Ast int 29: 23 urban, female).

State employees normally have lower incomes compared to private employees. But the state offers special housing programs for state employees. Thus this group can avoid high rents or mortgages in the private real estate market.

"We hope to get an apartment with help of the program of affordable housing. We don't have any special problems. Since both of us are budget workers, we can plan on a stable income although it is not so high like e.g. that of a private trader" (Ast int 25: 7, urban, female).

"It will be possible only with assent of every member of the household. We have to pay for flat rent 65,000 KZT (433 USD) per month. We have rented one-room small flat for 2 years. We have to pay for the utilities as well. This is about 10-15,000 KZT (66-100 USD) per month... The main thing is the housing problem. Our household doesn't have a private apartment and is not able to buy one. There are high prices for the flat rent and utilities" (Ast int 38:14 urban, male, 25 years).

In general, government benefits for civil servants are one of the causes of accepting low paid state jobs as opposed to taking private jobs. The savings from these benefits may lower expenditures.

"To tell the truth, earlier I worked in a private company, my salary was high enough. But I could not find an arrangement between my job and the kindergarten of my 3-year-old. I had to search for a job compatible with kindergarten. I am lucky now; my child goes to a state kindergarten on the left embankment" (Ast int 27: 11, urban, female).

While in a former paragraph we showed that pensions subsidize the household income, they may also be a cost factor. Pensions are not always high enough to pay for the expenses of the pensioners. In the following citation, the pensioner performs many traditional social responsibilities in the kinship network the costs of which exceed his pension, so that his daughter has to subsidize him.

"My father is pensioner. He does not work. He maintains his health (she is laughing). He goes to Ceragem (massage, performed on Korean apparatus called Ceragem, A.Z). He visits our relatives. Recently he has gone to Ust-Kamenogorsk. There was a wedding of his cousin's grandson. Earlier, it was the wedding of his brother's son. There are also ridden. He goes to all funerals. In general he always travels. Sometimes I pay for these trips. For example, he went to a wedding. And I think that he couldn't go there without presents, without money. I always buy him a one way ticket to visit his relatives. Our relatives buy him the return ticket" (Ast int 18: 44, urban, female).

Most respondents complain about the costs of living usually attributed to rising prices.

"The most important problem is high fees for transport, utilities, etc. and secondly the expensive gas. … The prices for coal, firewood, gas, electricity, consumer goods and spare parts of our car are rising. All prices are rising, but salaries stay on the same level. Therefore everything is getting more complicated" (Ast int 5: 24, rural, male).

"The most severe problem associated with life in the capital is high prices. The criminals too, but the biggest difficulty (…) is the price. Prices are higher in the capital than in the whole Republic (…) Prices are high, but nevertheless you can live. Other serious problems to live in the capital I don't see" (Ast int 30: 36, urban, female).

"The price of coal is always rising. We have paid 60,000 KZT (400 USD) for coal last year, this year we have paid 75,000 KZT" (500 USD) (Ast int 4: 13).

A considerable number of households complain about corruption. They have to calculate this cost factor in their household budgets.

"What can I say about corruption here? I should formalize my flat right now. I think with scary about the future informal expenses, because you have to either wait 3-4 months or pay a certain sum, the height of which I don't know" (Ast int 26:24, urban, female).

In all interviews, in one way or the other, people complain about the state of the health system and the expenses that might come up if somebody in the household gets ill. The treatment of illnesses quite often is a reason for getting indebted. Bank credits may result from this but most often family members feel obliged to help and pay for the expenses – totally or in part.

"I was ill. My husband gets rarely sick. He had a heart attack and he lay in hospital several times. Before, he got rarely ill. My younger sister helped us with finances during that period. She lives in the city. My husband was treated in an urban hospital. I was operated in that hospital too" (Ast int 4: 19, rural, female).

All respondents in our interviews have underlined the high importance they are ready to give to education of their offspring. Financing its education is a major concern of the households. As this topic is dealt also under the topics of credits and savings, there follows only one quotation:

"We send money to our daughter, who studies in A. city, twice a month and provide her with products, when it is possible. Mostly we help her with money. We send her 50,000 KZT (333 USD) monthly, because A. city is a big and expensive city. We also pay for her education. We pay 250,000 KZT (1, 667 USD) annually for her education, 15,000 KZT (100 USD) per year for her dormitory and as I have already mentioned 50,000 KZT (333 USD) per month for food, and other needs and expenses" (Ast int 13:13, rural, male).

Savings

Households try to protect themselves from everyday financial problems in many ways. Savings are one of the ways to overcome unforeseeable vulnerabilities and to plan one's future. According to a common definition savings are the positive balance between temporal incomes and expenses of households ... (Denizer, Wolf, and Ying 2002). Households in Kazakhstan have many choices for saving money; at home or in saving funds managed by the state or by private entrepreneurs. The state seeks to encourage households to make savings at banks and offers them incentives and help. For example the holders of deposits in Zhilstroysberbank can receive an annual additional interest rate of 10% to 20% from the state. There is also a state educational saving system (SESS) for parents, which offers a saving program for children's education. According to this program the state pays an additional bonus of 5% (7%) on a deposited sum every year from childbirth on. The Kazakhstani state tries "to teach" households to save money. But do households really follow these incentives and do they really try to protect themselves concerning future vulnerabilities or do they practice delayed need satisfaction in order to plan their lives more successfully? Is there enough trust in banks after de-evaluations and bank crashes in the past? And what about the soviet legacy which was not saving prone?

The opinions about saving are very much split.

"I think that the possibility of saving is an absolutely meaningless idea, because there are no guarantees that the money, which you save, will keep its value. I can say honestly, I don't trust banks, because our family lost a lot of money twice. My brother-in-law and my mother lost their enormous savings in bank deposits ... We all save our money in jars like in soviet time" (Ast int 26: 16, urban, female).

"We restrict our needs and save some money. For instance I am driving an old car, I wear this old suit, I eat this bread and I am going to eat that in future. Of course, I could eat this bread with butter or with cheese, but I am saving money. I am saving this money for necessities, for buying and updating, for maintaining our living conditions, we should save for marriage ceremonies of our daughters and our son. We don't want to be with nothing in the future. The matchmakers can come at any moment according to the Muslim customs and we have to prepare the dowries of our daughters and so on. But if there is wedding tomorrow and our savings are not enough for the celebration, we would have to ask help from somebody" (Ast int 5: 16, rural, male).

"I have an opportunity to save money. I can save about 5,000 KZT (34 USD) per month, but I don't do that. I do not know why" (Ast int 18: 28, urban, female).

Savings satisfy very different needs: consumptive needs by saving for household appliances, holidays, physical capital such as a car or an apartment, as means of general precaution or specific precaution such as health and old age costs, human capital formation of the children, or high expenses for weddings and funerals.

"I heard about deposits for saving money for the children's future. For example, my elder child is 5 years old now; this money will be ready enough for her education by 18-19 years" (Ast int 7: 17, rural, female).

"If we need to buy something, for example, a kitchen, it is not a problem to save money. I save money to buy things, to travel, for dinner. My sister also does so" (Ast int 30: 20, urban, female).

"Yes, we do it if we have some extra money. But we don't do it regularly. We save for the wedding of my children in the future. If it occurs during this year, we will have to take a credit for wedding" (Ast int 4: 17, rural, female).

It seems that age plays a role especially where people choose to keep their savings. Older people seem to prefer the 'jar' while younger people are more inclined to use bank deposits. This overlaps with the region. While people in the countryside prefer 'jar' or saving in kind, people in urban areas prefer banks.

"We save money for rainy days. We don't use bank services for saving money since I don't trust banks. If the bank bankrupts, I can lose my money. We are saving money for deaths, for some other events, my grandson is growing up; he needs clothes and other household necessities. We save money without commercial aims. My grandsons are growing up and soon they will receive higher education. I think our savings will provide them with a good education" (Ast int 8: 16, rural, male 51 years old).

"The most important decisions my elder sister makes, because my parents consult her. She has already been living in the city for a long time. She always offers decisions and the words are hers. Our parents say that we are smarter than they are. Therefore they rely on our opinions. Now we save money for an apartment. I plan to buy a car in winter, so I try not to make big expenses. I want to buy a car for myself. My dad has already one. My brother is going to buy a car on his birthday. Dad says that it is dangerous for me to buy a car in winter (she is laughing). My sister wants to visit Dubai this winter. So we save money for this purpose too" (Ast int 17: 18, 50, urban, female, 22 years old).

The market economy is a risky economy and with low social security offered by the state. Our respondents understand that they have to take precautions in order to render their lives more secure. Households act accordingly and save – many of them in banks. But other families save at home.

"Yes, we do that. We have these savings to have financial stability in critical situations, e.g. if our salary is late for paying the credits or for other urgent expenses. We save our money at home. We do that because this is not enough money for opening a deposit. If we had some urgent problems with finances or some expenses for anniversaries we could receive support from our parents once every three-four months" (Ast int 38: 16, urban, male).

"If I haven't spent all money I save this money for myself, make a stash. I have a piggy container. I put there coins (100 KZT). I never spend coins of 100 KZT. I have been saving about 6 months. When the piggy container is full, I will have 42,000 KZT (284 USD). I can make a big purchase. I can buy a gold ring or a cell phone. But I don't save money for special purposes" (Ast int 18: 24, urban, female).

Saving patterns seem to be influenced by age and location. The older age cohorts and people in the rural areas seem to prefer saving at home. The reasons for that can't be found by looking at the saving patterns alone. We also have to take into account different options for access to saving funds as well as other options to render the households more secure e.g. by relying on family networks.

Households save for many reasons as is done all over the world. Remarkable is the high number of households saving for the future education of their children (human capital formation). This is a new phenomenon, showing the change in saving habits under the new economic conditions (Denizer et al. 2002).

There is an interesting hypothesis by Denizer et al. that saving strategies of households depend on the occupation of their members. It seems that households with members, who work in state and budget organizations are less inclined to save compared to households with members engaged in the private sector. The reason could lay in the stable income of the former. But our material can't give a definite answer.

Rural households also save in cattle.

"If we get excess money, we immediately invest it to buy hay or cattle. That money helps more for our housekeeping than just put it into a bank with low interest rates. We do not trust banks because we can lose our savings in case of bankruptcy. It is better to invest in cattle, which can give more growth" (Ast int 1: 16, rural, male, farmer).

Credits

In order to be able to judge the living situation of middle class households in Kazakhstan it is also necessary to take credits into account.

Since independence Kazakhstan has reformed its banking system, supposedly to be in tune with the new market economy. Today there is a 2-tier banking system. The National Bank is the 1st tier bank and usually deals with the management of the entire banking system, printing the currency and implementing the financial and the economic policy of the government. Almost all 2nd tier banks are networks of commercial banks and other credit organizations, which include a lot of micro-financial agencies run by the state.

Currently Kazakhstani households can get a credit from 35 commercial banks (only Zhilstroysberbank is governmental among all 2nd tier banks) and from plenty of micro-credit organizations (Lombard houses, credit unions) (cf. Nazarbaev 2008b:195ff). In general, households may obtain credits from different sources: firstly from commercial banks; secondly, from organizations providing separate forms of banking services and thirdly from micro-credit organizations as well as special governmental programs for housing, education, against poverty and for rural development. The credits taken from credit programs supported by the government have the most profitable conditions. Organizational adjustment to a new financial and economic system does not automatically imply that the citizens know how to handle them appropriately. Given many evaluations from transformation research that claim that behavioral adjustments have to be counted in generations, we wanted to know how private households view the situation.

Today in Kazakhstan there are different ways of obtaining credits, some of which are not market oriented. Because obtaining credits may involve two institutions: kinship networks as a way of financing purchases outside the market economy, and financial institutions of the market economy. Let us begin with the first.

Borrowing money from acquaintances or relatives was already a well-known habit during soviet times. In ethnic Kazakh families it may be connected also to traditional norms. Nowadays such a way of taking credits is still preferred by many rural households.

"If we face with unexpected expenses like somebody's anniversary or necessity for medical treatment we can borrow this money from relatives or colleagues. We negotiate with them for lending this money until the next salary" (Ast int 7: 17, rural, female).

Urban households also borrow money, but they more often also use market oriented ways to solve their problems e.g. with help of banks or micro credit institutions.

"I assume that taking a credit from a bank in very hard periods is a wellfounded decision. I prefer this instead of asking help from my parents" (Ast int 38: 14, urban, male).

While until the early 1990s loans from relatives were – as far as we can judge – always interest-free independent from the time involved, times have changed with the advent of the market economy. Nowadays many people are commercially minded, and this may even touch the kinship sphere. Both urban and rural households may also borrow money with interest from acquaintances or from family members in certain situations or use other options. But not always, this kind of exchange goes without conflicts.

"I used to borrow often. It was from salary till next salary. I used to do that till May of this year. Currently I try not to borrow money, because there was one incident, which happened and ever since I never borrow money. I just promised myself that I will never borrow money again and better keep patience in some situations. In that case I returned the debt, but that person from whom I borrowed said that I should give her more money. I even didn't check in that situation and I just returned her all required money" (Ast int 26: 15, rural, female).

"Sometimes we use deferred payment as a credit. We often buy on tick; you don't need to redeem the whole sum at once. Once I bought the TV like this and redeemed the debt during the whole year. It is affordable. We use normal credits only when we don't have money for serious purchases. We don't take credits so often, for example once in three years. We take credits only for purchases of household appliances. The last credit was on 140,000 KZT (933 USD) at 10% of interest rate. It is normal, we are able to redeem it" (Ast int 8: 14, rural, male).

"I have never used credits, but my sister with her husband permanently takes credits and owing to their 'clean credit line' they do it without any problems. They always take credits, when they need to buy serious things like notebooks, a refrigerator, and a washing machine. There is one credit in our household now. Usually my sister and brother-in-law used to take a credit only for one year. They will redeem it in December of this year. They never took a credit longer than one year, and the sums of the credits were not enormous, therefore they somehow could cope. After the death of my husband my sister lives with us. Therefore that credit is possessed by our household. The last credit was for buying two notebooks and a mobile phone. I don't know the cost of the mobile phone, but I guess that two notebooks cost about 300,000 KZT. Unfortunately, I don't know the interest rates of these credits. I think this credit was not so necessary, because in our household there were already two computers, but it was a present of my brother-in-law to me and my sister for our birthdays" (Ast int 26: 13, urban, female).

"We take credits for urgent needs. Today our household has two credits. The first credit for 3 years we took for buying a car in April of 2011. At that time I worked and we got this credit from Halykh Bank. The second credit we took in January of this year (2012) from Kaspii bank through making a credit card for 2 years, but you can get additional money in debt from the credit card and your debt will be prolonged over the initial period. The first credit is 520,000 KZT (3,468 USD), and the second credit is 330,000 KZT (2,201 USD). To be honest, we even didn't pay attention to the interest rate of these credits owing to our living conditions in the rural area, where we haven't got any other choice. We take a credit when it is really necessary and then we take it from any bank, which is ready to give us the credit" (Ast int 15: 14, rural, female).

In the quotation above it is interesting that there is a certain amount of ignorance that excludes any comparison between more or less profitable credits. This hints at adjustment problems concerning market behavior. But often interviewees complain about informational deficits concerning the banks. But nevertheless even in these cases one can find a certain naiveté concerning market orientated behavior.

"For instance, I took one credit from Astanafinans and they informed me that the interest rate is 12%. I calculated on 12% of interest, but when they added expenses for their services and papers there were 21% of interest. Thus, the real interest was 21%. We all think that we are so clever. You take a credit; you have to pay for it. I took 350,000 KZT (2,334 USD) in credit and overpaid this money with interests. I noticed that there were no urgent necessities in taking these credits, but many people take out large sums in credits without thinking about the consequences. There was no necessity for this credit. My friend just asked to help him with a credit" (Ast int 10: 16, rural, male).

Further down, we shall discover more of such deficits.

"Now we pay for two loans. The first credit is a mortgage and the second is Daddy's loan of 500,000 KZT. We had financial difficulties, so my dad had to take it. As dad does bank services with Tsesna Bank, they offered him to take that credit. I help him with repaying the mortgage and my sister helps him with the payment of the second loan. Payment for the second credit is 18,000 – 22,000 KZT per month for 2 years. Papa (daddy) took the credit, because he needed the money urgently" (Ast int 30: 22, urban, female).

In many interviews we can find above mentioned involvement of all grown up members of the households in credit businesses thus combining market transactions with family centered help

But not all households take credits. Some have had bad experiences and therefore try to refrain from them. Others are stuck in their belief build up during soviet times that bank businesses are about speculation one should not take part in. Others believe that one should first save before buying and finally there are religious objectors.

"Muslims say that to give and take money with interest is a big sin. My parents told about this in my childhood. That we take a credit in a bank is a sin too. But after all, we are forced to it by hopelessness. We don't take the credit from a person but we take it from the state. At that time, when we took the credit, there wasn't any Islamic bank. I heard about this bank. I heard that the bank takes interest only from profit and that it doesn't press on the person with percentages. Which other banks do? You have to pay high interest rates before beginning the business. I think this is incorrect" (Ast int 19: 31, urban, female).

This religious objection to credits is very rare in our interviews. Objections stemming from the soviet legacy are revealed much more often. Older people grew up in soviet times with the objections concerning the banking business. Therefore this elder generation of "soviet people" seeks to refrain from taking credits due to distrust in credit institutions. We find this attitude also among different ethnics of the same age. But also bad experiences from the post-soviet past are named quite often. E.g. by an 'illegal' taxi driver from a rural area. He is a Tatar and explains that his whole family shares a negative belief, due to bad experiences.

"I told my children never to deal with credits. It was my admonishment to them. But she took a credit to buy a fur coat. I asked her about the necessity of that fur coat while she had nothing to eat. I abused her after that. She wanted to buy a fur coat immediately and thought that she would redeem the credit by installments, because the bank workers explained her everything in banking language, but perhaps she didn't understand their language (laugh) and instead of 200,000 KZT (1 ,334 USD), all in all she had to pay 600,000 KZT (4,002 USD). I was surprised about such big interest rates. We have closed this question. Currently the credit is redeemed, but I don't permit them to take credits any more. I don't approve taking credits. People talk about express-credits now. My daughter encouraged me to take such a credit for household appliances. I told her that we shouldn't buy anything on credit and should instead save money, because I'm working and the children are working too now. We shall have enough possibilities to buy something. We have what we have (Ast int 5: 14, rural, male, 58 years old, Tatar).

For a 49 years old female Russian taking out a credit is a very risky deal which she tries to avoid even in harsh times also due to a negative experience.

"If there are certain financial problems I will not be ready to take a credit from a bank any more. We don't use credits. We used to take credits. Credit is something, we avoid. It was a long time ago, bad experience. Currently we try not to take a credit, because it has high interest rates. It is better to cope with problems ourselves than to overpay to the bank" (Ast int 14: 16, rural, female, unemployed, 49 years old).

For many it seems hard to understand the essence and philosophy of the market.

"My husband studies by distant learning at the railway academy, since he has only a secondary special education. He has 2 credits – one credit we took for payments of his education, and another for a car purchase, a foreign car. It is difficult to live in a city with a small child without a car. However, our car credit nearly ended with a family scandal. We took this credit at random, without consulting and asking the permission of the parents of my husband. We were nearly expelled from the house (laughs). But then they have forgiven us and understood, that a car it not luxury, but transportation, that it is convenient for shopping and to visit relatives in the village" (Ast int 9: 17, urban, female, 46 years old).

The distrust in banks is quite strong and people tell astonishing stories, one can hardly believe.

"I don't trust banks. I lost 50,000 KZT (333 USD) in the Khalyk bank. My husband went to cash my money, because I was at work. He requested 63,000 KZT (420 USD) or 65,000 KZT at nearby 'Koktem' bazaar. The cash machine indicated that 'you can't cash this money' and he tried three times again, but there was the text message 'go to another cash machine'. So he went to the Khalyk bank 10 minutes away. There he dialed the requested sum again and noticed that there were only 13,000 KZT (86 USD) in my account. 50,000 KZT (333 USD) had disappeared. After that I applied to the Police of Financial Affairs and to the National Bank. I wanted to sue them, but I had problems with my heart and decided not to precede that any longer. They started to suspect my husband as if he had stolen that money. In short, the money disappeared unfairly. I know that it was the Khalyk bank" (Ast int 16: 16, urban, female).

Why do people take up credits? In general, there is a wide array of items for which households take credits: classical consumer goods as already mentioned above, credits bridge seasonality of incomes especially in agriculture, mortgages, credits for education and for traditional customs like weddings, funerals etc.

Consumer goods are usually bought with micro-credits. Although often termed as urgent need, the decisions are not free from elements of conspicuous consumption. People want to possess some modern, fashionable and expensive goods in order to gain in status or just to show their ability to consume (cf. Richards, 1995). Some households seek to equip their homes with appliances, technical and fashionable goods, which represent symbolic codes within the interaction with other households via their existence and via the consumption of credits (cf. Baudrillard, 1981). These households do not just consume credits, but with help of the credit they usually acquire some status and cultural positions within their environment.

"The last credit of our household was taken for some household appliances like TV, a new gas stove and a refrigerator, a computer and internet access for our children, helping them to learn. Also we didn't want to lag behind other households" (Ast int 2: 17, rural, female).

Additionally, by using credits, households are drawn into the rules of the contemporary market with its dominant organizational principle of consumption (Bauman 1998). This sometimes causes them quite some problems, as is to be seen in the following quotations.

"In any case we have to borrow money with interest from neighboring peasants or we have to bring all our gold to the Lombard house. With the latter we aren't able to repay the full credit. We will pay only the interest of the debt. So we can bridge the repayment period of this credit till summer holidays. Until then, we are not able to re-buy our gold from the Lombard house, therefore all our gold jewels is there. My husband will go on vacation in 3 months and he will get his holiday fees. Then we are going to redeem our gold jewels from the Lombard house (Ast int 15: 14, rural, female).

"I don't like to get indebted. When I had taken the mortgage and I couldn't pay, I took my gold to the Lombard house. But it was for 2 months only. When I took out the mortgage, there were service costs for it, in cash. Meanwhile, I only have to calculate with my salary, and I am no longer engaged with my gold garnish in the Lombard house" (Ast int 31: 38, urban, female).

The above quotation hints already at another important purpose for which people take out credits, that is to buy houses or apartments. Especially among ethnic Kazakhs, owning a house or an apartment has a very high value. The state has set up different schemes to help in obtaining mortgages to facilitate acquiring real estate property. But also commercial banks offer mortgages.

The governmental mortgage company is another popular type of credit institution among households[166]. The main difference of this program, if compared with commercial mortgage offers, is low annual interest rates. The governmental 'Zhilstroysberbank' offers mortgages with 4-5% of annual interest rates during a term time of 15 years for instance. The lowest and the highest annual interest rates of commercial banks we found were 13% (the program "express-alternative" of BTA bank for 3 years) and 45% (credit program of the Home bank until 4 years).[167] On average, for longer terms, commercial banks charge 11-14% of annual interest for 25-30 years of term time. The high interests of commercial banks make the government program economically very interesting.

"We handed over the documents to participate in the program of rental housing last year. That time my parents were assured that we would get an apartment by the program. Because of this we planned to move into the city. They extended the dates of the program until June because supposedly the apartment was not ready. Then we were told that the program was closed. People say that the program has been re-launched this year, but we haven't applied again. It's so time consuming. So many documents are needed. Moreover you should have acquaintances in this sphere. If you are just on the list, you will get a flat only after 2 or 3 years. It's such a long time! We decided not to wait any more. Our friends got an apartment in terms of the program. My parents wanted the same, they told us: 'Let's do it!' In comparison with a mortgage it is cheaper to buy an apartment under the conditions of this program. It is about 80,000 KZT (540 USD) per month. But as we could not g et an apartment with help of the program, we had to rent an apartment" (Ast int 17: 30-31, urban, female).

One reason, as explained above, of taking mortgages from commercial banks is due to the bureaucratic restrictions and to corruption observed by the interviewees concerning the state run program. And not everybody is eligible to it. Firstly, the program is only for state and budget workers. Secondly, other citizens can only get the special mortgage, if they can pay half of the price at the beginning. Due to these conditions many households take the risks of using long term commercial credits, being for 15-25 years on average.

"When the bank lifted the mortgage to 47,000 KZT ... the prices grew, inquiries and requirements grew as well ... it was necessary to pay for our son's sport training ... I tried to find another job. At that time I worked for the 'Rakhat' Confectionery Company.

166 Kazakhstan mortgage company. Available at http://kmc.kz/about/; access date 07-07-2013

167 http://prodengi.kz/cat/view_compare/loan/express~-- Comparative analysis of the express credital offers of 2nd tier banks; access date 10-07-2013]

I knew that some people received more than me in the company ... I asked to increase the salary, but it was refused. Therefore I resumed. And I was invited to work for another company and was given a big salary. In January 2006, I began to receive 40,000 KZT, in May I had 50,000 KZT, in June 70,000 KZT. The salary doubled and it became easier to pay the mortgage obligations. Yes, but again! The mortgage interest rate was raised! There was more than 50,000 KZT ... The bank somehow proved such sharp jump in payment. They told this is inflation. Therefore in October 2008 when I went to pay my previous 70,000 KZT, I thought that maximum would increase to 80,000 KZT. I was in tears ... but what to do? I braced my heart as there was no other ways. We paid the bank so much money! I heard about many cases that banks took away the apartments if people could not pay the mortgage. We have acquaintances who returned their apartment to the bank because they could not pay 200,000 KZT every month. I asked the bank twice to lower the percentage rate, but both times I was refused. Once, I was late with the payment for one day and I had to pay 300 KZT for it!" (Ast int 29: 24, 26, urban, female).

A large number of households, especially rural ones, have to use credits due to the lack of income flexibility and to bridge temporary money shortages. Often rural households have specific seasonal problems like large expenses for coal and annual stock of hay for cattle in autumn, which force them to take credits. Some do it regularly. For these households taking credits is no sign for lack of abilities to plan their budgets regularly and decently. Their money shortage does not allow them to act differently. And they learn to acquire a 'credit habitus' (Bourdieu 1986).

Established traditions concerning families and households are still practiced today and are reflected in the economic behavior of the households. To follow the traditional customs concerning birth, weddings and funerals represents still strong obligations especially for most ethnic Kazakhs. The obligation to supply children with a good education is also of high importance. With this parents aim at securing the habits also in the next generations building up moral obligations by the money paid for the education. Concerning this, a lot of rural households explained that they were in permanent financial crises during the time when their children were studying in the city.

"We didn't have any other sources where to take the money from. There were no other possibilities to borrow money, thus we had to take a credit. We made that decision jointly with my wife after discussing all details. We couldn't manage those problems without a credit, because currently education is very expensive and my daughter had not passed the exams to enter the university, otherwise we wouldn't have to pay for her education. I haven't thought yet about urgent expenses as anniversaries or weddings. I don't know what I will do in that case. Perhaps I will take a second credit, because I can't have money from somewhere else. I think that it is wrong to take credits for weddings and anniversaries, but nowadays we don't want to lag behind other people or the society, neighbors, acquaintances. Also the child will be deprived. Everything is for the sake of the children. We will look for banks with lower interest rates. Of course, the sum of the credit will depend on our salary" (Ast int 12: 15, 17, rural, male).

"I took a credit after the death of my wife in order to pay for the funeral" (Ast int 10: 16, rural, male).

"We have met difficulties for the last 5 years related to wedding. We have spent much money for our wedding. It was my fault and irrational from my side, my parents influenced me as well and we spent a huge sum for that wedding. We took a credit for this purpose and it was a shock for my parents. Because we lost much money irrationally. Credits covered only 40 % of the expenses, the rest was money, which was saved by my mom in a bank account. We had saved money, which we received from the sale of our cattle. Mum withdrew this money. A credit is good support for arranging weddings. If one has a job and is healthy, it will be certainly possible to redeem the credit. I think nowadays both urban and rural residents try to arrange luxury weddings at cafés or restaurants. Parents do everything for their children that they don't appear as old fogy among their friends. For instance, they think that all friends of their son made nice weddings and they want to make their son happy too by organizing him a nice wedding. We are Kazakhs and Kazakhnes influences us. Most households compare all weddings in the village and try to arrange the most respectful event for their child. Therefore they have to take credits. We are ready to take any risk because we feel obliged to have a good wedding despite of its costs. It is a matter of honor of my son. Especially as he grew up without father, and I sought to provide him with a sense that he didn't feel the absence of his father, who died 20 years ago. It was true intentions to take a credit for his wedding" (Ast int 3: 18, rural, female).

During transition to the market economy, credits have become a normal type of economic transactions. Most households in the Astana sample have experiences with credits. In general there is no difference between the rural areas and the city. For some households taking credits is similar to a fad or a fashion (cf. Akerlof 2010). But mostly the reason for credits is urgent needs concerning household necessities. Additionally, there seems to be a status element in taking credits. Cohorts seem to operate differently with credits. Among the elder generation there are more reservations towards credits. They overlap often with bad experiences, and – though rarely – with religious beliefs. Also a 'soviet way of thinking' is still prevalent, which fuels distrust in banks.

Most of the credits serve consumption needs, bridge temporary money shortages, are mortgages or serve traditional obligations. Many interviewees are far from a developed 'credit habitus' (Bourdieu). They are still learning how to handle this instrument of market transactions.

Aigul ZABIROVA, shortened and edited by E. DITTRICH and H. SCHRADER

Education

In market societies education has become an important factor that influences a person's position in society. It opens up chances in the labor market but also contributes to an individual's or family's position in social structure. Economists call education a 'human capital' investment, and the sustainable livelihoods approach takes it up as one of the capital forms which determine the vulnerability context. The sociologist Pierre Bourdieu went further by emphasizing the close linkage between education, culture and social position. He preferred the term 'cultural capital' and referred to the inheritance of such in families. We shall refer to this later on when trying to evaluate the vulnerability context.

The peculiarity of post-soviet societies, compared to other societies, is the high educational level of most citizens. Already in soviet times, the state put a large emphasis on education. Since independence, education and employment in Kazakhstan have experienced huge changes, which play significant roles in the everyday life of the households. The reformation of the educational system meant major challenges for the households. The state run system of education has been replaced by a mixed system. Today there are a lot of private schools, colleges and universities, which offer paid educational services. The contemporary Kazakh educational system offers different options, giving households a bigger choice. Therefore, some authors argue, that the attitudes of Kazakhstanis towards educational institutions have become more consumerist (Denizer et al. 2002:463–475). In any case, in the eyes of our respondents, education has become a factor defining one's position in society. Parents try to give their children the best education possible. According to cultural peculiarities of many Kazakhs, it is an important part of the duties of parents to give their children a good education. For them a good education is a litmus test for their present and future well-being. Education is also a status feature. Russian households seem to have a similar stance concerning education.

The analysis of this study shows that education both in rural and urban areas of Kazakhstan is perceived as important and of high value. In our sample there is no difference concerning the high esteem given to education by parents with higher education and lower education, by rural and urban respondents and by different age cohorts. Urban as well as rural households show a great willingness to pay for good education: from kindergarten to university.

Given the high importance education holds for Kazakhstanis, rural households are in a disadvantaged position as the institutions of higher education are in the urban regions and they have expenses for rents, commuting etc. For rural scholars there are special state grants to ease their burdens, but only few get these governmental scholarships.

"We conferred with ourselves and took that credit, because our child was supposed to study at the university and we had to pay for her education. We didn't have any other sources from where to take the money.... We made that decision jointly with my wife after discussing all details. We were not able to manage those problems without credit, because currently education is very expensive and my daughter did not pass the entry exams to the university; otherwise we shouldn't have to pay for her education" (Ast int 12: 15, rural, male).

"We changed the school. The level of education in the new school was better..... We hired tutors ... We paid a lot of money. I damned all tutors. Now my niece teaches English to my daughter because my niece studies at the university to be an English language specialist" (Ast int 31: 18, urban, female).

From the forms-of-capital approach human capital of households can be considered as potential for their members to access good education and later on positions in economy and society. To gain these not only individual skills but also internalized habits and goods that secure and help to achieve the positions are required according to Bourdieu's cultural capital approach. Kazakhstani households believe strongly in the necessity to give children a good education as already shown in the subchapters on employment, expenditure, and on the purposes of credits. Additionally, traditional beliefs among many ethnic Kazakhs especially make human capital an asset of outstanding importance with no particular gender bias. But the placement in society's job openings quite often is not based solely on educational achievements but also on the social capital candidates can mobilize in their favor. Additionally, human capital formation exceeds the sphere of formalized educational institutions. It also concerns the best studying facilities at home, or privately paid tutors, or the formation of habits by sports, artistic training etc.

"The last credit of our household was taken for some household appliances like TV, gas stove and refrigerator, computer and internet for children, which help them to learn" (Ast int 2: 17, rural, female).

"We changed the school. The level of education in the new school was better. .... We hired tutors... We paid a lot of money" (Ast int 31: 18, urban, female).

Apart from all remarks above however, high human capital is no guarantee for a good job in the labor market, as the following quotations show. Very often, applicants' qualifications and labor market needs don't match.

"We are the same age with my husband. He has a higher education, but he hasn't got a possibility to work according to his specialization here. He has absolutely inappropriate education for this location. He is specialist of geological explorations. Now he deals with most popular jobs here like construction and security" (Ast int 9: 7, rural, female).

"Our household comprises of 2 people: me and my wife. She is 50 years old too. She has higher education. She is psychologist. She doesn't work according to her diploma. She is operator in a control board... Usually I help her with duties if she has problems or she doesn't have enough time because her job is so difficult. She is an operator. She is tired on the control board, because sometimes she stays for 24 hours. Therefore it is hard" (Ast int 13: 6, 10, rural, female).

Vulnerabilities and Coping of Households

After having tried to outline the resource base of households concerning their incomes, their employments, their expenditures, their savings and credits, their conditions at home and their general beliefs, we now turn to their special vulnerabilities before we talk about sustainable livelihoods strategies. Vulnerabilities are related to the different practices taken or not taken, to their interconnectedness with the resource base the households can activate, as well as to the different contexts into which the practices are tied. Vulnerabilities may stem from a deficiency of financial capital for making an adequate living, which is the incompatibility between incomes and expenses. These are often overcome by credits. But vulnerabilities also imply experiences that differentiate the coping options people have. More than twenty years after the gradual introduction of a new order in society and a new economic system, we argue that adaptation to the revised conditions for making a living is still a problem. Does especially the elder generation which experienced a socialization during soviet times under a 'nanny state', have particular problems concerning the necessity for long term planning, of using credits properly, of calculating expenses against incomes etc.? This is what we want to consider now.

The contexts for such vulnerabilities may be very different as the following three quotations show:

"Our household always faces financial problems. The main problem is to live in the city with my disabled grandson. We don't have a house in the city. I stayed with him in the city since the 1-st quarter of the academic year and we have to rent the flat there. I rent the flat for 25,000 KZT (166 USD), but it costs me 35,000 KZT (233 USD) per month with utilities. My pension is not enough for these expenditures but with help of my son we try to overcome these shortages. We would like to buy a house in the city but we can't afford it" (Ast int 2: 14, rural, female).

"We still pay credits which certainly complicate our life even more. Part of our monthly income covers the credit. Half of my salary and part of the salary of my mother is spent on the credit. We pay over 50,00 KZT every month for credits. Since I work, I receive a constant salary monthly, half of which covers the credits. If I lost this job it will be a serious problem for our household" (Ast int 39: 14, urban, male).

"There are drug addicts; we know many of them... It's the guys who have stayed in prison ... If you do not give them, you will be an enemy to them. They knock and go home. You give them money and they come anyway... Yes, when my husband works at night, I stay alone and I'm afraid to sleep. I say him to lock the door. But if someone wants to enter, one will enter, having broken a window! Or for the first they will cut off the phone ... there is an area 'Shanghai', it is terrible there, always fighting, last night somebody was killed and brought away by the 'ambulance' car" (Ast int 6: 201-203, rural, female).

Vulnerabilities may also stem from the socio-economic transformation and may be expressed as differences in understanding the ongoing changes between the older and the younger generation.

"We tried to understand and support them even when they were children. Kazakhs have a proverb 'Till 7 years old hold children as kings, from 7 to 17 years old hold them as slaves, after 17 years old hold them as equal to you'. We try to treat them as equals without touching on their rights. For example if a problem isn't solved, we address the children and ask their opinion. This is because they are already adults and their thinking is modern and new (Ast int 19: 19, urban, female).

Vulnerabilities also result from the necessary amalgam of traditional orientations and new impositions of market related behavior. In the following quotations we find solutions to face these vulnerabilities. Many households seem to act like that.

"The most important decisions takes my elder sister, because my parents consult with her. She has already been living in the city for a long time. She always offers decisions and last words are hers. Our parents say that we are smarter than they are. Therefore they rely on our opinions" (Ast int 17: 18, urban, female).

"Sometimes the parents want to buy something. I can be against it. I am the eldest. Before they are going to make a big purchase, they consult with me. For example, a week ago we bought a car, a 'Toyota Camry'. They consulted with me, because we are still paying for the mortgage They asked me if I could help them to pay next month for the mortgage. I am young, they are old people. Sometimes some people try to trick them. They want my parents work in the network marketing. They offer them to buy something for 10000-15000 KZT. In this regard, I discourage them. Eventually, they realize that they were wrong. I don't want them to make a mistake and spend the money uselessly" (Ast int 30: 16, urban, female).

And also the new educational system is a context for coping.

"In two years our elder daughter will go to school. We hope that the credits will be paid off by that time and we can take a new credit to arrange the anniversary of going to school of our first child. It is a part of our culture. We will pay for this credit. After that we are going to buy an apartment on mortgage in the city through 'Zhilstroysberbank'. We will invest in real estate taking into account that our children will study in the city. Additionally, we are going to open a deposit and save money that way when our daughter will start her education at school. It will be a big sum by her graduation time if we put there at least 5,000 KZT (33 USD) per month. It would be good if she would be able to get a scholarship. But if she doesn't, we will pay for her university from this deposit. As for unexpected expenditures like invitations to weddings we overcome them relying on our family budget" (Ast int 15: 16, rural, female, 30 years old).

The new economic context represents special challenges. The endowment with assets may be unsufficient but also their handling in the new market related context may pose difficulties. A 55 years old male from a village 200 km far from Astana took one credit for himself and one for his friend without thinking about the consequences of the latter action. Bound to friendship as traditional habit, he could only reflect his decisions taken after he discovered the financial consequences for his own household:

"We have a stable financial position now, but there are still credit payments for 3 months. My daughter studied in a commercial department, my wife died and there was scarcity of money, therefore I took a credit; additionally, one of my friends asked me to help him with taking a credit. I gave him half of the whole credit's sum. I paid off my part of the credit, but he didn't have enough time for paying off that debt, because he died. The credit hasn't been paid off due to this. Today I am paying for that credit, because it was formally mine" (laughing) (Ast int 10: 14, rural, male, 55 years old).

A 45 years old self-employed businessman from Astana has positive attitudes to taking credits, but instead of accepting his miscalculations concerning his budget he complains about high interest rates (19%) which take away about 60% of the household's income.

"I took a credit of 25000 USD two years ago. But our credit has been stopped for the last six months; we took a break for half a year. Thus we don't pay for it now. Because we don't have possibilities to repay it. We have to balance our credit to our mortgage in order to reduce the interests. We must shift this mortgage to another person, because we haven't got the necessary stable income for taking it. Today our credit has 19% interest rate, we are going to reduce it to 125%-135% by shifting the mortgage. We must pay 60,000 Tenge (400 USD) per month for the credit. We took this credit to start a new business. We have hired workers for building the new small shop within my courtyard.

Building the shop costs 7000 USD. We are going to open this shop soon. The other part of the credited money was spent for different expenses like repair of the house, buying gates for the house etc. I think that taking a credit is possible and enough right a deal, but its interests are too high" (Ast int 27: 13, urban, male, 45 years old).

Quite a lot of respondents explain that they can't save but it is clear that saving as a kind of planning for the future has not evolved into a habit with which one can confront vulnerabilities. Their optimism prevents them from thinking about future difficulties. A 26 years old female from Astana lives with her parents and two siblings. They have recently moved there, but her household does not save:

"We do not have a chance to save. We have recently moved. We have a lot of costs. Now we constantly need the money. We have no possibility to save, because we need to cover our own needs, to eat, to dress up etc." (Ast int 30: 28, urban, female, 26 years).

But in some cases, especially among the elder generation, saving is not a preferable habit due to their claimed negative experiences during the crisis in the 90s. A 53 years old female from Astana does not support keeping savings as part of planning a family budget:

"You know, there are possibilities, but unfortunately we are not able to do that. If there are urgent needs and serious necessities, it will be possible. But we don't need it now. I think that the possibility to save is an absolutely meaningless idea, because there are not any guarantees that the money, which you are saving will keep its current sum. I can say honestly, I don't trust banks with savings, because our family lost a lot of money twice" (Ast int 26: 16, urban, female, 53 years old).

A proclaimed lack of money for living as well as for getting essentials is common for nearly all households independent from their location. Nevertheless in general, rural households have a weaker financial position if compared with urban ones. State statistics as well as our own quantitative data are very clear about this. Seasonality of incomes among the farming population plays the role of a constant challenge for calculation and a pressure to find solutions to overcome unforeseeable events e.g. The following household suffers from lack of money for fuel in winter and hay for cattle every season, which makes the household indebted again and again.

"Well, every month we pay 18,000 KZT (120 USD) for this credit. Besides this credit we take a seasonal credit of 200,000 KZT (1334 USD) every autumn for fuel and hay. Sometimes my vacation time fits with this period and in that case we don't need a credit" (Ast int 2: 17, rural, female, 59 years).

Some rural younger households like that of a 30 years old female with no cattle find other solutions for themselves. They have low incomes and fairly high expenses for childcare and for contributions for weddings and funerals of relatives. In fact, most young households seem to use credits more often and more freely. This household got confused about the overlapping of different credits to meet their expenses. They had to turn to a Lombard house (pawnshop) in order to consolidate financially:

"Therefore we aren't able to take a third credit having already our current credits. At least we can borrow money with interest from peasants as we put all our gold to the Lombard. We are not able to repay the full sum of the credit received from the Lombard and we can only pay the interest of this debt. So we will pay only interests and prolong the expiring date of this credit till summer holidays. We are not able to rebuy our gold from the Lombard, therefore all our gold, all jewelry is there. My husband will go on vacation after three months and he will get the holiday fees. We are going to rebuy our gold jewelry from the Lombard [pawnshop] from this money" (Ast int 15: 14, rural, female, 30 years).

Although seasonality of incomes may cause problems, many rural households seem to cope well with it. We already emphasized that rural households often save in cattle.

"Every year we have a growth of cattle, which we slaughter and sell as surplus. This money from the farming business is enough for us [...]. We take a credit when we do not have time to sell our cattle. Sometimes we take a bigger sum in order to make some repair works at home and to buy some household appliances" (Ast int 1: 12-14, rural, male).

"We sell the milk of cows, if we have surpluses. We make a stock of meat for winter. Sometimes we sell cattle. We sold cattle two years ago, but we didn't sell it last year. We did it for buying coal for 60,000 KZT (400 USD). Today the prices of cattle are higher. It has increased" (Ast int 4: 13, rural, female).

But to make a living from cattle implies a certain financial base not all households have.

"In other words, there are always financial problems. To sustain a livestock, it is necessary to buy hay, kombikorm (artificial food for cattle). You are always in need of money for maintaining livestock. It is a necessity. Therefore we always have to restrict ourselves. Otherwise, what is the reason for sustaining on livestock? That's why we don't have livestock" (Ast int 8: 12, rural, male).

Many rural households also practice subsistence production to decrease their living expenses. This refers to both garden/ agricultural produce and cattle or poultry.

"We don't sell them and their eggs as well, it is just for our consumption" (Ast int 3: 15, rural, female).

However, apart from subsistence production and agriculture, the rural areas are full of structural restrictions to put up one's own business, to find (adequate) employment according to specialization, and to get adequate salaries.

"We thought to open a shop and improve our living conditions owing to that new source of income. But we couldn't open it. Also we had to help other people. Of course, everything was not as we had planned" (Ast int 27: 13, urban, male).

"My problem is I couldn't find a job which would satisfy me. I can't work behind someone's back since I am old enough. My children graduated from university but they don't know what to do. All jobs are related to buying and selling. They didn't study for this purpose. I didn't invest all my means, energy, and savings in order that they get engaged in selling something. The monthly income is hardly enough for us. Of course, it would be nice if we had some additional source of income" (Ast int 5: 12, rural, male).

Therefore, for many rural dwellers, particularly young and well educated people, migration to the city is the better option to make a living. Regarding official statistical data, Kazakhstan's rural population is still moving to the cities[168] and also in our qualitative data, people report about their plans to move or about household members who have found employment in another location. Particularly older people whose children already left the villages would like to follow them.

"I thought about the housing problems in the city, where my children are going to move in the future. I plan to buy an apartment in the city. This is a matter of the future" (Ast int 3: 30, rural, female).

"... buying a house in the city in order to live with them will be the main task in the future. The problem is the lack of an apartment in the city. We can't afford to take a credit for mortgage, because only the salary of my son is appropriate for it. We are pensioners. I worry about this" (Ast int 2:29, rural, female).

"The only wish is to move to Minsk to my daughter. My daughter lives there. We buried our grandfather. We want to go there, but we are scared to leave Kazakhstan. Everything will be clearer soon" (Ast int 35: 19, urban, female).

But also urban households have problems mostly attached to housing costs: rents mortgages, utilities. A young teacher from Astana has a problem with his high rent

168 According to the 2009 Census in Kazakhstan, every 5th household in rural areas has changed the place of living in favor of cities.

for his 1 room flat, which takes about half of the household's income (approx. 500 USD for renting monthly:

"It will be possible only with assent of every member of the household. We have to pay for rent 65,000 KZT (433 USD) per month. We have rented a one-room small flat for two years. We have to pay for the utilities as well. This is about 10-15,000 KZT (66 – 100 USD) per month ... The main thing is the housing problem. Our household doesn't have a propertied apartment and we are not able to buy one. There are high prices for the flat rent and utilities (Ast int 38: 14, 26; urban, male, 25 years).

Some people seem to be seduced by the new options like credits and get indebted or at least burdened e.g. with credits. If they can't get new ones because of their financial situation, they turn to relatives for help.

"Recently, we had 3 credits, now there are 2 credits. I took one for wedding. We registered it on mom because my salary did not allow getting such a sum as credit" (Ast int 39: 23, rural, male).

"Then we had to take another loan and my brother had to go to work to help my mother repaying it" (Ast int 17: 54, urban, female).

"Our parents help us to pay for the mortgage. Certainly, they don't do it every month" (Ast int 23: 15, urban, male).

Given our sample, we can't definitely say, that the elder generation has more problems with facing the new economic conditions due to their soviet past and the bad experiences with the transition to market economy and the recent financial crises. Also younger households have problems to cope with their living conditions. Poorer households in general are exposed to greater vulnerabilities than better-off ones, because they lack the means to protect themselves. The same may be true when we compare rural and urban households. But vulnerabilities can be lessened when the households develop coping strategies and can, for example, compensate lack of financial capital by other capital forms.

Customs and education as well as unforeseeable life events like sudden illnesses also cause vulnerabilities.

"I was ill. My husband rarely gets sick. But he had a heart attack and he lay in hospital several times. Before, he got rarely ill. My younger sister helped us with money during that period. She lives in the city. My husband was treated in an urban hospital. I was operated in that hospital too" (Ast int 4: 19, rural, female).

"My wife is 56 years old. She has secondary education, but she is at home now, because she is a disabled person with 3-rd degree (the lightest form of disability with permission to work). Currently only our children work, they have higher education" (Ast int 5: 6, rural, male).

Despite the possibilities for some households to use state saving schemes for the future education of children, many households suffer from their wish to give children a good education.

"We send money to our daughter, who studies in Astana, twice a month and provide her with products, when it is possible. Mostly we help her with money. We send her 50,000 KZT (333 USD) monthly, because Astana is a big and expensive city. We also pay for her education. We pay 250,000 KZT (1,667 USD) annually for her education, 15,000 KZT (100 USD) per year for her dormitory and as I have already mentioned 50,000 KZT (333 USD) per month for food, and other needs and expenses" (Ast int 13: 13, rural, male).

Today a lot of urban and rural households show vulnerabilities, which stem from various social problems. Vulnerabilities of urban households are often caused by the housing problem in Astana. Also high prices, weaknesses in the social infrastructure (lack of kindergartens) and debts or even indebtedness through credits play a role. Rural vulnerabilities mainly stem from weak employment options and low salaries, unemployment, corruption, and seasonal problems of agriculture.

"I took 300,000 KZT (2,000 USD) in credit at the end of last year (2011) through the company 'Home credit', which is managed from Almaty. I redeem 20,20 KZT (134 USD) per month for two-and-a-half years. It is convenient for me. I don't know the interest rate of this credit, but I borrowed 300,000 KZT (2,001 USD) and I have to redeem 360,000 KZT (2,400 USD). All conditions are negotiated according to the paying schedule. I assume I will not have a problem with redeeming the debt if I will be healthy and receive my pension in time. It was my first credit" (Ast int 3: 18, rural, female).

"Our income is never sufficient, but we cope with problems owing to credits. There are not any other decisions. I can also make extra earnings. We used to borrow money, but currently nobody lends money at all. That's why I don't borrow money. We have a certain amount of additional income besides our salary. But this is not a significant amount. I would say this is nothing for us. We have a very hard working day at work, which lasts from morning to evening. Sometimes we have to stay at work until late evening. Sometimes we get fees for such additional working hours. For example, it could be 1/4 of the salary, but this is very small for us" (Ast int 12: 13, rural, male).

"We never count upon anybody. In winter, it happens that I go to work somewhere. There was a time that I made even cakes, pastries and sold them. Some of the necessary expenses I covered with money that I earned by selling cakes. We try to collect a lot of money and stuff to spend on daily necessities. When we have financial problems I bake cakes and pies in winter. My daily earning is 1,000 or 1,500 KZT. When we have a critical period in our life, we try not to borrow from anybody. Critical periods happen mostly in winter. In summer, my husband works, I'm at home, these difficulties do not exist then" (Ast int 21: 21, urban, female).

"If we urgently need to buy something, my dad takes a small loan. He has a good salary. But it has happened very rarely, because credits have some consequences. If we need some amount, we take the money from relatives. We take 100,000 KZT and return money in a month. We decide on life difficulties jointly. When there are such serious situations in life if someone is sick my uncle was shot dead we are going to help the family" (Ast int 30: 26, urban, female).

"We overcome these everyday problems owing to restricting ourselves from eating food in entertainment places and go out for leisure. For example: we can refrain from cinema and some delicacies and fruits. We have to refrain from going to cinema too often and also to premieres of new movies. Also we don't go to other entertainment places like bowling centers, restaurants, cafes, Spa and massage cabinets. I want to go to efficient English courses with high qualified teachers, native speakers, but I can't afford such expenses. We buy our clothes in 'Shanghai' (the bazaar at the outskirts of Astana), although we would like to do shopping in the trade centers and boutiques. We seek to economize the expenses. We restrict ourselves" (Ast int 38: 12, urban, male).

The urban-rural division imposes different types of vulnerabilities on the households. But it seems that in rural regions there are fewer options to overcome them than in the urban ones. Self-restriction is looked upon as the most adequate means to protect the households against the risks of the market. One can distinguish between long term and short term protection. Long term protection concerns education of the children and housing. Many households use or want to use the state programs that are offered for protection against these challenges.

Sustainability, Vulnerabilities and Coping

"Sustainability is the capacity to endure ... For humans, sustainability is the potential for long-term maintenance of wellbeing, which has ecological, economic, political and cultural dimensions" (Wikipedia, access date: 22-06-2013).

In literature, quite often different types of sustainability are distinguished: human sustainability (maintaining the level of education, health or improving human characteristics), economic sustainability (maintaining one's own economic situation), social sustainability (maintaining a certain status, social networks and relationships), environment sustainability (maintaining biophysical conditions, protecting natural resources and ecological conditions of living) (cf. Goodland, n.d.).

To reach sustainability and to overcome vulnerabilities implies to draw upon resources. Therefore we look at these resources in more detail. There are common financial problems for all households, but coping strategies and ways to overcome problems are strongly determined by distinctions of the households' place of living. Rural and urban households have access to different kinds of capital, due to the infrastructural and institutional possibilities.

Although Kazakhstan is meanwhile classified in international statistics as being a middle income country, most interviewees stress financial scarcity.

"I think there should be more money in the families and this would protect them from crisis. If you have money you will feel better" (Ast Int 21: 33, urban, female).

"There is one hope only. Our income is our hope" (Ast int 5: 20, rural, male).

How do households reach sustainability? Many households use several methods and ways to maintain sustainable situations. Often self-restriction of households in consumption and services is employed as already shown above.

Some households try to obtain more sources of income and to reach sustainability by additional employment. This kind of maintaining of sustainability is used primarily by urban households.

"I think, probably my husband will look for a second job. Generally, he works during day times and could work as taxi driver like many other men in our village in the evening. For example, he may work also as a guard. Basically I haven't got possibilities for additional work somewhere, because I spend all my time at work" (Ast int 26: 21, rural, female).

"I try to earn extra money, for example, now I sew at home and I do it for money to customers, I tailor and other more easy things. By the way, the sewing machine was given to me by my mother-in-law, she says, be useful in your life, study, don't sit on your hands. So I am busy and sew some dresses, skirts for myself, and also on orders from neighbors" (Ast int 9: 13, urban, female).

"We are ready for a subsidiary job. Therefore we are looking for part-time employment in the future" (Ast int 4: 21, rural, female).

As shown when discussing savings households also try to save money for rainy days at home or in bank deposits in order to be more sustainable.

"I manage the family budget myself and try to save a certain amount of money for urgent expenses or rainy days" (Ast int 2: 23, rural, female).

"I am saving money for necessities, for buying and updating, for maintaining our living conditions, we save for the marriage ceremony of our daughters and our son. We don't want to be with nothing in the future. The matchmakers can come at any moment according to Muslim customs and we have to prepare the dowries of our daughters and so on" (Ast int 5: 16, rural, male).

"I was even ready to get out from that situation. I have never asked help from anybody, also I don't even borrow ... I have a principle that I always make savings, hide money, and imagine as if this money doesn't exist" (Ast Int 28: 14, urban, female).

Others overcome financial scarcity by credits as already shown in the subchapter on credits.

Some rural households also achieve sustainability by putting their bills in local shops on the slate.

"One of the advantages of living in rural areas... is that you can put food and other things for domestic needs from stores on the slate till your next salary" (Ast int 15: 12, rural, female).

Achieving sustainability of households by using natural capital like cattle or gardening is widely used by rural households, who can reduce their own expenses by consuming their own products (milk, butter, meat, etc.) and eventually also sell them.

"I engage in gardening and cultivate some kinds of vegetables and trees. I planted potatoes in spring. It will be enough for us until December. We plant them in order to provide our household with food for everyday use" (Int Ast 27:11, urban, male).

Self-provisioning is widespread in the country side and most households also try to make a little income through their agricultural activities. Additional agricultural activities are also combined with formal incomes. Wealthier households convert their property into financial capital. Rural households raising cattle convert it into financial capital if necessary.

"If we would have to arrange a wedding for our children, we can just sell some horses and make this event immediately. Therefore we are not worried about the future" (Ast int 1: 16, rural, male; also Ast int 4: 13).

Urban households often apply another strategy. Two examples follow:

"We rent out another apartment we own. This is the subsidiary source of income, because we have a few flats and one of them we rent out" (Ast int 26: 11, urban, female).

"We are going to sell our house and I start my own business in the future. I am going to buy a plot of land. We are waiting for the decision of the government about this land. If the authorities sign the document, I want to start with a small brick plant in A. city. For this reason I am going to sell my house" (Ast int 27: 19, urban, male).

To sum up: Many households have understood that a market economy produces vulnerabilities against which one has to take action. These actions center on the means the Kazakhstani market economy offers itself but also around customs that traditionally bind many households together. Poorer households may often dream about their sustainability, but in fact they often do nothing to achieve this, or do not have the means to find adequate coping strategies (make savings, investments, second job, etc.). Sometimes they lack of knowledge on how to protect the households, sometimes they act risk-averse.

Reciprocity and Safety Nets among Kinfolk

Especially among ethnic Kazakhs, family ties are still very strong and are looked upon as a means to maintain wellbeing and to overcome unforeseeable life events. Those households consider sustainability as reciprocity and mutual help. Sometimes kinship networks are broadened and involve friends, neighbors, and colleagues. Reciprocity networks among relatives and friends (usually referred to as 'social capital'[169] or f-connections (cf. Ben-Porath 1980) in the literature) touch many spheres of the household. They concern monetary and non-monetary aspects and are based on cultural norms of mutual help, particularly in 'strong ties' (Granovetter 1983) relations.

In literature, mutual help is too often an idealized, 'over socialized' (Hirsch, Michaels, and Friedman 1987) conception of mutual 'insurance', and indeed it is among poorer households that such social capital has to be maintained. Some authors also refer to the norm of reciprocity (Gouldner 1960), i.e. the obligation to provide help, once being asked by close kinfolk, so that people cannot escape the claims of their kinfolk. Especially in crisis situations such mutual help can, however, become unbalanced. Those who are better off are obliged to permanently help their kinfolk and never will receive returns. Thus, spatial and emotional distancing is an opportunity to escape the claims of their kinfolk (cf. Evers, 1994). In our sample we also find some quotations supporting these arguments.

[169] Social capital is a result of interactions between individuals, families, groups, or communities, which offer an access to valuable resources and profitable positions (Bourdieu 1986). From the perspective of Coleman (1987), social capital requires maintenance work because otherwise it gets lost. From the perspective of social anthropology, social capital is strongly related to reciprocity in kinship networks (Gregory 1997) and patron-client relationships (cf. Eisenstadt and Roniger 1966).

Rural households usually have wider family-related social capital, which they can use to secure their living.

"I have prosperous brothers and sisters, who always seek to help my children. For example, each of them helped as he could afford that there was a good marriage of my elder son: someone paid for café, someone bought meat, someone bought all the drinks and I bought only clothes and gifts. They help us not so regularly, only during large events, but then they give us enough support. They arrange these events and I even don't think about it, because they are perfect specialists" (Ast int 16: 12, rural, female).

"The relatives help us when it is necessary. If I need some help, I will call our relatives. Even though I don't have parents, but my uncles and aunts have helped me" (Ast int 10: 14, rural, male).

The support of parents to their children and vice versa may be called 'intergenerational reciprocity'. The following quotation explains the concept.

"Kazakhs have a family concept: 'the first son is for support, the backbone'. Surely it is strange for some young couples always to be side by side with parents. But I consider this correct; I bring up my son this way. This is neither surveillance nor egoism of parents, but honors the children in relation to their parents. As a rule, on all family holidays we meet with our parents. This is tradition and a golden rule of Kazakhs" (Ast int 37: 15, urban, female).

"If you have money, you can help the family, parents, and then you will feel free ..." (Ast int 24: 32, urban, female).

But we find some mainly urban respondents who argue better not to have too close contacts to relatives or to keep monetary issues outside the sphere of reciprocity relations.

The reality of current Kazakhstan shows that social capital gradually splits up and disposable ties seem more preferable for organizing survival especially in urban area. E.g. lending money to relatives no longer is a self-understood custom.

"I had some disagreements with relatives. I always assume that if one has arms and legs, one always can work and earn money. My relatives offended me because I did not lend them money. I can't give them money; this is the main controversy with my relatives and friends. I do not agree with them. If you want to live with glamour, then you should work, if there is no money – sit at home. In this regard, there were disagreements" (Ast int 28: 30, urban, female).

"All our relatives live in other cities. There is such proverb: if one has no water, the fish has no water too. If you don't have anything, others will not have as well. Even those who live well don't live in affluence. Everyone has his own family and children. When they have problems or I myself, nobody will give anything. Even if businessmen have money, this money after all is enclosed in their business" (Ast int 19: 29, urban, female).

It seems to us that particularly lower middle-class households need this security support of their networks as a last resort to get help if they cannot help themselves, while for better-off households the security-aspect in their networks becomes an option among others, which gives them the choice to reflect on the utility of such networks. If such a reciprocity becomes too unbalanced, they might prefer changing strong ties into weak ones or even to 'escape' the clutches of demanding relatives by no longer maintaining or dissolving such networks.

But also a change in the network relations may occur in the urban setting. Among urban households friends and colleagues may replace relatives in such support networks. Perhaps it is easier to renounce the claim of a friend or colleague to be supported than the claim of a relative, due to Kazakh norms of strong family ties and family orientation.

"In many ways, our friends help us.... Because at one time my husband helped them also. My husband had his own firm, helped many to buy housing, assisted in the construction of houses. And thus everyone wants to help us as he can afford. Sometimes we laugh, because when starting to build, the house is already ready. We try to support each other [...]. In many ways, our friends help us. For example, my friends promised to help with the construction of a house, if we would build one. And another example, one friend assured me, that, if we build a house, he will shoulder the furniture of one room, and another one wants to shoulder the construction of something" (Ast int 24: 23, urban, female).

"We borrowed money from neighbors with interest. So, thanks to God, we have coped with all of these problems" (Ast int 28: 12, urban, female).

There are material and non-material, often obligatory, sometimes voluntary support mechanisms among relatives and friends. From the perspective of capital forms these can be considered as 'social capital', from the perspective of the household budget as incomes or expenditures because the ties have to be hold up – in form of money or in kind.

Education plays a special role in maintaining social ties with mutual help character between generations. Parents support their children in getting the best education or in finding a job in the city.

"Now the most important thing is the education of our child, we will take additional paid lessons at school..." (Ast int 25: 23, urban, female).

And children give back this 'investment' by supporting their old parents.

"When my brothers come, they leave money for my father. My sister is a pharmacist. She has her own pharmacy. So if our father needs expensive medication, my sister brings it. When my brothers or my sister have extra money, they send me money for a holiday e.g. – they don't send money monthly. They send drugs for my father and about 5,000-10,000 KZT (34-68 USD). If there is an anniversary or other holidays each family gives 10,000 KZT as a gift. We ask the birthday person, what he wants: money or gift" (Ast int 18: 46, urban, female).

The quotation above already shows reciprocity as a form of income. Non-monetary reciprocity is a source of income which often can be found in families with rural ties. Meat and vegetables or fruits are exchanged. Such a type of 'jar economy' (cf. Smollet 1989) helps households to reduce expenses and must be looked upon as a kind of income.

"Definitely, there were difficulties. We recovered from them by relatives' support. We have many relatives and we help each other, so we did cope with this problem. This is not every day help. If they are able to help you, they will do it when you don't find any other way. They help us regularly both with money and foods, it depends on their possibilities. I help them too. I have a vegetable garden and I send them vegetables when I have more potatoes. We have such kind of mutual supporting with relatives" (Ast int 8: 18, rural, male).

This exchange implies reciprocity but on a barely calculated basis (Turner, 2006, p. 184). Among many Kazakh families there are still strong obligations to help poorer relatives.

"I cannot say that in the case of financial problems there are people who can help us. Our parents help us, send food, meat. But they do not send us these products each month" (Ast int 24: 13, urban, female).

"The eldest son lives in a village, he helps us with products, oil, and meat" (Ast int 9: 13, urban, female).

However, norms of reciprocity exceed close kinship relations. Historically the Kazakh nomadic society consisted of different social classes as '*aq syek*' (kaz.; white bone), '*qara syek*' (kaz.; black bone) and '*jatak*' (kaz.; poor people), as well as two symbolically distinct status groups '*Qozha*' (kaz.; Qozha is a sub-group of Kazakhs who are believed to have descended from Arabs) and '*Tore*' (kaz.; Tore is a sub-group who is believed to have descended from Chenghiz Khan). For ethnic Kazakhs these social classes represent social capital even today. For them the relationships enshrined in these positions play an important role in organizing survival strategies and in gaining material and immaterial wellbeing. Networks, acquaintances, families, friends etc. often center on the traditional positions and the influence they impose on positioning. The difference to '*blat*', favors, sometimes corruption, is not always clear. People may refer to acquaintances to gain a position but detest corruption. Already in soviet times, blat and traditional ties were deeply intertwined. Of course, other ethnicities are also part and parcel of social competition.

Our interviews show that, first of all, social capital is important for rural-urban migration or relatives. The urban dwellers are expected to host relatives.

"As we live in the capital many relatives come to study or to work here. Surely it is very inconvenient for us, because we want to live for ourselves. Last year my cousin lived with us. He entered college. He had no place to live. His elder sister lived in a hostel. Later she wanted to live in an apartment. Now he does not live with us anymore. They moved to a rented apartment. In June my aunt came from P. She's not married. We hope that she will live with us until she finds a job. She came looking for a job, but so far unsuccessfully. She has a secondary special education. She does not pay anything. She eats with us. She spends her own money for her own purposes" (Ast int 30: 12, urban, female).

Furthermore, access to the labor market with good job conditions requires social capital.

"In the future, I would like to work in my original specialty as a financier or economist, but I need networks, acquaintances. My brother-in-law promised me to look for a well-paid and stable job for me. He has a lot of acquaintances in his job" (Ast int 9: 13, urban, female).

"I don't rely on our local administration. They don't support us like a young family. I think that the main problem for living in a rural area is facing 'blat' and informal relationships daily. All depends on the strength of your networks" (Ast int 15: 24, rural, female).

And finally, access to financial capital in the form of interest-free, sometimes low-interest credit is closely connected to social capital, as already discussed in the sub-chapter on credits. Where the ties are strong, one has to give and has to rely on the rule of reciprocity that seems to erode gradually.

4.3. Qualitative Report from South Kazakhstan: Almaty City and Almaty Region

Eckhard DITTRICH and Heiko SCHRADER[170]

The Setting

25 interviews out of 40 come from Almaty city, 15 from the rural area.

Almaty is the former capital of Kazakhstan and the nation's largest city, with a population of 1,472,866 (December, 1st, 2012).[171] The city represents 9% of the country's population and is the major commercial and cultural center of Kazakhstan, situated in the south close to a mountainous area, near the border to Kyrgyzstan. Almaty generates approximately 20 percent of Kazakhstan's GDP (or $36 billion in 2010). It is a key financial and business center in Central Asia. Apart from production, it hosts large shopping centers, various bazaars, and all the infrastructure and professional opportunities of a large city. The capital Astana as well as Almaty are key educational and research centers in the country. Almaty is still a magnet for many rural people looking for employment opportunities – people with higher education, as well as people with lower education.

In 2010 the ethnic composition was as follows:[172] Kazakh: 51.06%; Russian: 33.02%; Uighur: 5.73%; Korean: 1.9%; Tatar: 1.82%; Ukrainian: 1.24%; others: 5.23%.

Another 15 interviews were conducted in the following locations in Almaty region. The villages chosen represent special villages in order to have a broader variation concerning rural life.

I. S.: S. is an *urban-type settlement*, the administrative center of the K. district in the Almaty region. The settlement was established in the Soviet era. In 2012 the *population* was 13,401. The *ethnic composition* is: Kazakhs – 82.8%, Russian – 12%, others – 5.2%. The *distance* between Almaty and S. is 170 km. S. can *be reached* easily by road and by train. Travel time is approximately 2 hours 30 minutes by car or a private taxi[173] (fare – 1,500-2,000 KZT per person (10-13 $); close to 3 hours by public buses (1,000 KZT); and 4 hours by train (500 KZT).

---

170 The Almaty team taking the interviews and doing the transcriptions: Nazym Shedenova (coordinator), Aigul Beimisheva, Aigul Rismoldaeva, Aigerim Zhakipbek, Dinara Dusebaeva. Data analysis was done by Nigina Avganova, Batima Mambetalina, and Heiko Schrader.

171 Naselenie. Stat.kz. Retrieved 2013-01-11.

172 Archives 2000, Stat.kz. Retrieved 2013-03-25.

173 Taxi service without license.

Infrastructure: three schools, two kindergartens, a cultural center, a mosque, a hospital, Kazpost, Kazakhtelecom, a park, several personal services, a real estate agency, supermarkets, a bazaar, one bank, cafes, restaurants, an entertainment center, hairdressing saloons, one 'Technical Service Station (STO) for cars', a military compound. *Water and electricity* are in centralized supply, but not gas for heating. The population uses liquid gas in tanks, to be bought privately from a local supplier.

In the district the Korean International Cooperation Agency (KOICA) in conjunction with the Limited Liability Partnership (LLP) "Daegu Cite Gas" is engaged in a *developmental project* "Greening the villages and drinking water, using renewable energy sources for the village population of S".

Being an administrative center, S. has all public services: the district akimat (government), the settlement akimat (government), the settlement council, a citizen service center, a treasury, a tax committee, a district department of internal affairs (Police Department), the prosecutor's office. The *economy* in S. centers around these administrative functions and on transport and agriculture. Transport implies employment concerning the railway station and enterprises for rail transport. Agricultural businesses are engaged in grain farming and other produce. There is a silo for storing the grain.

Although the region of the administrative center is called rural, the settlement is no village comparable to those in northern Kazakhstan.

II. K. is a village in the Almaty region. The *population* in 2009 was 4,058 people. In comparison with the basis year 1999 it has now increased by 126.7%. The *ethnic composition* is Kazakhs (35-40%), Uighurs (50%), Russians, Germans, Turks, and others (10-15%). Some tension has been reported in inter-ethnic relations between Kazakhs and Uighurs. The village was founded in 1928. The *distance* between Almaty and K. is about 35 km, 45 minutes' drive by car. It is not possible to reach the village by public transport. Transport from Almaty is only to T. (fare 80-100 KZT; 30-40 min if not stuck in a traffic jam); from there people may hire a private taxi for 10 km. Taxi fare is 200 KZT. The village is within the reach of the city for daily commuting. This represents an exception from all other villages chosen for research. But as villages with different ethnic compositions exist we selected it for research.

Infrastructure: a Kazakh-Russian school, a kindergarten, a department of Kazpost, a small hospital, a well renovated cultural center and a mosque. There is no market, but there are about 10-15 grocery stores. The nearest bank is in another village. Only four streets are paved, the others are mud roads. Two thirds of the houses in the village are connected to the communal water supply. The rest use wells. There is a centralized electricity supply. Economically there are different options for the villagers. A few work for the government (administration, school, etc.) and in the small shops. Some younger people with academic credentials go to work in government agencies, banks, and etc. in nearby towns and some also in Almaty city. Less educated young people work mainly in Almaty in the security services, fire services, bazaars, etc. But most people earn their living in agriculture. Uighurs are mostly engaged in cultivating vegetables (potatoes, tomatoes, cucumbers, etc.). Kazakhs mostly raise livestock; they also slaughter and sell the meat themselves.

III. Z. is a village in the Almaty region, dominated by non-agricultural activities. The settlement was founded in 1953. It is located close to the K. reservoir. In 2009 the *population* was 16,527. Growth compared to the basis year 1999 is 119.2%. *Ethnic groups* are Kazakhs 60%, Russians 29%, Azerbaijanis 7%, Uighurs 3%, Germans 0.6%, and also Turks, Koreans and others. People have reported that in 1992-1993, there was a large and growing number of Roma in the village. According to this information, following some criminals' activity, internal security forces moved in and removed all Roma during one night. People maintain that the number of Roma was several thousand. The *distance* between Z. and Almaty is 37 km. People usually travel to Almaty by private taxi (350 KZT). There is also a bus (250 KZT). State services are mainly available in the district center 30 km away. It is normally reached by taxi (250 KZT). The time for a trip to Almaty is about 45 minutes by taxi. This means that it is possible to commute to Almaty from this village.

The *infrastructure* consists of 3 schools, 2 secondary, one primary one, one kindergarten, 3 post offices, a hospital with 25 beds and one medical dispensary, an orthodox church, a driving school, 2 bazaars – one daily and one on Sundays, 78 stores, 6 pharmacies. There is no bank. *Water* is in centralized *supply* for about 50% of the houses, the other half uses wells. The roads are in good condition and are regularly repaired. There is *centralized electricity* supply. The main streets also have electric lighting. There are many two and three story houses in the village because of non-agricultural activities of part of the population and due to the departmental military compound with four story houses. The "officer" houses and the "social" houses (special state program for housing) have been built in recent years according the program "Kazakhstan – 2020".

Geological explorations have been and remain the *main activity* of the population. Additionally, there is a factory, but it has been disused during the past year. It produced small metal items. There are several Limited Liability Partnerships (LLP) and Geological Survey LLPs, one Joint Stock Company (JSC) and a railroad repair shop. Agricultural activities are performed by 413 farms and two agricultural enterprises in the form of JSC. An international highway by-passes the village linking China and Kazakhstan; a station is planned but not working yet. It will produce additional employment. The village was chosen to host "oral-man" (Kazakh-repatriates), arriving from 2000 to 2008. Now immigration is in decline. The immigrants are mainly from Uzbekistan (Karakalpaks), Mongolia, and Turkmenistan. They work in construction and trade. Cattle rustling and occasional inter-ethnic tensions have been reported.

IV. A. is situated in a rural district in the Almaty region. Formerly it was dominated by a fishing kolkhoz.[174] The village is situated on the banks of the reservoir K. The total population in 2009 was 768 persons. Compared to the basis year 1999 it has increased by 156.7%. The population is mainly composed of Kazakhs (60%), Russians, and Koreans. The estimated average age of the population is 30 to 50 years. The *distance* to Almaty is 55 km, with no direct bus transfer. Residents mainly use private transport facilities – private cars or taxis – to get to Almaty city or the regional center. Some hire taxis and go to the nearby highway (6 km); from there, they use the public or private transportation available to the city.

The *infrastructure* consists of an ungraded high school with a total of 115 students, a first-aid post, a postman, a privately and recently built mosque, an evangelical church, and 3 private stores. The houses have telephones. *Centralized electricity* is in supply. The streets in the village are not paved. Engineering work for a mains *water supply* began in 2012, but this will take several years to complete. The road from the highway to the village (6 km) was paved, but due to newly opened 5 sand pits near the village, the 'kamazs' (big trucks) have destroyed the road. The *economy* of the village was dominated by a fishing kolkhoz that was relocated here in 1970 after the construction of a hydropower plant in K. In Soviet times, the farm employed about 150 people, including 80 fishermen, 25 crop growers, 20 machine operators and builders. There was a fully developed fish processing plant (dried, smoked) and other facilities to grow, harvest etc. ingredients for fish canning. This also explains the good infrastructure. Kindergartens were provided by the kolkhoz from 1970 to 1988. A cultural center and offices were also built. After the collapse of the Soviet Union, there was no further construction, except for street lighting and the recent start of building a water supply system. Additionally, a sewing factory had been operating in the village. Both sites, however, were closed down. Some people are still engaged in fish indepen-

[174] Collective farm

dently or join temporarily organized groups. An electrical transformer production plant, three km from the village, provides some jobs. A new plant for the production of cavity blocks has been built recently. This village represents the classical industrialized village as known from soviet times (cf. Dittrich, Oswald 2010).

Household Composition

Household Structure

We shall consider the following socio-structural parameters: household size and types of households (nuclear households, extended households).

Household Size and Household Types

According to the 2009 Census, the average household size was 3.6.[175] According to the Kazakh Census of 2009, 8.2 % were single households.[176] Interestingly, the smallest household seize in our sample is three members, the largest 7 members.

Table 59: Household size in the South Kazakhstan qualitative sample

Household Size	3 members	4 members	5 members	6 members	7 members
Number of households	7	13	12	4	4
Almaty Interview No.	5, 6, 7, 19, 24, 26, 31	2, 9, 11, 17, 18, 20, 22, 27, 29, 30, 32, 33, 39	1, 10, 14, 15, 16, 21, 28, 34, 35, 37, 38, 40	3, 4, 8, 13	12, 23, 25, 36

We want to distinguish two household types: nuclear households and extended households (more than two generations and/or other relatives). In the Census of 2009, the former constitute 45.0 %, the latter 35.5%. Furthermore, we consider the distribution according to location (urban/rural) and ethnicity.

For a nuclear household this means father, mother and children (here nuclear family and household overlap), for extended households this means a married couple in its middle-age and other people around them. As it is socially unacceptable, cases of unmarried people living together are rare.[177] The central position of

[175] The Agency of Statistics of the Republic of Kazakhstan, Results of the 2009 National Population Census of the Republic of Kazakhstan, Analytic Report Astana 2011. To compare, the household size in Germany in 2011 it was 2.02.

[176] In Germany, in 2011, this type of household formed the biggest group of all household types.

[177] The only case in our sample is Alm int 26: a young divorced Russian woman with child living

a married couple in the household, however, does not mean that a nuclear family and a nuclear household are the same, because often grown up family members no longer live in the household although they help to support it or they are supported by it. Also more distant relatives may live in the household.

In our sample and in Kazakhstan in general, we can observe a number of extended households, which are predominantly found among ethnic Kazakhs. Their existence seems strongly related to norms and responsibilities of children towards their parents. Among Kazakhs usually the youngest son and his family have the social responsibility to live with his parents.

Nuclear Households

14 investigated households are of the nuclear type, comprising a household size of three to five people. They mainly consist of parents and children. In two cases (Alm int 2, Alm int 33) the family is larger: the children study in the city or already live separately. The following table provides the distribution of nuclear households.

Table 60: Household size and household structure: nuclear households

Household Size	**3 members**	**4 members**	**5 members**
Number of interviews	4	7	4
Almaty Interview No.	5, 19, 24, 31	2, 9, 11, 17, 18, 20, 22, 27, 29, 30, 32, 33, 39	2, 11, 17, 18, 22, 33, 35

Nuclear households reside both in the city and in rural areas, but the majority of such households are found in the city. We have to admit that urban and rural interviews are unevenly distributed in the sample, but their number in the city significantly exceeds the distribution. Therefore, we assume that urbanization and urban living conditions (e.g. department size, housing programs etc.) as well as ongoing cultural changes favor the nuclear family type with one or two children.

together with her boyfriend who is Uighur. She explains, that she already made a proposal to marry, but her father is resistant to a Uighur marriage due to the ethnic and religious differences, being Muslim and Christian Orthodox and as she is divorced with a child from her first marriage. Although they are officially unmarried, the female respondent considers their relation as a marriage alliance, because they have a common household budget, and her boyfriend has assumed the role of father to her four-year-old kid.

Table 61: Household structure in the South Kazakhstan qualitative sample: nuclear households

	Almaty region		Almaty city	
Household Structure/Size	**No.**	**Interviews**	**No.**	**Interviews**
Nuclear family: 3 members	2	5, 31	2	19, 24
Nuclear family: 4 members	2	2, 33	5	11, 17, 18, 22, 35
Nuclear family: 5 members	–		3	6, 21, 38

Nuclear families are found among all ethnic groups, but in the sample, the majority (32) is Kazakh.

Looking at the household positions in the nuclear family, husband/father is usually looked upon as head. This holds true even in those cases in which the wife/mother is the main bread winner (Alm int 11, 16, 17, 18). Nevertheless, decisions are usually taken by the entire family, children included. However, the final decision is taken by husband/father if larger financial expenses are concerned (landed property, car, expensive furniture; e.g. Alm int 2, 5, 16, 17, 18, 19, 21, 22, 31, 33, 35, 38). Sometimes, one may conclude from the interviews, that this traditional decisional structure is more a hollow shell with weak grounding in reality. But in the majority of cases household head, main bread winner and main decision-maker correspond to each other. In some cases this is also due to the fact that female family members are on maternal leave or are housewives (Alm int 38, 33, 24, 21).

We want to provide an exceptional case here in which the household positions are reverse. The woman (Alm int 11) lives in Almaty, is 43 years old and Kazakh. She is the main breadwinner because her husband is a 'second-group disabled'. In this case, the husband takes the role of the housekeeper. The female respondent claims to be responsible for the financial issues. Nevertheless, she considers her husband to be the household head.

"I take the important decisions, because I am earning the money. But I am not the head of the family, because I have a husband, and together we make some major decisions; in most cases, I agree with his opinion. Therefore I believe I am not the head of the family" (Alm int 11: 8).

Extended Households

24 cases belong to the extended type. Ethnic Kazakh extended households represent mostly the orientation to traditional family ties, which includes a widespread integration of relatives of the family, of the tribe and of the 'juze'. This implies not only reciprocal exchange or cohabitation, but also occasional visits for a longer

or a shorter period. In our sample, we find the following constellations: people from three or four generations (grandparents, parents, and children) live together in one household; or close relatives from one of the spouses, mainly the husband, cohabitate. These two characteristics may also be combined. The census of 2009 reports that such 'composite households' have increased.

The following table shows the combinations in our sample.

Table 62: Household structure and size, extended households

Household Size	3 members		4 members		5 members		6 members		7 members	
	Freq	No of Int	Freq	No of Int	Freq	No of Int	Freq	No of Int	Freq	No of Int
3 generations	–		3	30, 9, 29	4	14, 28, 34, 37	1	8	–	
4 generations	–								2	23, 36
2 or 3 generations plus relatives	–		2	20, 27			3	3, 4, 13		
Relatives in the household	2	6, 7	2	32, 39	4	1, 10, 15, 40	–		2	12, 25

Note: Freq = frequency

Looking at the geographical distribution of extended households, they are found both in the city (15 from 25) as well as in the Almaty region (10 from 15). Urban extended households very often host relatives studying or being employed in the city (e.g. Alm int 12, 15, 25, 40), or unemployed (e.g. Alm int 20, 39). In general the hosting of relatives may also mean relatives being either unemployed (Alm int 1) or sick (Alm int 3, 4, 6, 22).

The majority of extended households belong to the Kazakh ethnic group. This may also be caused by the bias of ethnic Kazakh households in our sample, which are overrepresented. But we assume that this mirrors Kazakh traditions according to which e.g. the parents live together with the youngest son and his family, and according to which also the hosting of relatives is frequent and can also be explained by strong mutual help norms and responsibilities in the Kazakh ethnic group.[178] Because of that, in our sample Kazakh households are strongly represented among the large households and households hosting relatives, contrary to the Russian extended households, which have a maximum size of five in our sample. They comprise three generations but do not host any other relatives. Uighur,

178 In Kazakhstan we find the term '*asphaltniki*' referring to such people who live in the city and have lost their ethnic cultural norms and responsibilities.

Turk and Korean households may more closely resemble the Kazakh ones, but due to their small number, any reliable interpretation must be left open.

Three- and Four- Generation Households

Let us consider the three– and four–generation households in more detail. They comprise one fourth of the Almaty sample. Most frequent is the co-habitation of grandparent generation, parent generation and children – a three-generation household. In four cases (Alm int 28, 30, 34, 37) the household comprises a childless couple and the parents of the husband (Alm int 34: male, 27 years old, urban, Kazakh, Alm int 37, female, 72 years old, rural, Kazakh). In four other interviews (Alm int 8, 9, 14, 29) the household structure is a couple and their children, living together with the parents of the wife. Only one of these households is ethnic Kazakh – the daughter is the only child.

A reason for the comparatively large number of four-generation households is the increased life expectancy. Among the four-generation households there is a pattern of great-grandparent(s) living with their married son (grandparent generation), children of this couple one of which is married with children (e.g. Alm int 23: 11-15).

Four–generation households occur because people marry and have their first child quite early. According to the national statistics, the average age of marriage is between 20 and 24.[179]

Kazakh tradition implies the responsibility of the daughter-in-law for her parents-in-law who live with her husband and herself. Even if the children's generation founds separate households in the course of the family cycle, the time comes when the traditional responsibility has to be fulfilled: parents may become helpless or one of them is widowed, etc.:

"My wife insisted on living together with my mother, because my father died six years ago and my mother was left alone. That's why my wife suggested living together. Of course, at first it was not easy, because all of us have different characters. But now it is o.k.; everyone works, everyone has his own interests" (Alm int 23: 45, male, 39 years, urban, Kazakh).

In another case (Alm int 36) we can directly reconstruct the history of the extended household. Initially the household comprised three generations, but it was further

[179] To provide another example of the four-generation household and deliveries: In Alm int 36 the oldest generation is the mother-in-law of the female respondent who is 72 years old. The husband (her son) is now 49 years old. The respondent (wife of him) delivered her daughter with 20 years. This daughter – now 28 years old – has a five year old child.

extended because a daughter of the third generation divorced and she and her five-year-old daughter were integrated into the household.

How do household positions change in an extended household? How are the roles within the household distributed? Who is pooling incomes? Certainly in the Kazakh households age status is important. The oldest generation takes the role of advising the younger generations, even taking the decisions. In three-generation households the middle generation is the active income earning one. If the grandparents' generation consists of pensioners they receive transfer payments from the state. Whether or not the different incomes and transfers are pooled or whether the household members pool only a certain share for food and shelter, depends on the particular case. In Alm int 36 (female, urban, Kazakh), for example, pooling is organized according to necessity. Two of the three children with own income keep their money and only contribute to the household expenses in case of emergency. Then their mother – the respondent – advises them to contribute (§31-36)[180].

In another case (Alm int 23: male, 39 years, urban, Kazakh) the respondent is presently unemployed and makes some money through private orders in the black economy. His wife is the main breadwinner. Both husband and wife decide on the financial expenses. It remains unclear, if the mother of the respondent, a pensioner but still working as a teacher, pools her income into a joint budget. But during the crisis of the 1990s, when both husband and wife had been unemployed, the pension of the mother was the only income source of the household (§39).

While the males/husbands are usually considered to be the heads of the household, the females/women are often the housekeeper. In Kazakh three-generation households, the wife of the middle generation together with her mother-in-law decides on everyday issues. Other household tasks are distributed among the household members according to 'male' and 'female' gender obligations, age/generation and the availability of time. Concerning her grandchild a 48-year old woman states:

"I take her to the center and her greatgrandmother takes her outside for walks. I don't walk with her, I have plenty of domestic cares – ironing, laundry, cleaning, cooking. (Alm int 36: 14, female, 48 years, urban, Kazakh).

And she continues talking about the distribution of tasks in the household as follows:

"R: Basically I do all the housework – laundry, ironing, cleaning and cooking. My mother-in-law does laundry and irons her own clothes. My daughter irons her clothes by herself,

180 For § read "transcript paragraph"

but basically I do it all by myself. I cook by myself. If I am late or don't have enough time I can ask my mother-in-law to prepare something. My daughter doesn't have any responsibilities, we don't charge her, at the evenings and weekends she takes care of her child by herself, she baths her. Well, I stay at home so I can give her some free time.

I: Does your husband have any responsibilities at home?

R: What are you talking about?!

I: And do your sons have any responsibilities at home?

R: Only if I ask them to go grocery shopping or take away the garbage. The youngest son may vacuum. Otherwise we go grocery shopping with my daughter. We go to the supermarket and we buy a full car trunk and we return, and my sons unload the car. The men don't like doing shopping but they can unload purchases" (Alm int 36: 58-62).

As in many societies, the relation between wife and mother-in-law is not easy, sometimes extremely tense. Among ethnic Kazakhs, this is a major family problem. In Kazakh (and also in Uighur and Uzbek, but less in Russian) households a combination of age and social responsibility towards the parents of the husband makes wives subordinate to mothers-in-law. Usually the main burden of housework is put on them, while the mother-in-law takes command, sometimes over the education of children as well. To provide an example:

"My mother-in-law? We had lived together a long time, almost 7 years. I cannot say that it was the best time of our life [...]. She nagged constantly. Especially me. We have been living separately for a year now, and now I understand that she was the reason for our quarrels [...] She had no particular complaints, it was just endless whining. She also liked to grossly exaggerate, and liked scheming. There were endless problems. Also our apartment was too small for us. We lived in a two-room apartment, she slept over the wall. We could not invite anybody; because she always sat at home [...]. We have an easier life now. I noticed that our relationship has changed. Now everything is milder [...]. I think that her problem is that she has only one child, one son. If she had a few children, she would not 'cling' so much to Shuhrat (husband) and me" (Alm int 24: 20-28, female, 28 years, married, 1 daughter, urban, Uighur).

In the following case, the tensions between mother-in-law and respondent even caused divorce from her husband, although her mother-in-law did not live in the same household but close-by.

"Well, to tell the truth, [...] his mother came in between us [...]. Mother-in-law, in the truest sense of the word, controlled everything, what to buy. We even hid the purchases. Suppose we bought a refrigerator we hid it for half a year. [...] she dominated, always tried to control. She called every morning and asked why we were still sleeping, what we were cooking? Once again plow [rice]? Although it was cooked, suppose, two weeks ago. All the time it seemed to her that I cooked the wrong meals and so on, overbought, spent too much money. Of course, she controlled us. My husband – her only son, for some reason gave in to her. And I [...] thought that it was necessary to defend my own family [...] And you know I let her grumble, that is to say, I took a hands-off approach. I was engaged in business, was at work. At home everything seemed to be good, my husband loved me, lived in abundance, and children were safe and sound. ... I thought that everything was ok, she was a mother [...] There were no hard feelings; I didn't have any hostile attitude [...].That is to say, up to the situation when she went to Kazakh telecom, took the records of our phone expenditures, and showed them to him, saying that I called my parents [...]. The point is that my parents lived far from us, [...] three thousand kilometers; I saw them once a year [...]. In the end [...] we had such a cold war, he separated from me and then went to live with his mother, [...], that's all. As a consequence of all of above-mentioned, severance took place. Moreover, on his own initiative, he said that he wanted to divorce me that I should petition for divorce. I said to him that the divorce was not my idea, that the decision wasn't mine. And that I was not going to be liable for decisions not taken by me. Consequently, if he wanted to be divorced from me, he should petition for divorce by himself. [...] Without trial we were divorced"(Alm int 39: 75, female, 49 years, divorced, two children, urban, Kazakh).

The responsibility towards mothers-in-law can be so strong that some couples cannot found their own household:

"Of course, I would like to live separately, but it is impossible, because we can't leave my mother-in-law, because my brother-in-law does not work" (Alm int 20: 37, female, urban).

But of course there are also healthy relations between wives and mothers-in-law:

"She lives separately, but nearby our home. She is retired. We have a good relationship. Every day she picks up my daughter from school, prepares lessons. I think that we are beholding to her that our girl is a high achiever. Thanks to my mother-in-law for this" (Alm int 22: 78, female, 41 years, married with two children, urban, Uzbek).

"I mean my husband and I [take the decisions], because we both work. My mother-in-law probably feels ashamed to intervene in it [...]. Conflicts don't arise. My mother-in-law is a very loyal person. Even if she were offended she will not talk to me about it. There are no tensions between us" (Alm int 20: 23-25; female, married, 30 years, no children, urban, Kazakh).

As we shall see later in this chapter, structures of income and expenditure of households in the city and in rural areas differ from each other. In general, urban life is much more expensive, and this may explain why we frequently find other types of households.

Relatives in Nuclear and Extended Households

A common practice is cohabiting with relatives. A closer look at these relatives shows very different relations: brother or sister of the wife or the husband, children of the siblings of the wife or the husband, children of brothers and sisters of the parents (e.g. nephew of the husband in Alm int 1, rural, Kazakh; Alm int 25, urban, Kazakh), brother of the wife (e.g. Alm int 40, urban, Kazakh), sisters of the husband (e.g. Alm int 7, rural, Kazakh or Alm int 12, urban, Kazakh), or cousin of husband (Alm int 14, male, Kazakh), parent(s) of the wife, grandchildren, etc. Blood-relatedness to one of the household members seems to be the criterion that constitutes mutual responsibilities, reciprocity in help, and thus cohabiting. Usually such mutual support results from certain 'needs' of the hosted persons: sickness or unemployment, limited financial means for life in the city, insufficient time for their own children, old age and widowhood, divorce, etc.

Two interviews illustrate divorce as a reason of co-habitation. In both cases women are concerned. In one case (Alm int 39, female, urban, Kazakh), a woman with children takes her sister into the household, in another case (Alm int 10, female, urban, ethnicity unknown) a woman takes up her sister and her children. In the first case this is explained as an offer to the younger unemployed sister, in the second case to the sick and unemployed, even homeless sister and her children.

In some cases after divorce the former husbands do not care for their former wives and their children (e.g. Alm int 10: 22) although legally being responsible for alimony. In other cases divorced women are supported e.g. in the educational expenses for the children.

"Thank God, my ex-husband is sane in this issue. We have always aspired to provide our children with all the best. And we had paid all expenses in the school both official and off-the-record collections. We have been divorced for 4 years. Anyway he paid 6000 dollars for our daughter's education last year himself" (Alm int 39: 34, female, urban).

The incorporation of relatives into one's household is explicitly considered to provide support by the household members; in the city rent for an apartment is extremely high. In most cases the integration is only for some time, after which the guests will live apart again.

"[My wife's brother] has lived with us less than a year [. . .]. I do not feel very comfortable but support my wife. He works for a large firm. He is almost never here, he just comes overnight. [...He will stay until] spring probably" (Alm int 40: 37-40, male, 35 years, urban, Kazakh).

"At the moment my husband's nephew lives with us. When he studied at the university he lived in a dorm. Now he's just got a job. To rent an apartment is very expensive. Now he lives with us. How long he will stay? I don't know" (Alm int 25: 37, female, 34 years, urban, Kazakh).

"A. lives with us, she is my cousin. She is about 35 years, but not married. She's from my village, but is working in the city. She came to us in 2006 [...]. In 2008 she went to live alone, because she got accommodation in the place, where she was working. Then she left this job, came back to us and now has been living with us for half a year" (Alm int 12: 84, male, 38 years, urban, Kazakh).

Sickness and disability are other reasons to stay with relatives.

"We live in the apartment of my sister. She is a disabled person with first grade disability; and she requires physical and psychological care" (Alm int 32: 16, female, late middle age, urban, Kazakh).

"My husband lives here, my brother lives presently [in the household]. (...) he worked as a fisherman, came home rarely – once in 2 months, spent little time at home ... But then he got sick, he has tuberculosis" (Alm Int 6: 30-33, Alm, female, 49 years, rural, ethnicity unknown).

While these families support their sick relatives, they also get some support be it financially that they share the expenses, or by providing labor.

"The fact that they live here is not a burden at all to me. More hands in the house are always good. [...] Help in cleaning the house, somewhere to go. If I have to go somewhere I can leave my children with him. I am sure that my children are under the supervision of an adult male" (Alm int 25: 37-43, female, 34 years, urban, Kazakh).

Such a 'guest' says:

"I pay all utility payments, as I live here with my sons" (Alm int 32: 16, female, late middle age, urban, Kazakh).

"Yes, of course, once a month she [the cousin of the husband] buys the food. Also she helps us pay the rent. (...) [the cousin] helps her [the wife] with cleaning the house, cooking, looking after the children" (Alm int 12: 86-88, male, 38 years, urban, Kazakh).

"It is convenient for me [to live together with my sister and her children] and I think it's safer to live like that" (Alm int 10: 86, female, 40 years, urban, ethnicity unknown).

But such relatives in the household may also cause conflicts.

"My daughter doesn't like that my sister lives with us. She asks me when we will live separately. But she doesn't let on to her" (Alm int 10: 86, female, 40 years, urban, ethnicity unknown).

"The fact that he [brother-in-law living in the household] doesn't work is already a conflict. We did not find any relationship with him because we don't communicate with each other. He does not want to work. [...] Every time we try to start a conversation about work, he moves on to another topic" (Alm int 20: 37, female, 30, urban, Kazakh).

Another respondent prefers not to live with relatives. He refers to a Kazakh proverb saying:

"Our relatives live apart. Kazakhs have a saying, it is necessary to live with relatives at a distance from each other, but we, of course, communicate with them and we respect each other" (Alm int 5: 34, male, 52, rural, Kazakh).

Family Status

In our sample we find couples with children, those without children and widows with children. In the following we briefly discuss their household relatedness. The two latter cases are embedded in extended household constellations and will not be dealt here with. The majority of the sample (30 cases) is married couples with children, and even those who at the time of the interviews were childless expected children or were planning to have children. The results fit to the overall concept of "family" being in the minds of the people and being transported by politics. The analysis of the Almaty sample shows that none of the respondents lives alone. As a consequence of this, there is no single household or single – headed household, often being characteristic for higher vulnerability in literature (see Allan, Crow, 2001, 117 ff), living alone. Those having been divorced live in a new partnership. The following quotation provides an example. A 24-year-old rural divorced woman with one child lives with her boyfriend without being married; however, she considers this partnership as a non-official marriage and her partner as her "husband". From this interview, we learn that she wants to have a second child, but before she wants to remarry officially.

"I have a family, a child. I have a second husband, but we have no official registration. Of course, I want a second baby, but not now. Before, we will have to get married" (Alm, Int26: 13, female, 24, rural).

Only two cases represent married but childless couples. They explain that they postponed children because of the financial insecurity they live in. Only in one case of the sample, husband and wife live in separate places during the working week ("Sunday daddy") – it seems as a result of economic reasons (Alm int 32, female, middle age, Kazakh, urban).

The number of children in families is distributed as follows:

Table 63: Number of children in nuclear households

Number of children	1	2	3	4	5
Number of nuclear families	4	12*	5	6*	3

*) includes pregnancies

The statistical data on Almaty region[181] show a decrease of the average family size from 4.3 in 1999 to 3.7 in 2009, and for the urban population from 3.7 to 3.4 and rural population from 4.6 to 3.8. The sample data do not correspond to the statistical distributions since in our sample nuclear families with 2 and 4 children dominate.

The number of children in nuclear families corresponds to the reproduction age of the mother. Families with one child usually are rather young and expect more children in the future (e.g. Alm int 34, female, 27 years old, urban), or they "accidentally" have only one child, which is also semantically expressed in the interviews (e.g. Alm int 9: 9, female, 48 years old, Russian, rural: "but only one child"; Alm int 19, female, 46 years old, urban, Kazakh: "a late child"). In general, the age of the child corresponds to the age of the mother. Also women with young children usually have jobs while the children go to the kindergarten or childcare is done by the grandparent's generation if they live in the same house or close-by.

Families with children of course have much higher expenses that childless couples and this relates to almost two decades at least. This includes not only expenses for food and (fashionable) clothes, but particularly education fees, school books, transport of children to school etc. Expenses for education usually increase with the age of the child. The longer the education interval and the more overlapping the education of several children, the higher the financial expenses. Some children may be selected for scholarships, which eases the educational expenses. On the other hand, as we shall see later, a profound education will be topped by extra-curricular courses such as language courses, dance classes, sports classes etc.

[181] www.stat.gov.kz

While the majority of the sample households have the characteristics of double and more income-earning households, households with children require several incomes to be able to manage the educational fees, particularly in urban settings. In rural settings this relates to both monetary incomes and such in kind.

Older children, but also relatives from the grandparent generation may take over certain functions within the household, such as house and garden work or bringing the younger children to school or kindergarten. Usually these tasks are distributed according to gender roles.

There are seven cases of families with 4 or more children. Most of the wives support the households with income from jobs, from maternity leave, from subsistence production. We only found one household with a single income from the husband (Al mint 1). All other of these households had a differentiated income, e.g. monthly pension payments (Alm int 3), children's allowance, sale of livestock (Alm int 4), and incomes from formal and informal employments. Vulnerability particularly occurs because of seasonality of incomes as well as because of unexpected events (sickness or death of a relative; cattle raiding; and the breakdown of a car).

To sum up the family status: With the number of children the expenses of the households increase tremendously over a certain period at least where educational costs occur and overlap, so that these households may lack the financial means for other important expenses, particularly those for providing security for old age, unemployment or sickness. State transfers for such families are rather low. Double income earners and support by other relatives living in the households are important, and the lack of old-age security may in turn legitimize claims on the children's generation with regard to mutual intergenerational reciprocity. In urban conditions living conditions of large households/families in apartments are uncomfortable due to the sheer lack of space.

Household Positions and Decision Making

One question aimed at the identification of the social positions in the households. We wanted to find out who has the power over the household income(s), who takes decisions over the allocation of resources, and how decision-making processes occur.

Households with a Common Budget and Joint Decision-Making Processes

In the following we shall not talk about the cases with a sole breadwinner and a housewife without income. A first finding from the Almaty sample is that most households pool their incomes. The expenses are then covered from this household budget. While this is more or less obvious in a two-generation household with parents and children without their own income, this also applies to many extended households. To provide an example:

"Our budget is common. I receive my pension allocations and give it to the common budget. We all pay the food and utility services together. ... If they need something, they decide and buy it. ... If I have money in my pocket, I go to a shop and buy what I need: bread or milk. Certainly, I take money from our common budget. If anyone else needs to take money to go to work or to buy the necessary things in the shop, he will take money. It is a right order, I think" (Alm int 30: 27-30, female, urban).

But in some though rare cases, we find households with joint budgets and separate budgets; e.g. the main breadwinner may only a certain amount into the joint budget, according to his decision. He may also decide on the purchases (Alm int 27: 37ff., male, rural, Kazakh). In some households, often constituted of several generations with own incomes, household members may administer their own budget but pool money for particular occasions and for basic needs. In the following case brother and sister live together in the same place. They have their own incomes but share the rent and food expenses. For other expenses they support each other.

"When I was asphalting the courtyard, we clubbed together to do it. I'm building a sauna, but I do not have enough money for building materials. And she gives it to me out of her savings. Also we pay the rent together; and for food we have the same overall budget. Yes, in principle, she helps me well. When buying something big, she also pays half" (Alm int 10: 29-51, female, urban).

In the majority of cases we have at least two income earners per household, in other cases, however, only one. As in most societies, then, it is the women who stays at home and is the housewife.

But who takes decisions on what? We find different decision-making structures. In many cases husband and wife seem to decide jointly about larger expenditures and savings, while decisions on household utensils, nutrition and clothes for the children seem to be the wife's domain.

"We make the responsible decisions together, such as purchase of some large acquirements, though I am responsible for buying of food and general money distribution. We have no scandals at home, and if I bought a dress instead of sausage, everybody understands" (Alm int 29: 16, female, urban, Kazakh).

"Basically I am a kind of a person who considers spending only what I have. I am a foresighted person; for example, if I have to pay for my daughter's education, I save and pay for it in the first place. And then I live as I can. ... I do everything according to a plan" (Alm int 11: 38, female, urban, Kazakh).

Most husbands believe in the capability of their wives, sometimes also their children, to run the household budget what concerns everyday expenses.

"These solutions, not global, not related to the strategic issues, are taken by my wife and my children. I let them make these decisions" (Alm int 35: 42, male, urban, Kazakh).

"She buys food every time; I even don't calculate how much it cost" (Alm int 13: 95, male, urban 95).

"Therefore, in the case of uniform distribution of money, to plan the family budget my wife is master. We are still learning" (Alm int 18: 35, male, urban, Kazakh).

"He [husband] does not give me all the money – but the essential part. [...] It's my concern" (Alm int 36: 79, female, urban, Kazakh).

Sometimes husband and wife decide together about the everyday expenses or make a household budget plan, as the following quotation expresses.

"... we make decisions after joint discussions. For example, when we need to buy something for the house, because many affairs are associated with a woman, a woman executes them, but at that moment we discuss with my husband, decide them together, try to solve the affair" (Alm int 33: 13, female, rural, Kazakh).

"Sometimes we plan what we need to buy [for month] in advance" (Alm int 17: 34, female, urban, Kazakh).

The following quotation, an extraordinary case, is from a household with more financial capabilities. The husband explains that his wife and sometimes also the children decide even on more expensive consumer goods without consulting him as far as it does not concern "strategic" issues.

R: "Well, for example, to buy a refrigerator, television, or, for example, to buy something for New Year, etc. [...] I do not interfere" (Alm int 35: 42, male, urban, Kazakh).

In another case the husband even seems to hand over his full income to his wife.

"Now my wife is responsible for the distribution of money, I just earn the money and bring it to her" (Alm int 12: 88, male, urban, Kazakh).

These examples might suggest that the household is the realm of women and that the decisions are taken jointly or even by them. But a closer look at the material reveals that the husband, the eldest male etc. has the last word, at least over larger expenses

The following typical example shows this difference between daily household expenses and higher expenses in decision making. Additionally it hints at the mental orientation of many women, at first hand explaining that all are responsible for monetary decision making but in follow up questions then admitting that the last word is with their husband.

"I: Who in your family is responsible for the distribution of the basic family budget?

R: We together

I: For example, when you want to buy more expensive equipment for the home, who makes the decision?

R: Basically my husband" (Alm int 7: 62-65, female, rural, Kazakh).

The hegemonic position of men concerning the last word is not challenged by most of the females, even if they jointly discuss household issues.

"I: Do you solve issues together with your husband?

R: Honestly speaking, yes. I can say so. The male point of view is a sort of assurance and foresighted – it helps" (Alm int 29: 183, female, urban, Kazakh).

For this female speaker her "better half" is her husband whom she needs to assure herself in decision making what seems to be for her own well-being.

"We decide everything together, but my husband is an authoritative person, his word counts. I support him. We have no differences" (Alm int 31: 19, female, rural, Kazakh, similarly Alm int 39: 70-73 female, urban, Kazakh).

From most of the answers – having asked only one person of the households – nevertheless it seems clear, that consultation and negotiation do play a role but that the outcome is to the benefit of the males; be it that they have the last word or that women believe that it is to their best to integrate men's view into their decisions (see Allan, Crow, 2001, 88ff, who refer to the Western situation).

Households with Housewives

Housework is a "non-productive" work in the sense that is does not generate market values, and it does not engender a monetary income. Therefore it has a low status. The housewife's role has to be justified as it contradicts the societal role of women. Typical justifications are temporary non-employment due to decree leave, child-upbringing or health problems. Sometimes the reason is also lack of education:

"She is a housewife. She has a small three years' child, that's why she is sitting at home. She did not have time to study, because my son abducted her when she was 15 years old.[182] It is normal for Turk women... we study rarely" (Alm int 28: 39, female, 47years, rural, Turk).

"There was a time when she worked as a sales clerk. Now she is staying at home because of the problems with her health" (Alm int 27: 24, male, rural, Kazakh).

The housewife is busy doing the housework, looking after the children while particularly in rural regions the hard physical work around the house is a male affair. In three-generation households, often female pensioners take the role of the housekeeper and look after their grandchildren, as already shown above.

The low value of unemployment is mirrored in those interviews in which housewives don't want be compared with unemployed people.

"[When I was on child decree] I had (an additional job...). I sold cosmetics. I hadn't any considerable income from such trade. I myself also want to do something (...) I work due to this reason and to mix with people, so that no one can tell that I became a housewife (laughs)" (Alm int 33: 55-56, female, rural, Kazakh).

In the following example the role taking is a result of childbirth depression tensions in fulfilling different roles and the triple burdens as mother, (house)wife and laborer. This problem was already scientifically discussed during Soviet times, when ideology intended to make every adult contribute to the common good – independent from gender.

[182] Bride abduction happens more often than we expected not only in contemporary Kyrgyzstan from where it is often reported but also in Kazakhstan. If the wife is abducted without her consent she is pressed into marriage even by her own family, not to lose face (cf. Werner 2009). In two interviews we find reference to bride abduction. In the first case an old woman reports on village marriage practices at the time she was young.

"At that time women married early. Sometimes girls were asked for marriage, sometimes – abducted" (Alm int 37: 12). Also the second son of the 72-years old respondent abducted his wife. She and he graduated from KazNU. "She was going to celebrate her diploma, and my son abducted her. She is also a good daughter-in-law" (Alm int 37: 31, female, rural, Kazakh). In the second case a female Turk respondent also talks about his son's wife. "She did not have time to study, because my son abducted her when she was 15 years old. It is normal for Turks women... we study rarely [...]. My son fell in love. He was afraid that someone would steal her and stole her" (Alm int 28: 39-41, female, 47 years old, rural, Turk). From the last paragraph we may guess that bride abduction was rather frequent.

"I' have been at home for about a year. I had worked all my life. (...) It has advantages. I'm at home; the children are well-kept under control. (...) However, it is disadvantageous for your job. Slightly you lose your training. The more you sit, the more you lose. You're not practicing. In any case, you can go to enhance your competences. Go for further training. At the moment, my dream is to finish courses in English, go ahead. But now, it seems impossible.(...) On the one hand [I left my job because] it was like depression after delivery delay of two years. Have own problems, I' was tired of it. I was torn between home and work, and tried to find personal time for this and that. I decided to rest. And it was belated depression after childbirth. And so I think everything will be fine, in the future" (Alm int 25: 20-23, female, urban, Kazakh).

The Household Head

'Main breadwinner' and 'household head' are not synonymous. While from the position of 'main breadwinner' a high prestige and decision-making function may emerge, the 'household head' is a status position according to gender and age. No doubt, Kazakhstan is a patriarchal society. The role of the household head has traditionally been attributed to the oldest male member of the household, usually husband in two-generation households or (grand)father(-in-law) in three generation households or even grand-grand-father in four-generation households.

"Well, actually, according to Muslim tradition the head, the host, so to speak, at home is a man, who defines the policy, tactics and strategy of his family, his household" (Alm int 35: 22, male, urban, Kazakh).

"As a man, of course, I am the head of the family (...)" (Alm int 18: 33, male, urban, Kazakh).

"According to classical scheme, I am the head of the family" (Alm int 15, male, urban, Kazakh).

"I'm the head, of course. I have always been and will be. (Laughing)" (Alm int 12: 41-42, male, urban, Kazakh).

"My husband" (Alm int 28: 30-31, female, rural, Turk).

"I am not head of family, because I have a husband" (Alm int 11: 8, female, urban, Kazakh).

"The head of the family, in my opinion, should be the man, so the husband is the head of the family" (Alm int 19: 25, female, urban, Kazakh).

"Mmm, it is possible to tell, at home he is head, and the wife is the neck[183] (laughs)" (Alm int 1: 15-16, male, rural, Kazakh).

In the above cited cases the two status criteria do not conflict, as the male is the main breadwinner, too. Interesting are those cases where gender roles change, for example, when two- or three-generation households are incomplete as a consequence of divorce or death of the male household head. Let us consider the case of divorce. Although the woman in the following example has to play both the role of breadwinner and household head (female-headed household), she feels her incompleteness:

"In the context of upbringing, provision of material needs on a whole, I think it is difficult. (...) Nevertheless, I am able to provide for my children, practically independently. This is the first aspect. The second one: from the physical standpoint, I have time to pay attention to my children (...). At the same time it is my belief that the role of a father, role of a man in the family, is indispensable, in any case – somehow it is insufficiently... I cannot say that I'm so cool, that I supersede the role of a man, a husband, a father. Especially it is strongly affecting bringing up children. You know, lack of father's role, father's approach. Especially such lack I feel with my son. That is to say, nevertheless there is such a concept of a full family. I admit this fact, although from the other side it seems why I need a husband, a man? Everything goes smoothly. But in depth of my heart, nevertheless, it is a vacuum" (Alm int 39: 68-69, female, urban, Kazakh).

Now let us consider those cases where the oldest person in the household is a woman. Who will then take the position of household head and decision-maker? Does age range before gender or gender before age? The interviews show that sometimes age ranges before gender. The oldest woman can well take over the position of household head, even if she does not have her own income in addition to her pension. But it may also be the other way round that the parents are respected and approached for advice while the main decision-maker is the grown-up younger son, the main breadwinner:

"The main decisions are made by my younger son, but he comes to me for advice: 'May be I should do it in this way or that way' And I say to him: 'sonny, you are the head of our household, do as you think' If the questions are very difficult, then he will consult his elder brothers [living abroad]. If the question is extremely difficult, we rely on the opinion of the eldest son. All my children listen to him, seek his advice" (Alm int 37: 13-14, female, rural, Kazakh).

[183] This literally means that the wife (neck) follows the husband (head).

Here the oldest son – in cases of very difficult decisions to be taken – becomes 'head of the family' cutting across the role of 'head of household'. So, in general, age and gender have to be made compatible.

In some cases the women earn more than their husbands, but the respondents still attribute the household head position to the man.

"The head of our family is my husband, but the rate of his salary is 60 thousand KZT. I earn 90 thousand KZT per month" (Alm int 17: 32, female, urban, Kazakh).

"As a man, of course, I am the head of the family. I do not know what criteria you use to identify the head of the family. If we proceed from the one who earns more, then my wife earns more. Unlike me, she has been engaged in her activities for 15 years, and I did more creative activities at that time. From an economic point of view, of course, the head of the family is my wife, she has a steady income" (Alm int 18: 33, male, urban, Kazakh).

Also in the next case the wife is the main breadwinner, but she subordinates herself to her husband:

"I am not head of the family, because I have a husband, and together we make the major decisions; in most cases, I consider his opinion. Therefore I think I am not a head of my family" (Alm int 11: 8, female, urban, Kazakh).

"We decide everything together, but my husband is an authoritative person, his word counts. I support him. We have no differences" (Alm int 31: 19, female, rural, Kazakh, similarly Alm int 39: 70-73 female, urban, Kazakh).

Only in one case out of 40, the interviewee, a woman, considers herself as head of the household

"because I am responsible for all main purchases, expenses and the money distribution" (Alm int 29: 12-13, female, married, urban, Kazakh).

The role of household head sometimes is disputed. But this is rarely the case.

"Sometimes he starts muddying the water. But I do not pay attention. With the experience of life I do like this: I present that thing as if it was his idea. He came up with it, I seemed to just agree. In fact, it was my idea – mine" (Alm int 25: 27, female, urban, Kazakh).

"My husband and I – we both are the earners. All important decisions we make together, but in some cases I consider all possible options and then I propose them to my husband to choose one. At his choice, as the saying goes" (Alm int 32: 6-8, female, urban, Kazakh).

But in general the male dominance is still functioning and goes without saying. The "collective nature of much family life" (Allan, Crow 2001, 11) should not obscure this fact, overwhelmingly documented also by our interviewees be the male or female. Changes exist especially in the field of doing household chores but they rarely touch on the formal and informal roles of males being household heads.

We finish with some quotations that hint at democratic families and thus change. The case of consulting and negotiating is evident in our interviews in a number of households. The respondents in these cases talk about democratic families or e.g. of a 'family council' (cf. Allan & Crow, 2001:12):

"All is put to the family council. We come to a consensus" (Alm int 25: 27, female, urban, Kazakh).

"In this regard, we have a democratic family, all the issues we are taking together, discussing every detail" (Alm int 18, 35, male, urban, Kazakh).

"We are a democratic family, so we both take decisions. When it relates to major purchases, for example real estate or a car we always decide together. And the rest of little items, such as buying yoghurt, is usually done by us (laughing)" (Alm int 13: 14, urban, two respondents, so that gender unknown).

"In general we decide together about our economic affairs, finance, the budget.[...] Well, for example, it may be the purchase of property or purchase of furniture" (Alm int 35: 22-23, male, urban, Kazakh).

Conclusions

What conclusions can be drawn from the discussion of household structure and decision-making? The first conclusion refers to the theoretical concept. The data allow us to argue that the open household concept is useful in demonstrating the interrelatedness of household members by pooling incomes, by supporting children, the elderly and those being ill or handicapped. The income may come also from migrants working abroad but still counted as belonging to the household. The households can and should be looked at as a network constituted by various social actions. Those are based on norms and values. Quite often they represent traditional Kazakh beliefs. The second conclusion concerns the household positions themselves. While the conception of household head is in all cases except one attributed to males, it may either be linked with the age status or income status (main breadwinner) as a second criterion. Household head and male main breadwinner often but not always coincide. Sometimes women earn more than their husbands, but nevertheless, he is the household head. Women may cut across the gender hegemony of males concerning the position of household head in incomplete households where the oldest woman is a widow and steps into the role of her deceased husband. However, the other case is also possible, that her son will become the household head. The concept of 'family head' is also interesting, being usually the oldest living male. Here the family is a network cutting across different households. In general, however, women have a lower status than men, and younger women a lower status than older women.

The decision-making processes cover a wide spectrum, ranging from the household being the women's realm over the household (or family) as a democratic council to the labor division that women are concerned with household expenses and men with larger expenses, or even the autocratic household where the man has the last say or – in the strongest case- even decides everything with or without consultation of the wife and other female household members. As in many societies, the position of the housewife is critical, because she does not contribute to the household budget with an income and therefore is attributed a lower status. The status of housewife needs legitimation as it contradicts norms of structural equality existing since soviet times.

Major Problems in Almaty City and Almaty Region

When asked about specific problems, people will talk about them. This is especially true if people had to cope with challenges in their past, they had not experienced before and which represent major socio-psychological stress-factors for them: the breakdown of the Soviet Union. It implied the demise of a whole way of life, the development of a new national identity and the financial crises of 2007/8. It is against this catalogue of factors, built by people's experiences, that they view their current situation. The material concerning the topics addressed is extremely rich and can't be represented here in detail. We only illustrate certain topics.

Many problems reported are related to the general socio-economic situation. In addition to unemployment this concerns i.e. food prices, salaries, corruption, inflation, security and crime, infrastructure and some more issues. In general, the whole action frame that touches on vulnerabilities is a topic: policies, institutions, general conditions and processes. In describing these topics, we hope to enhance the understanding of the different areas of vulnerability prevailing in the Almaty region. The following chapters about employment and income expand the view given here.

The past experience

The transformation period from about 1991 to about 1998 was felt by most people as a constant crisis. A respondent nowadays working in real estate business and his wife working in a commercial enterprise remembers how his family managed everyday life by taking up many different income generating activities.

"There were the 1990s. [...] Crisis had been lasting until 1998 in Kazakhstan. He [the son of the respondent] lived most of his time with his grandfather and his grandmother, until the 1stgrade, and we lived here trying to survive, trading, selling and so on, trying almost everything" (Alm int 13: 85, male, urban, also Alm int 35, male, urban).

"I myself experienced this phenomenon, unemployment. [It happened] during the transition to the market in the 1990th, I was sitting a year without work, then in 2000, I was out of work again. At that time my spouse worked, she provided the family with income. Well, then I found a job in my specialty. At one time she too had no work" (Alm int 35: 31-33, male, urban).

The next respondent, a teacher in a public school and her husband also working in the public services reconsider the difficult times and the more recent developments.

"At that time [1990s] it seemed to me that we lived in a time of war. After independence, we have passed through the transitional period, reached a level of development, which we are observing now. There are people who worked for the state, and they were left with nothing, there are others that have gone into trade, business, and later became wealthy. If we grow at the same pace through 2030, we will achieve good results" (Alm int 16: 63, female, urban).

Not all respondents are equally optimistic concerning long term development; especially as crises returned for many in 2007/8 (e.g. Alm int 21: 152, female, urban; Alm int 23: 75, male, urban). Others see a new crises in 2013, due to high inflation (Alm int 19: 47, female, urban), but for many the situation today is different from that of the 1990^{s} and even if they complain about the loss of security of the soviet times, they see the recovery from the 90s.

Unemployment

Nevertheless, during the time of our interviews, the respondents looked upon unemployment as one of the most important problems in the rural Almaty region while we do not find any direct complaints concerning unemployment in Almaty city though there is anxiety for the situation in the future.

"Then we came with our diplomas here, to M village. But we couldn't find a job here..." (Alm int 31: 6, female, rural, married, 3 children).

"Unemployment happens here. If you leave one job, it is impossible to find another one" (Alm int 3: 27, male, rural).

The chances to find a job in the rural regions seem to be related to bribery, f-connections (Ben-Porath 1978),[184] '*blat*' (Ledeneva 2006) etc. That sets market criteria out of force. Furthermore, the working conditions (hard work, irregular and delayed payments) are considered to be a major problem (see further down).

Rising Prices, Low Salaries and Inflation

Prices are another topic that is tackled in all interviews.

"The prices have overtaken our salaries"(Alm int 5: 76, male, rural).

"For several years I have been watching and comparing fluctuations in food prices, which rise every year. I can say this with confidence. No matter how many times deputies discussed about it, there is no end to the rise in prices" (Alm int 17: 65, female, urban; see also Alm int 33: 63, female, rural).

People also mention that they suffer from costly rents and utility payments.

"Utility payments became much more expensive. Even in summer we pay around 20, 000 KZT. Even for these 58 square meters" (Alm int 32: 30, female, urban).

"There are problems. Because of the growing rates for rents, electricity, housing and utilities, the expenses are constantly growing. Problems grow, transportation costs increase, rising gasoline prices" (Alm int 35: 147, male, urban).

Lack of financial resources that means low incomes in combination with high prices is regarded by many of the respondents to be one of their major problems in the household's everyday lives. This argument often is combined with a reference to, inflation (e.g. Alm int 14, 27, 28) that eats up wage or pension increases.

"It does not matter what raises in salary we get, we are not able to catch up with the market. The prices have overtaken our salary" (Alm int 5: 76, male, rural).

So, the monetary budget is insufficient to make a decent living, sometimes chronically, sometimes periodically.

184 'F-connections' are a synonym for 'families, friends and firms'.

"Our budget fully absorbs our revenues. Our expenses exceed our revenues. We have to borrow" (Alm int 25: 53, female, urban, also Alm int 10: 66, female, urban).

"A difficulty [...] is the lack of money. Everywhere money is needed. For example, even taking a regular medical check-up. We pass the medical check-up for free in the place where we are registered (propiska), but in many cases due to lack of necessary equipment, we are compelled to apply to a private hospital. We spend about 30-40,000 KZT at once. This amount is equal to half of our wages. We buy food, clothing, appropriate for our revenues. If wealthy people are buying clothes for 100,000 KZT, we spend 3-5,000 KZT" (Alm int 16: 57, female, urban).

"From time to time we do not have enough money [...] As we have a family, we have a lack of finance. Now every problem is connected with money" (Alm int 2: 23, female, rural).

Sometimes we are short of money, short of 100 000. For example, we pay money for the livestock, for keeping our livestock, for cows, horses; then we may need money. One asks for money, another one asks, then children may want some new clothes. They may want to go to the resort; then they may be short of money. So, we sell the livestock, make use of this money. This is our situation" (Alm int 37: 45, female, rural).

The last quotation aptly demonstrates how livestock property is converted back into money when it is needed for monetary expenses. Lack of money in the rural area is extremely felt when high expenses occur in autumn to prepare for the winter.

"When the winter comes, there is not enough money. Because in autumn we prepare hay for the livestock. Also, we buy coal .... It is necessary for winter preparation. Besides, children go to study. Different clothes are necessary for them. At this time there are some difficulties. Relatives help in these difficult cases. We borrow money from them. Well, when there is a possibility, we return the money" (Alm int 1: 28, male, rural).

Some couples even postpone their wish of getting a child, due to financial constraints as indicated above (e.g. Alm int 27).

Bad Infrastructure

Bad infrastructure is particularly a rural issue, which is addressed by many respondents. This concerns comfort in the living place, public educational institutions, health services, water provisions, electricity and gas, internet, bad roads, transportation services.

"If we talk about infrastructure, we should say that we do not have such. We even do not have some of the channels shown in other villages, cannot install Internet. Plumbing this year has begun, but has not been finished yet" (Alm int 7: 80, female, rural).

"Although our village is close to the city, it is badly developed. There are only small shops, we haven't got any good service, and there is no pharmacy. Doctors tell us that they are not allowed to open one, because it is necessary to have a special pharmaceutics license and there is no premise for it, too" (Alm int 9: 25, female, rural).

"In our village they shut off the electricity; refrigerators got broken" (Alm int 9: 65, female, rural).

"There is still no gas... The roads have been destroyed by trucks (...). We are paying taxes for transportation, but we don't have normal roads, we should have facilities for disabled people" (Alm int 8: 138, 143, 159, 203, female, rural, disabled; similarly Alm int 27: 266, male, rural and Alm int 9: 93, female, rural).

The water problem is addressed in many rural interviews. This concerns drinking as well as irrigation water in quantity as well as in quality.

"Our district lacks drinking water. So many families lack drinking water. The situation has been the same for many years. Since we moved here. This problem has not been solved by anyone, and none tries to solve it. We draw water from a place 1 km away. In winter, our children and grandchildren bring water on toboggans. We have a small garden, but we have no irrigation water to plant it. Sometimes, we even can't find drinking water. There is an old water pipe, it breaks from time to time, and then there is no water in the village. It's difficult without water. Sometimes the drinking water is dirty, with clay. Just like the water in aryks [street water channels – typical for Central Asian countries]. In other words, in K. there is even water in some toilets, but we have no drinking water [...]. In 2003 drinking water should be laid. But that money was happily "eaten" [...]...it is still absent" (Alm int 4: 44, male, rural; similarly Alm int 5: 73, male, rural).

"We want to have a central sewage and plumbing. I am not sure whether we are drinking clean water" (Alm int 8: 139, 143, female, rural).

Women (Alm int. 9: 25, 114) report that they downsized their gardens because of lack of irrigation water. Some even can't drink the water from the well, because it is dirty and they have to buy expensive bottled water in Almaty. Other women (Alm int 6: 74, female, rural) report lack of irrigation water in summer, which severely affects their businesses.

And quite often our respondents make comparisons, especially those from the older generation:

"20 years ago conditions in our village were much better; we had irrigation water, pastures. We have a 18 hectare site, we could work a garden. We don't have such an opportunity any more, as there is no water [...]. Rangeland is also lost, because around our village some people bought land, a lot of private land, so we cannot keep cattle" (Alm int 7: 29, female, rural).

Many rural respondents also talk about the *bad transport system*, which affects them in many spheres of their lives.

"There is no bus to get away from this village. We all take taxis due to this inescapable situation. We survive on pensions, but taxis" (Alm int 4: 47, male, rural).

"Unfortunately, the situation with transport is too bad... We would like to have more buses. If I could bring my child to school by bus, not by car, it would be much cheaper. But now I have to do a roundtrip to K. by car. Thanks to my parents we have a 'Lada', they left it to us" (Alm int 9: 86, female, rural).

"We have difficulty with transportation in our village, also there are no pharmacies or hospitals. It is difficult for villagers" (Alm int 7: 81, rural, female).

While the vast majority of the rural respondents complain about lack or insufficient transportation and the costs accompanying this, the urban population complains about traffic jams.

"[The biggest problem] is traffic jams, because our son studies far from home. He spends one hour in the morning and in the evening to go to and come from school. Sometimes it takes him even more. For a child it is really complicated" (Alm int 22: 132, female, urban).

Interestingly enough, some people don't relate traffic jams to the large number of private cars or a malfunctioning of public transportation, but to bad control by the traffic police, or bad distribution of traffic lights, which implies that the administration does not keep pace with modernity, that is cars.

For villagers lack of*educational facilities and public medical services* is also a topic of common complaint.

"There is no kindergarten in our village, so I have to bring him to the kindergarten in K. [next larger center] in the morning and to take him out at 5 o'clock in the evening" (Alm int 9: 22, female, rural).

"Our village is located 14 km away from K. The village has no hospital, and in K. there are no qualified doctors, therapists, optometrists, they do not have modern equipment. Recently I had a sick relative; she had to go to examination of the stomach to Almaty, because the hospital did not have even a basic probe. An ophthalmologist is the same, there is no machine [...] The most important basic question for the people, it's health" (Alm int: 96, female, rural).

"It is even not possible to get ill. In the government hospitals there are no places, that's why people must use the private ones. I don't have money to pay 5,000 KZT per day. So, for me the main thing is not to get ill, because my children should go to school and eat normally" (Alm int 8: 201, female, rural; see also Alm int 26:114, female, rural).

But also in the city people complain about health services, because public health institutions are insufficient, and payment of private doctors is very costly.

"The state medicine service is [...] not good. There are lines in clinics constantly. You just need connections; then you will not have a problem" (Alm int 34: 153, male, urban).

"Everywhere money is needed. For example, even for taking a regular medical check-up. We pass medical check-ups for free in the place where we are registered to live [propiska], but in many cases due to lack of necessary equipment, we are compelled to apply for paid hospitals. We spend about 30-40,000 KZT at once. This amount is equal to half of our wages" (Alm int 16: 57, female, urban).

Internet connections in the rural regions do not exist is reported consentingly. Reported attempts to get connections failed. Thus also long distance learning on that base is not possible (Alm int 6: 23, female, rural; Alm int 7: 81, female, rural). In the city, internet is easily available.

Corruption

Corruption is a general problem in Kazakhstan. People are especially annoyed about favoritism and bribery in job search but also concerning public services.

"All is destroyed, no order. There is just only the name of our government left. Everything is done – theft, grabbing. Corruption is everywhere" (Alm int 4: 37, male, rural, shortly before pension age; see Alm int 2: 263, rural, male).

"There is much corruption. I left my job, because I did not want to be involved in anything. The police is also corrupt now.... They are only interested in money. Now you only have to trust yourself. No one else" (Alm int 38: 32, male, urban, 48 years).

"We celebrated the 20th anniversary of our independence in 2011. Our state is no longer young. If you remember all the events in the past, we have clearly reached a lot. But our government has something to work on. Because where corruption occurs, there will be no improvement of the social conditions of the population. Of course, the state is struggling with this social evil"(Alm int 16: 61, 65, female, urban, a teacher at the secondary school).

"In Kazakhstan, of course, corruption is rampant, all the time" (Alm int 7: 78, rural, female).

A woman, interestingly a lawyer, legitimizes favoritism and corruption in Kazakhstan as follows:

"We are from Asia, oriental people. In any case, we have corruption. Why? Because we have our own culture and another mindset. In general, the term corruption has an elastic notion. ... We are Kazakhs, and we are imbued with reverence, veneration, unity and mutual assistance. Imagine how I gained positions and I'm an akim [mayor]. For instance, you are my sister, a relative. Of course, I shall want to raise you into a post, and this is ok. There are my acquaintances, friends. Somebody drinks, somebody has a depression but I consider it my duty to render assistance to the future of that man. [...] with pleasure I make gifts to doctors, to my specialists. Or I give money. This is an expression of my gratitude or my confidence, or respect" (Alm int 39: 224, 230, female, urban).

This interviewee distinguishes between 'gifts' that can and should be given to teachers, doctors etc., because of gratitude and large scale corruption which she condemns.

Crime and Insecurity

High rates of crime are taken for granted by the respondents both in the city and in the villages. Parents usually do not allow their children to walk alone at night.

"We do not allow our children to go out at night. If the daughter A goes somewhere, she does it only with friends; we tell them that they have to bring her home till 12 at night. We call her from time to time. She reports when she comes back home. The younger daughter does not leave anywhere, generally she plays in the house yard"(Alm int 2: 45, female, rural, female, the elder daughter being 20 years old, see also Alm int 3: 54, male, rural, male).

"Although I love walking, I always try to take a taxi, even if there is only two quarters to go" (Alm int 29: 176, female, urban).

"It seems that it is safe here, but we try not to go out after 8 or 9 in the evening. Recently one guy was missed. He came home after work at 2 o'clock, somebody called him and he left the house. Nobody can find him since" (Alm int 12: 144, male, urban).

Not only walking but also driving seems to be dangerous at night (Alm Int 30: 234, male, urban). The next respondent reports about burglary.

"My daughter's apartment was robbed during three hours absence. She lives with her husband's parents. All together they went on a visit, during this time the apartment door was broken. They have taken all the gold and the computer. Police said that it was the eighth theft in a week. Now we are also afraid to leave the house unattended" (Alm int 38: 30, male, urban).

The next respondent feels safe in the new condominium which is watch-guarded while another one complains about safety in general.

"It was more criminality around our old house. Now we live in a new house with a safety zone, with entrance barriers. I feel calmer. Homeless people are not walking around here" (Alm int 21: 191, female, urban).

"Our country is not safe to live in. In terms of security, we probably are at the very last place among all countries, if such a rating exists" (Alm int 15: 73, male urban).

The feeling of insecurity is also negatively influenced by the belief in insufficient functioning of public security structures.

"No one protects me, the government is absent. If anyone kills me, someone would come and say 'This man was murdered, find out.' And that's all" (Alm int 4: 28, male, rural).

"As to criminality, there is cattle rustling, this is also a crime. 3-4 years ago somebody stole us a lot of beasts. [...] Nobody searched. We wrote an application. When we visited them for the second time, they couldn't find our first application. MIA (Ministry of Internal Affairs) does not work here. It's only a name. There is also no benefit from militia [police]. They just denude people of money" (Alm int 4: 41, male, rural).

Comparisons play a role in forming people's opinions because this neglect of the security forces is looked upon as different among nations, regions, and according to time:

"For example, in other places, the administration establishes complexes, the livestock is fattening, they grant credits, provide support. Mainly, in the North and the East Kazakhstan regions. The Russians predominantly live there, and where the Russians are, there is order. But where the Kazakhs live, there is always a 'but'. We think, if we say so, then may be tomorrow, someone always says 'but'" (Alm int 4: 41, rural, male).

Sometimes we find certain xenophobic worries:

"Sometimes I worry about the large number of newcomers from all the regions of Kazakhstan ... I understand why the people come to the big cities: to subsist with their families. On the other hand, the image of the city is rather spoilt concerning safety issues and in general esthetically. But I cannot say I dislike those people, although the criminal situation in the city has been worsening because of those people. But I did not face any such situation, thanks Allah. There are many rumors" (Alm int 29: 168, female, urban).

"Migration, there are many migrants in the city. Naturally, this affects the crime situation" (Alm int 35: 151, male).

Environmental Pollution and Degradation

In addition to the water problems already mentioned, environmental pollution and degradation takes place in many spheres and are mentioned as problems that affect the respondents both in the countryside as well as in the city.

"We would like the trash is not taken out of the city to where people live. This is harmful to the health of those citizens" (Alm int 19: 65, female, urban).

"For example, there are 4-5 brick factories in our village. Who needs them? It's just dust round us. And this is near A. resort. It will be impossible to live here in the future.... Earlier, in the Soviet period, there was a single plant in Y district in T, it was a brick factory. And now there are brick factories everywhere. There are ecological problems. All is destroyed, no order" (Alm int 4: 37, male, rural).

"The village was clean, tidy, we used to call it 'Little Switzerland'. Now we do not have a dumping ground, we pour our garbage everywhere, and that's not very good. Even when you drive [you see] fly garbage bags everywhere, it is shocking" (Alm int 6: 141, female, rural; see also Alm int 13: 229, male, urban).

"Ecology is a problem, I want to live in an environmentally safer city part" (Alm int 22: 132, urban, female, see also Alm int 35, male, urban, male).

Many people believe that it is healthier to live outside the city because of the cleaner air conditions.

"I work in the city and I think that it is wrong to breathe city's air all the time. The people should have a country house" (Alm int 39: 57, female, urban; see also Alm int 8: 200, female, rural and Alm int 34: 144, male, urban).

Deterioration of Living Conditions

Many respondents complain about the drastic deterioration of living conditions especially for youth, lacking decent employment and thus also a perspective for family foundation and for keeping up the intergenerational relationships.

"When I think about the future, I think not of myself, but about our youth. I am really concerned that this youth goes unemployed. As a lot of youth are now unemployed, they go single. A lot of them have not established a family, 'have not kissed children'" (Alm int 5: 79, male, 52 years, Kazakh, rural).

These people believe measures by the government like raising the pension age as counterproductive and also do not believe in programs to bring young people back into rural areas:

"Due to unemployment all people go to the city for earnings. The things are also difficult in the city, they need housing and registration. All problems of the youth have started exactly from this. For example, they say "with diploma to village"[185] Everything is wonderful on TV, everyone goes to the 'aul' [village]. But I see no youth in our village. There is no such perspective in our village... You are left alone, and you leave alone" (Alm int. 4: 18, male, rural).

Respondents, who talk about this topic believe, that the trend of outmigration from the villages will go on, due to lack of employment in the countryside leaving the older generation alone in the villages (Alm int 27: 238, male, rural; Alm int 4: 37, male, rural).

Social Problems

The problems of unemployment and the difficult rural living conditions are looked upon as related to alcoholism and drug addiction which are reported to be far-spread among the rural male population affecting both young and old.

"Our children and their generation drink a lot. These are children who cannot really find something to do. Before, we had a club and a disco, cinema. Yes, we do not have enough work" (Alm int 6: 143, female, rural; see also Alm int 8: 145, female, rural).

"There are also many unemployed people, drinkers, they steal, of course" (Alm int 9: 105, female, rural).

"...I have no idea from where they get the marihuana. Most of the local population is addicted to it. A lot of people just waste their time, they are unemployed" (Alm int 8: 180, female, rural).

To sum up: In general, most of our middle class households view their future optimistically especially if viewed against the transition period and against the financial crises of the past. Quite dispersed over all interviews we find comparisons especially with neighboring countries that seem at least partly to make for this

185 This is a special government project which started in 2009 and according to which in 2011, about 2,102 young professionals have received loans and 6742 got grants. The majority of credit-receivers are represented by professionals in Aktobe, West Kazakhstan and in South Kazakhstan villages: http://bnews.kz/en/news/post/114192/. The main goal is to keep resp. to bring young people into rural areas (see http://www.auezov.almaty.kz/page.php?page_id=896&lang=2).

view of their general living conditions. Nevertheless, there is a strong difference between people from the countryside and those from Almaty. The former view their future less optimistic and have stronger complaints in detail. Being optimistic does not mean that the respondents have no complaints about their living conditions. Most of them feel threatened by unemployment. Quite often, this refers also to those who have a job. That is, we believe, that the new economic conditions are felt as a general threat to many of the respondents. Prices and especially those for housing play a similar role concerning uncertainty among many respondents. People from the countryside very strongly complain about bad infrastructure quite often with an undertone of resignation. This refers also to corruption and includes the interviewees from Almaty.

Employment and Income in the Urban Situation

Employment is a major problem of all people being interviewed – even if they currently have a job about which they do not complain and even if they admit that the situation in Almaty is not bad in this respect. As the experience of life-long employment security has been lost, many respondents are afraid that their jobs might be endangered in the future, might not fit to labor market needs because of age or specialty (Alm int 29: 159 – 163, female, 37 years, urban; also Alm int 19: 38, female, 46 years, urban). The great anxiety is, that children, especially, will not find employment after graduation. Additionally, searching for jobs does not seem to be easy.

"My daughter recently graduated from university, and we went to look for a job. This is certainly a global problem. Economists are usually not required in small businesses. There is a chief accountant, and he or she is an economist as well; there is no need for economists. Therefore, it is very difficult now to find a job. I will tell you that labor law is disregarded in banks. That is: twelve-hour workday with a meager salary. And there is no guarantee that a kid will continue to work there. We have to pay for probation, for an internship, for a training [...]. An internship is worth 40,000 KZT; training 40,000 KZT just as probation. And still there's no security that the job is guaranteed. I was very outraged. One encounters such kind of problems now. I cannot say that is a special for a particular bank. This situation is in all banks. My daughter and I made the round in a few banks. Just where we go, the rate is the same everywhere. The unemployment problem is terrible, of course" (Alm int 11: 57, 59, female, urban).

"He's a lawyer by profession. We have spent a lot of money for his education, but now he cannot find a job. It is usually so in our country..." (Alm int 23: 33, male, urban).

Some people also complain that in job searching, it is necessary to have influential acquaintances, friends and relatives to get a job (e.g. Alm int 36: 98, 151, female, urban, Kazakh). To start certain businesses seems to be very expensive because of licenses and bribery to certain administrative departments.

"If I would like to leave my current job and start my own business, it would be very difficult to do so. You need a lot of money [...]. In our country, [...] licenses have to be paid for. So, such things slow down the process and put a spoke in one's wheel. The problem is that patents and licenses are expensive. Maybe it is worth telling about corruption, because some [inspecting authority] will find to cavil at something in any case. Doing business is only possible if a person has enough money" (Alm int 16: 59, female, urban, Kazakh).

However, the majority of respondents claim that they never had to ask someone to help them find jobs or to pay someone to get a job. Instead, they accentuate, that human capital and education play decisive roles for finding employment in the urban areas (e.g. Alm int 35: 117, male, urban, Kazakh; Alm int 14: 153, female, urban, Russian; Alm int 30: 105, female, urban, Russian; Alm int 29: 123, female, urban, Kazakh).

The topic of good education is explored further in the chapter on education.

Insecurity and Fear of Job Loss

Those who have a job in the private sector often fear losing it due to the next slump (e.g. Alm int 11: 66, female, urban; Alm int 20: 41, female, urban, Alm int 30; 22, female, urban). A sales-manager argues:

"We are employees: today we have a job, tomorrow they say goodbye to us. But I am not afraid of it. I have learned to believe in myself, this belief helps living" (Alm int 29: 188, urban, female, Kazakh).

Even state employees with a comparably high job security are afraid. The 47-year female teacher says:

"I always feel anxious, fear of losing my job. Being dismissed on grounds of redundancy does not allow me to relax. If we see it from another point of view, then we have no additional skills for anything. We are bound hand and foot to only one job, do not have any alternatives" (Alm int 16: 47, female, urban, Kazakh).

Badly Paid Jobs in the Public and in the Private Sector

Respondents complain about badly paid jobs in the public sector, especially in the field of health and education where there are no possibilities to make a second living.

"Teachers work from morning till night, and receive an average of 50-60,000 KZT. This does not correspond to the level and requirements of a market era, because life is becoming more expensive every day. We pay for educational materials from our own pockets. I believe that the amount of our salary is low. The state should raise wages for teachers and doctors, in the first place. There is no support from the state"(Alm int 17: 65, female, urban, Kazakh; also Alm int 16: 37, female, urban; also Alm int 19: 35, female, urban).

Therefore not a few have changed from the public to the private sector:

"My higher education is German language teacher, but now I work as an Import Purchasing Manager, that is, Import Manager in a large company in Kazakhstan with a net of shops" (Alm int 29: 6, female, urban, Kazakh; also Alm int 30: 10, female, urban, Russian; Alm int 22: 14, female, urban, Uzbek).

"Now a babysitter has a salary higher than a teacher. Babysitters have a salary of 80,000 KZT, that's why all babysitters are ex-teachers" (Alm int 14: 15, female, urban, Russian).

However, nowadays public employees have the advantage of receiving regular salaries on time, while salary payments in private businesses are sometimes delayed.

"... sometimes we face wage delays, sometimes we even don't have our salary paid. I had worked for many years in construction. There were many cases of exploitation. Employers deceived us" (Alm int 19: 27, female, urban, Kazakh).

"If people receive wages on time, they would not take food on credit. They have to feed the family" (Alm int 19: 57, female, urban).

Most interviewees stress, that private employment is better paid than public. But also in private enterprises some people are badly paid if they do not have higher education and profiles which are in high demand, or if they are migrants from other Central Asian states. The position of such people is very weak compared to the power of the employers.

"In private companies it is the same situation. People get a job without an employment contract; so for these organizations everywhere is 'green light', even if they decide not to pay, there is nothing to make them to pay [...]. This is especially true in the construction industry. Employers mobilize the Uzbeks, Kyrgyz, because if they employ our citizens, they will demand more money. For example, in Uzbekistan the products are 10 times cheaper than here. They say that they live for 10,000 KZT per month, for us this sum is enough only for 2 days" (Alm int 19: 66-71, female, urban).

Employment Types and Possibilities in the Urban Area

In the vast majority of urban interviews, the respondents indicate jobs and incomes for all adult household members before pension age. Many people prefer or would prefer to work in the state sector because in their eyes, it offers more employment security and secure pensions. The public sector is an important employer in Almaty for middle class households which aim at security. Such households typically do not aim at the maximization of financial capital but prefer stability and often prestige. Additionally, as the state still has a foothold in many companies, we find people working there:

"She [respondent's wife] graduated from The Kazakh State Academy of Construction and Architecture. Her specialization is "Design and Architecture". Now she is working in a cartographic company as a designer. The company has the status of Republic State Enterprise – partly state, partly private" (Alm int 34: 24, male, urban, Kazakh).

The urban labor market also offers a variety of jobs in private or semi-private companies, particularly in the service sector.

"My son is 42 years. He has graduated from our road-transport institute and now he works as a senior manager in a company related to transport" (Alm int 30: 8, female, urban, Russian).

"Then my son, he is 26 years, he works as an accountant" (Alm int 36: 18, female, urban, Kazakh).

Other, more entrepreneurially orientated citizens took their chance to build up their own company.

"My husband is 46 [...] He is founder and head of a small communication company. He is communications engineer" (Alm int 22: 33, female, urban, Uzbek).

"She [respondent's wife] is a self-employed entrepreneur. She has her own business" (Alm int 23: 18, male, urban, business type unknown).

"I am a lawyer. I have my own business: legal practice. Additionally, I am a partner in another legal company that provides services to one large company" (Alm int 39: 6, female, urban, Kazakh).

The next respondent and his wife are trained musicians but prefer self-employment in business.

"Presently, we do our private business, small business. We are self-employed people. I am the sole proprietor of a business that is involved in the delivery of audio equipment for the scenes of houses of culture, children's educational and cultural institutions [... My wife runs] her own business, is an entrepreneur. She has a store (boutique) in one of the markets of Almaty. She imports goods from Italy and Germany [...]. She does her job by herself" (Alm int 18: 22, 29, urban, male, Kazakh).

Self-employment or employment in the big markets offers many income opportunities in sales and transport for various people with different educational backgrounds. In the markets, not only women but also many migrants from Central Asia make their living as food sellers or sellers of Chinese imports, or as transport workers in the bazaars.

Interestingly enough, none of the respondents in our urban Almaty interviews mentions employment in production. It is trades, sales and services where they work.

To sum up: as we can see, employment opportunities in our sample cover nearly the whole range of the economy. With transformation to a market economy and nowadays growth, on the one hand many new employment opportunities emerged – in Kazakhstan particularly in the tertiary sector. Like Russia, Kazakhstan is a 'rentier state' (Brunnsweiler and Bulte 2009) that mainly lives from the extraction of natural resources (oil, gas) and commerce, while most items are imported from abroad. On the other hand, as some respondents explain, most new private enterprises require medium-trained people such as accountants but not specialists of higher education such as f. e. economists. Therefore, the market does not provide the labor absorption capacity for some people with higher education in their fields of training. But also the public sector is under pressure to economize in the new market economy, which seems to take much longer than in the private sector. Educational and medical services still provide a large number of jobs, while parallel private enterprises emerged. In government jobs payments are not very attractive, and even highly specialized people such as doctors prefer opening or joining a private medical center or even switch into another, better paid job.

Incomes

The data from Almaty city show that people's incomes are much higher than in rural regions. However, living expenses are also much higher, and therefore many people have or are trying to find an additional income generating activity in order to improve the household's sustainability. Double-income households are frequent, and often husband and wife have several jobs. We believe very much, that only thorough in-depth interviews can reveal the true amount of these economic activities. In comparison to the rural area, people in the urban area do not have the opportunity to raise cattle or practice subsistence production to decrease their living expenses – except if they have rural links to relatives or a dacha on their own. The former, however, happens frequently, as we will discuss later. Now we want to provide different examples of how urban households in Almaty make their living. In what follows, we present some cases in more detail in order to show the varieties of practices, households employ to survive. In general they mix different income sources in order to render their households stable. Usually the incomes are pooled and redistributed according to different needs and obligations. To achieve reproduction, the households in general may differentiate their economic practice including market options as well as non-market options. They may do this consciously or as a routine. Diversification of incomes is the major means to achieve sustainability in our regional area. But what can be diversified largely depends on the context, apart from the ability of the people to grasp their opportunities. The context is not only constituted by the location itself, it may also be relatives, living somewhere else, it may be migrants, who work abroad etc. Context is the social space that allows for interconnectedness of the households. The interconnectedness ranges from neighbors to migrants abroad, thus linking local economies with international ones.

Case 1: A middle-class three-generation household with different incomes from self-employment and a net of mutual support (Alm int 13: male, urban).

The respondent is a Kazakh male. The household consists of himself, his wife, two sons, his parents and his sister. They bought a big two-storied house to live together when moving to Almaty from the countryside. He, his wife and one son reside on the first floor, and his parents, the second son, and the respondent's sister live on the second floor. Furthermore, the house has enough space to host guests and relatives to stay and even live with them. This ensures very close relations and constant contacts with relatives (Alm int 13: 24-29).

The respondent and his wife are the main providers for the household budget, but also all other grownups share in it. Both main providers have good incomes. The wife works in a meat sales shop in a bazaar, and he is self-employed in the real estate business. The investment is based on saved money plus loans, mainly from family members but also from friends (§ 61; see also 72ff, 125ff, 152, 156-158, 220).

Interestingly, the respondent reports that the main reason for taking up self-employment was that he wanted to take his son to and bring him back safely from school. Somebody from the family had to make the sacrifice, and as his wife had a better income at that time, he quit his work in the security business. Education of children is the highest priority for the respondent:

"Mostly, there were circumstances, because my younger son went to the first grade and his school was far away in a big city. I wanted to bring him to school, as he was little and nobody could do so. My wife worked in a busy company from morning to evening; so I had to quit my job, and gradually became self-employed" (Alm int 13: 81, male, urban).

Today, the elder son is financially independent and has two good and stable incomes through his paid traineeship in a private-public Kazakh-Chinese energy company, and through his own business.

"He [the eldest son] has an education in construction, but he works in the energy sector. He works [in a paid traineeship) in a large company, a joint venture between China and Kazakhstan. He is a specialist. [...His job] is associated with energy, with electricity" (Alm int 13: 10, 105, male, urban).

His income from training is 65,000 KZT; the trainees

"are paid for their learning not for working. They practically don't work" (Alm int 13: 118, male, urban).

"His second income emerged out of his hobby: motorcycling. He imports and sells motorcycles and motorcycle equipment" (Alm int 13: 114, male, urban).

We may assume that the respondent's parents also attribute to the finances of the household making him an upper middle class household.

The respondent highly values family and family ties. He explains, that he constantly tries to help his relatives who study in Almaty, by inviting them to live in the house. Very often, the expenses of the relatives are also covered by the respondent's family. In general the household is embedded in a reciprocity net, that includes mutual crediting, housing for study purposes, employment search, supply with housing, visiting and moral support.

"[Our relatives] always live [in our house] because Z. [his wife] came from a large family and we have a lot of relatives. We are Kazakhs, open-handed people. There were many of Z.'s sisters who lived and studied in our home. They were the first generation and already got married. Now there is the next generation, which consists of grandchildren, nephews and nieces who are studying now. For instance, A. is studying at the medical school [... They live with us] as long as they need to study. [...] I financially support them if it is necessary" (Alm int 13: 39, 40, 45).

Reciprocity and mutual reliance as well as education play a very important role in the concept of life of the respondent.

"When you have many relatives, it's very good. They always help you in joy and sorrow. Anything can happen in life, so they are always able to help" (Alm int 13: 52, male, urban).

Family orientation goes hand in hand with mistrust in banks. Although – or perhaps because – both husband and wife are business people and have good knowledge of the economy, they do not trust in banks. They invest their savings in real estate, gold and jewelry.

"We do not trust in banks. We are mainly involved in deals with real estate and investing in gold and in diamonds, being honest [...] We have another place to store. We do not trust banks" (Alm int 13: 166, 168, male, urban; see also 177).

The network reaches beyond the family. The respondent's wife got an interest-free loan from her boss at work (§ 222).

In addition to investments, the main expenses of the household include the education of children, food expenses, and in the near future, expenses related to the wedding of the elder son (§ 255).

Case 2: A working woman with a handicapped husband and two daughters in education – the art of making the household survive (Alm int 11, female, urban)

The example of Interview 11 intends to show how a household dominated by a married woman with 2 daughters and a handicapped husband manages its survival. This household represents a poorer household. The respondent is the main breadwinner. Her husband receives a little disability pension (20,000 KZT) which is mainly used for his treatment. Both daughters study. Our respondent is a trained mathematician now working as a sales manager of advertisements in a daily journal (§ 8). She receives a fixed salary that may be supplemented by provisions according to the sold space (§ 27). The family owns a private house with four rooms and the plot on which it is built and a car (§ 10, 21). However, they do not raise products for subsistence. Since the education of the two daughters is costly, they have to economize.

"I pay for their education because they do not earn. So I am a provider. My husband doesn't work because he is a second-group disabled. Sure, he has his own earnings – disability grant about 20,000 Tenge. It's not much by today's standards, and the money goes mostly to himself: for medicine, for treatment, etc. You know what I mean" (Alm int 11: 9, female, urban).

Between herself and her sisters there is a reciprocal relationship: the sisters help with garden products and meat, while the respondent helps them financially.

"I have sisters, we support each other. They live in private houses with vegetable gardens. They help me with meat, vegetables and fruits. Generally, they help me, but if I have an opportunity, I help them too... I help with money. Usually it is not a big amount, about 15,000-20,000 KZT. If my niece or nephew, who study, need money or help, surely, I'm going to help them... Not so often, about once in a month or less" (Alm int 11: 30-35, female, urban).

Other expenses include traditional obligations related to weddings, funerals and etc. For this purposes the respondent tries to save with some difficulties (§ 43).

The household overcomes financial difficulties by planning and prioritization of resources. The respondents puts education and health of her family as the main priorities and economizes on other things such as food, beauty, etc. (§ 38). As the spouses cannot save bigger amounts, future housing of the daughters is thought of as constructing on the same plot, so that the two daughters do not need to move to their future husbands (§ 75) and one of them can take up the traditional obligation of caring for the parents.

The respondent trusts and uses only installment credits (which are often interest-free) and tries to avoid other credits (§ 40). She also avoids taking loans from relatives or friends:

"I also try not to take loans, as well as to give them. Because I do not have much money.... I live from paycheck to paycheck" (Alm int 11: 41, female, urban).

'Muddling through' from paycheck to paycheck in this case is combined with thorough planning and cautious management of the scarce resources. This implies prioritizing the expenses and avoiding all risks as loans, including those within the existing family network.

Case 3: A 3-generation household with two public incomes (medical doctors) and one pension (Alm int 14, female, urban)

The respondent is female, Russian, 72 years old, a pensioner. She has her own apartment but lives with her daughter, the daughter's husband (both surgeons) and their 2 children.

"I have my own apartment, but I help my daughter to nurse her children. I have been living with my daughter more than 11 years. I have come to nurse a baby for one day and stayed for 11 years. They both are surgeons. Their salaries are small. The government does not pay decently; therefore they cannot hire a nursemaid. I have to help" (Alm int 14: 5, female, urban).

The respondent is very unsatisfied with the salaries of her children, claiming that they as well as teachers, nurses etc. deserve more according to their qualifications (§ 9, 17). She explains that both keep their state jobs because of the relatively secure pensions (§ 21). However, they do have additional earnings from contract work in a private hospital (§ 19).

In addition to this, the respondent herself gets her own pension. She spends the money on gardening, food and on her grandchildren (§ 37, 42). The household has a dacha, and she owns a small apartment in a suburban area which is not used, leased, or cared for. Therefore, they do not have any incomes from this property (§ 14, 57).

Although the incomes of the respondent's daughter and daughter's husband are higher than average, the expenses for children's education eat their incomes completely up. One daughter studies drawing, and must be accompanied to famous art galleries in Russia and even Paris. Therefore there is no money for vacations. On the contrary, free time must be used to make additional income (§ 14, 27, 31).

In order to reduce the expenses for additional language courses for her grandchildren, the respondent tries to teach them English on her own, because she had English training in her own higher education (§ 37).

The family does not take on any loans. In order to be able to pay for the education which shall take place abroad, the respondent plans to ask her elder daughter for a loan, who earns much more in a private company, and who's only son has already graduated and has a well-paid job (§ 33).

This household, in our eyes, represents a mixture of ignorance and adaptation to market demands. For example on the one hand, the respondent does not rent out her apartment, on the other hand, she herself teaches English to her grandchildren. They opened up different income opportunities, but spend a lot of money on costly travels to support the education of one of the daughters. Grants are not a possibility to finance them.

Case 4: A lower middle-class household with three persons, three incomes and reliance on the state (Alm int 14, female, urban)

The respondent from Alm int 19 is female, married with one daughter. The family lives in a privatized two-room apartment in Almaty and has a car (§ 16-17). This household can be looked upon as representative of many lower middle-class urban dwellers working in the state sector and having average state monthly incomes.

All members of the respondent's household have jobs. The husband works in construction with unstable earnings. He has an additional income generating activity as an unlicensed taxi driver. She works part-time in the public sector, due to her health (§ 39). She had difficulties to get a job at all, although she has been living in the city for more than 25 years (§ 67). The daughter works in a state insurance company and earns 50,000 KZT (§ 28-33). The household's income is about 120,000 KZT, which according to the respondent is insufficient to make a living in the city (§ 35). Due to the low, and partly instable incomes and constantly rising prices the respondent perceives the current situation as a crisis (§ 17). She explains, that the family cannot save at all, which makes the household very vulnerable to unforeseen expenses and 'shocks':

"We are always short of money"(Alm int 19: 44, female, urban).

The household strategy is to economize on 'unnecessary' expenses:

"We have to limit ourselves in food, clothing. And we don't go for a visit" (Alm int 19: 54, female, urban).

The respondent suggests that the state should regulate the banks and reduce the interest rates for credits and loans.

"It would be desirable that the state somehow helps us, helps to reduce interest rates for loans in banks. [...]. I was recently in the bank. Banks offer 21%, 21.5%, and 23%. This is terrible. If I take a loan for 5 years at 23%, then I will have to pay on top of 115%. If I take USD 10,000, I should return USD 25,000" (Alm int 19: 55, female, urban).

This household is reliant on the state when it comes to making a living. Subjectively, this corresponds with claims for additional state subsidies to tame the market economy and to secure better opportunities in life i.e. by erasing corruption. If this represents a reminiscence of and identification with the Soviet Union and state-based welfare institutions and a mal-adoption to the current market conditions, must be left open. Although the household has three incomes, the respondent feels constantly short of money and is full of anxiety, which is also expressed through xenophobia against foreigners:

"Kazakhs get nothing, while the aliens (foreign migrants) get everything, what humiliates Kazakhs" (Alm int 19: 65, female, urban).

Summary

In general, we can observe that even in the city of Almaty most households do not rely on a single but on two or more incomes. The households use every opportunity to make a living. State employment has the advantage of being more stable, however, at the expense of comparatively lower incomes than those originating from employment in the market sector. Thus, even a double income from state employment is no guarantor for a good life. Self-provisioning hardly plays a role in the urban context but family networks do. These cut across the city into the countryside and through mutual help complement what is absent in the city or the village: in the first case subsistence produce from gardening or animal husbandry, in the latter case money. Sometimes the urban dwellers also rely on friends, but security is overwhelmingly organized by the family nets.

State jobs are also highly esteemed because of the prestige (at least in higher administration and higher education) and old age pension security. But these do not compensate for the income gap to have an adequate middle class lifestyle. It seems that higher income options can only be reached in the private sector. This explains why many former state employees with higher education switched into the latter as employees, or they may even try their luck by becoming entrepreneurial and self-employed in the business or service sector (lawyers, architects, etc.). But a case also exists, where the respondent prepares to go back to state employment due to the risks in the private sector. Vulnerabilities stem from the instability of incomes or from personal reasons. The market seems to be open for people from different educational backgrounds and ethnic groups, although nowadays the Kazakhization-cum-language policy promotes Kazakh civil servants.[186]

More or less, the sample households represent an urban middle class, which knows how to organize its life under the new economic conditions. Some are suspicious concerning banks and credit, but in case of need, many of them take bank credits, while others still rely on their family networks. Most of them are cautious concerning risky economic behavior.

186 For recruitment of civil servants Kazakh language knowledge is nowadays a pre-condition.

Employment and Income in Almaty Region

The living conditions of urban and rural households differ considerably as already revealed in our quantitative research. This is true also for the rural Almaty region. In 2010 the monthly income there was 27,474 KZT as compared to Almaty, where it was 80,210 KZT according to official statistics. In general, poverty in Kazakhstan is 2.2 times higher in rural areas than in urban ones (see Regional Report). Unemployment resp. underemployment is a severe problem, although official statistics don't mirror the reality. Many people have a part time job, are self-employed (43% in the Almaty region) etc. and thus do not show up in official statistics. Therefore, unemployment shows a lower rate in rural Almaty region than in the city itself. The majority of our respondents in the rural Almaty region do not have stable jobs. Under these conditions households combine different income opportunities such as wage labor and informal incomes, subsistence production, animal husbandry and transfers from pensions, or from migrant members of the family etc. This implies a high mobility of household members to cities, neighboring towns or other villages, where there is still some wage labor available. Underemployment in rural regions affects both highly educated as well as less educated people.

Disbanded Kolkhoz/Sovkhoz

The crisis of the 1990s and the current market economy are claimed to be one of the major reasons for rural underemployment, as well as the causes of the current misfortunes of the villagers. Both led to the dissolution of Kolkhozes and Sovkhozes, the closing down of industries and to rapid urbanization and to the loss of agricultural subsidies and support and developmental programs connected to them. This is the perception of the transition period, which is reflected in our respondents' answers. Furthermore, while in the cities state investments into infrastructure, housing, education etc. are visible, people in the village feel neglected and abandoned. One of our respondents, a 49-year-old woman explains:

"There is really no work like before. In Kolkhoz [...], fish processing plant, smoke, fishing shop, we had a service yard, a technician, and a mechanic, a locksmith. In general, everything was available, a joiner's shop, carpenters' machines, a sewing workshop. People could be drivers, turners, fitters, and mechanics. We had a prosperous collective farm. The Culture House was built... people were very energetic, interested, united. It is bad now that there is no work. But when a person wants to work, he will find a job, but it is very uncomfortable, when in the village there is no work and you should go and get it somewhere else. Yes, we do not have enough work. [...]. Now people who go somewhere [for work] need money for the trip, for food, they suffer from long overdue wages, it is also oppressive. People are dismissed. Labor is so heavy in the cold, the salary does not meet the work, I am disappointed too" (Alm int 6: 143, female, rural).

The woman further reports that as a result of the development, the whole village disintegrated, shops closed, services have disappeared, and if there is wage labor, then it is significantly underpaid. Another respondent points at almost the same problems when she reports from the closure of the old collective farm and the deteriorating infrastructure in the same village:

"Now all are leaving this place, because everybody searches for work. Women cannot work [for subsistence], because there is even no garden. Maybe they would like to go to work in K., but transport works only three times a day here. [...] I feel that there is a lack of services in the village [...] fish complex disbanded, the farm went bankrupt, all disappeared. Many businesses and, of course, our fishermen began to look for employment. Some of them went to K for work. Some organizations pay good salaries, but some of them don't, so [...] I can say that now we have difficulties, too, because my husband is still a fisherman. He doesn't have a fixed salary. [...] his wage depends on weather conditions. Buying the fishing nets, motor costs a lot, that's why we don't have a lot of money. [...] Generally it is difficult to live in the village, because there are no work places. If there was a job, no one would refuse it" (Alm int 9: 67, 65, female, rural).

Another respondent reports that with closure of the collective farm, irrigation fell into despair. This had a severe negative impact on their own arable land (Alm int 7: 29).

On a whole, the collective memory in the villages mostly represents soviet times as a time of stability, good infrastructure and general satisfaction; the market economy, on the contrary, as the time of major instabilities, lack of employment opportunities, deterioration of quality of life, and major vulnerabilities for households (e.g. Alm int 28: 77-79; Alm int 4: 31; Alm int 5: 62). Furthermore, nowadays people in search of labor are supposed to bribe or to have influential acquaintances.

"I looked for [another job], but it didn't turn out, because there should be some acquaintances" (Alm int 27: 98, male, rural).

"After they [children] finish education it is necessary to help them to get a job [...]. Money is necessary for that [...]. If you find it [job], it will also be necessary to pay a certain sum to get employed, people do so!" (Alm int 1: 49, male, rural).

"Don't you know?! [...] In some places you have to pay and for some work 50,000 KZT" (Alm, int. 8: 96-99, female, rural).

Bribery in search of employment is so prevalent that many people perceive it as something quite natural.

Working Conditions

Not only is labor insufficiently available in the villages, but the working conditions are very often not advantageous, including such facts as: irregularly paid salaries, significantly underpaid wage labor, long working hours, unhealthy working conditions, etc. (e.g. Alm int 6: 143). A woman reports:

"Before, I worked here in the village. In the factory [...] we made gears. I had really a small salary, only 10,000 KZT [per month]. But there it was very cold and I had to carry iron. I was not married at that time; I wanted to have a healthy child. So I left this job" (Alm int 26: 43, female, rural).

During transition also government salaries were delayed, as a teacher tells us.

"We didn't get our salary up to five months. But it was easier in the village, because I baked the bread myself; we had purchased livestock, etc. We sold the livestock, and so we survived" (Alm int 31: 42, female, rural).

But nowadays, people in government services predominantly have low but stable incomes. For those who are working in the private sector, the situation is different. Salaries are higher. But in construction it depends on the season. The unemployment periods have to be buffered by the households.

"Unemployment happens with our children. In winter mainly. Otherwise, one may find side building work in this village. If children get unemployed, and do not find another job within a month but one month later, they will receive the next salary in three months only" (Alm int 3: 43, male, rural).

However, occasional jobs can be found in agriculture. Several interviews mention that ethnic Koreans are practicing agriculture seasonally, hiring unemployed youth.

"Koreans hold the fields here. During autumn, for example, they employ non-working youth. I think it is good"(Alm int 9: 115, female, rural, married).

[They] attract our children, students who in the summer work in the field and earn [some money]" (Alm int 7: 87, female, rural).

As result of a South Korean Kazakhstan development cooperation, South Koreans offer special training programs in the villages on how to do business and generate incomes from subsistence production and cattle breading, with some elements of micro financing:

"We were visited by representatives from South Korea in the village, who lent us $ 500 and taught us how to do small business. I went to these courses and for the $ 500 bought the cow. We made a business plan, how to get income from this, of course, I tried a bit, selling milk, cheese, it was a good help" (Alm int 7: 75, female, rural).

Monetary and Subsistence Incomes

How then do households in the rural area make their living? What are their major sources of incomes?

One of the respondents gives a very comprehensive answer to this question:

"In the village, people work at school, in the kindergarten, the others survive by means of 5-6 sheep. Others have kitchen gardens. Also there are a lot of large families in the village, they draw allowances. People survive somehow" (Alm int 31: 79, female, rural).

In general, as the statement above indicates, and as further analyzed below, people in rural areas survive by means of the combination of the following types of activities: (1) employment in the state sector (schools, kindergartens, military service, state public structures, mining) or if available, private sector; (2) cattle/livestock breading, often as a combination of subsistence production and sale (3) subsistence production in kitchen gardens; (4) additional informal activities, which may include "raising and selling", "making and selling", repair works, seasonal salaried jobs, and some type of self-employment (i.e. fishing, informal taxi transport); (5) drawing on state allowances: pensions, child allowances, disability allowances, etc.; (6) transfers from relatives, friends and neighbors. Concerning the households, we may find combinations of these income sources in one way or another, depending on different factors such as household size and age of household members, type of major employment, income level and equipment with real estate, consumer goods, etc. If the combinations of incomes mentioned above are insufficient to make a stable living, shortcomings have to be overcome by temporary credits in various forms (consumer credit purchases, charging the bill in the shop, and financial support by relatives, friends and neighbors).

Private Sector Employment

As already shown, private enterprises and therefore wage labor is rare in rural regions. Entrepreneurs seldom invest in rural areas, probably due to locational disadvantages, although the government provides subsidies (Alm int. 31: 78, female, rural). They prefer investment in the city or the urban fringe.

To improve their living conditions rural people very often think about opening their own businesses, in order to make their income more or less stable. However, the lack of start-up capital (savings or credit) is always the main barrier to the realization of their ideas and plans.

"To start a business, you need a lot of money, such as 10,000 [USD] .... From whom to take? [...] My father doesn't have money ... There is no one to turn to..." (Alm int 8: 96-99, female, rural).

"But I want to work. Many times I thought about opening a [tailoring] studio here, but our village is not big enough [...] I have to take a loan to open my own business, to build the studio, but I'm afraid of it. We don't have good buildings in the village. I can take someone's home for rent, for example, but for this I also need to invest a lot of money" (Alm int 9: 65, female, rural, a dress-maker).

State Sector Employment

Chances of getting employment in the state sector depend on the level of acquired education. Those respondents with higher or vocational education have better chances as teachers, administrators in the civil service, in the military service or on the railway, and so on, and such labor is in high demand. Nowadays the advantage of state sector employment is a stable income. To provide two examples:

"I am glad, I am a teacher. It is good to get your salary every month" (Alm int 31: 23, female, rural, earning 65,000 KZT).

"My husband [working as a miner] has a good income" (Alm int 28: 71, female, rural).

One can observe a certain degree of satisfaction with state employment, mostly due to the regularity of payment, as well as perceived good pensions in the future.

However, those people employed in the state sector in the rural area, report having no time to realize additional income opportunities, except perhaps some subsistence production or cattle breeding:

"I work as a signaler in the Almaty's regional branch of the Kazakhstan railway in the small town S [the district center]. I receive a monthly payment of 50-60,000 KZT. I am not involved in any additional activity" (Alm int 5: 13, 24, 66, male, rural).

"As my husband works in state service, he can have no additional job. Of course, military men have no additional work. He leaves in the morning, then comes for lunch. He has his lunch and leaves for work again until in the evening. As he is a military man, the discipline is severe, is there a forming up in the evening his working hours continue, so he has no time for any additional work" (Alm int.33: 68, female, rural).

However, of course, there are some exceptions to this tendency.

The following, are examples to illustrate income pooling taking place in the rural areas:

Case 1: Income pooling: a better-off household (Alm int 31, female, 46 years, rural, Kazakh)

The household from interview 31 consists of a husband and his wife with three children, two of whom live in Almaty but return home regularly in order to help with work. The respondent and her husband have higher education.

"We work at the school [she is a teacher, he is a director at the same school]. Due to him, we know no misfortunes. And we receive our salary timely [...] Now I work 18 hours per week, I get 65,000. He [husband] gets 106,000. I am a teacher of the 13th category, he is of the 1th" (Alm int 31: 8ff, female, rural).

Thus, the general monthly income of this household is 171,000 KZT. This income is supplemented:

"We keep cows. And have milk for us. It is inconvenient, to live in a village and to buy milk. Herdsmen watch after our cows. We have three milk-cows. Herdsmen also watch after the horses for money. We have horses as well" (Alm int 31: 8, female, rural).

This additional income possibility generates even employment, in this case of herdsmen.[187] Otherwise, our respondent explains, there wouldn't be enough time for work and the family. The major expenses of the household are spent on the education of the youngest son, for the costs related to keeping the cattle, and for food products.

187 We find the same practice of hiring shepherds in other interviews. Thus, people can pursue their jobs in the city or the village (e.g. Alm int 37: 16, female, rural). Unemployed youth and even villagers with social problems such as alcoholism sometimes take over the role of shepherds to make some money (Alm int 9: 115, female, rural). Shepherds are paid according to the number of animals, and thus not everyone can afford a shepherd, but more often those who employ a shepherd have a larger stock of animals and therefore more capital. In one interview we find the following figures: "*200 Tenge per sheep, 10,000 for 50 sheep. 1,000 Tenge per cow, 5,000 for 5 cows, 10,000 – for 10 cows. The same for horses, 1,000 Tenge per head. Somebody says 1,500 per head, but we have luck, thank God, we pay 1,000. All is well, we have nothing in excess, but we have everything we need*" (Alm int 37: 50, female, rural).

Although the household has quite a good income, the family plans and economizes on the expenses.

"And mainly, I think about economizing, and bake the bread myself, and we slaughter, e.g. a lamb. We do all this, buy meat in summer time, slaughter livestock in winter. It's enough for winter, or we slaughter one fat cow" (Alm int 31: 26, female, rural).

Because of lack of time, the interviewee says, her family only grows some vegetables for self-consumption. Economizing also implies preservation for winter time.

"We lid pickles, from the middle of summer on. We put up compote. Make jams, sometimes autumn salads. [...] I can't say that it's all from our own produce. We lack some produce, we purchase it. Vegetables are cheap in our Chilik bazaar (§58)... [We grow] tomatoes, chives, potatoes, onions, eggplants. They gave us land in the village [...] For 5 of us they gave us 2 hectares. We plant wheat. We mow twice, press and gather" (Alm int 31: 56-58, 64, female, rural).

This kind of subsistence production and preservation for winter time is typical for rural dwellers and is also found among urban dwellers having a dacha. Produce our sample family cannot raise on its own, are purchased. Oil is also bought. The cheapest place to buy is always looked for (Alm int 31: 32, female, rural). Important to note here is, that this better off household also can employ a variety of means to secure their life. Higher income for example allows for the employment of herdsmen and to buy additional food for preserving. The different kinds of planning, described by the interviewee, show how people in rural areas with regular incomes can and do economize on their expenses.

From the interview (Alm int 31: 50, 52, female, rural) we can also learn that the husband of the respondent has an income-generating hobby that also implies informal income: making sculptures. However, due to the fact that this involves much work and makes the sculptures costly, the village does not constitute an appropriate market for them. They have to be sold elsewhere.

Additionally, the family receives support from their son.

"His salary is 80,000. He works as accountant in a private company in Almaty. Recently, he bought us a good TV set on installment. He pays from his salary 23,000. The TV set costs 250,000" (Alm int 31: 44, female, rural).

Supporting and honoring parents (even if one's own salary is not very high as in this case) is of high value in Central Asia. Additionally, in this example, we can observe that the context spreads into the region.

The relations to relatives are not only expression of family values but also a means to secure mutual material support, making the household a node in a web of relatives ... (Smith and Stenning 2006:202).

"We have good relations with them [with relatives]. If they ask for help, we help them. If we need help, they help us. We help each other. For example, we help on weddings, in money terms and with cloths. When we bought a car, my relatives helped us with money" (Alm int 31: 50, female, rural).

Such reciprocity relationships with relatives are reported in various interviews. They are very rarely reported from non-relatives. These relations seem to play an important role as "insurance mechanisms" to overcome financial difficulties and to finance costly family events such as marriages or funerals (see also the chapter on savings). But as discussed in social anthropology, the special aspect with reciprocity is its compulsory nature (Gouldner 1960; Gregory 1997; Mauss 1970) and might not be free from power 'geometrics'. Additionally, family relations – considered as social capital – have to be cultivated constantly to keep the reciprocity intact ((Coleman 1988).

The household in interview 31 follows practices of combining formal, informal and subsistence incomes. Additionally it economizes on expenses by doing subsistence production, by getting support from the son living outside the household, and by being involved in a family network as an "insurance mechanism" for material and also emotional support.

Case 2: Income pooling (Alm int 5, male, 52 years, rural, Kazakh)

The following example is of a rural Kazakh male respondent, married, with 2 children. The children are grown up, and both are employed. The son has a private business, and works and lives in Almaty city. The respondent, his wife and the daughter are employed at state facilities in the village, and therefore have regular incomes.

"I work as a signaler in the Almaty region's branch of the Kazakhstan railway in the small town S. [the district center].... My wife works in the Center of Population Services (CPS). My son R., 1984 year of birth, is engaged in a private business in Almaty city. My daughter is Z. D., 1986 year of birth. She holds a position as inspector of the CPS. I receive a monthly payment of 50-60 000 KZT. I am not engaged in any additional activity. With my wife together, we have a joint budget of the family based on our salaries" (Alm int 5: 13, male, rural).

In his eyes, state employment does not allow them opportunities to have a second job, but the family has a small garden, where they grow fruit and vegetables for subsistence, and thus have the possibility to reduce food expenses. But they haven't expanded into cattle breeding as the first household:

"As I work on the railway it is very difficult to have and be engaged in livestock, there is no time for it. We have a small piece of land. It is so-called subsidiary farming. There we raise some potatoes, vegetables, carrots, tomatoes, cucumbers; there are apricot and apple trees, cherry trees. We make different jams, we make compotes. It is a small garden in front of the house; thanks to it we do preservation for the winter. We do not receive earnings from it" (Alm int 5:24, male, rural).

However, the family plans to have some poultry after retirement:

"In the future, when I shall retire, I think, well, to get some poultry, little hens, house birds. Now, there is no time as I work for the state. Therefore we shall wait, until I shall retire" (Alm int 5: 13, 24, 66, male, rural).

This retirement planning can also be found in other interviews. Poultry can be used for subsistence production but also for sale. The same holds true for other house birds.[188]

Interestingly, in times of need – contrary to the former case – this household does not approach relatives for a loan, because the respondent believes that the overall situation of everybody is such that "*presently in Kazakhstan there are no people who would not take a credit*" (Alm int 5: 45, male, rural). They overcome financial difficulties by bank credit. This is possible, because of the regular incomes from the state that serve as security to banks. This allowed him a high credit of 500,000 KZT[189] that he repays regularly with 20,000 (Alm int 5: 50, male, rural). He is used to taking credits to finance foreseeable as well as unforeseeable purposes: purchase of a car, marriage of his children, university education of his son, family celebrations.

Case 3: Income Pooling (Alm int 6: female, 40 years, rural, Korean)

Interview 6 intends to show, how households with a mix of low state income and other multiple income-generating activities survive and overcome seasonal shortages and other vulnerabilities. The respondent is a 49-year-old Korean woman, married, with two sons working respectively studying at a university in Almaty.

[188] A similar orientation is found in Alm int 7, female, rural.

[189] He does not mention the purpose for that credit, however, with regard to earlier credits (§ 46) he mentions: for buying a car, for education, for marriage of his son, and for other family celebrations.

The respondent has no higher education and takes every job which is available. At present, she works as a flower seller, but not exclusively.

"Firstly I work as a seller on a farm, then in the SRT, then as fisherman"[...] I have no permanent job, in spring, in March, we dig the garden, plant flowers. We start planting the flowers, the flowers blossom in July; we carry them to Almaty and sell them in the green market. This is around 20-25 days, during which we sell flowers, and then the rest of the time I work in a shop in K. [...]. We try to plant early to sell before Oraza [Muslim fasting] starts, because at Oraza, flowers do not sell, you just have to throw them away" (Alm int 6, § 7, 44, female, rural).

This income from flower sales is seasonal, involves risks and also strongly depends on market demand.

"I receive a good income within 20 days; it can be said that we work 9 months, and the profit is received within a month. On the 1st of September, we do bouquets by ourselves to sell, before Teachers' Day" [early October] (Alm int 6, §47, female, rural).

The husband of the respondent has a permanent state job as watchman. This is one of the lowest paid categories (Alm int 6: 41, female, rural). The elder son has finished education and now works in Almaty; he financially supports his younger brother who studies at the university so that he can pay his living expenses (Alm int 6: 51, female, rural). The parents pay about 190,000 KZT per year for the tuition fees (Alm int 6: 19, female, rural).

The household makes additional income by other seasonal work. Interestingly, the payments are in kind.

"Sometimes, when my eldest son comes, we go to the fields to look for jobs, to cut onions or dig potatoes... if he comes, one or two weekends, we should prepare something for winter harvest – onions, potatoes [...] We do not take cash, if we go for onion harvesting then we take back home onions, if we go to harvest potatoes – bring potatoes, at least one sack" (Alm int 6: 51-55, female, rural).

Here we can observe that payment is by barter, which is also prevalent in other rural interviews.

Sporadic support for the younger son also comes from her ex-husband.

"At first, he didn't not help at all, but then began to help. When E. ended school, he gave money for his graduation celebration, and then he went to study. If possible he helps" (Alm int 6: 69, female, rural).

The household of the respondent does not keep or breed cattle or engage in other forms of subsistence production, although they have a plot of land where they grow flowers to have additional monetary income. To keep to the flower business, was a conscious decision.

"I had kept cattle before planting flowers. Kept a cow, a calf [...] And then, when I starting to plant flowers, if the cow accidentally runs into the garden, it's monkey work, all work will be useless. [...] We only kept the cattle for ourselves. In a farming region, nobody can sell milk, carrying it to K. is unprofitable. If you get 8 liters it will be 800 Tenge; this money you spent on the road" (Alm int 6: 57, 59, female, rural).

She also reports that raising cattle involves risks. If the climate is bad, no fodder is available and if there is no herdsmen – which they can hardly afford – there is danger of cattle raids (Alm int 6: 121, 123, female, rural). The climate also means risks for the flower business. Water scarcity is a major risk and there are additional growing problems (Alm int 6: 25, female, rural).

To overcome financial difficulties, the household relies on loans from friends and relatives (Alm int 6: 77-78, female, rural). She never takes credits from banks but in times of difficulty gets financial support from her relatives.

This household, though only relying on a small secure income, is very creative in organizing sustainability. All household members play their role in this. Its social space stretches out to Almaty where the eldest son supports his younger brother, who studies there and who works on weekends in the village during harvest time, producing his share for survival. And the household already thinks about the future, when the husband will be on pension. Unrecorded self-employment, subsistence production, reciprocal aid and a small, saved salary make up a pooled budget. But small incidents endanger the precarious situation as she describes when being asked about difficulties in the way they make their money:

"There have been very difficult times, it was very difficult, when the eldest son went to university and we still had two students. It was hard these 4 years. Especially when he finished last year, his graduation, and the graduation of junior in high school. That year I broke my arm, it was very hard. Because the younger passed UNT [Unified National Test], we needed money for the road and it was very difficult" (Alm int 6: 73, female, rural).

Case 4: Income Pooling (Alm int 26, female, 24 years, rural, Russian)

The example of interview 26 intends to show how non-state employees make a living in a rural area. The interview was conducted with a 24-year old divorced woman, ethnic Russian, with one child, living together with a Uighur man. She has secondary education. She makes her living as a seller in the bazaar being paid per day and receives alimony from her first husband. Her living partner, working in the city in a shop for non-alcoholic drinks, earns about 60,000 KZT, depending on the sales.

"Presently I work in the bazaar. I am just seller. Per day I take 1,000 KZT. [...] my friend helped me to find this container [from which she sells the goods]" (Alm int 26: 13, 19, 47, female, rural).

The respondent explains that she could not study because she and her parents could not pay for her education.

"I finished school here in J. I really wanted to go to college. [...] I wanted to enter "manager of tourism and hotel business". [Tuition fee was] 300,000 KZT per year. I started long-distance education. [...] my father came and gave me 15,000 KZT and told me that in the future I should live on my own. It was difficult for me, because I thought that I am alone in the world. I had no [higher] education, no job and no living place" (Alm int 26: 15, 35, female, rural).

This case shows how people without higher education have to live from what kinds of temporary jobs are presently available. Before she started self-employed market sales, she worked as a seller in a wedding shop, then in a shoe shop, then she did very heavy wage labor in the local gear-producing factory, then she sold household chemistry, then she worked as a baby-sitter. In general, one can say, that she belongs to the group of those unsecured people, having no choice in making a living but accepting any available job.

Regardless of her low incomes, she is satisfied with her job, because she can combine her family life and work. This is very typical for rural women in our sample and corresponds with reported women experiences in other countries (e.g. Charles & Kerr, 1999, p. 1991ff). Being responsible for family life, they are restricted in their mobility concerning search for better employment.

"Of course, I want something better. Every person would aspire to do something better than I am doing right now. But it is better for me, because I have a little child, I can take it to the kindergarten in the morning, then I go to work, and then I take it back after work. If I worked in the city (Almaty), I would not catch up with kindergarten openings. Now I can bring my child to the kindergarten at 7:45. I am in the bazaar from 8:00 to 17:00. I like my job in the village. I think that I am happy because I found the job here. If I worked in the city, I know that I would spend half of my salary for the trip. I like this job, because I have not any [higher] education" (Alm int 26: 21, female, rural).

Her partner spends a lot of money on commuting. From their pooled incomes they spend 12,000 KZT for the kindergarten, another 4-6,000 for electricity, and they live in an apartment which they had rented from her partner's father, but now they live there for free (Alm int 26: 59, 95, female, rural).

They do have a car, but they did not buy it. Her husband took this car as a pawn from someone, who owes him money (Alm int 26: 65, female, rural).

This example demonstrates how people make their living at the edge of poverty. Planning their lives seems hardly possible, saving only occurs for short-term purposes. They have educational limitations so that they do not get better jobs but have to work wherever and whatever possible. Accumulating property (e.g. own flat) seems to be difficult if not impossible. Also subsistence production is lacking, as they have no garden. But they must not pay rent for shelter. And the women can combine family obligations with her job. It seems that they can't really build on family relations for sustainability although they try to contribute to them. She saves only for short-term purposes:

"Yes, now in the end of July we want to go to R., to my relatives. We save money on this for 3 months. Have to wait. We could go now, but after returning we would not have money even for bread. We have to buy tickets beforehand. After we have saved, we can go. We need to save money on everything" (Alm int 26: 93, female, rural).

"I use another type of 'piggy bank'. But I can only save small sums and only for some aims. For example, before New Year or birthday I try to save money for presents for my son. But at present, we cannot save" (Alm int 26: 101, female, rural).

Case 5: Subsistence production, self-employment and additional small activities (Alm int. 2, female, 38 years, rural)

In interview 2 the household tries to overcome vulnerability as a result of unstable incomes by multiplying its income-generating activities in order to secure the household and spread risks. The respondent is a Kazakh rural 38 year old woman, married with 4 children. One daughter and one son study at universities in Almaty city, the other daughter is in the 3rd grade, and the fourth daughter is 1 year and 9 months. Her husband has secondary education. He works as an unlicensed taxi driver by transporting people. Additionally he makes deliveries with his truck (Alm int 2: 7, female, rural). She works as a vegetable-and-fruit seller.

"I bring them from the Almaty market "Altyn Orda" and I sell them in a market in S." (Alm int 2:13, female, rural).

The couple shares in subsistence production and production for sale (potatoes). In addition to these seasonal activities, the respondent indicates that she follows additional activities to increase their income. She takes orders to prepare food for sale and she sews special traditional rags and quilts.

"From time to time, I make noodles for lagman The girls of the hospital send me the orders by phone; I cook noodles for them for money. Besides, I do quilts [scrappy blankets] by request. They are presents for girls going to marry. So people come, say that blankets are necessary for the girls, so during the whole summer I wash wool, stretch it. My mother helps me. [...] We also do covers of rags, blankets by request. That's it. Although it is little money only, but we do it anyway. [...] I go to the city for the material" (Alm int 2: 25, female, rural).

On one hand, there is severe instability of the household's monetary situation. On the other hand, the different activities combined produce a relative stability. Thus, the household can even buffer, for example, bad times by transport service with a Kamaz (truck], unlicensed taxi driving between Almaty and S. or fruit and vegetable sales during the summer months.

Case 6: Vulnerability because of high expenses for sickness (Alm int 8, female, 38 years, rural)

The respondent is a rural, 38 years old disabled woman, ethnic Korean, married with two children. Her husband works as a security guard and earns 70-80,000 KZT. The household also includes her parents, who get minimal pensions (together 40,000 KZT; Alm int 8: 41-49, female, rural). They do some subsistence production, and her father makes some repair works.

The key vulnerability of the household is the disability of the respondent. Although she gets a small disability allowance (13,000 KZT), she has to spend a lot of money and time on her health treatment.

"There are only 13,000, for what to use them? One ampoule is 2,500, and there is 10 days to inject two times a day...I need this sum 3-4 times bigger. I'm getting treatment; there are injection costs of 180-200,000 KZT. I get them, but the most expensive drugs I buy by myself. I get treatment two times a year, and [...] not once in 3 months, because I have pain, and I was given only third group [classification of disability]. They believe that I'm fine. And the fact that my feet are constantly cramps. I am trying to hike with them, such a terrible pain and blood pressure 180-190 [...] After the surgery was done, I have such high pressure" (Alm int 8: 107-109, female, rural).

The respondent also reports on an emergency situation when she had to pay the doctors in kind by the help of a friend:

"You know what fish we usually catch, under 40 kg, 20, 10 kg. My husband asked his friend, he brought a fish that an adult man could barely carry" (Alm int 8: 90-91, female, rural).

Summary

Employment and incomes are diverse. Employment may be in the state sector or the private one, but additionally to the formal employment opportunities, there is a range of informal ones. Many household members in rural regions have a whole history of different employments after independence. All the households represent a kind of portfolio work to secure livelihood. This implies also migrant labor. The portfolio is additionally represented by domestic food production and self-provisioning. The 'subsistence' production is sometimes monetized or used for reciprocal gifts within the wider net of family relations. Keeping cattle means not only self-provisioning but must be looked upon also as a form of saving. Among ethnic Kazakhs it has deep cultural roots and implies a moment of esteem. Subsistence production occurs in almost all households whether they are richer or poorer. But richer households have fewer constraints in organizing their livelihoods, while for poorer ones even small expenses sometimes mean much effort to meet them, as i.e. collecting the money to go to Almaty for a graduation celebration of the son.

In many cases, family relations seem to play a role in economic practices. They seem to be more prevalent than relations stemming from the local neighborhoods or from the workplace. Economically, they serve different functions: they may be creditors for long term and short term necessities; they may be a general assurance for unforeseeable life events. But family relations are reciprocal ones and thus not free of costs.

People who are government employees as teachers, in the local administration or in state enterprises such as railway or mining have stable incomes. In some households it is supplemented by pensions of grandparents. Generally speaking, stability of income is a scarce resource in this rural area and therefore has high esteem. In search of security, many households refer to informal activities as sporadic taxi driving, outwork, seasonal selling of home grown products, of preserves and the like. But many interviewees complain about the scarcity of options they have to make a living. Usually, by this, they refer to private salaried jobs. There is scarcity of these jobs, many are only temporarily available and are underpaid as to be compared to urban jobs.

Therefore, for many rural households subsistence production is an absolute necessity to be prepared for job losses and unforeseen life events as marriages, funerals, illnesses etc. Even if they do not sell the produce, they can guarantee large parts of nutrition and therefore keep expenses for purchases low. Particularly cattle-holding is multifunctional. On one hand, it guarantees meat for subsistence, on the other hand cattle functions as a rural savings currency, which can be reconverted into cash. Cattle-breeding, furthermore, increases the capital. However, also cattle involve risks such as diseases which can destroy one's capital. But only those households that are better off, can use cattle for other purposes than mere survival ones.

Life in rural areas is quite often perceived as risky due to the scarce and bad job opportunities. One aspect of the economic practices therefore is always to reduce given risks or to protect of yet not seen or unforeseeable risks.

The immediate vicinity quite often is very unfavorable for making a living. Respondents complain about water scarcity for drinking and gardening, they complain about the bad public transport, about bad state services and in some villages also about criminality while in other villages lack of crime is seen as an advantage of living in a village.

Taking both the rural and urban investigations, we see a rural-urban migration particularly among younger people for studying and finding employment in the city; however, the material suggests that migration does not destroy the close family links and support networks. Left in the villages are older people and those who have no particular skills to offer for the urban labor market. But some pensioners plan to return to the village because of family ties, lower living expenses and less air pollution and noise.

While for entire Central Asia labor migration abroad is frequent to send remittances to the family at home, for the Almaty sample, we do not find evidence for such. This is probably due to the comparatively speaking much better living conditions in Kazakhstan than in i.e. Kyrgyzstan.

State Transfers

Kazakhstan is said to have the best social security system in Central Asia. Not much is known about how people experience it. We want to highlight this.

Pensions and Planning for Pension Age

Pensions provide a big problem because payments are low:

"I have two more years to pension age. My wife is on retirement she has a small pension – 24000 KZT" (Alm int 4: 7, male rural).

Therefore many pensioners take up or look for jobs in order to make some extra money. Pensions increased during recent years but also did retirement age what is not always appreciated (e.g. Alm int 5: 79, female, urban).

Some respondents pay into the state pension fund (e.g. Alm int 4, male, rural, a railway worker) and feel on the save side:

"Of course, we pay in the retirement accounts. The organizations where we work send 10% of our salary to the pension fund of the Bank of Kazakhstan and we are working on this plan. In addition to this, we do not think about it, [...] think about the children, how to arrange their future" (Alm int 35: 110-112, male, urban).

Another respondent does not trust into this retirement scheme because

"They are opened today, but tomorrow they will be closed" (Alm int 13: 179, urban, two respondents, gender unknown).

Respondents feel uncomfortable about their future concerning both the security and the amount of their pensions.

"I am afraid of poverty in old age. At present, our parents have retired, which is barely enough for them. And what will happen to us? Will we receive that money which we have accumulated in pension savings? How much will the bread cost in 20 years?" (Alm int 19: 79, female, 46 years, urban).

"My pension contribution consists of only 10% [of the salary]. And the educators don't have high salaries you know?" (Alm int 34: 52, urban, female).

"I am very concerned about whether I can get a pension in the future. The solution of extending the retirement age to 60 or more years is unsecure. In this case, the government should provide jobs and adequate social support like in European countries. So, I'm afraid that I cannot get a pension in my own right. It is not known whether I live to this age, and there is no guarantee that my retirement savings go to the right persons" (Alm int 17: 67, male, urban).

Many people do not have the money to plan for old age retirement beyond the obligatory state system. Some parents therefore rely more on the traditional intergenerational reciprocity within the family networks:

"We tell our children, that they will have to care about us, this must enter into children's perception, because we live our life for the sake of our children. [...] But, sure, we dream that our children-grandchildren will take care of us" (Alm int 33: 77, female, rural).

A basic argument for future insecurity of pensions is the belief that salaries and pension increases will be eaten up by inflation (Alm int 32: 62, female, urban). Therefore, these respondents orientate themselves at real estate in order to have some security for old age (see credits and savings), others in rural regions think about investing into cattle for old age security (e.g. Alm int 5: 66, male, rural).

Child Allowance

Parents receive a state allowance. However, it was cancelled at the end of 2012. Maternity leave allowance depended on the former income. A respondent explains:

"The allowances were not high, maximum possible 40,000 KZT. In that time, the allowances comprised 40,000 KZT, and I got it monthly [...] Maternity leave in Kazakhstan lasts for two months before and 2 months afterwards, and after this term the employer requires you to come to work again. [... But] According to Kazakhstan's legislation, a mother with a baby has the right to stay out of work for a period of 3 years. But in this case, a mother does not have any allowance" (Alm int 29: 130-132, female, 37 years, married with one daughter, urban).

A woman complains:

"We have to worry about every little thing – how to feed children. Why are so many orphans in society? Their parents leave them because they don't know how to feed them. Wealthy people do not leave their children. In Russia, I have found that $ 15,000 according to our money is transferred to the bank account of each newborn [by the state] immediately after birth. Why don't we have such conditions? There are many women in villages, which give birth in the hope to receive 15000-20000 KZT. But then, at the end of the year they do not get even that money any more. For example, my sister-in-law gave birth to five children. The Government canceled even those available 20000 KZT. Her husband earns 30,000 KZT, which is not enough to raise 5 children. This is wrong [...] Children grow up, they need to be educated"(Alm int 19: 81, female, 46 years, urban, married with 1 daughter, Kazakh).

One respondent is going to take only a short maternal leave because of economic necessity.

"I'll plan to work until childbirth [and will return to work] within half a year. I can't stay at home for long because of lack of money" (Alm int 24: 139-141, female, urban, married, 1 daughter and pregnant).

In four of our interviews the young couples with good and stable jobs in Almaty, invited their parents (usually the mother-in-law) to live with them for a certain period of time, especially after birth, in order to return to work immediately after delivery. The mother-in-law takes care of the grandchild during working time of the young couple. The main reasons are: (1) child allowance is/was low and limited in time; (2) babysitters are expensive and (3) the young women are afraid of losing their jobs if they take a long leave.

The anxiety of losing the job after maternity leave (Alm int 20: 41, female, urban) exists in spite of state legislation protecting the women.

Another respondent (Alm int 39: 201-204) had got 30,000 KZT in a lump sum after she gave birth to her child, but no monthly allowance was granted to her as she did not fall under the category of distressed people. Another respondent reports to have received 6,000 KZT per month from the state due to her four children (Int 25: 31-33, female, married with 4 children, rural).

Disability Allowance

Also disability pensions are paid by the state.

"It is disability pension. Last year I got about 13,000 KZT. I have been getting it since 2004. At first it was too low, but now it was raised. [...]Every year I also get free resort for 12 days. This year I received disability for life"(Alm int 12: 75-80, male, 38 years, urban).

But compared to the expenses being caused by disability this amount is very low and people complain (e.g. Alm int 8, female, rural, Alm int 11: 9, female, urban).

In general one may conclude from our interviews, that state transfers exist and help people to ease their situations but as they are fairly low they do this only in a very limited way. People therefore explain that these transfers don't compensate for the costs they have to shoulder in case of old age, of disability or of child birth.

Expenditures of the Households

Expenditures for Housing

The housing issue is the most acute problem for many respondents, especially from urban areas. The majority of the respondents spend large part of their incomes for rental payments.

"The cost of housing, of course. Very expensive. It is very hard for young professionals, who have no housing in Almaty. If you work the entire salary goes to accommodation. No one will immediately give you mortgage" (Alm int 34: 143, male, Kazakh, 27 years, urban).

"I think the problem is that young people cannot get an apartment; they always live with their parents. We would like to live separately, but this is impossible in our Kazakhstan conditions. Accumulate money? Even after 20 years it is not possible to make out. A mortgage is also costly, because you need something to eat, dress, and raise children. Not only young people cannot buy houses. My colleagues all live in rented apartments. Retirees are also affected. My mother- in-law wants to buy something, but cannot. We, of course, help her, but she cannot ask us every time. I feel that she wants to buy something, but cannot afford it" (Alm int 20: 39, female, Kazakh, 30 years, urban, married, no children).

If we assume that there is a tendency and a desire towards nuclear families in the younger generation of Kazakhs, the housing problem plays a key role in hindering the full realization of this.

Those who were able to buy a house or apartment spend a large part of their income on mortgages, interest and repayment of the principal (see chapter savings and credit). These return payments are very high and make up a large portion of middle class incomes.

"I can briefly describe our monthly expenses: $ 850 we pay for the mortgage [...]The main part of the income goes to repayment of debt and to buy food" (Alm int 18: 43, male, 44 years, urban, married with two children).

Indeed, there is a social housing program provided by the state (e.g. Alm int 32: 66; Alm int 15: 25; for details see report from North Kazakhstan), however, there are long waiting lists.

Housing rents in Almaty are so high, that sometimes young people, who are employed, still cannot afford paying for the rent; in such cases they live with their relatives in the city for some time (e.g. Alm int 25: 37). In other cases the parents pay for the rent (e.g. Alm int 29: 43 Alm int 31: 12; Alm int 6: 22; Alm int 8: 194, Alm int 7: 52-53). Others even quit their job in the city because they cannot afford to pay the rent.

"He [son] worked in a restaurant in the city, but we hadn't had the opportunity to rent him an apartment. That's why he quitted that job" (Alm int 28: 19, female, Turk, rural, married).

Expenditures for Utilities and Communal Services:

Payments for utilities (water, gas, electricity, central heating etc.) represent mandatory monthly expenses. In some rural places where there are no water pipes, people have to take water from the well or pay for bottled water; if there is no gas, they have to purchase propane gas for cooking. If central heating facilities are not available people in villages use furnaces and have to buy coal. High costs for utilities and communal services occur in both urban and rural regions and these are considered as a problem by the citizens.

"About 5-6,000 – electricity is very expensive" (Alm int 26: 103, rural, female).

"Utility payments have become much more expensive. Even in summer we pay around 20,000 KZT. For these 58 square meters. So this is the problem" (Alm int 32: 16, 30, female, urban).

Expenditures for Education of Children

The matter of educational expenses (human capital formation) is a crucial issue. We will talk about education as a high value in Kazakhstan in the ng chapter. Here it will be sufficient to say that the burden for tuition fees and other costs related to schooling and higher education is high, and often people save for that particular purpose in advance when the children are young or even take up credits to finance a good education.

Expenditures Food and Clothing

Expenses for food are lower in the rural regions than in the cities, because many people practice subsistence production.

"In the village we eat meat without any charge. In this regard, the rural life is better, because you have to buy everything in the city, you have to pay for everything, but when you live in a village, you have many things at home. Moreover, it is not necessary to wear fashionable clothes in the village, ordinary and clean clothes are enough. We save a lot" (Alm int 31: 18 female, rural).

All respondents, however, report on the high inflation on food and other consumer prices. Expenses for clothes are particularly high for those households with fast growing children in kindergarten or school age.

"They look at the social position at school. I do not want my children to be the worst off. The cheapest baby shoes cost 7,000, a jacket not less than 13,000, the school uniform costs 17,000" (Alm int 8: 103, female, rural, Korean).

Expenditures for Transportation

Payment for the own car(s) (mainly urban), for public transport and private taxis sums up during the month. Here also some unpredictable expenses occur for car repair. Due to the importance of family networks especially among ethnic Kazakhs, visits to close and more distant relatives on family celebrations frequently occur, and such trips may consume considerable parts of the income (e.g. Alm int 21: 106, female, urban). Some people even save for such occasions (see savings and credit). Transport of children to school or to extracurricular events may increase transportation costs.

Expenditures for Medical Treatment

Having health problems causes significant household expenses, and is therefore regarded as a financial burden for which the respondents have to spend their savings, borrow money from relatives and friends (e.g. Alm int 32: 54, Alm int 36: 110; Alm int 15: 39; see savings and credit).

State employees are better off, since they get a basic treatment from the state. Sometimes the private companies are also obliged to provide health insurance. However, this only covers the employee himself and not his family members. Due to bad medical equipment of the public system people turn to the costly private system. Additionally, corruption having severely evaded the medical system increases the costs.

Expenditures for Celebrations and Mutual Support Networks

In addition to transportation costs visiting relatives and family celebrations requires presents.

"We give as standard gift USD 100" (Alm int 40: 97, male, urban).

Presents of course will be reciprocated once such celebrations will take place in the own household.[190] If the household has to organize such a celebration on its own (weddings, funerals, births, *tois* etc.), it is a very high expense, because such family celebrations involve festivities with a large number of guests. To some extent they can be planned in advance, for example by saving for wedding. If they happen unexpectedly, such as the death of a main breadwinner, people have to cope with this vulnerability by taking up loans and finding other solutions (see savings and credit).

"We spent about 7,000 Tenge [for the wedding of my son]. It is a very large sum for us" (Alm int 28: 83, rural, female).

[190] Gouldner, 1960; Gregory, 1997; Kolm & Mercier Ythier, 2006

"You cannot imagine how many people came for celebrating Sundet toi (a special holiday celebrating females). ... I spent 40,000 Tenge. There were 30 guests. Dishes were plenty. From 100% of products 60% were left, the rest of products I gave to poor people" (Alm int 8: 115, female, rural).[191]

"By our tradition, after the wedding ceremony, the bridegroom's side has to invite the bride's relatives to their house. Usually we invite guests in our home or in the restaurant, if we have the financial possibility. And also we simply give big sums of money. For organizing events" (Alm int 21: 74, female, urban).

In such cases, the household's net which includes relatives as well as close friends also serves for the financing of such costly celebrations in the form of interest-free loans that have to be repaid in the shorter or longer run (e.g. Alm int 36: 92, female, urban; Alm int 27: 251-256, male, rural).

Such 'help' is in many cases not a voluntary act but can also take the form of mutual obligation.

"It is in the Kazakh tradition, if, for example, someone from the family is in need, we help, if we need, they help" (Alm int 35: 78, male, urban, Kazakh).

This mutual obligation also involves a 'legitimate claim' to ask relatives for help in case of such family events.

Particularly vulnerable in such situations are households, where the network for one reason or another is no more intact. This may happen i.e. in the case of divorce.

"It is terrible to think about my daughter going to get married, because there is nobody who can help me. I rely on myself" (Alm int 10: 55, female, divorced, 2 children, urban, Kazakh, a single income).

The passing of a relative has the same impact, as people are socially obliged to conduct the traditional ceremonies (Alm int 30: 91, female, urban).

The funeral of my father-in-law [...]. A big account, almost 1.5 million KZT [...] How did we divide the costs between our relatives? Initially all costs were directly from the family budget, because we had no savings for a funeral, it happened unexpectedly. Later on, our guests brought us some money [...]. The biggest part of money came from our friends – a relatively big amount. Our friends have high ranks .... It is usually so in our circle [of friends], because not everyone has relatives who can help" (Alm int 22: 119-123, urban, female).

[191] According to tradition food has to exceed the number of guests by far, as a matter of generosity. In the same way it is generous to nourish the poor.

The mutual assistance of network members is not only linked to monetary help.

"Sometimes it is a financial help, sometimes we help with food, for example, their children or grandchildren study and we help them, provide them clothes, stationery, bags, briefcases" (Alm int 35: 82-84, male, urban).

The network may also promote a regular support exchange between rural and urban households, often as a kind of conversion between cash, kind and services.

"I have sisters, we support each other. They live in private houses with vegetable gardens. They help me with meat, vegetables and fruits. Generally, they help me, but when I have an opportunity, I help them too... I help with money" (Alm int 11: 30, female, urban, Kazakh).

"Personally, I have assisted to a brother and my sisters, two of them... In the past year I helped him [the brother] to get his daughter married. Modestly, but with dignity. I helped with the apartment, he had no apartment in the city, he sold his house in the village, so it was only little money. One sister lives modestly, but she raises two daughters by herself, her husband has died long time ago [...]. Also we decided to organize the weddings together. The girls live well, they already have two children" (Alm int 38: 20, male, urban, Kazakh).

"For example, we sometimes send money to our brother, because my son lives with him. He's my younger brother and he has four children" (Alm int 10: 39, female, urban).

"Medicine, to my brother, to my sister. But now my sister lives here and does not need any help. I buy clothes for my younger brother once a year. But mostly I help my mom" (Alm int 24: 92, urban, female).

"We do all we can do to help him [brother]. With money, doing housework" (Alm Int 27: 103, male, rural).

Rarely Kazakhs have a critical attitude towards an extravagant spending for celebrations taking the form of generosity.[192] However, some have, emphasizing that people overspend their capacities and even cannot repay their loans.

"All is about money (...) They do not celebrate the event as modest as before. They lose their purse-strings for 'toi', go into debts, not even thinking of the consequences, because for them the main thing is to keep up with other people. We used to put up tents for important events. Now people have other requirements. They are willing to cheat. For

[192] While generosity in celebrations has extensively been discussed in social anthropology (Hamilton and Woolsey Biggart 1992; Mauss 1970; Sahlins 1963) and even been characterized as an agonic exchange of rivalry, Bourdieu linked generous expenditure and display to the capital form of symbolic/cultural capital.

example, they promise to repay the debt, but after a grand 'toi', they are not able to do so. (...) If we cannot invite 300 people, we automatically turn into miserable people. I was surprised to hear once that the wedding of one couple was held with the participation of two persons only, even the parents did not come, because they could not. The couple went for vacation with help of the collected money. I am talking about the Russians. Russians, for example, live for themselves, but, we [Kazakhs] live for the sake of 'toi'" (Alm int 19: 74, female, urban Kazakh).

Some respondents see this reciprocity as critical:

"As we (Kazakhs) say it, if you want to quarrel with a relative or friend, lend him money and you will produce it" (Alm int 35: 109, male, urban, male, Kazakh).

"We cannot go to visits with empty hands. If you do not go [...] even then it will be necessary to give money" (Alm int 19: 74, female, urban Kazakh).

Very often children take responsibility for the parent's health issues (e.g. Alm int 37: 43, female, rural; Alm int 39: 170, female, urban) thus fulfilling their moral obligation.

Credits, Loans and Debts

Paying for commercial credits or repayment of interest-free loans from relatives or friends represents a very large proportion of expenses of many researched households (see corresponding chapter).

Savings

Saving "*is the decision to defer consumption and to store this deferred consumption in some form of asset*" (Kotlikoff 2007)[193]. This asset can be used for future consumption, investment or risk management. Concerning poor people or poorer people, one of the illusions of development economics until the 1980s was that poor people can't save. But Esther Duflo explains: "*Poor people have less money, but they have a choice. They can decide whether they eat more today or tomorrow. If you have only little money today and you know that you will have no money tomorrow, then you save a little. There is no reason why a poor person proportionally should save less as a rich person*" (Duflo, 2012; systematically Banerjee & Duflo, 2012; Schrader, Prakash, & Jyothi K.K., 2005). Everybody can save though some do it more often than others. "*Research on savings has shown that*

193 http://www.econlib.org/library/Enc/Saving.html access 08.04.2013

transaction costs, market failures, and behavioral constraints limit poor people's ability to save".[194] Furthermore, savings occur both in cash and in kind: livestock, landed property, etc., and the latter can be reconverted into money.

In the communist societies, saving was not very far spread, due to the 'nanny' state. Under the new market conditions, one may ask whether the growing necessity to lead an autonomous life produces a new pattern of saving and thus helps to create and enhance sustainability under economically risky conditions. In other words, what are the costs, failures and constraints to save? Do the households save at all and why?

Of course, there are all variants concerning saving, one may think of: some people deny to be able to save, others do save, others would like to save more; some save in kind, some in money. Some do it for the 'goods of modernity', other for traditional purposes. Saving happens at home and in banks, it may be long-term or short-term, occasionally or constantly. And also the amount may be differently.

No Possibility to Save

The possibility to save depends not only on the income situation of the household but also on its expenditures. For both, the location is important. Living in the countryside is cheaper, for example by doing some subsistence production or animal husbandry, but also the salaries are lower. Furthermore, we have to keep in mind that not every household pools its different incomes, but perhaps only a certain sum for everyday–life expenses such as food. The individual living conditions of the sample households cover a wide spectrum ranging from the said incapability to save to long-term planning. Most of the interviewees, who explain not being able to save, have expenses, due to which they believe that they can't save.

"*Unfortunately, not*" says a male respondent from the countryside (Alm int 27: 233-236, male, rural). But he admits that they took a credit for purchasing consumer goods such as a refrigerator, a washing machine and a TV. The problem of behavioral discipline or subjective constraints to save is even clearer in the following case:

> "We do not have enough money. It is enough only for food. We have no opportunities to save money, for example, as our parents were making it by using the savings books [...]. For us it is unreal. We live from paycheck to paycheck" (Alm int 28: 66-67, 89, female, rural).

[194] http://www.PovertyActionLab.org/Finance-Microfinance, accessed 30.03.2013, 13.12 h

This household has five members. The respondent works as a cook and has additional income by selling vegetables. Her husband works in a mining company, the son in a construction company. His wife is housewife. Son and daughter-in-law have one child. As we learn from the interview, they spend a lot on consumer items as well as on family celebrations. They have never taken a bank credit, but they seem to 'muddle through', though not orientated towards future risks. This is a pattern, we find quite often.

Even in a household with three incomes, the female respondent denies to be able to save (Alm int 19: 43, female, urban).

"No, unfortunately not. We live without any saving" (Alm int 22: 112, female, urban).

reports this married woman with two children. The family has two incomes, and the woman complains about the financial instability. However, she explains, they can get help of parents and friends in case of urgent necessities. In fact, thus, they have a social capital enabling them to challenge possible risks.

Others can't save and even have to take a credit to finance expenses at the beginning of each new school year.

The ambivalence of saving and spending is best expressed in the following quotation:

"No, it is impossible. We spend all our savings on education for our children [...]. I have a list for each month. It is minimal. It is food products, education, sports. It is impossible to cut down on anything. I think we could save, for example, we could buy fewer things. Generally, I do not know. I don't want to confront myself with the task to save money" (Alm int 21: 138, 162, female, urban).

In other interviews, people look for cheaper educational possibilities for their children or cut down on sports activities.

No possibility to Save because of Temporary or Periodical Problems

Some interviewees would generally have the possibility to save, but they explain that it is difficult due to temporary or periodical problems. This may be children, who study (Alm int 18: 43, 45, male, urban), or housing construction. But they nevertheless accept the necessity to save, in money or in cattle as is often done in rural areas.

"When building will be over, I shall start to reserve money for ... [the marriage of my daughter]" (Alm int 10: 56, female, urban; divorced, two children and sister).

"I would not say that we have so much money, but we have some opportunities. So certain part of our income we can save. At this moment, we have some difficulties related to current expenses. But we try" (Alm int 15: 45, male, urban).

The following respondent is currently unemployed. He says:

"Not now. Our budget fully absorbs our revenues. Our expenses exceed our revenues. We need to borrow [...]. We are having friends, relatives, and can borrow money" (Alm int 25: 53, female, urban).

Occasional savings

Some of the sample households have savings but usually no larger amounts. The reasons are manifold: repay of credits, high mortgages, too many responsibilities. Richer as well as poorer households feel trapped in such situations.

"I use another type of "piggy bank". But only small sums and only for some aims. For example, before New Year or birthday I try to save money for presents for my son" (Alm int 26: 100-101, female, urban).

"Not always, but sometimes we do" (Alm int 17: 41-42, female, urban).

"Well, there is some possibility to save a little. Now my son in the city gives us money that exceeds his expenses. As I told you already, we save money in summer. We accumulate it from the monthly salary. Sometimes there is also additional work" (Alm int 1: 33-34, male, rural).

"We cannot save up substantial sums of money. For all the purposes, including apartment, wedding, funeral or old age. We cannot save for several purposes" (Alm int 32: 52, female, urban).

"But we increase the livestock number; they say the livestock is hard cash" (Alm int 31: 53-54, female rural).

After having so far described how far the sample households can save, we shall now consider the different purposes for which they save, and how far these purposes are related to coping with vulnerabilities.

Planned Savings

Some people save for undefined purposes, as general risk prevention: "*For the 'rainy days'.*" (Alm int 20: 28-29 female, urban). But interestingly enough, the same respondent admits: "*We have not learned yet to save money. We do a little, but not as much as we would like*" (Alm int 20: 28-29, female, urban).

But others have clear purposes in mind:

"In order to improve and meet the needs [...] For example – to buy a newer car, furniture, TV, car repairs, domestic appliances [...]. [For treatment] because a dentist is expensive. It requires money. At the given moment we don't have an insurance. [...] We should continuously think about this" (Alm int 15: 47, 49, male, urban).

And others do saving strategically (Kotlikoff 2007):

"I set the money aside and I bought immovable property to sell it if anything would crop up. The real estate brokers are doing it [the sale] now. Yesterday I talked with them about it; someone wants to buy [...]. It is land parcels in Almaty and Atyrau. Atyrau is the oil capital of Kazakhstan. My property is located in a good place. Well, I have made this investment in advance in 2003, because I knew I had children" (Alm int 39: 23-28, female, urban).

One respondent refers to a savings 'game', knows since Soviet times and played among good colleagues. In fact, it is a way of raising greater sums on the basis of reciprocity.

"Basically we ask our friends. In my working place, we, along with colleagues play 'Black Cash'. Thus, we are trying to collect a large sum. We play with 10-15,000 KZT each. Actually, I do not like to ask to borrow. The best option is to play the 'Black Cash' or savings" (Alm int 17: 46, female, urban).

Saving in livestock has a certain advantage compared to saving in cash: it is not so easily spent in everyday-life, but livestock is sold for particular planned expenses, as the following respondent explains:

"We have an opportunity for saving. But we don't save in money terms. We don't raise much in money. When we raise money, we spend a lot. For example, as we have livestock, we need to build the farmyard, the haymow. These are expenditures, then our house. We bought the house in this place. Near the house, we need to build a site hut, replace the roof of the house, and other trifles. In such case we just sell our livestock. If it's a cow – we sell a cow, if a horse – we sell a horse. We survive owing to our livestock. We have 15-16 horses, nearly a hundred of mutton" (Alm int 4: 29, male, rural).

Interestingly, micro financial institutions or credit associations that may organize savings are not mentioned at all, although they were set up by the state since 1998 in order "to combat poverty and unemployment" (Nazarbaev 2008a: 198). Maybe we can hypothesize, that, where strong family relations with their obligations to help each other do exist, these function as a kind of "family network insurance" so that participation in individual credit and savings schemes is less important.

Which special purposes of saving do the respondents mention? In general, in Kazakhstan people save for old age, real estate, for children's future, for obligations stemming from family relations, for the "goods of modernity" like cars, recreation, refrigerators and the like, as have been mentioned already above.

Old-Age Security

Pensions in the country are low and the complete introduction of the new system introduced in 1997/98 will only be fully established in 2038/40. Despite this, among large parts of the population it seems clear, that one should take provisions for old age. At present, pensions for many elderly are very low and force their offspring to help – apart from the moral obligations that go hand in hand with this. For many of our respondents, old age provisions are a topical issue.

Some of the working respondents, who have to pay 10% from their income for their future pensions, relate the obligatory deduction from their salaries as saving.

"Of course, we put the money in retirement accounts, the organizations where we work sent 10% of salary to the pension fund of Halyk Bank of Kazakhstan and we are working on this plan" (Alm int 35: 110, male, urban).

"As I work on the railway, I do pension accumulation. It then will help me, when I shall retire. At that time, I think, we will receive that pension which is due to us" (Alm int 5: 60, male, rural).

Due to the obligatory character of these deductions, other respondents probably do not consider these payments as savings for old-age security at all and do not mention them.

Real Estate

In the following quotation we find a direct relatedness between old-age security, old-age independence and apartment purchase.

"I would like to open a mortgage account for every son to provide them with their own living place [...] but we can't. For now we have been saving for one apartment. For 4 years so far since the autumn of 2008. But the housing prices in Almaty are very high, one of the highest in the whole world, because our citizens – Kazakhstani – can afford it. To buy a house abroad, in Bulgaria for example, is much cheaper. You live abroad, where you can buy a whole cottage. Just buy it. But even the amount that we saved for 4 years can't help. And I would really appreciate if each son had his own place to live in. My pension contributions consist of only 10%. And the university lecturers don't have a high salary, you know. There is not even one million Tenge, I suppose" (Alm int 32: 52, female, urban).[195]

The wish for apartments for the sons implies that the pensioner must not live with one of his sons in order to survive, as often done because of economic necessities and/or as part of traditional family obligations. Other respondents take a similar orientation, even if they can't afford buying (Alm int. 31: 65-66).

The respondent from Alm int 9 reports from his experience with real estate purchases as good economic investments:

"I'm for real estate, of course. Once I heard a conversation between two men, one said, that he had bought the land and paid USD 5,000, and another one had bought a Jeep for USD 7,000. I was young, but I evaluated the situation. The car can crack down tomorrow, but the land is a good investment. I already faced it. Once our aunt from Kyrgyzstan, my mother's older sister, moved to us. We bought her a one-bedroom apartment for USD 700 in Kapshagai, it was 7-8 years ago. Today, this apartment costs about USD 20,000. … She does not live there anymore But we still have this apartment. Therefore, I am for real estate, for keeping it there" (Alm int 9: 60-63, female, rural).

Children's Future

Investment in children's future is of high value for most citizens of Kazakhstan, as our quantitative results already showed. To provide some of many examples:

"I am a farseeing person; for example, as I have to pay for my daughter's education, I save and pay for it in the first place. And then I live as I can. In extreme cases, I am saving on food. I don't go to beauty salons or anything like this. I do everything according to a plan. Primarily, of course, tuition fees. After that, I can allocate the budget. May be I'm too economical to myself, but my daughters' health and education have always been in the first place. I'm not saving on them" (Alm int 11: 38, female, urban).

"I always think how to save the money for him, for his education and adult life. It is said that they have to achieve all themselves… but in our days money plays a very important role. You must dress good to go to work in a prestigious organization; you need to look all right" (Alm int 9: 57, female, rural).

[195] Here the respondent refers to the pension system in Kazakhstan where everybody pays 10% of the salary. See the more detailed discussion of the pension system in the regional description.

Celebrations/Visiting Relatives

Good family relations rank high as value. They are a major part of ethnic Kazakh culture.[196] But also for other ethnics they are important. Sociologists discuss social relations as social capital. Many households borrow money interest-free from close relatives or occasionally friends and help each other in cases of insecurity and big expenses like for funerals and weddings. Social capital, as discussed (... (Coleman 1987, 1988) consistently has to be maintained because otherwise it gets eventually lost. Marriages and funerals as well as visits play an important role in this. Funerals e.g., for Muslim believers, imply visits on the day of the funeral itself, after 7, 40 (50 in some regions), 100 days and after 1 year. People save for all these occasions.

"Yes, now at the end of July we want to go to Ridder [in East Kazakhstan], to my relatives. We have been saving money for this purpose for 3 months [... but for nothing else]. We can go now, but after returning we will not have money even for bread" (Alm int 26: 93, female, urban, Russian).

"I think that starting from September we will start to plan toi [family celebration]; we have to be as one family and we are going to Aktobe, it is also large costs back and forth" (Alm int 13: 254-255, male, urban, Kazakh).

"If there is a wedding, we will sell livestock. Our livestock is our saving. For wedding, we may sell a horse. The livestock now is expensive, if you sell one horse, you will receive 200,000 Tenge. If it is a dobbin – 100,000. We kill the livestock ourselves, totally 400-500,000 may be enough for wedding. Then this money returns. Our relatives, friends bring money. All expenses are met. Treasury is God given" (Alm int 37: 63, female, rural).

"There are weddings of relatives; both they and we have had funerals, so there was some spending too. Once in a month, I try to save at least two hundred dollars" (Alm int 11: 53, female, urban, Kazakh).

For the "Goods of Modernity"

The households also save for cars, for TV stations, for recreation and the like.

"She does not take a credit. She saves money, tries to sell the old car and then to buy the newer one [... It is] not exactly a new car. She sold her old car and now she doesn't have a car. She wants to buy a better one" (Alm int 36: 39-46, female, urban).

---

196 "Herrgott, lass uns nicht ohne Gäste sitzen, schick uns jemanden! dachte Kussen" (Muratbekow 1979), translated into English: "God, don't let us without guests, please send someone to us! Kussen thought".

The following household directly links purchases of higher value with the necessity to combine savings with a credit:

"We want to accumulate a principle part of the amount, and take a credit for the residual minimal amount [...] We have started to save money for a car: we have decided to do this first and only then, to start saving for a house..." (Alm int 29: 93, 98-99, female, urban).

Recreation is an important issue among middle class people in Kazakhstan. It concerns health, but to a larger degree, it concerns a lifestyle, the roots of which already date back to the Soviet period. Vacation at Issyk Kul and other places played an important role for the people. During the post-socialist period, middle-class lifestyles have replaced the Soviet ones. We find in some of the interviews (not discussed in this chapter) that visiting Issyk Kul is looked upon as normality, while travelling to Turkey is an expression of a highly appreciated lifestyle of the middle class. For most middle class people this may require discipline of saving for vacation.

"I generally prefer to follow the economic principle in my life, to save a certain amount and not to touch it. If I travel somewhere, I know, I have to have a certain amount of money. I do not like to travel using the last money. Having three children it is not adequate to act otherwise nowadays. I always count each penny" (Alm int 39: 46, female, urban).

"This year we are going to spend our vacation in Kazakhstan, where we have fine places, too. That is to say, in comparison I can say, as far as I have already travelled over the world, we have good places. Yearly, we had a rest with the children in Turkey" (Alm int 39: 171-172, female, urban).

"Every year, I tried to go abroad with my girls. Despite that we were saving money for buying a new car... for the old car's change exactly, because we already have two cars" (Alm int 23: 66-67, male, urban).

Tensions about Savings

Decisions and allocations of money may also cause tensions within the household if other household members do not agree to these and would like to do allocations in a different way. In the following quotation the situation is such that the household has a high income equally raised by husband and wife. They have problems with each other. The female respondent complains:

"I always save money. I can save, but he never saves money. I think he just spends it in restaurants or cafés or he has somebody [...]I have always observed, when we go somewhere with friends, he uses to spend a lot of money" (Alm int 24: 40-44, 48, female, urban).

"I wanted to buy a car, collecting money for a car for myself. I hide it. For example, I get 150,000 or 180,000. I hide half. Any working woman does so. This is normal" (Alm int 25: 54, female, urban, now unemployed, talking about the past).

These remarks are in line with research on micro banking (cf. Schrader 1997), that has shown that women at average are better householders than men and are even able to save small amounts of money if they are poor, while their husbands tend to waste and immediately spend money.

Where do the Respondents Save?

Saving in banks requires system trust (Misztal 1996; Schrader 2004). Trusting in banks requires a process of good experience, long-term stability of the domestic economic system but also the world financial system, as well as sound banking practices. It is well known that during the first decade of post-socialism the banking systems throughout the Soviet Union follower states were very fragile, often causing the collapse of private banks and the loss of savings of the customers. The banking crisis of 1998 plays a role in many interviews. But which attitude do the respondents take towards banks in a period of higher stability? Let's look into the interview material.

"We keep money in the bank" (Alm int 36: 82, female, urban).

"In the National bank" (Alm int 5: 58, male, rural).

"We keep money in a bank, for example, on deposit, etc. [. . .] We trust our banks, because our banks are now working steadily, for example, "Kazkommertsbank" or "CenterCredit". I think it is very interesting, because if we are served in those banks, our money will increase, it is an interest. We are planning and buy property from these savings, etc." (Alm int 35: 50-54, male, urban).

But we also find other positions:

"At home" (Alm int 20: 29, female, urban).

"I do not trust our banking system. I monitor the information about it, and I know as a lawyer what it means being rushed in some problems in Kazakhstan because of claims of the customers to the banks and financial institutes. I invest money in immovable property as a priority, and in gold. Anyway, the gold warrants. I have checked it by experience, and the gold is also valued as memory. Oh, girls, my daughter-in-law will be. . . " (Alm int 39: 42-44, 48, female, urban).

"[Trust in banks?] Not at all. Only in Narodniy bank. Afraid of Kaspii [bank]" (Alm int 8: 56-61, female, rural).

If we look at the answers concerning trust in banks, the opinions are mixed. Even those who trust in banks seem to have a preference to state banks, believed to be more stable. Those, who have higher incomes or are stronger involved in the business world or live in Almaty do not seem to have higher trust in banks. This may perhaps explain the strong incentive towards investing in, or saving for real estate (land, apartments, and houses). But, from a macro-economic perspective, the strong increase of prices for real estate in the cities is of course no guarantee for the future, as we have learned from many real estate bubbles. The incentive to save in gold has hardly been mentioned explicitly, although it existed traditionally also as dowry. How far this has been replaced by the purchase of consumer goods or even real estate (some of the respondents save for that purpose to purchase private property for their children) is difficult to assess form the material.

Credits

Now we explore into households' attitudes towards loans, credits, and mortgages. In English, the terms 'loan' and 'credit' are used interchangeably. Taking credits or loans makes a person a debtor to another person or organization. Many respondents don't distinguish between the two terms (e.g. Alm, int 10, § 51; 19, § 83). However, some of them do. By 'loan' those refer to non–commercial, mainly interest free borrowing, while they associate 'credit' with commercial borrowing from banks where interest payment is involved. Often, as we will see at the end of this chapter, this distinction is also connected with negative attitudes towards banks.

"I do not take credits. Sometimes I take a loan from friends, then I return it quickly" (Alm int 38: 22, male, urban).

"No, we did not want to take a bank's credit for building the house, we asked our friends for loans" (Alm int 23: 55, male, urban).

Another specific form of credits is mortgages, referring to the purchase of landed property by providing the property title as a security. Relevant from the perspective of households is not only, from whom one gets a credit but also the purpose of it, whether it is for investments or consumption. In scientific literature, the idea is, that credits for investments initially cause a debt but later on generate returns (capital finance accounting), so that the overall final outcome is a profit for the investor. Consumption credits are treated as a loss of financial resources from the perspective of the household which does not engender profits. While analytically such a distinction may make sense, in practice, however, it is not so easy to make a clear-cut distinction between consumer credits and investment credits (Schrader 1997, 2000a). A car bought on credit, for example, can be considered a consumer item, but when it turns out to make an income by informal taxi driving, the purchase becomes an investment. Additionally, it may as well represent simultaneously consumption and saving as other durable goods do (Bryant 2006: 87).

Credits in market economies increase the purchasing options by offering fresh money. They may be used for the fulfillment of long-term needs or e.g. for bridging short term scarcities. Options are installment purchases, higher purchasing credits and debit cards, special consumer credits offered by banks and shopping centers. These options represent only some of those means to make people spend money, although they presently do not have it. Taking credits needs experience and knowledge in order not to run into indebtedness traps by having problems to handle interest payment and return of the principal. To cope with credits requires planning capacities of households which, in the case of mortgages e.g. can span even a period of 30 years and more.

In consumption, monetary, social and cultural aspects overlap. Many authors have referred to the aspect of esteem connected with consumption, others have hinted at middle class lifestyles or tastes of distinction (Bourdieu 1986; Douglas and Isherwood 1996; Veblen 1953). The orientation at positional goods can imply very different items, but very often it refers to the possession of a house in the 'right' living quarter or the possession of a big foreign car (e.g. a SUV). In general, credits offer people the option to display a lifestyle which they would otherwise not be able to afford.

People take credits for different purposes. The first form of credit that we want to consider is *mortgage credits* for the purchase of land, apartments or houses or for the building of houses. In these cases there may be involved not only the creditor but also his/her children, as they may be the beneficiaries of the mortgage; or they take up a mortgage in their name to help their parents financing the purchase of an apartment. From the perspective of the people, landed property in the form of land, house, or apartment is an investment; it engenders security for the household, at present and for the future, it makes them rather independent from the residential market, however, at the expense of long-term repayment conditions.

"We have a mortgage [from KazCom bank]. Big credit. It was taken for our apartment, in which we are living now" (Alm int 22: 107-108, female, urban; married with two children).

"For a house. Still 20 years [repayment]. We have a mortgage" (Alm int 34: 58-60, male 27 years; wife, 1 child and his parents).

This respondent combines the incomes of three different jobs, his wife makes an income from design work, his mother receives a pension and his father (in addition to his pension) is looking for a job.

Also the next respondent reports that she and her living partner want to buy a house. They are both working in a bazaar and together, they make an income of only 90,000 KZT.

"We plan to buy a house" (Alm int 26: 99, female, 24 years, urban; Russian, divorced and a new relationship with Uighur man, 1 child).

But so far they were hesitant.

"We of course thought about a credit for an apartment. But there is a lot of papers [...]. Also we thought to buy the flat of my father. But if we paid about 200 USD per month [what we can afford], we would pay for 8 year. We do not want to pay so long" (Alm int 26: 95, female, urban).

Often, the debt burden is very high and exceeds the capacities of the people, so that they have to find ways to cope with this problem. In the above case, the couple would have to pay 31,200 KZT out of their 90,000 KZT monthly in a situation where they have hardly any job security.

"When we were building a house we had loans. We had got an apartment as public servants. We collected a lot of credits. We sat down and calculated all the time what we have to pay for the bank loans, even without repaying the principal amount. I have good wealthy friends. We took a large amount from them. We paid back all the loans. Now there rests to return the money only to one person. It's a very large sum. If we will sell that apartment, we can pay back a big amount of the debt. But we do not pay interest to a bank. The income that my husband earns is not spent for the repayment. This income fully goes to family needs. It will become easier to breathe" (Alm int 25: 61, female, 34, urban, married 4 children, and husband's nephew).

Also the next respondent reports about the difficulty of finding appropriate financing to build a house. Their solution was that different household members and/or relatives took up different loans.

"Five years ago we started to build the house. My husband took two loans, the eldest daughter and me one each. We have paid them off" (Alm int 7: 37-38, female, rural).

Some respondents report from friends who could not repay their mortgage credit or interest and lost their homes (Alm int 35: 106, Alm int 30: 22).

Credits for the *purchase of a car* are mentioned in five of the interviews, but unfortunately, the respondents do not refer to the reasons for the purchases. But also for car repair people take credits, as in the following example, where the truck is used to make an income.

"Yes, we take credits. We have taken 300-400,000, once we took 500,000. We took money for the repair of the Kamaz [truck]. We repaired the Kamaz, put it into operation, now we try to get profit from it. There was no way that we do not pay for it [credit] in time although the interest rate did not grow. But it is difficult to pay for it" (Alm int 2: 33, female, rural).

Credits for other *consumer goods* such as refrigerators, washing machines, TVs, computers, mobiles, play stations, etc. seem to be frequent, be it in the form of deferred payment credits or by loans.

Credits for *education*, e.g. tuition fees, other fees, books and dresses were already mentioned. Often they also involve related costs such as accommodation in the city, where the universities are situated – at least for the rural households.

Credits for *food purchases* (charging the bill) are very frequent in village shops to overcome financial difficulties until the next salary.

Another reason to take up credits or interest-free loans from relatives is important *family events* (Alm int 1, Alm int 55).

Credits as a possible option to *overcome difficulties and vulnerabilities* is mentioned in several interviews. Characteristic is the following quotation.

"Now, to overcome these difficulties, we took a little money on credit in a bank. As we pay money gradually every month, it is imperceptible. Now we pay it according to a monthly order when I receive the salary [...] We took a credit of 200-300,000 KZT. Monthly we repay 20-25,000" (Alm int 1: 29-33, male, rural).

Which attitudes do the respondents take towards credits in general? Some respondents who are experienced with consumer credits and who well managed the repayment consider it as advantageous. The following respondent compares the situation of paying cash or taking an installment credit. She argues that the latter is advantageous.

"Because the price is the same. Marketing of household appliances is not fully developed. It is not the case that, if you pay cash, the cost of the refrigerator is lower; the cost is absolutely the same. [...] Actually, it is more advantageous, not only for us, but even for any millionaire, because you do not pay additional money at all: no fees, no commissions, nothing. You pay only the good's price [...] No more. We can pay back, taking from each salary" (Alm int 29: 73, 81; 37 years, female, urban).

Above respondent's household has an income exceeding 250,000 KZT. She is a sales manager and her husband works in the IT branch. They seem to calculate very rationally, analyzing the different options. The last installment credits, she had taken, were for a TV set and a fridge two years ago (Alm int 29: 65, female, urban). For larger amounts of money, the household saves some money and pays the rest by credit (Alm int 29: 93, female, urban). The maximum credit amount, she has taken was 200,000 KZT (Alm int 29: 67) – which does not seem to be high as compared with other households having much lower incomes.

The next respondent reports on problems with loans among relatives in the past. He talks about changing his attitude and switching to bank credits instead of asking relatives for support. He favors the former.

"About money, nowadays, when everyone earns a living himself, such collisions do not occur. Now if there is no money, thank God, there is a bank, we take credits as all people do. After all, now, the economy works like this. Now it is not necessary to ask for help of relatives" (Alm int 5: 37, male, rural).

Other people do not trust banks, some made bad experiences. In any case, they avoid taking credits.

"No, we haven't. We are trying not to take. A credit is a trouble; a credit is an infinite hole. You have to pay back every month" (Alm int 38: 47, male, urban).

Another respondent says:

"In my opinion we should not take a credit. We want to sleep well, because all day and night you think about the loan. I try not to take a credit under no circumstances. But I took one time and pay off until today, although I haven't finished to build the bathroom" (Alm int 10: 68, female, urban, divorced).

Some avoid taking credits especially from banks.

"I do not take credits. Sometimes I take a loan from friends; then I return it quickly. Usually I take a small amount, but I calculate from what to give back from" (Alm int 38: 22, male, urban).

"I cannot say that I'm afraid of it. I just do not trust them" (Alm int 9: 57, female, rural).

Loans from friends or relatives are often interest-free – even if they run over long periods such as for housing.

"No, we did not want to take a bank's credit for building the house, we asked our friends for loans. Also, my brother lent me a large sum on a long time-term basis and without interest" (Alm int 23: 55, male, urban).

"Personally for me a credit represents bondage The only reasonable occasion to take a loan is the purchase of an apartment" (Alm int 36: 114 female, urban).

Some respondents report, that they themselves, close friends or relatives have had bad experiences with credits.

"We did such a stupid thing, applied to Kazpost, now we have to pay twice as much. [...] I shall pay for 2 years. ... Twice, if not two and a half We took 100,000; imagine how much it is for two years ... I will never address the bank for credit again. Better to be hungry, [...], I'll better die of hunger, will eat the fodder, but do not go to a bank again" (Alm int 8: 62-81, female, rural).

"The story of credits started with a loan for our apartment. Then I got a job at my present company. Employees of the company persuaded me to borrow $ 7,000, arguing that by doing so I would be able to promote my business [...] I made all my sisters go bankrupt. And in order to pay back the loan, I worked like a horse. In the end, I had not achieved anything. I wish I had spent the money on something else – for example, to build a house, or to buy land" (Alm int 19: 85-87, female, urban).

In the following quotation, children had taken a loan for the purchase of a car.

"After repayment they said that they won't take it again. They would better eat something simple and live simple. It is rather difficult to pay back a credit" (Alm int 30: 20, female, rural).

The same person rejects taking credits for herself. She is 68 years old and lives together with her son's family.

"We do not like to live with debts. I have never lived being indebted. In Soviet time, all credits were without charge of interest and it was a good thing. And now why should I loan from somebody? If I have no possibility to give back?! What's then...? Now real estate mortgage is a hard thing. So many people have no homes because they could not give the money back: today they work, the other day – they are fired. It is so, isn't it?" (Alm int 30: 22, female, rural).

The following respondent is aware of the ambivalence of credits. They may help to overcome financial problems or may cause even more.

"We did not run us in huge financial problems in the form of loans for ourselves; we have tried to earn enough to overcome our economic and financial problems. But I know friends who took loans to purchase apartments [...]. Some left without apartments, became homeless. [...] Many businessmen prospered through these loans, and many have lost everything" (Alm int 35: 106, male, urban).

Education

The Meaning of Contemporary Education in Kazakh Society

Transformation affected the uniform system of education in the former Socialist Republic. The system differentiated and commercialized. It became a much stronger means for personal economic improvement than before. Education turned into a new currency for social placements. Nowadays it is attached to the idea of achievement and of upward and downward mobility. Connected with remuneration, it has become a form of capital for ones position in social space. As we will see, it can take the form of cultural as well as of social capital. For many of the younger as well as the older generation, related to each other by traditional intergenerational obligations, it may be converted into economic capital in the form of remuneration as salaries as well as old age care. But also for the others education is strongly connected with future positioning. In addition education plays a role as symbolic capital in the sense of Bourdieu.

Transformation also meant job loss of many people in the stately employment system and the de-evaluation of their previous experiences and certificates as well as the loss of the lifelong job guarantee. They had to look for different employment opportunities, an experience never made before. The new economic system urged people to develop new skills and abilities in their working life as well as in other fields of their lives. The newer generation has to be aware of the necessary fit between their capabilities and the job market to secure their livelihoods. Furthermore, education is seen as one of the main and most important sources for national development (Nazarbaev 2008a:326 ff.).

The findings below seek to highlight the meanings given to children's education, the challenges for the households concerning expenses for education, and other related issues.

Access to Education

All respondents aim at providing their children with a good education. Parents invest in the education of boys and girls. Our local study does not reveal any gender gap concerning this. A statement of one respondent from the rural area of Almaty:

"The eldest son studied at the university in Almaty, now he is working in construction. He is 24 years old. The next child studies in a master program, she has graduated first level. She is 22. The next daughter has graduated this year from KazATC [Kazakh Academy of Transport and Communications]. She is 21. Both daughters have studied with help of state educational grants. Because of this it is much easier for us. Following we have a daughter, she has graduated 11th grade in a High School. Following is our younger son; he has finished 9th grade" (Alm int: 1, 12: male, Kazakh, 51 years old, rural, married; also Alm int: 39: 12, female, Kazakh, 41 years, urban).

How do parents explain their strong emphasis on education?

"I think this is very important especially for girls because if we take the period ten or fifteen years ago, or even take the psychology of the Soviet era, and psychology in general, for example in Eastern countries, Muslim countries. I believe that now, especially for girls, it is necessary to have education, so to speak, intellectual development, etc. [...] because if we, men, cannot always find a good, a stable job. So to say, as the examples of the Western European, American, Japanese women show, women can show more flexibility in job search, they can find good, interesting work, and when a man, for example, is unemployed, they can, so to say, provide him a little. [...] I know that many women are helping their families more than their husbands" (Alm int: 35: 27-29, male, urban).

Not all parents are likewise outspoken and farsighted, but care for children's education exists among all interviewees, be they richer or poorer, be they living in the countryside or in a town or city, be they man or women. Interestingly enough, in the above statement the respondent refers to social change, comparing the role of women in the past and now, as well as the traditional roles of women and the changes brought by current insecurities. A good education of the wife can become a survival strategy for the household once the husband loses his job. But even more: the speaker believes that women are more adaptable to jobs than men.

Quality of Contemporary Education

After the transition period, and especially in recent years, there were many reforms and policy changes in the system of education in Kazakhstan, seeking to raise domestic education to international standards. Kazakhstan is currently taking an active part in the international Bologna process, to improve the quality of education in the country at all levels. Regardless of all these efforts, most of the respondents claim that the quality of education is still one of the major problems and concerns for them and their children. The following quotations show the opinions of our respondents, who all value education high and are ready to sacrifice for it:

"I am worried about the education of my child, because I see the problems of the other parents at school, and I am frightened. In the schools the educational level is very low, unfortunately. So we have been talking with my mother about [a different] school" (Alm int 29: 180, female, urban).

"The level of education is very low here. If possible it is better to study abroad" (Alm int 34: 145, male, urban; also Alm int 11: 71, 72, female, urban).

Others complain about the mismatch between the educational and the employment system or about the lack of international recognition of Kazakh degrees:

"I think that our education has outlived its usefulness. Nowadays the competition has increased slightly, that is, the competition has changed, and the educational system not. There is overproduction in the professional fields. It is as if to build cars and keep them in stock. Unless we find buyers, they remain unused. The situation is the same with our skilled staff. Universities produce experts into the nowhere. So there's no demand in the labor market, but the universities still teach the people. Education is the most acute problem" (Alm int 15: 75, male, urban; also Alm int 11: 57, female, urban).

"The education system must have a lot of gaps, the fact that our diplomas are not recognized speaks for itself. Diplomas of Lomonosov University, Bauman University (Russian universities) are recognized internationally, in Europe. Minimum, students get a good technical education. After receiving degrees in these universities, students can easily get a job, at least here in Kazakhstan. Parents try to give their children a foreign education, at least in Russia" (Alm int 18: 78, male, urban).

Additionally many people complain about the number and quality of rural schools. Some criticize the Kazakhization policy with its favoring of the Kazakh language, what in their eyes has led to a lowering of quality in schools, while some others prefer a Kazakh language school because of their strong Kazakh identification.

Household Expenses for Education

About half of the respondents worry about the payments for their children's education. In Almaty, both public and private nurseries, kindergartens, schools, and universities are believed to be all too expensive. For many families from rural areas, higher education at least is only available in the city. This increases the household's expenses due to either commuting or housing in dormitories or other places.[197]

"I am thinking about my children's education. State tests are a big problem for children and for their parents. Education in our country is very expensive. Dormitories are not available for everyone [...] The age difference is three years; I have to pay for my children's education for 8 years. I have no idea how I will get 100000 KZT per month, I will also need money for food, for electricity etc. Still I prefer living in the village rather than in the city. Our income is 80000 KZT. We have a family, we have children, we must provide them with everything" (Alm int 8: 193-201; 207, female, rural; also Alm int 19: 35, female, urban; Alm int 32: 58, female, urban; Alm int 25: 67, female, urban).

In order to get an idea about the monetary sacrifices, let us look into the empirical material, what our respondents say about prices. For private nurseries 50,000 KZT per month, for public nurseries 22,000 KZT (Alm int 29: 89, female, urban) are mentioned, for kindergartens the equivalents are 15 000, resp. 12 000 KZT (Alm int 26: 82, female, rural). For prestigious state institutions of learning, the payments can mount to 240,000 KZT per year (Kaz GASA[198], Alm int 13: 98, male, rural). Private high schools are not cheap either:

"Now my daughter studies at the Kazakh Turkish High School providing one of the best education in Kazakhstan, so people say. And this education is rather expensive. [...]. Competition to enter there was very hard, notwithstanding that this education is very expensive: 5,000 USD [per year], which is 820,000 KZT" (Alm int 39: 20, female, urban).

Concerning colleges respondents explain:

"My daughter goes to college, in a paid department. Again and again, I myself paid for her school, but I am not complaining [...] Every month I'm paying 10,000 KZT for my daughter's education. It suits me. In summer time I have less customers and it affects me. Not to get into difficulties I'm trying to do my best and work a lot" (Alm int 10: 19, 53, female, urban).

"For college we paid 60,000 KZT per year for a period of three years" (Alm int 12: 26, male, urban).

And university education is not available without financial burdens:

---

197 The opportunity of evening schools or part-time courses, where students could study in the evening and work during day time, has been abolished in Kazakhstan. Therefore, students don't usually have their own income, which creates additional financial burdens for the households' incomes.

198 Kazakh Leading Academy of Architecture and Construction – Kasachskaya Golownaya Architekturno-Stroitel'naya Akademia; http://biblicalstudies.org.uk/pdf/rss/31-2_151.pdf

"I had to pay for my education. [It was] very expensive. Momentarily it is 250,000 KZT per year. We had no money, and we had to find it urgently" (Alm int 27: 248-50, male, rural).

"Education [of the elder son Emir] was worth 230,000 [KZT] per year. Junior goes to 'Turan' [private university], he went there with a discount as "Olympian" [special award for discipline competition], and studying costs are 192,000 KZT [per year]. He is a second year student now, and we have to pay in full" (Alm int 6: 15, 19, female, rural).

One can well imagine how much a family has to pay per year, if there are several children in the household. Education fees constitute the main block of expenses of the households, up to 50% of the incomes and sometimes even more.

"Sometimes, even their [parents] salary is not enough to cover the cost of tuition" (Alm int 16: 39, urban).

As tuition fees have to be paid in advance, households have to calculate these expenses. One option is saving in advance for educational costs:

"I am a far-seeing person; for example, if I have to pay for my daughter's education. I save, because this payment is in the first place. And then I live as I can. In extreme cases, I am economizing on food. I don't go to beauty salons or anything like this. I do everything according to a budget plan. Primarily, of course, tuition fees. After that, I allocate the budget. Maybe I'm too economical to myself, but my daughters' health and education have always been the in the first place" (Alm int 11: 37, female, urban; also Alm int 9: 57, female, rural).

Sometimes credits from banks or from relatives have to be taken up or other financial sources have to be activated in order to meet the financial obligations for education:

"For College we had to pay 60,000 KZT per year during 3 years. [...] We took loans from a bank, and then we were repaying them monthly. We had no other chance, because we had too low wages, it was not enough for paying. That's why we took a credit for 6 months, then another credit for a year" (Alm int 12: 26-28, male, urban; also Alm int 16: 46, female, urban; also Alm int 5: 45-46, male, Kazakh, 52, rural, married, 2 children; Alm int 7: 44, female, rural).

Some respondents underline, that education does not only mean tuition fees, but also additional clothes, books, 'voluntary' payments to the school and class funds etc. (Alm int 13: 96, male, rural; also Alm int 25: 33, female, urban; Alm int 14: 97, female, 72 years, Russian, urban).

Parents, especially in the urban, but also in the rural areas of Almaty, also pay for various extra-curricular activities. This includes swimming courses, additional English lessons, dance courses etc. These parents do everything to give their children an optimal education. Some of these additional activities aim at improving the chances in university entrance exams; others are orientated towards the ideal of an all-embracing personality.

"With grade 5 we are planning to sign him up for the sport section for swimming and for English lessons" (Alm int 13: 277, male, rural).

"She was studying with private tutors, we've spent a lot of money for this, and that's why her results are very good" (Alm int 23: 73, male, urban; also Alm int 39: 15, female, urban; Alm int 25: 33, female, urban; Alm int 25: 33, female, urban).

Education as human and cultural capital

Good education can be considered as investment in human capital. This includes successful completion of educational levels. To achieve them, parents and grandparents sacrifice financially, as already described above. In order to further explore the topic, we asked our respondents about their priority goals in live and about future plans. The majority of them named a good education for their children and/or grandchildren (more than 20 interviews) as their priority goal:

"The children are growing up. We need to educate my son, after that master degree. Perhaps, he will go abroad" (Alm int. 22: 136, female, urban; also Alm int 20: 37, female, urban).

"...Also, I would like to give a good education to my granddaughter. My son didn't get it, but maybe we can give it to her..." (Alm int 28: 91, female, rural).

"I want my child to get a good education, I want him to visit some extra-curricular courses too, but we haven't got them in our village. Today I've heard that they have opened a football-class [in the next urban center], but the time is not good for me. The football course is in the evening and it takes 40 minutes [to go there]. If we lived in Kapshagai, my son would have visited it, but in the village there is absolutely nothing. At school we have some music classes, but there is no sports class" (Alm int 9: 112, female, rural).

Analytically, following Bourdieu, education may be looked upon also as *cultural and /or symbolic* capital. With their care for their children's education, the families hint at institutionalized forms of cultural capital. Type of schools, colleges and universities and their degrees matter. But human capital can also be seen in the books bought, in the extra-curricular courses, the children attend or in general, the importance given to good education. Good education seems to have the value of a marker for distinguishing oneself from others. This includes employing tutors, going to dance and painting courses, but also doing sports (Nettleton, 2006; Wynne, 2002). And this includes a incorporated self-recognition as a best player often expressed by superlatives: "*my daughter is one of the best pupils*"; "*my child studies in the best school/university*"; "*that school gives best education in Kazakhstan*"; and so on. Additionally children, who are involved e.g. in sports or dancing courses can participate in competitions and receive rewards – markers of cultural capital for the family. Parents are willing to pay for these additional costs, even if the burdens and costs are high. In such cases financial capital is converted into cultural capital. Parents thus feel proud to let their children participate because educational cultural capital has been incorporated.

"This winter my son had the opportunity to take part in an international competition for computer physics. But this participation was costly. And we had no money because we had not anticipated this participation. We [asked] my parents for help. [It cost] about 2,000 USD" (Alm int 22: 40, female, urban).

"Now our granddaughter [who visits a drawing course] goes to Leningrad [St. Petersburg]. It's 200,000 KZT She goes to Kasteev's [Art Gallery], she studies drawing in her 4th year. Next year they will have to go to the Netherlands or Paris. Our dad[199] (respondent's son-in-law) must work hard to save some money. They even [respondent's daughter and her husband] cannot go for holidays, because they don't have money for that" (Alm int 14: 27, female, urban).

Going to the United National Test, passing it and thus winning a grant is highly esteemed (Alm int 16: 57, Urban). Additional courses for preparation or tutors are supposed to better the chances to succeed.

"This year A went to courses to prepare for the United National Test. It is not obligatory. We have paid 100,000 KZT for them; she visits the courses after 3 o'clock. The first month costs 30,000 KZT, the last three months 23,000 KZT" (Alm int 12: 92, male, urban).

Only 3 of 40 respondents stated that their children's higher education was on the basis of a full scholarship. Parents whose children get a grant, consider it as a very important achievement and support to the household budget (Alm int 1: 12, male, rural, Alm int 31: 12, female, rural).

[199] Dad – in this terms means that he is the only bread-winning male in the household, as the respondent herself is widowed. Therefore, she defines the role of her son-in-law, as the main male bread-winner of the family, and calls him "dad".

Needless to repeat: such scholarships are prestigious and increase the family's cultural capital. There are cases when mothers or even a father quit her/his job in order to be able to bring children to school in the morning (Alm int 13: 81, male, rural). In other cases, parents think about leaving the countryside in order to give better education to their children. In one case the mother-in-law takes over the care of her grandchild so that her daughter and her husband can save money for the children's education in future.

"I baby sit with my grand-daughter, I take her to the child center. I am very busy (laughing). This spring I have gone with her to the child center every day as if going to work" (Alm int 36: 9, female, urban).

Education and Social Capital

For our respondents, education is an asset they invest into in order to guarantee a more secure life in the future; for themselves and/ or for their children. They do this as a conscious practice or follow traditional obligations. To achieve high cultural capital for their children the households also mobilize their social capital that is relatives that can house their children and can help with loans or supervision etc. Housing is of special importance for rural households who send their children to Almaty for studying, because this may lower the costs for studying considerably.

"They [relatives] always live [with us] because Z came from a large family and we have a lot of relatives. We are Kazakhs, open-handed people. There were many of Z's sisters who lived and studied at our home. They were the first generation and already got married. Now there is the next generation, which consists of grandchildren, nephews and nieces who are studying now. For instance, A is studying at the medical school" (Alm int 13: 39, male, 50 years, Kazakh, urban, married, 2 children).

However, not all of the households do so. Some prefer to rent apartments in order not to become dependent on their relatives.

"Kazakhs have a saying, it is necessary to live with relatives in the distance from each other" (Alm int 5: 35, male, Kazakh, rural).

"So we rented a flat. It is uncomfortable to reside at relatives [in the city], so we rented a flat. Sure, they visited our relatives, but they lived separately. Sometimes they lived in dormitories. Like this our children grew up" (Alm int 31: 12, female, rural).

Human Capital Formation as a Value, an Investment or an Intergenerational Family Insurance Mechanism?

For young and old respondents, for male as well as female ones, for all nationalities in Kazakhstan children's education ranks first even when the household is short in resources. Is children's education a value by itself in Kazakhstan? Some respondents clearly refer to values such as independence and honesty and an all-embracing personality.

"After graduating and owning a profession they can take care about themselves, live honestly, that is enough for us" (Alm int 2: 15, female, rural).

From other respondents (more than 10) one might assume at first sight that they consider children's education as a strategic investment into their children's future. But a careful view at the interviews shows that the boundary between value and investment is blurred. In the following quotations, the idea of a good job goes hand in hand with the idea of an easier life because of better job opportunities and sometimes with the idea of an all-embracing personality.

"I, for instance, reassure my children, especially my daughters, so that after education if they study hard and try, then they will be able to get a good job and that life will be easier. We hope and believe in the future" (Alm int 16: 53, female, urban).

"Yes, I am very happy with the children, because that money which we have invested in the [language] training, for example, of the eldest daughter, is justified now. The eldest daughter is working in a company, work is stable, interesting, of course; in competition in the labor market she found the job very easily because of her knowledge of a foreign language [...] We had invested into the training, into the intellectual development of our child over five years. [...] Now we are investing into the development of the second daughter in order, so to speak, when she will finish her studies she can find her calling in life, interesting work, etc." (Alm int 35: 23-36, male, urban).

In the following paragraph we again see that combination of value and investment, here even enhanced by the element of strategic investment into a higher education which is in demand in the labor market; because, if not doing so, it would be an unprofitable investment. To put it another way, the value of "good education" becomes commoditized; it can be achieved by a purposeful monetary investment not only into the best school or university but also into a specialization which is in high demand.

"I think it is a holy obligation of the parents to give a foundation to their child in everything. I mean, define the intellectual values and provide good education. It is very important and I am ready to pay for it. This is an aim I aspire and I purposefully approach to this aim. Now, please God, my son has decided to be an IT specialist. I think this is very actual and perspective specialty. I am not ready to pay for the unimportant profession. A diploma of just an institute is not so important for me. First of all, it is important for me that my son likes the profession. Secondly, this profession must be in demand. I see that some children of my friends had studied for a translator, lawyer or economist, and they just walk around with their diplomas. It is a foolish thing to spend the money for a diploma and not to work using the acquired profession. This is a wrong position. This is a misbalance in behavior. That's why we had discussed this issue last year and defined the profession and the objectives, including the family's budget" (Alm int 39: 22, female, urban).

Whether value and/or investment; education involves careful planning of the households budgets, and strategic allocation of available resources as we already have shown: savings, taking credits, borrowing, or simply putting education fees as a priority, moving to the city, quitting a job and looking for self-employment, activating help of relatives.

Education is related to values and economic goals and behavior in the sense of a human capital investment but also to an intergenerational insurance mechanism, mainly having governed traditional Kazakh intergenerational relations. According to those, the youngest son has to care for his parents usually living together with them. This could even include the raising of the youngest son by his grandparents. Although rarely found some parents forward such arguments.

"It is necessary that for the first part of your life your parents take care of you and for the second one, your children" (Alm int 39: 167, female, urban).

"My children grow up, we helped them. I think that in the future my children will be more independent and they will have to help me" (Alm int 10: 81, urban).

But some also express their wish for more independence between the generations, thus turning the intergenerational 'contract' into a voluntary agreement.

"I see their education as a strategic stability in the future, so that they will have a job. I am really worried about the future of my children. So all this is for them to have a normal quality education, so that later they could provide themselves, without relying on me" (Alm int 11: 51-53, female, Kazakh, 43 years, urban married, 2 children).

"We tell our children, that they will have to care for us; this must enter into a child's perception, because we live our life for the sake of our children. But sometimes we say that in our age they should live for themselves, we are not going to leech you off. Because we have jobs, when we become old, we will have our pensions. But, sure, we dream that our children-grandchildren will take care of us" (Alm int 33: 75-76, rural, female).

The analysis of the interviews shows the high value given to education by respondents both from urban and rural areas, from all age cohorts, from those with high or low educational degrees.

Almost in each interview, the respondents explained that (1) they have or had to pay for their children's education and that this is/was their biggest budget share; (2) nevertheless, they were ready and willing to invest in the best education as possible and even into extra-curricular courses; and (3) they believed a good education to be a door opener for a good future of their children. Therefore, high, and sometimes "over-proportionate expenses" and even credits were accepted as means to achieve an optimal human capital formation for their children. Human capital is convertible into cultural capital, and our respondents relate it to social competitiveness, to class distinctions, and the like. We also find some hints that the importance given to education aims at intergenerational reciprocity as a family insurance mechanism. But if this assures the traditional intergenerational 'contract' prevalent mainly among Kazakhs, must be left open as some respondents claim to establish voluntary relations between the generations based on independence.

The current generation of parents considers the labor market in Kazakhstan as highly competitive, forcing their children to be "better" than others. Therefore, in their eyes, good schools, tutors for the passing of tests and extra-curricular courses, studying abroad and other value adding means increase children's chances for a good life in Kazakhstan or abroad. Many parents hope for upward social mobility.

The research also revealed a strong notion of responsibility for the education of the children combined with a taste for competition and distinction. Very often, parents compare themselves with others, and superlatives are used to define themselves as a strong player in this field. This orientation goes hand in hand with the public attention given to education by the government and especially by President Nazarbaev[200]. Given the attention for human capital formation, the orientation at competition and distinction, we conclude, that market values in this field have been internalized.

Reciprocity and Safety Nets among Relatives

The Almaty case study and also the other case studies show that reciprocity networks among relatives and friends (usually referred to as "social capital" in the

[200] http://www.scientific-publications.net/download/index{Education}educational-alternatives-2011-1.pdf p. 14; http://akorda.kz/ru/page/poslanie-prezidenta-respubliki-kazakhstan-n-a-index{Nazarbaev}nazarbaeva-narodu-kazakhstana-29-yanvarya-2010-goda_1340624693

literature) touch many spheres of the household. They concern monetary and non-monetary aspects and are based on cultural norms of mutual help, particularly in 'strong ties' (Granovetter 1983) relations.

While in the literature mutual help is too often looked upon as an 'over socialized' (Hirsch et al. 1987) conception emphasizing the 'insurance aspect' thus the necessity to maintain such social capital. Some authors also refer to the norm of reciprocity (Gouldner 1960), e.g. the obligation to provide help, so that people cannot escape the claims of their kinfolk. Especially in crisis situations such mutual help can, however, become unbalanced. Those who are better off are obliged to permanently help their kinfolk and never will receive returns. Migration may be an opportunity to escape the claims of the kinfolk (Evers 1994). In our sample we also find some quotations supporting these arguments. On one hand we find people particularly from rural regions who feel obliged to help. They do not scrutinize helping their relatives. On the other hand we find some urban respondents who argue better not to have too close contacts to relatives or to keep monetary issues outside the sphere of reciprocity relations. It seems to us that particularly lower middle-class households need this security aspect of their networks as a last resort to get help if they cannot help themselves, while for better-off households the security-aspect in their networks becomes an option among others, which gives them the choice to reflect on the utility of such networks. If such a reciprocity becomes too unbalanced, they might prefer changing strong ties into weak ones or even to 'escape' the clutches of demanding relatives by no longer maintaining or dissolving such networks.

But also a change in the network relations may occur in the urban setting. Among urban households friends and colleagues may replace relatives in such support networks. Perhaps it is easier to renounce the claim of a friend or colleague to be supported than the claim of a relative, due to Kazakh norms of strong family ties and family orientation.

4.4. Qualitative Analysis from the Kyrgyzstan Interviews

Galina GORBORUKOVA[201]

Introduction

Kyrgyzstan has a population of 5.6 million people with 66% living in rural areas. In terms of population Kyrgyzstan is one of the smallest Central Asian countries. As measured by the UN Human Development Index 2012, the country now ranks 125 out of 187 countries, which is the lowest amongst the Central Asian countries and the CIS. Economically, Kyrgyzstan belongs to the group of low income countries with a GDP per capita of USD 970 in 2012. According to the Kyrgyz National Statistical Committee, real GDP contracted by 0.9% in 2012, reflecting problems in the important mining (gold) sector. "The level of poverty in Kyrgyzstan, according to the UNDP reports, in the past two years has increased by 6%. If in 2009 the level of poverty was reported to be 31%, in 2011, the figure increased to 37%. Without remittances from labor migrants from Russia and Kazakhstan, 43% would have ended up below the poverty line".[202]

For many households remittances are a crucial source of income. According to World Bank statistics, workers' remittances and compensation received by employees amounted to about USD 1.7 billion in 2011, equivalent to 28% of country's GDP. This is an important source of external financing for the country; however, it also reflects suboptimal employment prospects.

According to UNCTAD in 2011, Kyrgyzstan ranked 64th out of 181 countries regarding the inward foreign direct investment performance. The investment climate is important for the Kyrgyz Republic to improve its energy sector. According to the latest Corruption Perception Survey conducted in 2012 by Transparency International,[203] Kyrgyzstan was ranked as 154th out of 174 countries; that is, it is among the worst 10%. Rent seeking slows down economic development. The literacy rate is still high, but the quality of education is declining.

The political situation in 2010 has unveiled the high degree of fragmentation of the Kyrgyz society into many elements characterized by ethnic, religious and social features. The most obvious division is the one between the urban and rural population. This has several effects on the political, social and economic trends in

[201] This chapter was revised by the editors.

[202] Kyrgyz National Statistical Committee, http://www.stat.kg/; access date 15-07-13

[203] Taken from Transparency International: http://cpi.transparency.org/cpi2012/; access date 29-08-13

the country. The rural population is the "main driving force of internal migration, because rural poverty is still widespread. Rural-urban migration puts pressure on urban infrastructure and leads to an emergence of poverty belts around the major cities. The revolutionary events of 2005 and 2010 had been driven by the rural population both in the provinces and the capital city. The political situation remains volatile, in particular due to the overall fragility of the governance system, and nationalist movements. The country is also geographically fragmented. The north is more developed thanks to fast growing service, trade and tourism sectors while the south is mainly agricultural.

Moreover, the population density in the south is high but has scarce resources (land and water) and inadequate quality of infrastructure and coverage. The area of Kyrgyzstan being a part of the Fergana valley (shared with Uzbekistan and Tajikistan) is considered to be a conflict prone area.

With regard to natural resources, livestock and pastures are significant factors for rural livelihoods in the Kyrgyz Republic. With the collapse of USSR, the livestock sector experienced a dramatic decline, but has now recovered its former level. However, the pressure on pasture land is now much higher than in the Soviet times because then complementary fodder had been imported, especially during winter. The pastures closest to the villages have deteriorated most and will continue to do so if no integrated management is practiced in the future. Agriculture in Kyrgyzstan accounts for about 20 percent of GDP and absorbs more than half of the country's labor force. With 30-40 percent of Kyrgyzstan's population living at or below the poverty line, poverty remains deeply entrenched in the rural regions. The most important sub-sectors for present-day subsistence agriculture are livestock farming and dairy production, in which some 90 percent of rural households are involved.

Bishkek, the capital of the Republic of Kyrgyzstan, with a population of about 1 million, is located in the Chui valley at the northern foot of the Kyrgyz Ala-Too mountain range, an extension of the Tian Shan mountain range, which rises up to 4,855 meters (15,928 ft.) and provides a spectacular backdrop to the city. It is situated on an inclined plain, at an altitude of 700-900 meters above sea level. The name is thought to derive from a Kyrgyz word for a churn used to make fermented mare's milk (*kumis*), the Kyrgyz national drink. Founded in 1825 as the Kyrgyz-Khokand fortress of 'Bishkek', then, in 1862, named as the Russian fortress 'Pishpek'; in 1926 the city was renamed Frunze after the Bolshevik military leader Mikhail Frunze. In 1991, the Kyrgyz parliament restored the city's historical name.[204] Bishkek is now a multinational city with over 80 nationalities. North of the city, a fertile and gently undulating steppe extends far north into neighboring Kazakhstan. The Chui River drains most of the area. Bishkek is connected to the Turkestan-Siberia Railway by a spur line.[205]

Socio-Demographic Profile of the Households

In this qualitative study we took 40 interviews. 25 of them took place in Bishkek, 7 of which were conducted with men and 18 with women. 15 interviews took place in villages, with 11 interviews taken from men and 4 from women. Villages covered in this project include 4 settlements. All of these villages are located in Chui region at the foothills of the mountains, and are within 50-70 km away from the capital city – far enough so that these villages do not form suburbs. There is a school, a small hospital (FAP), and a rural administration in each of them.

On average, every household consists of 4 to 6 people, with the majority of larger households in rural areas. Nuclear families are typical among ethnically Russian households, while extended families are common among Kyrgyz households.

Incomes

Assessment of household income in the study was entirely based on the subjective evaluation of the respondents. They named the following key sources of their earnings: salaries, pensions and benefits, incomes derived from purchase and resale of various industrial and agricultural goods, and finally remittances. The main source of income for all household types was the breadwinner's salary.

The majority of respondents noted low standards of living, difficulties of sustaining their livelihood in the present and rapid rise of prices.

"It is all expensive. It is only enough to feed ourselves, but not for profit, everything is expensive, and there is no governmental support … Because of the taxes, payment for water, you need pay for everything, thus there is a struggle for surviving" (B int 2: 23, male, rural).

"Now, the money is losing its power, everything becomes expensive, and money … several thousand Soms sounds like a big amount of money, but you can buy for it not many things" (B int 5: 124, male, urban).

---

[204] Wikipedia: http://en.wikipedia.org/wiki/Bishkek; access date 28-08-13

[205] Bishkek – the Capital of Kyrgyzstan, http://www.advantour.com/kyrgyzstan/bishkek.htm; access date 28-08-13

Contextualizing the addressed price increases, "According to the survey of food prices and food security, conducted by the World Food Program of UN in the Kyrgyz Republic, in January 2013, the retail prices of wheat flour did not change from the previous month and remained high. Thus, in the period between June 2012-January 2013, prices for flour rose by 56% in rural areas and by 48% in urban areas, making a 52% rise on average within the country. The retail price of flour in the domestic market in January 2013 was 27% higher compared to the same period in 2012, and only 4% lower than the maximum price mark, recorded in early 2011. The average price of potatoes in the country is 55% higher compared to January 2012. Economic opportunities for vulnerable households, which are already used to spending 61% of their total income on food, will be substantially reduced due to rising costs of gas, coal and firewood during the winter months."[206]

There are not many formal job opportunities in the country. Small scale trade has become an important source for making an income after the demise of the USSR. Trade is considered profitable in both urban and rural areas:

"There was one store, far away from here; people had to go there for foodstuff. Then, I decided to rent it, from my relatives. Earnings from sales at the store are sufficient; at least I can now contribute to the budget of my family, and stay at home" (B int 4: 9, female, rural).

In the light of shut downs of the majority of factories and plants in the aftermath of the Soviet Union's dissolution, Kyrgyzstan does not have a developed industrial production, and the majority of the population makes an income from trade.

"At the beginning I stayed at home, I didn't work. I got married and my husband didn't let me work. Our children were small. He was a taxi driver[207] and so he used to be out all night long. It was hard. We were worried about him all the time. We had hard times. The Soviet Union was destroyed and crime was growing. Then later my friend offered me to go to the bazaar to try working there and I went. I was purchasing goods and reselling them. It wasn't so bad. Then we saved some money and I sent them (my husband and my brother) to China, my brother used to go there and was importing sunglasses. (Then...) we both started working at the bazaar. Slowly we became more successful. Then I started bringing goods from Almaty, and my husband was selling them here" (B int 27: 166, female, urban).

The most common strategy of sustaining livelihoods in rural areas is the cultivation of produce for household needs (subsistence production):

206 UN notes a significant rise in prices for basic types of food products in comparison to 2012 – source: http://www.madein.kg/analytics/socio_economic access date 25-3-13

207 The woman refers to informal public transportation business of many males.

"Well, we are living in the big house of our parents. We live in a makeshift hut attached to the main house. There is a garden, bard and bath in the backyard of the house. There is also a garage. I have a large vegetable garden, 16 acres. In principle, I plant only tomato and cucumbers in the garden, and we've got raspberries, apple, walnut and apricot trees. What else... we own a cow, and four sheep" (B int 20: 5, male respondent, rural).

From the following quotation we can see that family members' labor in rural areas is usually taken-for-granted, and not considered in the estimations of the family budgets according to its market value, and hence is seen as free labor. It was common in respondents' answers, not to count their own labor in the household in monetary terms.

"My wife keeps the garden, and my mother and father take care of the livestock. It's my job to cut the grass, and pile the hay. But planting vegetables, collecting raspberries, those kinds of things are my wife's responsibility. She spends quite a lot of time in the garden" (B int 20: 6, male, rural).

Respondents claimed remittances to constitute a crucial part of their household budgets. Data from the Central Bank of Russia in 2012 show that USD 1, 859 billion were remittances, of Kyrgyz laborers in Russia, to Kyrgyzstan; the total amount of remittances from Russia to Central Asia was USD 11.7 billion.[208] It is important to note that these figures are drawn from formal reports from Russia; real figures may even be higher. Labor migrants from Kyrgyzstan also work in the neighboring Kazakhstan and other foreign countries. Hence, remittances play a significant role in households of the country, enabling them to purchase basic goods like food, clothes and to pay for utilities and other sectors' services, including education.

"There are not any other sources of income; our sons who work in the Russian Federation send us money" (B int 2: 25, male, rural).

Two of the main findings of the study include the prevalence of economic strategies that aim at compensating for the lack of sufficient formal income and the absence of investments in household strategies. On the one hand, the market offers a wide range of goods, services, and opportunities for spending personal and family savings. But on the other hand, the majority of households do not have sufficient resources that would enable them to make use of such opportunities. Low levels of income and an inability to make savings have catalyzed behavior

[208] The total volume of remittances from Russia to Central Asia equaled #11.7 billion. Source – http://stanradar.com/news/full/1280-obschij-obem-denezhnyh-perevodov-iz-rossii-v-srednjuju-aziju-sostavil-117-mlrd.html; access date 20-08-13.

where households try to make a living without saving and investing in the future. Strategies of avoiding zones of economic instability, unwillingness to compete for resources or to get into illegal or unfair businesses led many households to go back to subsistence production, spend all their savings and improve personal relationships / safety networks among relatives, friends and neighbors. The main objective for many households living in these conditions is to stabilize the current level of consumption and to make ends meet with resources in hand.

"But it is not my husband's fault; he is trying a lot, making some money on the side during the evening, taxi driving, and working during day time. I do not make some money on the side; I was recently hired on this job" (B int 12: 81, female, urban).

"There was an income, but little income. We cultivated sugar beet – cultivating sugar beet, I think now (...) there is much expenditure, but little income.... We cultivated sugar beet on 1 hectare of land, from which we got 20 tons of sugar beet. For 20 tons of sugar beet we were given 20 heaps, that is, 20 bags of sugar, at that time the price for it [20 heaps of sugar] was 20,000 Soms. And the expenditures for that, there were seeds, technical needs... we bought them and worked, fuel, if to sum up all of them, then the difference between expenditure and income was little" (B int 37: 64, male, urban).

"We sell children's clothes, winter and spring clothes. It happens differently, it is good when there is a job, if not we are waiting for the order. This is how we try to live and to do all in order to survive" (B int 7: 9, female, urban).

Very few households included in the study have shown opposite strategies. Such households can be characterized by a motivated and active approach to their economic activities and draw their primary earnings from entrepreneurial activities. Higher income levels of these households enable investments into education and consumption of durable goods that in turn make more resources available for family members so that they can obtain paid employment and receive additional income from existing savings.

"We do not have any big business with my friends, but we have a small one. For example, we deal with cars; we bring cars and sell them here in the market, such kind of small business that helps us" (B int 4: 111, male, urban).

"We save money for specific purposes. So recently we were planning to buy a new car for me (laughing) so we bought a car (Lexus RX 300, USD 12,000). Of course by husband didn't want to let me drive before, but then we decided that the car is not about showing your richness; it is for transportation. So it will take me less time to take the kids to school, sometimes I can go to the bazaar and buy something at the store. It is very comfortable. It saves me time with him. So he helped me to save money, we gathered together, but of course he gave more money because it was as a gift from him" (B int 31: 32 female, urban).

We can summarize so far that, at one extreme there are such households that become more deeply deprived, struggling for survival and taking every income opportunity offered, and at the other extreme we find those who improve their living very well and accumulate economic advantages and capital. While well-off households demonstrate investment-oriented behavior of consumption and savings, which will further strengthen their positions in the market and in society, poor households lean more towards 'the ethics of survival', where the earnings are spent for making a living and accumulated financial capital is spent within one generation's life cycle. The latter households live at the expense of formerly accumulated 'capital' of more successful years – a house, a dacha, an older car, etc. and many of them are also supplemented by remittances sent by relatives at work abroad.

The following two quotations represent such households that cannot or do not save at all.

"I cannot save, why? Because when the toi (holiday) starts, we spend money on it, when you spend on funeral, if you even spent on that, you will not have returns by the person, for other things we do not save. My grandmother can save; she does not spend much" (B int 12: 120, female, urban).

Before there was enough money which my husband used to earn, and also we could buy something, get something. But now we spend all money on food. Even now our children are working but still it is very hard to live. We can't even save some money to buy a house for our children" (B int 26: 43, female, urban).

These conditions are unfavorable in economic and social terms. Commonplace strategies discussed above reflect withdrawal of large segments of the population from the consumer market – a common way to cope with economic crises. Just as the resources in the economy as a whole have been redistributed from production to the spheres of trade and barter, households are expanding their informal economic activities. This survival strategy worsens the living standard of the household, and particularly of the children from these households, because they are not able to escape from that downward spiral. Subsistence production in the majority of the studied households only provides for the current basic needs of family members, instead of leading to the accumulation of material and human capital and further development of the household and, particularly, the children's generation.

Another typical issue in times of economic crisis is practicing barter exchanges, in full or partially at least.

"Well, sometimes people who hire me don't have enough money and then they pay me half in cash, and half in kind; I mean they can give livestock instead of money. Sometimes I sell this livestock or keep it in my household, feed it and then sell it, because in that way livestock brings more money. It is widespread practice in the rural areas" (B int 11: 31, male, rural).

Economic strategies of households have an urban/rural divide. More advanced "market-oriented" strategies of behavior are more common among urban households, while strategies of survival, that include subsistence farming and barter and aiming at sustaining the current consumption levels are more typical for rural households.

It should be noted, that urban households have more opportunities of employment in the urban economy. Furthermore, they obtain better educational and health services. Rural households are limited in their opportunities of employment outside the agricultural sector, and have a low level of access to the services of health and education. The ongoing migration of younger people from villages to the city and abroad, and aging of the rural population catalyzes rural-urban inequality and entails the so-called "poverty traps," adding to the serious institutional barriers to rural development.

"My husband worked in Moscow earlier. When we arrived in Moscow, we lived in a rented apartment, my husband worked and I didn't work [...] To get the working permission one needs money, and this money is not little. Their money is needed everywhere, not a step can be made without money. On the other hand the husband is jealous and he also didn't allow me to work. I sat at home, and my husband worked. I lived like that till April, and then in April I flew back to Kyrgyzstan. I came back because I had to study, plus there were family problems, besides that I got ill. I arrived in April, my husband came three months later at the end of July" (B int 16: 5, female, urban).

Our rural interviews show that (subsistence) agriculture remains the main source of livelihood for most villagers, due to lack of labor opportunities in the villages. Hence, such rural households have taken on a strategy of survival at the edge of poverty. Such can be lessened by remittances and transfers from family members.

The primary tendency of households' adaptation to the conditions of the market economy, may be formulated as 'strategies of primitive survival', where households do not simply make their ends meet within a new socio-economic environment, but also generate and reproduce a new system of values and norms, which end up constituting a 'culture of poverty'.

But also urban households may suffer from poverty, as the following quotation shows.

"We were economizing on everything. When we needed something we couldn't allow us to buy for ourselves; we had to pay our debt back. We were refraining from everything... We are trying to have all the time flour and oil, because if we hadn't them it would be a shock to our family. With flour you can bake bread and you will not stay hungry, you can toast bread on oil also. That is the most needed" (B int 26: 63, female, urban).

The situation of 'primitive survival' is characterized by a sharp decline in the households' income, as a consequence an economizing in expenses, even in food, an active use of natural environment (collection from nature, subsistence farming, livestock products, etc.), earning through temporary jobs, and involvement in areas of the informal economy, which includes second shifts, micro and small businesses, double-book accounting and using personal networks. As the following quotation illustrates, many households use this self-rationing regime in such periods:

"R. Usually I try to save on food.

I: Meaning that you don't buy all the food you'd like, in order to have enough money for other things?

R: Yes. Or simply buy stuff not in stores, but at the bazaar, this way I can save some cash... prices are lower at bazaars" (B int 12: 126-128, female, urban).

What has already become clear here and will also be seen in the subsequent paragraphs is that although we intended to exclude the poor from our interviews, many rural and also urban households in Kyrgyzstan are close to, if not in poverty. Nevertheless they can be called middle class.

Consumption

Households as an economic entity are characterized by the prevalence of informal inter-personal relations.

"The economic behavior of households is shaped by broader country-level economic conditions, traditions and shared cognitive frameworks, which evolve over time. The costs of refusing to comply with certain rules of economic activities, do not simply lead to financial losses, but may also have repercussions in the form of social exclusion, downward social mobility, and finally the disintegration of households" (Nureeva R.M. 2001).

Uncertainty is by far one of the most important difficulties that external conditions pose for households. Many households are muddling through their everyday life. They do not make a budget plan of their finances, which is why most of the respondents had difficulties in describing the structure of their income and expenses. As was noted above, recent years have seen a sharp decline in incomes in general. The impoverishment of the majority of the population goes in hand with rapid growth of wealth in the hands of few. Thus, one of the important social factors of the economy in Kyrgyzstan is segmentation and increasing inequality.

If the Soviet period with its lack of access to goods had produced certain strategies of disposing of money, the exact opposite problem is found nowadays in the market system where everything is available in the market against cash; however, most people are short of money, short of employment opportunities. Often women have particular problems finding jobs, since they had been out of work during times of child-bearing and child-raising.

"And for a long time I was sitting at home, I could not find a job, because everywhere I went, wherever I submitted my CV, they were asking for my professional experience. Therefore, that was a problem – experience – and it is right, because without experience, even nowadays (...) employers do not want to experience any difficulties with newcomers. They need an experienced worker" (B int 12: 86, female, urban).

"I would go, but because of my age my opportunities are getting worse. I can't work in my specialization, although my specialization is needed right now, a needlewoman. As so I didn't work when my daughter was born, while my kids grew up I didn't work either. Due to lack of practice I lost my speed. A needlewoman needs to have a speed she has to have a habit. Of course I forgot a lot of things and I will not have that speed which I used to have when I was young" (B int 26: 81, female, urban).

"(My wife) is from Kazak ethnicity. She worked as an economist... she stopped working because she had to raise the children. Now she is unemployed and I am a pensioner. I have a pension ... 4,020 Soms (85 USD, G.G.)" (B int 5: 14, 15, male, rural).

Under such conditions people have to develop strategies for making a living. When people do not find any opportunities in the formal economy to make an income, many of them pursue escaping 'the market'. Subsistence economy, barter between households, informal income opportunities, or mutual help systems which we can observe in our sample households are not oriented towards income generating, but towards a reduction of expenses to overcome the shortage in money. Such a strategy does not coincide with the logic of market relations; it has however often been observed in crisis situations.

We consider the instability of income and employment to be the primary factors for pushing the massive escape of the population out of the market. Rather than coping with the instability within the market economy, rural dwellers have chosen to leave this domain (the 'exit' option in terms of Hirschman (1974)). Exit from the market, however, also means exit from society, since participation in a market society is regulated by money (c.f. Luhmann, 1988).

Many of the respondents believe that subsistence production is a way of significantly reducing food expenses. As the following interview excerpt demonstrates, subsistence farming is not considered to be time and resource consuming. This is contrary to market behavior where opportunity costs are taken into consideration. But for those who have no formal income opportunities, time is no cost factor. The following respondent, whom we already quoted, practices subsistence production in his vegetable garden. He also owns a cow and four sheep.

"My parents are the ones who herd, they like it . . . all the other households in the village have sheep, cows and other cattle, we all take turns in taking the cattle to the pasture" (B int 20: 6, male, rural).

Most of the rural respondents note that they cannot take their harvest for sale in the local market; the spots in local bazaars are already taken by intermediary traders, who pay only little and make high intermediate profit.

"The harvest was good, but we sold it for nothing. We gave it to dealers because we could not sell it by ourselves. Nowadays, those who buy from the farmers cheaply, and sell in the market dearly take all the spots at bazaars. Production and harvest is devalued and the state does not control it. We have such situations . . . , let's say last year the corn overproduction made the price down to 50 Tyiyn (half a som) for one kilogram" (B int 5: 16, male, rural).

The keeping of livestock falls into subsistence production, once the produce is used for the household itself, and for trade, once the livestock or its produce (meat, milk, butter, eggs, etc.) is sold in the market. But in many cases this analytical distinction does not make sense. In the villages most people keep livestock for subsistence, but many of them sell a cow or a horse once they need cash (e.g. B int 5: 368; B int 37: 44).

The other method of coping with crisis is mutual support systems. This includes cash and in-kind assistance and exchange of services between several households that are usually related through kinship or close friendship ties.

"My parents helped us enormously, when we got married. We also got a lot of help from the relatives, in that period" (B int 39: 264, female, urban).

Such mutual help is based upon norms of reciprocity (Gouldner 1960; Hettne 1990), imposing the tacit obligation on the recipient, who will be expected in the future to offer support to the provider once he or she needs it. In addition to the support function mutual aid is a means of strengthening kinship and friendship ties, to keep such security networks intact (cf. Coleman 1987, 1988).

"Yes of course, my father helps us a lot financially, when we ask him. You know, actually we don't have any help from others, well some of them help us – they buy clothes for our children, it's usually relatives from both sides, however my father is the one who helps us the most" (B int 1: 36, female, rural).

"It is the support of family and friends. Well, let's say, five years ago, I was seriously ill, and I could not work, and there was a lot of money required for treatment. Also my husband had problems with work, his business was having problems, there were big losses. And it was a hopeless situation, I was ill, seriously ill, and my husband had no money, no job. We were helped by our family. Without their help, I do not know what would have happened to us" (B int 19: 27, female, urban).

Under stable conditions, reciprocity is balanced over a longer period. However, the crisis conditions and further stratification of households have made reciprocation more difficult, but at the same time the claims are even more necessary. A consequence of this is that such reciprocity networks have reportedly decreased in size, being confined to narrower circles of immediate relatives, who are then obliged to conform to these reciprocity norms.

Subsistence production and mutual aid are mechanisms of stabilization outside the market, but obviously strategies of households in or close to poverty within market societies. While in the literature they are often called 'traditional codes of conduct/traditional behavior' (cf. Max Weber), we consider such strategies as rational from the scope of the respondents (cf. Benda-Beckmann 2000). These strategies lower the dependency from the cash nexus and bring stabilization of the household budget (cash and kind) on a low scale. The problem with such a strategy is that it normally does not provide opportunities to escape from the situation.

However, subsistence production and mutual support networks are not the only strategies of low-income households to cope with everyday life. If the households possess some livestock, this livestock can also be converted into cash if necessary. Also credit from informal or formal sources is an option to cope with lack of cash. Often such coping strategies are applied simultaneously, as the following quotation of a rural dweller demonstrates.

"Well, of course we have trouble earning money like any other family. We faced unemployment of children – even with their degrees they couldn't find a long-time job. At first, they lived in Bishkek with my relatives, and then they started renting an apartment. It is very good that we have livestock – we could sell our sheep to pay for the education of my son and buy something for my daughter with that money. Recently, we sold all of our livestock to hold the funeral of my mother-in-law. We had to take a credit from a bank. Part of the credit I will invest in the goods for a shop, and the other part we will use to buy livestock. We have been taking credits during the past three years from several banks, the biggest loan was 60,000 Soms, which we got from 'Bai Tushum'[209]" (B int 4: 12, female, rural).

However, with the exception of interest-free loans from relatives, such a credit is a burden for the household: financially and emotionally. Often households face the risk of getting into indebtedness, meaning that they cannot pay off their debts in time or any more.

"Of course when you take credits, you can't sleep well. Sometimes, we need to take micro-credits from small microfinance companies like "Kompanion" and "Finka" in order to pay off previous credits, or to buy goods, something for the house, or sheep or cow. When we urgently need money we sell our cattle. The interest rates are very high, they are higher than 20 percent. Now we have credits from four different banks. These days, villagers also started lending money under 20 percent of interest, banks are better though. My pension is very small, about 1,050 Soms, it is actually enough for the two of us, but we also have relatives – I've got eight grandsons" (B int 4: 14, female, rural).

As a result of this project, we would like to recommend considering alternative estimates of livelihood than those usually applied in household studies. Material income of households is only an indirect, and not the most accurate measure of households' well-being. Well-being can be measured through the evaluation of household consumption behaviors and their access to resources necessary for achieving desired standards of consumption that may be prevalent in local communities. Deviations from these accepted standards of consumption, may add to deprivation. According to the interviews collected, the most common types of deprivation include the lack of financial means to replace durable goods, such as furniture and home appliances, and to hold regular family events. Payment for medical services is a common problem among rural residents, too. The conception of sustainable livelihoods used in this study is such an approach that goes beyond typical household income researches, by taking the different capital forms and the vulnerability context into consideration.

---

[209] 'Bai Tushum' is a micro-credit company.

The structure of household expenditure can be used for an assessment of households' well-being. For poor households food expenses constitute the largest share of household expenditure. As already shown such households try to avoid expenditure-related consumption. However, expenses on utilities and small purchases of basic goods also have to be paid by poor households. Virtually all expenses in the poorest households are directed towards the absolute necessities of survival. The expenditure structure of better-off households (owning small businesses or having stable salaries) is different. They develop their own consumer lifestyles, buying fashionable clothes and more costly food in the shops rather than in the bazaars, purchasing durable consumer goods (washing machines, furniture, electronics, car etc.), investing in human capital (education), saving for specific purposes and purchasing real estate. Segmentation and increasing inequality become visible in society, due to different lifestyles. Segmentation is stronger in the cities, while rural life is more egalitarian on a low level.

As the theoretical outline of this research shows we treat sustainable livelihoods considerations as being household considerations rather than individual ones. The households represent a pooling of survival options. Opportunities for households depend strongly on social-structural factors (incomes, place of living, education, etc.). In general only those who are better-off also have the opportunity to take more risks.[210] They can win from such risk-taking (e.g. investment), but they can also stand losses if necessary. Those who lack such a "financial buffer" avoid risks.

However, even among the lower-income households we may identify three types: 'coping with insecurity', 'adaptive' and 'expansionist':[211]

The 'coping-type' is passive in its adaptation ("we economize on everything"), with risk aversion, and a high level of subsistence production. This type is characteristic for many households residing in villages. Within this group "belt-tightening" is widespread. This type of households struggles with every day-life; there seems to be no way out of that struggle. The mental attitude sometimes tends to destitution. Rarely, such households have the means to migrate.

"No one helps, if emergencies happen, we save on food and clothing. We just try to survive that period" (B int 24: 29, female, urban).

---

210 An exception is forced migration of those who otherwise cannot survive (Castles, Office of the United Nations High Commissioner for Refugees, and Policy Analysis 2002; Raleigh, Jordan, and Salehyan 2008)

211 Galina Gorborukova chose that classification which is different from the one of the editors who follow De Haan/Zoomers (1999) in Chapters 5 and 6.

The 'adaptive type' is more active in its adaptation practices. It often has a better basic security, a save harbor from which it tries to improve the living conditions without taking too much risk (e.g., "taking an additional second job"). For such households the question of internal or even international migration may also come up. The following quotation is from a rural woman helping her husband in the largest bazaar in Bishkek in addition to her first work.

"I help my husband with his work at Dordoi since 2007, in parallel with my own primary job. Of course, there have been times when I couldn't sell much, and there are also times when there is no trade at all. Today is one of those days" (B int 24: 16, female, rural).

The 'expansionist type' willingly takes risks to get out of difficulties. This particularly involves new activities, new places to live, etc. E.g. shuttle trading and bazaar trade, often combined with leaving the safe but underpaid harbor of government employment. Even more than the adaptive type the expansionist type would be willing to migrate to improve his situation in life.

Interestingly, men and women have demonstrated similar tendencies in their involvement in the groups mentioned above. Both men and women are willing to take on overtime work within and outside of the places of their major employment.

"In 1991 I was having maternity leave, because I gave birth to a daughter at the end of May. In August USSR collapse happened. After that I stayed jobless, but we had to continue living anyway, because I have a son, he was 4 years old at that time. Everything collapsed and my husband didn't receive his wage for several months (...) We had a dacha, and my mother, in my mother's home we had farming and in the dacha we grew different plants, so we had some kind of natural farming. (...) Children had started attending school and I began to think that we have to change the place of living – before we lived in the Issyk-Kul region, R. town, and now it was time to move to Bishkek, anyway it is the capital, and there was some life boiling. Because in the place where we lived life was totally destroyed" (B int 35: 6-9, female, urban).

In R. this woman had had different jobs: baking, sewing, and mortgage business in a finance company. Then her first husband died, and a class-mate from Bishkek who occasionally visited her, recommended her to migrate to Bishkek. She settled in the suburbs and started one of her former jobs, baking rolls.

"Then I realized that this business is unacceptable for me, because Bishkek is a big city, and if you want to do this activity, at least you have to have the technical support and equipment, because my production didn't sustain the competition. I started thinking about another kind of activity, and when I distributed my production, I mean the rolls; I saw places where people do ritual services for funerals. (...) I decided to try this business, making funeral wreaths, I approached the head of a funeral agency and he told me to try it out. I had to learn a lot, because everything was new for me. And this was the city, absolutely different requirements, color palette, the sizes and a lot of other different things. My son helped me to start this business, he did the carcasses and bring thuja, the special plant for the decoration of wreaths. And my daughter helped me in housekeeping, so I had the time for my business. (...) Sometime later I had the occasion to buy the house (...). We borrowed money from everybody, from friends from relatives from everybody. And then gradually gave this money back, first for those people who asked to give them back money as soon as possible, for those who could wait gave back later, sometimes we borrowed from one and gave this money back to another. So, in this way we paid for our house"(B int 35: 6-9, female, urban).

Looking back to her jobs this interviewee argues:

"Of course I liked the fact that there was a growth of personality and I knew a lot of interesting communication with businessmen. It was a huge advantage to me; it has changed all my life, my way of thinking and views. It was a school of business, the school of life. People educated me and shared with me the secrets of their success. (...) Doing wreath business made us feel a financial stability, we had money, it was better than previously when I was doing bakery. Little by little we overcame some problems. We bought a house, however we had to repay debts for that particular period of time. Then we did renovation of this house. We started to buy supplies not just for one production, but as a reserve. But for that purposes we built additional premises as any developing business requires. One for business and the second one for our living. Literally we started to grow" (B int 35: 6-9, female, urban).

Savings

In recent years the problem of household savings has attracted considerable attention amongst economists, political scientists and sociologists. Savings provide present and future security to a household, a buffer for sudden risks and vulnerabilities, as well as for the pension age when incomes decrease. Furthermore, savings are necessary for larger expenses of durable consumer goods as well as for property, for children's education, etc. Ability to save or not and savings of a household indicate its degree of vulnerability.

Savings can be defined as deferred expenditures to be used for purposes in the future. Savings can accumulate (interest returns). When they are spent, spending is distinguished according to consumption and investment. From the perspective of micro economics, contrary to consumption, investment refers to higher returns (or lower expenditure) to the investor in the future but contains an element of risk. Keeping money "unemployed" (that it brings in no interest) means a loss. From the macroeconomic perspective the money of savers is directed to those in need of cash (for consumption and investment), and the intermediate function of financial institutions brings returns to the saver and profit to the intermediaries. Aggregated savings of citizens are traditionally a source of domestic investment in the national economy, and in this sense the share of savings of the population attracted by financial institutions, is a resource for economic development. At the same time, increases in the level of deposited and invested financial resources indicate the growth in levels of trust not only towards banks and financial institutions but also towards the state and the economy as a whole, providing institutional conditions for sustainable patterns of further savings and economic development.

We are concerned with the micro level, the ability of households to save. We predominantly talk about monetary savings, but from our interviews especially with rural households it is obvious that many of these keep their property as live-stock which brings returns by breeding, can function as a source of food (meat, milk, eggs etc.), and can be converted into money if required.

"Kyrgyz deal with cattle breeding, in the village everyone deals with it" (B int 5: 368, urban, male).

"In order to organize funerals I had to slaughter my only horse" (B int 37: 44, rural, male).

Let us now turn our attention towards monetary savings. Many respondents in this study explain that they usually do not have opportunities to make savings:

"Hm, I do not have opportunities to save money. My money is the cattle I have, the live-stock. If you sell them you get money, so they are my capital" (B int 35: 39, male, rural).

"No, there is no way to save. It's not really possible. The state does not help us. Saving does not work. We spend all of our earnings on basic needs. We also need to bring money to weddings and other occasions" (B int 35: 56, male, rural).

"Money is not the thing that can become rotten, spoiled and there is no need to save it in special boxes (kidding and laughing). There is a wallet of their mother, as you see, in the shelf, so there the money is kept. I cannot say that there is a big amount of money in the household (…,) every person saves money at home, money that is spent for the everyday expenditures, for the needs of children" (B int 4: 289, male, urban).

Indeed, a number of interviews show that people save at home. One reason for this is that they have only very little savings, another reason is that trust in banks is very limited especially among the lower-income groups.

"To invest in banks is a very risky deal. Today a bank exists; tomorrow it will no more exist. Of course we have to trust, but I don't trust our banks. To save money at home is dangerous too. To be honest I haven't thought about where I would put my money, may be because I don't have it" (B int 10: 143, female, urban).

After independence financial institutions had been mushrooming. There was aggressive advertising and promises of a "fast buck" in investment in special schemes. Many people were motivated to invest, but they were totally inexperienced. They were soon disappointed when myriads of pyramid schemes collapsed. Also the reputation of sound banks suffered during the 1990s and caused many people to distrust them when considering having savings accounts or other bank investments.

Keeping one's savings at home, often in foreign currency, is frequent. This brings no returns to the owner except a feeling of security from the financial market (whereas keeping cash at home bears the risk of losing it to burglars or in a fire). Macro-economically considered this savings attitude withdraws a lot of money from the economy, keeping it "idle". But due to the fact that real incomes have also decreased, savings activities have been reduced.

In general, saving activities of households in Kyrgyzstan are rather low. The main rationale for saving, according to the respondents, is investment in children.

"The reasons I save [...] are for the education of my daughter, the education of my children. Also, for some good and bad moments of life; as we are Kyrgyz we have many acquaintances for the good and bad moments of life" (B int 5: 435, urban, male).

"We save money because we have children, so, for children, for their future" (B int 6: 375, urban, female).

The vast majority of households do not have the ability to make large purchases without first having saved sufficient amounts of money. Some respondents mentioned "investments in their own business," "getting additional income besides primary salary" or "savings for vacation," as sources of cash, but the ratio of interviews where respondents explained to have extra disposable cash was very low within the whole group of interviewed people.

Credits

Formal credit is provided by banks and – particularly in rural regions – by micro financial institutions. Within recent years, in light of growing criticism about microfinance companies' potential to tackle poverty, there has been much said about the negative impact of micro-credit loans on the rural population, as well as about the lack of interest on the side of microfinance companies in financing income-generating activities of villagers (Bali Swain 2012; cf. Swain and Floro 2010). Within this study, we have added a block of questions in order to find out about access to credit and credit histories of households.

The majority of respondents are against the practice of taking credits – they emphasized high interest rates, lack of economic stability, which puts the collateralized real estate under threat, inability to pay off credits, and just a moral stand against taking commercial credits.

"Currently, as well as in 2011, we have a credit. We've put our house and my brother's house as collaterals, and got loans in the amount of USD 25,000. 20,000 was used to purchase a container at the bazaar. Our monthly payments to the bank are USD 620. We get about 200-250,000 Soms from the sales in the container. We pay half of the amount for the loan, and buy new goods for the rest of the money. Right now, we're starting to buy spring clothes' collections. At this point my husband is doing just that.

Q: So you put your house and your brother's house as collaterals, right?

A: Yes, we thought if our work gets better, we'll be able to pay back all of the credit, if not, then at least half of it" (B int 7: 31, female, urban).

The microcredit sector in Kyrgyzstan has very high interest rates, which is both due to the economic situation in the country and the higher cost of microcredits in general. The burden of interest and repayment of the principal is high for most debtors:

"My husband is totally against taking credits, because they all are predatory. They've got super high interest rates. Both my husband and I agree that it's awful; it's usurious, it is better to borrow money from relatives. Thank God there're people whom we can borrow from – my colleagues, family, friends, my brother in particular. My brother for example started cattle farming, he had no one to borrow the starting capital from, and he took out a loan. Well he paid back … of course it was difficult, but he did it" (B int 25: 22, female, urban).

"I think close to 95% of our population takes credits. There were times when we didn't know what it was like to take a credit, but times have changed. In 2009, we got our first credit. We got it after consulting with my husbands' friends, who bought a car on credit that same year. They told us we shouldn't be scared to do so. We soon came to realize lots of people take out loans, and in fact they can help you make profit. So my husband took a credit and bought a car. (…) The amount was 250,000 Soms, the interest 22%. And then we had to pay for three years. We were supposed to make monthly payments. So we've paid back in 3 consecutive years starting from 2009. During three years, each quarter we paid 35,000 or 32,000 Soms altogether. All the money earned by my husband, daughter and son used to go to pay back the credit and then we'd be surviving till the next month. Sometimes we had difficulty in making our monthly payments, so we had to take another credit to pay back the first one" (B int 5: 46, female, urban).

Looking back over the past 10-15 years, many people have had bad experiences in taking up credits. Sometimes taking out a credit put them into a worse situation than before. A respondent notes:

"Then notifications came from the bank that we had to make our monthly payments, but we couldn't pay on time. The interest rate doubled on penalties. Our house was taken by the bank. It was very difficult to lose our home and to find ourselves in the street" (B int 30: 78, male, urban).

The majority of respondents with experience in taking credits explained that they were very hesitant when they started to take out credits.

We already described cases about people taking a credit to repay another one. This seems to be a "new life style" of people close to or in poverty: "life on a loan." Such borrowers may end up in a vicious cycle of borrowing and impoverishment. Finding oneself in such a borrowing trap is widespread among both urban and rural residents. Sometimes people take loans from financial institutions as well as their relatives and friends. If they find themselves in such a poverty trap they may also lose their social capital. According to the respondents, the key factor in failures to successfully payback credits is the financial illiteracy of people – the lack of culture of making repayments in a disciplined and timely manner, as well as misuse of credits for purposes other than formally stated.

The following quotation shows the risk of getting indebted, but the family finally managed to get out of the threatening credit squeeze.

"Five years ago my family experienced a crisis – we took a credit and opened a shop. We thought that our life would improve. We opened a pavilion, brought products and sold them. But then our shop was robbed twice by thieves, we wrote applications to the police, but they couldn't find them, and so the payment for the products lay down on our shoulders. Then we went to FINKA (micro-credit institution). That credit had to be repaid every month. To pay this credit, we began to borrow money from different people who also took interest and it was also necessary to pay for them, so on our shoulders were many debts. Because of this we had to sell our own house in order to repay the debts and we had to move to another village where we live now (...). We bought land, built a house, all our relatives and both daughters helped us to become independent, and now there have passed already five years and we live here very well, now we are going into the fields to work" (B int 3: 86, rural, male).

The cousin of the next respondent was not so lucky.

"Yes, my cousin did. He lost everything and had to rent an apartment. He sold everything that he had and has nothing now" (B int 11: 69, rural, male).

In the following quotation a son and his wife even became liable for the debt of the son's father.

"They were demanding from us to repay his grandfather's credit; so it was not only the shock, but a stress. From one side I was glad for that experience to become experienced. There was a moment when you cannot do anything and asked 'Apa (father), such and such happened they came to us and demanded from us ...' It was from my husband's side. When we told about that directly to our relatives, they said (...) 'Let them come and repay by themselves'. But they came to us, apa did not understand, and he gave our address to the bank, and all of this was not a shock, rather than stress. I was like flying between the sky and earth, my husband was overloaded and angry, said 'I kill him'; but probably God helped us and we could solve it and repay" (B int 12: 118, 136, 137, female, urban).

Also in the next quotation the respondent took a credit not for herself but for supporting relatives.

"I often took credits. My father is working in a bank, and I also took credits at his bank. When I was short of money my father helped me to pay off the credit. As I told you, the father of my husband forced us to give money to other relatives, and we had to take credits in the bank. And we had to pay it off from our salaries, and it was quiet difficult for us, because our salaries were very low, and the interest was very high, and my father always came to help us" (B int 18: 36, female, rural).

The next respondent assesses micro-credits positively, although she and her husband are also in constant need of taking credits.

"Of course it helps but only temporarily. However, in the most difficult times FINKA helps. But then again, while paying back to FINKA we also had to pay for the major credit as well. In other words, if you, for example, take anything in credit it disappears in any way so that sometimes you have to sell. You just cannot make this money run around on time. You have to buy hay for cattle and pay back credit at the same time. It turns out that you deal with double interests, what you earn you pay for interests. So in three years we hardly made ends meet while paying for credits; yet we took another credit instead of... All together we took 250 000 Soms. And then again we had to work (for the repayment) together with the children. [...] It is said, whatever you think – everything can be solved when the family is united, and I do not even know what will happen next. In January of 2012 we paid off the last credit, but again in this year we signed up for another one. We thought of how we would be able to pay it back, but we had no other choice but to take it. Sometimes there is a job, sometimes not. It is no more like in the Soviet Union when we had no unemployment. Our jobs are not permanent. My son works for one firm then he goes to another one. There is not, as it is said, a permanent job" (B int 15: 39 – 42, female, rural).

Credits in rural households are primarily used for the purchase of seeds and cultivation of produce, purchase of cattle and sheep, or even land and for overcoming seasonality of income. Furthermore, respondents borrow money to pay for social events like *tois* (celebrations), weddings and funerals, sometimes also for the purchase of buildings and renovation of houses. Interestingly, borrowing larger amounts of money from relatives and friends is not very common among respondents, despite the fact that they discuss mutual aid among relatives when purchasing basic needs goods. Some explanations are found in our interviews. Relatives and friends in their networks may have a similar social and economic background, kinship and friendship should not be commercialized, and reciprocity decreases.

Urban respondents are more active in using credits to purchase real estate, household equipment and appliances, to covering expenses of various celebrations and ceremonies, and to pay tuition fees. Among the most often mentioned micro-credit companies and banks are: Aiyl Bank, Bai-Tushum, Finka and Kompanion.

Many interviewees jointly take a larger credit sum together with relatives or friends, and then they are jointly liable for the credit. Which is initially an advantage, because alone they might not get credit at all, however it may later become a very high burden or even a disaster. This is shown in the following paragraph.

"I, my sister, and her husband's sister took out a loan. We have taken a loan from the micro-credit company 'FINKA'. We got USD 30,000 and divided it into 3 parts, getting USD 10,000 each. I wouldn't have been able to get the credit but my sister helped me. In one year I have paid my share, which I have taken. Then my sister asked me to help her since she couldn't pay back on time and I was forced to pay instead of her. They bought a car for the credit and her husband got into an accident. It was impossible to repair the car… It was very hard. My house was put as collateral. Later my sister's husband found a good job though and paid all the rest of the money. I thought they'd never take credit again, but they took a new one. And my sister asked me to join the contract, but to give the money to her. I could not refuse them. After that one, I have taken one more credit and bought four bulls. Later I sold them at a profit and paid back half of the credit. My sister also tried to make profit by buying cattle, but she didn't succeed. There is a positive side of credits for sure, because we could buy furniture for example. I wanted to take a fourth credit, but my wife didn't allow me. I haven't got credits for the past 3 years, but my sister still relies on credits a lot. I tell them that it is dangerous, and they can stay with nothing. They have good jobs and it is unnecessary to take credits, they can save money by themselves. At the time when I wanted to take the fourth credit I happened to hear a story about one of the debtors in Osh. This woman took 200,000 Soms. She had sons and daughters and they decided to take this credit together. She was around 60-65 years old. She was disciplined the first year, but then she had 4-5 months of delay. The bank took her land and one month later took the other part of her 8-hectar land. She went to the bank and asked them to have a delay for 2 months. The bank agreed and she was supposed to pay the whole amount of money plus fines that accumulated in two months, but she was not able to do it on time. As a result, the bank took her 2 big houses, but it was not enough, she still owed 50,000 Soms to the bank. Two of her sons got into a car accident. She told the bank representatives about the emergencies, but the bank took the houses anyway. She gathered people and organized a strike. There were young people, women, and girls in front of the bank. Some women were crying and were telling similar stories. After that, I decided not to take credit anymore" (B int 40: 24, male rural).

We see that the respondent considers the bank behavior as a-moral, due to the fact that the woman from Osh was in an emergency situation but the bank nevertheless took her property. The "moral economy" (cf. Scott 1976) of the peasants conflicts with the economic rationale of the bank. Such episodes and personal experiences may result in renouncing bank credits and even the belief in the market system, because it is considered to be cruel and unjust.

Credits that are used for agricultural purposes, yield results only after 6 months (it takes 6 months on average starting from seeding to harvesting), and cattle breeding yields results in the period within 2 to 4 years. The longer the investment takes, the more risky it becomes, due to natural influences, cattle raiding, inexperience in market sales and unforeseen personal shocks.

"When we have our harvest or sheep, fruits and vegetables, surplus should be sold looking for points of marketing. The state cannot manage some marketing points for collecting the harvest from us, therefore we risk a lot; we do not know where to sell our harvest" (B int 2: 47, male, rural).

"Well, there are a lot of difficulties in agriculture that can happen, it is climatic conditions – we are always afraid of it" (B int 3: 106, male, rural).

"I used to keep horses and cows, but they were stolen I don't want to keep them anymore, because the thief wasn't found. Who knows what will happen tomorrow if I will keep them again. I don't want to keep big livestock anymore!" (B int 11: 139, male, rural).

Distribution of Power and Division of Labor

Tilly (1979) described the high correlation of individual family member's behavior with other family members. The author defines family strategies as a set of "tacit rules governing the behavior" of family members, within and between households. This does not mean that goals and motivations of family members coincide, because households and families are structured by power relations. Family and household studies show us the creation, reinforcement, modification and reproduction of unequal access to resources by families (cf. Blau 1998). Family strategies are shaped under the influence of prevailing power relations inside this social unit. Thereby, the vast majority of sociological work examines forms and causes of power distribution between couples. As a result, these studies isolate three types of power relations: (1) those with prevailing male dominance, (2) egalitarian; and (3) those with prevailing female dominance.

Since power relations within a family are a multidimensional concept, empirically they can be studied through explorations of how families make decisions, resolve conflicts and divide labor between family members. The results of our study show patriarchal discourses in describing the distribution of power and employment. Revival of traditional norms and practices in Kyrgyzstan bare influence on women's access to economic and power resources, further limiting women's capacity to gain benefit from interventions aimed at economic development. High rates of unemployment and labor migration among men are leaving women as heads and major breadwinners of households. Our study finds that, on the one hand, increasing numbers of women are coming to lead their households; but on the other hand, prevailing patriarchal discourses aim to make women conform to their traditional roles and prohibit women from becoming independent.

"Well, since we live in a Muslim country, I, as a father should be considered the leader of the family" (B int 29: 23, male, urban).

"Hm, according to our traditions and mentality, the man should be the head of the household, so of course I am" (B int 38: 78, male, urban).

Interestingly, women also emphasize their husbands' leadership, even when discussing family issues within the family.

"Every family member should know their own place in the family. Since our early childhood we were taught that women should stay at home and should know their obligations. Certainly, family is a small government and complies with the president. In our family too, we listen to my husband, he is the head. When we have family problems, we discuss them all together, including children. We never solve problems individually. For example, if my kids need something, like they need to go to their friends' place or go to a disco with girls, then they negotiate these things through me. First they would convince me, and then I'd convince my husband. If and when I need to leave somewhere, I ask my husband's permission. If he doesn't allow me to go, then I stay at home. My husband doesn't like it when someone in the family doesn't comply with him. But we make decisions based on discussions" (B int 5: 45, female, urban).

This is not only due to ethnicity in that Kyrgyz women subordinate themselves to their husbands. Also ethnically Russian families have the same practices, as the following excerpt demonstrates:

"Well, you know, I think that men are leaders, although my role as a woman is huge. I think it's normal that he as a man is stronger, smarter, I have a very good husband, he is honest and does not drink or smoke and is very caring. I think a lot rests on my shoulders though. Well, almost everything, yes, cleaning, repairing, shopping, these are all my duties. He does not like shopping. Of course I consult him and talk with him, but his word is the last. But since we are a family we stay together" (B int 25: 7, female, Russian, urban).

Children's upbringing is marked by gender roles, and activities beyond the family are segregated across gender lines. This usually means: differences in educating boys and girls; co-ed communication is limited and starting only from adolescence onward.

The educational sphere encourages different sets of traits among boys and girls, with the explicit goal of preparing them for diverse sets of adult roles. Within the family, children are involved in domestic work and carry out chores according to their gender. As one of the respondents stated:

"Our parents never washed the dishes, we, as the daughters in the family always used to do it. Men in the family were responsible for other tasks" (B int 7: 31, female, urban).

Most women and men take the usual division of labor as just given:

Well, men are performing work in the field, where we are engaged in watering, haymaking, we pack the hay supply, then we load packed hay on cars, and finally we sell all of this, sometimes we deliver to our customers' where we unload all packages of hay. (...). Other household chores are done by the women, (...) sometimes if we come early or have work to be finished, we are helping women and they helps us, men" (B int 3: 22, male, rural).

"Our responsibilities are within the household...how to say...for example, the tasks of men are outside tasks, they work in the garden...aaa, my sons do outside tasks...aaa, and the tasks inside of the house we do ourselves, me and my daughter" (B int 6: 192, female, urban).

Women continue to carry the triple burden of work: income-generating activities, housework and children's education. Traditionally, they retain their "right" to manage home economics, and remain to be the ones who carry out all the household chores like washing, cleaning, cooking and caring for children. Even when respondents said that the household chores are distributed evenly, they usually mean distribution across gender lines.

"Everyone has his or her own area of work. For example if grandmother is in the kitchen, so my brother's area is the garden, because plowing and doing other farm work demands physical strength. We try to share the responsibilities when it comes to cleaning the house. For example, it is my daughter's responsibility to mop the floor; my son's to vacuum clean. We are trying to teach them to do an equal share of work" (B int 32: 35, female, urban).

"My wife only washes the dishes, cleans, makes the laundry. For example, I can fix electric outlets at home. If the light bulb has to be changed I can ask my son to change it. He can take out the trash. Actually my son learned everything around the household and he can do everything. My wife has her own responsibilities. We have such a rule at home that everyone cleans his or her own room. For example my son cleans his own room, my wife cleans our room and the living room after guests, because we use the living room only when guests come to our house; there is a restroom, I sit there after I come back from work and one more room is my youngest son's room, where he has his toys and other stuff" (B int 30: 57, male, urban).

Similar divisions of labor are noted in interviews with rural respondents:

"We do everything in our household together. Those tasks that are related to the courtyard outside of the house in general, my husband and my son are responsible for that. They clean the courtyard. They work in the garden, plant the potatoes, gather our harvest, they do it together. Their second significant responsibility is to keep up the house. The rest of the work is on me" (B int 4: 9, female, rural).

Sometimes women even justify low participation of men carrying out household chores, while at the same time they are ready to take up new activities and learn them:

"You know, initially it seemed to me that my husband is very lazy in comparison to me. He was probably never taught to do household chores; he was led to believe that doing anything at home is not a tough man's job. Now, I do everything what I can, even if it's fixing an electric plug. Occasionally, I need a nail to be put somewhere, in those rare occasions I ask for my husband's help. Otherwise, I do everything else independently, since I got used to it anyway" (B int 7: 15, female, urban).

Another power-structure in Kyrgyzstan as in Central Asia in general is the strong position of mothers'-in-law, particularly when they step into the role of the oldest man in the household – the household head.

"In our family, our grandmother is the decision-maker in this regard. When we go to social events, she decides how to dispose of money. She is 65 years old. My mother is 42 years old. My father-in-law is 46 years old. Grandfather is very ill. So, grandmother makes decisions in our family. She orders, what to do with the money. She receives a pension. My husband hands all of his salary to her. He doesn't just spend his salary as he wishes" (B int 6: 27, female, rural).

Such practices are common among urban households too:

"Grandmother is the head! In our family grandmother has always been the head of the family, even when grandfather was alive, he passed away recently. Even though I'm 47 years old, but I give all of my salary to my grandmother, as I used to give her my scholarship till the last coin. It doesn't mean that she is controlling me, but I just can't spend that money myself. And yes, that she will dispose of all the money wisely. (In decision-making) we're coming to recommend, but hers is the last word! If my mother says "no" it means no! We will never go against her! Even if it is about little things, about the garden, the flowerbed, construction or even about installing gates – grandmother will decide!" (B int 32: 29, 30, female, urban).

"My mother-in-law kept most of the money, I didn't like to ask her, sometimes when it was needed I asked my mother for it, I always had a reserve of personal money, just in case. When it was so necessary I asked my husband, but his money was also kept by my mother-in-law, my husband always told me to ask the mother-in-law but I never did it. Never asked her, if you ask her she will hang you alive" (B int 16: 27, female, urban).

In some cases the household head and main breadwinner do not coincide, particularly when e.g. the husband is unemployed or has no constant income and the wife brings in the money. Female economic independence may, to a certain extent, influence the conditions of subordination. One of the respondents told us about how her husband who did not have a constant salary, tried to control how she dressed when she went to work, and to create obstacles in her career. However, she did not obey the requirements of her husband, because he was not the one who earned and therefore controlled the family budget. These cases occur but they are rare and indicate only a faint change.

Social Challenges

The most important challenges, which our respondents address, are poverty and harsh living conditions. Poverty continues to be a persistent social issue, although statistically at least extreme poverty has slightly decreased. "The level of extreme poverty in 2011 was equal to 4.5%, which was 0.8% less than in the previous year, thus bringing extreme poverty to 1.6% less in urban areas and 0.3% less in rural areas."[212] There is a big variation in levels of poverty across different regions of the country. "Kyrgyz Republic is an interesting case in terms of high socio-economic inequality that is predetermined by long-term regional differences, and the big rural and urban divide despite the economic development and overall poverty reduction"[213] For example in 2011, the poverty rate in urban areas was 31% compared to 40% in rural areas (National Statistical Committee). "The differences in the level of living standards are particularly noticeable among the growing capital city of Bishkek and other regions of the country. For example, the poverty rate in Naryn region is equal to 50% compared to 18% in the capital city."[214]

According to the research and information agency named 'Heritage of the Motherland' "the largest share of the poor is among households, where household leaders are older than 60 (50%), and lowest level of poverty is among younger generations. These figures raise one's hope – almost two thirds of young families (where household heads are in their 30s) are not poor, demonstrating that they were able to adapt to the existing harsh economic conditions. However, high rates of poverty among older generations point at the problem of less socio-economic adaptability among older cohorts. Of particular concern is the high rate of poverty among age groups of 30-50. At this stage of life, earnings of household heads tend to be at their height, enabling households to make savings, to invest in children's education, and to secure permanent housing. However, in the case of Kyrgyzstan, this age group has receding opportunities, for improving their financial situation, every year. A significant part of older generations are more likely not to benefit from the overall economic growth at all. In the light of the economic inefficiency of the system of social protection in the Kyrgyz Republic, this situation poses the threat of deprivation for many people of retirement age for decades ahead. The tendency of unequal consumption among households has been high in several recent years. In rural areas, where the basic agricultural sector is more or less self-sufficient, and consumption is less dependent on the local government budget, the poverty levels have not drastically declined. However, the overall difference

[212] Level of poverty in Kyrgyz Republic in 2011 – http://stat.kg/images/stories/docs/tematika/living/Ur.%20bedn.%202011.pdf; access date 09-04-13.

[213] Regional differences in living standards of the population in Kyrgyz Republic. À. Atamanov (The World Bank). http://www.undp.kg/ru/resources/e-library?start=50; access date 09-04-13.

[214] Ibid.

between the volume of consumption among the richest 20% and poorest 20% has increased by 9.6"[215]

Several housing and community living conditions can be identified as key indicators of modernization and civilization, namely: access to clean drinking water, sanitation, including sewage networks, as well as the effective heating system – gas and other alternative sources of energy. These indicators can also serve as criteria of socio-economic statuses among households, hence allowing us to classify some as poor, and others as better-off.

All households included in the study emphasized limitations in accessing all of the above-mentioned public goods. Hence, rural respondents noted a very low level of access to clean drinking water:

"Our drinking water is cut off very often. And the neighboring building has not water at all. Some people have connected their houses to the major water pipes themselves, some people who don't have water come to us. But we also have frequent cut offs. Garbage is another common problem. They have to take it out regularly, but they don't. There is always a bad smell in our neighborhood for that reason. As I already mentioned, the neighbors keep cattle, and that also makes our neighborhood dirty and smelly. Nobody cares to keep the neighborhood clean" (B int 3: 150, male, rural).

As can be seen from this quotation, garbage collection and disposal is yet another significant problem – as a rule, there are no garbage bins in most of the rural neighborhoods.

Uninterrupted electricity supply can serve as a litmus test in evaluating efficiency of the government's performance. Experts consider the following factors to be the key obstacles in making electricity available for the whole population: increasing the burden on the electricity network, technical depreciation and losses of electricity networks (partly due to unrecorded and illegal "pirate" consumption of energy by large segments of the population), and ineffective management of electric resources. As a result, the government officials and consumers of electricity find themselves in a vicious circle, where both sides accuse each other – and where the electric companies' budgets fall short of millions of Soms, due to large segments of the poor population consuming electricity illegally. For these reasons, the government and electric companies do not invest in the reconstruction of electric lines and improvement of services. This also leads to poor households' reliance on other natural resources that they utilize in heating their houses:

[215] Contemporary issues of poverty in the Kyrgyz Republic. http://old.nasledie.ru/politvne/18_31/kniga1/article.php?art=2, acess date 09-04-13.

"Well, we have problems; there are periods in the year when we do not get any electricity. It happens constantly during the winter period and also in summer we have water and electricity cut offs. We were told that the cut offs happen because of the damaged power lines and then because of the repair works. Although recently, it is more rarely that we get a water or electricity cut off" (B int 9: 110, male, rural).

Despite the lack of clear and unambiguous definitions of health in modern literature, indicators of health problems such as increased maternal and infant mortality, decreases on age of men and women; indices of mortality caused by diseases of the cardiovascular system indicate the presence of health problems, especially among the rural poor.

With the widespread poverty in the background, deterioration of the quality of healthcare available for the population, the absence and extreme weakness of preventive measures have all contributed towards the spread of so-called social diseases. Because of the lack of vitamins and poor nutrition, diseases associated with anemia and damaged thyroid glands are common among the poor. Moreover, regions with poor access to clean drinking water prove conducive for infectious diseases. As one of the respondents noted in his interview, brucellosis is a common infectious disease among those who raise livestock:

"During Soviet times, there were no diseases like brucellosis, there were cases when the cattle were sick with this disease, but it was rare. And now, there are many people who get brucellosis from their cattle. We never knew what aphtha's disease was all about. There are quite a few people who get these infections now. You could count people with mange on your fingers before and now there are many who get it" (B int 9: 98, male, rural).

In August 2013 it was also reported from rural Kyrgyzstan that cases of bubonic plague had been discovered.[216]

After several stages of reforms of the healthcare system, villages only retained low-level midwife stations that offer limited medical services. For a long period of time, a number of villages did not even have such medical centers, since the buildings were in poor condition and did not even have basic medical equipment.

"No, we do not have any problems in our family, our family is normal, we have some problems with health condition because of the age, but 90% of our villagers never went to hospitals because they do not have enough means for that. Moreover, they are afraid of going, because they think they will not even want to live once they find out the number of diseases they have" (B int 10: 77, male, rural).

---

[216] http://abcnews.go.com/index{Health}Health/wireStory/160-quarantined-plague-death-kyrgyzstan-20092763; access date 29-08-13.

What about the main urban problems?

"In Bishkek... now, in the current situation, the problems of Bishkek,..., there is the ecological problem... ecology becomes dirty, because many trees are cut for constructing houses, houses, detached houses; there is a problem of transport – (...) public transport... on the roads... there are small marshrutkas (mini buses) as we say, most of them do not meet the technical requirements. If our country was civil... civilized, a civilized country, then people would sit on their seats, and no more people were taken. And when you get into a marshrutka, you always get your destination standing on foot. They stop everywhere they want, although they must stop only on bus stops, whether there is a traffic light or not, they stop. There are too many transports, and they drive ... there are drivers who have driving licenses, learned this, but there are also those who buy them. There are many problems in Bishkek; there is the problem of roads... markets are too... if to think and look at Bishkek, Bishkek itself is like a big market, our city becomes like a big market, now, the dwellers of Bishkek, people who work at the government ... work ... I mean governmental workers, school personnel, who are based on budget, militia, medical personnel, workers of firms, firms, firms too, private firms are the one part of the market, the one part, and everything is a market. That is the problem. In the markets, it is called (...) anti, anti-sanitary, everything is dirty, there is a toilet, and next to it, there is food, and there is, for example, it is called trade neighboring, there are detergent, then next to it is food. And it should not be so, there are organizations which must control these things, but they do not work very well, but they get salaries. All these things are related to corruption, they should do – you can just write that – that everything is controlled and that everything is clean, but you go there and it is not so" (B int 37: 547 – 553, male, urban).

Respondents emphasized the unsolvable nature of such problems as unemployment, crime and corruption:

"We have particular problems that are related to employment. I have doubts that my children can find jobs for themselves when they grow up" (B int 29: 113, male, urban).

"We've got a lot of problems related to crime and corruption. I think as always and everywhere the governments and the systems are corrupted. It's not easy to live in Russia either, may be they have some advantages, you know that a lot of our citizens have left there already. My husband however is completely against the idea of moving somewhere. Well, he really likes this climate for example. We believe that this is our homeland. You know two years ago when there was a revolution, it was scary. Really, not even when there was the revolution itself, with all deaths, but especially scary during the aftermath events here that happened in Maevka, when ethnic conflicts appeared. That was pretty terrible, and I immediately began to write my friends in Russia. Well, I realizedthat only close people care about us here, only my brother. But eventually, things became right and it felt good" (B int 25: 62, female, urban).

Many of our respondents said that corruption permeates every aspect of their everyday lives. According to the results of the "Index of Economic Freedom" study, in the year 2013 Kyrgyzstan was positioned as 89th among 177 countries worldwide, coming one position down in comparison to the previous year. Thereby, "Kyrgyzstan has dropped out of the category of countries with moderately free economies and landed in the category of countries with mostly unfree economies. The main problems of the country are the protection of property rights, high levels of corruption, high costs of maintaining the government, and monetary policy as well as poor investment climate."[217]

In contemporary society, personal benefits from using one's official position take many forms. They vary from the interest rates that accrue from the state contracts (the so called 'otkaty' or "kickbacks"), to informal types of gratitude in-kind, that include children's education, recreation and treatment of oneself and one's relatives abroad, assistance in getting apartments and smaller "perfectly legitimate" gifts as flowers, liquors, chocolate and theater tickets as compensation for loyalty, monetary compensation for accelerating bureaucratic procedures, for assisting to evade penalties or for any other mediating role.

Corruption is deeply embedded in every aspect of life:

"R: Unemployment... now there are many educational institutions here, there are many educational institutions, yes, it is good to study, because youth who study in those places, at least improve their knowledge. They may not always be able to find a job afterwards, but at least they will become educated... they will have good thinking, critical thinking skills. However, there are no jobs, and this is another problem. We have many educational institutions, and students are graduating from them getting some professions, but there is no opportunity to work, and this is also a problem. Where can they go?

I: Is there much corruption in educational institutions?

R: Of course, there is. It is called "razvod" (the term used by students and professors in such situations when students give professors money for giving better grades, G.G.) (...) The advisor or some active students go to professors and give money saying 'this money is for this student, and this money is for that student'.

I: So, then, in your point of view what is the level of education in Kyrgyzstan? Do children get education?

R: No. There are people who get good education, but it is a small part out of all those who enroll in universities" (B int 37: 532-535, male, urban).

217 Kyrgyzstan on its way to economic slavery – http://www.freemarket.kg/analytics/kyrgyzstan-na-puti-ekonomicheskogo-rabstva.

According to a Swedish political scientist Johan Engvall, "all of Kyrgyzstan's government can be represented as a market, in which goods and services are bought and sold, government offices being one of the primary goods in the market." According to Engvall, "the standard political theories do not provide the tools to understand the processes in Central Asia, this is primarily because corruption is not one of the problems that the government encounters, but is actually a management tool that the government actively employs in its work. One of the starkest illustrations of this is the symbiosis between the law enforcement state agencies and organized crime, which was nurtured by the former President Bakiev and also by the government leaders that came later."[218]

Furthermore, respondents noted the complete withdrawal of government agencies from the regulation of agricultural production and the backwardness of the agricultural sector:

"We live in the 21st century, the era of cybernetics and automation, but our fields are still tilled with old-style tools, and use traditional methods in raising cattle. For instance, even when we have surplus produce, like fruits and vegetables – we still have to take care of finding a market place where we could sell it. The government doesn't bother helping us with that. Everyone takes his own risks. If you cultivated cabbage and potatoes, and then the border with Kazakhstan or other neighboring countries gets closed, then you won't have a market where you can sell the produce. Our country doesn't have the processing plants, so we sell all the produce to the mediators who buy our stuff from the fields. There are other cases, when the grain for example was expensive during the previous years, and all the farmers started cultivating grain, which led to lowering of prices of wheat this year – and many farmers couldn't earn enough to cover their initial expenses. All the farmers were at loss, and the government doesn't subsidize, doesn't protect its market, which means agriculture is really based on the enthusiasm of farmers, that's it" (B int 10: 47, male, rural).

It was very common for respondents to express feelings of nostalgia about the Soviet order of life:

I: "Does the instability of our country scary you?

R: Of course it scares us. We want to have stability. It is almost 20 years (the dissolution of the Soviet Union), but there is no stability here. That's why citizens live like that, they don't know if they should build or not, if they should run away or rather stay here. To run where? They don't know. Who needs us? If someone takes us with everything what we

[218] Corruption in Kyrgyzstan – it is not the government's problem, it is the government itself. http://www.adc.kg/index.php?option=com_content&view=article&id=317%3Al-------------r&catid=20%3A2011-01-17-05-51-32&lang=ru, access date 30-09-13.

have, what happens then? I think it is better to be a Kyrgyzstani citizen, and to develop here.

I: What about psychological difficulties?

R: All the time we have psychological difficulties. In communism, communist parties were thinking for you but now no one thinks for you. You have to think for yourself. No one needs you, if you're not capable of working. I think about it every day

I: Would you like to return back to those times?

R: Yes, I want to return back to those times. I don't know; I was born in that life. I liked it. We had collectives, we were friendly to each other. We used to gather all together in state farm's bases. We had a good life. We knew that we were going to work and then return home. No one had gates, doors, household was open, gates were open and no one would steal. But now everywhere, you see closed buildings, of course we don't want it. I wish people to be kinder" (B int 33: 214-221, male, rural).

In addition to a memory of communism, a turn to religion can be observed in some cases, too.

"Kyrgyz have Muslim holidays as Orozo Ait and Kurban Ait; Nooruz is a traditional Kyrgyz holiday; we celebrate them, we have guests during these days, also remember our ancestors and pray for them. Even if we did not invite people, we have to meet visiting guests, make food and read the Quran. We wear more modest clothes during such events. However, because we lived 70 years under the Soviet Union we also celebrate 7th of November, because we grew up in the Communist party – we cannot erase those holidays in one day, we do not have a right to do so. We explain those holidays to our children and on those days we go out and celebrate" (B int 35: 46, female, urban).

The increasing level of religious believers among the population does not pose any threats in itself, but the upsurge of Islamic fundamentalist organizations, which are new to the Central Asian region, raises concerns. The experts relate the danger of this to a politicization of Islam and potential emergence of a powerful political force against the weakness of the state and public institutions. It is already observed that Islamic organizations in Central Asia rely on ideologies resonant with masses in the region and use international financial and possibly military support.

According to experts, "political Islam in the region is still in its infancy: it is in the process of expanding its resource base, formulating policy requirements and developing social ground, gradually positioning itself as an alternative to the secular state and public vector of development. There are all the necessary social and political conditions (poverty, corruption, property differentiation) that are conducive for these processes. Formed as a political force, the Islamists will strive to create a new state union on the territory of Central Asia. While such a perspective is not yet taken seriously, it is only a matter of time."[219] Echoing this, some respondents express concerns about the spread of Islamic values and practices:

"First of all, I mean the Islamization of society, the factor, that's really very annoying me. Well, my husband is also annoyed, but less so. But it is annoying me very much. Because I see that with my eyes, this is changing dramatically and rapidly; even say 10 years ago, the picture was different. Now that's really a lot of people who adhere to Sharia law, who believe that we should move on to the state system of Sharia law. That is, well, of course, it's very annoying, because I would not want to live here in such a state... because, well, in general, I believe that Islam is an alien religion for us. Because I do not know ... it would be a step back to the Middle Ages. After all, we women are so ... no, of course, by law, we women have equal rights with men, and so on and so on ... but in reality, that judging from the statistics, we have women who on average receive only 60% of men's wages. That is, it turns out, women have earned less, very often they have been exposed to violence by men from the community... that is, in general, women in Kyrgyzstan are a vulnerable part of society. And then the Islamic factor, do not know if I am stereotyping, but I think that in an Islamic society, women do what is deprived of civil rights ... and I'm worried if it will grow, we will have to leave this country, even though we belong to ... well, We Kirghiz, we were born here, but we cannot live here, we have to leave from here. That's annoying, the Islamic factor first. Second ... yes more than anything to be honest. What else could it be? Well ... instability and that instability, we have already got used to it" (B int 19: 41, female, Kyrgyz, urban).

Respondents often mentioned the severe consequences of the two political upheavals, that happened in 2005 and 2010, along with the tragic events in the South of the country that happened in the aftermath of the second upheaval.

"These events did not only influence individual lives, but the whole Kyrgyz nation, 84 people died (during the 2010 upheaval)... this all influenced badly all Kyrgyz people. Also in Osh more than 1000 people died and some people's bones are still not found. That was a grief of Kyrgyz people, thank God we got out of that, now the head of the state is promising lots of new changes, but in reality they are robbing the Kyrgyz republic" (B int 59, male, urban).

Shocks, socio-economic instability, and migration flows, both external and internal, have led to a sharp stratification of the Kyrgyzstani population. At the upper end is the urban business elite, at the lower end the rural population, which lives at and even below the poverty line. In the past, the national elites were mostly con-

[219] V. Paramonov. Threats to the security of Central Asia and potential scenarios for the region's development. – http://ceasia.ru/forum/ugrozi-bezopasnosti-tsentralnoy-azii-i-osnovnie-stsenarii-razvitiya-regiona.html

centrated in the capital city and a large part of the rural population constituted by titular ethnic group representatives served as buffers for non-titular minority ethnic groups. These minority groups that used to be a "stabilizing" layer of the local population have been significantly reduced in size as a result of migration outflows. High outflows of non-titular ethnic groups contribute to multitudes of negative situations in the socio-economic, ethno-political, and ethno-cultural spheres of the society. The population begins to differentiate between those who are from the South vs. the North and between people of different tribal and national identity:

"R: There are no such big tensions; the only discord is the difference between the South and the North. I know this because the village of my husband is close to the border with Uzbekistan, and there are more strict laws and order. Close to the east, in relation to other regions, because we stay in Bishkek and there are a lot of nations and plus the Chui region it is more fertile. People are here more democratic, more understanding, not so rude than in the South but they are also not to be blamed...

I: As you know Kyrgyz people have clans, for example "Uruu" did you face with the claim that you are from another clan?

R: Yes! Yes I was! It is already such a norm here, for example my husband is called 'Oh, Oshskiy (from Osh), oshlyam, oshlyam' or even worse 'sart' and by 'sarts' they mean dishonorable Uzbeks. But when we go there they say 'Arkalyk' (those who were born in the North). The word is used in reference to the other side of the mountain for example, so when you are in the mountains, you can say 'Arkalyk', in reference to anyone that is on the other side of the mountain. People from the back side of mountain pass in this sense. Of course there was a case they said 'Aa, daughter-in-law Arkalyk came', and additionally they call me 'Orus kelin' (meaning Russian daughter-in-law) and it is because I didn't study enough Kyrgyz language in my school, and it began later, when Kyrgyz language was introduced into education. However in Bishkek there were few schools and as a result I can understand the language, but it is hard for me to speak with Kyrgyz and having an Uzbek accent. I could not understand nothing at all, I was saying 'A, who? Me?' ([her mimics demonstrated that she could not understand those who approached her in Kyrgyz and Uzbek accents). And they asked me in Kyrgyz, but I answered in Russian. From that time I was stigmatized as 'Orus kelin'" (B int 12: 66, female, urban).

Bride Abduction: Marriage Strategies

In the Soviet period arranged marriages by "parental consent" were common. In the interviews of our study, many respondents discussed bride abduction as a normal practice during these days. Five respondents from 40 mentioned this practice in their personal life.

"Talking about my daughters, they were also abducted The first was kidnapped ten years ago. She was a freshman and she was too young to get married, therefore we had to hide her in different houses for three days, but nevertheless she was kidnapped. Then relatives came and said that she is already a bride in the new house. The second daughter was kidnapped right from our house. About ten guys burst into our house, when my husband and I were out of the home, smashed up everything in the house, beat up my sons and took away my daughter by force. I was very angry and went to the house of that guy; there was already a wedding party. I didn't want to bother them and didn't want people think bad about me and didn't come into that house, I sent my son instead. However all guests started to ask not to take away my daughter and I was afraid of being cursed, because Kyrgyz say it is better to leave the daughter who was kidnapped because she might be cursed, and I also didn't want to offend my new relatives, and that is why I left my daughter as a bride in the new house. They now live well, have three children" (B int 4: 22, 23, male, urban).

Early marriages have serious implications for the independence and reproductive health of women. Young women who marry early are less likely to continue their education, they have less influence within the decision-making process in their husbands' families, and they are more vulnerable to domestic violence. They tend to experience early pregnancies and childbearing, which according to experts is one of the main causes of deaths among women within the 15-19 age cohort[220] in developing countries.

In the past several years, a wide circle of researchers, representatives of the media and policy makers in Kyrgyzstan have studied bride abduction. "Studies conducted in Kyrgyzstan, have shown that in the villages, where 96% of the Kyrgyz population resides, 80% of marriages are arranged through the bride kidnapping practice. 57% of them happened without bride's consent. In addition, 22% of women had never met their husbands before they were abducted. Only 8% of the abducted women refused to get married. In practice, marriages that were not registered by the state cannot be terminated through courts. In such cases, spouses do not share legally prescribed property rights and obligations, and often women's rights are infringed as a result of this. Issues such as sharing the rights over child rearing, aggravate property-related disputes. As was reported by the Ministry of Internal Affairs, a separate record of "bride abduction" and forced marriages is not kept, and accurate statistics for the 2011 – 2012 year are not available. There is only data from the Institute of the Ombudsman, which state that in 2011, there were only three criminal cases initiated for bride abduction of women under the

---

220 Millennium development goals. Gender diagrams for 2012, UN – http://mdgs.un.org/unsd/mdg /Resources/Static/Products/Progress2012/GenderR.pdf, access data 20-08-13

age of 16 and two were brought to trial. In the same year, there were 14 criminal cases initiated for forcing women into marriage (...) we may conclude that criminal cases have been instituted only in one case out of 700 cases of bride abduction, and a penalty was imposed only in one case out of 1.500 cases."[221]

"He abducted me. I was against it, said that I do not want to marry him, but my grandmother insisted that according to our tradition I must obey to it and stay at their home, so I stayed there as a daughter-in-law. At the beginning I didn't thought about the hardships of living with two fathers, and two mothers of my husband. When I faced it personally, I understood it. People hardly ever live with one mother-in-law. I was 19 years old when I got married" (B int 14: 15, female, urban).

Early marriage is also a widespread practice – about 12.2% of women in the country are married before they turn 18. In rural areas, 14.2% of women are married before they are 18. In urban areas, the percentage is lower – 9.7% – according to the study of the UN Fund for Population.

The majority of early marriages do not last long. According to a three-year monitoring study, conducted by the Ombudsman's office, more than half of the marriages arranged through bride kidnapping end in divorce.

The Ministry of Internal Affairs does not keep track of bride kidnappings. Although, according to the Ombudsman's Office Reports, in 2011 68 cases were reported to the law enforcement authorities, and only 6 of them were finalized with a sentence.[222]

Non-Governmental Organizations that aim to protect women's rights present their own statistics: "in Kyrgyzstan, there are 32 cases of bride kidnappings and 6 cases of rapes in one day, and the charges are pressed only in 1 case out of 700, with only 1 out of 1,500 cases of bride kidnapping ending in a penalty."[223]

Migration

Poor socio-economic conditions and extremely low standards of living are the main reasons that forced a significant part of the active labor force in Kyrgyzstan to leave the country in search of work. Regular "revolutions" additionally increased out-migration of the population from the country.

221 Myagchilova, À. Statistics is a stubborn and scary thing. http://www.polit.kg/newskg/479, access data 18-08-13; whether these numbers are correct may be disputed as also other numbers are cited; see below

222 Tradition of bride kidnapping is leading to deaths – who is in charge? – http://slovo.kg/2012/11/tradiciya-krazhi-nevest-vse-chashhe-ubivaet-kto-v-otvete/ access data 29-08-13

223 ibid.

According to the press secretary of the Ministry of Labor, Employment and Migration, Nazgul Murzaeva, in Kyrgyzstan every fourth family has one migrant – "Today, in Kyrgyzstan, the export of the labor force has turned into a separate branch of the economy. It is safe to say that every fourth household has at least one migrant worker."[224] Only in the first half of 2011 the number of arrivals to the country constituted 17,200 people, while the number of those who left the country constituted 34,900 people, with out-migration equaling to 17,700 people. According to the National Statistics Committee, "the highest level of external migration is usually observed in Chui (...) and Osh (...)."[225]

The cohort of young people between 18 and 35 is the most mobile and members of this cohort very frequently use migration as strategy to address the problems of employment and low income. As is stated by the study on "Labor migration and productive use of human resources – The Kyrgyz Republic," – "the majority of migrant workers from Kyrgyzstan is in the age group of 20-35 years." Given the mobility of young people, given the large proportion of children, adolescents and the elderly in the population, the real workload for the active labor force is very high. Also, children under 14 years are often included in the labor force, because they make a significant contribution to the household economy.

Migration issues were raised in 11 of the 40 interviews conducted. Kyrgyz often talked about labor migration:

"The citizens of Kyrgyzstan go to Russia and get the citizenship of Russia – I see this as a problem. And why do they do that? Because the living conditions are pretty bad here, speaking generally, broadly. If the living conditions were good, here, then the citizens of other countries would come here, instead. There are no such people who come and work here. There are no jobs to work, where, what factories are working, there are some, of course, like the flour factories, sewing factories. There is sewing, and it is good that the Kyrgyz have learned this thing, and across Central Asia, the clothes from Kyrgyzstan are valued in Russia and other places. Our clothes are sent even to China" (B int 37: 574, male, urban).

As many respondents noted, earnings of labor migrants comprise a significant part of household budgets:

"There are no any other sources of income; our sons send us money; they work in the Russian Federation" (B int 10: 25, male, rural).

---

224 In Kyrgyzstan, every fourth family has one migrant – http://www.kyrtag.kg/?q=ru/news/9255; access date 29-08-13

225 Ibid.

The Russian-speaking population of the country has different views about migration:

"But I'm afraid to imagine me here in pensionable age. I want to emigrate" (B int 18: 35 male, urban).

"My mother wanted to go to Russia as we have relatives there. Second, she will become a pensioner soon, and pensions in Russia are much higher than in Kyrgyzstan. Due to political instability as well... There is an illusion that this country has a future, and this illusion slowly becomes reality. I see it at my work. What do I do? I sell projects of our programmers. In particular, our company experiences a lack of specialists. Level of education is too low; universities do not prepare specialists with good level of knowledge. Our business cannot afford to support own students, it is not profitable for a company" (B int 32: 24, male, urban).

Future Problems

A quote from an interview with Johan Engvall shows how people in Kyrgyzstan perceive the future. "The majority in the country only live in the present moment without thinking about the future: what's the point if the rules change so often? They think that they must seize the moment to 'make a quick buck', since it is not rational to actually plan for the future."[226]

When the tomorrow is unpredictable and may either bring sudden ups or downs, living in the moment turns into a 'rational' form of behavior. Limited chances to plan their lives make the population focus on short-term goals in life. The analysis of the levels of anxiety and fear caused by specific social phenomena, events or processes among respondents enables identification of the following primary factors: poverty, increases in prices and rampant unemployment, declining educational standards and low access to health services, rising crime, terrorism, loss of moral values, corruption, arbitrary rule and lawlessness.

"You know how it works in Central Asia? They employ their people, whom they know. Simply I do not have a person, who could come and advise my candidacy without big difficulties. At the beginning I had difficulties because at that time I had little babies and could not arrange any kindergarten for them. Moreover, your employer asks how many children do you have and how old are they and immediately says no, because there will be cases when little children fall ill, he has to provide with leaves and absences, and they do not want it. A little normal job, you must not have additional loads and problems, now

226 Corruption in Kyrgyzstan – it is not the government's problem, it is the government itself. http://www.adc.kg/index.php?option=com_content&view=article&id=317%3Alr&catid=20%3A2011-01-17-05-51-32&lang=ru; access date 29-08-13.

I solved it, arranged my children, school, kindergarten, but have not found the job yet" (B int 12: 86, female).

"Well first of all, I never faced that, thank God. But I am worried about my children, because they have different clashes in school, close to our school there is a dormitory nearby the Lenin plant and there are different youth: normal, local, and strangers. And in order to secure them, I do not let my children go out in the evenings; secondly my teacher told me a story when children are kidnapped in Bishkek. Therefore, I and my husband inform them to be aware of strangers and not to talk to them. Somebody asks you, say I do not know, and go away. Better not to talk with strangers, my husband says. The eldest son picks up the younger if we are late. In the place where we live, all neighbors know each other. If something new, new car 'aksakals (aged respected people) notice immediately" (B int 12: 175, male, urban).

"I would like to tell that our Kyrgyzstan holds almost the last position in crime all over the world, because it is not safely in our country. You know clearly that it is not safe during day time and at night. I also read a statistic that in Middle Asia our country is the most unsafe country in Middle Asia. And also corruption in Central Asia it holds first place. Crime, corruption and unemployment are on high levels" (B int 32: 233, female, urban).

"Maybe here is a bigger chance to be fooled in comparison with the periphery. Here is a bigger chance to lay someone; I don't know how to answer. Here is more risk, more problems with living. The salary is not met with the payments for rent of apartments, not everyone can rent an apartment. Even if you are renting you try to find the ones which you can afford, you do not look into conditions, so you get the ones which you did not want to. But the financial problems push you to find the ones you can afford. But thanks God we do not experience that, we have our own apartment. Even owning an apartment there is further money to be spent on education, medicine, visiting doctors, etc. For instance when you go to the policlinic they say that since 5 years everything is free but not, they just write it but they take money. What I want to say is that even though you own a house there are many more problems. That's all I want to say" (B int 36: 48, female, urban).

Other hazards, such as drug trafficking, crime and terrorism are anthropogenic. From the 1990's, Kyrgyzstan has turned into the main transit point for drug trafficking in Central Asia, and as a result suffers from increased morbidity, crime and corruption. Hundreds of thousands of people in the region are suffering from drug addiction, and their number is constantly growing.[227] Kyrgyzstan as territory of Central Asia is located between the main centers of production (Afghanistan) and the main consumption centers (Europe, China, and Russia) of

[227] Report about human development in Central Asia. Into the future with no barriers: Regional cooperation in the sphere of human development and security – Regional Bureau of UNDP among European and CIS countries, 2005

drugs. While efforts to combat drug trafficking can give some results in limiting or redirecting the flow of drugs, experience has shown that the drug trade will continue, especially where the state is weak and governance is ineffective.

"Corruption,... corruption is at the very bottom... but I cannot say about... corruption... there is a good Kyrgyz expression 'balyk bashynan sasyit' (all things begin from the top), so if people on the top do good things and are pure in their deeds... Ishak Razzakov once said 'if you are pure, I am pure, then the society will be pure'. So if each of us would try to be pure" (B int 4: 553, male, urban).

"Today every citizen became a politician, for instance earlier states did not help the population by providing coal to houses, providing food. Before also every person worked to earn something What is actually needed from the government is water, people go and seek for water, there is no water for plants if we had water our air would have been fresher, it is 35degrees hot, soon will come Ramadan and we are asking the government for electricity, water, not expensive food and cheap transportation, that's all, people do not ask for something more" (B int 5: 87, male, rural).

Kyrgyzstan is also subject to the threat posed by terrorists, both local and from neighboring countries that are thriving because of mismanagement, political repression and revenues from drugs and crime.

The population is not confident about the future of their own families and the state's future as a whole:

"The most important one is peace, the main, the first thing. Now, in Central Asia, there is, now, ... many dangerous moments. Now, look to the Arabian countries, there are wars, aren't they? If to look at them, then it seems that someone makes them. There are wars in all Arabian countries; they are fighting with each other, fight for power. This thing was planned by someone, because such thing would not happen without it. For example, Muslim countries, Islam countries, they are close to God, they were far from stealing something, killing someone, so it was planned by someone. People say that it is planned by America. So, such things must not happen here. And the problem between Uzbek and Kyrgyz is also not the thing that people themselves have started, it was also was planned by someone, ordinary people do not need these kind of things. If ... why I say that it is a problem, because if there are tensions between Uzbek and Kyrgyz, then our closest neighboring country, Uzbekistan... the population of which is 5 times more than the population here... Ask God that this thing does not happen, because if something happens, then there will be a great fight not only within Kyrgyzstan but within Central Asia including Turkmenistan, Kazakhstan, within all countries, Afghanistan, Pakistan, Tajikistan, all countries will be involved. So, this is the situation in relation to peace" (B int 37: 576, male, urban).

Conclusions

The study of households and their members enabled us to identify and characterize the main stages through which households have adapted to the market economy: 'primitive survival', active adaptation to the new conditions of social and economic environment, and the sustainable reproduction of the new system of values and norms for behavior.

The majority of households in rural and urban areas classify as households that are in the "primitive survival" stage. These households are characterized by a sharp decline in household members' earnings and by their efforts to survive by any means, most often by very basic ways such as active use of the natural environment, subsistence farming, earning through temporary jobs, and involvement in areas of the informal economy. This includes second shifts, opening micro and small businesses, double-book accounting and using personal networks. The border between the formal and the informal economy gradually becomes blurred and partly does not exist anymore allowing especially for the expansion of a sector of illegal and informal activities that hinder the development of market orientated behavior.

Poverty has become a persistent characteristic of the society and produces new forms of culture – "the culture of poverty" – which can be characterized by the lack of access to the institutions of culture and sports, declining educational standards and increasing levels of religious adherence, the lack of plans for the future, and a sense of fear and hopelessness for the future of the children. Also our middle class households are touched by the problems of poverty and many are near the poverty line and constantly feel threatened falling below it.

Households cope with the declining economy and political crises in various ways, depending on the structure of the household, its resource base and other capabilities (such as income, social status, interpersonal relationships, interests, values, motivation, and individual characteristics). But a large part of the population does not demonstrate successful adaptation to the market economy, and instead, adopt primitive techniques of adapting to the market through non-market strategies.

Along with economic factors, a number of factors (such as traditionalism, collectivism, state paternalism, and high levels of corruption in all spheres) that had been shaped by preceding stages of the country's development have contributed towards the formation of the attitude of not thinking about the future, or to perceive it as hopeless. All these factors combined, have made the majority of the population adapt techniques that involve reduction of economic activities and “belt-tying” practices instead of self-development.

Thus, impoverished households have developed “passive” ways of adapting, which do not overcome poverty and create conditions for the emergence of effective institutions of the market economy but who help them to survive.

The household survey conducted in Kyrgyzstan, shows weak economic activity of the population; many complain that the state is no more a “nanny” state.

In the process of market transformation, the position of each household was largely dependent on the kind of social status occupied by household members in the social hierarchy of the previous administrative system. Thus, all other things being equal, individuals from households with a higher vocational or job status, or from more prosperous households, have a wider range of choices in the labor market as well as in the consumer market.

Most people have lost their hope for stability and social security. The old problem of "where to buy" disappeared, but a new problem of "where and how to get money?” appeared. Especially those, having lost their deposits in banks in the aftermath of the Soviet Union’s collapse, often find it difficult to make new savings. Constant delays and non-payment of wages, regular increases in consumer prices do not allow planning one’s budget. Micro-credit companies, with high interest rates are not conducing for business development and instead push people into the abyss of poverty.

A previously unknown problem of job search and constant search of extra earnings has become vital. Even those who were able to maintain the standard of living that they had ten years ago claimed to have reasons to be dissatisfied.

Migration poses a serious threat to countries like Kyrgyzstan. They lose their human potential (brain drain). Furthermore, ethnic and religious diversity is diminished and may cause polarization between remaining ethnic and religious groups. In the border areas – as we could recently see in other post-soviet countries – ethnicity may be misused from foreign political powers for autonomous claims or even dissolution.

The bad economic situation, the disastrous social security, crime, corruption etc. seem to be the seedbed for religious fundamentalism. A considerable number of respondents in the interviews note Islamic fundamentalism as a threat.

The economic, political, social and cultural deterioration of the country also seems to make acceptable a form of traditionalism, the symbol of which can be seen in the practice of bride kidnapping, that continues to be reproduced all over the country though more often in rural areas. Those households being confronted with bride abduction react to this with resigned acceptance.

All in all – and being pessimistic – the results of our household survey shows a constellation of middle income households in a society with a state near to failure. Therefore the economic behavior of the households implies a strong orientation at immediate survival with which the overall vulnerability is believed to be met.

5. Vulnerabilities and Livelihood Strategies

Eckhard DITTRICH, Denis GRUBER, Heiko SCHRADER

In order to better understand how households in Kazakhstan and Kyrgyzstan cope with their situation, we now try to find out about their vulnerabilities and their strategies we referred to already in the first chapter. Our interpretation is primarily based on the qualitative data; the quantitative data, the country and regional analysis forming the background. In accordance with the literature and with our previous results, we distinguish between urban and rural households. However, due to the methodology of the "household level approach" (Hess et al. 2000), we do not distinguish according to age cohorts, although other research and one of our research hypotheses referred to differences according to age (post-Soviet cohort – Soviet cohort).[228]

In the following we start by presenting three typical rural and three typical urban households from the three research regions that can best characterize and illustrate strategies. The households chosen were a result of lengthy intergroup discussions, by which we tried to overcome the different views in our intercultural group and to cope with the partly different regional and national results. We distinguish between three middle class households,[229] poorer, middle and better off households (while excluding the rich and the very poor). The distinction is based on a rough estimation of income of household members. By this we want to find out whether the three classes of households employ different strategies and what might be the reasons for that. Later on in our following interpretation, we ask for more general strategies and use the whole qualitative material to illustrate them.

The notion vulnerability as used in science was largely influenced by the ILO's definition on "vulnerable employment".[230] It defines vulnerability by lack of decent working conditions, inadequate earnings and informal work arrangements. But vulnerabilities for households comprise more than only employment. They are related to shocks or unexpected problems like sudden deaths, illnesses, to sea-

228 GALLUP Former Societ Union http://www.gallup.com/poll/166538/former-soviet-countries-harm-breakup.aspx; access 07-08-14.

229 For the usefulness of class theory in present-day sociology see Portes (2010).

230 UN-ILO Vulnerable employment: http://www.un.org/esa/sustdev/natlinfo/indicators/methodology_sheets/econ_development/vulnerable_index{Employment}employment.pdf; access 07-08-14

sonality, to infrastructures, changes etc. Vulnerability also has a subjective side – the reference points of judgment from the perspective of the agents – and can't only be measured in terms of percentage of the national households below the poverty line e.g. In general, the "objective side" and the "subjective" side both influence decisions about those arrangements that help people to cope with their life situation and to overcome vulnerabilities. The arrangements are outcomes of 'practices' ... (Smith and Stenning 2006: 19), "nested" livelihood strategies or "Lebensführung" in the sense of Max Weber, a "set of activities undertaken and used by individuals, households and communities in order to sustain livelihoods but also to sustain a sociality to economic life which requires mutual, reciprocal and embedded forms of economic activity" (Smith & Stenning, 2006, p. 192; Kleineberg in Dittrich, Oswald, & Voronkov, 2002: p. 25ff; Dittrich & Oswald, 2010). These practices may be routines (a "muddling through" in everyday-life) or may be conscious actions on the base of 'bounded rationality' (Simon 1982). As they borrow on past experiences and are building up by them, they do not lack continuity. Past experiences in our case are represented by the experiences and narratives of the interviewees during and about the Soviet times, for the older as well as for the younger cohorts. They accentuate that the socialist state was providing its inhabitants with security and stable incomes. And for both cohorts the experiences from the past 20 years of market economy are also meaningful with regard to privatization, economic crises, experiences with banks, the state etc. (Gallup, ibid). The strategies had to be learned. The households could not simply borrow on their past experiences under Soviet conditions. The new regime has exposed them to a new vulnerability context, new institutions, policies and processes and changed assets for survival.

Vulnerabilities are related to the different practices taken or not taken, from their interconnectedness with the resource base, the households can activate as well as from the different contexts into which the practices are bound into. We have tried to capture the resource base by using an extended version of Bourdieu' s forms of capital. In this chapter, we generalize them under the heading of strategies (see Figure 1, Ch. 1). We believe very much, that the following sustainable livelihoods framework has not only explanatory power for the group of the poor but also for middle class households.

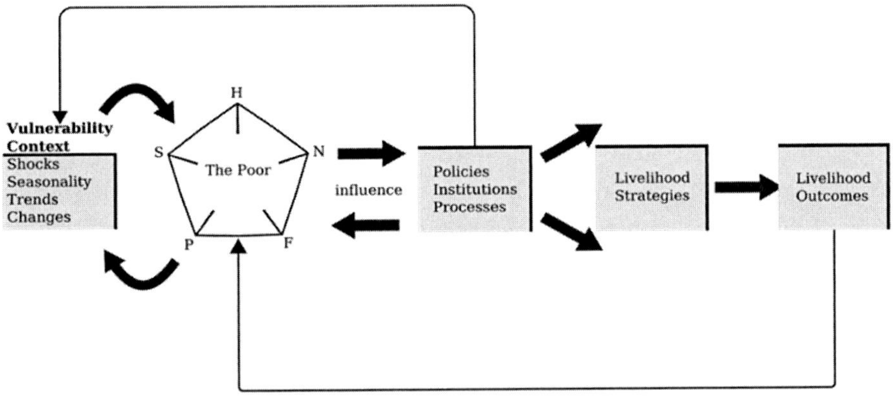

Figure 40: The Sustainable Livelihoods Framework
Source: cf. http://www.ifad.org/sla/; 22.03.13

Households near to Poverty – Rural Examples

Case A: Household of A.S. (A. village, Almaty Region, female, interview 9)

The household of A.S. is located in the Almaty region, close to the city of Kapshagay, in a village, 60 km from Astana. A.S. was born in 1964. She has lived in this village for 20 years. She has secondary education and worked as a seamstress, a cutter of women's clothing. At present she has no official job. The 48 years old woman gave birth to her first and only child when she was already 41. She has been married for 23 years, but lives alone in the household with her 75 years old mother, who is the owner of the house, and her 7 years old son who is enrolled in the first year of school. Her husband lives only temporarily in the household, because he is a labor migrant. The husband has secondary education too and also learned to be a seamster by specialty. After the couple had migrated to the village both found work in a small studio as tailors. After several years, the husband lost this job and started to work as a fisherman in a company located near the village. When this company was closed, the fishermen had to find a new job in another company. But there were no jobs. Thus, the husband became self-employed as a professional fisherman, but his business is not registered. The respondent worked in her profession until her son was enrolled in school.

Case B: Household of S.B. (E. village, Akmola Region, male, interview 31)

The household of S.B. is located in E. village, Akmola region, 80 kilometers from Astana. The household owns a privatized flat. S.B. is a 51 years old unemployed male. He has secondary education and worked in mining. The household consists of 6 persons (his wife, son, daughter-in-law, 2 grandchildren). A daughter left the household and lives separately. The wife works in a private company and has a steady, though low income. The 28 years old son works in a company, where he repairs computers. The daughter-in-law does not work at present because she is on maternity leave. Although S.B. is officially unemployed he works informally in construction. The household has a garden where they grow vegetables and fruits. They do not have livestock and due to the low household budget have to economize on consumption. The tense economic situation is of enduring character. Already four years ago, S.B. was forced to slaughter their entire livestock.

Case C: Household of E.E. (S. village, Alamedin district, female, interview 15)

The household of E.E. lives in a barrack-type house in a village in the Alamedin district, 20 kilometers from Bishkek. The general condition of the house is in a bad shape. The furniture is old and outworn. There is no kitchen furniture. The household owns one cow and a car, both being financed by credits. The household does not have any savings. There is no stove in the kitchen, therefore they cook on an electric hotplate. E.E. was born in 1959 in the countryside. Three persons live permanently in the household: E.E., her husband and the son who is a traffic controller at a taxi park. E.E. is unemployed; her main responsibilities are household chores and caring for two grandsons. The husband works as a driver for a private company. He does not have higher education. He started his study at a polytechnic institute, but dropped out. They have four children: three girls and a boy. One daughter, her husband and two children live separately. The youngest daughter has been working in Russia for a year now and stands on her own feet. At present, the middle daughter with her husband and 2 children live in the household. They used to live in Bishkek, but due to unemployment and insufficient income could not pay their rent any more. That is why they moved back to the wife's parents.

Reference points of judgment

Overwhelmingly, economic conditions are responsible for the current living standards of this class of households near to poverty. But the interviewees judge them in reference to the accomplishments of the socialist state, be the interviewees men or women, younger or older:

"I state this with good reason that our times were more or less better. The state secured us (...) At that time I received allowances for the kids: 35 rubles. So, in total I got 70 rubles for the two girls. At those times, that money sufficed. My husband, for example, was paid 70, and sometimes 80 or 90 rubles. This is how we lived" (B int 15: 22, female, rural, 53 years).

Respondents complain that there are no job guarantees anymore.

"Sometimes there is job, sometimes there is not. It is not like in times of the Soviet Union when we had no unemployment rate. Jobs are not permanent" (B int 15: 42, female, rural, 53 years).

Formal employment

After having worked in the same local company as her husband, and after having been dismissed and reinstalled a couple of times, A.S. started her own entrepreneurial career and registered her business as a seamstress.

"At first I worked in a studio, but then it was closed. There was a time I did not work at all, nobody did work, because there was no work available (...) Then we rented a room, three people began working in their own business" (Alm int 9: 103, female, rural, 48 years).

Until her son was enrolled in school she worked as a self-employed person from 8.00 a.m. until 5 p.m. five days a week. Besides the necessary labor migration of her husband, a second factor influences the low household budget: A.S. has interrupted employment for the period of one year as she wants to help her son with education.

"Now my son takes all my time. I want to have time for him while he studies in his first year. I was already 41 years old, when I gave birth. He is a late child and I want to have more time for his nurture" (Alm int 9: 21, female, rural, 48 years).

Households are vulnerable to poverty because quite often there is no stable monthly income. Often the only financial stability that households can achieve is provided by pensions. This is also the case in the household of A.S. Her 75 years old mother supports the household with her pension. With this, the instable incomes of the couple and a stable income are pooled, a strategy, to gain more security in everyday life and to reduce vulnerability.

Under these conditions, unemployment and wage arrears turn into shocks and crisis. Threatened are especially older persons. In these cases their situation gets aggravated if the household has to secure other responsibilities like paybacks or the support of children's education:

"This crisis just gets me down (...) nobody needs workers over 50. Looking for a job after 50 makes no sense. I cannot find a job, because with 50 I am too old for the labor market (...) It is impossible. For example, I do not consider myself a poor man, but I have enough common sense, to understand that my grandchildren should go to a decent school. And I am ready to pay for their higher education. Of course, it should not be too expensive. We have to consider our opportunities. If it is free education they can go. Anyway, we should think about it" (Ast int 3: 22, male, rural, 51 years).

Labor migration

Due to the necessity to earn cash and to contribute to the household's survival the husband of A.S. was forced to migrate to Balkhash, a village located more than 400 kilometers away from their home village. But his remittances, due to the seasonal nature of his work, are not of the kind that enhance the household's stability. In the cold season fish catches are poor.

"My husband is still a fisherman. He does not have a fixed salary and his wage depends on weather conditions. Buying the fishing nets, a motor for the ship, all this costs a lot of money. That is why we do not have much money" (Alm int 9: 33, female, rural, 48 years).

Labor migration of household members is a very important strategy of this rural household near to poverty in order to gain security in everyday life and to maintain the household's existence. But success is unsure. The husband had already tried to get a job in Zarechny, a settlement only 10 kilometers from the household's home, but all his applications were refused due to lack of qualifications and/or insufficient knowledge. A.S. puts it as follows:

"He works where it is possible to find a job" (Alm int 9: female, rural, 48 years).

Moreover, by starting his self-employment as a fisherman, the husband had to cope with vulnerability. His health was bad and he could not work for some time. Additionally, the necessary equipment for fishing ate up nearly all their savings, thus adding to the vulnerability of the household.

A.S. associates the difficult decisions they had to make with the role of men as breadwinners and thus reveals an internal, social psychological side of vulnerabilities through unemployment:

"Men are not as patient as women. If they have problems to work, they become nervous. Men are vulnerable. We support and care for them as best we can" (Alm int 9: 33, female, rural, 48 years).

As with becoming a fisherman, international labor migration is also not free from certain conditions. The decision alone does not make up for a job. In the case of E.E., relatives helped to find a workplace immediately:

"One relative from my husband's side lives there (in Russia) also. She is the daughter of my husband's younger brother. She lives there for three years already and works as a seamstress as well. My daughter works now together with her" (B int 15: 9, female, rural, 53 years).

Self-employment in the informal sector, selling food and property as strategies

Another strategy, rural households near to poverty pursue to secure survival is *self-employment in the informal sector*. In the case of A.S. not only the husband is involved in self-employment, but also A.S. herself works informally at home as a seamstress. S.B. works informally in construction.

"Sometimes I have an extra income. My friends call me if there are some works, where I can earn some money. These works are only manual jobs. For example, it could be to dig something or to cut something. The other household members don't have extra income" (Ast int 31: male, rural, 51 years).

To survive, sometimes drastic measures are necessary. S.B. was forced to slaughter the whole livestock four years ago in order to secure the household existence and to overcome financial shortages. It was necessary to sell the meat to have money, "no other way". Many informants report about *selling home-produced products* in bazaars or at crossroads. A.S. sells home-tailored clothes at crossroads. The necessity of such practices lies in the instability of incomes from wage labor or informal activities. Selling livestock or clothes or other property aims at crisis management to secure existence.

"The difficulties began 6 years ago, that is why we had to sell something. I had a foreign car, but we had to sell it, because of this crisis. We could not give back the money, which we had lent and had to sell our car" (Alm int 9: 53, female, rural, 48 years).

The danger of impoverishment can be so acute, that these households not only become indebted, but sometimes, as in the case of E.E. "even had no bread at home." The case of E.E. shows the sharpness of the daily struggle for survival as well as the necessity to look for any possibility of survival. At that time, E.E. started to produce the national drink *Jarma* and sold it at a bazaar.

"My husband's youngest sister lived in A. When I found some money, I used to go there and make this drink. At least we could buy bread then. I was trying to live as everybody did and did everything that I could.... We went there (to A. market) to sell 10 liters of jarma. The drink I made was so good and tasty, ... At that time one cup of jarma cost 3 soms, and 10 liters could be sold for 30 soms. ... At those times, the groceries were not expensive" (B int 15: 60, female, rural, 53 years).

After a short period of success, there was no demand for *Jarma* anymore and E.E. tried to sell *maksym* and later on *lepeshkas* and *bread*. She asked her neighbors for flour to produce these groceries at home. These attempts also failed and E.E. started to cook and sell plov. The failures continued. Also selling home-cooked *pelmeni* at the bazaar did not make any breakthrough. The last-ditch attempt to become a successful seller in a bazaar for E.E. was to produce alcohol at home and to sell it, but also selling *samogon* was unsuccessful. The vulnerabilities even increased when her husband was imprisoned after a car accident. Although, according to E.E., the husband was not guilty he was sentenced to three years imprisonment.

"The opponents had some friends who could help. My husband didn't have any support as he came from N. He didn't know anybody there (...) This was a hard time for our family and we lived in tense conditions" (B int 15: 18, female, rural, 53 years).

The imprisonment of the husband meant a huge shock for the household because E.E had to feed four children, had no money and could not work in a formal wage earning job because the children were too young. She asked her neighbors to help her out and used donor flour to bake pastries and toshoks and to sell it to neighbors. She describes this period as a daily battle for survival. By selling home-made food she received money and was "able to buy bread at least".

"Every day I would make toshoks and then sell them; this is how we survived, not lived. I have four kids, so imagine how hard it was to be without a husband. So, I kept on taking care of our kids and feeding them (...) There was also samogon. A bottle cost 15 soms (...) At home I was making bozo in 4- liter jars. I asked our neighbors to share some flour to make bread. Sometimes I couldn't pay back these debts" (B int 15: 70, female, rural, 53 years).

The cases of A.S. and E.E. can illustrate the danger of female-headed households becoming vulnerable to poverty, even if the context for their precarious situation is only temporary ... (Buvinic, Da Gupta, and Casabonne 2009). They are a good examples of muddling-through practices for making a living.

It is worth mentioning, that all these activities of self-employment are unregistered. In our whole sample, officially registered self-employment is a great exception. A last remark concerns old age. Members of these households normally don't accumulate high rights to a pension and thus will rely on their children concerning survival after their working lives.

Co-residence

Due to financial hardships these households try to minimize expenditures. A first option arises through permanent or temporary co-residence of extended household members. In the case of A.S. it is the grandmother, in the case of E.E. it is co-residence with the family of the middle daughter. The first one represent permanent co-residence, the latter a temporary one.

> "They tried to live on their own exactly four times. They always returned, living there for three months at maximum, because the apartments are expensive. You know how hard it is to live there. This time, they called me again and asked dad to help because her husband did not find a job, and there was no money; so they had to move out urgently. We helped them to quit from their apartments several times already, because they couldn't pay for the upcoming month" (B int 15: 54, female, rural, 53 years).

Within the wider family this causes quite some arguments and much shame on the side of the daughter being unable to live on her own feet together with her family. But the household members themselves seem to accept the situation.

Reliance on reciprocity networks

Another survival practice for rural households close to poverty is the reliance on reciprocity networks. This reliance may be based on family members and/or friends. This strategy is quite often combined with other livelihood strategies to overcome and/or to avoid crises and shocks. It is typical to ask F-network members for money and not to go to banks. Family members are often the first and often only addressees for financial support.

In the case of A.S., reciprocity exchange is among friends. They helped them when they were in need of cash:

> "Yes, because at that time we had money, it was six years ago. Now, my husband does not work permanently, but before that, he had a stable salary. We had enough money for ourselves to lead a normal life. Although we lived from paycheck to paycheck, we had

the opportunity to help out our friends. They always help us and we help them too (...) Our friends helped us with money. Fortunately, there are people, who are ready to help us, when we ask" (Alm int 9: 43, female, rural, 48 years).

S.B. asked for help because of funerals and the household got money from family members and friends. Relying on these reciprocity networks in one's life seems to be self-understood among this class of households.

"If there are some urgent celebrations and anniversaries and the current savings are not enough for expenses, we will borrow money from relatives and acquaintances. Usually we borrow money from somebody. It is better than going to a bank (...) We have many relatives and we help each other to cope with problems. It's not for everyday expenditures. If they are able to help you, they will do it if there are no other ways out" (Ast int 31: 16, male, rural, 51 years).

Households can rely on mutual (financial) support and it is a "no go" to deny help to friends or relatives if one is asked and the demanding person knows that there is money.

Another example for the reliance on reciprocity networks is the employment of grandmothers as surrogate housewives, e.g. to raise and educate younger family members at home and to share in household chores including e.g. gardening, animal husbandry and other outdoor work. Thus one can economize on expenses for nurseries, kindergartens and after school care centers and can improve self-provisioning and reach food security. Additionally, grandmothers allow mothers the opportunities to find employment, given the situation that child care options in the villages are not always available.

Subsistence food gardening and chicken keeping – both not identical with farming – are very important livelihood strategies for rural households near to poverty because they have a strong impact on the maintenance of food security.

The *exchange of food products* with family members even farther away in the city is important to secure one's existence. Family members, friends and acquaintances are at the same time receivers and senders of food products. S.B. describes it as follows:

"They help us regularly both with money and food, it depends on their possibilities. I help them too. I have a vegetable garden and I send them vegetables, when I have more potatoes. We have such kind of mutual supporting with our relatives" (Ast int 31: 18, male, rural, 51 years).

A.S. describes this exchange and mutual support with products as a local necessity for serving:

"We make this exchange with our neighbors. Thanks' god to that our village survives" (Alm int 9: 17, female, rural, 48 years).

Savings

Poorer rural households almost do not have any possibility to save money. The households' income is used to pay monthly living costs and to live from day to day. Their muddling through as a strategy is characterized by difficulties in finding suitable jobs with stable earnings, and by the inability to save constantly for risk factors and to exploit opportunities when they arise (e.g. for gifts in case of marriages or funerals; education of their children).

Credit-taking

As already mentioned, credits from commercial organizations don't play a relevant role in securing a livelihood among this class of poorer rural households. The three cases, we describe here in more detail have experiences with credits. But these taught them to avoid taking on new credits. In general, poorer households try to refrain from taking credits. To fulfill urgent needs or to bridge periods of scarce money reciprocity networks are favored:

"Firstly, of course, we go to friends. But when I do it, I always worry that I cannot give it back. I do not trust banks. I know people who took a bank credit and couldn't pay it back. I am afraid to take a credit, because there is no stability in my income. I am afraid that I cannot pay the interest. Of course, we thought to take a credit, to open a small business. But we decided not to do so. We try to live with our salary. You must have stable earnings to borrow money from a bank" (Ast int 31: 13, male, rural, 51 years).

The cash situation of poorer households may also make them unable to take opportunities for making a better living. Furthermore, their creditworthiness is low and thus credits are difficult to obtain. The cases of S.B. and E.E. show that although rural households near to poverty can be considered as risk-averse, taking a credit is often seen as the "last option". S.B. points out that "credit is an extreme step". The household of S.B. sometimes uses deferred payments to fulfill its needs:

"We often buy on tick. You do not need to redeem the whole sum at once. Once I bought a TV on credit for one year and redeemed the debt during the whole year. It is affordable. We use credits when we do not have money for serious purchases. We do not take credits so often, for example once in three years. We took credits only for purchases of household appliances. The last credit was 140,000 KZT (933 USD) at 10% interest. It is normal, we are able to redeem it" (Ast int 31: 14, male, rural, 51 years).

Also the household of E.E. lives with credits to "*become financially independent*" and see this as a "*very beneficial decision*". They took a credit of 250,000 KGS (5,000 USD) with an interest of 22 percent. For three years (2009-2011) they paid the credit back. As a result, each month, the incomes of the husband, the daughter and the son were used to pay back the credit and then they tried "*to survive until the next month*". From time to time, the household was in big trouble to "*find this money to pay monthly*" and finally decided "*to take another credit to pay back the first one*". They took a microcredit of 20,000 KGS (410 USD) from FINKA, a micro-credit organization. Also in this case, the reliance on reciprocity networks is crucial because "*without the help of the children*" the household wouldn't have been able to pay back. Thus, credits become an affair of the whole family be they taken with or without the consent of the other family members.

Credit pay back is a constant muddling through with help of friends and relatives. Although credit-taking is risky and although rural households near to poverty try to avoid this risk, some rely on credits to secure the household's existence. For example, the household of E.E. took a credit to buy a cow. This investment in livestock is used not only to provide the household with milk but also to sell surplus milk on the local market. The money from selling milk is used to pay back debts "*we had in the shop*". Thus, muddling through also implies taking on credits. This household as well as the one of S.B. mobilizes all opportunities for paying back. Mutual help, trust and credit taking are closely intertwined.

Evaluation of livelihood strategies of rural households near to poverty

In the following, we want to characterize the different strategies, rural households close to poverty pursue. We borrow also on the other interviews, not presented in more detail here in order to avoid overlapping.

The three cases of rural households, just as others of that class, are not poor per se. For example, people own property; this may be the house they live in or they even have a little real estate they keep for rainy days, they own land, but not much, they may also own livestock, but here too, it must be looked upon mainly as means for self-provisioning and little savings to cope with unforeseen vulnerabilities. But convertibility into cash is very limited. If the house is sold, the former owners must move out with their family, consequently they are without shelter of their own. If one sells the garden plot or has to kill ones livestock, self-provisioning becomes impossible and endangers food security of the household.

These households are characterized by pooling incomes, combining formal and informal employment, state subsidies, income from remittances and a high degree of self-provisioning, to cope with delayed payments, low wages, periodical unemployment and other vulnerabilities. Their budget is low and normally must be supplemented by subsistence production. The household members of this class usually have secondary education, but are often forced to work whenever and wherever there are jobs available. The gap between education and employment opportunities in the countryside makes them work in low paid, underpaid and less attractive jobs. In general, all household members are supposed to work in order to keep the household going. This includes migration if necessary. Many households are multigenerational ones.

These households pursue different kinds of strategies to obtain a certain level of security. If we follow de Haan and Zoomers' (2005) distinction of accumulation, consolidation, compensation and securing strategies, these poorer households in rural areas follow mostly security and compensation strategies.

Security strategies of these households refer to risk avoidance and diversification. A strong use of reciprocity networks is obvious as well as subsistence production. Security strategies are often combined with compensation strategies to overcome financial losses and shortages. By selling property (livestock e.g.) or home-made products these households try to compensate negative trends and/or shocks, e.g. because of a credit squeeze, sudden expenses for funerals or marriages. Quite often, the remedies taken, have a short term character and can be understood as a "next best" effort. Borrowing money is an encompassing system: People are ready to help out family members and friends and it does not matter how high the sum is. They are embedded in mutual-help-networks, mostly connecting family members but sometimes also neighbors and friends. These networks imply trust and reciprocity, and network members are aware that such networks have to be maintained. There is a certain pressure to reciprocate if others need help; otherwise one may lose this source of security provision. The reliance on such mutual-help-networks is basic for the survival of this class of households.

The diversification of activities pursued by rural households near to poverty is manifold and is characterized by the interdependence of both security and compensation strategies. This "search for security" on the one hand aims at sustainability, on the other hand it is characterized by risk avoidance, which mostly turns out to be more or less successful. The mix of labor migration, self-employment, informal labor and self-provisioning represents the 'normal' livelihood strategy for such rural households. Additionally, the reliance on social networks (mutual help, solidarity, trust, support, etc.) and household's decision-making concerning co-residence and the use of help of household and non-household members for child care (e.g. role of grandmothers) as well as the use of private and public transfers all belong to the pool of practices, that can be found in our sample and that aim at security and the compensation for 'stressors'. Risk avoidance is omnipresent for rural households near to poverty.

Security and compensation strategies have the goal of ensuring the economic, social and cultural security of the households. They have to be looked upon as flexible strategies, because people behave more or less strategically at different points during their life-course. At certain stages it is necessary to plan, e.g. for housing, children etc. and at other stages it is not very relevant to do so. Rural households near to poverty tend to rely more on soliciting help. Nevertheless, these households seem to have problems to consolidate their situation in longer terms, not to talk about improving their situation in such a way that accumulation and general betterment become possible. To use a term of Lindblom, typical for them are trajectories of muddling- through, of adaptation.

The extent to which households can adapt usually reflects their access to and their ability to use different types of assets. In areas where there are very few assets or people lack the capacity to utilize them, vulnerability will be higher. Many local and external factors influence it: the local markets, local infrastructures, political, economic, cultural and social environments. These features are themselves inherently dynamic and livelihoods are vulnerable to the shocks and trends, these factors may generate and that are beyond the immediate control of the households. The character of these internal and external forces represents the vulnerability context within which households develop their strategies. Rural households near to poverty are typically minimizers of risk and not maximizers of profits. They employ adaptive practices and not long-term ones. The empirical cases above make clear that successful crisis management in the past is often used anew to cope with their current problems. They are self-confident in the sense, that, if necessary, they will again sell home-made food, slaughter their cow etc. The traditional belief plays a major role in that the reciprocity networks will be strong enough to make them survive. And these networks seem to be quite intact so that such a trajectory is possible. The scope of their actions becomes directed more to solely overcome the present situation than also to plan for the future. Lack of assets, a special vulnerability context and a socio-cultural constellation seem to make up for trajectories of muddling through.

Middle Households – Rural Examples

Case A: Household of B.K. (K. village, Almaty Region, male, Interview 14)

The household of B.K. is located in K. village, 30 kilometers from Almaty. B.K. is married and has four daughters and one son. His wife is a pensioner and gets the minimum pension of 19,000 KZT (127 USD). All children are married. Six persons live in the household: B.K., his wife, a son of the youngest daughter, the daughter-in-law with two children. The son works as a foreman at the railway station Z. and lives in the household on days-off. The household has livestock: at present 100 sheep, 16 horses and 3 cows. Although B.K. and his family have been living in the village for 22 years they do not own the land which they cultivate. After their migration from another rural area they were refused permission to buy land because they are foreigners (Albans). The income of all household members is pooled. One of the main problems of the household is access to drinking water.

Case B: Household of N.S. (A village, Akmola Region, Astana, female, Interview 2)

The household of N.S. is located in A., 80 kilometers from Almaty. The household consists of three persons: N.S. herself, her husband and a child of one of the relatives who goes to school. They have a son and a daughter, both living in Astana. The son is just about to finish his university studies; the daughter has already graduated from university. N.S. is 42 years old and has secondary education. She works as a school teacher and earns a middle range salary. Most of household's income is contributed by her husband who works as an operator for a petrol station in a city nearby. They keep livestock: 3 horses, 10 sheep and cows. The household is characterized by having two employed adults with stable incomes and occasional income from selling livestock.

Case C: Household of A.L. (D. village, Bishkek region, male, interview 3)

The household of A.L. is located in D. village. It consists of four persons: A.L., his wife, the son and the youngest son of their first daughter. Both daughters are married and live separately. A.L. is 53 years old. He was born in the countryside. He is an accountant by profession. The household owns three hectares of land and a small garden. His wife is a housewife. She has a small pension. The family lived in Bishkek but lost employment. They sold their house in the city and moved to the countryside and opened an office where they planned to operate in business consultation. To open the office they took out a credit. Immediately after opening the business they were robbed twice and lost everything. At that time, the household of A.L. had extreme trouble in paying back the credit. Today A.L. is a farmer by profession (poultry and gardening).

Non-monetary and monetary exchange and market-based livelihoods

All three households combine stable incomes with farming. The monetary incomes stem from state transfers, state or private jobs. For all of them agriculture plays an important role. Partly the agricultural activity is nearer to subsistence, partly it is the biggest source for their income.

Also for this class of rural households non-market exchange of goods and labor is typical.

> "Of course, we help them too. We help them mostly with meat, milk, butter, other kind of foods, and meat of cattle in winter, meat of sheep in summer. We do it enough often. To provide them with meat is our duty. We give money to our son, when he visits us once in two weeks. We reimburse his expenses for coming and give him pocket money" (Ast int 2: 15, female, rural, 42 years).

Children and grandchildren support their parents in home gardening and preserving fruit and vegetables and the like even if they do not live in the households any more. Smollet (1989) has introduced the term "economy of jars" to describe how villages and cities are linked through familial, mostly intergenerational exchanges. The amounts of these exchanges are not small.

Food products are a part of a wider "economy of regard" (Lee 2000) involving reciprocal circuits of non-monetized exchange and, occasionally, become commoditized through sale in markets or on crossroads (Caldwell 2004). The first variant refers to barter mostly within the villages on a small scale. The second variant refers to selling food products for profit gain. Research on Russia (Clarke 1999, 2002a, 2002b), Bulgaria (Smith, 2000c) and Slovakia (Smith, 2000a,b, Smith & Stenning, 2006) has, however, suggested that subsistence food production with opportunities to monetize surplus for non- immediate purposes is not an activity undertaken by the very poor. "Rather, it is an activity that predominantly involves relatively affluent households that have enough land and the monetary resources to be able to afford to subsidize an inefficient form of food production. Domestic food production does not occur in this sense as the result of economic necessity but for other, more complex reasons. Household food production is an economic practice that bears great cultural significance to those practicing it. It remains an economic practice in the sense that it provides food for the household table, involves forms of use value production, and plays a role in social reproduction and expenditure patterns. But it is an economic practice that is culturally inflected by a variety of other rationales" (Smith, 2000a, p. 240).

All the three households pursue a survival strategy with a stronger foot in monetized or monetizable agricultural activities than the poorer households. Thus, we can also confirm the former research for Kazakhstan and Kyrgyzstan. It follows some illustrations:

"We have a garden where we are growing tomatoes, cucumbers. In autumn we sell potatoes and from sale of all this we have an income. This is how we survive" (B int 3: 80, male, rural, 53 years).

Nevertheless, such market orientated agricultural practices are based on kinship. The core unit of the local agricultural economy is still the household and its reproduction but the frame for this is kinship relations. Unpaid help is a necessary factor and precondition to pursue exchange and market-based agricultural activities because thereby households can minimize costs otherwise necessary to employ people.

"Well, our relatives help us, though it is not financial help, they help with their manpower (...) Well, that is how our relatives help us, I can say by using only their hands, but not money, they don't help us with money, because they are also in need of money" (B int 3: 48, male, rural, 53 years).

What distinguishes these kind of households from the poorer ones – apart from their stable incomes – is their way of thinking to keep their businesses alive. And these businesses are composed of their agricultural activities. Although there is scarcity of cash, these households look for possibilities to save and to plan saving. Entrepreneurial spirit and accounting principles can be found in the following quotation:

"All expenses are clearly calculated, we don't have anything superfluous to save Money always is scarce for us but we save, we are trying to save for the sows, for purchase of seeds" (B int 3: 42, male, rural, 53 years).

In these middle households livestock is planned to overcome possible losses, as by N.S., and used to make income e.g. by selling the milk of cows. These operations all need careful considerations. In the case of N.S. this also relates to the payment of a shepherd, who looks after the cattle because both adults work during daytime. If money is needed or big expenses occur, livestock can be converted into cash:

"If it is necessary we will be ready to sell livestock for some aims like buying a home for children (...) We usually sell livestock during this tough periods of stocking fuel and hays" (Ast int 2: 15, female, rural, 42 years).

Depending on financial necessities, the households are able to switch to market-based actions or just use their livestock for their own needs (self-provisioning). However, it is necessary to reinvest in livestock and to increase the number of animals in times of financial well-being to maintain the acceptable level of their livelihoods in the longer run.

To maintain their agricultural activities these households may also rely on other resources: additional money from the family network.

"The children in the city help us. They give us their vocational fee(...). The relatives of my husband, particularly his younger sister helps us with some expenses. They help us with finances and materials, when we ask them. For example, they gave us a certain amount of money for drugs when I was ill and went to hospital in the city. My elder daughter ... helps us with cash. For example, she gives us her holiday fees every year. Which is 100-150,000 Tenge (667-1,006 USD)" (Ast int 2: 15, female, rural, 42 years).

This provides evidence to the fact that only due to external monetary flow into the household's budget can the only temporal embeddedment in market actions (selling livestock and food products), be maintained. In other words: To sustain the ability to be only a temporary or partial market player, the household depends on external monetary flow. Nevertheless one should not forget, that foreseeable seasonal problems are tackled by planning and saving. Otherwise this type of economy would not function. Although these rural households also have to cope with financial shortages and losses e.g. from weather conditions etc. they are much more successful in making their living than the poorer households.

Rational planning and successful crises management

We have already underlined the ability of these households to plan. Now we want to take a closer look at this ability concerning animal husbandry. The case of B.K. is very interesting because here one can find evidence how this kind of households make a living by successfully managing livestock husbandry.

"We have an opportunity for saving. But we don't save in money terms. We don't raise much in money. When we raise money, we spend a lot. For example, as we have livestock, we need to build the farmyard, the haymow. These are expenditures, then our house. We bought the house in this place. Near the house, we need to build a site hut, replace the roof of the house, and other trifles. In such case we just sell livestock. If it is a cow – we sell a cow, if a horse – we sell a horse. We survive owing to our livestock. We have 15-16 horses, nearly a hundred of mutton" (Alm int 14: 29, male, rural, 53).

This household operates the livestock as a savings bank. For rural households saving in livestock is not just traditional behavior, but rational, since livestock is convertible into money, functions as a food store (meat and milk products) for everyday life and also for family celebrations, breeding increases the stock, and a big herd of horses, sheep or cattle is also prestigious for the owners.

Livestock helps with quite 'normal' expenses, but also in precarious situations.

"We faced shocks. After 1990, there was stagnation, no one had a job. ... There were a lot of difficulties during that time. But we had a few beasts. We survived through selling our livestock" (Alm int 14: 31, male, rural, 53).

In order to keep the process going, one should not eat up ones savings; that is the livestock has to be restocked or even extended.

"We have such difficulties. For growing the livestock, we need feed (...). We sell some beasts, and buy the things we need. We save, rise. Increase livestock, sell heavy beasts. So we make turnover. This is our economy. We sell one big mutton, and buy two little lambs, or sell ten, and buy 12 lambs. So we make turnover. If we do not make this kind of turnover, the livestock may end tomorrow. This is our second income" (Alm int 14: 35, male, rural, 53 years).

Of course this means planning, managing higher expenditures in preparing for the winter season, which also implies e.g. investing day to day incomes from fruit, vegetables and milk. Harvest depends on weather conditions, but nevertheless these households plan incomes and expenditures and relate the results to their practices. Planning means deliberately structuring further steps and thinking about the use of a certain capital amount to achieve a desired goal. Planning depends on the availability of capital: financial, social and human. These kind of households do not only muddle through as is the case for rural households near to poverty. Planning also involves thinking about possible dangers and risks and anticipating losses. For example, B.K. calls it "*these are also expenditures*" by referring to the case that

"last year, seven of my horses and two bulls were stolen. If you add up, it is about 2 million KZT" (Alm int14: 20, male, rural, 53).

Households that are characterized by planning activities are not *per se* stable and less vulnerable to poverty, crises and shocks. But they are much better able to cope with critical circumstances. As in the cases of rural households near to poverty depicted above, these households had to learn to adapt to new challenges in the post-Soviet period. Take e.g. A.L., who holds a degree in agricultural accountancy. He worked as an accountant during the Soviet period but had to change his job several times thereafter. He had to overcome the robbery of his start up business, when he decided to leave Bishkek for the countryside. He moved to another village to find a better place to make a living. He had to sell the house in the first village in order to repay debts. He took his destiny into his hands instead of being risk averse.

Such people have a tenacity to look for measures to make the household more stable and despite all unexpected problems in the past to overcome their problems.

"One needs patience and diligence if you labor, not to be lazy, endeavor, these difficulties may be overcome. We have to work in two jobs. There are persons, who cannot find even a single job in the village. Nevertheless, there is a small business, stock-raising. So we deal with it, grow livestock little by little" (Alm int14: 33, male, rural, 53 years).

With these people also the financing of weddings e.g. seems to be quite a normal challenge and not a further shock adding to their overall vulnerability as amongst poorer rural households:

"We wedded our children, sold livestock. We sold it because we had it. We paid for weddings by livestock. We were in hock to nobody, financed everything from livestock sale. We sold 6 horses and conducted our son's wedding" (Alm int14: 20, male, rural, 53 years).

These kind of households use experiences and human capital (knowledge, education, capabilities to adopt) not only to provide the household with sufficient income but also with rational agricultural planning and investment in the human capital of children. It was important for A.L. to support the education of his two daughters to make them "independent now" and he pays for the education of his son who is a student and lives separately.

Credit-taking and future planning

For the middle households taking credits is a crucial way to maintain livelihoods. But contrary to households near to poverty, credits are not only spent for buying necessary equipment for the house or the flat, but to deliberately invest in property and/or to keep one's business alive. These households do invest in long-term options and want to provide their children with their heritage:

"We now build sheds to contain cattle and leave it to the children. We will save money for it. If we would run out of money we would take a credit" (B int 3: 122, male, rural, 53).

Such farsightedness can't be found in the interviews of the poorer households. The middle households meticulously do book keeping and know about the household's budget allocation and expenditures. The repayment of credits are calculated in advance, and the obligations from them are usually met in time.

"To be more precise we save for the necessary sum differently; after all it is necessary to pay the credit. Only when we will pay off one credit, we may take a new credit. And additionally it must be possible to pay my son's education, to pay any other expenses and also expenses for those events like weddings or funerals, or any other unexpected expenses, like medicine. And still it is necessary to keep the money to pay the credit. As I already told you, every two months I have an income" (B int 3: 80, male, rural, 53).

Evaluation of livelihood strategies among 'middle' households in rural areas

As underlined in the introduction, households may pursue different strategies at different times. Nevertheless, the households near to poverty were characterized by us mainly by using compensatory and security strategies. Their timely orientation was short term to overcome sudden vulnerabilities and everyday problems in order to sustain their livelihoods. We argued that their type of "*Lebensführung*" (conduct of life) can be called muddling through. Also taking into account the middle households, we can see that both classes of rural households show a high diversity, implying the combination of formal and informal labor as income sources, and the use of additional or even predominant agricultural activities to make a living. The difference between the described households near to poverty and those of the middle type is that the latter are better able to absorb vulnerability impacts and/or respond to the opportunities their context offers. The scope of actions and the combination of mixed strategies carried out by these household show planning and future orientation even under the conditions of risks and shocks. Moreover, their practices are not mainly directed to self-provisioning of household members. While rural households near to poverty give greater priority to self-provisioning and to non-monetary exchanges, the opposite is true for the middle households. Monetary interactions move more into the center of their activities. The focus is on selling products and to combine this with self-employment and/or formal employment. The cases above give evidence to the fact that the use of family networks is no longer mainly a means to overcome vulnerabilities, but to improve the activities that stem from the seasonability of agriculture and to economize on labor and to secure aid for monetized activities. Nevertheless, reciprocity has to be served and products to feed and support the external family members are exchanged. The use of human capital is especially crucial for the strategic actions of these households. Intelligent and situational planning are important feature in the practices of these households.

Against semi-arid conditions and vulnerabilities that occur due to hailstorms, problematic provisions of irrigation and rustling etc., these rural households deliberately develop livelihood strategies to improve their living conditions. They combine different resources and organize themselves to implement a variety of activities to achieve short and long term objectives. To the latter belong support and education of children and grandchildren. Their scope of action is not only directed to overcome daily difficulties but to avoid vulnerabilities in the future and for the future generations.

Typical for them is a combination of accumulation and consolidation strategies (de Haan and Zoomers 2005:39f). This involves "establishing a minimum resource base and preparing for future expansion" as well as "investments to stabilize the household's wellbeing and improve quality in the short term". They can do so, because they know how to mobilize all kinds of assets, ranging from additional earnings, functionalizing the reciprocity network by employing unpaid labor, using credits and loans to overcome temporary shortages, etc. These households are to a much lesser degree self-sufficient than their poorer counterparts.

Households Better Off – Rural Examples

Case A: Household of R.Z. (M. village, Almaty Region, Interview 31)

The household of R.Z. is located in M. village, 100 kilometers from Almaty. R.Z. is 46 years old. She met her husband during her studies in Almaty. He is the same age. After his service in the Red Army, the couple married. They left Almaty in order to settle in a rural area. After several unsuccessful attempts to find jobs, they started to work as school-teachers in their present location. They have three children. The elder son graduated from university and works in his specialty. The second son studies social work in Almaty. The daughter currently is in her 6th school year.

Case B: Household of A.D. (B. village, Akmola Region, Interview 7)

The household of A.D. consists of five persons. A.D. is 46 years old, has higher education, and is a doctor by profession. She works as the manager of the village medical center. Her husband is the same age, also has higher education and is, by profession, a specialist in geological exploration. He works in well-paid fields, construction and security. The eldest child is 18 years old and studies in an elitist academy, where classes are taught only in English. She has a scholarship. The second child studies in 10th grade, the youngest in 4th grade.

Case C: Household of A.T. (Bishkek region, Interview 29)

A.T. is 49 years old, has higher technical education. A.T. has worked in business, engaged in production. At present, he has been working in the farming industry for the last 10 years. The household has a large livestock. A.T. is married and has four married daughters. Three daughters with their husbands and his grandchildren live in the household.

Reference points of judgment

Although for this cohort a high level of national pride is remarkable, they also pay attention to the fact that the Soviet welfare state has supported young families and students much more. Moreover, they emphasize that their current well-being is not a gift, but is based on hard work in the past and present day determination:

> "After separation from Russia, only Kazakhstan could withstand. A person, who is not lazy, may pasture, or make hay, and make money. So, people should not be lazy. People, who pasture private livestock, sell products from their gardens and kitchen gardens – they live better than we do. Government will never let people starve" (Alm int 31: 70, female, rural, 46 years).

Post-modern necessities and standards are important for all (extended) household members:

> "In Soviet times basically I didn't ask for help from my parents, but today anyway we should help our children (...) The elder child lives and studies in the city, in Astana (...) She needs internet, payment for telephone, food etc. (...). I entirely dress my daughter and provide her with all necessary things, which she needs. The kid tells me about her necessities, which I should buy" (Ast int 7: 13, female, rural, 46 years).

Formal employment opportunities

The household of R.Z. has two stable incomes from two official jobs. She and her husband work in the village school, he as the director and she as a teacher. They do not have to deal with wage arrears because salary is paid in time. As in other ex-soviet countries, salaries of teachers are on a relatively low level and many persons employed in the state sector belong to the losers of the transformation process. But this couple receives relatively high earnings due to the high wage groups, they are in: R.Z. earns 65,000 Tenge, her husband 106,000 Tenge.

The household of A.D. also has two stable incomes from two official employments. A.D. works as the manager of the village medical center and her husband works in construction and security. The average monthly salary of the household is 150,000 Tenge (1,000 USD). The eldest daughter gets a scholarship of 17,000 Tenge (113 USD) which is slightly more than a usual one (15,000 Tenge).

A.T. has an official agricultural business. He hires paid labor. His income is enough to make a living and to increase the well-being of the whole family. A.T. hires seasonal workers who he selects according to their work experience and vocational training:

> "That is, if not necessary, for example, in winter, when there is less work, employees do not have to be kept. In spring (. . .), employees are hired for specific jobs. For example, planting, mowing, harvesting, slaughtering cattle. Specifically. For each type of work, an employee is hired, pre-negotiated the amount and timing of work, and, accordingly, the payment" (B int 29: 14, male, rural, 49 years).

He avoids hiring family members as seasonal workers although he has a lot of conflict with his hired workers who are unsatisfied with payments. But he believes working with relatives would be even worse due to the emotional ties involved.

Additional self-employment in the informal sector

Although these rural households mostly have jobs in the formal labor market, the incomes of which suffice to make a living, many look for additional incomes by doing off duty activities. Typical is the household of R. Z. She also works as a private teacher for pupils and adults at home as well as at school in the evening hours. Another income source is her husband's work as an artist, both in sculpture and painting. Moreover, these households are able to compensate wage arrears by self-provisioning and selling livestock to survive.

> "They gave us land in the village. For 5 of us they gave 2 hectares. We plant wheat. We mow it twice, press and gather" (Alm int31: 64, female, rural, 46 years).

> "We sold the livestock, and so survived" (Alm int 31: 42, female, rural, 46 years).

A.T. owns a large herd of livestock: 150 head of cattle and cows, 200 sheep. A.T. rents about 100 acres of land. But he also cultivates a small plot to grow fruit and vegetables for his household's own use.

Selling products

Some of these households are also engaged in selling their produce in local markets. To be present at local markets depends on their specialization. Among this group we find agricultural entrepreneurs and households that are not engaged in agricultural businesses. The former either sell produce to their neighbors or other village inhabitants if they cultivate land and have surplus or they build up additional sources of income. But mostly produce from cultivation is for self-provisioning:

"Our vegetables in the kitchen garden are enough for winter (...) We grow tomatoes, chives, potatoes, onions, eggplants We lid pickles, from the middle of the summer. We put up compote. Make jams, sometimes autumn salads" (Alm int 31: 214, female, rural, 46 years).

For those respondents who have agricultural businesses ingenuity is a characteristic feature. A.T. even plays Kyrgyz music on a traditional instrument in order to increase the milk yield:

"Sometimes I go out at night, sit in a field, so ... well ... cows walking, I'm playing on komuz. (...) Folk melodies. Cows like it, and to say, even the milk yield increases by good music. It is not my idea, but from Japanese scientists. They used classical music, and the milk yield of cows increased by 30 percent. Using rock and roll, on the contrary, milk yield decreased. And from Kyrgyz tunes, there is more than 30 percent increase. I want to patent it" (B int 29: 48, male, rural, 49 years).

From reciprocity networks to "normalized" family relationships

This type of household uses reciprocity networks only due to the fact that family members support each other in specific situations (e.g. children in semester break or on vacation support parent's duties in home gardening or parents support children by providing them with produce from the countryside). The frequency of face-to-face interactions is much less compared to the other two groups of households. Moreover, it is obvious that the networks are used very pragmatically. For example, R.Z. points out that they did not only buy a car for fun for their children who are students in Almaty, but also to bring them back from the city to the village on weekends together with products which are cheaper to buy there.

"They come during holidays, we always welcome them, prepare meat dishes for them (...). They bring fodder, because it is cheaper in the city" (Alm int 31: 28, female, rural, 46 years).

Due to their better equipment with different forms of capital and the opportunities to convert them these households show a high flexibility for adaptation to different vulnerability contexts and life circumstances. They rely much more on themselves than do the other two groups of rural households. It seems especially, that social capital no longer includes extended family relations but is orientated towards grandparents, parents and children.

Planning consumption

Because these households have much better financial assets they do not depend on daily purchases e.g. for food. Moreover, as their mobility chances are much better they can use rural and urban places to buy necessary household products. They buy food and consumer durables in the countryside as well as in the city according to price calculations. These households know about market advantages and are able to plan their purchases on long-term.

"We make purchases in the (local) shop, but don't buy everything there. The meat is expensive in the shop; we buy there in summer only, because it's expensive to kill one's own livestock in summer. And the bread in the village is not baked by standard now; they make it fluffy, no one knows what they add to it. Mainly, I bake bread myself I have a miracle furnace, or I bake it in tandoori [oven]. We go to buy the durables on the wholesale market, as we have a car. (...) Vegetables are cheap at Chilik bazaar (...) In the village, such products are more expensive, we can afford to buy all on the wholesale market in the city" (Alm int 31: 32, female, rural, 46 years).

Future planning and improving well-being

The incomes of better off rural households are on a relatively high level; moreover, they are stable. Households can afford to improve their well-being and spend money to buy new furniture and up to date appliances. Besides, they are able to pay high monthly costs to sustain their livelihoods. For example, A.D. lives in a comfortable multi-storey apartment in a resort place, where many people spend their holidays. Due to the stable income of her household they can pay higher costs for habitation:

"This place is a very expensive resort center; therefore there are the most expensive foods and utilities costs in Kazakhstan. We pay about 15,000 Tenge (100 USD) per month for utilities like internet, electricity, water, payment for co-op apartment owners, heating etc. These monthly expenses range from 10,000 Tenge (66 USD) to 15,000 Tenge (100 USD) in winter" (Ast int 7: 13, female, rural, 46 years).

The well-being of A.D.'s household is visible: cars, new furniture, modern household appliances etc. They have a tenant in A.D.'s apartment in Astana. Moreover, A.D. has rented a flat in Astana in which the children live.

A.T. uses new methods in agriculture to stabilize his business and the well-being of his household. He makes use of scientifically improved methods in agriculture: forage for the animals, profit-yielding fertilizers, improved breeding. In his opinion, this is not only necessary to expand the number of cattle but also to improve the status quo:

"Do not expand, I'm telling you, but use more modern methods. The number is not transformed into quality. If a person has 100 hectares compared to one with 300 hectares, the latter will not improve his financial situation necessarily. It is necessary to make the best of the 100 hectares. Improvement on what you have. That is why I have so many cattle (...) This is the optimal number for me. With more, we simply cannot cope physically. Why torment yourself?" (B int 29: 64, male, rural, 49 years).

Investment in children's education

Better off rural households can afford to support their children. They buy good clothes and food for them and pay for higher education and accommodation in the city. They are also able to rent flats in the city for their children. Children are also well-equipped, not only with new mobile phones but also with computers. Some even have cars.

"Nowadays, you can't go without a car. So we bought them a car, and like that they live in Almaty" (Alm int 31: 30, female, 46 years).

Additionally, many children receive grants.

Investment in children's education is very important for all of these households. For example, A.D. worried about the "intellectual development of children" and hired a personal tutor who taught them in the afternoon in order to facilitate university entrance. Moreover, these households are very convinced that only a good education will lead to a successful future for their children.

"My child graduated from school with very good results and the English class was very useful for her in her further education at university. Thus I try to manage such issues of education" (Ast int 7: 5, female, rural, 46 years).

Savings

Better off rural households have the opportunity to save. They save e.g. in foreign currency (US-Dollar) to buy apartments for their children in the cities. A.D. opened a deposit for the education of her second child. What distinguishes them from the other two types of rural households is that they are able to secure long-term savings and that they save their money in banks but not at home:

"I think that saving money at home is a bad idea, although I don't trust banks in general. But I think that a bank is more reliable. An apartment is an apartment and everyone can rob you. Generally the police will never help you. Banks pay a certain interest and my money can increase" (Ast int 7: 17, female, rural, 46 years).

Other interviewees mention that they do not save in banks but invest in livestock:

"We increase the number of livestock; it is said that livestock is hard cash" (Alm int 31: 54, female, 46 years).

Credits

Although better off rural households have stable incomes their readiness to take credits is limited. The entire sample of these households shows that they are very aware of the risks to take and pay back a credit. Moreover, they know that high interest rates have a negative impact on household's practices. Mostly they try to use other resources to overcome vulnerabilities like their own savings or their livestock. Their credit averseness is also caused by distrust in banks and, in the case of Kyrgyzstan, the conviction of a financially instable nation state. The few cases of credit taking among this group of rural households show that credits are used to invest in households' appliances and new furniture:

"I took this credit because I wanted to update our furniture. I did it, but I suppose that we shouldn't have done so, because we would have been able to cope without that credit. That credit of 700000 Tenge (4669 USD) had an interest of 24% or 28%. That credit was taken for 3 years. We pay 19000 Tenge (126 USD) for the credit per month. I have repaid the credit twice since May. (...) I can't say that credit is not necessary at all. Sometimes you have such tough situations that you don't have any other choice. I think that taking credit in order to update furniture was not necessary. Of course, I will have to take a credit, if I don't have any other source, where I can take the money from" (Ast int 7: 15, female, rural, 46 years).

The distrust in banks is remarkable. Mostly due to bad experiences of their own, of relatives or acquaintances in the past, the majority of better off rural households avoids taking credits from banks. A respondent emphasizes that banks do not obey the laws:

"I took a loan to buy forage, to buy fertilizers, seeds, and so on and so forth. After six months collecting documents, I received a loan. That year we had a bad harvest (...). Under the law, if the year was lean, the district municipals give a certificate that yes, indeed, that was really a poor harvest due to weather conditions. And they give help. And according to current legislation, banks are obliged to give a delay and not to impose penalty fines. But no bank performs according to the Law of the Kyrgyz Republic. That is, they do not delay, calculate fines and penalties, (...) Although such legislation exists in Kyrgyzstan since 1995. That is, in the case of crop failure, confirmed by documents, references, banks are required to rollover loans. Required! But nobody does that. Therefore, I have disagreements with the banks. Strong differences" (B int 29: 54, male, rural, 49 years).

Evaluation of livelihood strategies of better off rural households

In general, in our sample, the better-off households in rural areas were rare compared to the two other classes, especially in Kyrgyzstan. These households do not only manage to secure their status quo to make a living but they are also able to expand their property and to increase their wellbeing. Although some of them could afford making a living in the city, these households believe that there are better options in the countryside and that they are free from urban "obligations" that hamper wellbeing. "Rural life is better", they argue.

"But we also benefit from our cows. In the village we eat meat without any charge. In this regard, the rural life is better, because you have to buy everything in the city, you have to pay for everything, and when you live in the village, you have many things at home. Moreover, it is not necessary to wear fashionable clothes in the village, ordinary and clean clothes are enough. We save a lot. In the city, this money is not at hand" (Alm int 31: 18, female, rural, 46 years).

Wellbeing of these households is visible. They own their houses or apartments which are well-equipped with furniture and appliances. Some have additional property. They have cars that enhance their mobility. For this kind of households the best possible education of children is very important and they can invest and do invest in their education.

Farming on a larger scale and paid labor in professional jobs are usually the basis of making a living in this group of better off households. But they do not restrict themselves to this. They usually combine f*ormal and informal activities* in order to better their living conditions. In doing so they not only benefit from their education and professions but also "sell" their knowledge and use their "prominence" (status as teachers e.g.) to gain extra-income. They are very industrious. Some of them can afford to hire shepherds and laborers who work for them. Thus they enhance their income options. Many do gardening or animal husbandry to additionally provide the household as well as family members with food. Rational and calculated behavior is significant for their survival practices:

"We think about economizing (...) We kill a lamb to have meat. We do all this, buy meat in summer time, kill livestock in winter. It's enough for winter, or we kill one fat cow" (Alm int 31: 26, female, rural, 46 years).

In difficult times these households were able to compensate e.g. for wage arrears by self-provisioning plus selling livestock. Some of these household are also taking their produce to markets although it is not necessary for them to trade and sell products on markets thus generating an additional income source. Especially, the latter is true for those households which have stable incomes and are not working in agricultural businesses as their first employment. The case of A.T. shows that he is successful as an agricultural entrepreneur in production as well as in sales. He improves his livestock and his land by the use of modern methods.

This constellation of enhanced options to make a living is different from the group of middle households for which e.g. a daily presence on local markets is important for their livelihoods. In the case of better-off rural households food produce does not have to be sold on bazaars, but is used for their own needs and as additional income. Agricultural businesses, operated by those better off rural households are professionalized and plan strategically according to market signals. They are able to cope with vulnerabilities like bad infrastructures, rural isolation and to compensate for losses like bad harvests, and financial burdens caused by funerals, marriages etc. To a large extend, these vulnerabilities are foreseen and precautions are taken (savings).

These households do not only have more assets to make a living, but are better able to convert the different sorts of capital they have. Reciprocity networks lose their crucial importance as security mechanisms unlike amongst the poorer and middle households in the countryside. They concentrate on making use of their human capital (the use of knowledge) and financial capital (opportunities to buy, invest and increase well-being). Reciprocity is understood rationally as a bilateral process by which somebody may do someone a favor but having an interest to get something back in the future. Relying on such a network becomes an option among others (savings in cash or cattle, e.g.). Reciprocity is no longer a traditional practice how to solve problems but a choice. As these households are relatively well-equipped and have a certain standard of well-being, they do not depend so much on mutual help, solidarity, barter and non-monetary exchange as it is obvious especially for rural households near to poverty. These use these networks to muddle through because they only have limited access to other resources and the middle households use, for example reciprocity networks to remain visible as market players and to sustain their livelihoods by caring for their network through 'hiring' relatives as unpaid laborers. Concerning better-off rural households, one can compare their livelihood practices with those existing in Western and Middle Europe, where two generations have a material well-being independent from each other, and where their relations are predominantly non-material but emotional though not free from advantages. It is also relevant to emphasize that for this type of household, their children are also in a much better situation compared to contemporaries who are the children of the two other types of rural households.

These households follow accumulation and consolidation trajectories. Accumulation quite often is fostered by additional incomes apart from their already good incomes. It is also based on rational planning and the rational use of their assets. The limited embeddedness in reciprocal networks allows for practices more orientated to monetary and contractual relations, also liberates these households from the burden of redistribution of property among kinfolk ... (cf. Evers & Schrader, 1994). Purposeful practices aim at consolidation of the households' wellbeing at present and in the future. Education for the children is supposed to secure intergenerational continuity of the property accumulated. None of the household members are forced to work abroad to help to secure sustainability.

Households near to Poverty – Urban Examples

Case A: Household of G.A. (Astana)

The household of G.A., male, is located in Astana. He has higher education and is 45 years old. As G.A. and his wife (27 years old) do not have children the household only consists of two people. The couple owns a house and rent out four rooms to tenants. The couple does not have jobs in the formal labor market and works only in informal jobs. They have huge problems to repay a credit and plan to sell their house in the near future and to look for new employment opportunities.

Case B: Household of O.D. (Almaty)

The household of O.D consists of five persons. O.D., female, is 40 years old, divorced and a mother of two children. The daughter is 19 years old and her son is 15 years old. O.D. works as a massage therapist. She has secondary education. She dropped out of an academic institute because she married. The daughter studies at a fee-based college. The son lives in the countryside with her brother. O.D. is the owner of a private house, which consists of three rooms. She also owns six acres of land. The house is located very far from her work place.

Case C: Household of N.A. (Bishkek)

N.A. is a female, 43 years old, and a teacher from Bishkek. She was born in the countryside. After her school years, she studied at the university and graduated as a teacher. Her first job was as a teacher for the Kyrgyz language and literature in a state school in Bishkek. Since 2009, she has been working as a teacher of the Kyrgyz language and literature at the Kyrgyz National University. N.A. is married and has two sons and one daughter. The elder son is a 2nd year student, the younger son studies in 8th grade and the daughter in 6th grade.

Reference points of judgment

Muddling through everyday life is an important characteristic for poorer urban households which have to cope with financial shortages, high urban prices, and diverse areas of vulnerability. These households have huge problems finding adequate employment and stable incomes in the formal labor market. The daily search for security is characterized by lack of financial means and uncertainties concerning the future. This uncertainty pervades their thinking:

> "Money became worthless and is not enough. Prices rise, for example rent (...) Everything that I have to do is to be at work from morning till evening; if I do, everything will be stable. I want that my daughter keeps studying in the university. But she said that she wants to work and pay for her education. My son is next. I can pay for his learning, if I stay at this work place. I want that he will be educated. I would like that he choose good prestigious work. But God knows what will happen every other year. Next year he will finish 9th form and he wants to enter college (Alm int 10: 62, female, urban, 40 years).

Formal employment opportunities

In the case of these three examples only the household of N.A. holds jobs in the formal labor market. N.A. works as a university teacher. The household suffered from financial and economic crises and had to cope with loss of earnings. After graduating from university and working as a school teacher her income was enough to make a living:

> "My category was high and that is why I got a good sum of money that was enough for us (...) It was 10,000 up to 15,000 Soms" (B int 6: 278, female, urban, 43).

Having changed her place of work, her income has decreased. N.A. explains that the loss of earnings is caused by a lower work load. Moreover, she mentions that it is very problematic for her to find a good job suited to her specialization and that one needs acquaintances and good connections in order to get good and well-paid employment:

"There are barriers to be hired for a job, for example. If you have a network of acquaintances, then you work, and if you do not have a network of acquaintances then you do not work, that is important. But, well, we have met such situations, for example, but I... in my personal life... mmm... after graduation from the university, I got a job because I was sent to work there, and after that, in order to be hired at the university, I sent my CV, and then I was hired. But if you look at our acquaintances, then you hear many words like "I work here thanks to my friends" and looking at them I am sure that it is like that" (B int 6: 562, female, urban, 43 years).

Her husband works for the Regional Department of Internal Affairs. Despite of the fact that the couple holds 2 jobs in the formal labor market the household's income is very low. N.A. earns 4,000-5,000 Soms (75- 95 USD) monthly; her husband only 8,000 Soms (150 USD). Both changed jobs with help of friends to get better placements, but their financial situation remained precarious. N.A. is conscious of the lack of financial means of the household and began to plan to start a private business but her husband objected.

"He did not support me... my ideas to start some businesses (...) For example, I wanted to open some shops... the saloon... and... I proposed him to open a sewing firm, but he did not support me at those moments (...) I do not know the reasons of his rejection... So, from that time on, I didn't talk to him about these things anymore, because if you talk all the time about the same things then it may bring conflicts about, and in order to safe my family, and a family is a small institution, I haven't re-opened the discussion about this topic" (B int 6: 334, female, urban, 43 years).

Self-employment in the informal sector

O.D. is a massage therapist. She runs her business together with her sister who is currently ill. The business success of O.D. depends on the demand of clients:

"Basically, the money we earn is for both of us. All financial decisions are taken together (...). All depends on having clients. If there are clients then there is profit. But now is a season, where clients are fewer. But I really try to make enough money" (Alm int 10: 20, female, urban, 40 years).

In the case of G.A. and his wife both persons do not have jobs in the formal labor market. Both spouses work on demand and do not have permanent incomes. Their jobs are based on their experience. G.A. is employed in housing construction as a designer of interiors. He does euro-repair works[231] and his wife works as a seamstress. After having migrated from a rural area in the Akmola region, he found a first job in construction and has ever since tried to specialize in the field.

"I had to make informal services like design and decoration of homes These design services weren't so popular in the first years of my coming, but later they became popular and people made orders for design. People called me and I made the design of their houses and flats. Also I do self-advertisements in newspapers" (Ast int 17: 17, male, urban, 45 years).

The average income of G.A. is 40,000 – 50,000 Tenge (266-333 USD) per month. Together with his wife's earnings the income is 80,000-100,000 Tenge (533-667 USD) per month, of course only in the case when their labor is in demand.

To stabilize the income, the couple rents out property. They are owners of a three-room flat and rent out each room to other tenants living themselves in the 'kitchen'. The whole income from rent is 50,000 Tenge (333 USD) per month minus utility costs.

Urban gardening, livestock in the countryside, and provision of food through social networks

For urban households near to poverty, self-provisioning by gardening is an important livelihood strategy. They either have their own small plot next to their house or flat or use social networks to provide them with products from the countryside. For example, O.D's household receives potatoes, vegetables and other garden produce from her brother's farm.

Gardening is also important for the household of N.A.:

"We have a garden, and there are apple trees, grapes, blackberries, and other things ..." (B int 6: 202, female, urban, 43 years).

Also G.A. is engaged in gardening and cultivating various kinds of vegetables and trees.

N.A. is engaged in cattle breeding to make additional money. Her household has income from cattle and horses. But they are not the only owners but share the business together with her brother who lives in the countryside.

"We do not pay him, he is one of our relatives and he just helps us in this way, taking care of the cattle (...) He supplies us with meat, milk, airan, kymyz from summer pasture, potato etc." (B int 6: 492, female, urban, 43 years).

[231] This means, major housing repair according to European standards.

Six times a year N.A. goes to the countryside to get produce. Moreover, her brother visits his sister five times a year in the city and supplies the household with agricultural products.

Vulnerabilities and overcoming shocks

G.A. mentions that his household had to cope with several crises during the last decade. Moving from the countryside to Astana was connected with the problem of finding an adequate place to live and work:

"I rented a room and worked in construction. It was a very harsh time for me. I worked very hard .... I remember these times well. I overcame the difficulties firstly because of my belief in Allah, and secondly I sought to cope with those problems. I think that it is due to my morale and psychological strength. Definitely, I had some constraints for realizing my life. It was very difficult to earn money; I was also unemployed" (Ast int 17: 17, male, urban, 45 years).

Moreover G.A. and his wife have to repay a large credit they took up, to open a grocery shop that failed. To overcome their difficulties, they plan to sell their house in the near future and to start up again with a new business:

"I am going to buy a plot of land. We are waiting for the resolution of the government about this land. If authorities sign this document, I want to start with a small brick plant in Astana. For this reason I am going to sell my house. If I do this and start with business it is going to be a good source of earnings. This brick plant will always be in demand due to the construction works in Astana. Anyway I have started this process. Since this will be my own business it demands finance and activity (...) I don't expect any subsidies or helps from the state. I have only applied for getting this plot of land for my brick plant. If they do help me, it would be the best support from the state. Definitely, I will face troubles. The first is money. If I have money the rest is a deal of the future. The brick plant is going to be the second source of income in my household in the future" (Ast int 17: 21, male, urban, 45 years).

O.D. is divorced and raises her two children without the help of her former husband who left the household and lives with his new wife. Her ex-husband does not support the household, neither financially nor morally. Moreover, O.D's. son lives with her brother in the countryside. However, the reason is not so much economical.

"I had problems with him. My son did not attend school, came in touch with bad company, police interfered. My brother has a good influence on my son" (Alm int 10: female, urban, 40 years).

Vulnerabilities in this group of respondents are often addressed in financial terms. O.D., particularly vulnerable as a female household head, explains:

"The difficulties are mainly related to finances. Everything depends on the clients. If there are many clients I have enough money. Now the difficulties are mainly related to the rent of my work place. (...), the landlord raised the rent (...) There are many difficulties and troubles, but I'm trying to solve them along the way. Problems like loans and rent are always in my head, I am not free of them. Seven years ago my husband and I became divorced. When I lived with him there were no troubles. He earned money; I sat at home and looked after the kids. I really don't care about money and products. But when I divorced I was left without a living. I searched any job. I worked at two or three jobs. The wage from my first job went for the rent, from the second to clothes for my kids and from the third I bought foods. It was a hard time. Sometimes I had no money for transport. In winter time I walked from one job, where I cleaned floors, to another and the distance between them was large. My husband didn't support our children and me. He bought neither food nor clothes. He didn't even come, but lay claim on the house. He suggested to sell it and to divide the money in half. But I was defending the house. These difficulties lasted until I found this job of a masseuse" (Alm int 10: 46, female, urban, 40 years).

N.A' household was confronted with dismissal. She lost her job as a teacher at a moment when her husband was unemployed.

"I was dismissed from my job, and the reason for that was that I missed two hours of lessons (...). On April 7th, (memorial day, ED, H.S.) on my way to work I met my friends and we decided to put flowers on the graves (...) I asked others to substitute me and they agreed to give classes for me, and then because of that, because I missed lessons, I had to leave my job. And at that time I was shocked, because from 1994 on I worked at that school, and I missed the lessons not on purpose... and, to put flowers on the graves of dead people I think is the duty of every person and I wanted to fulfill my duty and two hours were spent there... and because, as they said, I missed my lessons I had to leave my job" (B int 6: 400, female, urban, 43 years).

Co-residence

Like their rural counterparts, due to financial hardships, urban poor households try to minimize expenditures. Co-residence is one of the means in the urban context. O.D. e.g. lives with her sister and her children. Her sister pays for the cohabitation. G.A. rents out rooms from his flat.

Reliance on social networks

The social networks the households are embedded into are very important for survival. Already above, we mentioned the supply of food produce from relatives. But these networks are not only important for barter but also for cash.

"Sometimes we help our relatives, who live separately. Mostly I help them financially, if I have extra money. I do it, when I have opportunities to do that. The main problem of Astana is high prices, therefore in some cases our income is not enough even for us. Of course, if you have extra money you should help your relatives" (Ast int 17: 11, male, urban, 45 years).

It is a give and take process (mutual help, reciprocity with strong moral obligations. If you have extra money, that is money above your own immediate needs you have to give and the other has the 'right' to ask for that money. The rhetoric is 'help', but in reality it is a very strong obligation. O.D. connects it with gaining respect:

"As my close relatives live far away from me, we do not often have contact with them. Sometimes they visit us for short. When it's possible, both my sister and I try to help them. For example, we sometimes send money to our brother, because my son lives with him. He's my younger brother and he has four children. Thus, among ourselves we treat each other respectfully" (Alm int 10: 39, female, urban, 40 years).

In the case of N.A., parents and other family members supported the young family during their first years of living together in their own household:

"They helped us financially, if we were in need or when doing something; if our salaries were not enough, at such moments they gave us money (...) My sister helps me... my mother helps and the relatives help us" (B int 6: 324, female, urban, 43 years).

Investing in children's education

Despite all financial shortages the education of children is important for all households. O.D. is working hard to make money and to finance it:

"In praise of God, as long as I have a job I can cope with it. Every month I'm paying 10,000 Tenge for my daughter's education. It's ok. In summer time when there are less customers it really hurts me. Not to face too many difficulties I'm trying to do my best and I work a lot" (Alm int 10: 53, female, urban, 40 years).

N.A. has to pay 35,000 Soms for the education of her eldest son. Moreover, her household pays 1,200 Soms for English courses. Most of the household's savings are used to finance children's education:

"To educate our children money is needed, (. . .), so that they have a bright future, get good education and so that they can get everything they want" (B int 6: 382, female, urban, 43 years).

Savings

Urban households near to poverty can hardly save money due to financial shortages and/or repaying of credits. The household of N.A. saves money at home to be able to pay for anniversary gifts, wedding parties and funerals. According to the data it can be assumed that this money stems from husbandry. The others say that they do not save.

"We are not able to make savings. Our income is enough only for nutrition, clothes and for paying the credit. We don't have any extra money" (Ast int 17: 20, male, urban, 45 years).

"As I said above, at this moment I have no possibilities. (. . .) It is terrible to think if my daughter wanting to get married, because there is nobody who can help me. I rely on myself" (Alm int 10: 56, female, urban, 40 years).

In the latter case, the household is particularly vulnerable, because social networks cannot compensate for a lack of savings.

Credit taking

Before taking out credit, G. A. had long discussions with his wife, but finally decided to take the credit. They planned to open a grocery shop to have a better source of income. But the business plan failed because they did not have enough money to pay back the credit in time:

"Also we had to help other people. Of course, everything was not as we had planned (. . .) We took this credit to start the new business. We have hired workers for building the new small shop within my courtyard. Building the shop cost 7,000 USD. We are going to open this shop soon. The other part of credited money was spent for different expenses like the repair of the house, buying gates for the house etc. (. . .) I took a credit of 25,000 USD two years ago. But our credit has been stopped for the last six months; we took a break for half a year. I want to provide our mortgage as security. We don't pay for it now. Because we don't have any possibility. (. . .) I suppose that the reduction of credit interests would support improving the life of all Kazakhs. For instance, I pay the credit with 19% of interest. If I had the credit with 8% of interest, I could afford myself to pay the credit, improve living conditions and go out for leisure. The 19% is the huge sum for me. I am going to reduce the credit interest to 5-6% by this mortgage if it will be possible" (Ast int 17: 13, male, urban, 45 years).

Also O.D. suffers from repaying a credit she took for the improvement of her living conditions at home. For her credit taking is

"(...) a reason of nightmares, because all day and night you think about the loan. I tried not to take a credit under no circumstances. But I took one once and pay back now, although I didn't finish to build the bath" (Alm int 10: 68, female, urban, 40 years).

Only N.A. points out that she has no credit. To overcome difficulties concerning cash, she prefers the help of relatives and parents.

Evaluation of livelihood strategies of poorer urban households

As was shown for poorer rural households already, it can also be shown that poorer urban households are not poor per se. They have property, this may be houses or flats they live in or they even have their own land, but not much. Concerning expenditures and purchasing patterns, these poorer urban households spend most of their earnings to fulfil their basic daily needs, shelter and food. These households can only spend a very small portion of money for other needs like medicine, education, clothing etc. Their income is precarious.

Therefore, self-provisioning is basic for their survival strategy. These households near to poverty use their gardens for that purpose and have none or only little savings to cope with unforeseen expenditures. Many are indebted. For them having to repay credits means that there is hardly anything left for making a living. Most urban households near to poverty rely on gardening to avoid food insecurity. The garden and/or potato fields are usually directly behind the houses or flats or at least within walking distance, which indicates that such households live more at the periphery of the city and not in the expensive city center. In the cities, the produce from land constitutes a basic source of securing subsistence, but it can't be used for extra monetary incomes. All respondents grow vegetables and fruit, either on their own land or on that of their family members, e.g. in the countryside, or could rely on mutual help from those members of their families that have their own produce. These poorer respondents all emphasize how dependent they are on their plots for much of their daily food.

Poorer urban households are either employed in self-managed low paid jobs in the informal segments of the labor market that display a high turnover, or they have low paid jobs in the bazaars, shops or construction business. Sometimes their jobs are in the grey zone between formality and informality. Only a small portion of them work in government and semi-government organizations. And if so, they work in the low paid or underpaid fields. Many of them combine several jobs, formal and informal. The majority of poorer urban households frequently face unemployment due to sheer lack of employment opportunities, physical illness or limited mobility due to child care and other obligations. Making enter more household members into wage employment or finding additional employment opportunities is a major survival strategy for these households.

Working in the informal labor market is a risky strategy of survival, because respondents have to face varying demands of clients, possible wage arrears and low job security. Therefore combining jobs in the formal and the informal job sector is attractive for these households; it adds to their security. Because of their overall situation, the household members have to accept any available jobs. Temporary withholding of work in order to find better job openings is impossible for them. Members of the poorer urban households usually have low education but not always. Some have even a university background.

The chance to find a job in the cities is much greater than in the countryside – in both countries. This holds true for skilled and unskilled labor. Rural – urban migration is a result of this. The poorer job seekers try to find a position in the labor market. They make use of their human capital and use the help of acquaintances and family members to find initial accommodation and a job. Like poorer rural households, poorer urban households are also embedded in networks mostly connecting family members. But it also seems that in the urban settings, more often colleagues, neighbors, clients and friends belong to these networks. We assume the orientation towards kin networks is lower compared to poorer rural households. Nevertheless, our research suggests the pre-eminent role of relatives as social capital. Although family networks in both countries were important in general, interviewees assume an extra significance in today's period of post communism which they believe to be characterized by conditions of insecurity and unstable conditions for leading a decent life. In their belief, the family is an anchor of stability, even for those who have faced divorce.

Within our sample of poorer urban households female-headed households and one-parent households are over-represented. They seem to be vulnerable economically. Compared to their rural counterparts, female participation in the urban work force is considerably higher. Many of these middle-aged divorced and widowed female respondents who head these households, have to support unemployed family members, raise children alone, help ailing parents without sufficient back-up from relatives. Most of them have no financial support of ex-husbands who do not pay alimonies and do not take part in the education of their children.

It seems that among this group of households many have moved to the city from the countryside only lately. But they failed to build up a sustainable livelihood in the urban areas due to excessive indebtedness, divorce, bad or inadequate education, low paid jobs or diverse other factors.

For these poorer urban households, actual day-to-day survival is a struggle. Muddling through is their strategy to overcome the many uncertainties, financial shortages, bad working conditions, low paid jobs and the lack of upward mobility, and often this muddling through is the best strategy they can take. Often some entrepreneurial activity belongs to this strategy, because in the urban environment a certain amount of risk-taking is necessary for survival. But often the small micro enterprises for self-employment/family employment are very unstable. Social networking plays a vital role to cope with the daily challenges of urban life. As it was pointed out for poorer rural households, social capital is an important factor for the practices aiming at consolidation of their precarious situation. These households mainly rely on kin networks, but in the cities these networks may also include other people. Very often one problem is compensated for with the next. Emphatically one may coin their strategy: security, security, security above all.

"Middle" Households – Urban Examples

Case A: Household of L.D. (Astana)

L.D. is a 41 years old female. She lives with her husband and three children. At the moment of the interview, L.D. was on maternity leave. For L.D. it is her second marriage. Her elder son is from the first marriage, the daughter and the small child are from the second one. The elder son is 19 years old and graduated from a technical college. His specialty is machinist. He works in a trading company as the driver's assistant. The daughter is 10 years old and the youngest son is 6 months. The household lives in a two-room apartment, which they bought on mortgage in Astana.

Case B: Household of B.C. (Almaty)

Four persons live in B.C.'s household in Almaty. B.C. is a female, 43 years old and has higher education as a mathematician, but today she works in journalism. B.C. is married with her second-group disabled husband. They have two children. The younger daughter finished school and is a 1st year university student. The elder daughter graduated from university with a Bachelor degree and studies in her 1st year of a MA program. B.C. pays for their education because both daughters do not have any earnings. They live in a private and well equipped house, which includes four rooms and an big garden.

Case C: Household of T.B. (Bishkek)

T.B. is 48 years old. He was born in the mountains. He is married and has three daughters. The household lives in a well-equipped two-room apartment. After graduating from secondary school, T.B. was hired as a mechanic in a state enterprise. After serving abroad in the Red Army, he restarted working for his former state enterprise as a driver. In 1989, he entered the Kyrgyz State University to study at the Faculty of History. He holds a diploma, but his current work is not related to this specialty.

Reference points of judgment

"Middle" urban households are simultaneously planners and performers who want to improve their living situation and well-being. They are able to protect themselves against vulnerabilities and have overcome shocks in the past. They hold multiple jobs in both the formal and informal labor market. Moreover, a high degree of satisfaction with their living in the cities can be identified, due to their careers after the breakdown of the Soviet Union. Although they were successful in mastering crisis and overcoming shocks they are critical towards the political and social circumstances in their countries. They invest a lot of financial resources in the education of their children to provide them with future opportunities and to enhance their labor market chances. These households emphasize the good conditions for students during Soviet times and the difficulties to combine paying for children's education today as well as to make living more sustainable for all household members. B.C. summarizes these efforts as follows:

"I'll do well. I am a performer, a very good performer. I do not want any risks, because I am very afraid of them, as of all new things in my life. I love stability. In the future, I want to wish my Kazakhstan to be fair and supply children with good education, not with the one that exists now. I mean testing when you enter to the university. It's all formal education; I would like an education like in the Soviet Union when it was about quality (...) And it is education that does not suit me (...) And I hope that true democracy will be in Kazakhstan, so that we all will do all right, and the education will be, well, not free, but of high quality and with further employment. That is my wish and the problem to some extent" (Alm int 11: female, urban, 42 years).

Formal employment opportunities

A.D. has higher education and works in a large private trading company as a bookkeeper. Her husband works in a private company as a security guard. The husband holds 2 jobs. His salary is 120,000 Tenge, 80,000 from his first employment and

60,000 from the second. After paying taxes he has 120,000 Tenge. They spend money on repaying credits, gasoline, the car, utility fees and heating in winter. 30,000 Tenge remains monthly at their disposal. Moreover, A.D. has a small business and "*sometimes I make money there, I am engaged in a network business*".

T.B. married in 1989 and became a father for the first time. The young family rented a one-room flat in order to live in the city. In 1993, he began his internship at the Ministry of Internal Affairs. After graduating from university, he has worked in that ministry ever since.

"There, all my adolescence years were spent; I have made many friends, became part of the society, of the community. Also, I have made small contributions to the country, working there and providing people with security, also, making them to follow the road regulations, and many other things" (B int 4: 23, male, urban, 48 years).

Ever since, T.B. has worked in the ministry and made his career there gradually climbing up the career ladder. Today, he earns 5,800 Soms (120 USD) monthly. The second and bigger income is contributed to the household by T.B.'s wife who works as a trade dealer at a market. Before her marriage she worked as an accountant. After that she stayed at home to raise the children. When the children were grown up, she bought a container and started trading. She sells clothes. Her income is fairly high and maintains the well-being of the household. Her husband reports:

"Yes, it is good for now. 3-4, 5-6 years ago there was a higher income from her business. But, now, mmm, it is enough for our everyday expenditures (...) I have not calculated it, but it is enough for the education of our children, clothes (...) It is approximately 30,000 Soms (612 USD)" (B int 4: 127, male, urban, 48 years).

The establishment of the new business and the entering of the new field of activity was largely supported by acquaintances; that is social capital. T.B. explains:

"I bought the container (for sales in the bazaar, E.D., H.S.) for no high price; I bought it for the price of one horse, 16,000 Soms (327 USD) (...) It was cheap at that time, when containers began to be put up (...) We studied together with the guys who worked there and they helped me to buy the container" (B int 4: 529, male, urban, 48 years).

During the last year T.B.'s wife became ill and could not work on the market anymore. But the business did not die. They rented out the container for other traders to generate an income.

"One month ago she rented it out because of the deterioration of her health (...) per month 14,000 or 15,000 Soms (300 USD)" (B int 4: 199, male, urban, 48 years).

B.C. has changed her academic specialty. Today she works as the advertisement manager of a daily newspaper. She works five days a week outside of Almaty. The husband doesn't work because he has a second-group disability. He receives a disability grant of about 20,000 Tenge (130 USD). The largest part of this money is required to buy medicine.

Self-employment in the informal sector

T.B. has a second job in the informal labor market. Together with friends he sells foreign cars in Bishkek.

"It is not a big business with my friends, but we have a small one. (...) We look for cars abroad and sell them here on the market, such kind of small business that helps us" (B int 4: 111, male, urban, 48 years).

The money needed to buy the cars abroad is from the business of his wife.

"We do not get and sell many cars 100 or 200 or so; we bring 2 maximum 3 cars in the lowest price category (...) We try to get such cars, because we cannot afford to bring the cars of higher class with high price" (B int 4: 123, male, urban, 48 years).

B.C. also has additional earnings from different types of informal activities:

"(...) for example now I am making translations for the theater. In general, the additional income is equal to a half of the main one" (Alm int 11: 27, female, urban, 42 years).

Self-provisioning with garden produce and livestock

Self-provisioning with products from one's own garden or that of family members plays a negligible role among these middle households. Also saving through keeping of livestock is less important for "middle" urban households in comparison with their rural counterparts. Nevertheless, for some, it is an important income generating strategy. T.B. e.g. owns 100 sheep, 8 horses and 2 cows in a rural area.

"They are kept where my brother, my parents live, and they look after them" (B int 4: 161, male, urban, 48 years).

The combination of formal employment, informal job holdings and livestock is used to make livelihoods of the household more sustainable.

"I deal with cars, also with livestock. All these things are done in order to make the household stable" (B int 4: 535, male, urban, 48 years).

Vulnerabilities and overcoming shocks

"There were days when there was no money in the pocket, and we walked on foot from one place of the city to another. I went on my foot to the center of the city, you see, because of the lack of tyiyn (...) It was after the Soviet periods, before Soms, the days when, having no 5 tyiyns, I went on my foot. During the student days, there was no money even for bread, then we went to other rooms, to the rooms of girls, drank tea so that one did not stay so hungry" (B int 4: 387, male, urban, 48 years).

T.B. remembers the time when the Soviet Union collapsed and he had to find a job to feed his family. He and his wife lived in a rented room and the whole salary he earned was spent for rent and food. He expresses that it is important that

"(...) a person should not wait for someone's help, he should believe in himself, and he should say that I can overcome the difficulties, I should try to overcome them (...) Aiming in such direction, he should live (...) Asking for help because you cannot overcome some things is shameful for the Kyrgyz. It is not good to ask for help from someone like a beggar, it is not respectful. There were worse days than today, when our parents lived. Nowadays the time is good, everything at hand" (B int 4: 395, male, urban, 48 years).

T.B. not only overcame these political and economic difficulties, but also problems such as the theft of his car or his house being broken into. He survived due to his morale, but also with the help of friends and relatives:

"Kyrgyz people are very generous, mainly, kind, yes, hospitable, yes, when they see that a friend is in trouble they invite you to live in their houses, yes, if the relatives see it they also invite you to live in their houses, and I am very grateful for these actions of them" (B int 4: 399, male, urban, 48 years).

He explains that mutual help is important in order to make a good living today:

"For example, when I wanted to buy the apartment I took a credit from my relatives, also from my friend, my parents, relatives helped to buy the apartment, and the parents of my wife helped me" (B int 4: 403, male, urban, 48 years).

But sometimes, finding jobs does not happen smoothly and puts stress on households as B.C. describes:

"My daughter recently graduated from university, and we went to look for a job.(...) there is no need for economists. Therefore, it is very difficult now to find a job. I will tell you that labor law is not observed in banks. That is, a twelve-hour workday with a meagre salary. And there is no guarantee that a kid will continue to work there. We have to pay for a probation, for an internship, for a training (...) It is 40,000 Tenge. And still there is no guarantee that the job is sure. I was very outraged. I encounter these kinds of problems now. I cannot say that it is a situation in a particular bank. This situation is in all banks. My daughter and I made the round in a few banks. Wherever we went, the rate is the same everywhere. The unemployment problem is terrible, of course. It turns out that after two months of training and two months of internship, and something else, and we figured out that she is going to work for six months for free. Of course this is a big disadvantage for the family budget, because I have to feed her and pay for her transportation every day. A minimum of one thousand Tenge will be eaten up by this. And that is for every day. Therefore, these are big expenses for me" (Alm int 11: 60, female, urban, 42 years).

In the past, the household of B.C. has had to cope with the illness of her husband who had to stop working. It was a huge shock for the young family and they relied on the help of family members and friends to overcome the situation:

"Those were very difficult times (...). We could not afford anything, even walked in winter boots in summer. Relatives, of course, helped. I didn't take bank loans, but instead, I sold our old car and started my husband's treatment with this money. The family helped us and we saved, economized on everything; we even didn't go to the hairdresser. I worked for the medicine. My parents were still alive at that time. They received a pension and helped as much as they could. Those were some difficulties. But we didn't take loans, and I still try not to take them" (Alm int 11: 47, female, urban, 42 years).

The illness of B.C.'s husband also massively affected the education of their children, allowing for better higher education for only one of them.

"And the older daughter went to a prestigious high school; she went to a prestigeous kindergarten. It turned out this way that we have sacrificed our younger daughter" (Alm int 11: 49, female, urban, 42 years).

Future planning and improving wellbeing

"Middle" urban households are characterized by a high degree of planning activities and farsightedness. They calculate monthly income and expenditures. It is important for them to have a surplus of money at the end of the month. B.C. explains it as follows:

"I am a future orientated person; for example, if I have to pay for my daughter's education, I save and pay for it in the first place. And then I live as I can. In extreme cases, I am saving on food. I don't go to beauty salons or anything like this. I do everything according to a plan. Primarily, of course, tuition fees. After that, I can distribute the budget. May be I'm too economical to myself, but daughters' health and education have always been the in the first place. I'm not economizing on them" (Alm int 11: 38, female, urban, 42 years).

For all households of that class, it is very important to provide children with the best education possible. All respondents have children who go to school or are students or who graduated from universities. Urban "middle" households see the education of their children as "*strategic stability in the future, so that they will have a job*" (B.C.). They invest a very large part of their incomes for their education and thus – as they believe – their future wellbeing:

"By the standards of that time, it was a lot of money. This year, she graduated from Narhoz (Kazakh Economic University). I paid all three years. She never worked, I mean moonlighted during vacation time, so no income came from her" (Alm int 11: 37, female, urban, 42 years).

T.B. mentions:

"I try to give my children a good education, so that to make the household stable... and the household, the everyday life, are passing gradually, and a person should try to do his best for his happiness, stability, to behave in a proper way (...) We want our daughters to get the best education, and try to contribute all things we have, so that they can bring some contributions to the people, to the country and can be useful" (B int 4: 267, male, urban, 48 years).

Financing education not only means money for schools and universities, but also money for additional activities as e.g. learning foreign languages, taking part in software engineering courses or to go to fitness clubs.

"For language courses we pay 2,500 Soms per month. For the computer course we pay 300 Soms per visit. For fitness club we pay 1,300 up to 1,600 Soms" (B int 4: 201, male, urban, 48 years).

Savings

All households save in general. T.B. e.g. saves money at home for everyday expenditures and for payments in the case of illness.

"Also, for some good and bad moments of life, as we are Kyrgyz we have many acquaintances so for the good and bad moments of life. (...) children may become ill, and my wife is ill now, I can become ill, so money has to be spent for doctors. So for these things we try to save money" (B int 4: 435, male, urban, 48 years).

The education of children is also supported and made possible through the ability to save:

"Yes, of course. As we live for them, so that they can become good people, get a good education, a good knowledge... all these things ... parents, thinking about their children, aaa...do...try to save and spent money only for them" (B int 4: 285, male, urban, 48).

The money T.B. and his wife earn, also flows into the education of their children. The household invests in livestock and increases it, but has no monetary savings.

"I do not have opportunities to save money. My money is the cattle I have, the livestock. If you sell them you get money, so they are my money (...) The livestock was inherited from my parents and the number of it is gradually increasing on its own" (B int 4: 423, male, urban, 48 years).

L.D. argues that it is impossible for her household to save money but the 200,000 Tenge (1,300 USD) from the state for giving birth to her third child she has deposited in a bank. Additionally, her household wants to have their own house in the future for which they deposit 15,000 – 20,000 Tenge monthly.

The households also save for weddings, cars etc. In general, they are aware of everyday risks and try to equip themselves against them financially, by saving.

Credits

In general, credit taking in this group of urban households is done with caution. Credits are used for very different purposes: housing, appliances, weddings, funerals, education of children etc. But mostly, the households try to avoid credits and to save until they can buy. But there are rare examples where this attitude does not function.

"*All our life consists of credits*" mentions L.D. At the very moment, his household has a car on credit. In the past they took three other credits, besides the mortgage. They also used credits to buy appliances, furniture, and for repairs. L.D. bought their two-room apartment on a mortgage. It was very difficult for the young family to find an adequate space for living. Due to the high costs for apartments they decided to look for a two-room apartment on the outskirts of Astana which they could afford. When the interest rate of the mortgage increased they invited her husband's parents to live with them and to rent out their apartment in order to survive financially. Finally L.D. took a loan "*from one good person on the security of my apartment to redeem the credit*". Moreover, she received a loan from the company for which she works:

"When I had redeemed the credit I thanked Allah for that there are such people and I have met them (...) I have already paid off this person! I just left kind my salary there. It is

100,000 Tenge. Thus I paid 4 years (...) I paid 18 % interest rate for this borrower" (Ast int 21: 27, female, urban, 41 years).

But in general, middle urban households try to avoid becoming indebted and calculate their credit needs thoroughly.

"When my fridge broke, I bought a new one on credit. But it's not even a credit, I mean without interest, without any overpayment. For household appliances shops offer installments. And of course, I took advantage of it. In the course of a year, I paid back. I never took a credit, or anything else, for which I must overpay. I, generally, try to avoid such methods of spending money. I also try not to get indebted, because I do not have much money to give to someone. I calculate everything from paycheck to paycheck" (Alm int 11: 40, female, urban, 42 years).

Evaluation of livelihood strategies

In general, the more affluent a household is, and in particular the more assets it possesses, the more resilient it is to threats from unexpected problems and trends. The households of this group are well equipped. For many of them the transition was a disruption in their development, but it also gave them a fresh start. The flexibility these households show in coping with difficult situations is striking, be it the breakdown of the Soviet Union, divorce, illness, loss of property etc. They are ready to fight for better living conditions or standards in the future. Many of them reflect this even in stressing the kind of morale necessary to survive under difficult conditions and to keep households going and careers functioning etc. Education for the next generation plays an important role in their lives. They are ready to invest in it, but it also represents a kind of future orientation, supplementing the one already mentioned above. Education means continuity for the households, for their children as well as for their parents.

In these households, there are many members with multiple jobs. Starting a second job in the formal or informal labor market is a strategy pursued by both women and men – and it is often done. This group is very industrious and keen in making a better living. There seem to be hardly any restrictions which kind of second job is taken up, as long as it is compatible with the requirements of the first job. These household members not only look for jobs in which their special skills are demanded, but they also look for unskilled extra work to increase the household budget. For example, they may work as security guards, may do house and car repair, newspaper deliveries, car washing, construction work, sewing, repairing clothes, haircutting etc.

All three cities are heavily dependent on state sector employment. Although salaries in the state sector are comparatively low if measured against those in the "free" economy, for our respondents they represent a certain level of stability and security. It is a successful strategy to move sideways in the state sector concerning second jobs: into universities, schools, local governments, or police.

Moreover, migration was an obvious strategy for respondents to achieve a better living. Most of them migrated from the countryside to the cities to improve their living situation. Apart from better job opportunities, an important push factor for migration was also, and still is, higher education. Many of the respondents went to Astana, Almaty and Bishkek when enrolling in institutions of higher education. Very often they found their spouses in the cities. After graduation, some tried to make their living back in the countryside, before they went back to the cities. Others stayed in the cities after having graduated. But the relations between those in the cities and those staying back in the countryside stay strong and intact allowing for different forms of mutual exchange.

These households display a strong orientation toward upward mobility in terms of material goods and education for their children. For them human capital (skills and education) is one key to success. But also social capital (using the help of acquaintances) influences their opportunities and successes. Concerning Russia, Ledeneva (1998) argues that kin networks in the cities have become more important in the post socialist period and that the exchange of favors between acquaintances is more openly based on self-interest. If the observation is really a result of post-socialism, we can't answer as yet. But the phenomenon seems true for Kyrgyzstan and Kazakhstan as well, although among middle urban households kinship relations still dominate and are often explained by the national character. But in contrast to poorer urban households a tendency can be found that respondents' social networks also comprise friends, colleagues, and neighbors and that advantages or disadvantages are seen and discussed. We argue, that these networks are no longer pre-given and a necessary "insurance" mechanism but a choice to fall back upon for giving and receiving support. We can even observe that some of these middle households prefer to keep kin and friendship away from monetary relations. In any case, there can be no doubt, that social capital plays an important role in the households' strategies to organize their lives. In general, the strategies are orientated towards consolidation and accumulation.

The interviews show much success concerning livelihood strategies. But there is also stress. Stressors for the households are finances, corruption, and family relations. Strained relationships between women and men can be looked upon as an obvious consequence of the vulnerabilities of the households. There are a comparatively large number of households in our sample headed by divorced women. Gender relations are changing. Additionally, one can observe in this sample, that women show more flexibility in searching for jobs and in reorientation of life opportunities etc. Thus, in some households women have become the main bread winners.

"Better off" households – urban examples

Case A: Household of A.Z. (Astana, Interview 3)

A.Z. is 42 years old and has two higher education's degrees in higher education. She is a trained teacher and a lawyer. A.Z. rents a two-room apartment in Astana. She has two children and is divorced. Moreover, she has a step daughter who is the child of A.Z.'s eldest brother and his wife who died 10 years ago. They all live in the household. She receives a guardianship grant for the orphan and has become her lawful guardian. Her elder daughter is 22 years old and has already graduated from university.

Case B: Household of M.S. (Almaty, Interview 13)

M.S. has higher education in agriculture and is 51 years old. He is married. His wife has higher education in music, but works as an accountant. Two sons live in the household. The elder son graduated in architecture and construction and works as engineer for a large company, a joint venture between China and Kazakhstan. The younger son is 11 years old. The family owns a two-floor apartment in which the parents of M.S. are also living.

Case C: Household of M.M. (Bishkek, Interview 12)

M.M. was born in the countryside and came to Bishkek to study at the Polytechnic Institute, specializing in auto mechanics. After his service in the Soviet Army, he finished his education as an engineer. In 1992, he married his wife who came from the same rural region and they settled in Bishkek. The wife's family bought them an apartment and helped them in general. M.Ms. household consists of four persons: himself, his wife and two sons. The elder one is studying to become a lawyer. The younger son is enrolled in his 1styear at school. Today, they live in an 'elite' apartment in a closed compound a part of the city with high security standards and their own garage.

Reference points of judgment

Respondents stress the necessity of changes to adapt to post-Soviet conditions and the hard work that this meant. The idea, that if one works hard one can become successful, belongs to the strongest convictions of this group.

The divorced teacher and lawyer explains:

"It is necessary to improve constantly. I am such kind of person who needs to know, always to be cleverer than others. We are children of communist times, got used to plug. Consequently if I can't reach 100 %, I'll better give up. I can't work only 70 %. (...). Sometimes I come to work, and colleagues ask me: 'Why are your eyes so red?'. And I answer them that I worked nearly till 5.00 a.m. 3-4 persons at work know about my way of life, about my life. They tell me: 'Relax, get drunk once in a life?'. I answer them: 'What for? Tomorrow I will be ill; I must be in different places tomorrow. I don't presume to relax'" (Ast int 3: 103, female, urban, 42 years).

In this respect, concerning useful activities, these respondents see a generational gap between those having grown up under Soviet times and those afterwards.

"When I was a child, mom and dad scolded me. I was wondering why she or he does remark, why she or he scolds only me. And now it all turns out to be repeated. The problem of fathers and children has not been canceled, the interests are different. Our generation grew up in different time, the internet, television, all of this was not present at our lives, we were more physically developed, and we had more game types, for instance asyk [folk game with bones]. All time is different. I say, why do you always sit in front of TV, go out for sports, walk, run, do not sit in the internet or watch TV" (Alm int 13: 195, male, urban, 51 years).

Formal employment opportunities

M.S. is self-employed and runs a small company which deals with real estate sales and trading. He has flexible working hours. He started his business two years ago. Before, he worked in a high position in the security service. He decided to become self-employed after his younger son was enrolled in school and somebody had to bring him there. His wife has a well-paid job in a private company and works from early morning until late evening. In contrast to this example, members of this group of households are mostly multiple job holders. Outstanding is this respect is A. Z. She holds five jobs in the formal labor market. The first job is as teacher at the university. Additionally, she works as a sports manager for the university. She is a trainer in a children's sports school. All of these three positions are part of state organizations. Moreover, she trains people in self-defense. The fifth job is related to drawing up legal contracts. She earns 120,000 Tenge (810 USD) as a teacher at the university, which is her main income. In total, her average monthly income is 250,000 Tenge (1,700 USD). A.Z. benefits from her two professions and shows high organizational abilities to coordinate all her professional and private activities. Not only does A.Z. contribute to the household's budget, but her eldest daughter does also. Already during her studies, she worked as a sales assistant in a clothing store. She gets a monthly salary of 60,000 Tenge (390 USD). She contributes half of her salary to the common budget. The step daughter is a 2nd year student and receives a grant of 15,000 Tenge (100 USD) and as an orphan she has a grant of 15,000 Tenge (100 USD). Given this budget, it is no problem for the household to pay for the fashionable apartment (70,000 Tenge (475 USD)) and the utilities, internet access included.

Also M.M.'s career shows adaption to different fields of activities. After having graduated as an auto mechanic with good qualifications, he couldn't find a job. Having his family in the countryside and having moved to the city only lately, he had no 'contacts' that could help him to get a job. He married just after the collapse of the Soviet Union. His wife's father bought an apartment for the young couple and they had a first son. M.M.'s wife started to work after she graduated from university, her specialization is accountancy. M.M. took care of his son until he went to the kindergarten. He found work at the Academy of Science, where he met a lot of people who until today make up his network of relationships. From this network there stemmed the idea of opening up a restaurant. This idea was achieved and M.M. became its director and co-owner on a fifty-fifty basis. This enterprise prospered and M.M. could buy his first car and a house. In 2005, health problems occurred and finally he had to leave this business to undergo medical treatment. During a period of unemployment, in which only his wife worked although she was pregnant, he began his own new business. The prosperity of the household started to grow further. In 2010, he changed his occupation and took over a position in the presidential administration, where he works to the present day. His wife is a director and chief accountant of a real estate company. M.M. also plans to extend his business activities. He wants to build one more restaurant as he believes himself to be a professional in this business and to be able to withstand the competition in this field.

Self-employment in the informal sector

In general, these households are not forced to combine employment in the formal sector with informal activities. Their formal jobs – the majority in higher positions – are sufficient for making a living and the relations and the kind of jobs of the interviewees allow for additional incomes from jobs in the formal sector. One of the few who combines formal with informal activities is A.Z. who apart from her five jobs in the formal labor market, works as a spin doctor.

"There are many rich people who can't dress well. All began when my female friend married a businessman. It was small growth. They went to have a rest in the mountains. We went to a shop, I picked up a smart suit for him, which hit his shortcomings and emphasized the advantages. Then, I began to earn with this occupation. So sometimes I have earnings by working as image consultant. I help people to dress correctly, people with a non-standard figure, but it takes me much time. Sometimes a person needs to dress with limited means. Sometimes a person needs to be clothed for different occasions: to dress with classic clothes, to dress with sports clothes and to dress in official style. I am engaged in this occupation during weekends (...) It depends on the sum the people spend. If the person buys clothes for 5,000-10,000 USD I can earn 300-500 USD" (Ast int 3: 45, female, urban, 42 years).

Livestock

Gardening to maintain a living standard does not play any role in this group, which is perhaps also due to the fact that such households live in the city centers. Very rarely are there respondents who keep cattle in the countryside where they usually come from and where family members can take care of the herd, the breeding and the sales. Partly it is to support this part of the family and it is also prestigious to do so.

Vulnerabilities and overcoming unexpected problems or shocks

A.Z.'s life story is characterized by overcoming unexpected problems and constantly looking for resources to make living more sustainable. During her divorce, she lost her apartment because she could not pay for it any more. Moreover she had to raise the children by herself. For a short time she lived with relatives in a one-room apartment. She was in debt and had to repay the credit on an apartment she did not own:

"Practically, at that time, my life started from scratch (...). When I lost everything as that grandmother in the fairy tale, I didn't hang down my head as she did" (Ast int 3: 107, female, urban, 42 years).

To overcome vulnerabilities she started different jobs. The breakthrough came with her car.

"We had no car that time but I decided to buy one. (...) It seems that a car is a luxury, but without a car it would be unprofitable now. I couldn't be in time anywhere. Without the car I can't do it. Clients call me and ask to come to their office, to make a contract, to help, to check something, to make remarks, to advise etc. I must to be there. I am in time thanks to the car" (Ast int 3: 95, female, urban, 42 years).

M.M. also mentions financial difficulties, at the time when his second son was born and when he left his job. But the family had savings they used to cope with the situation:

"It was hard to live. Our friends helped us. They supplied me with some ideas and I started to work on them. But before I opened our own business; we were living on our savings" (B int 12: 207, male, urban, 43 years).

M.M. was also confronted with damages through looting, burglaries, and blackmail concerning his restaurant business.

"These organized criminal groups always were visiting us and asked for some amount of money per month so secure us with all problems. But now everyone is in jail. Now it is quiet. Even in Issyk-Kul every resort was giving money to organized criminal groups, but now it is quiet, all of them are in jail" (B int 12: 285, male, urban, 43 years).

Today his household is rich and stable enough to absorb financial shortages. He can even support family members:

"Help comes from my friends, offering different ideas, looking for projects, businesses, help just like this. I don't need any help from my relatives and I don't ask, because I live well (...) I give help to my own relatives, to cousins not much. As I told you last year I bought a car for my sister. I always help with household appliances, sometimes I help financially. My second sister lives well and they don't ask any help, but if they lived badly I would help. I help my younger sister sometimes too" (B int 12: 131, male, urban, 43 years).

Investment in children

Within this group of households education is of utmost importance. This is not looked upon in an abstract way, in the sense that the well-educated child will have a good job and will thus be able to sustain themselves and will support their parents as is traditionally done in both countries. In this group, some parents look upon their children as their possible successors in the businesses, they have built up. Thus, their business activities automatically become linked to the future.

M.M sends his sons to private schools. That costs him considerable personal and financial engagement. He sees his eldest son as his personal successor in his business, and therefore he should be well educated to secure it. It is very important for M.M. that his son will have suitable training for his business.

"I want him to become a lawyer, because we don't have any lawyers in our family. (...). I think later I will leave him my own business and he will control it" (B int 12: 163, male, urban, 43 years).

M.S., who has his own business, is happy to spend as much time as he can with his youngest son.

"It is very important not to miss this time from the 1st to 4th grade and to help him to feel comfortable. He has already finished 4th class and now he is in the 5th class Now I have more free time for him" (Alm int 13: 83, male, urban, 51 years).

He compares this privileged situation with the problems during the 1990s when the family raised their elder son. He lived most of the time with his grandparents and M.S. and his wife "*lived and tried to survive*" by trading, selling, "*trying almost everything*". He looks upon the high fees they had to pay for their son's studies as a good investment having so far led to a sharp rise in the career of this son.

Charity

Charity is not unknown in this class. It expands the family and includes relationships with friends. It is also looked upon as a social commitment to society.

"Once, one boy needed help getting surgery, so me and my 10 friends we gave 3,000 USD each, so we gathered $30,000. Surgery cost $60,000 (...) His parents said thanks, now he is feeling good" (B int 12: 135, male, urban, 43 years).

Renting out property

M.M. has an apartment in Bishkek which he rents out. Moreover, he is the owner of a shop which is run by a tenant. Also M.S. rents out an apartment. In this group, investment in apartments is a means of security and of making additional income. For some of these households renting out has become their main source of income. Real estate property has turned into an investment and business strategy as well as a household strategy.

"We have several apartments in different areas of the city. It is the main income of the family. We have 1, 2 and 3-room apartments" (Alm int 13: 150, male, urban, 51 years).

Lifestyle

Repair works at home are not done by the household members any longer, but by specialist firms:

"I earn money and don't do something around the house. Well, in such an apartment there is no work to do. If something goes wrong, we call a plumber, if we need to repair electricity, water supply the same. We use the benefits of civilization, and give work to specialists" (Alm int 13: 59, male, urban, 51 years).

Although transportation by car is not absolutely necessary in the city, it is nowadays a sign of belonging to the better-off class. As in the West cars also function as status symbols.

In this group of households people go on holidays, have a 'lifestyle', dress up fashionably.

"We went to the Emirates. In Turkey I was with my wife only shortly, because our youngest child was small and the oldest son stayed with him at home. I also go to China because of my business (...) We go to Issyk-Kul, we have a rest in Avrora always. We go to the mountains. In summer time when it is very hot in the city we go to Ala-Archa" (B int 12: 175, male, urban, 43 years).

"I prefer to relax in Kazakhstan, I'm afraid of heights, afraid of airplanes. We have the possibility to fly to Turkey, Hainan, but I'm afraid of airplanes" (Alm int 13: 216, male, urban, 51).

Most of these households refer to a decent dress code, to fashion standards they have to comply with.

Furthermore, these urban households with higher incomes accentuate how much money they spend for spa and health. A healthy lifestyle is an important code for better off urban households. A.Z. gives the following explanations:

"My main aim is to be healthy. Besides different difficulties, I always try to keep my health and the health of my children. In spite of the fact, that the children have already reached grown up status. I always correct their health. I accustom them to a healthy diet. Earlier I didn't worry about it (...) The most important fact why today many people don't have enough money is because they drink Coca-Cola, eat hotdogs, hamburgers. Our family doesn't consume these drinks and junk food. We don't drink Coca-Cola, we don't drink lemonades, we don't eat hotdogs, we do not go to KFC etc. We protest against all this food. Two years ago my daughters wanted it. Now I have accustomed her to a healthy diet. It is said that to eat healthy food is very expensive, it is not true. We always have eggs, sausages, and cheese for breakfast. We buy 10 kg of meat for a month to have something for a dinner. We make 5 kg of minced meat and the other 5 kg is just left over. We always have a hot meal. If there is no hot dish, money is spent wrongly. There should be a hot dish at home; therefore I do preparation in the evening. In the morning I wake up at 5-6 o'clock and I finish cooking. So we always have a fresh hot dish for dinner and supper" (Ast int 3: 24, female, urban, 42 years).

Of course, not all respondents are as strict as that. But for most of these households a healthy lifestyle is associated with their status.

Savings

Also in this group of households as in all groups, there are considerable reservations concerning private banks.

M.S. does not trust banks at all. For him it is much more relevant to deal with real estate and investing in gold and in diamonds than to save money in banks or to put money in pension funds.

"It is don't trust the banks; it is better to save at home, somewhere else to keep the savings. I think the financial situation is still unstable (...) There is no stability in the banks (...) Gold is growing all the time, it is a good investment too, I recommend it (...) (pension funds) have opened today, but tomorrow they will be closed" (Alm int 13: 177, male, urban, 51 years).

Also M.M. mentions that he does not put any money into banks. He gives half of the money to his wife who saves it in her office at work. The other half of the money he stores in his safe.

"I don't trust such organizations (...) Honestly I don't put money into the bank. I don't have any relations at all with them" (B int 12: 159, male, urban, 43 years).

But M.M., who makes sure that he did not take any credit all his life, gives money on credit to different persons:

"To be honest, one of my cousins needs to give me back 2,500 USD. Also one other person whom I know, owes me money. Actually I have a lot of debtors" (B int 12: 225, male, urban, 43 years).

Contrary to these two cases, A.Z. has been saving money in a bank deposit for many years. She also takes part in a special state program to buy her apartment, which she now rents. She is involved in different saving activities, all channeled through accounts in banks. By saving in advance she also covers the expenditure for her holidays.

"Most important is a good distribution of the budget. It doesn't mean that we don't go to have a rest. We do it. On Nauryz we went to have a rest for a week. We spent some money. In the summer we will have a rest too. In addition we can go to have a rest with friends on weekends" (Ast int 3: 93, female, urban, 42 years).

Credits

The sample shows that these households are aware of the risks of credits and try to avoid high interests. Nevertheless, sometimes these respondents take credits to satisfy needs. We already learned that a car was vital for A.Z's different activities. She bought it on credit with an interest of 13,4 percent. She is completely aware of all payments and the time schedule she has for repayment. In the whole sample of this group of households, we do not learn about a single case that comes near to a credit squeeze as in poorer households:

"Earlier I was afraid of credits. But then I understood that it is impossible to live without a car (...) We have a small sum for repayment, (...) 38,000 Tenge is no big sum for me. (...) I plan to close it in a year" (Ast int 3: 83, female, urban, 42 years).

Evaluation of livelihood strategies of better off households

Due to their high and stable incomes "better off" urban households can afford to have their own flats or houses or to pay high rents for their fashionable and well equipped apartments. Income is used to create stability and to improve wellbeing. Many respondents migrated from the countryside to Astana, Almaty or Bishkek. They prefer to live in the cities and to use the opportunities for making money there. All of them are 'nouveau riches', who started their careers after independence. Multiple job holding mainly in the formal sector is a significant marker for this group. Most of the respondents combine their several jobs intelligently and report on their high workload, about which they seem to be proud. They display a high degree of flexibility concerning jobs and making money. They mastered overcoming shocks and times of hardships (financial shortages, death of household members, divorces, unemployment) and make plans to improve their livelihoods. Better-off urban households were not all the time in privileged situations. They are newcomers in their present positions. Most of the respondents only consolidated their households after the end of communism and had to cope with the challenges of the post-communist transformation period during the 1990s. They argue, that they gained their position due to strong assertiveness.

The career of these better off urban households may highlight the importance of human capabilities. Most of them were not successful because of their formal education and professions alone but because of their ability to recognize and to use their chances and opportunities. Their activities are bound into networks of kin and other persons, be they friends, colleagues or others. Kin relations are still strong, but they are rationally calculated and supplemented by relations to others, which are important for success in making money. The stories of success are characterized by overcoming unexpected problems and by being able to avoid risks and vulnerabilities. These households found resources and made use of capital to make their living more sustainable and to improve their well-being. They pay special attention to saving which is mostly done not in banks but at home or in other places. They adapt to living standards as in Western and Middle Europe; they are owners of houses or apartments. They rent out property, renew household equipment and utilities. Prosperity of the better off urban households is not only visible with regard to houses or private apartments in very good shape or luxurious utilities, but also for example with regard to large fashionable cars. These households can afford to have holidays abroad or in expensive spa resorts. Moreover, most of them display a healthy lifestyle. Home-made repairs which are frequent among poorer households, are not a part of their live style; they call for specialists to do these repair jobs. Moreover, they are able to provide their children with a high standard of modern up to date goods (fashion, cars, electronics etc.). They invest a lot of money in children's education. They often pay for private education of them because many believe the educational system of the state as being bad or unsufficient concerning success in real life (payments for private schools, private teachers for afternoon lessons at home or additional language courses etc.). Many of the respondents see their children as their heirs in their businesses.

These households are able to support their kin not only emotionally but also financially. Some are engaged in charity. Social commitment is a characteristic feature for this group; they help other persons in difficult circumstances. Often they argue that this is attributed to their national character, be they Kazakhs or Kyrgyz.

As it was already pointed out for better off rural households, also better off urban households use credits with caution and some of them refrain from taking them completely. They rely on savings, family or wider network support in organizing their economic activities. Also among this group of better off urban households a comparatively high level of distrust in banks prevails. Usually it seems to be connected with doubts about the financial stability of the nation state. The latter is much more prevalent among Kyrgyz respondents who usually refer to the several financial reforms during the last 20 years.

In short, the household strategy of this group may be characterized by the term accumulation.

6. Summary and Conclusions: A New Variant of Capitalism?

Eckhard DITTRICH and Heiko SCHRADER

This chapter does not only sum up our research findings but also draws some general conclusions including the country and regional studies, the quantitative and the qualitative results.

Our research concerns households. Its intention was to interview middleclass households with an open household approach (Allan and Crow 2001: 3ff). By interviewing those who were supposed to know best about housekeeping, we believed to gain good information to answer our research questions concerning:

- the process of transformation on the micro-level of households and its relatedness to macro-level transformation;
- the adjustment of the households to economic insecurity as an important trait of capitalist societies in general, and developing post-socialist countries in particular;
- the differences between the households in Kazakhstan and Kyrgyzstan, representing two countries with very different economic conditions and transformation paths;
- the differences between rural and urban households and those between age cohorts;
- the assets of the households (forms of capital) by which they can make their living and develop strategies of coping with insecurities.

Concerning our interview partners it turned out, that most of our respondents, especially in the qualitative part of the research, are females. In our view this already represents a first result. Addressing the households to name the one who knows best about the household, the respondents usually named women. We argue this is due to the fact that in both countries, it is usually women who keep the household emotionally together, who have important functions in budget management, and who keep strong links to family members who left the household (migration, marriage, education, etc.). We may even speculate that in both societies – at least in the urban setting – women gradually gain a greater say and better chances of participation This can be seen also in response to the question about the head of the household. Of course, male as well as female respondents, explain at first glance, that the eldest male is the head of the household, what represents the tradition in these Asian countries. But a closer look into the interviews reveals, that in many cases, both, men and women, often even the entire family, decides about household affairs and investments, although it is often argued that the male partner has the last say. Sometimes even the woman is the major breadwinner and not her husband. In some cases, men have deliberately transferred the budget authority to their wives. Only rarely we find strict traditional orientations concerning decision-making in the households, that is the grandfather in the patrilineal order being in charge and if dead, his wife has the budget power in households that pool their income as normally done.

The changes in women's roles can be found also in other fields of family and household lives. E.g. in our sample we have lone-parent households, all headed by women. A considerable number of respondents has been divorced and has then mostly remarried. Discussions concerning alimonies seem to be a conflicting topic in these cases. Single women migrate to the city for the purpose of work or education. In families the role of men in the education of the children often is a topic in the households as well as their contributions to household chores. More generally, at least in the urban settings, our results are in tune with those observations, that discover a growing diversity of family arrangements in modernizing societies (Allan and Crow 2001; Beck and Beck-Gernsheim 2002; Beck 2011). Soviet tradition was different from the western one as the soviet model of families was not based on the male breadwinner model as in Western societies especially after the Second World War. But even though women were more equal in obtaining education and in working life than in Western European societies, women were therefore not necessarily stronger emancipated in private life. The 'double burden' (if not even triple burden) of women as employees and housewives (cum educators) is well known as having coined also Soviet family life. But we believe that the present role of women in public and private life is to some degree path-dependent from Soviet times. The soviet model has a positive effect on gender issues. This can be seen in our quantitative as well as in our qualitative research: joint responsibilities are accentuated and are balanced in family affairs, life long relationship loses its normative power and divorce is less stigmatized, girls have the same educational chances as boys, and the "responsibilities of both parents towards their biological children" (Allan and Crow 2001: 15) are stressed. In both countries,

Islamism as a countervailing power to women's equality is weak and in Kazakhstan and at least North Kyrgyzstan there are no signs of a 'counter-revolution' against the public role of women. Nevertheless, there are also practices that hint at trends contradicting growing equality of women, notably bride abduction. In 4 of our 40 qualitative interviews in Kyrgyzstan, women reported of having been abducted, with and without their consent. It seems, that this "represents a break with the Soviet past. During the Soviet period, the state promoted gender equality and Kazakh (and Kyrgyz E.D., H.S.) women were encouraged to make their own decisions about whom they wanted to marry. And many of the people who married in the 1970s in particular insist that brides were only abducted with their consent during this time period (...). At that time, the act of abducting a bride without her consent would have been shameful for the groom" (Werner 2009: 330). We can't judge about this assumption about a complete break with local traditions. Werner reports that nowadays the situation is changing. There seems to happen a 're-narrativization of the past' (ibid: 315 quoting Anagnost (1997)) aiming at a legitimization of this practice. A report of the Asian Development Bank argues similarly: "The (re)emergence of traditions and customs, including bride theft and polygamy, are a real concern for the Kyrgyz Republic and the significant levels of violence against women are increasingly understood as a serious health as well as a social issue. Moreover, female poverty and its specific vulnerabilities are increasingly manifesting themselves in the growing numbers of women and girls trafficked each year and the seasonal flow of (illegal) female migrant women to labor in neighboring countries" (Asian Development Bank 2005: XI). Because of our small number of cases we can't evaluate about the far reaching assumptions about the changes in women equality. But one should not oversee these cases and their threat to the trend as described above. Also there may be differences between Kyrgyzstan and Kazakhstan.

In the rural setting traditional gender roles are more common insofar that the core household issues in the house are related to women – wives and their daughters, sometimes also grandmothers – while the chores around the house and heavier work in subsistence production are related to male household members, predominantly the husbands. But also in these settings most women are income earners. Also here we can see path dependency from the Soviet past where wages in the "industrialized villages" (Dittrich and Oswald 2010; Oswald, Ernst, and Dittrich 2005) provided the major incomes stemming both from men's as well as women's work. However, as is well-known from the literature and also supported from our research findings, this structure of industrialized village has collapsed. Only a limited number of public jobs in administration, education and health and private jobs in commerce and production have remained or replaced them, while the majority of rural dwellers have to be socially creative to make an income from various opportunities in the formal and informal sector as well as in subsistence production (cf. Elwert et al. 1983).

But at the same time – and this is a striking difference to modernization processes in Western societies – the majority of our urban and rural cases suggest a strong orientation towards family and kinship despite new family arrangements as described above. Family relations are preserved even if the families are no longer located in one particular place as a result of migration, housing, etc. This orientation seems to be strongest among ethnic Kazakhs and Kyrgyz. We shall address this specific topic later in this chapter.

The organizations of a market orientated capitalist economy have been established since independence of the two countries. And both have also experienced what also belongs to the reality of this type of economic regime: economic crises. But while one may describe Kazakhstan as having gone through a more or less continuous development which was only shortly interrupted by the global financial crisis of 1998 and 2008 – due to the richness of oil and gas –, the economic and also the general situation of Kyrgyzstan appears quite different. The transformation shock of the early 1990s was quickly overcome if one looks at the establishment of basic organizations of a capitalist market economy. At that time, many observers heralded Kyrgyzstan the forerunner of a liberal market orientated economy and society in Central Asia. But economic development did not really take off. Today Kazakhstan can be described as a rather successful middle income country with strong traits of a resource-based state (Howie 2014: 71ff.) and a mild authoritarian rule aiming at top-down developments like e.g. Singapore (Nazarbaev 2008a: 23ff.). Kyrgyzstan belongs to the poorest countries in Central Asia and even on the world scale, that has run through a series of "revolutions", that all resulted in state capture of new groups and a constant situation of instability. State authority is weak what makes some authors classify the situation as near to a failing state. Economic output is very weak causing a high amount of outmigration from the country and remittances as being a base of survival of many households. A recent representative poll by Gallup mirrors this history of transformation. While Kazakhstani citizens overwhelmingly vote the breakdown of the Soviet Union as beneficial (45% against 25% as harmful), Kyrgyzstani citizens vote the breakdown overwhelmingly as harmful (61% against 16% as beneficial) (Gallup, acc 10.04. 2014, 21.34). Consequently, most Kazakhstani citizens in our sample view their future in bright colors while their counterparts from Kyrgyzstan mostly look at it as gloomy. All evaluations from our research have taken this general difference into account. This shows us how the collective perception of the present is always mirroring the past as a comparative folio.

If we examine the development and the current situation in the light of our empirical data on households, we can conclude, that in both countries, middle class households of the different types (poorer, middle, better off) have adapted to the established capitalist market conditions. They know about the necessity to make their own living and to rely on oneself in doing so. They know about the reduced role of the state in supplying citizens with means to make a living, although many particularly older people complain about this and bemoan the Soviet past.[232] They look for jobs in the formal and informal sector and have learned to use all their assets to make a living. Many are ready to change their location for job opportunities. Most households have direct or indirect migration experience. But while Kazakhstani households overwhelmingly migrate from rural to urban areas, Kyrgyzstani households quite often have members abroad, notably in Russia and Kazakhstan. It is a fact that the Kyrgyzstani economy does not offer many options – even not in the capital. This is quite different in the booming economy in Astana, Almaty and some more secondary cities. For Kyrgyzstani it means that the networks into which the latter households are bound into are international ones, with all the typical effects of diaspora communities, stigmatization and social exclusion in the host countries and repercussions of those in the home country. The migration of Kazakhstanis is often connected with education. Many of the younger generation go to Almaty or Astana for studying, marry fellow students and stay in the city. Some of the well-off prefer studying in Europe, the USA or Russia. On a very limited scale such an orientation can also be found in Kyrgyzstan. Of course, we can't prove this with representative numbers but the biographies of our respondents allow arguing for such a country-based distinction.

The analyses also show that the citizens in both countries are well aware of the risks of capitalist regimes, namely unemployment. They use diversification of income sources to lower the risks and they use options of subsistence production and of self-provisioning to render their households more stable. Networking aims at the same goal. Intergenerational relations are strong and are combined with mutual help. Kin represents an important social capital that is nourished by various celebrations and ceremonies like birthdays, marriages, funerals etc., and families often visit relatives living in distant locations. In urban areas and among better off households, these networks on the basis of kin or clan seem to

[232] Here we have to admit that our intended cohort analysis could not be applied, due to the chosen household approach where we sometimes changed the interview partner during the interview, as a result to major expertise in certain fields.

be more open socially including also friends, neighbors and colleagues. This tendency seems to be stronger in Kyrgyzstan than in Kazakhstan, which is due to the fact that kinship among ethnic Kazakhs particularly matters. Coherent with the literature is that for poorer households such kinship networks provide an essential insurance mechanism for themselves, however, with the obligation to reciprocate (Evers and Schrader 1994). However, when wealth increases, household members begin reflecting about advantages and disadvantages concerning this survival arrangement. The preservation of kinship networks becomes an option. Thus, many evolve into purely social networks that help in economic transactions but lose their traditional self-evident character.

The households mainly represent two or three generations. The incomes of the household members are normally pooled even if children are grown up and have their own salaries. Also pensions go into the pool. Purchases and investments are taken from that pool. Sometimes in the city this pool is confined to buying necessities of everyday life, while every contributing household member keeps a certain individual part as "pocket money". Sometimes, also the young contributing generation hands over its entire salary to the parent generation.

In addition to contributing to the household with their pensions, the grandparent generation often serves the households with gardening, child care etc.. Usually, the former is a welcomed input also if the grandparents – or relatives – don't live in the household. In some cases grandchildren spend their entire childhood with their grandparents, while the parents, father or mother are working.

Family members living outside the household are often supported also financially. This holds true for children in the process of studying, but also for pensioners. In general, family members represent a social capital that can be activated if necessary. First of all this concerns monetary or labor contributions to the household budget in case of emergencies and sometimes even on a regular or permanent basis. This is the case especially with poorer households and to a certain degree also with middle households. And this concerns also the help of urban relatives when the children of rural ones study in the city and become cohabitants of them. This may imply not only a short period of entry into studying but often lasts the entire study period, and sometimes lasts even longer when graduates are looking for or enter their first job. We have to emphasize that the hosting of kin in limited space of urban apartments (usually one to three rooms) provides a burden for the host family. In this way quite often, rural-urban locations are thus bridged and family relations are upheld.

In general, our research affirms the differentiation of economic practices and thus the existence of portfolio budgets based on portfolio work to secure the livelihoods of the households. The economic practices imply "those involving market relations, those involving non-market relations and those concerning alternative market relations" (Smith and Stenning, 2006: 193). For the economy as such, the exchange networks predominantly among kinfolk, sometimes extended to friends, which we investigated in our empirical study seem to be a structural element for these two economies. If they represent only a temporary element on the basis of the still ongoing transformation process or if they represent one further "variety" of capitalism[233] is difficult to judge on the basis of our data and needs further research. We are inclined to argue that this is a variety of capitalism, not only because of the described processes but also because of the traditional role of families and households in the two societies. Traditionally orientated Kazakhs as well as Kyrgyz claim that this is their way of living, which is different from Western societies. They hold that even modernization in the cities has no eroding effect on the larger family and kinship network. Putting this issue into the context of modernization theory this would indeed be a different modernization path. However, twenty years of rapid modernization after independence is of course a period which is too short to draw such far-reaching conclusions, although we have to admit that also the communist experiment, which had enormous consequences for family and kinship, was not able to break the family tradition, as cultural practices from every day-life in Central Asia during the Soviet period highlight (cf. Kamp 2007).[234]

The households also have accommodated to saving and to credit. Credits may be taken from financial organizations or from kin or rarely others. Taking them can be a normal economic action or expression of bare necessities. Poorer households quite often declare their inability to save in cash. For them subsistence production or the help in kind by members of the network are of utmost importance to decrease living costs and to survive. For many rural households cattle represents savings, investments and insurance against risks. But also some urban households with rural network links own cattle, sheep or horses that are managed by their kinfolk in the countryside. Some of them emphasize the multiple functions of this: to accumulate by breeding, by reaching stability against inflation, by selling to

233 The Variety of Capitalism discussion from economic sociology discusses cultural specifics of Anglo-Saxon/US-American and continental European, as well as East Asian and post-socialist forms of capitalism (cf. Hall and Soskice 2001; Hancké, Rhodes, and Thatcher 2007; Myant 2012; Orruì 1997).

234 Kamp shows on the basis of articles from a journal from the 1930s in Uzbekistan how a compromise between the time and cost-cutting of marriage practices in Soviet time was found with the cultural practice to celebrate extensively. Although this is only an example even from another Central Asia state it indicates to the strength of cultural practices concerning kinship and family.

obtain cash, by reaching food security through slaughtering in possible worst case scenarios of world economic crisis or civil wars.

In general, savings and credits serve different means. But it is obvious, that households save for provisions, the states and the state security systems do not or insufficiently supply them with: housing, health care, pensions, and (higher) education. Another reason for saving and credits is orientated towards the maintenance of kinship networks. Orientations towards savings and credits may be more traditional, normatively orientated or more economically, rationally orientated. The occasions concerned are births, marriages, funerals, visits of relatives etc.. A third purpose for savings and credits is more economically motivated and refers to consumptive and investment issues like vacation, cars, repairs, cattle, land, business activities, housing, etc.. One specialty concerning savings and credits is worthwhile mentioning here. Many Kazakhstani citizens but also some of their Kyrgyzstani counterparts save and take up credits for the education of their children, and this preference ranges very high among the reasons being mentioned in our quantitative and qualitative data. They consider this as an investment in the future of their children – this is what economists call 'human capital formation' – but also for themselves. The latter is attributed to the ethnic Kazakh and Kyrgyz traditional obligations of help for the elderly parents – with clear-cut norms who of the children will take responsibility to do so. This contributes to the stability of the kin networks. And there is hardly evidence in our sample that this norm is undermined by modernization. Only few respondents who according to birth had to take this role complain that their older brothers and their families are better off and could contribute more. But the support as such is not scrutinized by them.

How far are savings, credit-taking and insurance provisions of private households in our sample related to the new market organizations? We have already emphasized the importance of security networks among kin as a distinct form of economic practices. We have to mention that the organized insurance business for life, old age, health etc. is negligible from the perspective of private households – apart from the obligatory forms, that exist. But what about banks?

High amounts of saving on a savings account or in financial instruments such as stocks could not be observed in our sample. This can be due to the fact that transformation happened only two decades ago and within that rather short period middle-class households invested in real estate and higher consumer goods rather than in financial products. Besides, however, much saving is done at home. Not that banks do not offer such accounts for middle-class households, but the majority in the sample, both urban and rural, takes a negative stance towards banks. This holds true for both savings and credit offers. Only few households also emphasize the positive aspects of credit taking from banks. The majority of respondents use their kinship networks for taking – mainly interest-free – credits, while others also report having bank credit(s) or – in rural regions – micro credits from micro credit organizations. Concerning banks, some of the respondents declare state banks more reliable than private ones. In general, credits serve the same means as savings. But the majority reports either own negative experience with bank credits (too costly, too complicated) or refers to negative experiences of friends and relatives. If the negative attitude towards banks is a more general attitude prevailing from Soviet times and its rhetoric or if this is a more time bound reaction from the past financial crises or from bad experiences in general is difficult to judge. Looking at the whole sample, we would hypothesize that remnants of the past are blended with a general critique towards capitalism, banks being believed to represent the 'bad' side of it.

A considerable number of respondents especially from poorer and middle households report difficulties in handling credits. For sure, some of the poorer households are indebted: they can only repay one credit by taking up another one. Many respondents, however, emphasized that they only realized the cost of their credit once the contract was running for some time and they had to repay much higher amounts than taken. This may account for the negative stance towards bank credits. Additionally, we have to keep in mind the general practice to ask for credits from relatives that are often interest-free. Even the financing of apartments occurs via kinship networks. With regard to religion we can't prove more general objections against commercial banks stemming from Muslim belief against *riba*, interest (cf. Schrader 2000b) or a vivid flourishing of Islamic banking practices in Kazakhstan or Kyrgyzstan. And also the absence of interest in borrowing from kinfolk seems to be more a social than a religious phenomenon. Only in one interview out of 450 quantitative and 150 qualitative one woman referred to religious beliefs concerning credit and interest.

Overbridging short term cash squeezes by credits can be found among certain rural households and certain urban jobholders because of the seasonality of their incomes. The purchase of an apartment or house is very common in Central Asia, since there is no real market for renting, and since from the perception of the interviewees "investments in concrete" are safer than bank investments. Like in the West people who take up credits for financing the purchase of an apartment or a house have high debts and can only repay these over a longer period. Only some of the better-off households in the sample discovered the investment in houses or apartments as a source for generating a constant flow of income. This may indicate that sooner or later a housing market for rent will develop in the cities, since the prices for purchases have been increasing considerably.

In order to judge the households' endowment with assets, we used the sustainable livelihoods approach SLA[235] referring to physical capital, financial capital, human capital, social capital and natural capital. In Ch. 1 we discussed the relatedness to Bourdieu's analytic model of the forms of capital We argued that the SLA is under complex when it comes to resources, power and class aspects. Therefore we referred to such aspects in our data analysis, and particularly in Ch. 5 where we aggregated copings of households into types of middle-class: poorer, middle und better-off. Aspects of reproduction of household class status and therefore class became visible. For example, with regard to human capital we found the tendency that in addition to the best affordable education middle-class households have an enormous expectation to their children not only what concerns their later professions but also what concerns class representation. For example, we found that in addition to the high workload at schools many middle-class children visited ballet (girls) and music schools (boys and girls) – a typical expression of cultural capital of the "*intelligentsia*", the higher educational but not necessarily economically better-off class. Others prefer sports clubs. In the same way wealth is nowadays displayed in expensive lifestyles This may be interpreted as representing cultural capital and symbolic capital in Bourdieu's terminology

For a view on the endowment with capitals, rural-urban differences are very important. On one hand, rural households are more vulnerable concerning cash but food scarcity plays only a little role while in the urban contexts, the latter finds more concerns in urban households due to high (and rising) prices for food in the supermarkets and shops. Of course, this difference is closely related to the component of subsistence production as natural capital what we find far more spread in rural areas than in urban ones. Compared to urban households rural ones complain more often about scarcity of and low paid, inadequate jobs not allowing them to gain a sufficient income thus causing them to organize survival with help of different forms of self-provisioning. This finding shows up in the qualitative as well as in the quantitative research. Some rural households also complain about the endowment with physical capital, especially the bad transport and schooling facilities. They argue that this situation hampers their wellbeing and the betterment of their households. The job situation, the need of subsistence production as well as bad physical capital make up for push factors concerning

[235] cf. Asian Development Bank 2008; Chambers 1992, 1994; Espling 1999; Evans 2002a, 2002b; Morse and McNamara 2013; Mukherjee 2001; Tacoli 1998.

migration. They seem to be very prevalent among poorer groups of our middle class households in rural areas in Kazakhstan as well as in Kyrgyzstan. Some households in the qualitative sample reported about family members working in different locations others about their planning to move.

Especially the educational options in the countryside seem to be a motive of considerable concern in general and concerning moving options. In these cases kin relations play an important role of support as pull factors. Relatives in the cities may house, finance or generally help youngsters, thus enhancing the options for a better education. The difference in educational options between the countryside and the cities is one major element that upholds and stabilizes kin relations of the households. In all qualitative interviews education played a major role in the middle class households underlining its central role for social positioning. Achievement in society – one may conclude – is predominantly regarded as provided by human capital. All households bother about the necessary investments in human capital. With savings and credits the households try to stabilize and enhance intergenerational options. Investments and disappointments lead to strong criticism about the state of education in the countries of the interviewees. To give an example: parents report that they made their children study economics believing this to be a good investment in the future. But having finished their study children and parents had to learn, that there were only job openings for accountants. Among these parents, this example represents a more general insight, the misfit between the educational and the employment system. And many of these parents report that access to jobs depends on parents' position and on 'acquaintances'. Furthermore, we have to take the macro-conditions of both countries into consideration. Even the Kazakhstani economy which is booming is a predominantly commercial economy with limited production. Also in Kyrgyzstan which has been stagnating or even deteriorating with regard to the economy, production came to a standstill in the post-socialist period. As a consequence of this, bookkeepers are in higher demand than economists which are often overqualified for commerce.

The endowment with financial capital does not only mean to have more money and a better equipped household but also to have more favorable options for social positioning in society. To follow Bourdieu, we would like to stress, that these households are able to display a high degree of convertibility of their assets. All capital forms taken into account, the favorable class position of the better off households is responsible for the stability of them, chances for upward mobility included. The better off households have more choices: better access to different and multiple job holdings making cash available, thus enhancing their options to render their households more secure by a multitude of means that help to avoid risks. Some report e.g. that they keep a herd of cattle in the countryside for possible bad days, what additionally implies high esteem among ethnic Kazakhs and Kyrgyz, both countries strongly referring to their nomadic origins. These households can invest strongly into human capital to secure their future and that of their offspring. Not only with these educational titles but also with help of 'acquaintances', that is the network the household is bound into, these households have better access to state positions as well as to private business life. That means not only the households themselves are better equipped in societies' social struggles but also their networks. On the other side of the social ladder we have to conclude that especially among poorer households convertibility of capitals is low and thus risk avoidance is structurally limited and vulnerability is high. With our analysis we can confirm the findings of network theory and theories on social capital that households in a higher social position have broader, more diverse and more 'valuable' network relations, expressing themselves in better access to chances. (cf. Coleman 1988; Portes 1998)

Social capital is not only a valuable means to enhance household options for economic wellbeing through mutual help. In both countries, it is deeply connected with 'blat' (Ledeneva 1998, 2006), favors, 'gifts' etc., all forms of briberies and corruption. Households speak out quite freely about briberies and blackmailing. They report about corruptive practices like gaining jobs, having access to subsidies for housing, finding kindergarten places, paying for the access to and good results in the educational system, getting justice, being fairly treated by the police and by public officials and civil servants, getting medical treatment according to their entitlements etc. That is, all spheres of their lives and practices are touched. This is very much in tune with the results of the 2013 global corruption barometer as issued by the NGO Transparency International.[236] Despite the complaints of the interviewees about corruption, most give and take bribes. The practice belongs to their normal behavior in everyday life. The explanations for this behavior are different. Some see it as a pure necessity without which certain services or positions are not available. For them it is part of the struggle for survival on all levels of society. Others differentiate, naming as corruption only the immoral behavior of the rich and the persons of influence in society.[237] Others explain it as a national characteristic thus downplaying its harm to society. For them it is a form of gratitude and mutual gift exchange with high appreciation. One medical doctor illuminated this orientation by explaining that she would never go to another doctor without a

[236] http://www.transparency.org/gcb2013/report, access date 05-05-14)

[237] Similar argumentations we found in our research on small enterprises in Russia, the Czech Republic and in Bulgaria (Dittrich, Schrader, and Stojanov 2006; Dittrich et al. 2008).

gift showing her gratitude for the treatment. Mostly, the evaluation of corruption is contradictory. In general, it represents a structural component by which positions, titles, options and chances in the two societies are distributed. The practice and the justifications sharply contradict to all ideas about achievement by education and personal abilities strongly articulated as basic social values by the members of this middle class and found in our research. Meritocracy as ideal is challenged by the practice of corruption.

In our quantitative sample, nuclear families were dominant and their members strongly expressed their way of living as devoted to themselves as individuals. Only a limited number of households were embedded in broader exchange relations with others especially kin. We don't want and we can't refute this result. But we have to conclude from our qualitative results, that social capital is a very important asset for the households. Social capital implies networks of mainly kin relations and those of a broader group of people. According to our qualitative interviews these networks are of eminent importance for all respondents. Individual action is turned into a network based action. This relational orientation concerns the identity of the interviewees, especially if they were ethnic Kazakh or Kyrgyz. Many respondents explain this orientation towards kin relations as an ethnic trait. Some declare it as an element of national identity, thus excluding other ethnics from the nation. Individualism may be getting stronger in both societies as observers have argued hinting at the spread of nuclear families, growing divorce rates and lone parent households or selfishness in behavior. But the daily conduct of life, '*Lebensführung*' in the sense of Max Weber, is strongly organized along kin relations at least among ethnic Kazakhs and maybe to a lesser degree among ethnic Kyrgyz and ethnic Russians. In general, conduct of life is organized along the lines of the support networks of which we find numerous examples in our interviews[238] These kin networks have to be nourished. In our qualitative material we find all different modes of exchange, anthropological literature since long has revealed: symmetric and direct, with reciprocal delay or as generalized reciprocity (Lévi- Strauss 1969; Mauss 1970; Sahlins 1965). To provide some examples: cash against a promise (credit) or meat against money of the same value or help in house building under the condition that later this help is given back by equivalent help or in another equivalency (all being forms of balanced reciprocity, the "gift" as a way of continuous reproduction of kinship networks; or intergenerational exchange e.g. by grandparents as a form of generalized reciprocity. Households

[238] For an interesting account showing how modern family arrangements go hand in hand with kin relations see Hofferth (1984: 791ff)

practice this networking extensively. For them, it implies a chance to keep or better one's position in society. As traditional practice it is founded in the inheritance rules among ethnic Kazakhs and Kyrgyz (but not among ethnic Russians): the youngest son inherits and has to care for the parents; brothers and sisters have to help and must be helped. This implies a network of mutual trust and exchanges. These networks sometimes may be extended by 'acquaintances'. This orientation towards network orientated social and economic exchanges means normality of life for many of our interviewees. For some this even implies cohabitation as highly esteemed form of living. The importance of networking does not correlate to specific household groups of the middle classes in Kazakhstan and Kyrgyzstan although the power of these networks may change as already shown. From our qualitative research we can't judge whether networking is more prevalent in rural or urban areas. What we can say is, that some networks comprise more members than others, some hardly expand nuclear families, some are nearly restricted to one locality, others are spread all over the nation state or are even bridging national borders, some are more economically driven, that is are orientated more to economic benefits and are based on rational calculations, others are more traditional and are deeply enshrined in the general belief system of its members but nevertheless constitute aspects of security provision, also in economic matters. Although there are tendencies towards nuclear families with self-orientated individual interests, we argue that the developing economic system is largely connected and maybe even based on networks mainly from kin. That is, transformation in Kazakhstan and in Kyrgyzstan has evolved into an economic system with a special element that is kin networks. Economic exchanges are processed partly through them. They refer to direct economic transactions, to transactions aiming at social security, to transactions that impinge on the reproduction of social structure and inequality of society. The latter may particularly hold true for Kazakhstan. While also in the West we may observe a reproduction of classes through marriage and educational practices, there is a political will of Kazakhization of society, which is a break with the Soviet past and a seamless following of real or imagined Kazakh nomadic culture and tradition. Equivalents exist also in Kyrgyzstan but maybe not so strongly. This reorientation includes a strong reference to family genealogy originating from clans and hordes, the knowledge of kinship links into the 7th generation, a tendency of endogenous marriage among ethnic Kazakhs, etc.

Households develop enduring practices in order to create sustainability. They take into account life events like births, marriages, anniversaries, funerals etc., but also shocks that stem e.g. from criminal actions, bad harvests etc., and they react to the risks of capitalism as perceived by them. These strategies are deeply intertwined with the assets, the forms of capital, the households can build upon and their convertibility (see Ch. 1). In his research, Zoomers found four class based strategies. We follow his orientation is discussing these strategies. We believe that these strategies may be found on all levels of the social hierarchy, although differently distributed. With regard to sustainability of private households, Zoomers (Zoomers and Kleinpenning 1996; Zoomers 1999) distinguishes four strategies: accumulation, consolidation, compensation and security.

- Accumulation is a long-term strategy to create a resource basis in order to enable future actions of the households being more 'profitable' than the present one (e.g. by deposits, investment in children's education etc.).
- Consolidation aims at security of existing resources and efforts by purposeful investments (e.g., in house building, purchases of cars, buying hay in summer, etc.).
- Compensation describes how negative developments or shocks are compensated through e.g. the use of social capital or the sale of economic values.
- Security is a sustainable strategy especially for those households that are near to the subsistence minimum. We assume that through diversification of activities, by referring to subsistence production, by using close reciprocity networks, and resorting to successful past crisis management etc. the households organize their survival. This kind of preventive risk management may be looked upon as a rational strategy of action if it is reflected upon or if it represents a relatively successful "muddling through" against the background of "limited rationality" in regard to the complexity of everyday life. These households use past experiences as guidelines to secure their survival. But their chances to change their social position are very limited.

In general, we also addressed these issues in our household study, but these four issues are predominantly relevant in a micro-level household approach. However, missing in Zoomers' contribution is the link to the meso and macro-levels which we aimed at by introducing the class aspect. Therefore, we put more stress on the convertibility of the forms of capital. On the micro level convertibility implies flexibility that is a general orientation in the life course that helps households to adjust to different constellations they may enter or be pushed into. Convertibility is especially important for crisis situations. But already in these micro-level strategies meso and macro aspects come in. Households e.g. may resort to (re)activating of private security networks they have invested into in the past. Here, different networks may provide different chances not only to cope with insecurity, but also to overcome it in the long run, e.g. by setting up another business with advice and the financial help of relatives or friends. Or, they may reactivate subsistence production to make themselves more independent from the market by slaughtering cattle they have kept with kinfolk in the countryside. Or, they may close their deposits in order to pay for expenses stemming from a marriage or a funeral.

Accumulation strategies, we hypothesized, would more often be used by better off households while poorer middle class households would more often use security strategies to reach sustainability. To give an example: we assumed that also poorer households save and accumulate but their assets only allow for few chances to do so and the realization of these chances is often endangered by unforeseeable events like sudden job losses, by personal shocks like deaths or urgent need of relatives they can't repudiate. And indeed, we found many examples that can be taken as proof about these restricted possibilities of poorer households even when they try and are aware of the necessity to accumulate in order to fights risks and vulnerabilities of their households. In general, poorer households live in more precarious constellations; their vulnerability is high, if compared to better off households.[239] But because of this vulnerability, many of such households cannot gamble about chances and losses; they show a more risk-averse behavior like households from lower classes but therefore do not sustainably change their living conditions. To give another example: all middle class households have a high appreciation of education to render households more secure by transferring better life chances to the next generation. They also explain that under the present situation – capitalist market economies – this attempt is one of the most important aims in their lives. Therefore also many poorer households try to save, take up credits, sometimes getting considerably indebted and use all their social capital. Most struggle hard to reach their aim. Nevertheless, their assets, their exposure to vulnerabilities, their life practices, their chances to position their offspring in better jobs only allow for limited realization of chances with help of educational achievements.

Poorer households only dispose over few assets with low convertibility. Usually they have no choice among job openings; they have to take those jobs that are available or develop their own creativity to survive in the informal sector. Access to jobs with a long term perspective is limited. Most frequent is that the inter-

[239] In the following we often compare better off and poorer households in order to better illuminate the different strategies.

viewees combine a job with subsistence production. Consolidation mainly stems from this, or additionally from pensions that may go into the budget or from the multiplicity of activities bringing some limited income as basis for the household budget. Their job holdings supply them with little cash and payment may even be irregular. Especially those working in the informal sector are threatened by frequent job losses. The histories of their job holdings they told us reveal a tendency towards job hopping, making consolidation unlikely. Other members of the households or the networks, who contribute to the household budget, often show the same characteristics concerning the endowment with capitals. Informal activities are strongly represented among this group. They are characterized by low protection of contracts and often by give-and-take transactions. Titles and credits, mostly from secondary schools, do not only account for lower cash returns but also for a higher exposure to replacements if we compare the three groups of middle class households. In rural areas of both countries, cash orientated activities are so scarce, that nearly all households of our qualitative sample reflect about the chances of migration, be it for themselves, their children, or for single members of the households. Some of the households in the sample were preparing to leave. E.g.. they took part in the state housing program in Kazakhstan in order to move to Astana or Almaty or they were about to send a grown up child to Russia to join others working there already. Subsistence production for self-provisioning is a security option in these households they all use. The reliance on subsistence production decreases with the affiliation to higher groups in the middle class. The poorer households rely on garden plots, poultry, sheep etc. for their survival strategies. Those who do not have direct access to subsistence production use their kin network and exchange their manpower for produce from relatives' gardens and meat. Some poorer urban households also keep some cattle with relatives in the countryside. All these different types of self-provisioning are essential for the survival of the households. This contrasts strongly to some urban households who keep cattle in the countryside to show a certain traditional standing. In the qualitative sample, all interviewees underline the importance of kin relations in their lives. But most strongly poorer households rely on them. Among the other two groups we find reflections about the side effects of kin relations in doing business, concerning the traditional obligations and concerning individual choices, intergenerational problems included. Among middle and better off households some respondents even argue that the elder generation and the younger one should live apart. Few take provisions that this can really happen by supplying the younger generation with housing at a different location. All poorer households employ certain compensation strategies to protect themselves against risks or to overcome sudden shocks or events that could not be foreseen. That is they follow a precautionary principle. They may sell cattle, they have raised or even household appliances; they may borrow money from people belonging to their network; single household members may migrate for a short time or for longer to overcome the dilemma they are in. Also savings and credits are used to overcome the situation and to fight their vulnerability. But these households are not only poorer than the others in monetary terms but also their means to protect themselves, to develop compensatory strategies are limited. They don't possess larger herds of cattle, they own few household appliances; the people, they know from their network are mostly in similar economic situations; their savings are small and their creditworthiness is low. Based on all of our research material, we conclude that the networks of poorer households are more closed and often rely solely on kin, while among the other groups also colleagues, friends, acquaintances etc. belong to the network. Together with their relatively limited other assets, this accounts for our conclusion, that their compensation strategies rely on less options if compared with those of other households. Poorer households are disadvantaged also in this respect.

Their very limited chances to accumulate and to consolidate their households given, the main strategies of poorer households rely on means to compensate for vulnerabilities they experience and to build up a basic security for their households. All in all, it is clear that the strategies of this class of households mainly result in keeping their present position, upward mobility being rather improbable. Furthermore, in our interviews we can find good reasons for arguing that the present position of these households in the social hierarchy becomes socially inherited to the next generation. Children move back to their parents and join the household of their parents again because of failure to build up a household of their own. Migration does not decouple from the household and migrants move back to the parents' households. And in case of unemployment, people live in those households that might help them to stay on their own feet again. In all these cases, it is kin relations that represent security between generations.

Better off households are not only able to compensate for losses, shocks and vulnerabilities in general but they are able to consolidate their households and thus to live complete different lives than the poorer households. A better off farmer e.g. will buy hay in summer and will do it on credit as a quite normal, calculable established practice that implies routinized relations with his bank. It is an economic transaction not to worry about. As already mentioned above, the endowment with capitals and their convertibility is much better in this group than in the poorer one. Some households report about taking up a second job even in the state sector in order to render their incomes bigger and steadier. This allows them to look for better options for profitable accumulation. Real estate investments are widespread among this group. And as in the two other groups, education plays an important role concerning intergenerational consolidation and chances for upward mobility. Their possibilities allow them to send their offspring to the best schools and universities and to find them favorable jobs. If they don't find grants, financing education is self-evident for these households. Usually these students don't live in state dormitories but in rented or owned apartments. The financial capital of these households allows for regular vacations in the country or abroad while among the poorer households vacation often means to go to see relatives while the middle group of households has to labor in order to get enough savings for vacations. The networks of these better off households support their accumulation strategies. They do not mainly represent kin relations but also include colleagues, people from the administrations and from politics etc. Some of these households report about considerable savings and investments that document their financial power. They display a lifestyle near to affluence: big SUVs, housing in well protected fashionable regions, accentuation of a healthy diet and a healthy lifestyle, use of service providers. Some donate and thus take a public role. The accumulation strategy often combines positions in the state sector with activities in the private one. As in all other groups, all grown up members work. There were no reports of unemployed members of the households of this group of middle class households. On average, all members of the household have good positions with good monetary incomes. These households have fully accommodated to the risks of the present capitalist market societies, the well reflected use of their options included. Their orientation is usually long term while especially the poorer households only can calculate short term. Their protective options in respect of vulnerabilities, shocks, seasonality etc. are good and their coping abilities are based on thoroughly calculated investments, deliberate organization of network support, and by an orientation at the future. Better off households have made their ways into the new economy and the new society. Their household strategies aim at consolidation and further accumulation.

All in all, Zoomers' survival strategies have proven to be a good instrument to research survival strategies of households; their particular value lies in the linkage of the micro-level, the household analysis, to different social groups and classes, as has been shown in the two last chapters.

7. Literature

Akerlof, George. 2010. *Animal Spirits: How Human Psychology Drives the Economy, and Why It Matters for Global Capitalism*. Princeton N.J.; Woodstock: Princeton University Press.

Allan, Graham and Graham Crow. 2001. *Families, Households and Society – Sociology for a Changing World*. Basingstoke [u.a.]: Palgrave. Retrieved February 28, 2013 (http://www.gbv.de/dms/hbz/toc/ht013488830.pdf).

Anagnost, A. 1997. *National Past-Times: Narrative, Representation and Power*. Durham,N.C.: Duke University Press.

Anderson, Benedict. 1983. *Imagined Communities. Reflections on the Origin and Spread of Nationalism*. London: Verso.

Asian Development Bank. 2005. *The Kyrgyz Republic. A Gendered Transition. Soviet Legacies and New Risks*. Manila.

Asian Development Bank. 2008. *The Sustainable Livelihoods Approach (by Olivier Serrat)*. Retrieved (http://www.adb.org/sites/default/files/publication/27638/sustainable-livelihoods-approach.pdf).

Bali Swain, Ranjula. 2012. *The Microfinance Impact*. London;New York: Routledge. Retrieved August 29, 2013 (http://www.worldcat.org/title/microfinance-impact/oclc/712124057&referer=brief_results).

Banerjee, Abhijit V. and Esther Duflo. 2012. *Poor Economics: A Radical Rethinking of the Way to Fight Global Poverty*. New York, NY: Public Affairs. Retrieved April 3, 2013 (http://www.gbv.de/dms/bowker/toc/9781610390934.pdf).

Baudrillard, Jean. 1981. *La Société de Consommation: Ses Myths, Ses Structures*. [Paris]: Gallimard.

Bauman, Zygmunt. 1998. *Work, Consumerism and the New Poor*. Buckingham, Philadelphia: Open University Press.

Beck, Ulrich. 2011. *Fernliebe: Lebensformen im globalen Zeitalter*. Berlin: Suhrkamp.

Beck, Ulrich and Elisabeth Beck-Gernsheim. 2002. *Individualization: Institutionalized Individualism and its Social and Political Consequences*. London; Thousand Oaks, Calif.: Sage.

Becker, K. F. 2004. *Fact-Finding Study -The Informal Economy CDIP/11/INF/5 Annex, Page 12 P. World Economic Outlook Database*. Stockkolm. Retrieved (http://www.imf.org).

Benda-Beckmann, Franz and Keebet von. 2000. *Coping with Insecurity: An "Underall" Perspective on Social Security in the Third World (2nd Ed.)*. Yogyakarta: Pustaka Pelajar.

Ben-Porath, Yoram. 1978. *The F-Connection. Families, Friends and Firms in the Organisation of Exchange*. Rand Paper Series P-6323. Santa Monica, Cal.

Ben-Porath, Yoram. 1980. *The F-Connection. Families, Friends and Firms in the Organisation of Exchange* . Population and Development Review6(1):1–30.

Bensmann, M. 2007. *Viel Zensur, Wenig Freiheit. Medien in Zentralasien.* Osteuropa -Stuttgart- Deutsche Verlags Anstalt- 57(8/9):531–42. Retrieved December 27, 2013 (http://www.worldcat.org/title/viel-zensur-wenig-freiheit-medien-in-zentralasien/oclc/212191213&referer=brief_results).

Blau, David. 1998. *Labour Force Transitions of Older Married Couples in Germany.* London: Centre for Economic Policy Research. Retrieved August 30, 2013 (http://www.worldcat.org/title/labour-force-index{Transition}transitions-of-older-married-couples-in-germany/oclc/39759864&referer=brief_results).

Bohle, Hans. 1993. *The Space of Vulnerability: The Causal Structure of Hunger and Famine.* [Emmitsburg MD: National Emergency Training Center]. Retrieved June 10, 2013 (http://www.worldcat.org/title/space-of-index{Vulnerability}vulnerability-the-causal-structure-of-hunger-and-famine/oclc/503616824&referer=brief_results).

Bonnen, K. et al. 2007. *Sustainable Livelihood Approach und das Konzept der Vulnerabilität.* Retrieved (www.geographie.rub.de/ag/rur/methoden_der_ef_pahs/sla_bonnen_jaensch_messink.pdf, 04.07.2009).

Bourdieu, Pierre. 1986. *The Forms of Capital.* Pp. 241–58 in Handbook of Theory and Research for the Sociology of Education, vol. 241, edited by John G Richardson. Greenwood Press.

Brad, A. 2008. *Der Sustainable Livelihood Ansatz.* Retrieved (http://othes.univie.ac.at/3054/1/2008-10-07_0008994.pdf, 16.07.2009).

Brück, Tilman et al. 2012. *Household Survey Data for Research on Well-Being and Behavior in Central Asia.* Berlin.

Brunnsweiler, C. N. and E. H. Bulte. 2009. *Natural Resources and Violent Conflict: Resource Abundance, Dependence and the Onset of Civil Wars.* OxCarre Research Paper No. 2009-18.

Bryant, Wilfried. 2006. *The Economic Organization of the Household.* New York [etc.]: Cambridge University Press. Retrieved June 3, 2013 (http://www.worldcat.org/title/economic-organization-of-the-index{Household} household/oclc/781479974?referer=br&ht=edition).

Burt, Ronald S. 2004. *Structural Holes and Good Ideas.* American Journal of Sociology 110(2):349–99.

Buvinic, M., M. Da Gupta, and U. Casabonne. 2009. *Gender, Poverty and Demography.* World Bank Economic Review 23(2).

Castles, Stephen, Evaluation Office of the United Nations High Commissioner for Refugees, and Unit Policy Analysis. 2002. *Environmental Change and Forced Migration: Making Sense of the Debate.* Geneva: Unhcr.

Chambers, Robert. 1992. *Poverty in India: Concepts, Research and Reality.* Pp. 301–32 in Poverty in India. Research and Policy, edited by B et al. Harriss. Bombay et al.: Oxford University Press.

Chambers, Robert. 1994. *Poverty and Livelihoods: Whose Reality Counts?.* New York, N.Y.: United Nations Development Programme.

Charles, N. and M. Kerr. 1999. *Women's Work.* in The sociology of the family: A reader, edited by Graham Allan. Oxford: Blackwell.

Clarke, Simon. 1999. *New Forms of Employment and Household Survival Strategies in Russia*. Coventry, UK: Centre for Comparative Labour Studies, University of Warwick.

Clarke, Simon. 2002a. *Making Ends Meet in Contemporary Russia: Secondary Employment, Subsidiary Agriculture, and Social Networks*. Cheltenham UK; Northampton MA: E. Elgar.

Clarke, Simon. 2002b. *Sources of Subsistance and the Survival Strategies of Urban Russian Households*. in Work, Employment and Transition. Restructuring Livelihoods in Post-Communist Eastern Europe, edited by A. Smith, A. Rainnie, and A. Swain. London: Routledge.

Coleman, James. 1987. *Norms as Social Capital*. in Economic Imperialism – The Econmic Method Applied Outside the Field of Economics, edited by G Radnitzky and P Bernhold. New York: Peragon.

Coleman, James. 1988. *Social Capital in the Creation of Human Capital*. American Journal of Sociology 94 (Suppl.:95–120.

Demszky, A. M. 2005. *Alltägliche Gesellschaft. Netzwerke alltäglicher Lebensführung in einer großstädtischen Wohnsiedlung*. München: Hampp.

Denizer, C., H. Wolf, and Y. Ying. 2002. *Household Savings in the Transition*. Journal of Comparative Economics 30:463–75.

Dittrich, Eckhard. 2001. *Wandel, Wende, Wiederkehr. Transformationen – Gesellschaftlicher Wandel*. Würzburg: ERGON.

Dittrich, Eckhard and Ingrid Oswald. 2010. *Jenseits Der Städte: Postsozialistische Lebensweisen in ländlichen Regionen Mittel- Und Osteuropas – Gesellschaftliche Transformationen = Societal Transformations; 16*. Berlin [u.a.]: LIT-Verl. Retrieved April 29, 2014 (http://www.dandelon.com/servlet/download/attachments/dandelon/ids/CH0014A58E3F442614FDEC12579530044615B.pdf).

Dittrich, Eckhard, Ingrid Oswald, and Viktor Voronkov. 2002. *Einleitung: Wandel alltäglicher Lebensführung im postsowjetischen Russland.* Pp. 7–24 in. Retrieved April 29, 2014 (http://gso.gbv.de/DB=2.1/PPNSET?PPN=573449376).

Dittrich, Eckhard, Heiko Schrader, and Christo Stojanov. 2006. *Von Wirten und anderen Entrepreneuren: Kleinunternehmen in Bulgarien, Tschechien und der Russischen Föderation*. 1. Aufl. Berlin [u.a.]: LIT.

Dittrich, Eckhard, Heiko Schrader, and Christo Stojanov. 2008. *The Development of Small Enterprieses in Bulgaria, Czech Republic and Russian Federation*. Journal for East European Management Studies (JEEMS) 13(2):129–53.

Douglas, Mary and Baron Isherwood. 1996. *The World of Goods. Towards an Anthropology of Consumption (repr. 1979)*. London: Routledge.

Duflo, E. 2012. *Armut*. Süddeutsche Zeitung 220 (22-23 Sep).

Eisenstadt, S. N. and L. Roniger. 1966. *Patron-Client Relations as a Model of Structuring Social Exchange*. in The Social Anthropology of Complex Societies, edited by M Banton. London.

Elwert, Georg, Hans-Dieter Evers, und Werner Wilkens. 1983. *Die Suche nach Sicherheit.*

Kombinierte Produktionsformen im sogenannten informellen Sektor. Zeitschrift für Soziologie 12(4):281–96.

Espling, M. 1999. *Women's Livelihood Strategies in Processes of Change: Cases from Urban Mozambique.* Göteborg Univ., School of Economics and Commerical Law.

European Bank of Reconstruction and Development. 2012. *Crisis and Transition. Transition Report 2011.*

Evans, P. 2002a. *Introduction: Looking for Agents of Urban Livability in a Globalized Political Economy.* Pp. 1–30 in Livable Cities? Urban Struggles for Livelihood and Sustainability, edited by P Evans. Berkeley / Los Ageles: University of California Press.

Evans, P. 2002b. *Political Strategies for More Livable Cities: Lessons from Six Cases of Development and Political Transition.* Pp. 222–46 in Livable Cities? Urban Struggles for Livelihood and Sustainability, edited by P Evans. Berkeley / Los Angeles: University of California Press.

Evers, Hans-Dieter. 1994. *The Traders' Dilemma. A Theory of the Social Transformation of Markets and Society.* Pp. 7–14 in The Moral Economy of Trade. Ethnicity and Developing Markets, edited by H.-D. Evers and H Schrader. London: Routledge.

Evers, Hans-Dieter and Heiko Schrader. 1994. *The Moral Economy of Trade. Ethnicity and Developing Markets.* London: Routledge.

Fuller, G. E. 1994. *Central Asia. The Quest for Indentity.* Current History 93(582):145–49.

George, Julie A. 2009. *Expecting Ethnic Conflict: The Soviet Legacy and Ethnic Politics in the Caucasus and Central Asia.* London: Routledge.

Gilster, A. and H. Hättich. 2007. *Niedergang, Stagnation, Aufstieg, Bildung und Gesundheit in Zentralasien.* Osteuropa 57(8/9):511–30. Retrieved December 27, 2013 (http://www.worldcat.org/title/niedergang-stagnation-aufstieg-bildung-und-gesundheit-in-zentralasien/oclc/212191211&referer=brief_results).

Goodland, R. n.d. *Sustainability: Human, Social, Economic and Environmental.* Washington D. C. Retrieved (www.balticuniv.uu.se/index.php/component/docman/doc_download/435-sustainability-human-social-economic-and-index{Environment}environmental).

Gouldner, Alvin. 1960. *The Norm of Reciprocity. A Preliminary Statement.* American Social Review 25(2):161–78.

Granovetter, Mark. 1983. *The Strength of Weak Ties: A Network Theory Revisited* edited by P V Marsden and N Lin. Sociological Theory 1(1983):201–33.

Gregory, Chris A. 1997. *Exchange and Reciprocity.* in Companion Encyclopedia of AnthropologyHumanity, Culture and Social Life, edited by T Ingold. London: Routledge.

Gubhaju, Bina and Gordon F. De Jong. 2009. *Individual Versus Household Migration Decision Rules: Gender and Marital Status Differences in Intentions to Migrate in South Africa.* International migration (Geneva, Switzerland) 47(1):31–61.

De Haan, Leo and Annelies Zoomers. 2005. *Exploring the Frontier of Livelihoods Research.* Development and Change 36(1):27–47.

Halbach, Uwe. 2007. *Das Erbe der Sowjetunion. Kontinuität und Brüche in Zentralasien.* Osteuropa 9(21):77–98.

Hall, P. A. and D. Soskice. 2001. *Varieties of Capitalism. The Institutional Foundations of Comparative Advantage.* Oxford: Oxford Univ. Press.

Hamilton, G. G. and N. Woolsey Biggart. 1992. *Market, Culture and Authority: A Comparative Analysis of Management and Organisation in the Far East.* in The Sociology of Economic Life, edited by M Granovetter and R Swedberg. Boulder: Westview.

Hancké, Bob, Martin Rhodes, and Mark Thatcher. 2007. *Introduction: Beyond Varieties of Capitalism.* Oxford u.a.: Oxford Univ. Press.

Haug, Sonja and Sonja Pointner. 2007. *Soziale Netzwerke, Migration und Integration.* Pp. 367–96 in. Retrieved August 16, 2013 (http://gso.gbv.de/DB=2.1/PPNSET?PPN=557167159).

Hess, Jeniffer and et al. 2000. *The Effects of Personal Level Versus Household Level. Questionnaire Design on Survey Estimates and Data Quality.* Public Opinion Quarterly 65:574–84.

Hettne, Björn. 1990. *The Contemporary Crisis. The Rise of Reciprocity.* in The Life and Work of Karl Polanyi, edited by Kari Polanyi-Levitt. Quebec: Black Rose.

Hiro, Dilip. 2009. *Inside Central Asia. A Political and Cultural History of Uzbekistan, Turkmenistan, Kszakhstan, Kyrgyzstan, Tajikistan, Turkey, and Irian.* London, New York: Overlook Duckworth.

Hirsch, Paul, Stuart Michaels, and Ray Friedman. 1987. *'Dirty Hands' versus 'Clean Models' – Is Sociology in Danger of Being Seduced by Economics?.* Theory and Society 16(3):317–36.

Hirschman, Albert O. 1974. *'Exit, Voice, and Loyalty': Further Reflections and a Survey of Recent Contributions.* 13(1):7–26. Retrieved August 29, 2013 (http://gso.gbv.de/DB=2.1/PPNSET?PPN=489024440).

Hofferth, Sandra. 1984. *Kin Networks, Race, and Family Structure.* Journal of Marriage and the Family 46(4):791–806.

Hollingsworth, J. Rogers and Robert Boyer. 1997. *Contemporary Capitalism: The Embeddedness of Institutions.* Cambridge: Cambridge Univ. Press.

Holzmann, Robert. 2003. *Risk and Vulnerability: The Forward-Looking Role of Social Protection in a Globalizing World.* Pp. 47–80 in Poverty and Social Exclusion in North and South, vol. 1, edited by Paul Mosley and Elizabeth Dowler. London: Routledge.

Howie, P. 2014. *Resource Boom and Inequality: Kazakhstan as a Case Study.* Resources policy. 39:71–79.

Ibraimova, Ainura. 2011. *Kyrgyzstan: Health System Review.* Copenhagen: European Observatory on Health Systems and Policies. Retrieved December 27, 2013 (http://www.worldcat.org/title/kyrgyzstan-index{Health}health-system-review/oclc/774092550&referer=brief_results).

Inglehart, Ronald. 2003. *Human Values and Social Change: Findings from the Values Surveys.* Leiden: Brill.

Kamp, Marianne. 2007. *The Wedding Feast: Living the New Uzbek Life in the 1930s.*

Pp. 103–14 in Everyday-Life in Central Asia: Past and Present, edited by Jeff Sahadeo and Russell G Zanca. Bloomington: Indiana Univ. Press.

Kandiyoti, Denis. 1999. *Poverty in Transition: An Ethnographic Critique of Household Surveys in Post-Soviet Central Asia.* Development and Change 30(3):499–524.

Kollmorgen, Raj and Heiko Schrader. 2003. *Einleitung: Postsozialistische Transformation und Transformationsforschung*. Pp. 7–18 in Postsozialistische Transformationen: Gesellschaft, Wirtschaft, Kultur. Theoretische Perspektiven und empirische Befunde, edited by Raj Kollmorgen und Heiko Schrader. Würzburg: Ergon.

Kolm, Serge-Christophe and J. Mercier Ythier. 2006. *Handbook on the Economics of Giving, Reciprocity and Altruism*. Amsterdam; Oxford: Elsevier.

Kotlikoff, Laurence J. 2007. *Saving*. in Concise Encyclopedia of Economics, edited by David R. Henderson. Retrieved (http://www.econlib.org/library/About.html#CEE).

Kraay, Aart. 2010. *The Worldwide Governance Indicators: Methodology and Analytical Issues*. Washington, D.C.,: The World Bank,. Retrieved November 11, 2013 (http://www.worldcat.org/title/worldwide-governance-indicators-methodology-and-analytical-issues/oclc/778847528&referer=brief_results).

Kuehnast, Kathleen R. and Nora Dudwick. 2004. *Better a Hundred Friends than a Hundred Rubles? Social Networks in Transition – The Kyrgyz Republic*. Washington, D.C.: World Bank.

Ledeneva, A. V. 1998. *Russia's Economy of Favors: Blat, Networking and Informal Exchange*. Cambridge: Cambridge University Press.

Ledeneva, Alena V. 2006. *How Russia Really Works: The Informal Practices That Shaped Post-Soviet Politics and Business*. 1. publ. Ithaca, NY [u.a.]: Cornell Univ. Press. Retrieved (http://www.loc.gov/catdir/toc/ecip0617/2006023279.html).

Lee, R. 2000. *Shelter from the Storm? Geographies of Regard in the Wolds of Horticultural Consumption and Production.* Geoforum 31(2).

Lévi- Strauss, Claude. 1969. *The Elementary Structures of Kinship*. London: Eyre and Spottiswood

Lindblom, Charles. 1969. *The Science of 'Muddling Through.'* Pp. 154–73 in Readings on Modern Organizations, edited by Amitai Etzioni. Englewood Cliffs, NY: Prentice Hall.

Lokshin, Michael et al. 2001. *Household Strategies for Coping with Poverty and Social Exclusion in Post-Crisis Russia.* Washington, D.C.: World Bank Development Research Group Poverty and Human Resources and Europe and Central Asia Region Poverty Reduction and Economic Management Sector Unit.

Luhmann, Niklas. 1988a. *Die Wirtschaft der Gesellschaft*. Frankfurt: Suhrkamp.

Luhmann, Niklas. 1988b. *Familiarity, Confidence, Trust. Problems and Alternatives.* Pp. 94–107 in Trust – Making and Breaking Co-operative Relations, edited by D Gambetta. Oxford: Basil Blackwell.

Marat, Erica. 2006. *The State-Crime Nexus in Central Asia. State, Weakness, Organized Crime, and Corruption in Kyrgyzstan and Tajikistan.* Retrieved December 27, 2013 (http://www.worldcat.org/title/state-index{Crime}crime-nexus-in-central-asia-state-weakness-organized-index{Crime}crime-and-index{Corruption}corruption-in-kyrgyzstan-and-tajikistan/oclc/166472803&referer=brief_results).

Marat, Erica. 2009. *Labor Migration in Central Asia. Implications of the Global Economic Crisis.* Retrieved December 27, 2013 (http://www.worldcat.org/title/labor-index{Migration}migration-in-central-asia-implications-of-the-global-economic-crisis/oclc/428541443&referer=brief_results).

Mathijs, E. and E. F. N. Swinnen. 1998. *The Economics of Agricultural Decollectivization in East Central Europe and the Former Soviet Union.* Economic Development and Cultural Change 47(1):1–26.

Mauss, Marcel. 1970. *The Gift. Forms and Functions of Exchange in Archaic Societies.* Glencoe, Ill.: Cohen and West.

Mayring, Philipp. 2010. *Qualitative Inhaltsanalyse. Grundlagen und Techniken.* 11., akt. Weinheim [u.a.]: Beltz. Retrieved (http://www.content-select.com/index.php?id=bib_view&ean=9783407291424).

Meuser, Michael and Ulrike Nagel. 1991. *Experteninterviews – Vielfach erprobt, wenig beachtet.* in Qualitativ-empirische Sozialforschung. Konzepte, Methoden, Analysen, edited by Detlef Garz und Klaus Kraimer. Opladen: Westdeutscher Verlag.

Misztal, Barbara A. 1996. *Trust in Modern Societies. The Search for the Bases of Social Order*. New York: Polity Press.

Morse, Stephen and McNamara, Nora. 2013. *Sustainable Livelihood Approach: A Critique of Theory and Practice*. Dordrecht: Springer.

Moser, Caroline. 1996. *Confronting Crisis: A Comparative Study of Household Responses to Poverty and Vulnerability in Four Poor Urban Communities*. Washington, DC: World Bank.

Mukherjee, A. 2001. *Perspectives of the Silent Majority: Air Pollution, Livelihood and Food Security. Indepth Studies through PRA Methods on Community Perspectives in Urban and Peri-Urban Areas of Varanasi and Faridabad, India*. Aldershot: Ashgate.

Muratbekow, S. 1979. *Kussen-Kusseke.* in Die weiße Aruana, Kasachische Erzählungen, edited by L. Weist. Berlin (DDR).

Musabaeva, A. 2008. *Internal and External Migration in Kyrgyzstan.* in Kyrgyzstan Today, Policy Briefs on Civil Society, Migration, Islam, Corruption, edited by American University of Central Asia. Social Research Center. Bishkek.

Myant, Martin. 2012. *International Integration, Varieties of Capitalism and Resilience to Crisis in Transition Economies.* Europe-Asia Studies 64(1):1-33.

Nazarbaev, Nursultan. 2008a. *Kasachstans Weg*. Berlin: Schiler.

Nazarbaev, Nursultan. 2008b. *The Kazakhstan Way*. London: Stacey International.

Nettleton, Sarah. 2006. *The Sociology of Health and Illness*. Polity. Retrieved April 9, 2013 (http://books.google.com/books?id=lqPQyS067qsC&pgis=1).

North, Douglass C. 1988. *Theorie des institutionellen Wandels*. Tübingen.

North, Douglass C. 1995. *Structural Changes of Institutions and the Process of Transformation.* Prague Economic Papers 4(3):229–34.

Nureeva R.M., ed. 2001. *Economic Subjects of Post-Soviet Russia (institutional Analysis).* Moskovskiy Obshestvennyi Nauchnyi Fond.

Orruì, Marco. 1997. *The Economic Organization of East Asian Capitalism*. Thousand Oaks Calif.: Sage Publications.
Oswald, Ingrid. 2000. *Die Nachfahren des "Homo Sovieticus". Ethnische Orientierung nach dem Zerfall Der Sowjetunion*. Berlin: Waxman.
Oswald, Ingrid, Frank Ernst, und Eckhard Dittrich. 2005. *Das industrialisierte Dorf: Zur Transformation ländlicher Lebensweisen in postsozialistischen Gesellschaften*. Münster: LIT.
Panarin, S. 2008. *Contemporary Kazakhstan Social and a Cultural Factors Change in the Provisions of the Russian Language*. Bulletin of Eurasia 4.
Portes, Alejandro. 1998. *Social Capital: Its Origins and Applications in Modern Sociology* edited by Eric L. Lesser. Annual Review of Sociology 24(1):1–24.
Portes, Alejandro. 2010. *Economic Sociology. A Systematic Inquiry*. Princeton, NY: Princeton Univ. Press.
Putnam, Robert D. 2007. *E Pluribus Unum: Diversity and Community in the Twenty-First Century – The 2006 Johan Skytte Prize Lecture*. Scandinavian Political Studies 30 (2): 137–74.
Raleigh, Clionadh, Lisa Jordan, and Idean Salehyan. 2008. *Assessing the Impact of Climate Change on Migration and Conflict*. World 24(3):1–57.
Reeves, Madeleine. 2005. *Of Credits, Kontrakty and Critical Thinking: Encountering 'Market Reforms' in Kyrgyztani Higher Eduction*. European Educational Research Journal 4(1):5–21.
Richards, Jeffrey. 1995. *The Rise of Consumer Society in Britain, 1880–1980. By John Benson. New York: Longman, 1994. Pp. Viii, 245. £32.00, Cloth £11.99, Paper*. The Journal of Economic History 55(02).
Ronsijn, Wouter. 2006. *Coping During Transition in Rural Areas: The Case of Post-Soviet Kyrgyzstan*. Working Paper No 4. Conflict Research Group Ghent University.
Roy, Olivier. 2000. *The New Central Asia: The Creation of Nations*. London [u.a.]: Tauris.
Sahlins, Marshall D. 1965. *On the Sociology of Primitive Exchange*. in The Relevance of Models for Social Anthropology, edited by M Banton. New York: Praeger.
Sahlins, Marshall David. 1963. *Poor Man, Rich Man, Big Man, Chief. Political Types in Melanesia and Polynesia*. Indianapolis: Bob Merrill.
Sancak, M. 2001. *Intra- and Inter-Ethnic Relations in Central Asia*. Report, ISSN 1618-8683, Bd. 1999/2:38–39.
Schrader, Heiko. 1997. *Changing Financial Landscapes in India and Indonesia. Sociological Aspects of Monetisation and Market Integration*. New York: St. Martin's.
Schrader, Heiko. 1999. *Ekonomitscheskaya Antropologija*. Saint Petersburg: Zentr "St. Peterborgskoje Vostokovedenje."
Schrader, Heiko. 2000a. *Lombard Houses in St. Petersburg: Pawning as a Survival Strategy of Low-Income Households?*. Münster: LIT.
Schrader, Heiko. 2000b. *Modernization between Economic Requirements and Religious Law: Islamic Banking in Malaysia*. Internationales Asienforum 1-2/00:36–59.
Schrader, Heiko. 2004. *Spheres of Trust, Social Capital and Transformation in Russia*.

Pp. 79–102 in Trust and Social Transformation. Theoretical approaches and empirical findings from Russia, edited by Heiko Schrader. Münster: LIT.

Schrader, Heiko and Eckhard Dittrich. 2012. *Households in Central Asia. Research Findings from an Explorative Study in Kazakhstan and Kyrgyzstan.* Working Paper No. 62. Magdeburg: ISOZ.

Schrader, Heiko, Kamini Prakash, and Jyothi K.K. 2005. *Thrift and Credit Groups and Community Development: The Hope Project in New Delhi/India.* Asien94:59–72.

Schuler, Martin. 2009. *Migration Patterns of the Population in Kyrgyzstan.* Espace populations societées (2007/1):73–89.

Scott, James C. 1976. *The Moral Economy of the Peasant.* New Haven, Conn: Yale University Press.

Simmel, Georg. 1978. *The Philosophy of Money.* Boston: Routledge and Kegan Paul.

Simon, Herbert A. 1982. *Models of Bounded Rationality.* Cambridge, Mass.: MIT Press.

Small, Lee-Ann. 2007. *The Sustainable Rural Livelihoods Approach: A Critical Review.* 28(1):27–38.

Smith, A. 2000a. *Culture/economy and Spaces of Economic Practice: Positioning Households in Post-Communism.* Transactions of the Institute of British Geographers 27(2).

Smith, A. 2000b. *Economic Practices and Household Economies in Slovakia: Rethinking 'survival' in Austerity.* in Work, Employment and Transition. Restructuring Livelihoods in Post-Communist Eastern Europe, edited by A. Smith, A. Rainnie, and A. Swain. London.

Smith, A. 2000c. *Employment Restructuring and Household Survival in Postcommunist Transition: Rethinking Economic Practices in Eastern Europe.* Environment and Planning, 32(10).

Smith, Adrian and Alison Stenning. 2006. *Beyond Household Economies: Articulations and Spaces of Economic Practice in Post-Socialism.* Progress in Human Geography 30, 2 pp. 190–213 30(2):190–213.

Smollet, E. 1989. *The Economy of Jars.* Ethnologie Europa 19(2):125–40.

Soucek, Svat. 2001. *A History of Inner Asia.* Reprinted. Cambridge [u.a.]: Cambridge Univ. Press.

Stren, Richard. 1986. *The Ruralization of African Cities: Learning to Live with Poverty.* Toronto: Institute for Environmental Studies University of Toronto. Retrieved August 19, 2013 (http://www.worldcat.org/title/index{Rural}ruralization-of-african-cities-learning-to-live-with-poverty/oclc/320855433&referer=brief_results).

Swain, Ranjula Bali and Maria Floro. 2010. *Reducing Vulnerability through Microfinance: Evidence from Indian Self Help Group Program.* Uppsala: Uppsala Univ., Dept. of Economics.

Szporluk, R. 1994. *National Identity and Ethnicity in Russia and the New States of Eurasia.* Armonk, NY: Sharpe.

Tacoli, C. 1998. *Bridging the Divide: Rural-Urban Interactions and Livelihood Strategies.* London: International Institute for Environment and Development.

Tilly, Louise. 1979. *Individual Lives and Family Strategies in the French Proletariat (Downloadbares Archivmaterial, 1979) [WorldCat.org].* Journal of Family History.

Retrieved August 30, 2013 (http://www.worldcat.org/title/individual-lives-and-index{Family}family-strategies-in-the-french-proletariat/oclc/742751966&referer =brief_results).

Tu Dang. 2008. *Vulnerability to Poverty in Select Central Asian Countries.* Retrieved June 7, 2013 (http://www.worldcat.org/title/index{Vulnerability}vulnerability-to-poverty-in-select-central-asian-countries/oclc/836970657&referer=brief_results).

Turner, B. S. 2006. *The Cambridge Dictionary of Sociology.* edited by B.S: Turner. New York: Cambridge Univ. Press.

Veblen, T. 1953. *The Theory of Leisure Class* (reprint from 1899). New York: Mentor.

Wallace, Claire. 2002. *Household Strategies: Their Conceptual Relevance and Analytical Scope in Social Research.* Sociology. Retrieved (www.hwf.at/downloads/open_area/ pdf_reports/pdf_report_1/hwf_r1_01_literature_overview.pdf).

Werner, Cynthia. 2009. *Bride Abduction in Post-Soviet Central Asia: Making a Shift towards Patriarchy through Local Discources of Shame and Tradition.* Journal of the Royal Anthropological Institute (N.S.) 15:314–31.

Wynne, Derek. 2002. *Leisure, Lifestyle and the New Middle Class: A Case Study (Google eBook).* Routledge. Retrieved April 9, 2013 (http://books.google.com/books?id=2U 5c0A4G_-UC&pgis=1).

Yurkova, Irina. 2004. *Der Alltag der Transformation: Kleinunternehmerinnen in Usbekistan – Bibliotheca Eurasica; 2.* Retrieved June 10, 2013 (http://gso.gbv.de/DB=2.1/ PPNSET?PPN=376342781).

Zoomers, Annelies E. B. and Jan M. G. Kleinpenning. 1996. *Livelihood and Urban-Rural Relations in Central Paraguay.* 87(2):161–74.

Zoomers, Annelies and Elisabeth Bernhardine. 1999. *Livelihood Strategies and Development Interventions in the Southern Andes of Bolivia: Contrasting View on Development – Cuadernos Del CEDLA; Nr. 4.* Amsterdam: CEDLA, Centro de Estudios y Documentaci6n Latinoamericanos. Retrieved June 10, 2013 (http://gso.gbv.de/DB= 2.1/PPNSET?PPN=466683286).

Zweynert, Joachim and Nils Goldschmidt. 2005. *The Two Transitions in Central and Eastern Europe and the Relation between Path Dependent and Politically Implemented Institutional Change.* Retrieved (http://opus.zbw-kiel.de/volltexte/2005/3192/pdf/31 4.pdf).

Internet Sources (International and Local)

Agency of Statistics of Kazakhstan: Demography Bulletin for 2010. Online: http://www.stat.kz/publishing/DocLib4/2010/%D0%94%D0%B5%D0%BC%D0% BE%D0%B3%D1%80%D0%B0%D1%84%D0%B8%D1%8F/Bull_Hsany2010.rar; access 24-10-2013

Agency of Statistics of the Republic of Kazakhstan (2011): Living standards in Kazakhstan, 2006-2010. Astana. Online: http://www.stat.kz/publishing/20111/UrovJizni End.pdf; access date 22-10-201

Agency on Statistics of the Republic of Kazakhstan: “Migratsia naselenija. Itogi Nacionalnoi perepisi naselenija Respubliki Kazachstan 2009 goda” [Migration of the population. Results of the census in the Republic of Kazakhstan in 2009]. Edited by Smailov A.A., 2010 p. 192. Available at http://www.stat.gov.kz/faces/wcnav_externalId/p_perepis?_afrLoop=16797994110690#%40%3F_afrLoop%3D16797994110690%26_adf.ctrl-state%3D1agozx3if5_186; access date 10-11-2014

Agency on Statistics of the Republic of Kazakhstan: “Osnovnye pokazateli differenciacii dochodov naselenija za 2001-2010 gody” [Principle indicators of income differentiation of the population for the period of 2001-2010], Bulletin. Astana, 2011

Agency on Statistics of the Republic of Kazakhstan: “Results of the 2009 national population census of the Republic of Kazakhstan”, Analytical report. Available at http://liportal.giz.de/fileadmin/user_upload/oeffentlich/Kasachstan/40_gesellschaft/Kaz2009_Analytical_report.pdf; access date 10-11-2014

Almaty for 20 years of independence of Kazakhstan (Almaty za gody Nezavisimosti Kazakhstani) Almaty, 2001 – p. 153 http://rus.almaty.gorstat.kz/stat_sborniki/page/4/#).

cng.kz/wp-content/uploads/.../ecoprogramm.doc?

Epidemiology of malignant tumors of the child population of the Republic of Kazakhstan (review)//Bulletin KazNMU. – November 16, 2011

Forbes Kazakhstan: “Nazarbaev: V Kazachstane neobchodimo prinjat’ socialnuju programmu vozrozhdenija sela” [Nazarbaev: It is necessary to adopt the rural revival program in Kazakhstan], Interview as of 11-04-2013. Available at http://forbes.kz/news/2013/04/11/newsid_24756; access date 18-07-2013

Galat, Irina: “Infografika: Korrupcia v Kazachstane” [Info-graphics: Corruption in Kazakhstan]. In: Vlast, 17.04.2013. Available at http://vlast.kz/?art=1606; access date 10-11-2014

http://data.un.org/CountryProfile.aspx?crName=Kazakhstan; access date 27-07-2013

http://demoscope.ru/weekly/2002/057/analit04.php; access 24-10-2013

http://epp.eurostat.ec.europa.eu/statistics_explained/index.php?tittl...; access date 20-08-2013

http://i-news.kz/news/2011/04/13/4397910.htm

http://interfax.com.ua/news/political/156312.html; access date 22-10-2013.

http://knowledge.allbest.ru/index{Economy}economy/2c0a65625a3bc68b4d43b89421316c37_0.html; access date 20-08-13

http://web.worldbank.org/WBSITE/EXTERNAL/EXTOED/EXTM, 20-08-2013

http://www.akorda.kz/ru/page/page_poslanie-prezidenta-respubliki-kazakhstan-n-a-index{Nazarbaev}nazarbaeva-narodu-kazakhstana-mart-2006-g_1343986805; access 23-10-2013

http://www.eng.stat.kz; access 25-10-2013

http://www.euromoneycountryrisk.com/Wiki/Kazakhstan; access 27-7-13

http://www.gnpf.kz/1369; access date 28-08-2013

http://www.indexmundi.com/facts/kazakhstan/poverty-gap#SI.POV.GAP2; access date 19-08-2013
http://www.indexmundi.com/facts/kyrgyz-republic/poverty-headcount-ratio; access date 19-08-2013
http://www.kyrtag.kg/?q=ru/news/18870; access date 20-08-2013
http://www.mga.kz/uploads/prog_2011-2015.pdf; access date 21-10-2013
http://www.nationsonline.org/oneworld/kazakhstan.htm, access date 30-07-2013
http://www.nationsonline.org/oneworld/kyrgyzstan.htm; access date 03-09-2013
http://www.perspektivy.info/oykumena/krug/demograficheskije_uspehi_kazahstana_2011-02-21.htm;
http://www.primeminister.kz/page/article_item-110?lang=en; access date 28-08-13
http://www.stat.gov.kz/publishing/Pages/demo_2011.aspx; access date 24-10-2013;
http://www.transparencykazakhstan.org/eng/content/8.html
http://www.who.int/countries/kaz/en/; access date 27-07-2013
http://www.zakon.kz/100059-utverzhdeny-strategija-razvitija-almaty.html; access date 21-01-201
http://www.zakon.kz/4570615-v-kazakhstane-sozdan-edinyjj.html; access date 21-10-2013
https://en.wikipedia.org/wiki/Provinces_of_Kazakhstan; access date 27-03-13
Ikonnikov A.//Center for Asia. – 2009. – 13 (13)// http://asiakz.com/rus/article/305
Kazinform, Astana, 13 April 2011, online: http://med.zakon.kz/209323-samyjj-vysokijj-uroven-prestupnosti.html; access date 21-10-2013
Law of the Republic of Kazakhstan No 126-I as of 16.06.1997 "O gosudarstvennych social'nych posobijach po invalidnosti, po slučaju poteri kormi'lca i po vozrastu" [On state social benefits for disability, loss of the provider and the old age]", Article 12. Available at: http://online.zakon.kz/Document/?doc_id=1007927; access date 10-11-2014]
National Agency of Statistics of the Republic of Kazakhstan 18-09.2013 http://www.stat.kz/digital/pravo/Pages/default.aspx; access date 15-09-2013
National Agency of Statistics of the Republic of Kazakhstan; http://www.eng.stat.kz/digital/index{Environment}Environmental%20protection/Pages/default.aspx; access date 15-09-2013
Ohrana okruzhajushej sredy i ustojchivoe razvitie Kazahstana/Ecology and sustainable development of Kazakhstan. – Astana 2010. pp. 117-147; http://www.stat.kz/publishing/2010/%D0%9E%D1%85%D1%80%D0%B0%D0%BD%D0%B0_%D0%BE%D0%BA%D1%80%D1%83_%D0%B8%D0%BD%D1%82.pdf; access 21-20-2013; http://www.meta.kz/60555-gazovaja-ataka.html; access date 21-10-2013
Panarin S. Contemporary Kazakhstan social and a cultural factors change in the provisions of the Russian language. / / Bulletin of Eurasia. – 2008. – 4.
Regions of Kazakhstan – Astana: The Agency of Statistics of the Republic of Kazakhstan, 2009. Online: http://www.eng.stat.kz/publishing/DocLib/Region_%D0%B0%D0%BD%D0%B3%D0%BB_09.pdf, access date 25-10-2013

Regions of Kazakhstan in 2010/ Statistical yearbook, in ed. Smailov A.A. / Agency of Statistics of the Republic of Kazakhstan, Astana.
Results of the 2009 National population census of the Republic of Kazakhstan. Analytical Report. The Agency of Statistics of the Republic of Kazakhstan. Astana 2011. http://www.eng.stat.kz/publishing/DocLib/2011/,%D0%90%D0%9E%20%D0%BD%D0%B0%20%D0%B0%D0%BD%D0%B3%D0%BB%D0%B8%D0%B9%D1%81%D0%BA%D0%BE%D0%BC.pdf; access date 21-20-2013
Shakirova, S. M. 2007: "Middle class of Almaty: quality of life, gender differences, identity". Almaty, 2007. P.18-25.
Shaukenova, Z.K./Morozov, A.A./Buluktaev, Ju.O. (2010): Uroven' social'noj konfliktnosti: potencial'nye riski I ugrozy (na osnove sociologičeskogo issledovanija). Almaty: KISI pri Prezidente RK. Online: http://kisi.kz/img/docs/5048.pdf; access date 21-20-2013.
Social-economic development of the Republic of Kazakhstan/ Statistical yearbook, in ed. Smailov A.A. / Agency of Statistics of the Republic of Kazakhstan, Astana, 2010 – Vol 1. – p. 130.
State development programme for Almaty in 2010-2015. Online: http://www.mga.kz/uploads/prog_2011-2015.pdf; access date 20-05-2013
State development programme for Almaty in 2010-2015. Online: http://www.mga.kz/uploads/prog_2011-2015.pdf; access 21-10-2013 and http://www.zakon.kz/100059-utverzhdeny-strategija-razvitija-almaty.html; access date 21-01-2013
Statisticheski bulletin Ministerstva Financov Respubliki Kasachstan(Statistical bulletin of The Ministry of finance of the Republic of Kazakhstan) / in ed. Parusimova L.I., Astana No 1 (133), January 2012.
The National Agency of Statistics of the Republic of Kazakhstan http://www.eng.stat.kz/digital/index{Health}Health%20care/Pages/default.aspx; access 15-09-2013
The population of Almaty. Department of Statistics. 19 May 2009
Zhen'shchiny i muzhchiny Kazakhstana (Men and women in Kazakhstan) Statistical yearbook, in ed. Smailov A.A. / The Agency of Statistics of the Republic of Kazakhstan, Astana, 2010
Zhusupov B.S./Alimbekova G.T. 2002: Medical service in Kazakhstan: realities and evaluation. http://ciom.kz/assets/files/Nashi%20publikacii/Med_obsluzhivanie.pdf; access date 23-10-2013

8. The Authors

Aigul Beimisheva, PhD, is Senior Lecturer at the Department of Politology and Law at the T. Ryskulov Kazakh Economic University, Almaty, Kazakhstan. She obtained her PhD from the Kazakh National University named Al-Farabi in Almaty. Research interests: Urban Studies, Social Stratification and Inequality, Social and Economic Inequality, Quality of Life.

Contact address: aigulb777@gmail.com

Eckhard Dittrich, PhD, is a retired professor of Macro Sociology at Otto-von-Guericke University Magdeburg, Germany, where he was the co-founder and director of the 'Center of Transformation Research' devoted at research of the post-soviet countries. He studied in Gottingen and won his PhD from the University of Hannover. He received his second doctorate (habilitation) from the University of Bielefeld. The main locations of his professional career were Gottingen, Bielefeld, Madison (Wisconsin, USA) and Magdeburg. Fields of activity in his long career were Labor Relations, Sociology of Work and Organizations, Ethnic and Race Relations, Rural Sociology and Transformation Research. Since the breakdown of the former Soviet Union he has been doing research and teaching in many post-socialist countries, mainly Poland, Bulgaria, Russia and Kazakhstan.

Contact address: eckhard.dittrich@ovgu.de

Galina Gorborukov, PhD, is Chair and Associate Professor at the Department of General Education and Liberal Arts and Science at the American University of Central Asia, Bishkek, Kyrgyzstan. She finished her PhD at the Kyrgyz State National University in May, 2005. Her research interests are Ethnic and Cultural Identity, Ethnic Studies, Memory and Trauma, Social Stratification and Inequality, Social and Economic Inequality, Social Migration and Movies.

Contact address: wisdom20gg@gmail.com

Denis Gruber, PhD, was lecturer at the State University of St. Petersburg/Russia before he entered into local politics in Saxony Anhalt/Germany recently. He won his PhD at Magdeburg University with an empirical study on Russian minorities in Estonia.

Contact address: gruber.denis@web.de

Daurenbek Kuleimenov, PhD, is presently Junior Researcher at the Nazarbayev University Graduate School of Education. He won his PhD at the Dpt. of Sociology, L.N. Gumilev Eurasian National University, Astana. The topic of his PhD research project was "Households in the Republic of Kazakhstan: social-territorial differences of adaptation to the market". His research interests are Economic Sociology and Labor Sociology among others.

Contact address: deekurec@mail.ru

Heiko Schrader, PhD, is professor of Macro Sociology, Sociology of Development and Transformation and presently head of the sociological department at the Otto-von-Guericke University Magdeburg, Germany and the "Centre of Transformation Research" (ZTF). He has been teaching and doing research in India, Russia and Central Asia. During 1997-1999 he was professor of Economic Anthropology at the State University of St. Petersburg, Russia, and before 1997 reader in sociology at the University of Bielefeld, Germany, where he also took his first and second PhD (habilitation). He is an economist and sociologist by training. His major research interests are in Economic Sociology, where he covers the spectrum of the people's economy, small-scale businesses, informal sector, micro-finance, and slum research. Together with Eckhard Dittrich he led the research on livelihoods in Central Asia.

Contact address: heiko.schrader@ovgu.de

Nazym Shedenova is a professor of Economic Sociology at Al-Farabi-University, Almaty, Kazakhstan. Her first PhD concerned the topic of "Women labor under the conditions of market relations: Social issues". Her second PhD (Dr. nauk) was on"The institutionalization of social-labor relations in the Republic of Kazakhstan: Gender aspects". Her major interests concern Sociology of Work, Gender Sociology, Demography and Political Sociology. She participated in different research projects and had several visiting professorships in the USA.

Contact address: nshedenova@hotmail.com

Aigul Zabirova is professor and holds a chair for Urban Sociology, Identity and Migration Studies at the Faculty of Social Sciences at the Eurasian National University, Astana, Kazakhstan. She studied in Moscow and received her degree of Doctor of Sciences from the Institute of Sociology of the Russian Academy of Sciences (2004); she has been Research Fellow at the School of Oriental and African Studies, London, UK (2011), at Lund University, Sweden (2008), at Warwick University, UK (2007); and Indiana University, USA (2002). Her research and writing focuses are on Identity Policy in Post-Soviet Space, Urbanization and Migration in Central Asia. Her current research focuses on Power, Identity Policies and Modernist Architecture in Kazakhstan. She is a member of the International Sociological Association since 2010.

Contact address: zabirova@hotmail.com

Appendix 1: Questionnaire

Questionnaire for the Project

Livelihoods Strategies of Private Households in Central Asia.

A Rural-Urban Comparison in Kazakhstan and Kyrgyzstan

Participating Institutions:

L.N.Gumilev Eurasian National University, Dpt. of Sociology, Astana
Al-Farabi Univ., Dpt. of Sociology, Almaty
American University of Central Asia, Dpt. of Sociology, Bishkek
Otto-von-Guericke-University, Dpt. of Sociology, Magdeburg

This interview will take 45-60 minutes. We, the research team, would like to invite you to participate to tell us about the living conditions of your household. We assure you that data are kept anonymous and confident and are used for scientific reasons only.
We would like to thank you for your participation.

Questionnaire Header

AS 001-150 AL 151-300 BK 301-450	AS=Astana AL=Almaty BK=Bishkek	Location Name L1 ____________________	
No of Int.	Interviewer Name	Urban Rural L2	Date DAT
		1 ☐ 2 ☐	

Location: Please write down name and tip U=Urban, R=Rural

Respondent(s)	Sex m=1 f=2 RS	Age RA	Respondent Codes A1-An see Tab. 1 RC
1.			
2.			
3.			

What is the Nationality of Your Household?

Note: In case the household consists of several nationalities, please indicate which (several answers are possible)

Nationality	Kazakh 1	Kyrgyz 2	Russian 3	Uzbek 4	Tajik 5	Other 6
NAT1,2,3	☐	☐	☐	☐	☐	☐

Appendix 1: Questionnaire

Part 1: Household Composition, Activities and Revenues

1. 1: Household Composition, Activities and Monetary Incomes

Household Pos. *Please fill for those positions that belong to household*	Code	Sex M=1 F=2	Age	Highest Educ.	Activity 1	Activity 2	Activity 3	Monetary Income 0=No 1=Regular 2=Irreg.	Transfers from State 0=No 1=Regular 2=Irreg.	Transfers From NGOs 0=No 1=Regular 2=Irreg.
Code		S	A	E	I1	I2	I3	M	T	N
Grandfather	A1	X								
Grandmother	A2	X								
Father	A3	X								
Mother	A4	X								
Child 1	A5									
Child 2	A6									
Child 3	A7									
Child 4	A8									
Other 1 ________	A9 A10									
Other 2 ________	A11 A12									
Other 3 ________	A13 A14									
Other 4 ________	A15 A16									

Note: Among others write e.g.: brother of grandfather

Appendix 1: Questionnaire

1.2. Monthly or Annual <u>Household</u> Income in Cash

Note: Please tip category either for monthly or annual income for Kyrgyzstan or Kazakhstan Please recalculate for the data matrix into monthly incomes

Codes Kyrgyzstan **IKR**			**Som**		**Codes Kazakhstan** **IKZ**			**Tenge**	
Monthly			**annually**		**monthly**			**annually**	
1	<1500		< 18000		1	<5200		62400	
2	1500-3000		18000 –<36000		2	5200-<10400		62400 - <124800	
3	3000-7500		36000 - < 90000		3	10400-<27000		124800 - <324000	
4	7500-14000		90000 - < 168000		4	27000 –< 75000		324000 - <900000	
5	14000-28000		168000 - <336000		5	75000-<120000		900000 - <1440000	
6	28000-42000		336000 - <504000		6	120000 - <155000		1440000 - < 1860000	
7	More than 42000		More than 504000		7	155000-<310000		1860000 - <3720000	
					8	310000-<465000		3720000 -<5580000	
					9	465000-<620000		5580000 - <7440000	
					10	More than 620000		More than 7440000	

1.3: People Living Outside Household but Contributing to Household Budget.

Note: If there are not such people please leave blank

Type of Person, please mention relatedness (e.g. husband)	Place of Living (e.g. town or Russia)	Activity 1	Activity 2	Activity 3	Transmittance Cash No=0 Regular=1 Irregular=2	Transmittance Non-Cash No=0 Regular=1 Irregular=2
P	PL	A1	A2	A3	TC	TK
P1						
P2						
P3						
P4						
P5						

1.4: Household Support to Dependents

Note: This shall identify people who are living outside the household but who are depending on it. If there are not such people, please leave blank

Status of Supported Person 1 pupil/stud. 2 pensioner 3 invalid 4 widow(er) 5 Other	Support in Cash No=0 Regular=1 Irregular=2	Support in non-Cash No=0 Regular=1 Irregular=2	Living Place (Please mark urban=u or rural=r and write name
S	TC	TK	L1 L2 (Name)
S1			U☐ R☐
S2			U☐ R☐
S3			U☐ R☐
S4			U☐ R☐
S5			U☐ R☐

1.5: Subsistence/Natural Revenues

Definition: Subsistence/natural revenues shall be produce and natural resources that make household expenditure decrease. Not falling into that category is produce and resources for regular sale in the market

Importance of Subsistence Revenues for Your Household	0 no access/no importance 1 little importance 2 importance 3 strong importance	Code
Animal products		SR1
Garden/agric. Products		SR2
Drinking water (pipe/well)		SR3
Collecting from nature (incl. fishing)		SR4
Grazing land		SR5
Other ________________		SR6,7

Appendix 1: Questionnaire

Part 2: Household's Living Conditions, Main Problems and Assistance, Vulnerability

2.1: Basic Expenses

Can the household cover the expenses for making a living (food, shelter, education = basic needs)?

Code	BE

No ← Yes

-3 -2 -1 0

2.2: Self-Assessment of Household's Economic Status

How do you consider the household's living conditions?

Code	SAE

Worse than average ↔ Better than Average

-3 -2 -1 0 +1 +2 +3

2.3: Self-Assessment of Improvement of Economic Status

Please compare the present economic situation of the HH with that 10 years ago

Code	SAI

Much worse ↔ Much better

-3 -2 -1 0 +1 +2 +3

2.4: Self-Assessment of the Economic Status of the Household in One Year?

Code	SAF1

For the future of the HH I expect

Strong deterioration ↔ Strong improvement

-3 -2 -1 0 +1 +2 +3

Why? (Please write)

Code SAF2

____

Appendix 1: Questionnaire

2.5: Infrastructure

In the Location of Living there is Access to (please tip/several answers possible, yes=1, no=0)

Heath services	Doctor D☐ Med. Centre M☐ Polyclinic P☐ Hospital H☐	IS1... (e.g. IS1D)
Educational Services	Pre-Primary K☐ primary P☐ secondary S☐ vocational V☐ University U	I☐.. (e.g. IS2K)
Banking Services	Yes ☐ No ☐	IS3
Market/Shops	Yes ☐ No ☐	IS4
Transportation Service	Yes ☐ No ☐	IS5
Cultural Services	Library L☐ Cinema C☐ Theater T☐ Music Entertainment M☐	IS6... (e.g. IS6L)
Sports Facilities	Yes ☐ No ☐	IS7
Internet	At Home H☐ Internet Café/Shop S☐	IS8... (e.g. IS8H)
Post Office	Yes ☐ No ☐	IS9
Access to Phone	Yes ☐ No ☐	IS10
Gas	Yes ☐ No ☐	IS11
Regular Electricity	Yes ☐ No ☐	IS12
Free Access to safe drinking water	Yes ☐ No ☐	IS13

2.6: Which are the Main Problems that the Household has been Confronted with in the Last Year?

Go through the list and tip strength of problem!	0 no	1weak	2medium	3 strong	Code
Unemployment					HP1
Illness of family member/medical treatment					HP2
Death of family member					HP3
Divorce					HP4
Marriage					HP5
Food price increases					HP6
Price increases in general					HP7
Prices of communal service					HP8
Prepare kids for new academic year (clothes, books etc.)					HP9

Payment for Education					HP10
Criminality					HP11
Natural disaster					HP12
Transportation					HP13
Problem with neighbors					HP14
Other ____________________					HP15/ 16
Other ____________________					HP17/ 18
Other ____________________					HP19/ 20

2.7 With whom are the Following Household Problems Discussed?

Please go through the different problems and relate them to the different people (codes 0-11). Only one answer is possible. In case that several people or institutions help, please mention most important!	0=with nobody, 1=all hh members 2=male hh members 3=female household members 4=oldest male/female 5=husband/wife 6=brother/sister 7=parents/step parents 8=father in law/mother in law 9= friends 10=colleagues 11=Others ________________	Codes
Financial problems		HPD1
Health problems		HPD2
Education problems		HPD3
Problems with relatives		HPD4
Problems with friends		HPD5
Marriage issues		HPD6
Labor problems		HPD7
Family/cultural traditions		HPD8
Problems with neighbors/community		HPD9
Other ____________________		HPD10,11

2.8: Who Provides the Household Members Assistance when They Have the Following Problems?

Please go through the different problems and relate them to the different people (codes 0-12) Only one answer is possible. In case that several people or institutions help, please mention most important!	0 = nobody 1 = family, relatives 2= friends 3= neighbors 4= colleagues 5= employer 6=local administration 7=educational administration 8= doctors/nurses 9= religious leaders 10=financial institutions 11=NGOs 12= Others ___________	Codes
Financial problems		HPA1
Health problems		HPA2
Education problems		HPA3
Problems with relatives		HPA4
Problems with friends		HPA5
Marriage issues		HPA6
Labor Problems (including unemployment)		HPA7
Family/cultural traditions		HPA8
Problems with neighbors/community		HPA9
Other ________________________		HPA10,11

2.9. Are there any Tensions between the Generations in the Household?

Code TG	
No tensions	0 ☐
Some tensions	1 ☐
Strong tensions	2 ☐

2.10: Are there any Tensions between Males and Females in the Household?

Code TS	
No tensions	0 ☐
Some tensions	1 ☐

2.11 Are there Tensions between different Nationals in the Household?

Note: Skip this question if it is not a nationally mixed household

Code TN	
No tensions	0 ☐
Some tensions	1 ☐
Strong tensions	2 ☐

2.12 Are there any Tensions with Relatives outside the Household?

Code TP	
No tensions	0 ☐
Some tensions	1 ☐
Strong tensions	2 ☐

2.13: Which are the Three Major Problems Living in the Countryside/the City?
Note: only fill for the specific context!

Problem	Code
	MP1
	MP2
	MP3

2.14: Private Property and Living Standard

The household owns...

Please go through the items and mark yes/no	Yes=1 No=0	Code
House/apartment		LS1
Land		LS2
Car/motor cycle		LS3
Refrigerator		LS4
Washing Machine		LS5
Music Centre		LS6
Computer		LS7

LCD or Plasma TV		LS8
Euro Remont		LS9
Datcha (summer house)		LS10
Livestock		LS11
Agricultural Machinery		LS12
Other ______________________________		LS13,14

2.15: Living Space

The household shares __________________sqm living space Code SQM

Part 3: Savings, Credit and Security

3.1: Decisions Concerning Savings, Credit and Security

How are the Following Decisions Treated? (Note: Tip only one answer)

Please tip box	Code	Household affair 1	Nuclear Family Affair 2	Individual Affair 3	The question is not relevant for the household 4
Savings	DSS	☐	☐	☐	☐
Consumer credit	DSC	☐	☐	☐	☐
Investments in housing	DSA	☐	☐	☐	☐
Other investments	DSO	☐	☐	☐	☐
School Education	DSE	☐	☐	☐	☐
Higher Education	DSH	☐	☐	☐	☐
Migration	DSM	☐	☐	☐	☐
Insurances other than car	DSI	☐	☐	☐	☐

3.2: Who is the Main Bread Winner for the Household?

Note: The main bread winner for the household may also be somebody living outside the household sending remittances; please write down as text.

Code	**MBW**

____

3.3. Who is the Household Head?

Code	**HHH**

____*(Please write down according to the following codes from question 1.1*)

Code	
Grandfather	A1
Grandmother	A2
Father	A3
Mother	A4
Child 1	A5
Child 2	A6
Child 3	A7
Child 4	A8
Other 1	A9
Other 2	A11
Other 3	A13
Other 4	A15

3.4: For which Purposes Household Members have Taken up Credit and from Whom?

Note: If there is no credit for any household member, please leave blank

Purpose of credit *Please write down for which purposes credit is presently taken*	Amount Acc. to Category In US-$ <15=1 15-50=2 50-99=3 100-499=4 500-999=5 1,000-4,999=6 5,000-20,000=7 20,000-50,000=8 >50,000=9	Credit Source 1= shop 2=bank 3=relative 4=friend 5= colleague 6=employer 7= State 8= Micro credit institution 9=Money Lender 10=Other *(if other, write 10 and write down source)*	Interest Rate in % *Write down interest rate and tip monthly m or yearly y. If they do not know, leave blank* *For data matrix please recalculate per month*
C P	CA	CS	CI

			% m y
1			☐ ☐
2			☐ ☐
3			☐ ☐
4			☐ ☐
5			☐ ☐

3.5 Ability to Save

Whether the Household Prepares for the Future?

Note: If people say they are too poor to save, use 0 in every category

	Code	0=No 1=Yes
For crisis situations	ACR	
For old age	AOE	
For next generation	ANG	

3.6 Please Mention the Three Most Important Priorities for Which the Household Saves (ranking)

Note: If there is no saving, please leave blank

1st rank HS1	
2nd rank HS2	
3rd rank HS3	

3.7 Lending to Others outside the Household?

Note: If there is no lending please leave blank. If there is no interest rate please write 0%. If people do not know interest rate please leave blank

Category:	Purpose	Amount	Interest rate in %	Short term or long term?
1=Relative 2=Friend 3=Neighbor 4=Colleague 5=Other *(if other, write down who)*		Acc. to Category In US-$ <15=1 15-50=2 50-99=3 100-499=4 500-999=5 1,000-4,999=6 5,000-20,000=7 >20,000=8	*Write down interest rate and tip monthly m or yearly. If they do not know leave blank.* *For data matrix please recalculate per month*	1=<1 month 2=1-<3 months 3=3-<6 months 4=6-<12 months 5=12-<36 months 6=3-<10 years 7=10 years and more

LC	LP	LA	LI % m y	LT
1				
2				
3				
4				
5				

3.8: Savings and Investments

Does any Household Member have Savings and Investments in...

	Code	0=no 1=yes
a savings account in a local bank	HSI1	
a savings account in a foreign bank	HSI2	
bank account abroad	HSI3	
bank investments (shares, stocks and other financial investments)	HSI4	
investments in livestock	HSI5	
investment in private property (land, apartment)	HSI6	
savings at home (i.e., cash, gold)	HSI7	
Other ____________________	HSI8,9	

3.9: Household Savings Purposes

Which of the Following Savings Purposes are Important for Your Household and for Which do You Save/Which do You Possess?

	Code	a 0=unimportant 1=important	b HH saves=1 HH possesses=2
Wedding/funeral	SP1		
Other family events	SP2		
Apartment/house	SP3		
Jewelry /Gold	SP4		
Land	SP5		
Livestock	SP6		
Health insurance	SP7		
Private old age insurance	SP8		
Life insurance	SP9		
Children's education	SP10		

Vacations	SP11		
Perform Hadj	SP12		
Other___________	SP13,14		

4. Values and Future

4.1: How Important are the Following Goals for the Household or Individual Household Members?

	Code	Not important 0	Less important 1	Important 2	Very important 3
Keeping the household together	VF1				
Building new independent Households	VF2				
Earning much money	VF3				
Improving the living standard	VF4				
Enhancing the competences	VF5				
Giving best education to children	VF6				
Buying a house/an apartment	VF7				
Being healthy	VF8				
Being happy	VF9				
Performing Hadj	VF10				
Other ____________________	VF11, VF12				

4.2 What is Your Most Import Aim in Life?

AIM1 *Note: Please write down in a few words what the respondent says!*

Note: Please note age_______ AIM2 and sex (male 1 female2)AIM3 of respondent

4.3 Assessment of Responsibilities

Who do You Think Should be Responsible? Multiple answers possible, please tip?

Please tip box; for codes in matrix: 1=yes, 0=no	State	Family network	The Individual	Insurance companies	Charity organizations
For old age security	ARS1	ARF1	ARM1	ARI1	ARC1
For child care	ARS2	ARF2	ARM2	ARI2	ARC2
For unemployment	ARS3	ARF3	ARM3	ARI3	ARC3
For healthcare prov.	ARS4	ARF4	ARM4	ARI4	ARC4

For the poor	ARS5	ARF5	ARM5	ARI5	ARC5
For school education	ARS6	ARF6	ARM6	ARI6	ARC6
For higher education	ARS7	ARF7	ARM7	ARI7	ARC7

Thank you very much for your attention!

Appendix 2: Interview Guide for Qualitative Research

Introduction

May I introduce myself: ...

Thank you very much for your readiness to participate.

This is joint university research from Europe, Kazakhstan and Kyrgyzstan. All information we receive is strictly confidential and only used for our purposes. After this interview, your name and all data that can reveal your identity are no longer used. In our research, persons get a number, so that the information can't be traced back to them. This means that you can openly express your opinion.

In this research we want to understand your life and the ways of making a living. This is important for us to better understand livelihoods and to make proposals to enhance personal capabilities, improve living conditions and give more stability to them. We believe that official statistics lack the view from the people. Therefore we make these interviews.

Do you have questions or can we start with the interview?

1. *Can you please introduce yourself?*
   Inquiry in: gender, education, professional career, household position (head?) Concerning 'household position' try to find out the real position not only the formal one: who really decides, who really earns the income and who is the formal head etc.
2. *Please describe the household you are living in?*
   Inquiry about size and structure (members, incl. migrants in and out, helpers, adopted children, dependent elderlies, etc.)
3. *Please describe who does what in your household*
   Inquiry concerning allocation of tasks and responsibilities. If possible refer to the answer in Question 2 and find out the tasks of children, men/women, other members.
4. *If you think about what you have told me up to now, are there any tensions in the household?*
   Inquiry aiming at finding out what kind of tensions are there living and working together in the household. Tensions concern f.e.: young/old, male/female, different nations, insiders/outsiders, mother in law/daughter in law, clan.
5. *Is the household confronted with weaknesses in making a living?*
   Inquiry aims at the vulnerability of the household. This does not necessarily aim at economic/financial issues but also solidarity, networks of friends and relatives, clan etc.
6. *If you think about these weaknesses. How do you protect yourself against them?*
   Inquiry aims at coping and adaption activities concerning f.e. savings, credits, selling assets, assistance in general by persons, institutions, clan etc.

7. *Do you have the possibility to save?*
   Inquiry aims at how and for what purpose people save: f.e. for marriage, funerals, credits, study etc.
8. *If you think back 5 years or so, have there been shocks the household had to cope with?*
   Inquiry into these shocks (personal, economic, what ever). Make sure that the mechanisms to overcome the shocks are explained and make sure to have described the major obstacles
9. *What could make your household more secure in general?*
   Inquiry aims at all kind of activities to increase sustainability: f.e. 2nd job, neighbourhood help, sending children to school, savings etc.
10. *If you think about these activities, what are the key constraints for their realization?*
    Inquiry aims at barriers to enter, money, level of skills, social capital etc.
11. *What are the major problems living here in ....?*
    Inquiry aims at lack of security, trust, corruption, crime etc.
12. *If you think about your future, what kind of problems do you see?*
    Inquiry aims at long-term aspects of livelihoods
13. *Concerning the household, is there anything you would like to mention and you did not talk about yet?*
    Inquiry open

Thank you very much for your help in this research!

Index